P9-AOU-164

EMOTION
IN MAN AND ANIMAL

EMOTION IN MAN AND ANIMAL

ITS NATURE AND DYNAMIC BASIS

SECOND REVISED EDITION
by PAUL THOMAS YOUNG

ROBERT E. KRIEGER PUBLISHING COMPANY
HUNTINGTON, NEW YORK

Originally Published 1943
SECOND REVISED EDITION 1973

Printed and Published by
ROBERT E. KRIEGER PUBLISHING CO., INC.
BOX 542, HUNTINGTON, NEW YORK. 11743

Library of Congress Catalog Card Number 72-83380
ISBN 0-88275-084-4

Printed in U.S.A. by
NOBLE OFFSET PRINTERS, INC.
NEW YORK, N.Y. 10003

Preface

This book is an outgrowth of more than thirty years of teaching university courses dealing with feeling, emotion and motivation. The book is intended to serve as a text and for reference in these and related areas. It is intended for students who have had introductory courses in psychology and who possess some background in physiology and general biology.

Since the first edition was published, in 1943, there has been an explosion of scientific research on feelings and emotions in man and other animals. There is a vast experimental literature dealing with emotional behavior, the neurophysiology of pleasantness and unpleasantness, the neurophysiology of emotional reactions, different forms of emotional excitement, and related topics. I have not attempted to review this literature but have given references with excellent bibliographies. In Chapters V and VI I have considered the bodily basis of emotion and in Chapter VII, the conscious aspect. Other chapters deal with the nature of emotion, emotional development, and various emotional problems of living.

A personal reason for writing this book has been to bring together the most recent findings from my laboratory studies on hedonic regulation of behavior and development. Details of these studies can be located through references to experimental papers and reviews listed in the bibliography.

In the present book the central point of reference is to the human and animal organism that experiences emotion and reveals it in overt expressions and behavior. The basic assumption underlying every part of the present work is *biological monism*: the body and mind are not separate entities, but rather aspects of a single psycho-biological unit. The approach to the study of emotion is phenomenological and multidisciplinary. This eclectic approach makes it possible to consider the topic from various angles. I believe that the more ways we can view and study a complex event the better will be our understanding of it.

The present edition of *Emotion in Man and Animal* is based upon facts which appeared in a first edition in 1943. I have retained the bulk of original content, insofar as it is factually sound and for historical reasons have preserved the original references. The original plan of organization has been changed somewhat and the overall size of the volume has necessarily expanded. Much has been deleted to make a place for recent up-to-date materials.

In revising *Emotion in Man and Animal* I have drawn heavily from the more recent work, *Motivation and Emotion,* especially from those chapters that deal specifically with emotion. Through a special arrangement with John Wiley and Sons, Inc., it has been possible to reproduce, in this book, many of the illustrations and parts of *Motivation and Emotion* (1961) that are relevant to the topic.

Credit for the illustrations and for quoted material has been given at the place of citation.

My obligations are many. Among teachers and colleagues who through the years have influenced my research and thinking (mentioned in chronological order) are: Edward Bradford Titchener, Karl S. Lashley, Wolfgang Köhler, Curt P. Richter, Carl Pfaffmann, and William E. Kappauf. In my studies of the hedonic regulation of behavior and development I am indebted to a long line of research assistants and students who have faithfully carried out experiments and contributed ideas and suggestions beyond the call of duty. Among these helpers (again in chronological order) are: John R. Wittenborn, James P. Chaplin, Edna A. Maisner. Janet C. Schneider, Mrs. Mary Massey Bauman. Mrs. Joanne Patterson Leonard, Harold W. Richey, John T. Greene, Emir H. Shuford, Jr., John L. Falk, David Asdourian, Kent R. Christensen, Richard H. Schulte, Richard G. Burright, Charles H. Madsen, Jr., and Clinton L. Trafton.

In the preparation of the first edition, my wife, the late Josephine Kennedy Young, M.D., gave unstintingly of her time to improve the readability of the text and to advise on medical aspects of the topic. During preparation of the manuscript for this second edition I have been greatly aided by the competent help of Mrs. Thelma Kramar.

My continued research on hedonic processes has been made possible through a series of grants from: The Rockefeller Foundation, The Research Board of the University of Illinois, The American Medical Association, The Quartermaster of the United States Army, and the National Science Foundation. I am grateful to these organizations for sustained financial support of this research.

Paul Thomas Young

Claremont, California
January, 1972

Contents

Table of Illustrations

Chapter I

The Nature of Emotion

A child darts out from behind a parked car directly in front of an approaching auto. Brakes are jammed. The wheel is whirled. The car misses the child by inches. An instant later the driver emerges. He is pale; sweat is on his brow. His breathing is irregular. His muscles are limp. His heart palpitates. "A close call," he says hoarsely.

During this crisis the driver acted automatically and adaptively, in the fraction of a second making the correct moves. The brief crisis over, he became aware of bodily changes; there was a disturbing emotional excitment. Here we have, disjointed in time, several major aspects of emotion: habituated adaptive behavior during a crisis, involuntary bodily changes, cognitive awareness of a critical situation, a disturbed conscious feeling.

An emotion is a complex *event,* a natural process, not just a subjective feeling and much less some mysterious "mind stuff." An emotion is a natural occurrence as truly as a sunrise is, or an earthquake, or swaying of a tree in the wind. All such events are complex processes within a natural setting. Because they are complex an analysis must be made piecemeal and from different points of view.

Aspects of Emotion. As with all complex events in nature, what is observed from one point of view differs from the facts as they appear from another standpoint. Subjective and objective facts may even appear to be contradictory as with the well known optical illusions.

From the point of view of an experiencing individual an emotion is a conscious event. Such words as *fear, anger, joy, grief, excitement, jealousy, disgust, embarassment,* and the like, carry the meaning of subjectively felt experience. From an objective point of view, emotional behavior can be recognized and named when the inducing situation is known. An individual may weep, scream, pace the floor, wring his hands, strike an enemy, run; he may shuffle his feet, frown, or show other signs of emotional disturbance. An astute observer can notice the pallor or blushing, the trembling, perspiration, irregular breathing, the changes in facial expression. These are objective signs of emotion. The subject, of course, may be aware of these bodily changes. In everyday life the behavioral changes are commonly called "expressions" of emotion.

In everyday life emotional processes are viewed in the context of environmental situations that elicit the affective processes. There is an enemy feared, a sweetheart loved, a job lost, a game won, and so on. To understand the emotional event a dynamic psychology is needed. One must understand the motives, attitudes, values, beliefs, frustrations and conflicts of individuals in order to understand their feelings and emotions.

The task before us in searching for understanding of human and animal emotions is complex and difficult. Various approaches and points of view are required. There are the points of view of the psychologist who is interested in conscious experience, the behavioral scientist, the physiologist,, the neuropsychologist, and the view of developmental biology which takes account of evolution and ontogenetic development. There are also the views of common sense psychology.

IMPORTANCE OF EMOTION IN HUMAN LIFE

Emotion influences profoundly, and in countless ways, the lives of men. An understanding, therefore, of the nature of the various emotions is a matter of practical importance.

Down through the centuries there has been a practical. moral, interest in emotion. This is seen in eighteenth century discussions of egoism and altruism, hedonism and standards of conduct. In current psychiatry, psychosomatic medicine, clinical psychology, and other disciplines, there is an emphasis on the importance of emotion in relation to health and human welfare.

Emotion and Mental Health. Back in 1876, Dr. George M. Beard read a paper before the American Neurological Association in New York City entitled, "The influence of mind in the causation and cure of disease and the potency of definite expectations." Dr. Beard maintained that disease might appear and disappear without influence of any other agent than some form of emotion. Fear, terror, anxiety, grief, anger, wonder, or a definite expectation, he regarded as mental conditions likely to produce disease. Dr. Beard argued that certain emotional states could neutralize therapeutics and increase the effects of drugs. At the time, his ideas were new and startling. Later the ideas were recognized in a movement known as psychosomatic medicine.

Today it is widely accepted that persisting emotional states are an important factor in certain disorders: peptic ulcers, essential hypertension, rheumatoid arthritis, ulcerative colitis, bronchial asthma, hyperthyroidism, neurodermatitis, and other disorders. The health of a patient is strongly influenced by conditions of living which produce emotional traumata: financial failure, bereavement, injury, insult, unrequited love, threatened divorce, loss of self-esteem, feelings of guilt and remorse, chronic physical disease, and various other factors of stress.

Psychoanalysts have long recognized the importance of emotion in the etiology and therapy of neuroses. Unresolved conflicts, persisting anxieties, phobias, repressed hostility, loss of self-confidence and self-esteem, and similar conditions, underlie neurotic symptoms. To reveal unconscious motivations and alleviate mental disorder psychoanalysts resort to free verbal association, aided recall, interpretation of dreams, all the while observing emotional expressions. The clinical aim is to elicit thoughts that accompany the emotional reactions. A dominant emotion is associated with something important to the patient, something that affects him deeply. Just why it is important can be learned only be getting the patient to talk, to express his thoughts and feelings.

Free emotional expression plays an important role in psychotherapy. Psychotherapy is not merely an intellectual process. An intellectual understanding of the patient's life-situation is helpful but not sufficient to effect a cure. Psychotherapy operates in the sphere of emotion. The aim of psychotherapy is to provide corrective emotional experiences by relaxing the subject's defenses and permitting him to reappraise the situations that produced anxiety or hostility or depression. In the major methods of psychotherapy the subject is encouraged to *feel*, to express his emotions. Emotional expressions are of primary importance; they can be supplemented, of course, by rational suggestions, arguments, persuasions.

It is a matter of interest that words designating physical disorder and words designating feeling have been derived from the same Greek root (παθος). There are thus medical terms such as *pathology, psychopathic, pathogenic,* etc., and psychological terms such as *sympathy, empathy, apathy*, etc.

Reason *versus* Emotion. The contrast between reason and emotion is widely recognized. We hear such phrases as "intellect and emotion," "reason and emotion," "mind and emotion." The implication of these phrases is that intellect, reason, mind, are rational processes; emotion is non-rational. A man with a towering rage and uncontrolled impulses is said to be temporarily "out of his mind," "irrational," "unreasonable."

One hears a great deal about controlling the emotions. There are varying degrees of rational control. In some psychoses and under the influence of drugs there is a condition known as dyscontrol or complete loss of control by rational processes.

No one can argue that human behavior is completely rational. Affective states of hunger, thirst, pain, fear, rage, terror, lust, disgust, joy, euphoria, apathy, and the like, simply exist. They are *not* the products of logical reasoning. They depend upon intraorganic and environmental conditions that simply exist. They are non-rational.

Human nature is in part rational but only in part. Any practical project that deals with human beings should recognize this fact. It is important, therefore, to understand the non-rational dynamic and emotional, aspects of human nature.

Emotion in relation to the educative process is considered in Chapter IV that deals with emotional development. See pages 192-4.

Feeling and Emotion in the Control of Human Behavior. In a readable book entitled *Motivation in Advertising*, Pierre Martineau (1957), who is Research Director of the *Chicago Tribune*, argues on the basis of his vast experience in advertising that feeling is much more effective than argument in making people buy. People are not wholly rational. The *reason-why* type of advertisement is less effective than one which arouses feeling. In other words, feeling is more evocative of action than logic.

Martineau illustrates his thesis by many examples. For instance, in successful advertisements of Coca-Cola there is little or no argument. There may be a picture of happy, healthy people at the beach or in a mountain resort or in a home-like room. There may be a few words like *delicious* and *refreshing* but that is all. A person looking at the picture puts himself empathically into the situation and gets a comfortable, relaxed feeling. The positive feeling tone is associated with the product and that is enough to bias him favorably towards Coca-Cola. With such a feeling people are more likely to buy the product than if they were exposed to a *reason-why* type of advertisement.

Writers, musicians, actors, parents, politicians, and salesman have understood for centuries the primary importance of feeling in shaping human judgments, beliefs, and actions. In political campaigns argument is less effective in winning votes than baby kissing and other emotional appeals. There are some, however, who do not admit this but argue that man is governed by reason and intellect; feelings are pushed out of sight. Today scientists and other thinkers recognize that man's complete rationality is a fiction. Writes Martineau: "If we reconstruct our own lives for an hour or a day—our daydreams, our irrational actions, our behavior influenced by associations and attachments, our fondness for our children and pets, our escapes into hobbies and movies, our preference for pretty secretaries—we should be honest enough to realize that there is probably no mental action and no behavior in which feeling does not play a central role."

Again, the average motorist isn't sure what "octane" in gasoline actually is. He doesn't know whether there is peppermint octane or chocolate octane; but he does know vaguely that it is something good. So he orders "high-octane" gasoline because he wants this essential quality behind the meaningless surface of jargon.

The idea that human action can be controlled by logical reasoning has limitations because man is only in part a rational creature. In advertising, propaganda, evangelism, political oratory, salesmanship, and other practical arts for controlling action, the emotional appeal is more effective than cold logic. An emotional appeal creates loyalties, commitments, motives, attitudes, ideals, and beliefs. To get action one needs to create a feeling that the suggested action is right and reasonable. This principle is important in the control of human behavior.

Anyone who is concerned with the government of men should start by recognizing human nature as it is. There must be a frank recognition of the emotional, non-rational, aspect of behavior. This is expecially important in the social sciences.

Does man's survival on the earth depend on the dominance of rationality over emotion? Does *homo sapiens* face extinction because he is not sufficiently sapient to overcome his animalistic tendencies? Will emotional dyscontrol of psychopathic leaders determine the fate of man? I do not know the answers. But anyone concerned with pressing social problems—war and peace, population control, eugenics, race relations, economic conflict, polution of the environment, education, religious tolerance, and others—should consider the nature of man as it is.

On the social importance of emotion, R. W. Leeper (1970) has written:

> . . . the most important problems of modern society are, in many respects, emotional problems. Both directly and indirectly is this so. Directly because of the fact that, in our modern world, there are such powerful and widespread feelings of aloneness, rejection, insecurity, discouragement, alienation, and resentment, rather than the positive emotions which people might well prefer to have. Indirectly in that, if it be protested that the crucial problems of modern society are problems of international conflict, economic waste and exploitation, racial discrimination, population explosions, and the like, the answer that might well be made to this: what underlies these other problems, in considerable degree, are emotional factors such as fears of other nations with different ideological orientations, difficulties in making emotional readjustments regarding what constitutes a satisfying, heart-warming size of family, and emotional commitments to special privileges on the part of far too many groups within society. [151]

THE IDENTIFICATION AND CLASSIFICATION OF EMOTIONS

The use of the term *emotion* by poets, philosophers, psychoanalysts, psychiatrists, psychologists, and others, has been so varied and confused that some have suspected that *emotion* means exactly nothing. Thus Bentley (1928) asked, "Is 'emotion' more than a chapter heading?" And Duffy (1941) in her critical article wrote: "I can therefore see no reason for a psychological study of 'emotion' as such. 'Emotion' has no distinguishing characteristics. It represents merely an *extreme* manifestation of characteristics found in some degree in all responses."

Relative to the concept of emotion, Sheer (1961) wrote:

> The concept of emotion has had a much-maligned but ever-present place in the history of psychology. There is an extensive literature to indicate that emotion, both subjectively in its experiential or feeling aspect and objectively in its expressive or behavioral aspect, involves the organism at many levels of psychological and physiological integration. It is primarily because of this widespread influence and interactions with other psychological processes (before emotion finds expression in behavior) that the concept has been so difficult to deal with. Also, its close association with the clinic in the various forms of anxiety, frustration, hostility, and so forth, has served to complicate matters further. Everyone knows something of what is meant by emotion, but not precisely what. [433]

In view of such misgivings it is important to inquire how emotions can be recognized, distinguished, classified and defined.

Identifying and Naming the Emotions. How can specific emotions be recognized and distinguished from each other? A good many people believe that they can identify emotions on the basis of facial expression. As a test of this please observe the photographs in Figure 1 and attempt to name the emotions portrayed. In the first illustration the inducing situation is not known; the photograph can be used to compare the judgments of different persons. The situations producing the other expressions are described in the legend.

The problem of identifying emotions from facial expressions has been studied by a good many investigators. Landis (1924) studied the problem experimentally. He aroused genuine emotions in human subjects and then photographed the disturbed individual. To evoke emotion the following situations were employed: listening to music, reading the Bible, smelling ammonia, hearing a loud noise, writing out a *faux pas*, viewing pictures of skin diseases, pornographic material, art studies, reading sex case histories, handling live frogs, decapitating a rat, experiencing electric shocks, and, finally, relief from these various ordeals.

As an aid in the analysis of facial expressions dark marks were placed

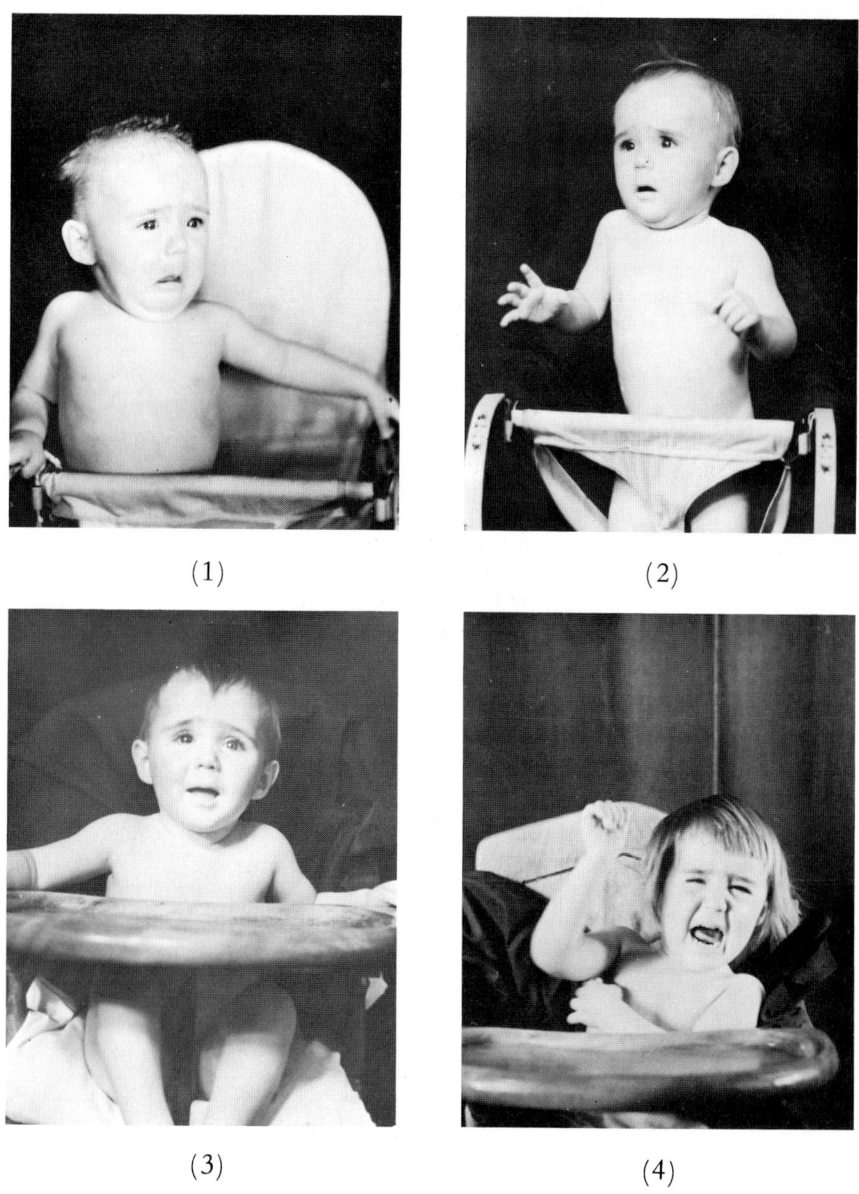

Figure 1. Emotional expressions of a child. The photographs are those of a female child at these ages: (1) Age six and a half months; the inducing situation is not known. (2) Age nine and a half months; attending to a toy or object about to be revealed. (3) Age twelve months; an expression of interest or pleasant attention which is a response to an adult talking to her, trilling the tongue, etc. (4) Age thirty months; angry crying in response to being pinched. *Courtesy of* Myrtle B. McGraw.

upon the subject's face. Measurement of the distances between these marks on the photographs revealed the degree to which different groups of facial muscles were contracted in emotional states and at rest. The subjects also gave verbal reports of their emotional experiences.

After measuring the photographs and studying the verbal reports, Landis made the following generalizations (his statements are not quoted literally):

1. For each experimental situation wide individual differences existed in the facial expressions evoked. For the total group of twenty-five subjects no fixed pattern of expression was common to any single situation.
2. Each individual tended to use some particular group of facial muscles habitually, to the exclusion of others. This tendency gave certain characteristic facial patterns to each person.
3. With not one of the emotions reported did a muscle or group of muscles contract sufficiently to be considered as characteristic of the stated emotion.
4. When the subjects were instructed to imagine some emotion, no uniform relation could be found between the facial expression and the emotion which was imagined.
5. When the emotional expressions were ranked according to the gross amount of facial musculature involved, the rank order was found to be: pain, surprise, anger, exasperation, crying, disgust, sexual excitement, revulsion.

On the basis of these and other generalizations, Landis concluded that an emotion, as it is observed in the face, is not a true pattern of response as is, for example, the wink reflex. He suggested that the common names of emotions typically refer to *situations* which induce them rather than to the pattern of facial response. Also, he stated, the *degree of general disturbance* may be a factor which aids one in naming emotions, but *not* the facial pattern nor the subjectively experienced reaction.

This negative result is contrary to findings of other psychologists who have utilized photographs of facial expressions posed by skilled actors, instructing the subjects to name the emotions represented. Landis believes that *posed* expressions are conventional and that they are used in communication much as the spoken word is employed. The conventional expressions differ from culture to culture. Landis distinguished between *social* and *emotional* expressions. The latter are reflexive patterns of response but, as pointed out above, the common names of emotions do not designate stable patterns of facial expression.

In general, then, the "emotions" that we recognize and name in everyday life are *interpretations* based upon experience. These interpretations involve a dynamic relation between an organism and its environment. There are specific forms of adaptive behavior that grow out of different forms of emotional upset and the "emotions" are recognized and named, in good part, by the adjustments that restore complacency.

How do we recognize and distinguish emotions? First, we rely upon our knowledge of the inducing situation and, second, upon our knowledge of the subject's history—his characteristic ways of responding to stimulus-situations. We also rely upon the observation of adaptive behavior that appears in the disturbing situation as well as upon the objective signs of emotional disturbance—patterns of reflexive response and indications of visceralization.

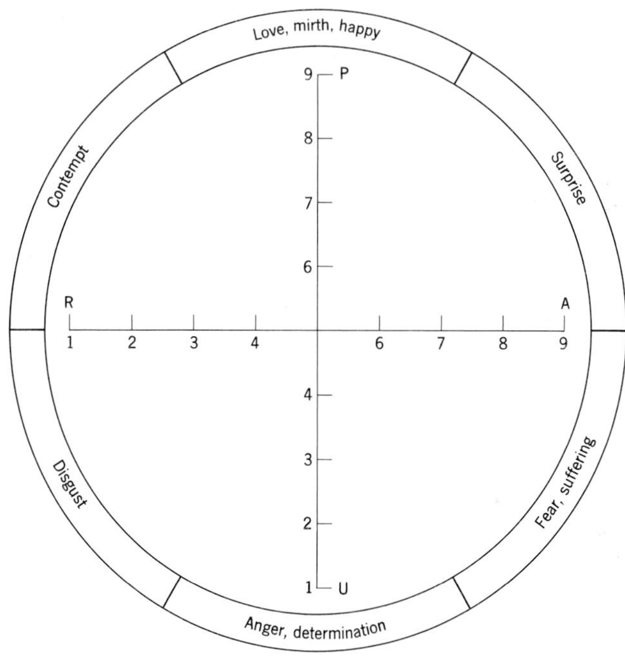

Figure 2. Frame of reference for scaling facial expressions. *Modified from* Schlosberg (1952).

Facial Expressions of Emotions in Man. Schlosberg (1941, 1952) studied patterns of facial expression by instructing subjects to sort photographs on the basis of similarity and difference. Seventy-two pictures of facial expressions were chosen from the Frois-Wittmann series. Three sets of these (a total of two hundred and sixteen pictures) were shuffled and given to the subjects for sorting into seven bins.

The bins were arranged in a row and labelled, from left to right, with names of the six categories of facial expression used in Woodworth's scale: (1) love, mirth, happiness; (2) surprise; (3) fear, suffering; (4) anger, determination; (5) disgust; (6) contempt. The seventh bin, named "Scattering," was used for pictures that did not seem to belong in any of the other bins.

Analysis of scale values and overlapping of categories showed that Woodworth's scale is not a straight line but rather a circle with categories 1 and 6 near together. Figure 2, modified from Schlosberg (1952, 1954), shows the categories arranged in a circular series.

There are two scales in the center. The vertical scale is an hedonic continuum extending from pleasantness (P), through indifference, to unpleasantness (U). The horizontal scale extends from rejection (R), through neutrality, to attention (A).

The subjects readily placed all Frois-Wittmann pictures upon the surface determined by these two axes. The expressions did not cover the entire area but they fell within an oval-shaped area inside the circle.

The major dimension of facial expression is hedonic–expressing pleasantness or unpleasantness. A minor dimension is related to the fact that some facial expressions indicate attentive observation while others indicate rejection and avoidance.

The Basis for Identifying Emotional Expressions. One difficulty with the use of photographs in identifying the facial expressions of emotion is that these pictures show only a portion of the data which is available in actual life. Photographs are static; they do not reveal the constant changes in expression which occur.

Kanner (1931) noted that still photographs lack features which are observable in reality. They do not reproduce the blush or the pallor (vasomotor features); they show inadequately the secretion of lacrimal, sudorific, and salivary glands–which are frequently affected during emotional excitement. Activation of the hair-raising (pilomotor) muscles, too, is less visible in photographs than in actual life. Gestures and postures are often left out of the picture. Respiratory disturbances are incompletely shown by the momentary position of mouth and nostrils presented in the photograph. Further, a photograph of the face gives little or no clue to visceral and general somatic responses. Most important of all, perhaps, is the fact that the situation which induces an emotion is entirely left out of account in a still photograph of facial expression. Later studies by Schachter and Singer (1962) have demonstrated the great importance of the psychological situation in determining the emotional state. Hence, as Kanner states, to judge an emotion from a still photograph of the face is at worst a guessing game and at best an art which tests the ability of the judge.

Some of the experiments upon recognizing emotions from facial photographs have isolated part of the face for judgment, as the eyes or the mouth. In this connection, Arnheim (1928) showed that we can judge with greater consistency when observing the total configuration of a face than when making a judgment on the separate features. By extending the principle of *Gestalt*, we can assume that the more complete the data which are available to the judges, the more consistent will be their identifications of the emotions.

Consistent with this principle are results obtained by Sherman (1927). Instead of stills he used motion-pictures and also gave his judges the opportunity of making first-hand observations of the emotional behavior of infants. In this work several groups of judges were employed, all presumably qualified to pass upon human behavior—graduate students in psychology, medical students, nurses in training, and normal-school freshmen.

To induce an emotional state Sherman used the following techniques: a delay in feeding (hunger); dropping (fear); restraint of movement (anger); sticking with a needle (pain). Unfortunately the conditions to produce pleasing emotions—smiling and laughing—were not represented.

After taking motion pictures of the responses, Sherman prepared films to show: (1) the stimulating circumstances and the ensuing responses in the infant; (2) the responses only; (3) each stimulating circumstance followed by the response to a different situation. In addition to presenting motion pictures to the judges, Sherman used a more direct method. Infants were stimulated behind a screen which was then removed. This last technique made it possible for the judges, without seeing the actual stimulating situation, to hear the outcry, see the color of the skin, and get other clues lacking in the motion pictures, as to the nature of the emotional response.

Sherman rightly concluded that knowledge of the inducing circumstances is a major factor in identifying emotions. An emotion is not recognized solely by the observed pattern of facial response but rather by the situation-response relation. It is the response as back-acting on the situation that is important. The infants' emotions were differentiated by Sherman's judges in terms of the response pattern *plus* a knowledge of the situation that induced the response.

Sherman's findings corroborate the statement of Kanner that the more complete the information about the emotional response plus the situation which induces it, the greater the consistency of recognition and naming. Other psychologists, too, have questioned the view than an emotion can be recognized solely by its specific pattern of response. For example, Dashiell (1928), after reviewing the experimental facts, expressed doubt as to the existence of specific emotional patterns.

There are, he said, referring to experiments dealing with this problem, two possible explanations of the negative results: (1) There *are* emotional patterns in the organism which correspond to the conventional names—despair, love, joy, grief, anger, fear, ecstasy—but the visceral core of each remains to be discovered. (2) A very different explanation is that names conventionally used to designate different emotions refer to varying forms of viscerally facilitated or inhibited *overt behavior patterns* that have been classified and labeled more in terms of their *social* significance than in terms of their visceral components. (Landis, also, it will be recalled, distinguished between social and truly emotional expressions.)

In addition to the two explanations suggested by Dashiell, there is at least one other possibility: (3) There *are* emotional patterns of response which do not correspond to the conventional names. In Chapter V we shall describe patterns of response which appear during emotional excitement—the rage pattern, crying, smiling, laughing, the sexual patterns, and others. There can be no doubt as to the existence, uniformity, and primitive nature of these patterns; and there can be no doubt that the list of authentic patterns is far removed from the conventional lists of emotions. (One difficulty in identifying and naming emotions from the pattern of response is that the term *emotion* commonly designates attitudes such as hatred, resentment, fear, love, liking, and disgust rather than actual patterns of response.)

That there is an innate core of emotional response for certain emotions has been claimed by Goodenough (1931). She photographed the emotional responses of a ten-month-old infant and presented to the judges still photographs which were to be matched with statements describing the circumstances calling forth the expressions. She found that, on the average, the judges were able to match the photographs and situations correctly in 47.2 percent of the judgments, which is 5.7 times the percentage of successes to be expected by chance. Goodenough remarks that, as the infant develops, his primitive emotional responses are inhibited, modified, and changed by social experience.

Goodenough's work does not necessarily prove that there are innate emotional patterns, which can be recognized from still photographs, for the following reason: The judges were given statements descriptive of the inducing situations and thus had more information than that obtainable from the photographs alone. Matching facial expressions and situations is very different from recognizing and naming emotions on the basis of facial expressions alone. Sherman's work demonstrates that a knowledge of the inducing situations makes for greater consistency in identifying and naming emotions. In view of this finding, Goodenough's result is not surprising.

But despite this minor criticism of her interpretation, it may still be true that for certain emotions there is an innate core of response whose surface manifestation serves as the basis for recognizing and naming emotions.

The most likely illustration of this is the basic contrast between pleasant and unpleasant emotions. Pleasant emotions were not aroused in Sherman's experiment, and they were inadequately represented in the investigation of Landis. Thus an enlightening point may have been missed.

That some facial expressions can readily be identified as pleasant and others as unpleasant is shown by the following bit of evidence. The writer selected at random a series of fourteen photographs portraying various emotional expressions. On several occasions these were rated by advanced students of psychology in terms of the pleasantness or unpleasantness revealed. All told, 133 students rated the pictures.

Results are ranked and tabulated in Table 1. From these results one can see that there is almost unanimous agreement that photograph N represents a pleasant feeling and photograph D an unpleasant feeling. Between these extremes there are all gradations in the frequency of judging pleasant and unpleasant feelings.

TABLE 1
Judgments of photographs of facial expression in terms of pleasant and unpleasant feeling

Photograph designation	Frequency of rating		
	Pleasant	Indifferent	Unpleasant
N	132	0	1
C	131	2	0
G	100	17	16
F	89	32	12
E	55	60	18
K	35	57	41
I	12	64	57
B	10	34	89
A	2	37	94
J	6	22	105
H	1	16	116
L	3	2	128
M	0	4	129
D	0	1	132

To illustrate the fact that there are certain patterns of positive and negative facial expression that can be easily distinguished, consider the pictures shown in Figure 3. View 1 shows neutral or interested visual attention. View 2 is the pattern of crying, with rectangular mouth. View 3 is laughter. If these facial patterns are judged in terms of pleasantness and unpleasantness, there will be practically unanimous agreement that view 2 portrays unpleasantness and view 3 portrays pleasantness. Opinions will differ as to whether view 1 expresses neutral attention or mildly pleasant interest.

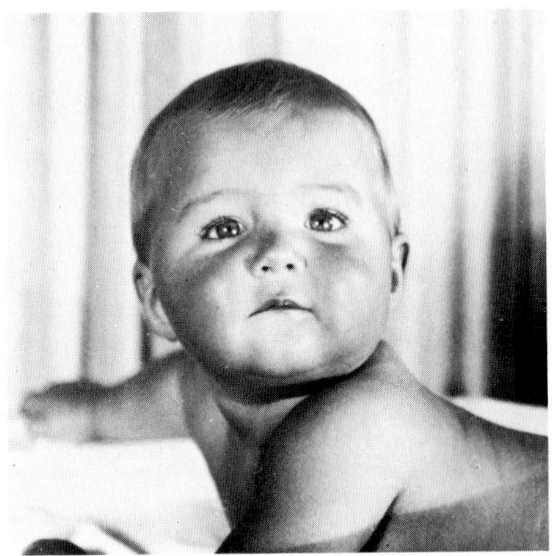

1

2

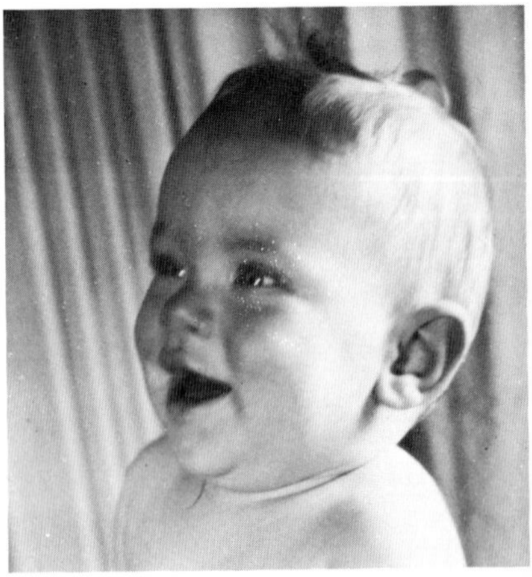

3

Figure 3. Three views of facial expressions in an infant, age nine months. *Courtesy of* Nancy Bayley.

Recognition of Emotional Expressions in the Chimpanzee. Since the behavior of the chimpanzee is similar in many respects to that of man, it is of interest to compare emotional expressions in these two primates. Although the recognition of emotions in animals is difficult and gross errors are commonly made, still a certain degree of success can be obtained.

Before the reader is familiar with the following descriptions, let him examine the photographs in Figure 4, and jot down on a scrap of paper the names of the emotions portrayed. The descriptions below can be used to check the ratings as right or wrong.

These photographs were presented by Foley (1935) to 127 subjects. He instructed them to select from a printed list of names the particular emotions shown in the pictures. Foley found that there were wide individual differences in judgment. Confusions were especially frequent between weeping (tearless), anger, and laughter.

The confusion that arises in attempting to judge the facial expressions of the chimpanzee may be illustrated by reference to a popular film entitled, *School Pals*. In this picture curious antics of the chimpanzee are depicted. At the conclusion of the picture when presumably the chimpanzee had "played a trick" upon his adversary, it was desired to convey to the audience the impression that the chimpanzee was laughing. The animal's hand, hidden from view by a board fence, was pinched or otherwise painfully stimulated. This at once elicited the typical expression of anger (5) which, in the context, was interpreted by the audience as joy or laughter.

The photographs in Figure 4 represent six facial expressions of Joni, a five-year-old male chimpanzee: (1) quietude, (2) sadness, (3) laughter, (4) weeping, (5) anger, (6) excitement. These expressions and the situations which typically arouse them have been described by Foley approximately as follows:

1. The expression of *quietude* is the usual aspect of the chimpanzee when he is inactive, undisturbed, and remains in his customary environment.
2. *Depression* or *sadness*. Slight protrusion of tightly compressed lips, lifting of eyes. Observable when the ape is slightly depressed or saddened. Takes place when there is some slight delay in supplying his wants, such as in giving him food, drink, or sleeping accommodations. Noticeable upon refusal to comply with some of the chimpanzee's desires, such as to be taken into one's arms, to be given some desired object, to be permitted to escape from the cage. Also seen when experimenter or guardian for whom he feels particular affection shows signs of withdrawing. Such evidence of sadness is usually accompanied by extending of arms and soft whimpering.
3. The expression of *joy* is marked by facial movements entirely opposite to those of weeping (4). A kind of smile can be seen; the corners of the lips are slightly lifted; the mouth is open, and panting can be heard (but no laughter is ever to be observed). The joy-causing stimuli are exactly the opposite of those

Figure 4. Facial expressions of the chimpanzee. These photographs were originally taken by Mrs. Nadie Kohts (1935), of the Darwinian Museum, Moscow, U.S.S.R.; they are reproduced here with her special permission. The photographs were provided by the late Robert M. Yerkes and *courtesy of* Yale University Press.

causing depression or sadness, viz.: permission to leave the cage; the arrival of a guardian; a caress from him; playing or wrestling with him; being tickled by him. All such stimuli invariably evoke a smile or broad grin accompanied by "bustling" movements and invitation to play or "enticing" gestures.

4. *Weeping.* The infant chimpanzee begins to cry when his desires definitely fail to be granted, especially when his guardian withdraws, leaving him alone, or when he is confined to his cage in seclusion. He also cries in the presence of frightening stimuli (e. g., a stuffed wolf, a panther skin, large live animals, such as horses or cows). He opens his mouth wide so that the teeth and gums can be plainly seen, and tilts his head slightly backwards. The ape emits a continous deafening roar, somewhat resembling the crying of a child but incomparably louder. *No tears are ever to be seen.* This seems to be a characteristic feature of weeping in the chimpanzee. The paroxism of crying behavior is marked by complete closing of the eyelids and wrinkling of the upper part of the face.

5. The chimpanzee's *anger* is characterized by a wrinkling of the upper half of the face with a straining of the lips downward, so that not only his teeth but also his gums are plainly visible. The provoking stimulus may be the appearance of some supposedly offending animal or object which the chimpanzee is likely to attack, such as a hen, dog, or cat. Angry behavior is also to be observed toward strange people or in connection with protecting the objects which the ape understands to be his property. Again, anger usually appears when the chimpanzee is being punished, and is always present when some attack or assault is made upon the ape. Anger is expressed by a short hallooing sound, a threatening gesture of the hand, clenching of fists, and finally by striking the offending stimulus.

6. *Anxiety* and *excitement* are expressed in a trumpet-like projection of the lips, a bristling of the hair on face and body, and the vocalization of long, modulated, "oh-oh" sounds, which are a sixfold repetition of higher- and lower-pitched tones taken over a tierce within the octave.

A less pronounced form of excitement is expressed only by bristling of hair and protrusion of lips and is a common preliminary to the onset of the usual affective emotions of the ape: anger, fear, tantrum, buoyant joy, despair. When in extreme excitement the ape usually stands vertically erect and extends his arms toward the intriguing stimulus. If the emotion is not interrupted for some time the ape will repeatedly crouch down and again stand erect.

Conditions likely to call forth maximum excitement are as follows: an especial unexpectedness or novelty of the exciting stimulus; also, ignorance of the exact purport of the stimulus and concomitant absence of a specific response on the part of the ape. A concrete example: The chimpanzee was confronted with the sham fight of two men armed with truncheons and seemingly attacking one another. The make-believe combat was accompanied by loud shouting and much rattle and noise. The chimpanzee responded by plainly expressed maximum general excitement. [43-44, modified]

Hebb (1946*a*, 1946*b*) pointed out that a long-time acquaintance with chimpanzees is necessary to interpret their emotional behavior. Animals have characteristic ways of responding emotionally and an observer must know the history of the animal, for example, to distinguish between *rage* and *hate*. Temperamental traits and specific emotions are recognized as deviations from the normal base of behavior but that base must be known before the momentary emotional states can be recognized and interpreted.

Words Indicating Emotion. The word "emotion" is derived from the Latin *e* (out) and *movere* (to move).[1] Originally the word meant a moving out of one place into another, in the sense of a migration. Thus: "The divers emotions of that people [the Turks]" (1603). "Some accidental Emotion . . . of the Center of Gravity" (1695). The word came to mean a moving, stirring, agitation, perturbation, and was so used in a strictly physical sense. Thus: "Thunder . . . caused so great an Emotion in the air" (1708). "The waters continuing in the caverns . . . caused the emotion or earthquake" (1758). This physical meaning was transferred to political and social agitation, the word coming to mean *tumult*, popular disturbance. Thus: "There were . . . great stirres and emocions in Lombardye" (1579). "Accounts of Public Emotions, occasioned by the Want of Corn" (1709). Finally the word came to be used to designate any agitated, vehement, or excited mental state of the individual. Thus: "The joy of gratification is properly called an emotion" (1762).

In describing emotional states, writers have commonly referred to the parts of the body presumably determining those states. In the Bible one reads the phrase "bowels of mercy." Shakespeare in *Lucrece* writes: "To quench the coale that in his liver glowes." In a record from Waltham Abbey dated 1554 are these words: "This bishop was bloody Bonner, that corpulent tyrant, full (as one said) of guts and empty of bowels; . . . " Modern slang contains similar phrases: "He has plenty of gall"; "He got his spleen up"; "He could not stomach it"; "Have a heart"; "He lacked the guts"; "Es ist ihm etwas über die Leber gelaufen (He is peeved)."

It is surprising to find how many words in the English language today are used to designate emotions and attitudes. In an experiment upon the judging of emotion from facial expression, Kanner (1931) projected upon a screen a series of thirteen photographs, each of which portrayed the facial expression of some human emotion. Students in six classes were instructed to write "the best" descriptive term for each facial expression. Ignoring duplicates, the students used 365 terms descriptive of emotion and attitude—a term for each day of the year!

The words obtained were then grouped according to similarity of meaning. For example, the words *anxiety, apprehension, fear, awe, terror, horror* were placed in one group because they designate related

[1]This discussion of the etymology of emotion words is based upon the article "emotion" in Murray's dictionary. The first two paragraphs of this section are copied from the writer's book, *Motivation of behavior*. For a psychological discussion of terms which designate emotions and sentiments, see the book by Shand (1920).

emotional states and attitudes. No two of these words, however, have precisely the same shade of meaning. This is true also with the following group: *disfavor, resentment, anger, rage, temper tantrum.*

Kanner found that the terms could not all be placed in exclusive groups such as the two cited above. *Fear*, to illustrate, is related to *shyness* and *timidity*, but these two words are classified with *self-consciousness. Anger* is related to *hate* and *intolerance,* but these two words are placed in a separate group with *dislike*.

Kanner attempted to relate these 365 terms on the basis of their significance by drawing a line between two related terms. He produced a verbal maze within which one could easily get lost.

A major difficulty with emotion words is that an emotion, being complex, presents many facets to the observer. This point has been brought out in a brief note by Hunt (1935). What, he inquires, is *fear*? To one it is a sensory experience, "an awful feeling in my stomach, and cold, clammy hands." To another, fear is the attempt to escape from some danger such as a wild animal or a fire. It can be expressed: "Something is present which I would like to avoid." To yet another, a fear is the object which induces the emotional response, as when one says, "The thunderstorm is something I am afraid of." To someone else, fear is the awareness of danger with an ill-defined affective accompaniment.

The word *feeling* with its distinctly subjective connotation is even more broadly and confusingly used than *emotion*. On the use of the word *feeling*, Titchener (1924) wrote:

> The word "feeling" is used in a great variety of meanings. A thing feels rough or smooth, hard or soft, sharp or blunt, firm or shaky, warm or cold, elastic or brittle, thick or thin, clammy or oily. We ourselves feel hungry or thirsty, fresh or tired, energetic or lazy, strong or weak, well or ill. We also feel comfortable or uncomfortable, we feel at home or strange, at ease or ill at ease, natural or constrained; we feel happy, cheerful, restless, angry, irritable, eager, calm. We feel hopeful, despondent, grieved, hurt, injured, relieved, contented, gloomy, anxious, annoyed. We feel indifferent, and we feel sympathetic; we feel the difficulty of an objection, the truth of an argument, the nobility of a character, the sacredness of a belief. "Feel" and "feeling" seem, indeed, to be psychological maids of all work; they can do, in the sentence, practically anything that a verb and a substantive can be called upon to do. There is little hope, one would think, of turning them to strict psychological account, and of giving them a place in a list of technical terms. [225]

It is obvious from this discussion that there is little hope of obtaining a sound psychology of feeling and emotion from words alone!

Classification of the Emotions. In reviewing the systems of emotions which have been worked out by philosophers and psychologists, Kanner (1931) lists, among others, the following:

Descartes specified six primary emotions: admiration, love, hate, desire, joy, sadness. Spinoza mentioned only three: joy, sadness, desire. In more recent times Jorgensen claimed that there are six fundamental elements: fear, happiness, sorrow, want, anger, shyness. Watson, the rigid behaviorist, described three primary emotions: fear, rage, love. Mehran K. Thomson, in a lengthy list, enumerated dozens of "compound emotions" which he analyzed into their components. Shand listed seven primary emotions: fear, anger, joy, sorrow, curiosity, repugnance, disgust. For McDougall the primary emotions were: fear, disgust, wonder, anger, subjection, elation, tenderness. Allport reduced the facial expression of emotion to six elementary roots: pain-grief, surprise-fear, anger, disgust, pleasure, and intellectual attitudes such as doubt. Stratton described a system of emotions including undifferentiated excitement, elation, depression, and differentiated fear, anger, and affection. Yerkes gave a scale of moods, weak emotions, strong emotions, passions. James distinguished between the coarser emotions (grief, fear, rage, love) and the subtler emotions (including moral, intellectual and aesthetic feelings). So it goes.[1] There is some agreement but there are more discrepancies!

Instead of discussing the merits of existing classifications it would be more profitable to consider the nature of emotion and its relation to dynamic processes.

THE NATURE OF EMOTIONAL BEHAVIOR

In its primary meaning, *emotion* is an intense feeling, an affective consciousness. But this is only one aspect for there is more to emotion than purely subjective experience.

In terms of behavior as well as in experience, an emotion is an event, a process. Further, emotions have profound effects upon the development of dispositions, traits, and temperaments. When we speak of emotional conflicts that persist, of emotionalized attitudes, of emotionally maladjusted individuals, etc., we imply that some continuing states are emotional more than others. Viewed objectively, however, emotional behavior is an observed process and emotional states are postulates. The postulated states are revealed repeatedly in behavior.

A basic question for the objective scientist is this: How does emotional behavior differ from non-emotional behavior?

[1]If the reader cares to turn to the excellent survey of Gardiner, Metcalf, and Beebe-Center (1937), he will find there further evidence of the diversity of classifications of feelings and emotions. An account is given of the speculations which have been made through the centuries upon affective and motivational processes.

Try to think of the most non-emotional process that exists. You may think of sleeping or of some automatic and thoroughly habituated activity such as twiddling the thumbs or knitting. Perhaps you will think of reflex reactions or of logical reasoning about some problem. In these and similar examples the course of behavior moves smoothly with little or no interruption or disturbance.

Now try to think of the most highly emotional processes and states that you know. You may think of excited activities of a child who laughs, jumps up and down, claps his hands; or perhaps he cries, strikes another child, complains vocally. You may think of a biological crisis such as a primitive man met when he encountered a wild carnivorous predator—a cave bear, a lion, a leopard—and had to attack or defend himself and his dependents. You may think of bereavement, of grief and weeping, or of joy, hilarity, merriment, or of shame, guilt, remorse, embarrassment. All these conditions are highly emotional.

Now ask yourself: How do highly emotional activities differ from non-emotional? What adjectives best describe the contrast between emotional and non-emotional behaviors?

I think emotional behavior can be described as a perturbation, a departure, from a normal level of non-emotional activity. Although some forms of emotional behavior are highly excited, others are extremely quiescent as in deep depression. Although some forms are pleasant. others are unpleasant; and there are hedonically neutral or nearly neutral emotions that differ in the level of excitement or arousal. But all emotional reactions depart from a normal level of activity.

One basic contrast between emotional and non-emotional behavior is between organized, integrated, processes, on the one hand, and more or less disorganized, disintegrated, disturbed processes, on the other. This same contrast between integrated and disintegrated, organized and disorganized, aspects of emotional behavior applies to persisting states which we characterize as emotional or as non-emotional.

The Signs of Emotional Disorganization. Emotional behavior is frequently characterized by such terms as *disturbance, disruption, disorganization, upset, turbulence, outburst, perturbation, stirred-up state*, etc. These terms imply that when emotion arises, integrated activity is hindered or impaired in some way.

The view that emotion is a disturbed state or process is implied in everyday language by a variety of phrases. Thus when there is impending danger such as meeting a grizzly bear in the mountains, a city dweller may "go to pieces," "lose his head," "be unable to collect himself," "not know what to do." An experienced mountaineer would meet the situation calmly. An inexperienced man "gets rattled," "loses command of himself," "freezes in terror," or "runs wildly."

When emotion arises there is a disorganization of smooth, adaptive, behavior. In rage, great excitement, horror, elation, and other intense emotional states, there is a disruptive effect. Again, a man may be "beside himself" with joy or grief. The emotional seizure hinders whatever adaptive behavior is in progress when the emotion occurs.

What are the signs of emotional disorganization? Consider the following:

First, the performance of rats in a maze is impaired by anger and fear. Higginson (1930) evoked anger by pinching an animal's tail and stimulating the nose. Fear was evoked by placing the rat in a cage with a cat, the rat being confined to a small inside compartment which the cat could sniff and explore. The rats were tested for maze performance immediately after emotional stimulation and their behavior was compared with that under quiescent, non-emotional conditions. Higginson found that the emotionally excited animals showed an *increase* in the following measures: time spent in running; total time required to learn the maze and the number of trials required to master it; variability in performance from trial to trial; the total distance traversed; the number of errors made in learning the maze. In general, the emotionally excited rats were more prone to enter blind alleys than quiescent animals. They were more variable in performance and slower in maze learning.

Second, when rats are frightened there are two patterns of behavior that may appear. In a strange situation there may be increased exploratory activity with emotional urination and defecation (Hall, 1934). In fright, rats and other animals may "freeze" remaining immobile. See page 239.

If a rat is greatly frightened or injured, he may dash for shelter and remain quietly under cover. If mildly frightened, the level of his activity may be lowered. An example of this is found in an experiment by Patrick (1931).

In this experiment ten rats were placed, one at a time, in a Dashiell maze—an apparatus that invites exploration. Under quiescent conditions the amount of random behavior in the maze was measured. Other rats were placed in the maze under different conditions: two electric buzzers placed on opposite sides of the apparatus were sounded continuously. When the buzzers sounded the animals crouched, quivered, and moved about very little in the maze. Their behavior suggested caution and timidity. If the random behavior of the first group is taken as a basis for comparison, the activity level of the frightened group is found to be lowered by 27 percent. From this we conclude that noise from the buzzers produced a lowering of the exploratory activity of the animals and that relative inactivity is a sign of fear.

Third, during emotional excitement there are changes in motor manifestations, such as speed of movement, muscular coordination, and steadiness. Some of these changes can be illustrated by reference to a study of "razzing" by Laird (1923).

Laird utilized a fraternity initiation to study the effects of "razzing" upon a group of eight pledges. Tests were given under two conditions. The tests were first given under conditions of friendly competition, the members of the chapter and other pledges watching the performance with respectful silence. Two nights later the tests were repeated in a similar way except that there was free-for-all "razzing" of the pledges which consisted of personal remarks, ranging from mildly disparaging to highly uncomplimentary ones—even to actual insults.

The tests measured speed of tapping, muscular coordination (three-hole-coordination test), and steadiness of movement. Results demonstrated that for all subjects there was a loss of steadiness during "razzing." In results of the tapping test and the muscular-coordination test, there were changes in the scores of all subjects but the changes were not uniform within the group. In speed of tapping, five subjects showed a gain and three a loss under "razzing." In muscular coordination, three subjects showed a gain in scores and five a loss; for the group as a whole the average showed a loss.

These individual differences in scores are not surprising. We know from other evidence that excitement sometimes facilitates a skilled performance and sometimes interferes, depending on the degree of excitement and varying from person to person. Persons react differently to a social situation.

Fourth, during emotional excitement there are obvious changes in the level of neuromuscular arousal. In joy, a child jumps up and down, claps his hands, laughs, and makes excessive muscular movements which appear to be random and aimless. In pain and agony there are writhing and struggling, vocal outcries, slashing with the arms, and various other manifestations.

In the calm, asthenic, emotions—sadness, grief, depression—the level of arousal is abnormally low. In many emotional states, therefore, the level of activity clearly departs from that of the non-emotional condition.

Fifth and finally, during emotional disturbances there are marked bodily changes in the activity of glands and smooth muscles that are controlled by the autonomic nervous system. Many of these bodily changes are outwardly visible during emotional excitement. Others are hidden from view but can be measured by physiological techniques. These bodily changes will be considered in detail in Chapters V and VI. A single example will suffice for purposes of illustration.

In a report of studies of emotional behavior made by Soviet physiologists, Simonov (1969) gives a small bit of evidence. He measured the frequency of heartbeats per minute of Russian cosmonauts shortly before the lift-off and compared this with their normal pulse rate. His figures follow:

Cosmonaut	8 days before flight	4 hours before flight	5 minutes before flight
U. Gagarin	64	65	108
G. Titov	69	69	107
A. Nikolaev	64	72	112
P. Popovich	58	56	117

It is important to add that no one of the above-mentioned signs of emotional disorganization is invariably present during all emotional disturbances. But if the above signs are considered collectively, they give a picture of the kind of phenomena designated by the terms *disorganization* and *disturbance*.

Dissociated Function during Emotion. It should be pointed out that emotion disrupts the activity in progress at the time an emotion occurs.

Everyone has heard accounts of someone who in the face of danger acted wisely with a high level of energy expenditure and little disorganization, thus saving the situation from total disaster. In a critical situation the organism becomes re-integrated for defense or attack or some other activity that is biologically adaptive.

Two examples of human behavior during a crisis have been given, from first-hand information, by Stratton (1925). One of these illustrations is described below. The account is that of an aviator during a hair-raising experience when his airplane was temporarily out of control.

There are two remarkable features of the incident. First, during the immediate danger and crisis there was no general disruption of behavior—no breakdown of motor integrations, no confusion or blurring of consciousness. On the contrary, the quick thinking and delicate movements needed to gain control of an airplane in a tail-spin and to discover the source of trouble remained available and were utilized. Second, all the time this exciting activity was going on, there was a vivid re-living of early experiences, an imaginal reinstatment with astonishing detail and rapidity. The mental imagery was functionally dissociated from the skilled and habituated activities required by the situation.

The account of the incident, as given by Stratton, follows:

> During my service as an aviator I had two accidents which were of psychological interest. [Only the first is here described.]
>
> The first of them was at Dallas, Texas, in June or July of 1918, while I was doing that part of my training which is known as "stunts." Before going up on this particular day I, as usual, examined carefully my controls, and found that they were working right. I then went up to a height of about 5,500 feet, having planned the order in which I should go through my stunts, so that I should make as good a showing as possible to my instructor on the field below. My first stunt was a loop, and this I went through all right and straightened out. Then I found that my elevator-control was stuck. I went up on the rise for a second loop, but instead of letting my ship whip-stall and thus running the risk of permanently damaging my controls, I kicked the rudder to the right and dropped into a tail-spin.
>
> It was at this time that a dual personality came into play. I had a rapid survey of my life, not as though I were looking at scenes of my past, but as though I were doing and living them again.
>
> Yet I was conscious at the same time of having to manage my ship. For as soon as I started down in the tail-spin I realized that I had a certain amount of time, and I went carefully over the different controls. I tried the rudder and found that it worked all right. I then moved "the stick," and its movements showed that the ailerons were working, but that the elevator was stuck. I thought that the elevator-wire might have become entangled in the leather slot where the elevator-wire goes through the covering to the outside. So I pushed the stick slowly and steadily forward to overcome such an obstruction. In shoving forward on my stick I felt the tension on my belt, which showed that the control was in some way entangled with the belt. So I reached around and found there the loose end of a wire used to support the triangle of the safety-belt, and which had been left too long and had become entangled in the wire which worked the elevator. I pulled this loose end out, and my elevator then worked perfectly, and I straightened out my ship. I was then at a height of about 1,500 feet, having fallen about 4,000 feet since the accident began. (The aviator estimated the rate of his fall to have been about 150 feet a second, giving a total duration of about 27 seconds for the 4,000 feet.
>
> During this fall I re-lived more events of my life than I can well enumerate. These were in an orderly series, very distinct, and I cannot recall that anything was out of its place.
>
> 1. One of the first things that I remembered was learning my ABC's. My grandfather was sitting in a tall easy-chair with castors attached to a frame upon which the chair rocked. I remembered him sitting as I am sitting now; and I was on the floor. That was between the Christmas when I was over two-and-a-half years old and the February when I was three. That was the first picture I had.
>
> 2. Another was when I had to stay home when my mother had to leave me and teach school for a while. It was late in the fall, and I was looking out of the window and I saw her pass the window and go off to school. (The original of this occurred when he was about three-and-a-half years old.)
>
> 3. Next I was playing under a grape-arbor in the back yard at my grandmother's. In throwing things at the little chicks, I accidentally killed one of them. Then I buried it, feeling very sorry over what I had done. (When he was about three-and-a-half or four years old.)

4. Another one was during a very cold winter, when I went up to my grandmother's, and had a long drive with a horse and buggy from the station, about seven miles, and there was a great family reunion. (When he was about seven years old.),

5. Another was a very cold night in Kansas City when we were coming home from a play and got stalled on the street cars because the snow was so heavy. (When he was about nine years old.)

6. Another was of fishing for small cray-fish in a little slough in a park in Kansas City. (At the age of nine.)

7. Another was when I was on a journey, and my folks told me that we were coming to California. I thought we were going from Kansas City to somewhere else in Kansas. It was when we were out some distance. I remember the isolated group in the stationhouse when they told me where we were going. (At the age of nine.)

8. Another was when I was cutting some wood in the back yard in El Paso, Texas, after I had left California. It was a very clear moonlit night. It happened that at this time I was wondering what I was going to do some five or ten years later. It was just like I was there again. I cut the wood, and distinctly saw the moonlight, the axe, and the block again. (at the age of eleven.)

9. Another was very distinct. It happened just a year before I went into the service. I went up here to Lake Tahoe with a party. We arrived about twelve o'clock, Sunday night, having come over a foot and a half of snow at the summit. There was hoar-frost all over the rocks, and ice on the edge of the lake. [Then follows in minute detail an account of swimming in the icy lake at midnight, as the result of a "dare"] I was doing it again; I felt the cold air, and saw the hoar-frost. [48-50]

The aviator's experience can be paralleled by that of others who have reported re-living their past while constructively meeting a serious crisis. In an emotional situation the individual is stirred not only to swift adaptive action but also to a lightning chain of thought. There is consideration of the present problem, of the prospects that one or another course of action will succeed, and at the same time a detailed recollection of the past. The chain of memories from the past really indicates a temporary dissociation of the thought processes. (Possibly, temporary dissociation should be added to the foregoing list of signs of emotional disorganization.)

This illustration shows that in times of danger an individual may be capable of acting in a well-integrated adaptive manner. Thought processes can move more rapidly than under normal conditions. Ideas appear in great number; some are accepted, others rejected. The process of sifting goes on with almost lightning rapidity while the excited individual is carrying out some course of adaptive action.

Stratton's example, however, clearly indicates a degree of mental dissociation during the great excitement. The aviator's thoughts of childhood, reviewed rapidly during the crisis in the air, have no conceivable utility in solving the immediate problem. The truth seems to be that during the great excitement there was excessive mental activity.

Adaptive thought and action occurred simultaneously with mental activity that was not serviceable in the face of danger. There was functional dissociation.

Emotional Disorganization *versus* **Organized Activity.** During an emotion the organism is for a time "out of" or "away from" integrated, planned, purposive, activity. This state of emotional disorganization may be acute—brief, intense, disruptive—or it may be a chronic maladjustment of long duration. Psychiatrists, clinical psychologists, and others who are concerned with human welfare, commonly speak of persisting emotional conflicts, emotional disturbances and maladjustments, affects such as anxiety, hostility, depression, euphoria, and others. These terms designate more or less persisting states of disorganization within the individual. The aim of the clinician is to restore composure, complacency, peace of mind, balance, adjustment to an environmental situation.

Acute emotional upsets are produced by such dynamic conditions as frustration, insult, failure, bereavement, unexpected news (good or bad), etc. An animal is emotionally excited by the appearance of a predator, the threat to his security, invasion of his territory, infliction of injury, pain, enticement by a mate, and other conditions of vital importance.

Now it is true that emotional disturbances frequently lead to highly energized, integrated, directed, behavior such as flight from a threatening situatiom, attack upon an enemy, pursuit of a mate, or defense of the young. Well-organized built-in patterns of attack and defense are present in many animals, including man. Organized, goal-oriented behavior is commonly the immediate outcome of an emotional upset. The resulting behavior is biologically useful, highly adaptive, as Darwin pointed out.

Leeper (1948) challenged the view that emotion is a disorganized response. Young (1949) defended the view that emotion is an acute or persisting affective disturbance of psychological origin.

Bindra (1955) wrote that disorganization and organization are successive stages in the development of all behavior. Consider, for example, the behavior of a rat in a maze. At first the naive animal is frightened when placed in a strange environment as shown by emotional defecation and cautious exploratory activity. With successive trials in the maze the animal's behavior becomes increasingly goal-oriented, smooth, organized ; signs of emotional disturbance disappear.

Smith (1958) slightly changed Bindra's interpretation. Smith took a broader view of motivation. If *all* behavior is motivated (in the sense of being causally determined), then behavior is emotional to the degree that it is (*a*) highly motivated, and (*b*) poorly organized. The degree of organization, Smith stated, can be defined in terms of the strength of habit that develops out of an initially disorganized state. The thoroughly habituated rat is not at all emotionally disturbed.

I will add that some emotional disturbances persist indefinitely and that from a developmental point of view individuals with unsolved emotional conflicts must be regarded as emotionally immature or unstable. Further, emotional disorganization is not a necessary condition for learning to occur. For example, in the acquisition of a human skill, such as typewriting, there is increasing integration with practice. The entire process of learning can be free from emotional disorganization. Duffy (1941), I am sure, would agree.

Integration, organization, within the nervous system, occurs at different levels. Sherrington (1911) demonstrated integration in the reflexes of the spinal dog. Some of our experimental studies of food preferences demonstrated hedonic integration at the level of the limbic and related neural systems. Total integration involves the cerebral cortex and cerebral dominance over the built-in patterns of response that appear during emotional excitement. If there is a conflict or blocking at the cortical level, integrated patterns of behavior at some lower level may appear. Possibly this is what happens during emotional upsets.

Emotion as Facilitative. Opposed to the view that emotion is a disorganized, disturbed, affective process and state, is the view that "emotion" facilitates and furthers adaptive behavior. For example, Carl Rogers (1951) writes:

> *Emotion accompanies and in general facilitates such goal-directed behavior, the kind of emotion being related to the seeking versus the consummatory aspects of behavior, and the intensity of the emotion being related to the perceived significance of the behavior for the maintenance and enhancement of the organism.*

The view that emotion facilitates goal-directed behavior is very different from the view that emotion is an acute affective disturbance. But there would be little room for argument if for "emotion" we substituted terms like *affective process, interest, mood*, and the like. Positive forms of affective processes *are* facilitative and organizing rather than disrupting. Feelings of self-confidence and assurance come from success and achievement and are not at all disruptive; they are facilitative. Negative affectivity also may lead to adaptive behavior.

The matter boils down to a question of terminology and definition. "Emotion," as Rogers, Hilgard, and others, have used the term, is equivalent to "affective process." We know that some affective processes are associated with facilitation and others with inhibition. Hence "emotion" may either facilitate or inhibit performance. But I have followed a tradition in defining emotion as a special form of affective process—a form that is described as an acute affective disturbance, a departure from normal activity.

Emotion and Motivation. Bindra (1959), in considering the classification of motivational phenomena, wrote:

> The term *emotional behavior* is used as a collective name for the behavior of anger, fear, joy, and the like, and *motivated behavior* as a general label for the phenomena such as hunger behavior (food seeking and eating), sex behavior and drug addiction behavior. Now, although emotional behavior and motivated behavior are often treated as if they were distinct classes of behavior, they are not so in fact. Over twenty years ago, Duffy. . . painstakingly started to examine the various criteria that had been suggested as the differentiating marks of emotional and motivated behavior. . . She found all such differentiating criteria to be inadequate, for they failed to set apart unequivocally the phenomena which, conventionally, are grouped together either as emotional behavior or as motivated behavior. . . .

Bindra argued that the distinction between emotional behavior and motivated behavior, on the basis of degree of goal directedness, is untenable. Emotional behavior is commonly regarded as disorganized, lacking goal direction. Motivated behavior, in contrast, is regarded as organized, goal-directed activity. But, Bindra argued, disorganized and organized behavior are different developmental stages. The same sequence of development appears (from disorganized to organized behavior) when we consider emotional behavior and motivated behavior. Lack of organization is an early stage of development; organization and goal direction, a later stage. We cannot distinguish between emotional and motivated behavior in terms of goal direction. That is because the degree-of-goal-direction dimension cuts across the traditional categories and cannot be employed as a differentiating criterion.

Again, Bindra argued, we cannot reliably distinguish between emotional and motivated behavior on the basis of external and internal origin. It is true that conditions that evoke motivated behavior appear to be mostly internal, whereas those that evoke emotional behavior seem mostly environmental. It can be shown, however, that both types of response patterns are determined by both internal and environmental conditions and can be controlled by manipulating either one of these sets of conditions.

The outcome of Bindra's argument is that *there is no single criterion that can be used reliably for distinguishing between emotional behavior and motivated behavior*. This view is unquestionably sound.

Emotion is an exceedingly complex event. Perhaps psychologists should study separately the very real differences between emotional and non-emotional forms of behavior. Five such differences are the following:

1. Emotional behavior is disturbed, disorganized. Non-emotional behavior is organized and frequently goal directed. Reflexive patterns, however, are organized but not goal directed.
2. Emotional behavior typically originates within a *psychological* situation which always contains an environmental factor. Many forms of non-emotional behavior originate from internal tissue conditions.
3. Emotional behavior is characterized by visceral changes regulated by the autonomic nervous system. In non-emotional behavior there is a lower degree of visceralization and autonomic involvement.
4. Emotional behavior is characterized by a weakening or loss of cerebral control and the appearance of response patterns that are integrated at subcortical levels. Non-emotional behavior is characterized by a higher degree of cerebral control and dominance.
5. Emotional behavior, whether viewed subjectively or objectively, is characterized as intensely affective. Non-emotional behavior is more neutral, indifferent, affectively.

Now if Bindra, Duffy, and others are correct that no one of these contrasts can serve as an adequare criterion for distinguishing between emotional and non-emotional behavior, it may be necessary to replace the concept of emotion with five or more specific concepts. But if we can combine all of these contrasts, we arrive at a complex picture of emotion: *When an individual is affectively disturbed by the environmental situation to such an extent that his cerebral control is weakened or lost and sub-cortical patterns and visceral changes appear, that individual is emotional.* The emotional disturbance is a real though exceedingly complex, event.

Regarding the complexity of emotion, Lindsley (1951) has written:

> Emotion is one of the most complex phenomena known to psychology. It is complex because it involves so much of the organism at so many levels of neural and chemical integration. Both subjectively and objectively its ramifications are diffuse and intermingled with other processes. Perhaps therein lies the uniqueness, and possibly the major significance of emotion. [473]

Instead of regarding "motivated behavior" and "emotional behavior" as separate classes, or categories, of activity, as Bindra and other psychologists have done, I prefer to state that *all* behavior is motivated (causally determined) and that behavior is more or less emotional according to the degree of affective disturbance that is present in the arousal.

EVALUATION OF FEELING AND EMOTION

The view that feelings and emotions are biologically useful is a teleological interpretation implying, in Darwinian terms, that the prime value of life is simply to survive. Similarly, the view that emotion is a disturbed process or state—a disorganization or perturbation of purposive behavior—is evaluative. This view carries the implication that emotion is a harmful or undesirable or, at best, a useless process.

Pure science deals with *facts* and not with *values*. Despite this distinction, men of science have been much interested in and concerned about questions that involve value. Weinberg (1970), a scientist and administrator, wrote a paper entitled, "The Axiology of Science." He pointed out that when limited funds are available, administrators and government agents must make value judgments and decisions. Questions like this must be answered: Which is more important—a research project in oceanography or an exploration of space or a search for a cure for cancer or an agricultural experiment, etc.? Limited funds must be allocated among many requests.

In the practical affairs of living, also, evaluations are inevitable. Parents, ministers, propagandists, men of science, and others, instill in children and youths ideas of good and bad, right and wrong, good taste and bad taste, truth and error, etc. We evaluate many things: musical performance, paintings, political ideas, traits of character, the quality of food, services, and so on. We cannot escape evaluative behavior. The man of science may claim that his research is value-free. But despite this claim he values truth, clarity of statement, logical consistency, objectivity, integrity. These are intellectual values.

In the discussion of a paper presented by Howard (1928) at the Wittenberg symposium of feelings and emotions is the following question and answer:

> *Professor Thompson*: Is it not the biological and physiological purpose of emotion to protect the person rather than to confuse him?
>
> *Dr. Howard*: I have always been interested in that question, as to the value of emotional states, and the conclusion to which I come is that they have absolutely no value at all, but represent a defect in human nature. I cannot see any other conclusion you can come to. [147]

The Utility of Pleasantness and Unpleasantness. Various writers have associated pleasantness with processes that are beneficial to the organism and unpleasantness with processes and conditions that are harmful and resisted. See, for example, the views of Troland and Arnold (pages 107-8.)

In an important series of experiments Cabanac (1971) has shown that a stimulus can feel pleasant or unpleasant depending upon its *usefulness* in maintaining homeostasis. He made a series of experiments with temperatures, tastes, and odors. I will consider the work with temperatures.

In the thermal experiments the subject was immersed in a stirred water bath while making affective reports after a 30-second thermal stimulation of the left hand. The responses differed according to the thermal state of the subject. When the internal body temperature was high (hyperthermic), the cold or cool stimuli were pleasant and the warm or hot stimuli were unpleasant. When the internal body temperature was low (hypothermic), the cold or cool stimuli were unpleasant and the warm or hot stimuli were pleasant. The temperatures of the bath (15° and 45° C) were between the lower and upper thresholds of pain so that pain was not involved in the response.

A given nonpainful thermal stimulus could be perceived as either pleasant or unpleasant according to the internal thermal state of the subject. A hypothermic subject will *like* a hot, even slightly burning, stimulus; a hyperthermic subject will *like* a biting cold stimulus even when the temperature is slightly painful. Therefore, Cabanac argues, pleasure occurs when sensation indicates the presence of a stimulus which helps to maintain homothermia—a relatively constant internal temperature (which for man is about 37° C). The affective reactions are useful when considered in relation to the homeostasis of temperature.

Cabanac's subjects could readily discriminate temperatures and could easily distinguish between sensation and the affective response. The affective-motivational component of perception, Cabanac states, depends upon signals from inside the body since one and the same physical stimulus can be perceived as either pleasant or unpleasant depending upon the internal state of homothermia.

During fever the set value of the internal body temperature is higher than in the healthy state. Cabanac found that the affective reactions to thermal stimuli during fever are relative to the internal body temperature.

Cabanac proposed the term *alliesthesia*, coming from *esthesia* (meaning sensation) and *allios* (meaning changed), to indicate that a given external stimulus can be changed, i.e., perceived as either pleasant or unpleasant depending upon signals coming from inside the body. The hedonic processes, therefore, are physiologically useful in so far as the temperature-regulating processes are involved.

Alliesthesia was also demonstrated for tastes and odors as well as for temperatures. Cabanac found that sweet-tasting sucrose and an orange odor were pleasant when the subjects fasted, but the gustative and olfactive stimuli were unpleasant after the subjects had ingested 100 grams of glucose in water. The internal signals, during satiation, that produced these hedonic changes are not known.

The Utility and Inutility of Emotional Behavior. The responses of escape and defense, as we observe them in nature, are not reactions to actual injury so much as they are responses to situations that are premonitory of injury or pain. Thus the deer is startled by rustling leaves, by a moving form, or by a strange odor; and he flees before the lion gets his fangs into the flesh. The terrified cat climbs a tree (let us hope!) before the dog catches her. The utility of these activities in protecting the organism is self-evident.

The utility principle was extended by Cannon (1929) and collaborators to include the internal bodily changes that occur during emotional excitement. During a biological emergency the internal changes mobilize the energies of the body for a vigorous fight or a prolonged race for life.

Darwin (1872) interpreted outward expressions of emotions in terms of their utility in the struggle for existence. But Darwin, importantly, also noted that many emotional expressions have no apparent utility in the vital struggle. Thus:

> When animals suffer from an agony of pain, they generally writhe about with frightful contortions; and those which habitually use their voices utter piercing cries or groans. Almost every muscle of the body is brought into strong action. With man the mouth may be closely compressed, or more commonly the lips are retracted, with the teeth clenched or ground together. There is said to be "gnashing of teeth" in hell; and I have plainly heard the grinding of molar teeth of a cow which was suffering acutely from inflammation of the bowels. The female hippopotamus in the Zoölogical Gardens, when she produced her young, suffered greatly; she incessantly walked about, or rolled on her sides, opening and closing her jaws, and chattering her teeth together. With man the eyes stare wildly as in horrified astonishment, or the brows are heavily contracted. Perspiration bathes the body, and drops trickle down the face. The circulation and respiration are much affected. Hence the nostrils are generally dilated and often quiver; or the breath may be held until the blood stagnates in the purple face. If the agony be severe and prolonged, these signs all change; utter prostration follows, with fainting or convulsions. [69]

In this description of agony are listed many useless, random activities–grinding of the teeth, staring of the eyes, perspiration, changes in circulation, in respiration, etc. According to Darwin, such bodily changes are quite useless, of no service to the animal. When the nervous system is highly excited these excessive bodily changes occur. They should be explained in terms of the structural organization of the nervous system.

Excessive and useless activity is present not only in the unpleasant emotions of painful excitement and agony but also in pleasant emotional states. Consider, for example, the useless activities present in the emotion of joy. Darwin described some of them in these words:

> Under a transport of joy or of vivid pleasure, there is a strong tendency of various purposeless movements, and to the utterance of various sounds. We see this in our young children, in their loud laughter, clapping of hands, and jumping for joy; in the bounding and barking of a dog when going out to walk with his master; and in the frisking of a horse when turned out into an open field. Joy quickens the circulation, and this stimulates the brain, which again reacts on the whole body. [75-76]

Thus in emotional upset there are excessive, useless movements.

One final instance of the inutility of the bodily changes of emotion is found in those authentic instances of death from terror. A clear example of this was observed by the writer.

A pet rabbit had been reared from birth to maturity in a small cage. Occasionally he had been allowed to play upon a fenced-in lawn. On one such occasion the rabbit escaped under the fence and began to nibble the grass on the other side. A barking dog approached. The rabbit ran to shelter under a spreading, thorny shrub. The dog barked loudly and jumped excitedly about the shrub while the rabbit crouched in an inaccessible place. It was several minutes before the dog could be chased away and the rabbit rescued. Examination of the latter showed that there had been no injury of any kind–no bone broken, no blood shed. Placed in his cage, however, the terrified rabbit crouched quietly in the corner without moving, and in a few hours was dead. It is reasonable to assume that the rabbit, young and healthy but greatly sheltered as a pet, literally died as a consequence of the bodily changes which occurred during the fright and following it. The surgeon Crile, incidentally, has demonstrated that terror produces observable changes within the cells of a rabbit's brain.

Critique of the Utility and Inutility Doctrines. When one attempts to evaluate emotional excitement as useful or useless, certain basic facts must be kept in mind. Utility always means usefulness for some definite end. Utility is relative. An act which is useful from one point of view may be useless or even injurious from another. This is illustrated in the field of surgery. A wounded soldier has to decide whether to let the surgeon amputate his leg or save it and run the risk of losing his life. The amputation may be useful in saving life but most detrimental to locomotion following the operation! An illustration in the field of psychology is that of the child jumping up and down with delight over the promise of a picnic. He is performing an act that has no usefulness from the standpoint of purposive activity but which gives the child a useful release of energy.

Again, the so-called expressions of emotion which lack utility in terms of individual survival may be regarded as having *social* utility so far as they are signals to other members of the group. In man, there are facial contortions, gestures, vocalizations; and, in animals, erection of fur or feathers, drawing back (or erection) of the ears—all of which serve to communicate to others the existence of danger. The emotional expressions, in fact, may have developed on account of their utility in controlling the behavior of other members of the social group, as Craig (1922) pointed out in a note extending Darwin's utility principle.

Psychologists and others who have stressed the utility principle in emotion have been at a loss to discover any use for the responses of laughing and weeping. As forms of overt behavior they are useless. On this point Crile (1915) wrote:

> Even superficial analysis of the phenomena of both laughter and crying shows them to be without any external motor purpose; the respiratory mechanism is intermittently stimulated and inhibited; and the shoulder and arm muscles indeed, many muscles of the trunk and extremities are, as far as any external design is concerned, purposelessly contracted and released until the kinetic energy mobilized by excitation is utilized. During this time the facial expression gives the index to the mental state. [102]

Yet, from another standpoint, laughing and weeping are useful so far as they provide an outlet for the bodily tension present in joy and grief. To illustrate, if a mother has anxiously watched the course of a serious illness in her child, while expending the maximal amount of energy caring for him, she may continue in a state of tenseness until the child either recovers or dies. If sudden relief comes, as when the child passes the crisis of pneumonia the mother will readily smile and laugh; if tired, she may cry. If death occurs, there is a sudden withdrawal of the necessity for further action, and the mother may now cry aloud and even continue to perform various acts which no longer are useful in the physical care of the child.

Outcries and writhing in pain or weeping in grief may similarly be interpreted as useful in that they furnish a motor outlet when the organism is highly excited. In a word, many emotional processes may have *physiological* utility even when they lack *behavioral* utility. Hence, as noted above, an emotional response which is useless when viewed from one standpoint may be useful when considered from another angle.

A point in the critique of the utility and inutility doctrines is this: An emotional disturbance which is wholly useless at the time of its occurrence may result in the formation of an attitude or motive which is of definite utility. For example, it is said that Abraham Lincoln, when a youth, saw slaves being sold on the New Orleans market and was so greatly disturbed by the experience that he said, "If ever I have the chance, I will hit that thing hard." The emotional disturbance, while apparently useless at the time of its occurrence, left him with a definite attitude against slavery. Lincoln's later decision to free the slaves was doubtless determined in part by this attitude, resulting from his early emotional experience.

The Science of Axiology. In another chapter I have asked, "Is a science of values possible?" See page 107. This question turns Weinberg's title (The Axiology of Science) around.

Since science deals with *facts*, a *science of values* must observe and analyze evaluative processes on the factual level. I have argued that when a rat accepts one food and rejects another he is making evaluative reactions (Young, 1968). If the animal develops a consistent preference between two foods, this behavior implies that one reaction (accepting food A) is better in some way than another (accepting food B). These primitive behaviors imply evaluation. They can readily be observed, without straining a point, as *facts* of evaluative behavior. If a science of values is possible, it must rest upon a matter-of-fact analysis of evaluative behavior. I am sure that, apart from food preferences, animals, including man, repeatedly make evaluative reactions and judgments.

Axiology as an *art* is something different. The control of human behavior is a practical *art* that deals with values, attitudes, desires, interests, aversions, beliefs, habit systems, and the like. The educator, propagandist, advertiser, politician, evangelist, and all the rest of us, more or less clearly realize that the *art* of influencing behavior and getting along with people depends upon a practical understanding of human feelings and motivations. We know that the appeal to feeling and emotion is more effective in producing action than a coldly logical argument. See page 56.

A *science of values,* as distinct from the art of controlling human behavior, deals with the *facts* of evaluative behavior and development. Evaluative reactions are empirical facts.

What can be expected from a science of values? Certainly not a computerized oracle that will tell people what they *ought* to do! Erik H. Erikson, the psychoanalyst, has said that *is* and *ought* are different sides of the same cloth. This could mean that there are both factual and evaluative ways of looking at the same events. I believe, however, that some forms of behavior (acceptance, rejection, preference) can easily and correctly be observed as evaluative behaviors.

A science of values describes the evaluative behavior of organisms, including children and human adults. It describes the development of evaluative attitudes, the establishing of goals, the learning of habits that are instrumental in goal-oriented behavior. It studies the evaluative aspects of feelings and emotions and the nature and role of affective arousals in the regulation and development of behavior. It examines human evaluations in the social context—their nature, acquisition, conflict, and the stabilizing of systems of values including the hierarchical relations. It describes what happens *as a fact* when values and purposes conflict. All this and more can reasonably be expected from a genuine science of values. Axiology, I believe, is an important part of dynamic psychology.

Values are not purely subjective phenomena. As I noted, they can be observed objectively in subhuman animals. And evaluative hierarchies can be manipulated experimentally in the laboratory.

THE DEFINITION OF EMOTION

I will define emotion as *an affectively disturbed process or state of psychological origin.*

To clarify this definition a few comments will be helpful. Emotions are exceedingly complex phenomena. They are revealed in various ways—in conscious experience, in behavior, through internal bodily changes. It is necessary, therefore, to consider the nature of emotion piecemeal from several points of view.

Rapaport (1950) wrote that a great deal of the confusion concerning the definition of emotion has been due to failure of investigators to distinguish between the *phenomena* of emotion and the underlying *dynamics*. The phenomena of emotion are complex and can be analyzed from different points of view. The underlying dynamics are postulated to explain the facts.

The phenomena of emotion present three main aspects. First, an emotion is a conscious experience that is *felt* and directly reported. All of us *feel* anger, fear, joy, sorrow, love, grief, shame, guilt, disgust, amusement, and other affective experiences. Second, an emotion is a bit of behavior. Everyone has observed *emotional behavior* in animals and human beings: hostile excitement, friendly vocalizing, excited jumping about, lustful approach, terrified flight, cries of fear and pain, joyful behavior, and other patterns. Third, an emotion is a *physiological process*. During emotion there is marked activity in the autonomic nervous system and viscera, electrical and chemical changes in cortical and subcortical centers. The physiological psychologist is concerned with this vital aspect of the emotional event.

It is an article of scientific faith that these diverse aspects reveal a single underlying emotional event. We believe that the different facts, no matter how complex, can be fitted together into a single account.

There are a number of criteria which are useful in distinguishing emotional from non-emotional conditions. Several of these will be considered in the following sections. It should be said in advance, however, that no single criterion, considered by itself alone, is fully adequate to define the concept of emotion. But when the first three of the following criteria are met simultaneously, the process or state under consideration *is* definitely an emotional one.

These three criteria are the following: (1) An emotion is an *affectively disturbed* condition of the organism. (2) An emotional reaction involves *visceral changes* mediated by the autonomic nervous system. (3) An emotion originates within a *psychological situation* which includes dynamic processes instigated by perception, memory, imagination, and related cognitive precesses. The psychological situation includes the experiencing individual in relation to his total life-situation.

Emotion as an Affective Disturbance or Upset. The above definition describes an emotion as an affectively disturbed process or state which is revealed in various ways.

This aspect of emotion has been widely recognized. An apt illustration is found in a paper by Howard (1928). To bring out his point he uses the case of a man unexpectedly meeting a bear in the woods.

> In the disruptive state called emotional the victim can be said, in one sense, "not to know what to do." The bear is too much for him. He has no ready-made responses to draw upon, and too little resources in the way of reaction patterns to enable a reconstitutive process to build up an appropriate response. From another point of view the victim can be said to think of too many things to do. For, upon sight of the bear, he tends simultaneously to yell, to climb a tree, to run away, to throw a stone, to grasp a club, and what not. All of these impulses seek motor expression, get jammed in the process, and the result is a state of discoordination. Accompanying this disruptive condition we have those strange visceral and vegetative phenomena commonly recognized as characteristic of the emotional condition.

Also emphasizing the disruptive nature of the emotional state, Claparede (1928) wrote:

> Emotions occur precisely when adaptation is hindered for any reason whatever. The man who can run away does not have the emotion of fear. Fear occurs only when flight is impossible. Anger is displayed only when one cannot strike his enemy. . . . The uselessness, or even the harmfulness of emotion, is known to

> everyone. Here is an individual who would cross a street; if he is afraid of automobiles, he loses his composure and is run over. Sorrow, joy, anger, by enfeebling attention or judgment, often make us commit regrettable acts. In brief, the individual, in the grip of an emotion "loses his head."

Watson (1929), who has emphasized the view that an emotion is a pattern of response which can be conditioned and reconditioned, wrote:

> There would seem to be no question but that the immediate effect of the exciting stimuli upon organized activity . . . is always disruptive. If an individual is preparing a lecture or writing a book or rendering a musical selection, any strong emotional stimulus at least temporarily disrupts and blocks the organized activity.

Dockeray, in the 1936 edition of his *General Psychology*, discussed the topic of emotion under the heading of "Disorganized Response" and contrasted organized and disorganized (emotional) behavior.

Morey (1940) has identified emotion with bodily upset and has distinguished between integrated behavior and upset. The contrast is illustrated by what we commonly call love. The condition of being in love may be an emotion *(upset)* or a highly integrated, intelligent reaction. "To avoid upset," Morey continues, "people can be taught how to make love gracefully, as the Loma teach their children in the bush school as soon as they reach puberty, with the result that Loma men and women are seldom upset by love situations."

Although disturbance of the individual is a *necessary* condition of emotion as here defined, it is not a *sufficient* criterion for differentiating it. One difficulty with the definition of emotion as a disturbed or upset state is that one cannot always, on superficial observation, determine whether such upset exists. An example of this has been cited by Morey. He writes:

> Upset of physiological processes is provoked by numerous sets of forces. Emotions are as numerous, therefore, as the sets of forces that elicit upset. Patterns of forces eliciting upset differ from one group of people to another, and vary with the past experience of the subject on which such forces play. A set of forces will elicit upset in some people and smooth responses in others. This is doubtless the reason that some people judge a situation to be emotional whereas others judge it to be non-emotional.
>
> For example, six years ago a climber set out from a Swiss mountain hut at 3 a.m. to climb the Matterhorn. He was alone, cold, and half asleep. Less than 100 yards from the comfortable safety of the hut, he had to climb an overhang of rock. Foot- and hand-holds suddenly could not be found.
>
> The climber was cold. He seemed unable to concentrate his activities; his

> attention swerved from essential details. His strong wish and tendency to move quickly up the mountain was blocked. He experienced bodily upset, and for a moment was unintegrated, emotional. If asked, he would have said he was afraid. This fear might appear at first to be something inside him. Fear, however, was present only insofar as an essential combination of two conditions was present: upset inside the climber and a situation which is thought to be conducive to upset.
>
> Later in the day, when the climber's blood was circulating freely, he concentrated wholeheartedly on each successive movement. His responses were well integrated and harmonious as he climbed up and down places much more difficult than the one that had stirred upset within him when he was cold.
>
> A few times at the top of cliffs he hesitated, and looked out at the sun playing on the glaciers of the neighboring mountains. An observer, who was watching through a telescope, said, "*He seems to be afraid. He'll turn back now.*" The observer was referring to the situation in which the climber found himself, not to a particular pattern of invisible physiological processes inside the climber. The situation together with the climber's hesitation meant to the observer, fear. It was a fearful situation and hesitation at a critical point might be a sign of upset, which would have been precipitated if the climber's deep-seated wish to climb to the very tip of the summit had been blocked by an impassable cliff.
>
> To the observer, hesitancy on the edge of a precarious cliff meant block of integrated climbing responses entailing upset. To the climber, hesitancy on the edge of this cliff meant a moment's rest for a fine view. The observer judged all of the factors visible to mean fear; the climber was completely integrated, however. The same items were judged by one observer to be emotion, by another to be non-emotion. Such misinterpretations of signs indicating upset are common. Judges interpret these signs by referring to their past experiences, which differ from group to group, person to person, and differ in the same person at different times. [344-346]

It is clear that conditions of disturbance, disruption, upset, may occur in other than emotional situations. To illustrate, if the telephone rings when one is writing a letter, one stops to answer. The process of writing is wholly disrupted (at least for a moment) by the phone call; yet this disturbance of behavior is not necessarily an emotion. Again, if a man is lost in a strange city, he may roam about the street, quite unperturbed, asking questions of pedestrians. He is definitely disoriented but the disturbance of his activity is not necessarily an emotional one.

If one attempts to recognize emotional disturbances by the presence of excessive movements, one may be led astray by the excessive movements in various nervous and mental disorders. Thus, tics and convulsions are present in Saint Vitus dance (chorea), in hysteria, in epilepsy, in certain neuroses, etc. Technically, pathological conditions are not emotional in character, although to the inexperienced observer some of them look like emotional disturbances.

Clearly, then, one cannot claim that all disturbed states are emotions.

The concept of disturbance is broader than that of emotion. We postulate, however, that all emotions are states of *affective* disturbance or upset. Since *disturbance* alone is not fully adequate as a distinguishing characteristic of emotion, we must seek other criteria to delimit the concept. A second criterion follows.

Visceral Processes in Emotion. An outstanding characteristic of every emotional state is the presence of profound and widespread visceral changes (in smooth muscles, glands, heart, and lungs) due to increased activity of the autonomic nervous system. Secretion of sweat, flow of tears, inhibition of saliva, a wildly beating heart, irregular respiration, dilation of the pupils, erection of the hair, frequency of urination and defecation, pallor or flushing of the face—these are only a few of the externally observable signs of internal bodily changes in emotion.

But changes in visceral processes appear also in calm undisturbed behavior. If, for example, a man is fatigued and overheated by hard work, or if he is in a room which is too hot, secretion of the sweat glands is increased. Vigorous excercise is associated with quickened heartbeat, deeper respiration, increase in adrenal secretion, and other bodily changes which regulate energy expenditure. In hunger the smooth muscle fibers of the stomach wall contract, giving the painful hunger pang which is spoken of as a *feeling* or *appetite*, not as an emotion. Similarly there are visceral changes associated with all the basic needs of the body—the needs for water, sleep, elimination, etc.

Again, in pregnancy and in various diseased or otherwise abnormal bodily conditions, there are marked changes in the vegetative processes (functioning of smooth muscles and glands). One can legitimately argue that an attack of pneumonia or some other serious illness is a disturbed state of the organism which profoundly involves the vegetative processes. Yet neither physician nor psychologist would designate such a condition as an emotion.

It is clear, therefore, that the presence of visceral changes cannot in itself serve as an adequate criterion for defining emotion. Some additional criterion is needed.

The Psychological Origin of Emotion. Perhaps the most important criterion of all for defining emotion is the requirement of a psychological origin for the affectively disturbed condition. Emotion is a *psychological* and not a purely physiological event.

When we say that an emotion has a *psychological* origin and basis, we mean that the affectively disturbed condition arises from a dynamic relation between an organism and its environment. The environment stimulates the organism and the organism in turn responds to the stimulating environment. A psychological situation is not in the environment alone nor in the organism alone; it implies a dynamic relation between the total surroundings of an experiencing organism and his total life history. The psychological relations, of course, can be viewed in different ways—from the points of view of behavior, subjective experience, physiological process, development, psycho-dynamics, and so on.

Sokolov (1960), a physiological psychologist, postulated a "neuronal model" which is a kind of biological filter or sieve that acts selectively upon sensory imputs. The "neuronal model" is a mechanism, established by habituation, which senses differences between present and previous inputs and provides a stable background against which incoming patterns of excitation are matched, tested and responded to. For example, if a dog, in a laboratory situation, has become conditioned to a signal tone of 1000 cycles per second, another tone will arouse an alerting reflex which appears as a tonic change in skeletal muscles followed immediately by an orienting reflex. The difference in sensory input may be one of frequency, intensity, duration, or some other parameter; even the failure of a tone to occur is sensed by the "neuronal model" as a difference. This is a mechanism that underlies expectation, anticipation, and the recognition of differences. A novel stimulus-pattern elicits a discriminative response but not necessarily an emotion. Habituated behavior is free from emotion. Sokolov's "neuronal model" is quite similar to the Test-Operate-Test-Exit (TOTE) mechanism postulated by Miller, Galanter, and Pribram (1960).

Pribram's (1967*b*) comprehensive theory of emotion considers the *affective* component of emotional disturbances in a way that Sokolov's theory does not. For Pribram an emotion is defined as an affective perturbation, or disturbance, during which the organism is temporarily "out of" or "away from" planned action. An organism becomes emotional when there is a sufficient discrepancy between the present situation and a baseline grounded upon memory of previous experience. The discrepancy is felt as a mismatch between expected and actual (including visceral) processes; See page 273.

The psychological situation definitely involves affective and cognitive memory as Rapaport (1950) demonstrated. Common sense explains emotions in terms of memories of previous traumatic experiences, persisting motives and attitudes, personal identifications, unsolved conflicts, unrelieved frustrations, unexpected rewards, and the like. This view of the psychological origin of emotion (which is also taken in psychoanalysis) is far removed from the reflexological and neurophysiological accounts of physical behaviorists.

Schachter and Singer (1962) have emphasized the importance of congnitive and social factors in the causation of emotion. A strictly physiological account is inadequate. See pages 308-9.

Finally, from the biological point of view an organism's perception of unfamiliar and potentially dangerous surroundings is a primary cause of emotional behavior. Emotions arise while an organism is coping with threats and dangers in its environment. The result of such coping may be beneficial or harmful. In man, emotions also originate in memories of past experiences.

Other Possibile Criteria of Emotion. In addition to the above three criteria there are at least two other characteristics of emotion. These are briefly considered below as possible criteria of emotion.

One of these characteristics is the *weakening or loss of cerebral control.* During calm, non-emotional behavior the organism usually functions as a unit, the cerebral hemispheres dominating activity of the lower neural centers. During excitement, conflict, frustration, or sudden release of tension, however, the cerebral control is weakened or temporarily lost. When this occurs, the reflexive response patterns, which are integrated at subcortical levels, partially or wholly dominate behavior. The individual may laugh or cry, show rage, startle, disgust, or some other pattern. The appearance in behavior of some reflexive response pattern which is integrated below the level of the cerebral cortex, may serve as an index of the loss of cerebral dominance. This loss or reduction of cerebral dominance has been considered as a criterion of emotion. A practical difficulty, however, is the fact that such loss of control is not directly observable but has to be assumed on the basis of the response patterns which are observed. A second difficulty is that a loss of cerebral control occurs in some states other than emotion, as in sneezing and coughing.

Another possible criterion of emotion is a *marked change in the level of general activity.* In excited, energizing emotions the activity level rises markedly. The individual makes excessive, aimless movements in great excitement, rage, fear, pain, injury. Such excessive activity occurs also in joy. Sometimes in fear there is a complete paralysis of action instead of heightened activity. And in grief, as well as in other depressive states, the level of general activity is low.

One difficulty with using the change in activity level as a criterion of emotion lies in the fact that the activity level also changes with a variety of non-emotional states. In fatigue, sleepiness, and in many illnesses, the activity level drops; in vigorous health and a well-rested condition, and in certain diseases, the activity level rises.

In conclusion, *an emotion is an acute affective disturbance of the individual, psychological in origin, involving behavior, conscious experience, and visceral functioning.* Or, more concisely as stated above, an *emotion is an affectively disturbed process or state of psychological origin.*

CONCLUSION

Emotion has been defined as an affectively disturbed process or state of psychological origin. The process is an acute manifestation which is observable in different aspects as a conscious experience, a behavioral pattern, or an internal neurophysiological event. The emotional state is a persistingly disturbed condition which can best be understood in the light of an individual's complete psychobiological history. A view of evolution and ontogenetic development is needed to understand the significance of a specific emotional reaction.

Emotion arises when an organism is coping with environmental conditions. In this process of coping there are frustrations, blocks, conflicts, painful stimuli, which disturb homeostasis and smoothly running activity. There are also successes and victories which are affectively disturbing.

Emotion is one of the most complex events examined by scientific psychology. It is so complex, in fact, that an interdisciplinary, eclectic, approach is required to gain fair understanding and control of emotional activity.

The more information one has about the conditions that produce emotion the better is one able to recognize and identify emotional upsets and to discriminate among different emotional conditions. Facial expressions alone do not provide fully adequate cues for recognizing and identifying emotions. Facial expressions become stereotyped for different individuals. Further, it is possible to control expressive behavior voluntarily for purposes of social communication.

The direct observation of behavior is helpful in identifying emotional disturbances. But a knowledge of the inducing situation and a long-term acquaintance with the subject are of prime importance as a basis for recognizing and naming emotions.

Emotions are of great practical importance in relation to health, education and social welfare. On the one hand, emotions are dependent upon motivation and psychodynamic relations. On the other, emotions are importantly related to adjustment and to mental development. To deal practically with problems of emotional maladjustment and development one must understand the basic dynamics. In Chapters II and III we will consider motivation and the dynamics of affective processes.

GENERAL READING SUGGESTIONS

Most up-to-date textbooks of general, experimental, and physiological psychology contain chapters on the affective processes including emotion. References for further study can be found in such texts.

An older work of merit is C. A. Ruckmick (1928), *The Psychology of Feeling and Emotion*, I have not surveyed the extensive medical literature dealing with emotion but a survey of older studies, by Dunbar (1935), is available.

There are three symposia which contain a miscellaneous collection of papers on the affective processes by various authors. The articles vary in interest and merit. The *Wittenberg Symposium on Feelings and Emotions*, edited by C. Murchison and M. L. Reymert, was published in 1928. The *Mooseheart Symposium on Feelings and Emotions*, edited by M. L. Reymert in cooperation with the University of Chicago, was published in 1950. The *Loyola Symposium on Feelings and Emotions*, edited by M. B. Arnold, was published in 1970. For purposes of orientation and because of the many problems they raise, these symposia are worthy of perusal.

My textbook entitled, *Motivation and Emotion*, contains several chapters on emotion and places the discussion of emotion within the broader context of motivation (Young, 1961). Also I have in press a chapter entitled, *Feeling and Emotion*, to appear in B. B. Wolman's (1972), *Handbook of General Psychology*.

Chapter II

Motivation, The Dynamic Basis of Emotion

As with any complex event in nature, an emotion can be observed and analyzed from different points of view and in different contexts. As a matter of fact, what one observes depends upon the position of the observer in space as well as his beliefs, desires and general outlook on life.

A striking example of the importance of point of view in space is seen in Figure 5. A goldfish in an aquarium was photographed from three positions in space. When the camera or human eye is located at the side of the aquarium, a single fish is seen (Figure 5*a*). When the point of observation is raised above the upper edge of the aquarium, two fishes appear (Figure 5*b*). When the viewpoint is near the corner, three fishes are observed (Figure 5*c*). Not only the number and position of the fishes, but also their shape is dependent upon the position of the eye of the observer or the camera.

Consider another exanple. If a house is on fire, the conflagration appears very differently to a person on the inside and observers on the outside. The appearance, moreover, varies with the position of the observer. The fire presents different aspects when seen from the north, south, east, west, or from an airplane. Despite the different points of view, we believe that the various aspects are relevant to a single, complex series of events. Taken together, the different views give a more complete account of the event than that obtained from any single point of view. The person on the inside, for example, can tell about an explosion in the furnace that started the fire. No outside observer has this view of causation.

Moreover, different onlookers have diverse interests in the burning house. To one the conflagration is an exciting spectacle; to another it represents an economic loss; to a third it is a tragic loss of keepsakes or of a home with treasured memories. There are not only different aspects of the burning house as seen from different positions in space, but also different evaluations and interests in the event.

(a)

(b)

(c)

Figure 5. Three views of a goldfish in an aquarium. *Adapted from* pictures by the Photography Department of Harvard University.

PSYCHOLOGICAL RELATIVITY

Points of View in Psychology. The phenomena of human experience are always relative to the point of view, outlook, motives, or attitude and cognitions of the experiencing individual. Human experience includes the perceptions, memories, feelings, desires, beliefs, intentions, plans, and the like, of which the individual is aware.

In viewing and analyzing the physical world the observer simply takes it for granted that the universe has an independent, real, existence. This is the objective point of view. An observer, however, may fail to distinguish clearly between physical bodies and events, on the one hand, and subjective phenomena—after-images, dream objects, hallucinations, thoughts, fantasies, etc.—on the other. All exist within the phenomenal experience of individuals.

The dynamic relations between an organism and its environment can be observed and studied from the physical point of view without reference to conscious experience. Behavior includes gross bodily movements, such as running, the movements of the speech mechanisms, and the facial expressions of emotion. In non-human organisms behavior also includes physical changes like production of light or electric shock or a change in pigmentation or color pattern, etc.; but human behavior is based upon two kinds of bodily changes—muscular movements and glandular secretions. There are chemical and neural bases of behavior.

The physiologist observes bodily processes from an objective point of view. The behavior which it outwardly observed depends upon processes in the nerves, sense organs, muscles, and supporting tissues. These changes can be described in physicochemical terms. The physiologist does *not* observe color qualities, feelings of pleasantness, beliefs, loyalty oaths, and the like, within the brain. He observes physicochemical processes.

The three kinds of phenomena—experience, behavior, physiological facts—are shown in Figure 6. The horizontal line in this figure indicates a basic distinction betweeen the facts of observation, or phenomenal experiences which are above the line, and the inferences drawn from those facts, below. Although the psychologist also deals with social, cultural and historical facts, the three kinds of facts shown in the illustration are of major importance to him.

Below the line is a circle that represents the psychologist's concept of an organism. The arrows connecting the organism with the facts of observation indicate a two-way relation: hypotheses about the organism are based upon these three kinds of facts, and these hypotheses are tested by further observation and experiment.

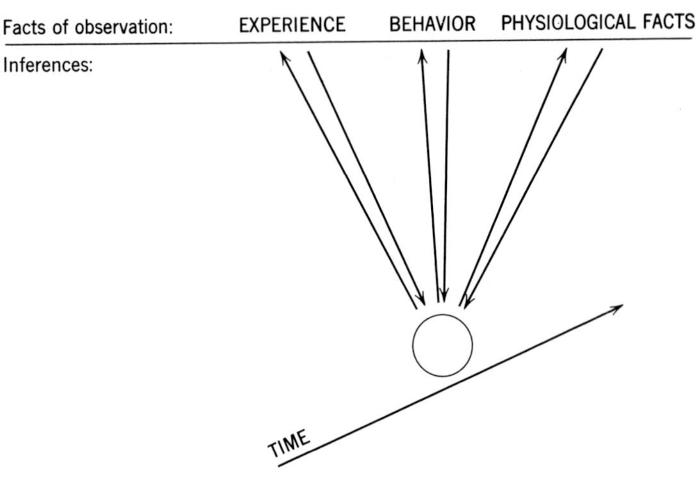

Figure 6. Representation of facts and inferences with which the psychologist deals.

The organism has the characteristics attributed to it in order to explain the facts above the line. A complete understanding of the organism rests upon at least these three kinds of facts.

Please note that the postulate of a *single* organism is an inference. It is an inference in the sense that the postulate of a single goldfish in the above aquarium (Figure 5), is an inference.

Philosophers and psychologists have sometimes postulated two individuals—a mind and a body—but the doctrine of biological monism postulates only one individual—the psychologist's organism. This organism wakes and sleeps, perceives, remembers, imagines, thinks, feels, desires, and acts, i.e., it is the subject of conscious experience. Moreover, psychologists attribute to the organism certain abilities, traits of personality, interests, attitudes, and motives, as well as conflict states, neuroses, good and bad adjustments, and the like. These characteristics of the organism are attributed to it on the basis of the facts of human experience, the facts of behavior, and physiological facts.

Dynamic processes like repression, dissociation, unconscious motivation, and the like, are also inferred; but whether or not these inferences are sound is another problem.

The concept of a single psychological organism needs to be extended to take account of developmental changes that occur in the course of time. The organism lives through a life cycle extending from conception to death. During this life cycle the organism matures, learns, solves problems, acquires traits of personality, attitudes, motives, interests, motor skills, information, etc., as well as emotional conflicts and neuroses. A temporal dimension must be added to the illustration to take account of these changes. An arrow below the organism symbolizes the temporal dimension.

A Fixed Point of View *versus* Eclecticism. A student of psychology when confronted with so many points of view may be at a loss not knowing what to do.

One way out of the difficulty is to hold rigidly to some fixed and well-defined point of view. This was Titchener's way out. He defined psychology as the science of experience. By experience he meant something that exists, that is observable or reportable, that depends upon neural processes. Watson, the radical behaviorist, held to a fixed objective point of view. He defined psychology as an objective science of behavior of man and brute.

Skinner, Spence, Snygg and Combs, and others, have met the complex situation differently, but all have done so by defining and holding to a fixed point of view. A good case can be made for this procedure. It can be argued that holding to a fixed point of view is necessary to make progress in this age of scientific specialization.

A fixed view, however, necessarily restricts the scope of a science and makes it difficult to appreciate the merits and relevance of other viewpoints.

The eclectic, within psychology, frankly faces this situation and shifts his point of view according to his immediate interest or aim. The eclectic, as Boring pointed out, is not wedded to any fixed point of view but changes readily from one view to another as a matter of convenience.The eclectic, within psychology, develops facility in changing from one view to another as a musician, in playing a piece, shifts from one key to another.

An Alternative to Eclecticism. Eclecticism may lead to despair in the face of complexity. It is unsatisfactory to students who are looking for unity within psychology. One alternative to eclecticism, noted above, is to hold firmly to a fixed point of view. But there is another possible way to escape from the complexities of a multiaspect situation. This way begins by frankly recognizing the relativity of facts of observation to a point of view or bias. To begin with, it can be recognized that man is the kind of creature who can readily shift from one point of view to another. He can change his orientation, his attitude. It is a remarkable fact that the human being is capable of changing point of view, and of considering diverse aspects of phenomenal experience.

In the area of social behavior a frank recognition of the relativity of facts to points of view has important implications. If a man *believes* something to be true, that makes it true for him. A man's belief influences his perception of the world, his remarks, his overt actions.

For example, consider the circles in Figure 7.

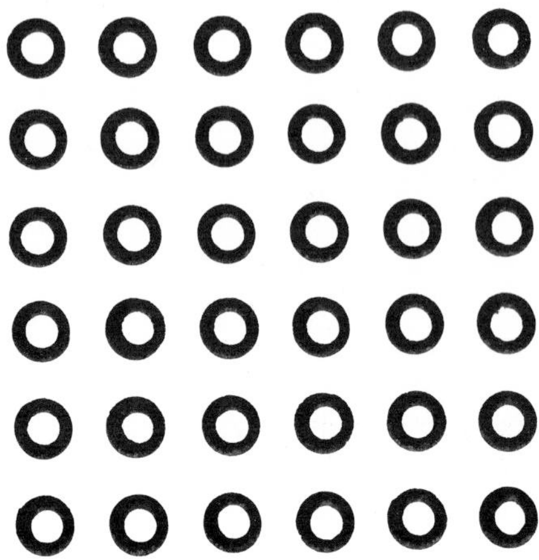

Figure 7. A figure to demonstrate how perceptual groupings depend upon mental set. *Slightly modified* from Schumann (1900).

Assume that these circles are arranged in groups of four with spaces between them, and look fixedly at the circles from the standpoint of this assumption. The circles appear to be grouped into nine groups of four circles in each group. Now assume that they are grouped by nines; they *are* in groups of nines. Again assume a grouping by sixes first in a horizontal and then in a vertical arrangement; the various groupings appear. A wide variety of patterns can be perceived merely by assuming that they exist while persistently looking at the figure with a particular mental set. Practice makes the observation more striking and facile.

The doctrine of psychological relativity is important in the area of religion: Many a man takes his religious faith seriously. Wars have been fought to defend a faith. Men with the same faith feel a kinship to each other. Yet a calm study of comparative religions reveals the upsetting truth that there are many faiths, many systems of religious beliefs that differ in theology and eschatology, sometimes radically, from each other. This means that one's most cherished faith is just one specimen of religious belief. It is fortunate that we have religious freedom in the U. S. A.!

Much the same can be said about political and moral beliefs. There is a high degree of relativity among everyday beliefs and practices. It is not surprising, therefore, to find different views of psychology and different views concerning the nature of motivation and emotion. The serious student may well ask: What should I do in the face of this complexity and relativity?

One alternative to eclecticism is to study the psychological origin and nature of points of view, beliefs, attitudes, orientations, motives, emotions, and the like. One can ask about origins: How did this particular disposition develop? How does it influence behavior and experience? How can it be changed? Such questions are of central psychological importance in the study of motivation and emotion. They are questions that admit psychological relativity yet move beyond this doctrine into the realm of determinants and mental development.

Psychological relativity is recognized by the propagandist and advertiser. The quest of a propagandist is for *psychological* truth. The propagandist does not ask, "Is this objectively true?" He is an opportunist who asks: "Is this believed and believable?" "Will this appeal evoke the kind of action I want?" "How does this item make people feel and act?" Such questions go to the heart of dynamic psychology. They presuppose a relativity of the facts of observation to psychological orientations. They recognize that spoken words are motivated and also motivating.

The concept of relatively stable dispositions—attitudes, interests, motives, states of conflict, and the like—is at the center of dynamic psychology. An approach to psychology through the study of dispositions might be called *dispositional* or *attitudinal* psychology. Such a study can include the predispositions laid down by the genetic code. This kind of approach recognizes the relativity of phenomenal experience to the hypothetical underlying conditions. A doctrine of psychological relativity is essential to any integration of psychological principles in the complex field of emotion and motivation.

BELIEF, DESIRE AND FANTASY

Determinants of Belief. In an investigation by Lund (1925-6) the subjects were instructed to rate propositions, first, in terms of their belief that the propositions were true and, second, in terms of their desire that they be true. Lund was primarily interested in the determinants of belief—what it is that makes people believe as they do.

After the subjects had rated the propositions in terms of belief-disbelief they were asked to indicate, so far as possible, the basis of their ratings. Lund instructed his subjects as follows:

> We may take as a primary assumption that beliefs all have their antecedents, and are directly determined either by certain propensities inherent in the individual or by influences brought to bear upon him from without. With this in mind reconsider each proposition and along with its number state as briefly as

possible—preferably in a word, phrase, or short sentence—what you think has been the main *determinant* for your rating of the proposition. The question is—what led you to rate it as you did? What (perhaps in your past experience) conditioned your rating? In some cases you may be able to think of no such condition or reason, in which event state that it is simply an opinion for which you can give no account.

Lund found eight principal determinants of belief. They are listed below in order from the one most frequently mentioned to the one least frequently mentioned. The frequencies are the total frequencies for thirty-five subjects after they had rated thirty propositions on a scale of belief-disbelief. See Table 2.

TABLE 2

DETERMINANTS OF BELIEF

Frequency	Determinant	Description of Determinant
317	Teaching and training	Belief conditioned by instruction received at home, through the church, school and similar institutions.
142	Personal experience	Acceptance engendered through sensory experience or observation.
116	Personal opinion	Beliefs for which no real account can be given except that one thinks it is so.
92	Personal reasoning	Acceptance determined by a rational process, a definite "thinking it out."
54	Desire and satisfyingness	Beliefs embraced because they satisfy or embody conditions that are desired.
46	Authoritative opinion	Acceptance determined by the prestige given through official or authoritative attestation.

TABLE 2 (cont.)

Frequency	Determinant	Description of Determinant
44	Public opinion	Beliefs fostered through a general attitude of acceptance by people at large.
28	Axiomatic principle	Principles which cannot be doubted, being imperative in commanding belief.

After Lund (1925-1926).

The list indicates that the determinants of human belief are both rational and non-rational. Of the eight determinants, at least two or three can be described as rational: personal experience and observation, personal reasoning, and possibly axiomatic principle. But apart from these the remaining grounds for assent contain a large non-rational element. We have beliefs for which we can give no explanation. We assent because others do; we believe what we desire to be true, what satisfies us; we agree to what we are taught in the home, church, school, especially do we believe opinions which are expressed by persons of authority and prestige. Our beliefs are thus formed not only through the senses and through intellectual processes but by our wishes, feelings and other non-rational determinants such as hearsay, statements by other persons, and a desire to conform.

The most frequently mentioned determinant of belief is teaching and training at home, through the church, school, and similar institutions. Children tend to accept the religious, political and ethical beliefs of their parents. The things we are taught are rarely determined by a process of reasoning.

Long ago Alexander Bain used the phrase "primitive credulity." He argued that a child tends to accept whatever he is told until something in his experience gives him the shock of contradiction. Doubt, produced by contradiction, leads to thinking and to a critical attitude; but if contradiction is lacking, the child is primitively credulous. Small children, for example, readily accept the stories about Santa Claus.

An understanding of the determinants of belief is tremendously important for the educator, the politician, the propagandist, the psychiatrist, and others who are practically concerned with human relations. Man is only in part a rational animal.

The Fiction of Rationality. Aristotle said that man is a *rational* animal. The modern psychologist would be inclined to say that man is a *rationalizing* animal.

Martineau (1957) wrote:

> Most people accept the religion of their parents. But it doesn't sound very rational for an adult to admit this. So he sells himself on the proposition that his belief rests on completely logical grounds. He has examined, he says, numerous faiths, but his own is the one that makes the most sense to him. He would angrily deny the actual reason.
>
> So would the attention getter deny heatedly that he was telling off-color jokes and serving vodka and wearing a back-yard chef's costume so that he could occupy the center of the stage. So does the social striver deny the true but not acceptable reasons why he has changed churches, changed friends, and changed neighborhoods.

The alleged reasons for our actions are not necessarily the true determinants. Freud made the point clearly in his emphasis upon unconscious motivations. What we say may be only an attempt to make ourselves appear reasonable and correct.

We have seen above that our beliefs rest upon both rational and non-rational grounds. The important point for a student of psychology is that beliefs regulate our actions and experiences. The point has been well stated by Britt (1949) in a chapter upon the psychology of irrationality: "*If people believe things to be true, then they are true for them and have social consequences.*"

The propagandist aims to change beliefs and attitudes, starting with what people already accept. The unfortunate thing is that beliefs and attitudes can be changed by various techniques and without regard for objective truth and reality.

Belief and Desire. Human beliefs are determined to some degree by wishes or desires. The phrase *autistic thinking* refers to imagination, like that in day dreaming or building castles in the air, which is dominated by a wish rather than realistic logic.

The extent to which belief is dependent upon desire was investigated by Cronbach and Davis (1944) during World War II. In their work sixty-one college students were instructed to rate fifty statements about living conditions during wartime. The statements dealt with matters of importance to the subjects.

The statements were rated on a five-point scale, first as to the probability that an effect would occur and second as to the desirability of the effect. The instructions for the belief-disbelief ratings were as follows:

> You are to indicate what effects you think the war will have on the United States as a whole. Each item in the test states an effect some people have said the war will cause. You are to show how likely you think each effect is by circling the proper key letter on the answer sheet. Circle:
>
> CY (certainly yes) if you think the effect is *certain to happen.*
> PY (probably yes) if you think the effect is *more likely to happen than not.*
> E (equally likely) if you think the effect is *equally likely to happen or not to happen.*
> PN (probably no) if you think the effect *probably will not happen.*
> CN (certainly no) if you think the effect is *certain not to happen.*

Four days after the belief-disbelief ratings the questions were again presented, without previous warning, and the students were instructed to indicate how desirable the effect was, using a similar five-point scale. In the scale for desire CY meant *certainly desirable*, PY meant *moderately desirable*, E meant *neither desirable nor undesirable*, PN meant *moderately undesirable*, CN meant *certainly undesirable.*

Cronbach and Davis found that for some statements there was a wide discrepancy between the ratings of belief and desire. For example, consider the statement: *Food will become so scarce after the war that civilians will go hungry*. Fifty-six of the sixty-one students believed this statement to be true, but not one of them desired it to be true. In general, however, there was a positive correlation between the ratings for belief and for desire. Lund had found a high positive correlation ($r = +.88$). Cronbach and Davis found a lower but definitely positive correlation ($r = +.41$). The reasons for the discrepancy need not be considered here.

Cronbach and Davis found marked individual differences in the extent to which persons are dominated by wishful thinking. For individual students the correlations between belief and desire ratings on the fifty propositions ranged from +.74 to −.27.

It was found that the degree of correspondence between belief and desire varied with the nature of the proposition rated. Several factors were demonstrated. (1) The *ambiguity* of a proposition leads to greater correspondence between belief and desire. If there is no ambiguity—if the objective facts are clear—even those with strong wishes are likely to believe what the facts imply. But if the facts are unknown or uncertain, desire is relatively more influential. (2) The *familiarity* of a statement affects judgment. If a statement that is unsupported by evidence has been frequently discussed, it is likely to be believed even if it is not desired. Familiarity breeds consent. The propagandist, as we know, may secure acceptance of a statement simply by reiteration. (3) If both ambiguity and novelty are present, the *plausibility* of a statement is a factor determining the agreement between belief and desire. A statement may be plausible that is not necessarily true; but if a statement is extreme, desire may be powerless to make one accept it. (4) The *importance* of a statement to the individual is likely to lead to correspondence between belief and desire only when there is no possibility of acquiring information on which to base a realistic judgment. If there is no basis of experience for making a judgment, the majority of persons tend to agree to a proposition. They show a tendency to acquiesce, to agree, to conform.

The tendency to believe what one desires is associated with optimism. Perhaps optimism can be defined as a tendency to believe what one desires. A person who is over optimistic may refuse to face reality, being influenced largely by his wishes.

Belief and Perception: A Study of the So-called Canals on the Planet Mars.[1] During the years 1877-79 an Italian astronomer, Schiaparelli, at Milan, observed a remarkable network of broad curved lines and narrower straight ones of a dark color on the surface of Mars, which he called *canali*. His ability to observe those canals improved from year to year. As he repeatedly gazed through his telescope, these lines appeared straighter and more numerous. One evening he observed a remarkable phenomenon—the twinning of one of the canals. There were two parallel canals where but one had shown before. He suspected some optical illusion and so changed his telescope and eye-pieces; but the phenomenon was apparently real.

Upon still further observation one canal after another became two until some twenty of them had doubled. This increased his wonderment as well as the incredulity of other people. At this time nobody else had succeeded in seeing the canals at all, much less in seeing them doubled.

It was not until 1886 that anyone else saw these canals of Mars. In April of that year, Perrotin observed them in the observatory at Nice. The occasion for his observation was the setting up of a great glass with a twenty-nine-inch aperture. His first attempt to see the canals resulted in failure; so, later, did a second. Perrotin was on the point of abandoning the search when on the fifteenth of the month he quite suddenly detected one of the canals. His assistant, M. Thollon, also saw it immediately afterward. Then they managed to make out several canals, some single, some double, substantially as Schiaparelli had drawn them.

Since these earlier observations other persons have been able to see the canals; but, in 1895, the astronomer Lowell remarked that the number of persons who had observed them might almost be told on

[1] See note at end of chapter.

one's hands and feet. Lowell himself repeatedly observed the canals of Mars from his observatory at Flagstaff, Arizona. As seen by Lowell, the canals are straight and they make geometrical patterns; the markings are very fine and at the intersections are "oases." Lowell observed about four times as many canals as had Schiaparelli in 1877. Other astronomers were skeptical but Lowell merely replied that to observe the canals of Mars one must have still steady air such as exists at Flagstaff.

In 1907, E. S. Morse reported as follows his experiences in attempting to observe the canals:

> Professor Percival Lowell, of Flagstaff, Arizona, finally gave me the opportunity I so much desired and, through his courtesy and kindness, I was enabled to observe Mars every night for nearly six weeks through his twenty-four inch refractor, the last and probably the best telescope ever made by Clark, mounted in one of the steadiest atmospheres in the world and at an altitude above sea-level of over 7,000 feet. Imagine my surprise and chagrin when I first saw the beautiful disk of Mars through this superb telescope. Not a line! Not a marking! The object I saw could only be compared in appearance to the open month of a crucible filled with molten gold. Slight discolorations here and there and evanescent areas outlined for the tenth of a second, but not a determinate line or spot to be seen. Had I stopped that night, or even a week later, I might have joined the ranks of certain observers and said "illusion" or something worse. And right here it was that my experience in microscopic work helped me, for, remembering the hours—nay, days—I had worked, in making out structural features in delicate organisms which my unprofessional friends could not see at all, I realized that patient observation would be required if I was to be successful in my efforts. My despair, however, was overwhelming when Professor Lowell and his assistant, looking for a few moments at the same object, would draw on paper the features which had been plainly revealed to them, consisting of definite shaded regions, a number of canals and other markings, of which, with the utmost scrutiny, I could hardly detect a trace. . . . [80-81]

Later, however, Morse saw some canals and drew a diagram of them.

The objective existence of the so-called canals of Mars rested wholly upon direct human observation, for they have never been photographed. The failure of so many observers to see them has led to a wide disbelief in their objective existence. But despite uncertainty regarding the existence of canals upon Mars, interpretations have been rife. Lowell in 1895 summarized his complete argument as follows:

> We find, in the first place, that the broad physical conditions of the planet are not antagonistic to some form of life; secondly, that there is an apparent dearth of water upon the planet's surface, and therefore, if beings of sufficiient intelligence inhabited it, they would have to resort to irrigation to support life; thirdly, that there turns out to be a network of markings covering the disk precisely counterparting what a system of irrigation would look like; and lastly, that there is a set of spots placed where we should expect to find the lands thus artificially fertilized, and behaving as such constructed oases should . . . [210]

In later publications Lowell elaborated the argument for the existence of intelligent beings on the planet Mars. He furnished maps and charts and arguments favoring his hypothesis. Life on Mars, he wrote, is becoming extinct. It will soon go, cosmically speaking. Evolution produced a single species which exterminated or subordinated the others. Members of this species had to cooperate in order to get water and survive.

From the psychological angle there are special problems centering around the perception of something barely visible. In this connection there are also problems based upon the influence of belief and desire, of suggestion and self-hypnosis, in perceiving objects.

In 1907, the astronomer Douglass, after stating certain recognized physical facts about Mars, went somewhat out of his field to give a psychological explanation of the controversy over canals. He wrote:

> There is no doubt that there is a complicated plexus of markings on the planet; but as to the general canal interpretation, I have much doubt. In investigating visual work done on the limit of vision, from the viewpoint of experimental psychology, I have found several peculiarities that, under similar conditions, produce just such lines, whose sole existence is in the eye, and is due to the well-known phenomenon of rays. Black rays appear around a black spot, just as white rays around a star, and are due to the same cause—irregular refraction in the lens of the eye . . . These rays are actually present around every small dark marking; and when one is looking for such markings on the limit of vision, he is apt to see rays, the more care, patience and industry he uses.
>
> In this ray phenomenon we have the explanation of the multitude of radiating canals, which to a number of observers characterize the "lakes" and "oases" of Mars. . .
>
> Another class of canals is due to a halo phenomenon. To illustrate this, I have devised the following experiment: Make a small spot of ink on a blank card and place it at a distance of six to twelve feet from the eye. Around it appears a white area surrounded by a dark ring, which presents the appearance of a halo around the spot. This halo explains at once canals parallel to the limb or to large markings. Since white spots may produce a ring, or secondary image, as well as dark, light areas within dark markings may merely be the secondary image of adjacent light areas. Here we have an explanation of those curious results of Schiaparelli in his map of 1888, where he shows not only a considerable number of canals, but also some of the seas, as double.
>
> Another class of canals really exist, but derive their form through misinterpretation. From various causes, irregular areas appear to the eye to be canal-like in form, when on or near the limit of vision. This I have studied extensively by means of naked-eye views of the moon. I find that such errors apply only to markings so large and conspicuous that there is no doubt of their reality.
>
> And lastly, the study of artificial planets reveals the fact that on a perfectly blank globe rays sometimes appear radiating from near the center. . .
>
> From the foregoing, it will be seen that what I have to add to the literature of this subject, by supplying a psychologic origin, destroys most of those canals upon whose artificial appearance rests the strongest habitation argument. But it shows that the investigation of the canals has been done in a conscientious belief in their genuineness, and that work in the future should be free from such errors. [116-118]

The interesting psychological argument of Douglass is based solely upon optical effects, but there is much more to the psychological interpretation of the Mars controversy than this. We know that a verbal suggestion to observe a particular effect plus repeated attempts to observe it may result in the observation of the suggested phenomenon. The facts of normal suggestion and self-hypnosis need only be recalled in this connection.

It may be taken for granted that the astronomers who observed canals on Mars were sincere and honest human beings. Their observations were genuine. Today, of course, the surface of Mars has been photographed by satellite television and no canals or signs of life have yet been found. The problem of possible life on other planets can well be left to the astronomers and biologists, but apart from physical reality the historical controversy concerning the existence of canals on Mars bristles with factors of psychological interest.

Perception and Imagination. The line of demarcation between imagining and perceiving, between reality and fantasy, cannot be very sharply drawn. With some children and with some demented individuals the distinction does not exist.

In support of this statement consider the classical experiments of Perky (1910). She instructed subjects to imagine some object, such as a tomato or an orange or a banana, upon a ground-glass screen. On some of the trials she silently signaled to an assistant in an adjoining room who with a stereopticon projected a faint optical image of the suggested object on the screen. The optical image was hazy in form and dim in color but frequently it was definitely perceptible to an outside observer. The subjects did not suspect the trick. They described the perceived object as if it were truly an object of imagination, similar to the imagined object which was observed when no physical image was present. Even when the colored form was distinctly above the color threshold (clearly perceptible) the subjects did not detect a difference between the imagined and the perceived objects.

If this confusion between imagination and perception can be demonstrated in the laboratory, without hypnosis, it is clear, for example, that belief in the existence of canals on Mars could easily lead to the perception of such canals through the eyepiece of a telescope.

THE NATURE OF MOTIVATION

In the literal meaning of the word, *motivation* is a process of arousing movement. Factors which initiate, sustain, or change the pattern and course of bodily movement are, by definition, *motivating*. And this is true regardless of the point of view from which these factors are observed and analyzed. Psychologists have conceived and described the process of motivation in various ways: (1) To one, a motive is a stimulus–physical energy which excites a receptor or nerve cell. (2) To another, a motive is a physiological state, such as thirst or fatigue, which influences the excitability of the nervous system in a specific way. (3) To still another, a motive is a determination to act, an intention or set which activates and channels the course of behavior. (4) There are psychologists who explain behavior by assuming tensions and forces which drive the organism, such as the *libido* of Freud, the *elan vital* of Bergson, the *hormic force* of McDougall, the *tension* of Lewin. (5) Down through the centuries has come a doctrine of psychological hedonism which holds that conscious feelings of pleasantness and unpleasantness are human motives (the "pleasure-pain" principle). (6) Finally, there is a widespread belief that perception and memory are motivating in so far as they arouse action. For example, if a man sees the roof of his house on fire, he does something about it.

Although these, and other, concepts of motivation are divergent, in each there is the implication that motivation is a process of arousing the movement of an organism. Motivating factors, in whatever frame of reference they are described, in whatever terms conceived, are those which initiate bodily movement, sustain the activity in progress, or change its course. This implies that motivation is a process that liberates physical energy within the tissues of an organism.

This definition of motivation is so inclusive that it raises a question: *Are there psychological factors which do not motivate behavior*? The answer is plainly in the affirmative. Every individual carries around with him inert "possibilities of action," as Woodworth (1918) called them, which are not motivating so long as they remain latent and inert. At the present time, for example, the reader doubtless has habit organizations which can direct and regulate such behaviors as driving an automobile, solving a problem in geometry, carving a beef steak, speaking in some foreign language, singing *The Star Spangled Banner* (at least the first verse!). None of these activities, I assume, is in progress or even incipiently aroused right now. The latent habit organization is inert, non-motivating, although it can direct and regulate the course of behavior when an environmental situation or an inner intent activates the latent structure. Similarly, the reflex neural arc regulates the pattern of response when the appropriate stimulus is present.

Actually there is not always a clean break between motivating and non-motivating conditions. For example, if I have determined to take a plane to Chicago, this motive intermittently appears when I buy a ticket, pack a brief case, take a bus to the airport, etc. Possibly I dream about the trip. (We know that brain cells are always active even during deep sleep.) Later I recall events of the flight. The intent to travel, therefore, continues to exist until the trip has been completed; it is aroused or latent in varying degrees of intensity.

Latent Structure and Motivation. Most psychological structures are latent a good deal of the time. Only when a problem, task, environmental situation, or other motivating factor, is present is the latent structure tapped and utilized in behavior. Here is an obvious example:

How much is 8 times 9?

You reply: 72.

Structural organization of your nervous system determined this response. *Seventy-two* popped up into your mind. The organization was acquired years ago in the school room. The organization has been repeatedly exercised and utilized, but a moment ago it was latent. The structure was aroused, activated, by the statement of a problem. The question came unexpectedly and aroused a bit of latent habit organization.

Social attitudes are often latent. A mother was particular that her young daughter be well chaperoned when in the company of boys. While the daughter was away at a supervised boarding school, the mother had no worries. The attitude concerning importance of chaperonage was latent. Then her daughter came home for summer vacation and, on the first night, wanted to go out for a date with a boy friend. This situation instantly activated the mother's latent attitude.

Passive organization, by definition, *is* passive; it does nothing. It merely exists as quiescent structure until aroused by an activating situation. But if the necessary structure is lacking, the reaction obviously cannot occur.

Suppose someone asks you to give a lecture in Chinese upon Einstein's theory of relativity! You smile at the compliment (or perhaps the joke) for this is impossible. You know neither the Chinese language nor the theory of relativity. Your capacities for performance are limited. Yet there are actually a few individuals who could explain Einstein's theory in Chinese.

Motivating factors liberate energy while arousing certain segments of latent neural organization, producing movement in a specific performance. At any given period of time the motivation arouses only certain patterns of movement out of innumerable possible patterns, the selection depending upon the exact nature of the motivating factors. Why this is true and how particular behaviors are motivated at a given moment are basic problems for the serious student of motivation.

Motivation as a Quantitative Variable. In the psychological literature there are frequent references to the *degree* of motivation. Motivation is regarded as a quantitative variable.

To define motivation quantitatively one must specify the criteria by means of which differences in degree, or intensity, can be measured. Some of the criteria which have been used in human research are increments and decrements in: (1) speed of movement, (2) strength of muscular contraction as measured by a dynamometer, (3) speed of learning, (4) precision and coordination of movements, (5) quantity of work performed per unit time, and (6) quality of the work accomplished.

In animal research the level of general activity has been used as a criterion of the degree of motivation. To measure activity level the animal is placed in an activity cage. A common form of this apparatus resembles the rotating drum, seen in zoölogical gardens, for exercising squirrels and other small animals. The number of revolutions of the drum per hour or per day is counted mechanically. The level of running activity is found to vary with such physical conditions as age of the animal, temperature of the environment, approach to feeding time, satiation, stage of the estrous cycle, surgical removal of a ductless gland, and other conditions. In some experiments, the level of motivation has been measured by the amount of work accomplished, e.g., in pressing a bar or running back and forth in a shuttle box, to attain a goal. An increase in the activity level, dependent upon factors defined as motivating, is a *motivational increment*, and a decrease a *motivational decrement*.

Quite apart from laboratory measurements, in everyday life we recognize marked differences in the degree of motivation. Mary is lazy, easy-going, languid; she lacks "motivation." John is vigorous, energetic, full of "pep"; he has a high degree of "motivation." Such differences depend in part upon the condition of health but, whatever the cause, it is widely recognized that individuals differ in the degree of motivation.

Motives are commonly regarded as internal determinants and incentives as external factors that influence behavior. Motives and incentives are interlocking variables. Increments and decrements of motivation are shown with both.

Praise a school child for his correct spelling and he will more vigorously attack the next spelling list. Words of praise give added incentive to performance. Whip a horse or use the spur; the animal jumps forward with much release of energy. Such quantitative differences in the level, or vigor, of activity depend directly upon factors defined as motivating. Motives energize behavior and, in the ordinary use of the term, motives direct and regulate the course of activity.

The Reticular Activating System. The anatomical and physiological basis for quantitative variations in the *degree* of motivation is found in the reticular activating system of the brainstem. The neurology will be considered elsewhere, but the general principle of activation can be made clear by reference to a figure which has been borrowed from Bindra (1959). See Figure 8.

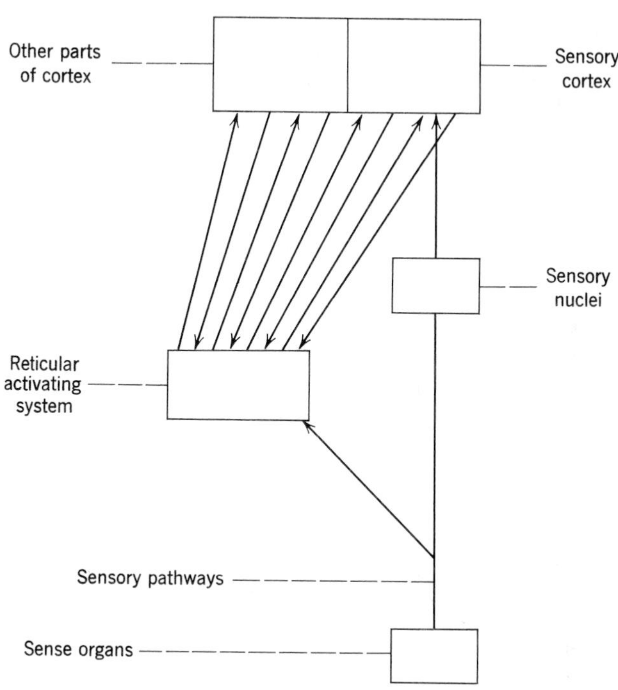

Figure 8. Schematic diagram of the reticular activating system. *After* Bindra (1959).

The primary sensory systems conduct nerve impulses from the various sense organs to sensory nuclei in the thalamus and from there over the classical projection pathways to the sensory areas of the cerebral cortex. Conduction through the primary sensory systems is direct, fast, and specific. The inputs into the sensory system convey information; they provide sensory cues or messages. The direct pathways have a discriminative or cognitive function in every perception.

Every sense-organ stimulation, however, initiates two kinds of neural input. Impulses, as noted above, are sent directly to specific cortical areas where they provide cues for discriminative reactions. And impulses from the same stimulations are fed by collateral fibers into the reticular activating system where they serve to tone up or alert the total cortical area. Impulses from the reticular activating system are conducted over devious multisynaptic pathways and are transmitted diffusely to all parts of the cortex. This system has been called the *non-specific* sensory system to distinguish it from the *specific* sensory systems.

The non-specific sensory system furnishes a diffuse background of cortical excitation which profoundly influences the way incoming primary sensory impulses are dealt with. Low levels of activation are correlated with sleep; moderate levels with relaxed or alert wakefulness. The highest levels of excitation are shown in the strong, or sthenic, emotions; they are often accompanied by a lowered efficiency of performance.

The reticular activating system is not limited to one-way conduction from sensory nerves to the cortex. The system is excited by cerebral action which, in turn, produces further effects via motor efferent pathways. It is likely, for example, that when we anticipate pain or injury the cerebral excitation arouses the reticulum. There is thus a two-way interaction between cortical and subcortical mechanisms. This possibility is indicated in Figure 8 by arrows from the cortex to the reticular activating system.

The reticular activating system also influences lower neural centers (not shown) and the outflow to various motor organs. Here again the effect upon motor function is non-specific—affecting the level of tonus rather than specific patterns of response. And, of course, the sensory feedback from all reactions has a dual effect: it conveys specific information in the form of sensory cues and it changes the level of arousal via the reticular activating system.

Activation and Drive. In his book upon *The Organization of Behavior*, Hebb (1949) argued that his neuropsychological principles were adequate to explain the phenomena of motivation. The term *drive* did not appear in the table of contents of Hebb's exciting book.

The physiological experiments of Moruzzi and Magoon, Lindsley, and others, upon the activating systems of the brainstem, forced Hebb to revise his view of drive. Hebb (1955) pointed out that there are two kinds of pathways from receptors to the brain. This changes the view of sensory function:

> In the classical conception of sensory function, input to the cortex was via the great projection systems only: from sensory nerve to sensory tract, thence to the corresponding sensory nucleus of the thalamus, and thence directly to one of the sensory projection areas of the cortex. These are still the direct sensory routes, the quick efficient transmitters of information. The second pathway is slow and inefficient; the excitation as it were, trickles through a tangled thicket of fibers and synapses, there is a mixing up of messages, and the scrambled messages are delivered indiscriminately to wide cortical areas. In short, they are messages no longer. They serve, instead, to tone up the cortex, with a background supporting action that is completely necessary if the messages proper are

to have their effect. Without the arousal system, the sensory impulses by the direct route reach the sensory cortex, but go no farther; the rest of the cortex is unaffected, and thus learned stimulus-response relations are lost.

Lindsley has stated, and Hebb agrees, that the diffuse excitation of the cortex provides a physiological basis for the concept of arousal or energizing that is essential in most studies of motivation and emotion. There are, Hebb points out, two functions: One is a *cue function* related to the guiding or steering of behavior. The other, less obvious but no less important, is an *arousal or vigilance function.* Without a foundation of arousal, the cue function cannot exist.

Arousal, in this sense, is synonymous with general drive. Drive, as *energizing*, can now be identified anatomically and physiologically. Drive is an energizer, not a guide; or engine, not a steering gear; a propeller, not a rudder. Drive gives impetus to behavior but it is always related to the cue (directive) function.

The Activation and Direction of Behavior. Lindsley (1951) formulated an activation theory of emotion based largely upon his researches in electroencephalography.

According to Lindsley, the electroencephalograms (EEGs) show different degrees or levels of activation as indicated in Figure 9. These different levels can be described in different ways: (1) in terms of the activation pattern of brain waves, (2) in terms of awareness, (3) in terms of the level of activity, and (4) in terms of the efficiency of performance.

Highest possible activity
Excited emotion
Alert attentiveness
Relaxed wakefulness
Drowsiness
Light sleep
Deep sleep
Coma
Death

Figure 9. Continuum showing levels of activation. *After* Lindsley (1957).

In terms of brain waves: The highest levels of activation are characterized by desynchronized waves of low to moderate amplitude with high mixed frequencies. Lower levels, like the level of relaxed wakefulness, are characterized by synchronized waves with an optimal alpha rhythm. At the level of drowsiness and sleep the alpha rhythm is reduced and larger slower waves appear. In deep sleep there is great synchrony. In coma there are irregular large, slow waves; sometimes the brain is completely inactive electrically as it is in death.

In terms of awareness: On the level of strong excited emotion, awareness is restricted or it may be divided or there may be confusion and haziness. Alert attentiveness is characterized by a controlling set or concentration. In states of relaxed wakefulness, attention wanders; this state favors free associations. Drowsiness is a borderline condition with partial awareness; there is reverie and dream-like consciousness. In light sleep there is reduced consciousness and some loss of consciousness; but dreams occur and may be remembered. In deep sleep, coma, and death, there is complete loss of awareness.

In terms of the activity level: The continuum agrees well with observed differences in the level of general activity from the highest levels of emotional excitement down to the lowest levels of deep sleep and coma. It should be remembered, however, that activation is an internal physiological process and differences in the level of general activity are observed as behavior or performance.

In terms of efficiency of performance: The level of strong excited emotion is characterized by lack of control, freezing up, or disorganized behavior. Efficiency of performance is poor at the highest level of activation. Efficiency is maximal at the levels of alert attentiveness and relaxed wakefulness. Efficiency is very poor at the level of drowsiness. And it doesn't make sense to talk about the efficiency of performance during deep sleep and coma because these are purely vegetative states.

Lindsley's activation theory of emotion is more accurately described as a physiological theory of *activation*. The theory does not take account of quiescent affective states, moods and sentiments. Moreover, the important relations between positive and negative hedonic processes, on the one hand, and complex emotions and motivations, on the other, are not considered.

Duffy (1957) pointed out that the term *activation* has a wide range of applicability within the psychology of motivation and emotion. In Lindsley's sense, the term is closely related to *excitatory level, level of energy mobilization, intensity of drive, degree of arousal*, and other dynamic concepts. According to the dictionary, however, the term *activate* also means *to make active* or *to render capable of reacting* or *to promote reaction*. In this last sense, activation is almost synonymous with motivation.

In one meaning of *activation* (which must not be confused with Lindsley's usage) a psychological determinant can be said to be latent or activated. For example, when a latent emotional conflict is activated there can be an acute affective disturbance—a manifest feeling or emotion. The phrase "Let sleeping dogs lie" implies that emotional dispositions can be dormant or activated. Psychologists know very well that music, words, odors, and other kinds of stimulation, can arouse affective memories and redintegrate emotional disturbances.

In her book *Activation and Behavior*, Duffy (1962) makes a thorough review of the concept of activation as a variable underlying behavior and individual differences. Duffy proposes that the traditional category of emotion be eliminated and all behavior described in terms of approach or avoidance. Her so-called "activation theory," however, does not adequately relate activation to hedonic values.

Other psychologists have identified motivation with diffuse activation, or general drive. For example, J. S. Brown (1961) in his book *The Motivation of Behavior*, identifies motivation with activation. Instead of describing different drives (hunger, thirst, sex, pain avoidance, etc.) he speaks of different sources and conditions of activation (stimulation). To explain the direction and patterning of behavior Brown points to the structural organization of the organism, particularly to neural structures laid down by the genetic code and to structures acquired through learning.

Brown shares the view of Lindsley, Hebb, Duffy, and others, that there is a diffuse, non-specific, process of activation or arousal. Hence, he argues, an explanation of the direction and regulation of behavior must be sought elsewhere than in the processes of activation.

I have argued to the contrary, in an unpublished manuscript entitled *Hedonic Regulation of Behavior and Development*, that the positive and negative hedonic processes are both activating and directive, that hedonic changes away from the negative and toward the positive valences *reinforce* the behavior upon which these changes are contingent, and that there is sound evidence for the existence of non-specific forms of positive and negative excitations.

One thing can be said with certainty: The common, everyday view of motivation recognizes that one of the prime attributes of motives and incentives is the direction and regulation of behavior. It is also recognized that motives differ in degree or "emotional" intensity as well as in the persistence and fixity of a determination.

A Directive-Activation Theory of Motivation, In the fall of 1953, Dr. James Olds was experimenting with electrodes implanted in the brains of healthy, normal rats. He was interested in stimulating the brain within the reticular formation to discover whether such stimulation would increase alertness of the animals and thus facilitate learning.

Quite by accident, an electrode was implanted in the region of the anterior commisure. When the rat's brain was stimulated at this point the animal acted as if he liked it. If the brain was electrically stimulated when the rat was at a specific place in an open field, he would, sooner or later, return and sniff around that area. Repeated intracranial stimulations caused him to spend more and more time at the place where the brain stimulations were received.

Later Olds found that the rat could be trained to go to any spot in a maze if his "pleasure center" was consistently stimulated when he arrived at that spot. For example, in a T-maze the animal could be trained to turn consistently to the left or to the right if he was rewarded solely by brain stimulations. A hungry rat with food at both ends of the T-maze would stop at any point where he was rewarded by electrical brain stimulations. It became apparent that stimulation alone at certain points in the rat's brain is rewarding or reinforcing. This early work has been described by Olds and Milner (1954). See Figure 10.

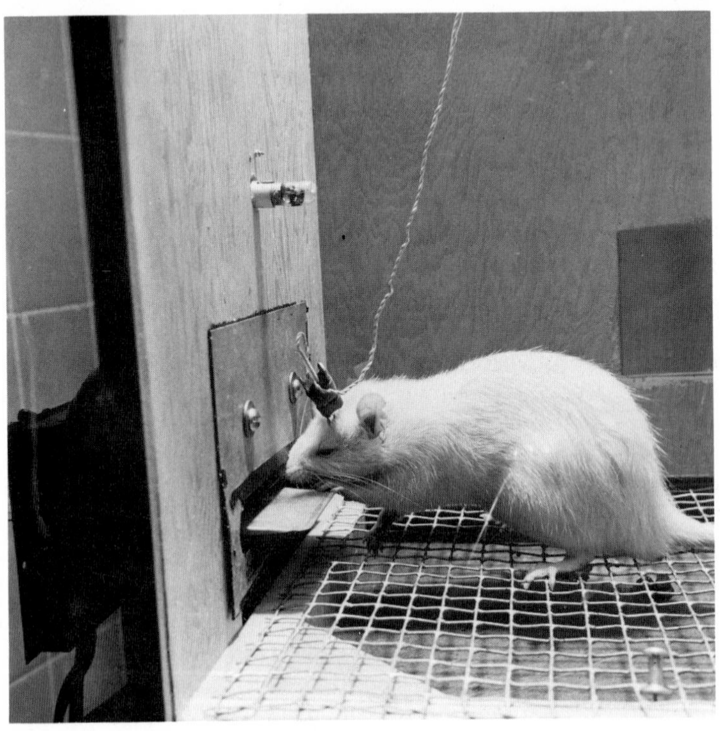

Figure 10. Photograph of a rat pressing a bar which stimulates a point in the septal area of the brain. The rat is "plugged in" to a light flexible cord that is suspended from the ceiling and is free to move about the apparatus. Through implanted electrodes points in the brain are stimulated directly. *Courtesy of* J. Olds.

At about the same time Delgado, Roberts and Miller (1954) were experimenting with electrodes implanted in the brains of cats. In one experiment five cats were trained, before the operation, to rotate a wheel at the end of the cage in order to turn off an electric shock delivered through a floor grid. A buzzer anticipated the shock by 5 seconds. The cats learned to rotate the wheel when the buzzer sounded thus avoiding the frightening buzzer and the painful shock. Training continued until all animals learned to respond to the buzzer and avoid the shock.

After this training, the electrodes were implanted and the cats allowed to recover from the operation. When the animals recovered they were healthy and normally active. Then they were tested with electrical brain stimulations. Some animals turned the wheel immediately at the first stimulation of the brain. Others appeared to be confused by motor side effects of the intracranial stimulation, but learned in a very few trials to turn the wheel and avoid the punishment. The habit of turning the wheel thus transferred readily from external to internal punishment.

Following these pioneer studies the research upon intracranial stimulation has mushroomed until today there is an immense literature upon the brain centers for reward and punishment, for pleasantness and unpleasantness. (The neuropsychology of hedonic processes will be considered in another chapter.)

The Hedonic Continuum. Quite apart from this physiological research I had for many years been studying the affective processes with human and animal subjects. My work showed that pleasantness and unpleasantness differ in sign (positive or negative), in intensity or degree, and in temporal course. These early studies demonstrated that *felt* pleasantness and unpleasantness do not normally coexist and that so-called "mixed feelings" involve a confusion between cognitive and affective aspects of experience. The relation between pleasantness and unpleasantness can be represented by a biopolar continuum.

Figure 11 is the hedonic continuum extending from maximal distress at the negative pole through neutrality or indifference to maximal delight at the positive pole. Arrows indicate important directions of hedonic change.

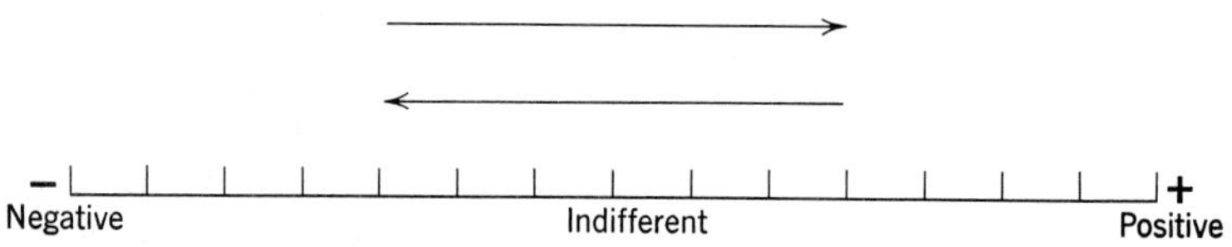

Figure 11. The hedonic continuum.

Figure 11 implies that positive and negative hedonic processes are incompatible, antagonistic. Hedonic values can change from negative to indifferent, from indifferent to positive, or in the opposite direction. They do not normally change simultaneously in opposite directions! Felt pleasantness and unpleasantness, as components of awareness, do not coexist.

In some objective psychophysical studies, I presented rats with compound taste solutions that differed in sign and in level of palatability (Young, 1967). These studies showed that positive and negative hedonic intensities combine algebraically when solutes that are normally positive are combined in a single compound solution with solutes that are normally negative. The rat either *accepts* or *rejects* the mixture. The level of acceptability depends upon the relative signs and hedonic values of the component solutes. Hence, with rats, the positive and negative effects of gustatory stimulation are dynamically opposed, reciprocally related, and they summate algebraically.

Neurophysiological Antagonisms. This same dynamic opposition and reciprocal relationship appears when one turns to current findings in neuropsychology and physiology. From the physiological point of view there appears to be much evidence that diffuse, non-specific, excitatory and inhibitory processes exist in close proximity within subcortical neural structures. For example, Olds and Olds (1963) in self-stimulation experiments observed a positive system that includes large portions of the rhinencephalon and hypothalamus, and some portions of the thalamus and tegmentum. Aversive effects were observed from only a few sites in the posterior and lateral diencephalon and lateral tegmental regions. Negative locations, however, were found in the hypothalamus in the immediate vicinity of the most effective positive sites. Both the positive and negative systems were affected by self-stimulations through implants in the posterior hypothalamus.

There is general agreement that non-specific positive and negative activations are reciprocally related. This relation is similar to that described by Sherrington (1911) in his classical experiments on the integrative action of the nervous system. Sherrington demonstrated that when an extensor muscle contracts, its antagonist actively relaxes its tonus. In flexing a leg, for example, the flexor muscle is excited while the tonic innervation of the opposed extensor is inhibited. Again, the pairs of muscles that move the eyes to the right or to the left react in a similar way with "reciprocal innervation." The muscular systems of the whole body, in fact, are organized in pairs of opposed groups. Sherrington's principle of reciprocal innervation applies to the non-specific, diffuse, excitations and inhibitions that underlie the positive and negative integrative action of the nervous system as well as to the simple reflex.

Activation and Hedonic Regulation. Now Lindsley's linear continuum of activation does not provide for diffuse positive and negative excitations that are reciprocally related. A single continuum ignores the hedonic processes and the regulative influences of non-specific positive and negative arousals.

Figure 12 shows two variables of motivation: activation level and hedonic value. At any given level of activation the motivation may be hedonically positive or neutral or negative. The facts are clear.

One could easily speculate about the placement of different affective processes within the area determined by these two variables: States of ecstacy, rapturous delight, euphoria, and the like, are positive and highly activated. The sexual orgasm, feelings of joy, are high in hedonic value and also highly activated. Cheerful moods and relaxed satisfactions are positive and at a relatively low level of activation. On the negative side of the area are highly activated states of agony, intense

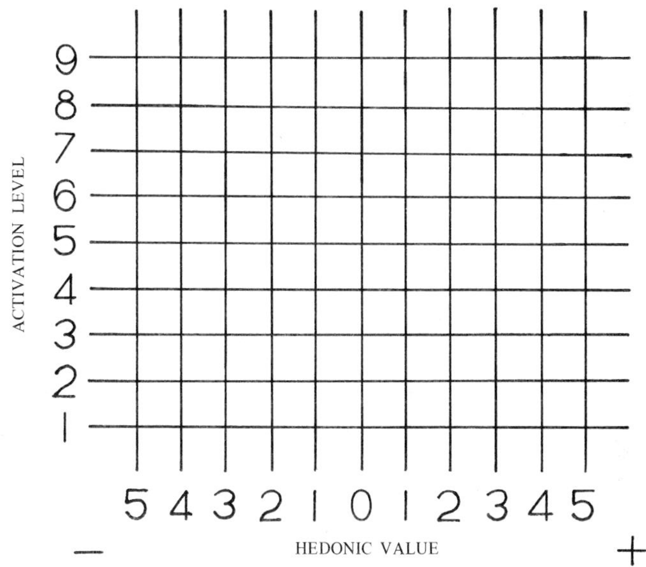

Figure 12. Two dimensions of arousal: Hedonic value and activation.

pain, disgust, and other unpleasant reactions. At lower levels of negative activation are moods of depression, grief, disappointment, and the like. Neutral states of hyperactivity, manic excitement, and the like, are well known, There are thus normal levels of neutral alertness some of which, perhaps, can be described as interesting (mildly positive) or boring (mildly negative). There are also states of calm relaxation and quiescence which are not appreciably negative or positive.

With the sthenic emotions such as anger, rage, fear, terror, great excitement, agony, and others, an essential feature is the adaptive behavior that can result from such emotional states. The adaptive behavior is something different from the hedonic values and activation levels represented by Figure 12.

Now the final point must be made that positive and negative activations are directive as well as activating. The differences among GO and STOP and CAUTION are clearly directive. They are the red, green and yellow traffic lights of behavior. The primary non-specific positive and negative motivations are *directive* and also *activating*, i.e., according to a directive-activation theory of primary motivation.

Reinforcement and Extinction through Hedonic Changes. One point should be made clear: Excitation and inhibition are widespread physiological processes that have both a chemical and a neural basis. These processes occur in different forms. As noted above, there is a reciprocal relation between excitation and inhibition in the simplest reflex and in voluntary movements. Also there are diffuse, non-specific, forms of excitation and inhibition which are dynamically opposed and reciprocally related. There is *hedonic integrative action* of the nervous system.

It would be misleading, however, to identify pleasantness with all positive excitation and unpleasantness with all negative excitation. Yet the affective processes are clearly related in some way to the non-specific forms of positive and negative activation.

The concepts of reinforcement and extinction are related to *changes* in hedonic value. The arrows in Figure 11 indicate two dynamically opposed directions of hedonic change. If the hedonic change is away from the negative pole and toward the positive pole, the behavior that produces such a change tends to be repeated, reinforced, learned. If the hedonic change is away from the positive pole and toward the negative pole, the behavior that produces such a change tends to be terminated and, in future situations, extinguished, avoided. As a matter of fact, in many experiments the reinforcment or extinction of a behavioral pattern is a sound index of change in the intensity or sign of hedonic processes.

In another chapter we will see that the hedonic changes that lead to learning occur during the early stages of development and that dispositions are organized that become autonomous guides to action. These dispositions (habits, attitudes, motives, sentiments, traits) take over the directive function of the original affective arousals. There are clearly non-hedonic forms of direction and regulation.

There is one final point: Pleasantness and unpleasantness are monitors, not plans. The affective processes instruct and guide behavior. Plans and purposive determinations give specific direction to activity.

PURPOSIVE BEHAVIOR

Tolman (1932) pointed out that purposive behavior in animals and man is a fact of observation and not an hypothesis. Persistent goal-oriented behavior develops within a stable environment. The course of its development can be observed and analyzed.

Goal Orientation in Behavior. When a man finds himself suddenly plunged into the icy ocean, he struggles to reach the air, to keep afloat. From the standpoint of biological need, such a struggle is necessary for survival. The man must reach the air to live. Even with sufficient air he cannot survive unless he maintains a stable internal temperature. Vigorous activity in the water aids in accomplishing both results.

At first he swims about with no particular goal; but while he is struggling upon the surface of the water, he sights a life boat not far away. At once he swims in the direction of the boat. Behavior becomes boat oriented, clearly purposive. Now the man is not merely keeping afloat. His activity is directed toward an object. As the boat moves, the man's behavior changes to keep his body constantly oriented toward the goal. His actions illustrate the appearance of specific goal orientation in the course of random activity.

A gradual development of goal-oriented behavior can be observed in the laboratory. If, for example, a rat is placed in a maze, he explores it. Activity is not entirely aimless, however, for every pattern is organized. Such activities as sniffing, looking about, entering this blind alley and that one, manipulating an object, preening—all these activities are already patterned. When, by chance, the rat finds food in the maze he eats it. On successive runs behavior becomes more consistently oriented toward the food until finally the hungry animal runs directly toward the goal box without stopping to preen or to enter blind alleys along the path. A new goal orientation has been built into behavior.

Under normal conditions all behavior is patterned; only certain activities are goal oriented, the rest being reflexive patterns. To illustrate, a chicken with its head chopped off dashes wildly about the barnyard for a few seconds, bumping into obstacles and flapping its wings. This behavior has no goal orientation but it is none the less patterned, organized. The physiologist calls such activity reflexive and points out that running and wing flapping depend upon coordinated contractions of pairs of muscles and that such integrations depend upon neural structures within the spinal cord of the decapitated bird.

In contrast with reflexive behavior of the headless-chicken type, goal-oriented activity is observed to be persistently directed. Ordinarily when a goal is reached, i.e., when the consummatory act or goal response is made (a thirsty animal, for example, finds water and drinks it) a need is met and the degree of motivation is lowered. The goal response consummates or brings to a close the goal-oriented act.

The goal orientations of an individual change frequently. When a motive has been reduced, another motive dominates behavior in such a manner that a new goal orientation appears.

Goal orientation is a fact of observation just as truly as is the fixed direction of a steel ball when it rolls down an inclined plane. It is a fact, for example, that a child, in chasing a ball, follows it in whatever direction it may go or bounce—to right or left, up or down. The child remains oriented toward the ball.

Goal orientation can be *observed* in two forms: first as a persistent and consistent direction or trend in behavior; second, as an overt posture or bodily attitude toward some object. In addition to these observable forms, goal orientation is also *assumed* to exist. A mental set to act, a specific intention, implies an orientation of the subject toward some end result; but this determination is only at times revealed in overt behavior.

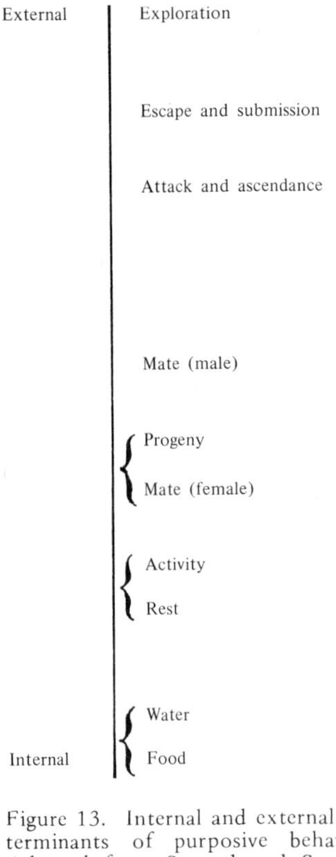

External — Exploration
Escape and submission
Attack and ascendance
Mate (male)
Progeny / Mate (female)
Activity / Rest
Internal — Water / Food

Figure 13. Internal and external determinants of purposive behavior *Adapted from* Seward and Seward (1937).

Internal and External Determinants of Purposive Behavior. Although every purposive activity is determined by both internal and external factors, the balance between these two groups of determinants is variable. Typical purposive activities can be grouped as in Figure 13 according to the internal or external location of the principal stimulation which originates the behavior.

Seward and Seward (1937) have pointed out that the vegetative drives on the whole are cyclic because they are determined by recurring organic states such as hunger for food or filling of the bladder. External determinants of purposive behavior, by contrast, are non-cyclic; they appear and disappear with the inducing situation. For example, if a white rat is placed in a strange environment, he explores it; but, when he has become familiar with his surroundings, exploration ceases and does not return unless he is again put in an unaccustomed place. Similarly, when a man is working out a puzzle, he has an urge to persist until the puzzle is solved. When this is achieved the man's interest and motive ceases.

Although no sharp line can be drawn between purposive activities which are exclusively internal in origin and those which are exclusively environmental, the foregoing distinction between internal and external determinants of behavior is serviceable in any analysis and classification of drives and incentives.

In addition to the cyclic or non-cyclic character of drives, there is a further contrast between drives of organic and incentives of environmental origin. With organic drives the typical order of causation is from chemical change to neural excitation, but with environmental incentives the order (at least in part) is from neural excitation to chemical change. For example, states of hunger, thirst, sexual excitement, fatigue, sleepiness, and others, are describable as chemical and neural conditions which motivate the organism through changing the excitability of nerves. As an illustration of an external factor which evokes internal chemical changes, it may be noted that almost any situation in which there is a biological emergency—danger, for example—excites the organism in such a manner that the adrenal glands secrete. Adrenal secretion, in turn, evokes a variety of internal neural and chemical processes.

Biological and Social Determinants of Purposive Behavior. Malinowski (1941) has listed a series of basic impulses, with their resulting acts and satisfactions, which are incorporated into all cultures. These primitive impulses rest upon well-known organic states. There are, however, other conditions (those which call forth maternal behavior and those present in certain specific food cravings and aversions) which might be added to the list. Malinowski's chart is worthy of careful study:

Impulse	*Act*	*Satisfaction*
Drive to breathe; gasping for air	Intake of oxygen	Elimination of CO_2 in tissues
Hunger	Ingestion of food	Satiation
Thirst	Absorption of liquid	Quenching
Sex appetite	Conjugation	Detumescence
Fatigue	Rest	Restoration of muscular and nervous energy
Restlessness	Activity	Satisfaction of fatigue
Somnolence	Sleep	Awakening with restored energy
Bladder pressure	Micturition	Removal of tension
Colon pressure	Defecation	Abdominal relaxation
Fright	Escape from danger	Relaxation
Pain	Avoidance by effective act	Return to normal state

When we turn our attention to the environment we find there a countless number of situations which induce purposive behavior. Some of them are *social* and others are *non-social*.

The analysis of social motivation is a large and complicated task. The following tentative list of social motives which are present in the chimpanzee, and presumably also in man, is taken from Tolman (1941).

Gregariousness	i.e., Returning to company of others of the group.
Loyalty to group	i.e., Defending other members of the group against attack.
Imitativeness	i.e., Copying actions performed by other members of the group.
Dominance	i.e., Dominating over another individual.
Submission	i.e., Submitting to another.
Competitive acquisition	i.e., Piling up material for the future—such activity being enhanced by the presence of other individuals.
Sharing with and soliciting from others	i.e., Giving to another individual. Receiving from another individual.
Cooperation tendencies	i.e., Working with another individual for a common goal.

It is interesting to note that every one of the social motivations ascribed by Tolman to chimpanzees is also well-developed in human beings. These broad generalizations of behavior are based upon a great variety of detailed observations by Köhler, Yerkes, and others. The generalizations are socially significant, but they are not to be regarded as explanations of behavior.

The specific factors within the social environment which induce behavior are protean. In animals a few examples are: A blow administered by the master, the latter speaking in a soft and low voice, the presence of a stranger, a rival competing for food or for the possession of a mate. With children, a reward presented by teacher or parent, a punishment, an insult, words of praise or reproof, a blow from another child, and the approach of a strange dog, are all environmental factors which induce behavior. In each of these examples it is a specific stimulation which motivates behavior.

Examples of non-social motivating factors within the environment are: the novelty or familiarity of a situation, a danger or threat to one's safety (such as fire or rising flood water), and physical stimulations from cold temperature or heat or from the lack of air.

SET, TENSION, AND THE BALANCE OF MOTIVES

In view of the close relationship between motives and emotions, it is important to consider the nature of those sets and postural tensions which underlie the manifest outbursts of emotion.

Overt Posture and Mental Set. When a man or an animal is prepared to carry out some specific act he sometimes betrays his intention by posture and behavior. Thus the deer, when startled by a noise, stands with head erect, sniffing the air, and poised to run. The cat remains crouched before a mouse hole, ready to spring when the victim appears. Human examples of such preparatory attitudes are frequently observed. The diver before jumping off the springboard maintains his stance. The runner toes the line awaiting the gun.

These explicit bodily attitudes prepare the individual for a specific action. There are also implicit mental sets which are preparatory but which are not outwardly observed. For example, when the members of a committee meet to discuss some particular topic, a predetermined plan dominates the discussion of the meeting. In social gatherings, by contrast, where there is no fixed plan of discussion, the conversation usually wanders from topic to topic with little direction. Thus a conversation recently overheard by the writer at a dinner table thoroughly covered the topics of snakes, funerals, airplanes, bridges, and Billy Sunday!

A mental set is a fixed determination to respond in a particular manner to a stimulus-situation. The set may be released in a variety of ways. Thus if one intends to mail a letter, one can release this tension by dropping the letter in a mail box, by handing it to a friend for mailing, or by offering it to the postman. The mental set is the same regardless of the specific way in which it is released and revealed in behavior. As Lewin (1927) pointed out, activities which are very unlike in their superficial appearance may have a common motivation.

It is also true that activities which are superficially alike may be very unlike in their motivation. Two boys, both known to the author, returned lost dogs to their owners. One boy returned the lost dog out of sheer kindliness. The other boy's motive was the hope of collecting a reward. Another instance is that of an actor who, in affecting a burst of anger upon the stage, is very differently motivated from the man who reveals genuine anger when insulted; yet anger on the stage may very closely resemble the genuine outburst. The important consideration is the motivating set, the intent.

A word of warning is in order about the use of the phrase *mental set.* This phrase is employed in diverse ways by psychologists today. Gibson (1941), in a critical review of the experimental literature, has pointed out that the term *mental set* and its variant forms are employed by psychologists to designate a variety of processes. Among other meanings the term *set* may signify: (1) a prearoused sensory expectation, as the awaiting of another beat in a rhythmical metronome sequence; (2) an intention to respond to a situation by making a specific movement, as a set to switch on the lights when entering a dark room, or, in the reaction experiment, a set to press the key when a light flashes; (3) an inner determination to perform a familiar operation, as to multiply or add or subtract or divide two numbers; (4) a wholly non-voluntary (spontaneous) readiness to return to some incomplete task and complete it; (5) the perseverance of a recent, vivid experience, as the running through one's head of a catchy tune or the re-living in imagination of a social event. The existence of these diverse meanings shows the importance of a clear definition of the concept of *set* whenever the term is employed.

Postural Tension and Behavior. Physiologists have drawn a distinction between the tonic reaction of muscles and the phasic reaction. A tonic reaction is of relatively long duration; a phasic reaction is brief and transient. Almost any quick, brief movement, as tipping one's hat, waving a hand, or taking a step, is a phasic reaction. The phasic reaction supplies direction and pattern to behavior. Tonic reactions supply persistent motivation.

The persistent motivation comes from the stimulation of receptor organs in the muscles, tendons, and joints when a postural tension has been established. To maintain a bodily posture and muscle tonus, as to hold out the arm against gravity or to pose as a statue, requires constant excitation of the muscle fibers and an expenditure of bodily energy. But the posture also stimulates the proprioceptors and is thus a source of persistent motivation. Freeman (1939) pointed out that at any given time there is a background of tonic excitation which to a considerable extent determines the intensity of an overt reaction.

There is a basal level of postural tension, Freeman states, which varies from individual to individual and which is characteristic of a given person. This level varies with age, with the metabolic state of the organism, and especially with the degree of external stimulation. External stimulations—from lights, sounds, contacts, odors—force the individual above his basal level. Increments of tonic activity from these and other sources are superimposed upon the existing level of postural tension. Internal stimulations—increased bladder pressure, for example—also heighten the general level of postural tension; the increased tension persists until relieved by an appropriate act. Further, a conflict-situation or the frustration of any goal-oriented activity heightens the level of postural tension. The heightened tension from conflict or frustration persists until some adjustment can be made.

There is a level of postural tension which yields the most effective performance of any skilled act. Below this level the quality and quantity of work varies directly with the degree of stimulation from the postural set. If the tension level exceeds a certain degree (that required for optimal performance) there is excitement and a breakdown or disorganization of the skilled act. The relation between muscular tension and performance is reviewed by Courts (1942).

In some respects the view of Freeman is similar to that of Kempf which will be presented briefly in the next section.

Kempf's Doctrine of "Segmental Cravings" in Relation to Attitude and Feeling. The importance of autonomic functions can hardly be overstated. Kempf (1920, 1935) writes: "The autonomic apparatus is constituted of all the vital organs, including the ductless secretory glands, unstriped muscles and the ganglionic nervous systems that have to do with *assimilation, conservation, distribution* and *expenditure* of energy-giving metabolic products and the *elimination* of the waste products. This includes the entire digestive, circulatory, respiratory, and urinary systems, sex organs, glands of internal secretion, glands of external secretion, and the autonomic nervous system."

Changes in postural tonus involve not only the skeletal musculature but also the glands and smooth muscles regulated by the autonomic nervous system. Thus, when an individual turns toward some part or phase of his world of experience with an attitude of "love-acquisitiveness," or "fear-avertiveness," or "anger-hate-destructiveness," this is not merely an attitude of the cerebrospinal nerves and the skeletal muscles. Along with the overt behavior and posture there are changes in the respiratory, circulatory, and gastrointestinal musculature, which have become tied up with the total response through conditioning and reinforcement.

Further, the tonic changes in smooth muscle of the body excite cerebrospinal nerves. Thus from alimentary, urinary, genital, and respiratory functioning there arise afferent nerve impulses which have a more or less dominant effect upon the posture of the body as a whole. The gastric griping for food, the rectal griping for evacuation, the sexual tension, and the tensions and distensions of the circulatory systems are readily distinguished from each other. Kempf refers to these specific changes of visceral tonicity as "segmental cravings." They arise from any or from all of the great visceral segments: the bronchi, arteries, somatic muscle, esophagus, stomach, ileum, colon, rectum, bladder, internal genital organs, and others.

The afferent neural excitations arising from the viscera contribute not only to the maintenance of postural tonus but also they furnish the organic groundwork for various conscious cravings and feelings. The feelings of well-being and comfort and the enjoyment of living, as well as the various experiences of organic distress, are conscious representations of the tonic conditions in visceral organs.

According to Kempf, the general law of attitude (postural tonus) is this: The form or pattern of attitude which exists at a given moment determines what the reactions will be to stimuli. That is to say, attitude determines the thoughts and movements which occur in response to an external situation.

Visceralized attitudes and visceralized intentions are known to play a vital role in human conflicts. The important conflicts of life, Kempf states, are those in which the cerebrospinal system opposes the autonomic. A person's desire for social esteem, to illustrate, may conflict with his sexual appetite. If he suppresses his sexual appetite for the sake of social esteem, a variety of nervous symptoms (indigestion, irritability, etc.) may develop, owing to the increased tension continually present. If he satisfies his sexual appetite and sacrifices social esteem, he may be classed as a delinquent, or an anxiety neurosis may develop. Thus, among people who engage in autoerotic practices it is not an uncommon complaint that for several hours or days following the indulgence they suffer from a severe sense of inferiority, fear of discovery, and shame. This is followed by a firm resolution (compensation) to prevent a similar recurrence. After several days the sexual tension is again built up and the "segmental craving" becomes more intense until finally this craving again dominates the entire organism. The resolution to maintain self-control and win social esteem is again overcome, and the cycle repeats itself unless, of course, some reorientation (sublimation, according to Freud) can be effected or the person's situation can be so altered that the normal autonomic tensions can find release under conditions which meet with social approval (in our culture, marriage).

Anxiety Tension as a Form of Motivation. If an individual has been pained, injured, or humiliated in a given situation, he will anticipate a similar misfortune when again placed in that situation. To give a concrete example from the laboratory: If a dog has received a painful shock on the foot after the sounding of a tone, he will prepare himself for another pain on the foot when the tone begins to sound or when he is again placed upon the conditioning apparatus.

Mowrer (1939) regards anxiety as a *learned* response which can be explained by the established principles of conditioning. Through the process of conditioning, certain signals (conditioned stimuli) become premonitory of pain or injury (unconditioned stimuli). After an individual has been conditioned, the signal leads to the anticipation or expectation of pain-injury.

Anxiety, as distinguished from fright, is a state of heightened tension with a specific expectation of some pain, injury, or humiliation to one's self or to another. The expectant set of the organism includes not only the skeletal musculature but the visceral organs as well. The expectation is not necessarily conscious; it may be a purely physiological preparation for the impending traumatic stimulus. This principle may be illustrated by reference to the experiment of Blatz (1925). His subject was seated in a chair, which, without any warning, could be made to fall over backward until stopped by a door-check. After a subject had experienced one fall in this chair his heart rate increased when another fall was anticipated. This was found to hold true in fifteen out of eighteen subjects. There was, we might say, a visceral preparation to meet the impending emergency. The worries of everyday life are of the same nature as this experimental anxiety.

Anxiety plays an important role in neurasthenia and in many psychoses. Sometimes there is a prolonged foreboding of harm or injury without any specific reference to a dreaded object. This is called an anxiety neurosis. More commonly, however, the anxious individual finds some object—real or imaginary—for his anxiety, or a whole succession of objects.

Anxiety tension is a very important form of human motivation. Whatever adjustments succeed in reducing the general level of anxiety of an individual are likely to be repeated—reinforced. And whatever responses raise the level of anxiety are likely to be eliminated from future behavior. The struggle for economic security or the struggle to maintain one's social status is accelerated when something happens to raise the level of anxiety in either of those specific areas.

Motivational Balances and Antagonisms. The second of the three classical principles of emotional expression formulated by Darwin (1872) was designated the principle of antithesis. This was described by Darwin as follows:

> Certain states of the mind lead to certain habitual actions, which are of service, as under our first principle. Now when a directly opposite state of mind is induced, there is a strong and involuntary tendency to the performance of movements of a directly opposite nature, though these are of no use; and such movements are in some cases highly expressive. [28]

Darwin illustrated the principle of antitheses by describing the behavior of dogs and cats. See Figure 14.

> When a dog approaches a strange dog or man in a savage or hostile frame of mind he walks upright and very stiffly; his head is slightly raised, or not much lowered; the tail is held erect and quite rigid; the hairs bristle, especially along the neck and back; the pricked ears are directed forwards, and the eyes have a fixed stare. These actions . . . follow from the dog's intention to attack his enemy, and are thus to a large extent intelligible. As he prepares to spring with a savage growl on his enemy, the canine teeth are uncovered, and the ears are pressed close backwards on the head. . . . Let us suppose that the dog suddenly discovers that the man whom he is approaching, is not a stranger, but his master; and let it be observed how completely and instantaneously his whole bearing is reversed. Instead of walking upright, the body sinks downward or even crouches, and is thrown into flexuous movements; his tail, instead of being held stiff and upright, is lowered and wagged from side to side; his hair instantly becomes smooth; his ears are depressed and drawn backwards, but not closely to the head; and his lips hang loosely. From the drawing back of the ears, the eyelids become elongated, and the eyes no longer appear round and staring. [50-51]

Hostile behavior in the cat presents a contrast to that in the dog. When the cat is threatened, she arches the back in a surprising manner, erects the hair, opens the mouth and hisses. This familiar response indicates terror or, at times, an emotion which combines terror with rage. The response of pure hostile attack is seen when two cats are fighting each other or when a cat is being plagued by a boy.

In hostile attack the animal assumes a crouching position, in which the body is extended. The tail or just the tip is lashed or curled from side to side. The hair is not erect as it is in fear. The ears are pressed backward; the mouth is partly opened, showing the teeth; the forefeet occasionally strike out with protruding claws; the animal utters a fierce growl. All these responses are preparatory to actual attack upon an enemy.

The bodily set of the friendly cat is directly opposite to that of a hostile animal. The friendly cat stands upright with her back slightly arched. The hair appears to be rough, but it does not bristle. Her tail is stiff and stands straight up; her ears are erect and pointed; her mouth is closed. She rubs against her master with a purr instead of a growl.

Friendly behavior is thus the antithesis of hostile attack, appearing when hostile attack is inhibited or counterbalanced. Darwin regarded antithetical expressions (such as friendly behavior) as useless in a fight or flight, but he suggested that they are serviceable so far as they communicate friendliness to other animals and to man. They have social utility. The neural structures for exhibiting friendly behavior and those for hostile attack are always present, but the two patterns are opposed and incompatible. Friendliness is a correction, an over-

Figure 14. Hostility and friendliness in animals: (1) Hostility in the dog. (2) Friendliness in the dog. (3) Hostility in the cat. (4) Friendliness in the cat. *Redrawn by* Mrs. K. H. Paul from Darwin (1872).

compensation, for hostility. There is, of course, much behavior which is neither hostile nor friendly.

Fright in the cat is something different. The cat terrified by a barking dog is poised between two impulses. She can attack the dog and, in fact, the bodily expressions of rage are present or she can run for a tree to escape from her enemy. These two emotional reaction patterns are balanced against each other and the environmental situation can trigger either reaction.

There are many other examples of motivational balances and antagonisms. I have seen a child, when hurt, balanced between laughing and crying. A slight change in the behavior of the mother can result in either laughing or crying. Also in some instances of hysteria the patient may alternately laugh and cry. The environmental situation apparently determines which reaction will occur.

In the sphere of social behavior there are antithetical attitudes and corresponding forms of behavior. For example, attitudes of courage and bravery are built into the developing individual through social training. These attitudes in the soldier are directly opposed to the inborn impulse to escape from a threatening and dangerous situation. The courageous man, however, enters the burning house or jumps into the foaming sea to make a rescue; in battle he fights on unaware of serious bodily injury; or he endures the desert heat to reach a friend.

Now one cannot at the same time react positively to a threatening situation while avoiding it and escaping from danger. Consequently, in terms of human values, there is incompatibility between courageous and cowardly conduct. Courageous behavior implies facing danger and accepting the risks; cowardly behavior is negative—running away or escaping from the threat.

Again, antagonisms exist in the sphere of sexual behavior. Promiscuity is opposed, in our civilization, by ethical standards of chastity and monogamous marriage. In psychological terms this means that an urge for promiscuous sexual expression is blocked by opposing inhibitions based upon a desire for the esteem of the social group, upon fears of pregnancy and venereal diseases, and upon an acceptance of the ideology of monogamous marriage with its special satisfactions and restraints. There are thus conflicts between a fundamental biological urge, on the one hand, and sex-inhibiting attitudes, on the other. This conflict may be satisfactorily resolved through redirection of the biological urge into channels of indirect expression acceptable to the mores of the social group. On the other hand, it may become the source of emotional disturbance and even of neuroses, as Freud observed.

Sex-inhibitory attitudes sometimes overbalance the sex motive to such an extent that prudery appears. Prudery is the negation of sex, as friendliness is the negation of hostility. Prudish behavior is the opposite of natural and spontaneous sexual activity. The prude is easily shocked by situations which an emotionally balanced individual does not find objectionable. The prude, in extreme cases, acts as if he or she were denying the existence of sex in the world.

Another motivational balance which is important, especially in social psychology, is that between self-display, including self-assertion and expansiveness, on the one hand, and self-abasement or subjection, on the other. McDougall (1926) more than any other psychologist has stressed the self-regarding motives. Self-display and self-assertion, he wrote, exist in the behavior of children. The child will act so as to draw attention to himself. Frequently he will command, "See me do this," "Watch while I do so-and-so," "See how well I can turn a somersault." Adults are less obvious in calling attention to themselves, but whole segments of adult behavior can be epitomized by the words, "Here am I! Look and admire!"

Successful self-display is experienced as pride, self-confidence, and assurance. When self-display is unsuccessful, there are likely to be feelings of shame or failure or inferiority. McDougall, to describe these feelings, has used the terms *positive* and *negative* self-feeling.

There are a good many other examples of the dynamic balance between opposed motivating systems. For example, the positive appetite for food is opposed by disgust aroused by foul food objects or odors or even by an offensive topic of conversation during a meal. Again, nausea is suppressed by fear. It has often been the experience of persons who are seasick that a storm which becomes severe enough to be dangerous quickly banishes the nausea of seasickness.

Cannon (1929) pointed out that during fear and anger the digestive processes are inhibited; the secretion of gastric juice is diminished and the peristaltic movements of the stomach are checked. Subjectively, the hunger pang vanishes when strong fear or anger is aroused. Hungry persons, when suddenly confronted with grave danger, report that the hunger disappears when they experience fear.

Thus there are various counterbalanced systems of motivation. The balance can swing from side to side, but it is not possible for an organism to move simultaneously in opposed directions. This is a physical fact of nature and of life to which the organism must become adjusted.

CONCLUSION

In this chapter we have considered the psychologist's relativistic approach to the study of motivation and emotion. The study of motivational factors will be continued in the following chapter and elsewhere because feelings and emotions must be analyzed within a broad dynamic context.

The psychologist examines all phenomena from different points of view: experiential, behavioral, physiological, developmental. With such a complex event as emotion an eclectic, multidisciplinary, approach to the study is essential. The different aspects of emotion are found to be wholly congruent, however, and to supplement each other.

What a person sees, believes, desires, does in an environmental situation, varies with his outlook on life, his *Weltanschauung*. Feelings, emotions, attitudes and motives, are all relative to an individual's past experience, to his developed mental structure. There is psychological relativity of the phenomena of emotion to the current structural organization of an individual.

Motivation is the basic process of arousing, directing, and sustaining activity. Purposive, goal-oriented, behavior is an essential aspect of the process. A directive-activation theory of motivation has been described. The theory takes account of activation of behavior through non-specific, diffuse, neural excitations and the directive and regulative aspects of behavior through positive and negative hedonic arousals. The developmental and physiological aspects of this theory will be considered in other chapters.

An organic *set* is outwardly observable as a bodily posture in preparation for some specific action. The *set* corresponds to an intention, plan, or specific purpose. This *set* directs the course of behavior. Psychoneural structures may remain latent for indefinite periods of time and then be aroused, or activated, by an environmental stimulus-situation.

Behavior shows many dynamic balances. Motivational balances and antagonisms are prominent in emotional behavior. Thus friendly behavior is the antithesis of hostility. On the social level, attitudes of courage and bravery are opposed to the basic impulses of fear which lead to escape from a threatening, dangerous, situation rather than to face it positively. The sexual appetite is opposed by various no-sex attitudes. Other antagonisms are implied by the following pairs of words: *love-hate, liking-disliking, interest-aversion,* etc. Attitudes and motives are continually balanced against each other. Circumstances can tip the balance one way or the other.

READING SUGGESTIONS ON MOTIVATION

There is a vast and complicated literature dealing with human and animal motivation. For an introduction see the writer's text, *Motivation and Emotion* (Young, 1961) and the scholarly compendium by Cofer and Appley (1964) entitled, *Motivation: Theory and Research*. There are many other texts.

The dynamic principles which have grown out of Freudian psychology and current psychoanalysis are considered, for example, in books by Symonds (1946, 1949).

Studies of motivation within the personality and in the social context have been made by McClelland (1951, 1955), by Atkinson (1958), and by McClelland, Atkinson, Clark and Lowell (1953) in *The Achievement Motive*.

For advanced study see reports of the *Nebraska Symposia on Motivation* which have been conducted annually since 1953. These symposia are published by the University of Nebraska Press under the editorship of Marshall R. Jones (Vols. II-XI), David Levine (Vols. XII-XV, XVII) and William J. Arnold (Vol. XVI). The many papers deal not only with motivation but with closely related psychological topics.

All of these works contain numerous references to the literature. So the task of the student is to decide what *not* to study!

Note upon the canals of Mars

Discussion of the canals upon Mars is based upon portions of the following works: E. M. Antoniadi, *La Planète Mars, Étude basée sur les Résultats obtenus avec la grande lunette de l'observatoire de Meudon et exposé analytique de l'ensemble des travaux exécutés sur cet astre depuis 1659* (Paris: Librairie scientifique Hermann et Cie, 1930). A. E. Douglass, Is Mars Inhabited? *Harvard Illustrated Magazine*, 1907, 8, 116-118. P. Lowell, *Mars* (New York: Houghton Mifflin, 1895; pp.x + 217); *Mars and its Canals* (New York: Macmillan, 1907; pp. xv + 393); *Mars as the Abode of Life* (New York: Macmillan, 1908; pp. xix + 288). E. S. Morse, *Mars and its Mystery* (Boston: Little, Brown and Co., 1907; pp. xi + 192). W. H. Pickering, The Planet Mars, *Harvard Illustrated Magazine*, 1907, 8, 115-116. A. R. Wallace, *Is Mars Habitable?* (London: Macmillan, 1907; pp. xii + 110).

Chapter III

Needs, Values, Appetites and Aversions

No survey of motivation is complete which ignores the needs, values, appetites and aversions that underlie the affective life of man. In this chapter we shall continue the analysis of motivation by considering these basic factors.

EVALUATIVE AND DYNAMIC DEFINITIONS OF NEED

In everyday life the concept of *need* is evaluative. When we say that a child *needs* a spanking we mean that punishment would be good for his development. When we say that the soup *needs* more salt we mean that it would taste better if salt were added. When we say that a man *needs* a new coat we probably mean that the garment would improve his appearance, comfort and self-esteem.

In scientific literature the concept of need is frequently met. A *need* is an evaluation relative to some criterion. Various criteria have been used. When we have agreed upon a criterion, we can then agree that a specific need exists. For example, the principle of homeostasis provides an excellent criterion for an objective analysis of organic needs. To maintain homeostasis the organism *needs* (requires) oxygen, water, protein, carbohydrate, fat, minerals, vitamins, a certain range of temperatures, etc. If these needs fail to be met, homeostasis is impossible.

Survival of the individual is another criterion closely associated with maintaining homeostasis but a somewhat broader criterion. To survive an organism must not only maintain homeostasis; he must successfully fight enemies and avoid physical dangers. He *needs* adequate means of defense and offense to remain secure.

Reproduction of the species is still another possible criterion. For example, it can be said that chicks, mice, and other laboratory animals, *need* vitamin E since a deficiency of this vitamin impedes reproduction. Also from this point of view it can be said that sexual behavior is needed, and the need is quite apart from sexual motivation.

Another possible criterion for defining *need* is normal growth and function. If normal growth and function are known, then there is a criterion for specifying organic needs. for example, the avitaminoses are defined by describing the physical defects that appear when a specific vitamin is removed from the diet.

Possibly health is a criterion. The state of health has many aspects but if one can state objectively what is meant by "being in sound health," one can then specify the needs of organisms to remain healthy.

In general, a *need* is an evaluation that is made by reference to some criterion. The needs of an organism are the requirements for maintaining homeostasis, reproducing, growing and functioning normally, keeping healthy, and, in fact, for surviving in a hostile world.

Visual Sensitivity as Measure of a Need. Since the usual concept of need is evaluative, and not factual, it is possible to dispense with the concept. To illustrate this possibility consider an experiment by Russell and Younger (1943) upon the relation between the differential threshold for visual intensity and a vitamin A deficiency in the diet.

It is well known that vitamin A plays an essential role in the photochemical processes of vision. Vitamin A is a precursor of visual purple (a photosensitive substance) as well as a product of its decomposition.

On the basis of available evidence, Russell and Younger predicted that avitaminosis-A would raise the differential threshold for visual intensity and that restoration of vitamin A to the diet would lead to recovery of normal visual discrimination. In laboratory tests it was found, as predicted, that the differential threshold for visual intensity increased to three or four times its original level when rats were maintained upon a diet deficient in vitamin A. When the rats were returned to a complete diet the threshold decreased to its normal level. Only 4 or 5 days were required for the threshold to return to normal.

In reporting this work the investigators did not mention the concept of need. They simply described the functional relation between two variables: (1) the duration of dietary depletion of vitamin A, and (2) the differential threshold for visual intensity. It would be easy, however, to introduce as a criterion of need: "The ability of the rat to discriminate visual brightnesses." With this criterion one can readily demonstrate a need of the depleted rats for vitamin A.

There is a large and growing literature that deals with the impact of diet upon behavior. Many examples can be found of relationships between behavior and specific dietary deficiencies. But all such relationships can be described in a matter of fact way without introducing the concept of need, as in the above example.

The Dynamic Definition of Need. A dynamic definition of need is in sharp contrast to the evaluative concept. There are psychologists who employ the term in a dynamic sense by equating need with drive, force, or motivation. The view that need is a *tension, force,* or *drive*, is commonly held within contemporary psychology. Thus Murray (1938) writes: "A need is a construct (a convenient fiction or hypothetical concept) which stands for a force (the physicochemical nature of which is unknown) in the brain region, a force which organizes perception, apperception, intellection, conation and action in such a way as to transform in a certain direction an existing unsatisfying situation."

Murray distinguished two knids of needs: viscerogenic (primary) and psychogenic (secondary). The viscerogenic needs include the needs for air, water, food, sex, lactation,urination, and defecation—all of which have a known physiological basis. The need for food, Murray explains, could be broken down into separate needs for different kinds of foods. The viscerogenic needs also include harm-avoidance, nox-avoidance, heat-avoidance, cold-avoidance, and sentience. The last (sentience) includes the needs for sensuous gratification as contact, taste sensation, tactile sensation, e.g., as seen in thumb sucking.

The viscerogenic needs can be grouped in a number of ways. The grouping in Table 3 calls for division of the need for air into two needs: the need for inspiration and the need for expiration.

TABLE 3
Classification of Viscerogenic (Primary) Needs

Need	
A. Lacks (leading to intakes)	Positive
1. *n* Inspiration (oxygen)	
2. *n* Water	
3. *n* Food	
4. *n* Sentience	
B. Distensions (leading to outputs)	
Secretion (life sources),	
5. *n* Sex	
6. *n* Lactation	
Excretion (waste)	Negative
7. *n* Expiration (carbon dioxide)	
8. *n* Urination	
9. *n* Defecation	
C. Harms (leading to retractions)	
10. *n* Noxavoidance	
11. *n* Heat avoidance	
12. *n* Cold avoidance	
13. *n* Harm avoidance	

After Murray (1938)

Murray also recognizes a need for passivity (not listed in the tabulation) which includes needs for relaxation, rest, and sleep.

Murray's classification of the primary viscerogenic needs as positive or negative does not, of course, reflect *hedonic* values. The "*Lacks*" of oxygen, water, food, sensory stimulation (which are classified as positive), can become very unpleasant. Deprivation of these essentials, however, often leads to positive, seeking behavior that normally relieves the viscerogenic distress. The "*Harms*" are negative reactions to environmental conditions that generally lead to hedonically negative processes and to avoiding behavior. The "*Distensions*," some of which are classified as positive and some as negative, can be anything hedonically depending on conditions. It would be better, I am sure, to classify the primary motivations as hedonically positive, neutral, or negative than to follow Murray's classification.

Murray goes on to discuss the psychogenic needs which, he states, are derived from the primary viscerogenic needs. He lists twenty-eight secondary needs including: acquisition, order, achievement, recognition, exhibition, dominance, aggression, affiliation, play, cognizance, and others.

Such needs appear to originate in the *social* environment rather than intraorganic conditions. Murray does not specify the criteria by which these secondary needs can be defined nor does he show exactly how they are derived from viscerogenic conditions.

It seems to me that some needs are *social* in origin, e.g., being accepted by one's group, conforming to group standards, security within the group, recognition by others, etc. There are also *personality* needs: a need for self-esteem, for self-expression, for intellectual freedom, etc. The basic question, however, remains as to how such social and personality needs can be defined and whether they are static evaluations or dynamic processes—motives. What are the criteria of social and personality needs?

Needs and Drives. In contrast to *need* is the concept *drive*. In so far as *need* is an evaluation—an extrinsic appraisal—a need may exist without having any effect upon behavior. As a matter of fact, nutritional needs may exist which are entirely unknown to the needy organism. Such needs are revealed in various ways—by abnormalities of growth, failure to reproduce, deficiency in learning, activity, etc. The concept of *drive*, contrastingly, is always dynamic. Physiological drives are motivating, activating. In so far as a need is regarded as a tension or force that instigates activity, the concepts of need and drive are synonymous. Homeostatic drives like thirst, hunger, pain avoidance, fatigue, somnolence, etc., are always motivating. These drives organize adaptive behavior.

Homeostatic needs and drives are of tremendous human importance. Certain biological conditions of survival are common to mankind in all societies, in all parts of the world, at all times. People everywhere *need* air, water, food, a livable temperature, etc.; they need to acquire basic patterns of behavior that meet the requirements of life. Some primary needs and drives are obviously common to man and non-human animals.

Drives, according to Tolman, are of two kinds: appetitive and aversive. Appetitive drives are shown by seeking behavior; aversive drives, by escape from noxious stimulations and avoidance of threatening conditions. Appetitive drives are organized and developed on the basis of hedonic changes in the positive direction—away from discomfort and toward comfort. Aversive drives are organized and developed through the same kind of hedonic changes—typically away from painful discomfort toward relief and restoration of comfort.

There are, of course, many behaviors which are hedonically neutral. Observant, exploratory, manipulative, problem-solving forms of behavior are typically neutral—neither intensely pleasant nor unpleasant. Such ongoing behaviors imply neural activation, as does all sustained activity, but the direction and regulation of behavior comes from the ever-changing environmental situations, combined with the skills, habits, attitudes, and motives that have been acquired by the organism.

HOW PRIMITIVE MAN MEETS HIS NEEDS[1]

In building a brick wall, the mason *needs* mortar. When an artist paints a portrait, he *needs* canvas and pigments. If an organism is to survive, it *must have* oxygen, water, protein, fat, carbohydrate, mineral salts, vitamins, a moderate range of external temperature. *Need* is always a requirement for some result. Where need exists, it is a need *of* something *for* some end or goal.

Primitive man acts to meet the biological requirements of his existence even though he has but hazy understanding of their nature. Beautiful illustrations of this principle can be drawn from the field of anthropology.

Actinic Rays and Vitamin D. Within recent years it has been discovered that the actinic rays (those that produce chemical action,

[1]Of the following eight illustrations, the first six were brought together by the anthropologist, Dr. C. S. Ford, in an unpublished paper presented to the Monday Night Group, 1939-1940, at the Institute of Human Relations, Yale University, and are reproduced with his permission.

especially the violet and ultra-violet rays) of the sun aid in the manufacture of vitamin D in the human body. These rays filter through bodily skins of a light color, but darker skins serve as insulation against them.

In tropical regions the quantity of actinic rays transmitted through the atmosphere is enormous indeed, whereas, toward the polar regions, the concentration of these rays diminishes rapidly. Within the arctic circle very few actinic rays filter through the atmosphere and reach the inhabitants. The rays of the sun, which meet the earth's surface at right angles in the tropics, are very slanting at the poles, and this is an important factor in determining the concentration of actinic rays.

An excess of actinic rays means an excess production of vitamin D, which, in turn, leads to nervous disorders such as neurasthenia, while lack of the rays—unless vitamin D is supplied in some other way—is conducive to rickets. The illnesses resulting from excess of vitamin D or from its deficiency, although injurious to tissues and depleting to strength, are not ordinarily fatal. They do, however, hamper childbearing. It follows, therefore, that darker-skinned people have a better chance of reproducing in the tropics than those with lighter skins; and lighter-skinned people are better able to perpetuate their kind in the artic circle.

But in the North there are some relatively dark skinned people. How, then, do they persist? In seeking an answer to this question it was discovered that the Eskimos, although they cook some of their food, follow the custom of eating raw fish. The practice, according to vitamin experts, supplies them with the necessary vitamin in a form not dependent upon actinic rays for its effectiveness.

Turning now to tropical and semitropical regions, we find some relatively light-skinned people. With them, protection from the sun's rays has been through artificial insulation in the form of clothing. The turban of the Moslem. the Turkish fez, the hooded veil of the Tuareg people who inhabit the Sahara, for example, all prevent an excess production of vitamin D. Yet none of these people, probably is any more aware than are the Eskimos of the relationship between its headdress and the meeting of its need for a controlled amount of vitamin D.

These and many other well-known examples show how customs exist which serve to adjust peoples to their environment and which permit reproduction of their species even under very adverse conditions. The customs have developed in the absence of any scientific understanding of the need which they meet.

Climatic Conditions. All over the world men have protected themselves against the extremes of cold and heat. An excellent illustration is afforded by the Polar Eskimo dwelling.

In the arctic circle existence depends upon a highly developed adjustment to climatic and geographic conditions. The temperature averages 34°F in the summer, 16°F in the autumn, –11°F in the winter, and –7° in the spring. Snow falls every month of the year, but especially in the spring and autumn.

The winter house, usually situated on the sloping beach just above the ice foot and overlooking the sea, represents an ideal adjustment to the climate and to the available materials.[1] The typical house accommodates one or two families.

> The main part of the dwelling is pear-shaped, wider in front and narrower behind. In dimensions it rarely exceeds twelve by ten feet, with an internal height insufficient for an average man to stand erect. No wood, bone, or ice enters into its construction. Heavy stone walls support cantilever beams of stone, upon which rest flat slabs of slate. The whole is covered with earth and an outer layer of stones. This marvel of engineering is entered by a low-semi-subterranean tunnel, ten feet long, lined and covered with stones and turf, and protected at the entrance by a wall of snow. The tunnel opens into the single room of the dwelling by a narrow door less than two feet in height. The floor, nearly level with the roof of the tunnel, is restricted in area, paved with stones, covered with grass and skins, and flanked by raised platforms on both sides and on the rear. In front, over the door, a window overlooks the sea. It consists of a skin, in which is inserted a square pane of animal membrane with a tiny peephole in the center. . . . The small platforms on either side of the floor hold food and household articles. On each stands a blubber lamp, over which are suspended a cooking pot and a frame for drying clothes. The rear platform, covered with dry moss and bearskins, occupies at least half the room. Here the members of the household sit and sleep, each in his special place, the housewives at the sides within easy reach of the lamps. The problem of ventilation is admirably solved. The air enters through the tunnel in a quiet stream and spreads out over the floor where the temperature is nearly always below the freezing point. It is not warmed until it reaches the level of the lamps, where it streams over the raised platforms. Here the temperature, though constant, is so high that the occupants regularly divest themselves of all clothing except their trousers, the men frequently even these. Under the roof the heat is stifling; the Eskimos therefore assume a reclining position as the most comfortable. However warm the room may be, the air is always fresh and pure, for all fumes and odors escape through the peephole and a tiny opening in the roof. [203-205]

This winter house is amazingly expedient as an adjustment to a rigorous climate. Some of the dwellings in other parts of the world seem less adequate. For example, the Australian aborigines build a simple lean-to hut or *wurley* which, from our point of view, is a

[1]The following description of the Eskimo dwelling is taken with permission from the work of G. P. Murdock (1935), of Yale University.

relatively poor adjustment to a climate in which the temperature often drops to 20° and rises to as high as 115°F is the shade.

But by and large, people have made relatively good adjustments to climatic conditions with the materials they have had at hand.

From the standpoint of psychology, this kind of adjustment is easily understood. Each activity which increases the comfort or decreases the pain experienced by individual members of society is likely to be repeated. Successful methods of constructing dwellings are retained by members of the group and become established as customs.

The Cooking of Food. The cooking of food is an almost universal custom. Despite the labor involved and the frustration through delay imposed by the extensive preparation of food, cooking is quite generally regarded as a necessary preliminary to consumption.

The advantages of cooking must be but poorly understood by the people themselves. To the physiologist they are better known. Cooking amounts to a sort of predigestion. It breaks up and softens foods to a greater degree than milling or even chewing. Although a few foods are less digestible cooked than raw, on the whole a raising of the temperature of food in the presence of moisture amounts to a shortening of the processes which precede intestinal assimilation.

Cooking thus makes the nutrient properties of food more available for body use by their more complete digestion. Also, cooking makes foods more appetizing (this is especially true of meats), increasing the flow of gastric juice and making the individual want to eat more. In these ways the cooking of food helps to build up the energy reserves of the organism, freeing them for activities other than the digestion and assimilation of food. Moreover, cooking has the additional advantage of destroying harmful bacteria that may be living in raw foods. Though all this is obvious to modern science, it is not so obvious to primitive peoples. Finally, in all the ways just described, cooking provides food better suited to the needs of infants and young children. The practice lessens infant mortality.

Apparently the practice of cooking food has been found, through trial and error, to be advantageous in the struggle for existence and—perhaps on account of its biological advantages—has received the sanction of the mores of the group.

But this must not lead us to think that cooking is advantageous in every respect. Under modern conditions cooking destroys some of the vitamins which are needed for the adequate nutrition of the body. These vitamins must be supplied through concentrates or in other ways.

Infant Care. Among primitive peoples, except where the infant is deliberately put out of the way, he is given exceptionally good care during the first week after birth. In many societies he is completely isolated from contact with all other members of the group, with the exception of the mother and a few elderly women who take care of both the mother and her child. This seclusion is commonly terminated with the dropping off of the umbilical cord, which occurs, among some primitives, between the third and the seventh days after birth.

From the medical standpoint, there are good reasons for such care of infant and mother. Until the navel has healed and the cord has come off, there is danger of infection. Further, the newborn infant is in great need of rest and warmth while making a profound biological adjustment to living in the outer world. The functions of respiration, temperature regulation, and food ingestion are all becoming established for the first time in a new environment.

It is a recently discovered medical fact that vitamin K, which is one of the factors regulating the coagulation time of the blood, is deficient in the normal infant during the first five or six days of life. This means that there is more danger from bleeding during the early days of infancy than later. In this connection it is worthy of note that although infant mutilations are common among primitive peoples, those involving the possibility of bleeding are not performed until after the first week of life. Circumcision, too, is not ordinarily performed during the first few days.

There are doubtless other biologically sound reasons for the isolation and care which the newborn infant receives, but primitive man explains the matter differently: A spirit mother hovers nearby to snatch the soul of the infant if it is not carefully hidden, or perhaps someone with an evil eye may harm the baby. The practices are biologically useful despite the explanation given.

Storing Food against a Future Shortage. Another practice of obvious utility is the storing of food as a precaution against times of drought and natural disaster. Although the Bushmen of South Africa, the Australian aborigines, and the Veddas of Ceylon hardly ever hoard for the future, most primitive peoples throughout the world store food for their future wants. The Hopi Indians, for example, store a reserve supply of corn for two years.

In Fiji, Dr. Ford reports, the community ate yams that had been stored for a year, and the yams from the new harvest were stored in their place. When questioned about the practice, the natives explained that the chief made them store a certain proportion of yams for each person—regardless of how poor the crop was. In support of the wisdom of this procedure they cited the hurricane of '31 and pointed out that all would have perished had not the chiefs for many years past forced them to conserve their food supply in this way.

To store food for future use imposes a self-denial which may be contrary to the wishes of certain members of the group. For example, among some of the New England Indian tribes the women had to hide the seed corn from the men lest they devour it all. This is a case in which some individuals are forced by the tribal mores to subordinate their biological impulses to the survival needs of the group.

The storing of food is supported in various ways: by ceremonial rites in times of plenty, by the authority of the chief, by the desire of certain individuals to obtain prestige through acquiring property. But it is really danger of starvation which is being combated by this practice.

Although the utility of food storing as a means of meeting biological needs is obvious to us, and to some primitive peoples as well, there are those who conform to the group practices without understanding their biological significance.

Avoiding Contact with the Dead. Among primitive peoples there is a widespread conviction that the ghost of a man who has died is dangerous. Fear of ghosts is shown by practices which aim at warding off the danger with which the dead threaten the living.

One technique for avoiding the ghost is that of attempting, by various magical practices, to recall the dead to life; if the ghost re-enters the body, it is no longer a source of danger. But the commonest custom of all, one which is almost universal, is to avoid contact with the ghost. Avoiding contact with the ghost is accomplished by avoiding contact with the corpse.

In some societies this is carried out by every member of the group. Among the Veddas, for example, the body of the dead man is left lying in a cave, and the tribe moves to another location to resume its living. But in the majority of social groups certain individuals handle the dead, burying, burning, or otherwise disposing of them. By various procedures the attempt is made to prevent the return of the ghost.

There is also the custom of taking a corpse out of the house through a hole in the wall or some other unnatural exit which is thereafter blocked up—the theory being that the ghost will be unable to find his way back. Keeping silence is another way thought to avoid the return of the ghost; not to mention his name is another.

But, to come back to the persons who act as undertakers, we find almost universally that they are obliged to purify themselves after handling a corpse. Very rarely are they allowed to return to normal group life until they have thoroughly washed and purified themselves. In some societies they are forbidden to handle food until extensive and prolonged purification ceremonies have been carried out.

Our modern sciences of pathology and bacteriology make it clear that there are real dangers of infection from a decaying corpse. The human body in a process of dissolution can be a source of disease. Thus there are genuine advantages in the self-imposed quarantine of primitive peoples.

But to assume that primitive man has an understanding of disease transmission is to miss the point. Illness and death (in these cases) are explained by him in terms of the return of a vengeful ghost and not in terms of pathology or bacteriology.

Tea Drinking in China. That tea drinking is a universal custom in China is well known. A laborer will carry along his pot of steaming tea in its well-padded "cozy" unless the liquid can be obtained where he is working. Along the road are countless places for getting tea. In temples the Chinese will leave the ceremonies from time to time to sip their tea. They do not drink water at all but take all their liquid (except what is in their food and their wine) exclusively in the form of tea. The Chinese insist that tea must be taken very hot, and actually they often drink it at temperatures which the uninitiated foreigner cannot tolerate.

This practice of tea drinking is so ancient that no one knows where it started or how.

The fact is that the water in thickly populated parts of China is usually unsafe, being contaminated with typhoid or cholera germs or other dangerous bacteria or with an amoeba which is the source of dysentery. Americans traveling in China are warned to boil their water before drinking it as a precaution against bacteria and amoebae.

But the masses of the Chinese know nothing of bacteriology and infection. The more intelligent ones realize that tea is safer to drink than water but do not realize that it is the *boiling* of the water rather than the tea itself which makes the liquid safe to drink. They believe, too, that tea must be taken very hot to be safe, not realizing that cold water which has been boiled is equally safe.

Here, then, is an instance of a universal custom which meets an important need and which is carried on without appreciation of its hygienic significance.

The Meeting of Sexual Needs in a Primitive Society. The Trobriand Islanders of northeastern New Guinea (or northwestern Melanesia) are an interesting group to study because they are ignorant of the facts of physical paternity. According to the anthropoligist Malinowski (1927), the natives, although they know in a general way that a virgin cannot conceive, have no idea whatever of the fertilizing influence of the male semen. Children, in native belief, are inserted into their mother's womb as tiny spirits, generally through the agency of the spirit of a deceased kinswoman of the mother.

Kinship is recognized only through the mother, i.e., kinship is matrilineal. The mother's brother exercises a good deal of the authority which, with us, is assumed by the father. He requires obedience of his sister's child and, especially with a boy, cultivates traits of ambition, pride and social worth which go to make life meaningful for the Trobriander.

Now this ignorance of physical paternity carries with it a lack of all sense of moral responsibility for the procreation of children. So sexual impulses, from infancy to maturity, are given uninhibited expression much as they are with many animals. Throughout the lifetime, the development of sexuality is free from repression, censure, and moral reprobation. For this reason the Trobrianders well illustrate, in their practices, the meeting of sexual needs in a primitive society where scientific knowledge of reproduction does not exist.

At the ages of five to seven the children in the Trobriand archipelago begin to form small groups within the community. These juvenile groups roam about in bands, play on distant beaches or in secluded parts of the jungle. In all this, though they obey the commands of their child-leaders, they are relatively independent of the authority of their elders. They gradually become emancipated from the supervision of their families.

At an early age these children are initiated by each other, or sometimes by a slightly older companion, into the practices of sex. Usually they content themselves with various games in which the dominating interest is genital. In the more elaborate husband-and-wife games sensual pleasure alone does not seem to satisfy them; it must be blended with some imaginative and romantic interest. The parents take these plays for granted and do not look upon them as in the least reprehensible.

At the age of puberty in most primitive societies, initiation rites are performed which serve to train the youth in adult sexual pratices but which completely mask the normal biological developments of the period. The Trobrianders, however, have no such initiation ceremonies.

During adolescence there is a period of general promiscuity, but eventually every man and woman in the Trobriands settles down to matrimony, which is usually monogamous except for chiefs, who have several wives. In marriage the girl goes to join her husband in his house, migrating to his community. Matrimony is a permanent union, involving sexual exclusiveness, a common economic existence, and an independent household.

In a Melanesian home the mother invariably shows a passionate devotion to her child, and the surrounding society fosters the maternal inclination and idealizes it by custom. The father, too, plays an active role in the physical care of the children. He is obliged to protect and cherish them, to "receive them in his arms" when they are born; but they are not regarded as his in the sense that he has had a share in their procreation.

Thus, among the Trobriand Islanders the biological needs of sex and reproduction are met in a way which is free from all restraint, by people who are ignorant of the basic facts of biological science.

Concluding Statement. The foregoing illustrations were selected to make clear one basic principle: Primitive man somehow manages to meet the basic needs or biological requirements of his existence—growth, reproduction, and physical well-being—even though he lacks scientific understanding of the reasons for his conduct. The savage may explain in terms of ghosts or evil spirits, the man of science in terms of bacteria or vitamins; but both continue to carry out their adjustive activities. Innumerable customs and taboos have grown up in primitive societies as aids in meeting biological needs which are common to mankind everywhere.

Although this proposition is true in general, there are some primitive customs and taboos which are directly opposed to the meeting of biological needs. For example, in ceremonial dances the men may continue to dance until they drop exhausted; or widows may be put to death at the time of their husbands' demise. Again, the headbinding of infants and the various mutilations of face and body (practices required by the mores of some peoples) have no biological utility. Hence, although group practices do in general tend to meet the requirements of existence, this principle is not a universally valid one.

Nevertheless, it should be stated in a positive way that primitive behavior tends to meet the cultural standards of the group. By and large, the cultural reguirements do minister to the various needs of individuals within the group. The fact that man has survived, that we are here today, is sufficient evidence for the truth of this general proposition.

FACT AND VALUE IN PSYCHOLOGY

It has often been said that science deals with *facts* and not with *values*. I have pointed out, however, that the primary hedonic reactions of animals and human beings are intrinsically evaluative and are also observed directly as a matter of fact (Young, 1966).

The acceptance or rejection of a foodstuff by a rat or a man is a primary evaluation which could be verbalized by such words as *good* or *bad, acceptable* or *unacceptable*. Verbalizations, of course, are not necessary because hedonic reactions by their very nature are evaluative. Felt pleasantness is equivalent to GO, continue, more; felt unpleasantness, to STOP, terminate, no more. A preferential discrimination between two foodstuffs is a *relative evaluation* implying that one reaction (accepting food A) is, in some respect "better than" another (accepting food B).

On the basis of hedonic effects organisms acquire evaluative dispositions which tend to become autonomous. These dispositions take over the evaluative role of primary hedonic reactions. And in man there is also a cognitive basis for appraisal, estimation, decision, as well as a hedonic basis. In man there are various forms of evaluation implied by pairs of words such as: *good-bad, right-wrong, beautiful-ugly, true-false, appropriate-inappropriate*, etc.

Rewards and Punishments. In everyday life parents, teachers, animal trainers, and others, offer rewards and apply punishments to control the performance and learning of their subjects. Rewards are bestowed and punishments inflicted to guide the behavior of children and pets, and to force upon adults conformity to social norms. A reward implies *good* performance; a punishment, *bad*. The evaluations are extrinsic—made by the trainer. The subject may or may not concur.

In countless experiments the investigators have utilized rewards and punishments. Intracranial stimulations are currently being used as "rewards" and "punishments." Actually these brain stimulations produce positive and negative excitations which can facilitate or impede behavior. I had to smile when a colleague in a scientific discussion referred to a "punishment" center in the brain!

Are the concepts of reward and punishment necessary? In considering the question a distinction must be drawn between the facts of observation and the interpretation of those facts. Positive and negative behavior, approach and withdrawal, can be observed directly without evaluation. When a bear climbs a tree to raid a bee hive, the tasting of honey is positive whether or not someone regards the gustatory reaction as a reward or as pleasant. The sting on the nose by a bee is negative whether or not someone calls it a punishment or unpleasant. Positive and negative behavior are directly observed. So are the many facts of preferential discrimination. So also are the human experiences of pleasantness and unpleasantness. These affective processes are empirical realities on the psychological level.

Sequences of Hedonic Evaluations. With animals, one can sometimes observe sequences of hedonic evaluations. For example, when an animal approaches a food object he is attracted or repelled by the odor. There is often a preliminary olfactory exploration prior to contact with the food. If the smell is positive, the food is taken into the mouth and tasted. If the hedonic effect of food-in-mouth is positive, the food is chewed and swallowed. Sometimes there is a delayed postingestional evaluation in terms of comfort (positive) or distress (negative). It has been shown that postingestional physiological effects can regulate intake and at times dominate or even obliterate the palatability effects.

Sequences of behavior, therefore, can and do become organized on the basis of successive hedonic reactions. After a sequence has been learned there exists a regulative disposition that controls the pattern of behavior.

Underlying the hedonic organization of behavior is a general principle: Positive and negative reactions give *direction* to behavior according to the principle of maximizing the positive and minimizing the negative. Subjectively this appears as an organization of activity to attain and enhance pleasantness and to avoid unpleasantness.

The Study of Values. Human values can be studied objectively on the level of gross behavior and also through verbal tests of relative values. If a person values something, he will work and spend money for it. He believes his actions are worthwhile.

All of us have standards of evaluation. We judge things in terms of right or wrong, good or bad, true or false, beautiful or ugly, etc. We judge human conduct in terms of strength or weakness, morality or immorality, and we take account of such general values as efficiency, power, safety, possessing goods, respect, heroism, mercy, loyalty, etc. Our standards of value are related to the goals of life. People value money, love, social position, advancement in a career, health, happiness, power, fame, reputation, prestige, rightness, religion, and other ends.

Philosophers have written many volumes about value. Spranger (1928) argued that personality can best be known through a study of values. He described six main types of man, corresponding to six dominant values.

1. The *theoretical* man has a dominant interest in the discovery of truth for its own sake. He is an intellectual—a man of science or a philospher.

2. The *economic* man is characteristically interested in what is useful and practical. He is interested in the business world—in production, distribution, and consumption of goods, and in the accumulation of wealth.

3. The *esthetic* man finds his highest value in beauty—in form and harmony. He may be a painter, a musician, a poet.

4. The *social* man values people. He has a love of people, which may be conjugal, filial, friendly, or philanthropic.

5. The *political* man places a high value upon power. He seeks to dominate others not necessarily in politics but in any and all human relations.

6. The *religious* man is a mystic who seeks to comprehend the unity of the cosmos; or he may be an ascetic who finds the experience of unity through meditation and self-denial.

No person is dominated by just one kind of value to the exclusion of the others; in everyone there is a mixture and balance. Within a given person the above values have different weights, or relative influence.

Allport, Vernon, and Lindzey (1960) devised a test of values based upon Spranger's philosophical work. In taking the test the subject is instructed to choose between two items as in this example;

> The main object of scientific research should be the discovery of pure truth rather than its practical application. (a) Yes. (b)No.

If a person checks *Yes*, he has placed theoretical value ahead of economic. If he checks *No*, he has placed economic value ahead of theoretical. Of course, there is no objectively correct answer; it is all a matter of the subject's evaluation. The procedure forces the subject to make a choice but he may not be aware of the fact that his choice reveals relative values.

With this type of item the Allport-Vernon-Lindzey test of values reveals, for each subject, a value profile which shows the relative importance of the main types of value for the individual. The test has been extensively used, criticized, and revised, but space will not permit further details.

Human values are acquired through experience. The individual learns to conform to society, to judge according to the standards of his group. He learns to discriminate between what is beneficial and harmful, useful and useless, practical and impractical, beautiful and ugly, true and false, right and wrong. He acquires these evaluative dispositions from his social world through a process of social learning.

A psychologist would like to discover how evaluative dispositions develop and upon what they rest. Chandler (1934) argued that most forms of esthetic value rest upon affective experience. The value of a painting rests upon the enjoyment of colors and forms. In music, pleasantness is derived from tones, harmonies, melodies and rhythms. In the dance, delight is from free rhythmic expression and graceful movement. In the culinary art, the value of food rests upon pleasing flavors (odors, tastes, tactual qualities). A primitive form of evaluation is simply expressing the attitude of liking or disliking the object evaluated.

Philosophers have argued that science deals with facts and not with values; but if values, in some sense or other, are determinants of human behavior, the science of psychology must take account of them. Guilford (1959) regards the values that are revealed by the Allport-Vernon-

Lindzey test as broad interest categories. If he is correct, we do not need two categories—value and interest—but only one.

Is a Science of Values Possible? In a philosophical treatise, Hilliard (1950) attempted to establish ethics as a science of values. He recognized that a scientific axiology is closely related to psychology and especially to hedonistic psychology. "Hedonism provides a single, simple, and consistent set of postulates under which the entire range of phenomena involving the concept of *value* may be unified, interconnected, and explained." Pleasantness and unpleasantness furnish the empirical basis for a science of values.

I agree with Hilliard's emphasis on hedonic processes as at least one basis for a possible science of values; and I agree with his relativistic view of values. I do not agree, however, that affective processes constitute the *sole* basis for a scientific axiology. Reasoning, reflection, deliberation, rational decision, are an important part of decision-making and in the setting of goals and priorities. Further, Hilliard's concept of an *organism* (which includes all living things and even a state or a society) is much too broad. Nevertheless, Hilliard's proposal is interesting and suggestive.

In considering this matter I think it is important to ask, "Who does the evaluating?" In his book, *The Fundamentals of Human Motivation*, Troland (1928) developed a hedonic theory of behavior. He defined several terms which imply evaluation:

Beneception: A process in a sense-organ or afferent nerve channel which is indicative of conditions or events that are typically beneficial to the individual or species.

Nociception: A process in a sense-organ or afferent nerve channel which is indicative of conditions or events which are typically injurious to the individual or species.

Neutroception: Any kind of sensory process which is neither beneceptive nor nociceptive.

Troland gives many examples. Beneception includes erotic excitations which lead to reproduction, gustatory stimulations from sugars which lead to the detection of carbohydrates that are sources of energy, etc. Nociception includes pain excitations from damage to the tissues, organic stimulations from such bodily conditions as hunger, etc. Examples of neutroception are found in the many excitations from lights, sounds, odors, etc., that are neither beneficial nor harmful in a direct biological sense.

Now in his analysis of hedonic motivation Troland himself is the evaluator. Troland interprets sensory stimulations in terms of benefit or harm. Although Troland is a man of science, I doubt whether a science of values can be based on his personal evaluations or upon the evaluations of any other individual. Science deals with *facts* and not with values, but evaluative behavior is a *fact* of observation.

In contrast with Troland's view is that of Arnold. Arnold (1960, Vol. I, p. 74) defines feeling as "*a positive or negative reaction to some experience. Pleasure and pleasantness are positive reactions, varying only in intensity. They can be defined as a welcoming of something sensed that is appraised as beneficial and indicates enhanced functioning. Pain and unpleasantness are negative reactions of varying intensity and can be defined as a resistance to something sensed that is appraised as harmful and indicates impaired functioning. What is pleasant is liked, what is unpleasant, disliked.*" [Italics in original]

In Arnold's view it is the *experiencing individual* who feels the pleasantness or unpleasantness and who appraises the stimulating situation in terms of benefit or harm. The individual subject rather than the psychologist does the evaluating! I agree with Arnold that direct reports of pleasantness and unpleasantness by human subjects should be taken at face value and that such reports indicate appraisals in terms of rudimentary good (GO, continue) or bad (STOP, terminate).

Arnold distinguished between rudimentary appraisals of sensory stimulations in terms of felt pleasantness and unpleasantness, on the one hand, and higher level (cognitive) appraisals and estimations, on the other. It is certain that most human appraisals, evaluations, estimates of priorities, decisions, evaluative judgments, and the like, involve the highest levels of cerebral function.

Arnold examined in detail the neurophysiology of an "estimative" system. I agree with her that there is a difference between rudimentary hedonic evaluation of sensory processes, on the one hand, and the cognitive evaluation of complex situations, on the other. Cognitive evaluations involve perception, memory, expectation, and related noetic processes.

It is my belief that the positive and negative hedonic reactions are *intrinsically evaluative* and that they are also observed and reported as facts of experience. Evaluative behavior can be dealt with scientifically on a factual level. Hence a limited science of axiology, at least, is possible.

In general, the evaluative behavior of animals, including man, is observed *as a matter of fact* and such behavior can be examined objectively, experimentally, quantitatively, statistically. A science of values, therefore, can be based on the *facts* of evaluative behavior and evaluative experience. Some of these facts are considered below.

EXPERIMENTS UPON THE HEDONIC VALUES OF FOODSTUFFS

I have made a good many experiments, with laboratory rats, upon the palatability of foodstuffs. Rats are excellent subjects since they have no culture and cannot talk!

Palatability can be defined as the hedonic response of an animal to foodstuffs (Young, 1967). Our experiments have revealed some of the fundamental principles of hedonic regulation of behavior and the role of hedonic processes in psychological development. Some of the more important findings are considered in the following sections.

Hierarchies of Hedonic Values. Studies of preference with natural foods, fluids, and compound solutions have consistently shown that test foods arrange themselves into hierarchies from low to high hedonic values. The series are transitive: If A is preferred to B, and B is preferred to C, then A is preferred to C. Exceptions to this rule of transitivity are assumed to indicate some change in the conditions that determine the acceptability of test foods.

TABLE 4
Preferential Hierarchies of Ten Rats Tested with Six Foods

Rat	Preferential Hierachy										
40	S	>	M	>	W	>	D	>	B	>	F
41	M	>	S	>	W	>	D	>	B	>	F
42	M	>	S	>	D	>	W	>	F	>	B
43	M	>	S	>	D	>	W	>	F	>	B
44	M	>	S	>	W	>	D	>	B	>	F
45	M	>	S	>	W	>	D	>	F	>	-*
46	M	>	S	>	W	>	D	>	F	>	B
47	M	>	S	>	W	>	D	>	B	>	F
48	M	>	S	>	W	>	D	>	F	>	B
49	M	>	S	>	W	>	D	>	F	>	B
Group	M	>	S	>	W	>	D	>	F	>	B

*Died before B vs F test.

From Young (1933)

I have found that when the conditions of maintenance are constant for a group of rats the preferential hierarchies for different animals are strikingly similar (Young, 1932, 1933). The hierarchy for a group of animals is remarkably stable. This can be illustrated by the record in Table 4 in which the letters symbolize the following test foods:

M= fresh milk standardized at 4% butterfat
S = granulated cane sugar, extra fine
W= whole wheat powder, freshly ground
D = dehydrated milk (commercially known as KLIM which is milk spelled backwards!)
F = commercial white flour made from wheat
B = pure butterfat prepared for the experiment

Individual differences in preferences are always between foods that are close together in hedonic value—between M and S, W and D, F and B. There are no individual differences with test foods that are more widely separated in the group hierarchy.

Hedonic Equivalence of Sodium-Saccharin and Sucrose Solutions. Experiments with common foods demonstrated the difference between the sensory and hedonic attributes of foodstuffs. Two foods may be very different in appearance, texture, taste, and yet be equal in hedonic value. Two simple or compound solutions, contrastingly, may look alike and feel alike to the human subject and yet differ widely in taste and hedonic value.

Studies by Young and Madsen (1963) demonstrated the hedonic equivalence of solutions of sodium-saccharin and sucrose. For a sodium-saccharin solution with constant concentration it is possible to determine the concentration of a hedonically equivalent sucrose solution. The method, known as the up-and-down psychophysical method, requires that the concentration of sucrose in a series of solutions be varied up and down during repeated preference tests. From the data it is possible to compute the sucrose concentration that is isohedonic to the constant saccharin solution.

The hedonic-equivalence function for solutions of sodium-saccharin and sucrose is shown in Figure 15. Vertical lines crossing the curve indicate the range of individual measures of hedonic equality for a group of eight rats tested individually. The solid curve is the mean hedonic-equivalence function for the group as a whole. On the basis of this curve I estimated that the optimal concentration for solutions of sodium-saccharin is located at about 0.5 grams per 100 ml of solution. This optimal is hedonically equivalent to a sucrose solution with concentration of about 3.5 grams per 100 ml of solution. Incidentally, human observers report that sodium-saccharin solutions are sweet and pleasant up to a concentration of about 0.5%; higher concentrations become sharp (bitter?) and unpleasant.

The curve shows, as a reference point, the sucrose preferential threshold (0.32) as determined by Burright and Kappauf (1963) who used a method based on choice. This is the concentration at which rats distinguish preferentially between sucrose solutions and distilled water.

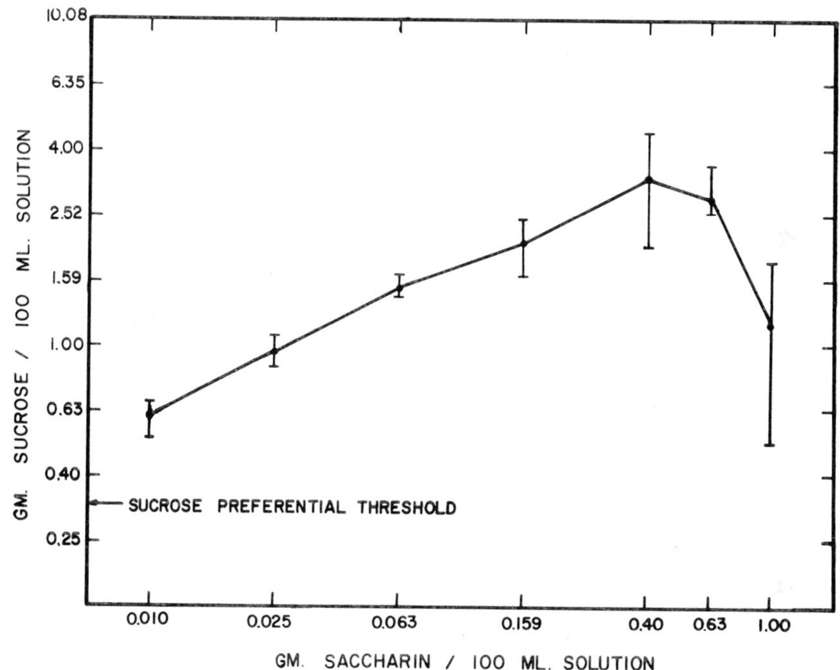

Figure 15. The hedonic equivalence function for solutions of sodium-saccharin and sucrose; based on preference tests with a group of eight rats. *From* Young and Madsen (1963).

Isohedonic Contour Maps. When two solutes are combined in a compound solution, the varying concentration of each solute can be represented upon a line of coordinates. Two perpendicular lines can then form a stimulus-area which represents an infinite number of compound solutions containing two solutes. Such a stimulus-area for solutions containing sucrose and quinine hydrochloride is shown in Figure 16.

The hedonic value of these compound solutions varies with the concentration of sucrose and also with the concentration of quinine in the mixture. The higher sucrose concentrations are consistently preferred to the lower (Young and Greene, 1959). This is also true in compound solutions.

If we take a pure sucrose solution of known concentration as a standard, it is possible to determine the sucrose-quinine mixture, containing a constant concentration of quinine, that is isohedonic to the standard. This is accomplished by varying the sucrose concentration of the *mixture* up and down during a series of preference tests.

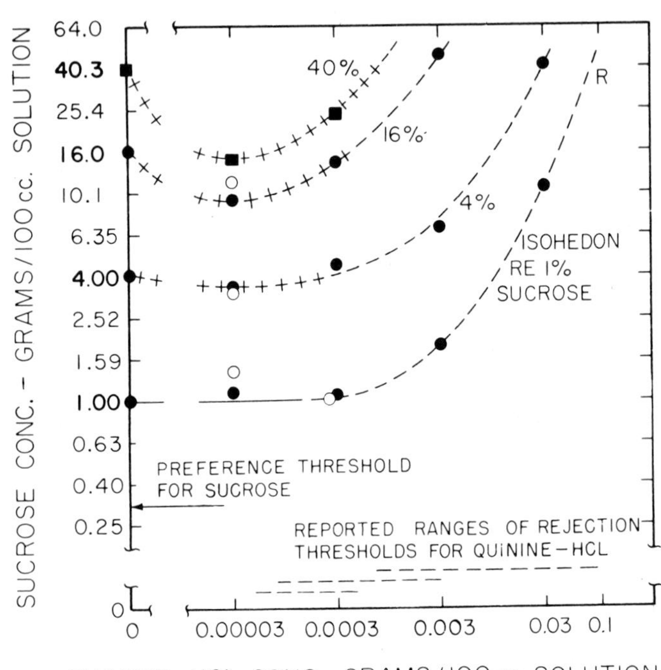

Figure 16. Isohedons in the sucrose-quinine stimulus-area. *From* Kappauf, Burright and DeMarco (1963).

An isohedon is a series of points upon a curve with each point representing hedonic equality of a standard (sucrose) solution and a compound comparison (sucrose-quinine) solution. Figure 16 shows a series of four isohedons in the sucrose-quinine stimulus-area with sucrose standards of 1%, 4%, 16%, 40%.

These isohedons show that when very low quinine concentrations are combined with relatively high sucrose concentrations the compound solutions are more palatable than the simple sucrose standards. Kappauf et al. (1963) have represented this enhancement effect by "+" signs on the isohedons. With higher concentrations the quinine impairs palatability and this is indicated by "–" signs.

It is interesting that these exceedingly low concentrations of quinine can facilitate acceptance of the compound solutions. Thus a mixture containing 0.00003 gr/100 of quinine + 16 gr/100 of sucrose is hedonically equal to a sucrose standard of 40.3%. This finding is interesting because, as Kappauf et al. pointed out, in various experiments as well as in their own work, the response to pure quinine solutions is consistently negative, aversive. The facilitating influence of quinine is at a concentration (0.00003 gr/100 ml) which is below the rodent detection threshold for quinine hydrochloride (0.0005 gr/100 ml) as reported by Koh and Teitelbaum (1961). How can subthreshold concentrations of quinine enhance palatability? The question needs further study.

Isohedons with similar properties have been plotted in the following stimulus-areas: sucrose-sodium chloride, sucrose-saccharin, sucrose-quinine hydrochloride, sucrose-tartaric acid. In these areas low concentrations of the non-sucrose component enhance palatability and high concentrations impair.

The Locus of Hedonic Indifference. If an isohedon dips below the hedonic level of the pure sucrose standard at low concentrations of the non-sucrose variable and rises above that level at higher concentrations, there is implied an intermediate (indifference) concentration. At the indifference concentration the sucrose standard and compound solution are isohedonic but they differ in sensory quality.

In an exploratory study of the sucrose-tartaric acid stimulus-area Young and Schulte (1963) determined, at five sucrose levels, the concentration of tartaric acid in the compound that would make the compound and standard isohedonic. Results are shown in Figure 17.

In determining the locus of hedonic indifference the sucrose concentration was the same in standard and comparison solutions while the acid concentration was varied up and down from trial to trial. Horizontal lines show the range of acid concentrations that were varied up and down in each test. With concentrations at the left ends of these lines all rats in the group preferred the compound (tart) solution to the standard (sweet). With concentrations at the right ends of these lines all rats preferred the standard (sweet) to the compound (sour). The points of indifference were computed by formula for the group as a whole.

The locus of hedonic indifference divides the stimulus-area into two regions. To the left of the locus are concentrations of tartaric acid that enhance palatability; to the right, concentrations that impair palatability. The line itself shows the locus of compound solutions that are hedonically equal to the pure sucrose standards at the same sucrose concentrations. The compound solutions and the simple sucrose standards are *hedonically* equal at each level but differ greatly in *sensory* quality.

The locus of hedonic indifference, of course, is not an isohedon. Every point upon the locus, however, is also a point on an isohedon which has a standard at the same sucrose level. This fact is illustrated by the curve at the right of Figure 17 which is *part* of an isohedon with standard of 1% sucrose (1 CHO). It is *part* of the isohedon because the curve does not dip into the region at the left of the locus where low acid concentrations enhance palatability.

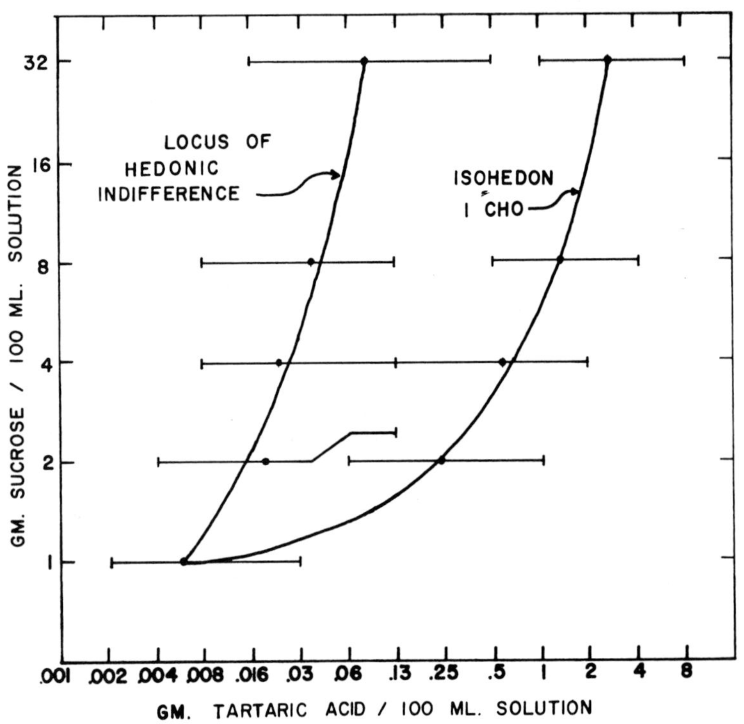

Figure 17. The locus of hedonic indifference in the sucrose-tartaric acid stimulus-area and part of an isohedon. Plotted from data by Young and Schulte (1963).

The apparatus used by Young and Schulte was the electronic preference tester which is pictured in Figure 18. The apparatus records separate contacts of tongue with fluids presented in pairs or singly.

Algebraic Summation of Hedonic Intensities. In tests of preference with a brief-exposure serial technique, Young and Christensen (1962) found that the addition of 0.75% NaCl (a nearly optimal concentration of sodium chloride for rats) to a solution containing low concentration (0.50% - 2.00%) of sucrose, produced a mixture that was preferred to either the sucrose component or the saline component. Hence this early work demonstrated that two positive hedonic values summate when the solutes producing the hedonic effects are combined in a single compound solution. The algebraic summation of positive and negative hedonic values was easily demonstrated by adding 4.0% NaCl (hedonically negative) to the sucrose solutions. The summation of two negatives presented a problem because all negatives *ipso facto* are rejected by the rats.

Figure 18. An electronic preference tester used at the University of Illinois for testing preferences simultaneously with squads of six rats. Animals are offered a continuous choice between a pair of simple or compound taste solutions. Separate tongue contacts with the fluids are counted electrically or recorded cumulatively on moving charts. Photo shows the author placing a rat in one of the testing units.

Following this early work the principle of algebraic summation of hedonic intensities has been repeatedly confirmed. For example, the studies of isohedonic contours and the locus of hedonic indifference (described above) consistently demonstrate algebraic summation of positive and negative hedonic values when positive and negative values are combined in compound taste solutions.

Algebraic summation of hedonic intensities was clearly shown also in a series of tests upon the rate of licking simple and compound taste solutions. Young and Trafton (1964) measured the amount of licking of simple and compound solutions presented one at a time and hence without the possibility of choice. Tests were made in the same stimulus-areas and with some of the same solutions that had been presented in mapping isohedonic contours.

In this work a single solution was exposed for two successive 60-sec periods with a minimal pause of 30 sec between exposures. The tests were made with 32 healthy, need-free (nondeprived) rats, tested in squads of 8. Separate tongue contacts were counted electronically with a "drinkometer" circuit, relays and counters.

A sample of results in the sucrose-sodium chloride stimulus area is pictured in Figure 19. The figure shows a tridimensional activity surface based on the single-stimulus data. Fine vertical lines indicate mean rates

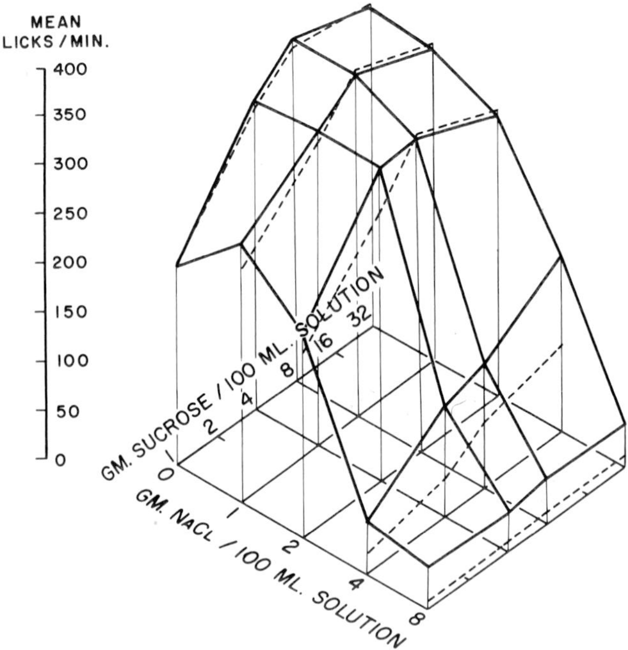

Figure 19. A tridimensional surface showing levels of tongue activation (mean licks/min) with simple sucrose solutions and mixtures containing sucrose and sodium chloride. Plotted from data of Young and Trafton (1964).

of licking (licks per minute) at points within the stimulus-area where the activity tests were made. Solid lines describe a tridimensional surface based on mean rates of licking during the first 60-sec exposure. Broken lines show mean rates of licking during the second 60-sec exposure. The floor of this chart is identical with the stimulus-area used in plotting isohedons with compound NaCl-sucrose solutions.

This tridimensional chart clearly shows certain relationships between level of tongue activation (mean licks per min) and composition of the stimulus-solution. I will be specific: (1) For any constant sucrose concentration above 1% the rate of licking *declines* as the NaCl concentration increases. This implies that an inhibitory effect of NaCl increases with a rising concentration of the saline component. (2) When sucrose concentration is held constant at 1% there is a maximal rate of licking at the NaCl concentration of 1%. This agrees with findings in various studies that show optimal palatability of NaCl solutions near 1%. (3) The rate of licking increases with rising sucrose concentration. Not shown too clearly is the fact that when some sucrose solutions are combined with low saline concentrations the rate of licking is slightly higher at 8% sucrose than at 32% sucrose. (4) On the second 60-sec test, when sucrose concentrations are high and NaCl concentrations are relatively low, the rate of licking is slightly higher than on the first 60-sec test. This suggests a warming-up or "learning to like" effect. Contrastingly, when NaCl concentrations are 4% and 8% there is a marked retardation of the rate of licking on the second test which suggests increased rejection with experience or a "learning to dislike" effect. Admittedly, these findings are complex and all are interrelated.

The main conclusion from the above studies is clear: *There is in fact an algebraic summation of positive and negative hedonic processes.*

Hedonic Integration. The foregoing studies demonstrate that positive and negative hedonic values summate algebraically to produce a final level of activation, positive or negative, at an intensity that depends upon the signs and hedonic intensities of the separate components. The algebraic summation of positive and negative hedonic values is a principle of major importance. The principle implies that there are two kinds of hedonic activation: positive and negative rather than a single form of neutral activation. There are, of course, neutral (non-hedonic) activations, or excitations. Intense positive and negative affective arousals are *occasional* events.

Hedonic integration occurs across sense modalities. The palatability level of common foods is influenced by their taste, odor, temperature, texture, and other sensory components. Hedonic values can be equal despite wide variations in sensory properties.

In an unpublished experiment Dr. Clinton L. Trafton demonstrated hedonic integration across sense departments. He found that a food preference can be changed by giving rats a shock on the foot every time they touched the preferred solution.

Normal naive rats developed this preference:

8 CHO > 8 CHO + .01 QHC1

in which CHO symbolizes sucrose; QHC1 symbolizes quinine hydrochloride; numbers indicate grams of solute in 100 ml of solution.

When rats were given a footshock every time they touched the pure (preferred) 8 CHO solution they steadily developed the following preference:

8 CHO + .01 QHC1 > 8 CHO + footshock

Therefore, the footshock had the same negative influence upon the original preference as addition of a quinine solution of relatively high concentration. The rats integrated hedonic intensities arising from a multi-sensory gestalt.

Years ago Sherrington demonstrated the integrative action of the nervous system with reflexes of the spinal dog. Now it is clear that there is integrative action at higher levels of the C. N. S.: diffuse, non-specific, positive and negative excitations from different receptors are integrated and lead to a single adaptive reaction.

SPECIFIC APPETITES AND BODILY NEEDS FOR FOODSTUFFS

The foregoing objective studies with gustatory stimuli show how taste solutions *affect* the organism. Man and other animals also react positively or negatively to stimuli in all sense departments and especially to environmental, including social, situations. The affective processes are *felt* subjectively as pleasantness, comfort, or unpleasantness, discomfort.

In a different category from these sense feelings are appetites and aversions. In appetitive behavior the organism goes out to seek something: food if hungry, water if thirsty, air if deprived of air, sexual gratification if excited, rest if fatigued, sleep if deprived of sleep, defecation or urination if the physiological tensions are present, sensory experience if deprived of sensory stimulation, etc. An appetite is experienced subjectively as a craving or desire. Persons who have become addicted to a narcotic—opium, heroin, morphine, or other—develop a craving for the drug so intense that they sometimes engage in criminal acts to obtain it. Persons who are addicted to nicotine or caffeine experience discomfort when they cannot get a cigarette or a cup of coffee.

Aversive behavior shows repulsion, repugnance, dislike. An aversion is a negative appetite. Aversions are expressed by withdrawal, escape from the stimulating situation, avoidance.

In so far as appetites depend upon internal bodily conditions they tend to be cyclic because those conditions recur. There are several stages. In the first stage of the appetitive cycle there is restlessness and uneasiness coupled with seeking the objects or conditions that satisfy the appetite or reduce the tension. This stage is accompanied by discomfort and, in developed organisms, by purposive behavior. In the second stage the appetite is satisfied by consummatory behavior. Typically, a state of agitation is followed by quiescence. Occasionally there is a third stage of oversatiation, for example, when the sight of food produces nausea and revulsion. Finally, there is a stage of indifference with relative freedom from the appetite. The appetite then gradually increases and the cycle is repeated. Thus there are stages of arousal, satisfaction, possibly overindulgence, and freedom from the appetite.

Aversive reactions occur sporadically when an organism encounters painful stimulation, bitter tastes, foul odors, and threatening environmental situations. Hence aversions are typically non-cyclic. But under some conditions, as noted above, organic states can generate aversive nausea and disgust.

The following sections are concerned mainly with specific appetites for foodstuffs.

Examples of Specific Appetites. The following appetites, occurring in man and animals, depend upon specific depletions and excitations. They are also called specific hungers.

Air hunger. The body has no means for storing oxygen as it has for storing protein, fat, carbohydrate, water, minerals, and certain other substances which are essential to life. The biological explanation of this fact is probably that air-breathing animals are so constantly surrounded by air that no necessity exists for them to store oxygen within the body. When, however, a man is trapped beneath the water or in a room filled with injurious fumes, the need for pure air is all too obvious. He struggles to reach the air, and his failure to do so will result in speedy death.

Anatomically, the respiratory apparatus is so distinct from the structures of the alimentary tract that air hunger has often been regarded as an appetite different in kind from the cravings for solid food and for water. Fundamentally considered, however, air hunger is just one of the group of normal appetites.

Thirst. Cannon (1934) described the experience of thirst as a condition of dryness in the mouth and throat region. Subjectively, thirst is referred to the inner surfaces of the mouth and throat, especially in the root of the tongue and to the back of the palate. The subjective experience, in severe cases, is highly unpleasant. The mouth is perceived as dry or sticky. During intense thirst the tongue cleaves to the teeth or to the roof of the mouth. A lump seems to be present at the back of the throat, where it remains despite repeated attempts to dislodge it by swallowing.

Mild thirst can be temporarily relieved by moistening the mouth and throat or by placing against these parts a dry rubber sac containing ice. But such measures bring only brief respite from the discomforts of thirst.

In a significant experiment, Bellows (1939) made use of a sham-drinking technique by means of which water was passed through the mouth and pharynx of dogs and thence outside the body in a tube. Sham drinking moistened the mouth and throat of the animal and thereby brought temporary relief from thirst, indicated by the fact that the dog would momentarily stop drinking. But when a quantity of water (equal in amount to the water deficit of the body) was introduced by tube directly into the alimentary canal, a more permanent satisfaction of thirst appeared ten to fifteen minutes after introduction of the liquid.

In other words, in thirst the bodily need for water is a general one, which can be met only by supplying the tissues with the needed liquid through drinking or in an equivalent way of removing the water deficit.

In addition to air hunger and thirst, there is general hunger for food, which can be factored into a group of appetites for specific food elements—fats, proteins, carbohydrates, the different mineral salts, and the vitamins. Normal appetites are sometimes transformed into abnormal cravings when the body is deprived of an essential substance for a long time. A study of some of these abnormal cravings demonstrates the existence of the separate food appetites and shows that they are independently variable. Examples of some abnormal cravings will follow.

An unusual salt hunger. There has been described the case of a boy who had an unusually strong hunger for salt which persisted until death at the age of three and a half years. During his life he ingested great quantities of salt.

When about a year old, he started licking the salt off crackers and asking for more. He would chew soda crackers until he got the salt off and then spit them out. Although he didn't speak at this time, he had a way of letting his parents know what was wanted. At eighteen months, he started saying a few words, and *salt* was among the first that he learned. Practically everything that he liked very well was salty: crackers, pretzels, potato chips, salt mackerel. His foods were all very much saltier than those of his parents and, in addition, he ate about a teaspoonful of table salt per day. He drank large amounts of water and showed a marked preference of water to milk.

At the age of three and a half this boy was admitted to the Harriett Lane Home for Children and placed upon the regular diet of the ward, which contained only a normal amount of salt. As a result of salt deprivation, seven days after admission he suddenly died. Post mortem examination, according to Wilkins and Richter (1940), revealed deficient tissue in the cortex of the adrenal glands.

This finding is significant because it is known from laboratory experiments that, if the adrenal glands of rats are surgically removed, the animals die within ten to fifteen days when maintained on the ordinary stock of laboratory diets. Death occurs largely because of excessive loss of salt through the urine. But the survival time of these adrenalectomized rats can be increased by adding sodium chloride to the diet until it approximates the amount of salt lost in the urine. Further, it has been shown that, if adrenalectomized rats are given free access to a salt solution, they ingest large amounts of it. As a consequence, they keep themselves alive indefinitely and free from the symptoms of insufficiency.

Apparently the boy with deficient adrenal glands had kept himself alive by ingesting great quantities of salt. The boy's appetite was an accurate index of his bodily need.

Phosphorus deficiency and "depraved appetite." In certain areas of South Africa and also in some parts of the United States the soil is deficient in phosphorus as well as in other mineral elements. Consequently, cattle of these regions are limited to a forage which is deficient in phosphorus.

Green (1925) has described how phosphorus deficiency in the diet gives rise to a "depraved appetite." The cattle eat bones which they find lying on the plains or in the carcasses of animals. It is reported that they become carnivorous to the extent of capturing small animals and eating their bones.

This "depraved appetite" has been produced experimentally in cows by feeding them a diet which is deficient in phosphorus. The craving for bone, however, is only one symptom of the bodily deficiency (osteomalacia). Other symptoms are loss of weight, stiffening of the joints, softening of the bones, disturbances of reproduction and lactation. Feeding cows bone meal or giving them phosphorus in some other form corrects the disorder and removes the appetite for bone.

As the bodily condition produced by phosphorus deficiency becomes more and more severe the animals grow less discriminating in their choice of foods. A cow not only will eat bone but also will chew wood or eat leather if it can be obtained; or she will pick up and swallow stones, dirt—almost anything. From one standpoint this indiscriminate eating is the mark of a "depraved appetite," but from another point of view it is nature's desperate attempt to obtain for the body a much needed dietary element.

An unusual appetite for calcium. When the parathyroid glands are surgically removed, rats ordinarily lose weight, develop symptoms of tetany, and die unless they have access to an adequate supply of calcium.

In one experiment, Richter and Eckert (1937) found that parathyroidectomized rats, when given a choice among a variety of food elements, ingested large quantities of calcium solutions (lactate, acetate, gluconate, and nitrate). The selection reduced mortality to zero, greatly improved the tetany, and eliminated or reduced the loss of weight.

After the removal of the parathyroid glands the appetite for calcium was definitely increased with seventeen out of eighteen rats. The average daily intake of a 2.4 percent calcium lactate solution was nearly four times as high after the operation as before. Parathyroid implants in five animals caused the calcium intake to return to its normal level.

The experiment shows clearly that the intake of calcium varies with bodily need for that substance. If given an opportunity, the operated animals select calcium and survive.

Appetite for a fatty acid. In her readable book on nutrition, Adelle Davis (1970) describes her experience in feeding an infant linoleic acid.

> In my opinion, deficiencies of these acids are more common than is appreciated. For example, babies are rarely given vegetable oils until old enough to eat mayonnaise. I recall a boy of three whom I first saw at eighteen months of age. His father had been an All-American football player and wanted an athletic son more than anything else in the world. Instead, this pathetic child was smaller than most one-year-old children and had been covered with severe eczema since he was three weeks old. The boy was lethargic and seemed dim-witted. A diagnosis of "allergy" had been made, and thousands of dollars had been spent seeking correction. After a few minutes conversation with the mother, I placed the boy in a highchair and offered him a tablespoon of soybean oil. At the first taste, the child became alive as if electrified. He leaned across the tray, mouth wide open, and even a moment's delay caused him to scream for more. He must have had six or eight tablespoons of oil before his mother, fearing he would be ill, made me stop. I suggested that she give him several tablespoons every hour if he wanted it and seemed to tolerate it well. Within three days, the eczema was almost gone, and in a week his skin was beautiful. After that the child blossomed. His bone development became particularly excellent; he grew muscular and has now achieved normal size and weight. If there is one man in the world willing to die for me, it is probably the boy's father. I strongly suspect that such eczemas, appearing so soon after birth, are caused by mothers avoiding fats during pregnancy, being unaware of their need for linoleic acid.

> Linoleic acid has been shown to help prevent or cure eczemas resulting from a lack of any one of several B vitamins, possibly because this fatty acid stimulates the growth of intestinal bacteria which can produce these vitamins. Even the stubborn eczema-like condition known as psoriasis usually disappears rapidly when salad oils and lecithin are added to the diet. [44-45]

Appetites for vitamins. Richter, Holt and Barelare (1937) made some obervations on rats that were deficient in thiamine (vitamin B_1). When tested with pure vitamin crystals or with aqueous solutions the animals' behavior revealed an overwhelming appetite for the substance:

> This is shown by the fact that the rats found the bottles at once, even when as many as twelve other containers filled with different foods or solutions were present in the cage at the time. It was difficult to stop the animals from drinking the substance, once they had tasted it. Efforts to remove the bottles were met with fierce resistance. The bottle was held tightly with both paws and even with the teeth. By reaching far into the bottles the rats made an effort to obtain every remaining drop of the vitamin.

In ordinary foods the distinctive flavor of a vitamin may be masked by other dietary components. Such foods commonly contain a small but sufficient amount of the B vitamins. Harris, et al. (1933) found that vitamin-deficient rats *learn* to select a vitamin-containing food in preference to others that lack the vitamin.

Scott and Quint (1946) developed a technique that bypassed the head receptors and introduced the vitamins directly into the stomach. They trained rats to swallow daily a pill that contained vitamins in controlled amounts. By removing from the pills a specific vitamin (thiamine or riboflavin or pyridoxine or pantothenate) they could produce a specific vitamin deficiency. Scott and Quint found that when rats were depleted of thiamine or riboflavin or pyridoxine they *learned* to select vitamin-containing foods in preference to foods that lacked the vitamin. Pantothenate differed from the other three vitamins in that a specific appetite for it developed only when the vitamin-containing diet was labeled with a distinctive odor. Even then some pantothenate-deficient rats failed to acquire an appetite for the food that contained the needed vitamin. Scott and Quint concluded that the preferential selection of a vitamin-containing diet is *learned* since preferences developed gradually with repeated tests. Importantly, however, preferences developed only under conditions of nutritional need.

Scott and Verney (1947) suggested two possible explanations of the acquisition of specific appetites for vitamins: (1) A preferential habit is set up on the basis of association between the feeling of well-being and some sensory properties of the foodstuff. (2) There is an increased stimulus to eat, presumably derived from and associated with a persisting feeling of well-being. Both suggestions agree with the original hypothesis of Harris, et al., that a *feeling of well-being or comfort* (an affective process) underlies the development of specific appetites for the B vitamins.

There has been a great deal of research upon the appetite for thiamine and other vitamins. An excellent review has been made by Rozin (1967).

The Independent Variability of Appetites and Aversions for Food. The foregoing examples demonstrate the existence of specific appetites for nutritive substances. Hunger, in contrast to appetite, is often regarded as a demand for food produced by privation. General hunger and thirst are poignant realities.

Cannon (1934) distinguished between hunger and appetite. Hunger, he said, is a physiological state characterized by contractions of the empty stomach which are correlated with subjective hunger pangs, and by changes in the level of blood sugar, etc. Appetite is something different. We eat sweets and dainties from "appetite" at the close of a meal when hunger no longer exists. We develop "appetites" for specific kinds of foods. Such "appetites" are based on the pleasantness of taste or the internal comfort they yield. An "appetite," I believe, is a specific craving or desire that develops on the basis of hedonic change in the positive direction (enjoyment or relief from discomfort).

Appetites become dominant motives that are independently variable. There is sound experimental evidence for the existence of appetites for protein, fat, carbohydrate, water, sodium, phosphorus, calcium, thiamine, riboflavin, and other substances. There are doubtless other independently variable food appetites which have not yet been demonstrated in the laboratory or clinic--appetites for other minerals and vitamins (although several researches upon vitamin D have given negative results). They have been called "specific hungers."

The intense cravings developed by the victims of addictive drugs such as heroin, further illustrate specific and independently variable appetites. These cravings, of course, do not belong on the list of food appetites. The drugs impair health.

Special aversions should also be considered. Both man and animals show an aversion to putrid meat and certain other spoiled foods. Some dogs have an aversion to dog's flesh as food. Cattle are said to refuse toxic vegetation growing in their grazing lands. In liver disorders an aversion to fat develops.

There are also perversions of appetite, among the more common of which (in animals) are: coprophagia (eating of feces), infantophagia (eating of the young), osteophagia (bone eating), the grass eating of dogs and cats when sick. In chlorosis, girls sometimes show a craving for sour and highly spiced foods. In diabetes, the patient may have an intense craving for sugar. Pregnancy is accompanied by unusual food cravings which vary from individual to individual. In hookworm disease, the patient may indiscriminately eat earth, paper, chalk, starch, hair, and clay.

In view of the available facts it is reasonable to assume that general hunger can be factored into a group of partial hungers of appetites which, within certain limits, vary independently of each other. Actually, the independent variability of certain appetites is not merely an assumption, but a known fact. Further evidence for independently varying appetites has been revealed by experiments which are described in the following sections.

Self-selection Feeding and Preference Experiments. It has been found that when animals are given a free choice among a variety of food elements, they select a diet which is adequate in calories and balanced with respect to the dietary elements ingested.

In one such experiment Richter, Holt, and Barelare (1938) gave rats complete freedom of choice among eleven pure food elements (three solid foods and eight liquids), each presented in a separate container. The foods were:

Casein (protein)
Sucrose (carbohydrate)
Olive oil (fat)

Sodium chloride, 3% Dibasic sodium phosphate, 8% Calcium lactate, 2.4% Potassium chloride, 1%	Mineral solutions
Dried baker's yeast Cod-liver oil Wheat-germ oil	Sources of vitamins

Water

Daily measurements were made of the quantities of each element ingested. It was found with self-selection or cafeteria maintenance that the daily quantities of food elements ingested were fairly uniform. With some foods the intake was relatively constant from day to day. Other foods revealed cycles of intake. The daily intake, moreover, varied with such conditions as pregnancy, lactation, removal of a gland, deprivation of an essential food element.

To illustrate, during pregnancy, according to Richter and Barelare (1938) and Barelare and Richter (1938), under the self-selection feeding system there was a change in the balance or proportions of food elements ingested. The quantity of protein and fat consumed was definitely increased. Also, there was increased intake of sodium and calcium. Rats were observed to take, on the average, more than twice as much sodium chloride solution (3 percent) in the ten-day period following conception as in the previous ten-day period. Carbohydrate intake did not change appreciably during pregnancy.

Appetite as a Guide. All of us know, in general, that wild animals somehow manage to locate suitable food and to select an adequately balanced diet from the *edibilia* of forest and plain. How is this possible? Is there a food-selection instinct? How far is appetite, in man and animals, a dependable guide in the selection of foods? Given a choice among a variety of foodstuffs, can an individual select a diet which is complete, balanced, and adequate to meet the biological requirements of existence?

Dr. Clara M. Davis (1928) described a self-selection feeding experiment carried out with three infants. At the time of weaning, these infants were given a choice among a variety of simple unseasoned foods—some cooked, some raw. All told, there were thirty-three kinds of food presented to the infant on a tray. He was allowed to eat in any way he could, using fingers, a spoon, or the more direct method. He was not corrected for table manners! With two infants the experiment lasted six months; with the third, a year.

Before each meal the foods were weighed separately, and after a meal the residue was again measured. In this way the daily intake of each kind of foodstuff was determined.

Dr. Davis reports that the infants, from time of weaning, were able to select, from a list of simple natural foods, quantities sufficient to maintain themselves with apparently optimal digestive results and in excellent health. They were happy, energetic, full of "pep," and their growth curves were slightly ahead of the norms prepared by the Children's Bureau in Washington.

The infants were omnivorous in their eating and ingested a quantity of food sufficient to give them an approximately constant number of calories from day to day. At the start, food selection was seemingly haphazard. With habituation the infants developed definite food preferences which, however, changed from time to time and were unpredictable.

The babies tended to eat certain foods in waves or cycles. After eating cereals, eggs, meats, or fruits in small or moderate amounts for a number of days, there would follow a period of a week or more in which a particular food or a class of foods was eaten in larger and larger quantities until astonishingly large amounts were taken. After this, the quantities would decline to the previous level. Such waves were recognized in the diet kitchen and came to be known as "egg jags," "meat jags," "cereal jags," etc. These "jags" were not accompanied by symptoms of overeating, nor were the waves followed by a period of aversion for and neglect of the particular food.

A practical test of the self-selection system of feeding has been made in the orthopedic ward of the Children's Memorial Hospital of Chicago. Under the self-selection or cafeteria plan, food from the kitchen was placed in containers on a long cart, which was also used for carrying the trays. This cart made its rounds through the rooms of the ward. In a given room the nurse slowly and distinctly recited the menu for the meal. Each child was then served the items he selected in whatever quantity he wished. The youngest, who could not talk, were served some of everything, but no child was urged or obliged to eat.

Result: No appetite problems occurred. The children were enthusiastic and, when they left the hospital, regretted having to stop the self-selection feeding plan. Incidentally, there was less waste of food than in any other ward of the hospital. Each child ate what he selected himself and enjoyed the process.

Later, Davis (1939) published the account of a similar self-selection experiment with fifteen children in which thirty-four foods (including water) were served daily. She reports that during a period of six months the diets chosen by the children were adequate as judged by nutritional standards and in terms of health, growth, and vigor of the children.

Dr. Davis' advice on feeding the infant and child does not exactly agree with the common practice of preparing a meal and requiring the child to eat it. We all know the results of forced feeding in children and can readily sympathize with little Mary Jane's predicament, described in A. A. Milne's poem:

> *What* is the matter with Mary Jane?
> She's crying with all her might and main,
> And she won't eat her dinner—rice pudding again,
> What *is* the matter with Mary Jane?
>
> *What* is the matter with Mary Jane?
> She's perfectly well and she hasn't a pain,
> *And it's lovely rice pudding for dinner again*!
> What *is* the matter with Mary Jane?

Dr. Davis' advice in feeding the infant and child is this: Give the individual a variety of foods. Let him select the ones he will eat and reject those he does not want. Let him eat as much as he will of each element and hold to this procedure.

This work upon self-selection feeding is interesting and important, but it does not answer satisfactorily questions about the dependability of appetite as a guide. For one thing, Dr. Davis used such a wide variety of wholesome foods that the infant could scarcely go wrong. From such a diversity of foodstuffs dozens of combinations could yield a nutritionally adequate diet. Moreover, for obvious reasons toxic substances were omitted from the list.

Self-selection feeding methods, however, have been repeatedly tested in experiments with pigs, cows, chicks, rats, and mice. The net result of these researches is that, when animals are given a free choice among the components of an adequate diet (protein, carbohydrate, fat, water, vitamins, minerals), they tend to make a selection which leads to normal growth, reproduction, health, and vigor.

Moreover, animals commonly reject injurious foods. It has been claimed that range cattle recognize poisonous plants and eat only the normal or the least toxic forage. Further, if a small quantity of the toxic element (selenium) in this vegetation is placed in the food of rats, they avoid the toxic food or prefer other foods which lack the toxic element.

There is, however, another side to the argument upon the merits of self-selection feeding. Many children, and adults too, overeat sweets or rich cream desserts and avoid vegetables and fruits which are rich in important vitamins. It has been said by a nutrition expert that most Americans are overfed. The resulting overweight condition predisposes, in middle life, to organic diseases. Then too, people ignorantly eat poisonous fishes, mussels, toxic mushrooms, castor-oil beans, and poisonous berries. Insects, rodents, and the higher mammals, including man, actually do accept the poisons which have been prepared for their destruction. Doubtless the toxic elements are tasteless or present in amounts below the taste threshold; or perhaps their taste is completely masked by other tastes and odors. In view of all this, one cannot argue that appetite is an infallible guide.

The fallibility of appetite may be further illustrated by the story of the discovery of vitamin B. When some inventive genius found a way to scour the bran coat off rice, making it pleasing to the eye and easy to masticate, this polished rice came to be preferred to the unpolished variety. To many oriental peoples who subsist mainly on rice and fish the result was disastrous; they developed the deficiency disease known as *beriberi* (a multiple neuritis). This disease took its toll until two

Dutch physiologists (Eijkman and Grijns) discovered a vital factor (vitamin B) in the bran. This vitamin had been scoured off and fed to the pigs, and the human sense of taste was inadequate to warn the orientals that the new polished rice was deficient in a vital ingredient.

Further, laboratory experiments upon other vitamins (G, A, and D) have shown that animals cannot discriminate among foodstuffs which contain an adequate amount of these essential elements and those which lack them. In this connection it should be noted that vitamins are probably present in amounts so small that they do not affect the taste receptors. Also, the complex state of natural foods often allows one taste element to mask another, just as the full chord from a pipe organ masks a weak partial tone which could be heard if presented alone.

In view of the above facts, it is clear that the sense of taste is no more infallible a guide in the selection of foodstuffs than organic appetites are. Nevertheless, the bulk of evidence indicates that, when laboratory animals and the human infant are offered a variety of foods from which to choose, to an amazingly high degree they can and do automatically select a diet which is balanced, adequate in calories, and one which leads to normal growth, health, and reproduction.

There are obviously two sides to the controversy concerning the fallibility of appetites as guides to sound nutrition and health. The editors of *Nutrition Reviews* (1944), after reviewing the availible evidence, published a blast against the view that appetites are dependable guides to sound nutrition. In view of this blast no one today would have the temerity to claim that the food choices of animals are infallible guides to correct nutrition and health. Nor would any one be so rash as to claim that the food selections of animals have no relation at all to organic needs. The question to be answered lies between these extreme views: To what extent do animals select and accept foodstuffs which meet their metabolic and nutritional needs? This is a question of fact. The answer must come from further observations and experiments.

The question involves several basic problems. First, there is the problem of defining physiological, metabolic and nutritional needs. Second, there is the problem of accounting for the organization and development of appetites—their psychological and physiological bases and nature—and their relation to the meeting of needs. Third, there are problems relating to the formation of dietary habits and the influence of such habits upon the choice of foods. Finally, in man, there are problems relating to cognitive influences from the social environment. These factors are all complex and closely interrelated.

THE HEDONIC ORGANIZATION OF APPETITES AND AVERSIONS

The primary hedonic processes from sensory stimulations are *in themselves* appetitive and aversive in that pleasantness is GO and unpleasantness STOP. The primary affective processes are both activating and directive.[1] Subjectively they determine direction away from distress and toward relief, comfort, pleasantness, complaisance.

The primary hedonic processes are also *organizing* in that they lead not only to immediate approach-avoidance patterns of behavior but also to the acquisition of dispositions which regulate and control the positive and negative patterns of behavior. These dispositions are variously known as motives, habits, attitudes, expectancies, etc.

Reinforcement, Extinction and Expectancy. An experiment was made by Dr. C. L. Trafton in which four groups, each of 8 naive rats, were given opportunity to ingest pure sucrose solutions. The experiment is reported by Young (1966, p. 79). The percent concentrations (weight/volume) were: 1%, 4%, 8%, 32%. The rats were tested individually. During each trial the numbers of licks (tongue contacts with sucrose solution) at the nozzle, during a single 60-sec exposure, were counted electrically.

The mean numbers of licks for each group during successive days of the experiment are shown in Figure 20. During the first five daily tests (apart from two minor inversions on Day 3) the mean numbers of licks per minute were proportional to the sucrose concentrations. These curves show, however, that after the first 5 days, Groups 4%, 8%, and 32% do not differ significantly. These activity curves cross and re-cross. On days 10 and 11 the mean rate of licking was slightly (not significantly) higher with the 8% animals than with the 32% group. Although all groups show a day-to-day increase in the rate of licking with practice, the 1% group consistently and significantly licked the fluid at the lowest level of tongue activation. The influence of hedonic intensity upon performance is, therefore, most clearly shown during the early stages of habituation.

After 11 days of acquisition, all rats were offered for 5 days, in the same nozzle, an incentive of distilled water. There was no other change in experimental conditions.

For all rats the substitution of distilled water for a sucrose solution

[1] For an account of the methodology and rationale of research upon food acceptance see: J. L. Falk, Determining changes in vital functions: Ingestion. In R. D. Myers (Ed.), *Methods in Psychobiology: Laboratory Techniques in Neuropsychology,* Vol. I; London: Academic Press 1971 (in press). And P. Teitelbaum, Motivation and control of food intake; in C. F. Code (Ed.), *Handbook of Physiology,* Section 6, Vol. I, Food and water intake; Washington D. C.: American Physiological Society, 1967.

brought an immediate decrease in the rate of licking. During the 5 days of extinction, the 1% group showed the *least* change in level of tongue activation and the 32% group, the *greatest* change. After five days of extinction the amounts of licking were inversely proportional to the prior sucrose concentrations and to the initial levels of tongue activation.

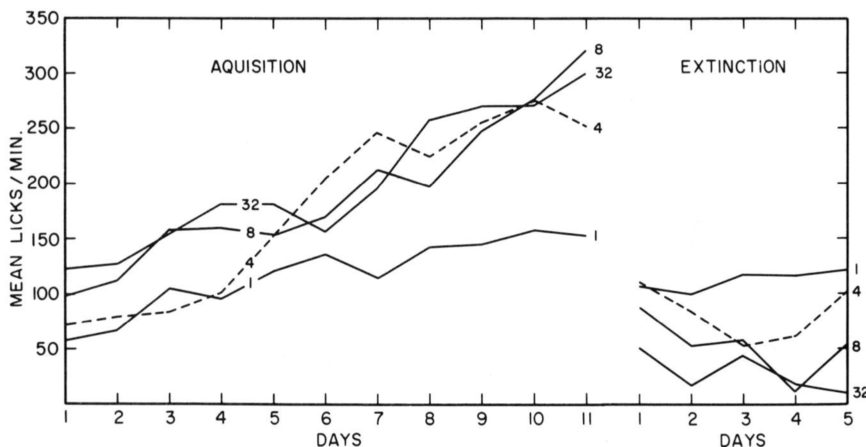

Figure 20. Levels of tongue activation, plotted in mean licks per minute, as related to concentration of sucrose solutions during habituation stages of acquisition and extinction. Data by C. L. Trafton, reported by Young (1966).

It is obvious that performance during extinction is a function of an expectancy developed during acquisition. Each rat had developed an expectancy of reward with a definite sweet taste and hedonic intensity. The performance during extinction was a function of the *difference* (discrepancy) between the expected hedonic effect and an actual hedonic effect. With the 1% rats the discrepancy was minimal; with the 32% group, maximal.

These findings agree with results from other experiments. For example, Guttman (1953) did a bar-pressing experiment with rewards of sucrose solutions that differed in concentration. He found that during extinction the biggest drop in rate of bar pressing occurred with rats that had been trained with the highest sucrose concentration and the least drop with rats that had been trained with the lowest concentration. Again, Young and Shuford (1955) observed the same phenomenon of inversion during extinction of the habit of running down a 6-foot straightaway for daily 1-sec sips of sucrose solutions.

Reinforcement during Magnesium Deficiency. Lest anyone associate all reinforcement with relief from intraorganic need, consider for a moment the effect of magnesium deficiency.

There is evidence that magnesium deficiency in the diet actually leads to avoidance of the needed mineral! Scott, Verney, and Morissey (1950) reported that rats maintained on a magnesium-deficient diet *avoided* foods containing adequate amounts of magnesium despite the fact that this mineral is essential for health and ultimate survival. We cannot, therefore, assume that an animal's behavior is always instrumental in meeting nutritional needs.

In a speculative attempt to explain this finding, Scott et al. commented:

> The most plausible explanation of these results is that the avoidance of magnesium is learned. It is well-known that a feeling of well-being is not always associated with the best possible physical status nor the ultimate welfare of an individual. Examples that may be cited are those of alcoholism, narcotism, and the euphoria that may occur in high altitude anoxia. Magnesium-deficient animals are nervous, highly excitable, and likely to go into convulsions on slight stimulation, while magnesium is a nervous system depressant. It is possible that the highly excitable stage of magnesium deficiency is pleasurable to the rat, and that he learns to avoid a diet that represses this pleasurable state. [199]

This speculation concerning pleasure may or may not be correct but at least it can serve as a warning against the assumption that every state of need is associated with hedonic negativity and that all pleasurable states lead to health and well-being.

It occurs to me that the magnesium-containing food may have been unpalatable and that possibly rats would learn to react positively to weak solutions of pure magnesium. In any event, a further study of the problem should be made.

Gustatory and Intragastric Controls of Intake. Experimental studies by Miller and Kessen (1952), Mook (1963), Stellar (1967), Borer (1968), and others, have clearly demonstrated that appetitive behavior can be learned on the basis of intragastric effects alone quite apart from gustatory stimulations.

Epstein (1967), however, in an excellent review of the literature dealing with the role of oropharyngeal factors in selection of foods and regulation of intake, pointed out that oropharyngeal factors contribute to: (1) the identification and choice of nutrients; (2) the motivation of feeding and drinking, and (3) maintaining internal homeostasis. Oral processes thus supplement the intragastric controls.

According to Epstein, animals are drawn to food by smell and taste rather than driven to it by hunger. Palatability, writes Epstein, is the dominant factor controlling intake of food and drink. The nutritionist and laboratory scientist have been inclined to ignore the fact that man selects food and fluids mainly for their appearance and flavor rather than for nutritional value. The gourmet tradition is largely one of refinement and exaggeration of palatability. The food and beverage industries encourage consumption by emphasizing flavor and acceptability. Calories, proteins, vitamins, weight control, health and nutritional adequacy are intellectual concerns that the food specialist imposes on food selection, especially when obesity or nutritional deficiency threatens; but when food is abundant and choice wide, man eats primarily for palatability and secondarily for nutritional benefit.

An example of the oral regulation of intake is prandial drinking. Prandial drinking is taking small drafts of water immediately after dry food has been taken into the mouth. The reduction or removal of saliva by chewing dry food is temporarily relieved by taking water into the mouth; this facilitates swallowing. Prandial drinking is obviously mouth-regulated rather than regulated by an internal water deficit and intragastric conditions.

In general, the available evidence indicates that there is a dual sensory control over the selection and intake of foodstuffs. Stimulations of receptors of taste, smell, temperature and touch, in the oropharyngeal region, and physical intragastric conditions play separate but interrelated roles in regulating the feeding process. Research today is centered upon the interrelations of the central and peripheral determinants of food preference and intake and the relation of both to habit formation.

The Distinction Between Palatability and Appetite. The term *palatability* refers to the hedonic value of a foodstuff that depends upon taste, aroma, texture, temperature, appearance, and other sensory properties, and upon the surroundings of a foodstuff (environmental setting). In need-free organisms a preference between two taste solutions reveals a difference in palatability.

The term *appetite* refers to desire or craving. The positive hedonic effects of contacts with foods are in themselves appetitive and lead to the development of appetitive, goal-oriented, behaviors. Negative hedonic effects are intrinsically aversive and lead to rejection and to the development of aversive dispositions and behaviors. In so far as preference and intake are influenced by deprivation or satiation, by surgical operations, by special organic conditions such as pregnancy and lactation, diseases, etc., the appetites for foods are determined by factors that are extrinsic to palatability. In some diseases, for example, there is anorexia. Intraorganic conditions clearly influence appetites and aversions.

When an animal eats a food continuously there are appetitive changes. Again, the eating of salted nuts and other tidbits before a meal is said to whet the appetite. The French have expressed it in an aphorism: "*L'appetit vient en mangeant.*" The *hors d'oeuvre* before a meal are appetizers; they increase the desire to eat.

The distinction between palatability and appetite does not imply that there are two kinds of affective processes. I would postulate only one kind of affective process, with positive and negative signs, but a variety of conditions that influence affectivity.

An experiment by Shuford (1959) will be considered in some detail because it illustrates the validity of the distinction between palatability and appetite as objective concepts.

Shuford studied the relative acceptance of sucrose and glucose solutions by need-free rats. He arbitrarily selected for study three concentrations of glucose solutions, namely, 5, 15 and 35 percent. For each of these solutions he computed, on the basis of preference tests of the intake type, the concentrations of sucrose solutions that would be equally acceptable. The three sucrose concentrations, respectively, turned out to be: 2, 9.6 and 27.6 percent.

During the main experiment thirty animals were given, individually, a 20-minute drinking test with each of the six sugar solutions (three of glucose and three of sucrose) presented singly. Each rat was given one test per day. The six solutions were presented according to a counterbalanced Latin square design.

The curves presented in Figure 21 show the cumulative mean intake for each of the six solutions as a function of drinking time. It is obvious at a glance that the six solutions do *not* yield identical curves of intake. The greatest quantities of fluid consumed during the 20-minute test were for the 9.6 percent sucrose solution (9.6 S) and the 15 percent glucose solution (15 G). The lowest fluid intake was for the pair of solutions with the highest concentrations (27.6 S and 35 G).

A careful study of these three pairs of isohedonic curves reveals an interesting fact. The initial rate of acceptance is practically the same for the two fluids in each pair of equally palatable solutions. Compare the curves for 5 G and 2 S during the first 12 minutes; and the curves for 9.6 S and 15 G during the first 5 minutes; and the curves for 27.6 S and 35 G during the first 1 or 2 minutes. If the initial slopes of these pairs of curves are studied by noting the angle of a curve to the vertical, it will be seen that the highest rate of acceptance was for the pair with highest concentrations; an intermediate rate was obtained for the pair with intermediate concentrations; and the lowest initial rate was for the pair with the lowest concentrations.

In an earlier study, McCleary (1953) failed to find a positive relation between initial rate of acceptance and concentration of solution. His

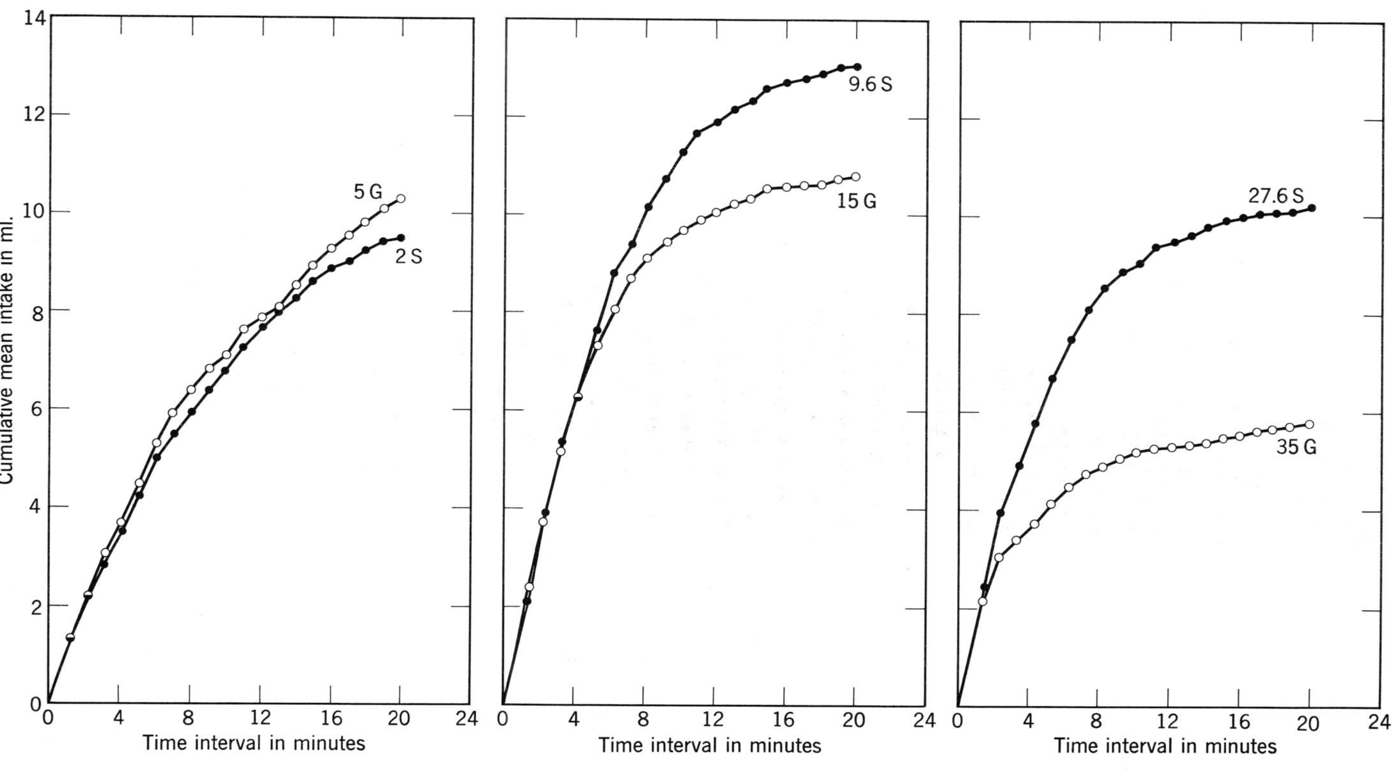

Figure 21. Pairs of curves for isohedonic solutions of glucose (G) and sucrose (S) with need-free rats. *From* Shuford (1959).

rats, however, were thirsty and doubtless drank at a maximal rate of acceptance throughout the tests. Shuford's rats, by contrast, were not thirsty, hungry, or deprived in any known way. With the need-free animals the initial rate of ingestion was positively related to concentration of the sugar solutions.

McCleary recognized a distinction between two groups of factors that regulate intake: taste factors and postingestion factors. The postingestion factors serve to check ingestion. He demonstrated the importance of postingestion factors by introducing solutions through a small tube directly into the stomach of the rat—thus bypassing the taste receptors. McCleary found that preloading the stomach with glucose depressed the ingestion of glucose after the stomach tube had been removed. He showed that the depression of intake is related to the osmotic pressure of the fluid in the stomach. Preloads of urea, sodium chloride and glucose, when matched for osmotic pressure, produced equivalent amounts of depression of ingestion.

Shuford's work confirmed the distinction, drawn by McCleary, between a taste factor and a postingestion factor in the regulation of intake. Shuford showed that the taste factor regulates the initial rate of acceptance; but sooner or later a postingestion factor checks the intake. It is the postingestion factor that accounts for the difference in Shuford's curves after the first few minutes.

To test the influence of osmotic pressure upon intake Shuford plotted his data in the form shown in Figure 22. Osmotic pressure (in atmospheres) is represented along the baseline and the four sugar solutions that are hypertonic are placed upon the baseline according to their osmotic pressures. The illustration gives the cumulative mean intake (in milliliters) for the four hypertonic solutions, plotted after 1, 4, 8, 12, 16, and 20 minutes of drinking.

It is obvious from this illustration that the quantity of fluid ingested during a fixed period of time is a decreasing function of osmotic pressure of the solution as well as an increasing function of the drinking time. If drinking time is held constant, at 4, 8, or 20 minutes, the quantity of fluid ingested decreases as the osmotic pressure increases.

In general, these experiments demonstrate the validity of a distinction between the peripheral and internal determinants of ingestion. Since both sets of determinants regulate intake, it would be confusing to interpret the amount of fluid ingested as an index of either appetite or palatability. There are at least these two determinants that operate jointly in the regulation of ingestion. They can be experimentally distinguished.

Hedonic Regulation in Specific Hungers and Poisoning. Rozin and Kalat (1971) have reviewed a great deal of careful research on specific

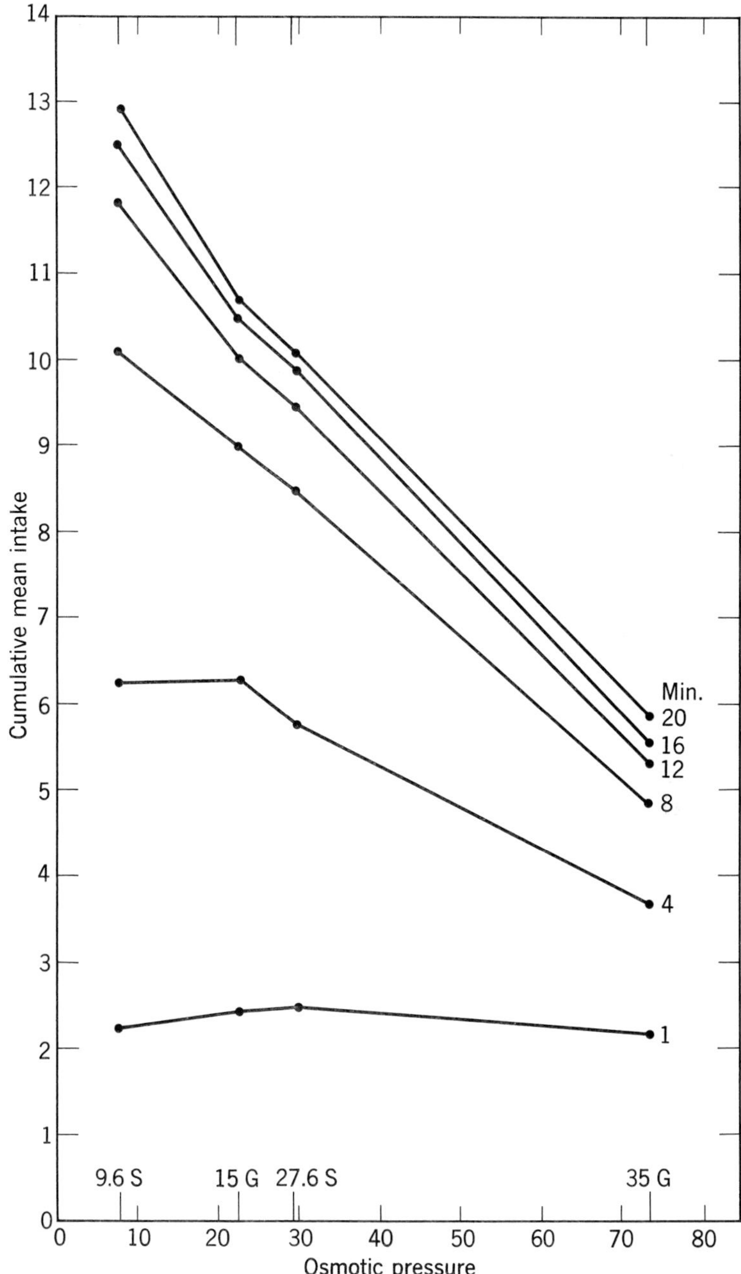

Figure 22. Cumulative mean intake of sucrose (S) and glucose (G) solutions as a function of osmotic pressure and drinking time. *From* Shuford (1959).

hungers. They have emphasized the biologically adaptive nature of food selections and especially the regulatory influence of delayed intra-organic effects upon ingestion and preference.

Under conditions of wildlife it is highly important that animals select their foods wisely from the available supply. Rozin and Kalat report that laboratory rats maintained on a deficient diet prefer a novel food, even though it is deficient, to a familiar food. There is a "neophilia"—a fondness for a novel food that appears especially when a familiar food is inadequate. If the novel food is adequate and meets a need, rats continue to accept it. If inadequate, they develop an aversion to it and prefer the familiar food.

If rats are offered a poison, such as lithium chloride, they develop an aversion to it on the basis of some deferred negative after-effect. Specific aversions to inadequate foods influence preference.

Wild rats when poisoned become bait-shy. They sample available foods but, if poisoned, show an aversion (a "neophobia") to novel foods. They prefer a familiar safe food to a novel food that might prove to be toxic. It is not easy to poison wild rats. They sample available foods and associate a particular food with its deferred after-effect.

Diets are recognized by their odor, appearance, taste, feel, and associated perceptual properties. Rats somehow learn to associate the sensory properties of a food with its deferred long-term after-effects. Rozin and Kalat point out that this long-term memory cannot be explained in terms of classical conditioning in which the interval between CR and UCR is very brief. They believe that the facts of specific hunger and poisoning require the postulate of a special kind of adaptive learning in which there is a factor of "belongingness." The intragastric after-effects of an ingested food *belong* to the specific kind of food. In other words, the after-effects of a food become associated with the perceived food. The interval of delay between eating a food and its after-effect may be eight hours or more. Hence long-term associative memory is involved rather than classical conditioning.

Much of the data on food preferences, Rozin and Kalat state, can be explained as the development of aversive behavior to a non-preferred food on the basis of deferred negative after-effects. Positive and negative palatability effects are minimized.

I believe, however, that there is only one kind of learning (learning through associated arousals) and that positive and negative hedonic effects are present not only in association with peripheral stimulations of the head receptors but also in association with intragastric and other internal after-effects. The relief from internal distress is an hedonic change away from negativity and toward neutral or positive affectivity. Relief is a change in the positive direction.

Rozin and Kalat point out that some specific hungers are more "salient" than others and that this difference in "salience" can explain food preferences. Doubtless internal organic states do differ in the intensity of hedonic negativity and such intensive differences could easily influence adaptive behavior. Positive and negative hedonic changes, whatever the source, can regulate adaptive behavior and development.

I would like to point out that the concept of hunger, whether general or specific, contains an ambiguity. The concept does not clearly distinguish between *need* (metabolic requirement or nutritional deficit), on the one hand, and *activation*, on the other. Hedonic effects of stimulation are of two kinds: positive and negative. Behavioral drives are of two kinds: appetitive and aversive. Purposive behavior is of two kinds: approach and withdrawal. Conscious feelings are of two kinds: pleasant and unpleasant. Reinforcement effects are of two kinds: rewards and punishments. This dynamic polarity must be reckoned with in any theory of learning. Activation is both positive and negative. The concept of specific hunger confounds need and the facts of affective arousal.

The basic problem of explaining the regulation of food intake and preference involves an understanding of the relation between palatability and post-ingestional effects. The affective processes are in evidence internally as well as at the periphery.

FOOD PREFERENCE, BODILY NEED AND DIETARY HABIT

In an experiment by Young and Chaplin (1945), groups of rats were maintained in cafeteria cages upon a self-selected Richter diet. The animals were given unlimited access to a fully adequate diet, the components of which were presented in separate containers. Repeated tests of preference were made between two of the dietary components: sucrose and casein. A brief-exposure serial technique of testing preferences was employed. The need-free rats developed and maintained a uniform and consistent preference of sucrose to casein. This preference, we assumed, was based upon palatability. For some reason the rats do not like casein very well; they prefer the sweet-tasting sugar.

After a preference for sucrose had been established we removed casein from the cafeteria cages. Then protein starvation steadily increased day by day but the rats continued to select sucrose on the preference-testing apparatus. The preferential habit was definitely and obviously opposed to the nutritional needs of the rats for protein.

At this point in the experiment we tried another method of testing preferences. The sucrose and casein were presented in separate containers, widely separated and in fixed positions as in a Y- or T-maze. To demonstrate a preferential discrimination the rats had to *learn* to take a path to one food or the other. Under these conditions all rats learned to take a path to casein. For a while there were two incompatible and simultaneous preferences! When the animals were placed on the preference tester with test foods close together and positions alternated from trial to trial they preferred sucrose. When tested on the apparatus with foods widely separated and in fixed positions they consistently developed a preference for casein! Now simultaneous incompatible preferences require an explanation.

After several control experiments I concluded that the choice of sucrose was a preferential habit that had developed on the basis of palatability under need-free conditions and that persisted as a habit during the period of protein starvation. The developing preference for casein, contrastingly, was based upon relief from a severe and increasing nutritional need.

One can speculate that the need for protein enhanced the palatability of protein so that casein "tasted better" than sucrose to the protein-starved rats. But why, then, did the original preference, observed on the foods-together apparatus, not change? Our answer was that preferential habits tend to persist as independent determinants of choice. Preferential food habits, however, do tend to form in agreement with metabolic and nutritional needs as well as on the basis of palatability. There is thus a dual basis for habit formation.

Anhomeostatic Habits of Choice. Harriman (1955), using a 2-bottle continuous-exposure technique, tested the preference of rats with a 1.2% sodium chloride solution versus 8.0% sucrose solution. The normal rodent preference for sucrose developed.

Then the rats were adrenalectomized. It is known that adrenalectomy increases the homeostatic need for sodium. Despite the increasing need for sodium the adrenectomized rats persisted in their preferential selection of sucrose. Failure to select the needed NaCl resulted in death of some animals and marked loss of weight in the survivors. The persisting choice of sugar was obviously unwise, opposed to bodily needs, anhomeostatic. Harriman's observations confirmed a principle recognized by Harris et al. (1933) that a habit of choice may persist even though contrary to metabolic needs. The above study by Young and Chaplin also confirmed this principle.

A different result, however, was obtained by Cullen and Scarborough (1969) who used another method of testing that made it difficult or impossible for rats to establish a stable position habit. In their work the rat was presented with two levers in a Skinner box. Each lever operated a dipper that presented a small amount of test solution. To obtain a taste of 1.5% (w/v) NaCl or 13.5% (w/v) sucrose the rat had to press one of the levers and then move to the appropriate dipper. There were daily 20-min tests. Relative positions of the containers were changed from day to day. During a test the rat had to discover which lever produced a saline taste and which a sweet taste. These conditions required animals to be alert and actively discriminating. Stable position habits could not form.

Under these conditions (which are radically different from those of Harriman) the *preoperative* rats preferred sugar to salt. This normal rodent preference persisted despite the fact that the animals were maintained on a sodium-deficient diet. The dietary deficiency did not of itself change the normal preference of sugar to salt.

Then the rats in one group were adrenalectomized. The preference immediately reversed: the rats then preferred salt to sugar in agreement with their metabolic need.

In a control experiment with a group of adrenalectomized rats, the stomach was loaded twice daily with 5% NaCl so that no need for sodium was present despite the operation. These animals developed and maintained for 15 days the normal palatability preference of sugar to salt. When the technique of stomach loading was discontinued there was an immediate mutation of preference: The rats promptly preferred salt to sugar in agreement with their need.

The experiments of Cullen and Scarborough demonstrate that choice is controlled by homeostatic need despite persisting habits of choice. Further, the experiments show a palatability preference in the need-free condition. The experiments also show that in the absence of homeostatic need the palatability effect dominates choice.

Saline Preferences and the Need for Hydration. Young and Falk (1956) ran a series of preference tests between distilled water and sodium chloride solutions of different concentration, and between pairs of sodium chloride solutions. They found that need-free (nondeprived) rats revealed optimal concentrations for NaCl within the range of 0.75-1.50 percent (w/v) NaCl. With concentrations below this range, rats preferred the *higher* concentration; with concentrations above this range, they preferred the *lower* concentration. Within the *optimal* range there were marked individual differences in preference and much indiscriminate behavior. The experimenters concluded that there is a *range of acceptance* within which the level of acceptability rises with increasing concentration of NaCl and a *range of rejection* within which the level of acceptability falls as concentration rises.

It was found that need-free rats occasionally accepted solutions of NaCl with concentrations as high as 3 or 6 percent. We wondered whether making the rats thirsty would force them to show a preference between pairs of hypertonic saline solutions. Actually, we found that thirsty rats would not touch such salty fluids. The thirsty animals, when offered a choice, tended to prefer the weaker saline solution of a pair or distilled water to hypertonic saline. Moreover, there were indications that thirst disturbed the system of hedonic values which had been established under need-free conditions. There were mutations of preference, failures of the hierarchical principle, indiscriminate behavior, and pronounced inhibition of running activity on the apparatus. Apparently the need for hydration dominated preferential behavior and disrupted the value system established under need-free conditions.

Young and Falk used a brief-exposure serial technique for testing preferences with the test fluids side by side and their relative positions interchanged from trial to trial.

Different techniques were used by Deutsch and Jones (1960) in their experiments with saline preferences. Their data are unique in that they demonstrate incompatible simultaneous preferences with the same rats, the same pair of test solutions, the same conditions of deprivation, but with different methods of testing.

I will disregard the "diluted water" hypothesis of Deutsch and Jones and consider only their data and methods. (For details see Young, 1968, p 233.) Deutsch and Jones tested the saline preferences of rats with two kinds of apparatus: (1) a T maze and (2) a cage with two nozzles that provided a 20-min continuous choice between a pair of test fluids. In tests with both forms of apparatus the animals were offered a choice between two (hypotonic) saline solutions: 0.2% NaCl and 0.8% NaCl. In both experiments there was water deprivation of 20 hours. The only difference between the tests was the apparatus and the criterion of preference.

In tests with the T maze the rats steadily learned to turn to the *weaker* saline solution–to 0.2% NaCl rather than to 0.8% NaCl. This choice makes sense because it is known that saline solutions are dehydrating and increase thirst. The weaker saline solution or distilled water is better for reducing thirst than the stronger saline solution. But with the intake test, with nozzles near together, the animals showed a significant preference for the 0.8% NaCl. This is the normal rodent preference for saline solutions–a preference based on palatability. The 0.8% solution is nearly optimal for need-free rats.

In general, it seems that the traditional T maze with test foods widely separated in fixed positions is better for testing choices based on intraorganic need and the foods-together continuous-choice technique when exposures are brief especially, is better for testing palatability. The striking thing about the data of Deutsch and Jones is the demonstration that preference is a function of the method employed in testing.

Studies with Saccharin Solution. Studies with saccharin are interesting because saccharin meets no known metabolic need. Saccharin tastes sweet at low concentrations but passes through the body unaltered by metabolism.

Sheffield and Roby (1950), however, report that rats learned to run down a straightaway when their only reward was the sweet-tasting saccharin. Sheffield argued that eliciting a consummatory response rather than reduction of need and drive is the prime factor in reinforcement. Again, Young and Madsen (1963) found that need-free rats show clear and consistent preferences for saccharin solutions that differ in concentration. The isohedons are strikingly uniform. The motivation, they believe, is hedonic.

Strouthes (1971) tested the effect of water deficit on the saccharin preference of rats. He found that a great need for hydration obliterates the preferential selection of saccharin solutions. He concluded that rats must first drink water in order to reduce their water deficit to some threshold value before saccharin is drunk. When saccharin solutions are accepted postingestional and oral factors, according to Strouthes, together become responsible for ingestion of quantities of saccharin.

These studies are interesting because no one can argue that saccharin meets an intraorganic need yet the palatability effect is pronounced. And, further, Strouthes' experiments suggest that an internal need for hydration disengages the entire machinery for preferential discrimination.

Now if we review the above experiments on food preferences, bodily need, and dietary habit, it becomes clear that there are at least three interdependent determinants of choice and the intake of foods: (1) The hedonic (palatability) effect that arises from stimulations of the receptors for taste, smell, touch, vision. (2) The positive and negative motivating effects produced intraorganically by bodily needs. (3) Dietary habits that are established through (hedonic) reinforcements from either the oral or intragastric regions.

The experiments show that a habit based on palatability may dominate choice despite metabolic and nutritional needs (Young and Chaplin, Harriman). But when habits cannot be established on the basis of fixed positions the intraorganic need may control the selection of nutrients (Cullen and Scarborough, Young and Chaplin, Deutsch and Jones). Further, the peripheral and central determinants of choice interact in determining preferences (Young and Falk). Also an intense intraorganic need may obliterate and completely obscure preferential behavior (Strouthes). And, surprisingly, two incompatible and dynamically opposed preferences may exist simultaneously side by side (Young and Chaplin, Deutsch and Jones).

We must conclude, therefore, that there are at least three independent and interacting determinants of the selection and ingestion of foods: the palatability effect, the hedonic (or other) effects of intraorganic need, the habits established on either or both of these bases. In man there is a fourth factor: the beliefs, attitudes, knowledge, derived from the social environment and from past experience.

CONCLUSION

In the present chapter we have extended the study of motivation by examining needs, values, appetites and aversions. The purpose of the chapter is to give a dynamic setting for analysis of affective processes in man and other animals.

The concept of *need* is ambiguous. In one meaning, *need* is an evaluation made by a judge. There is always a criterion or standard by which a need is appraised or estimated. In a second meaning, employed by some psychologists, *need* is a force, drive, or motive. In this dynamic sense, *motive* and *need* are synonymous.

Primitive man lacks scientific knowledge to appraise all of his needs but nevertheless finds ways to meet the biological requirements of existence. Techniques for meeting needs differ from group to group but somehow man and other animals have survived.

The concept of *value* is also ambiguous. The source of ambiguity becomes clear when we ask: Who does the evaluating—the man of science or the organism he observes? I postulate that the evaluative behavior of rats is a *fact* of nature. It is also a *fact* of nature that philosophers make value judgments which differ from person to person and from time to time. A *science* of values is possible if and only if we start from observed behavior which is regarded as evaluative and also as factual.

Acceptance or rejection of a food can be observed as an evaluative reaction; preference, as a relative evaluation. Studies of food preferences have revealed: hierarchical value systems of laboratory rats; that positive and negative hedonic values summate algebraically; that dynamically opposed hedonic processes are integrated when an organism responds to a complex sensory presentation; that behavior is regulated according to a principle of maximizing the positive and minimizing the negative hedonic values, etc. Experiments on food acceptance demonstrate that the hedonic values of taste solutions can be analyzed quantitatively, objectively, experimentally, statistically. This constitutes a sound basis for a (limited) science of values.

Available evidence indicates that food preferences and dietary habits are organized and developed on the dual basis of excitations from the oropharyngeal and intragastric regions. Investigators who have studied the adjustments of intake to dietary deficiencies agree that hedonic effects (comforts and discomforts) from internal regions play a basic role in the development of appetitive and aversive behavior and in the acquisition of food preferences.

In following chapters it will appear that frustrations, interruptions, conflicts, failures, and other disturbances, elicit feelings and emotions, and that success, achievement, reward, and other satisfying conditions, have positive affective consequences. An understanding of psychodynamics is necessary in explaining these complex events.

Chapter IV

Emotional Development

Before turning to the study of emotional development it will be worthwhile to consider briefly what is known about the genesis of behavior in the embryo. Systematic observations of the behavior of the *human* embryo have not been made. The first responses of the human fetus to stimulation can be observed only on relatively rare occasions of surgical operation. But with animals the life of mother and embryo can be sacrificed in order to observe the beginnings of behavior. There is dependable information upon the behavior of non-human embryos. What are the characteristics of the earliest responses of the embryo?

The following account of the beginnings of behavior in the embryo serves at least as a background for consideration of this question.

First Behavior of the Embryo. During the first months of uterine existence, the behavior of the animal fetus can be described as a diffuse and aimless "mass activity." Movements involve gross portions of the body. As the fetus grows, however, patterns of specific activity, similar to those employed in walking, swimming, and feeding emerge out of this diffuse mass action. After birth a process of differentiation proceeds, the patterns of response becoming increasingly specific, definite, precise, until finally they can be recognized as the forms of adaptive behavior which characterize the mature organism. For an elaboration of this view see Irwin (1932).

In a remarkable account of behavioral development in the embryo salamander, *Amblystoma*, Coghill (1929), in discussing the relation between behavior and bodily structure, shows how specific patterns of activity develop out of more general patterns. At a given stage of development, he states, the general patterns of behavior dominate the then-existing specific patterns. To illustrate the point two examples of the developing behavior of the salamander will be cited.

1. In the development of *walking*, the first movement of the leg is part of a postural reaction of the trunk. Before the limb can respond separately to stimulations from the outside, it responds to internal

stimuli arising from a particular posture of the body. The movements of each limb are coordinated with gross movements of the trunk in such a way that as one flexure after another passes from the head of the animal tailward, the limbs adjust themselves to the dominant position of the trunk. Even at later stages of development—when each leg has acquired a certain degree of functional independence and can respond to external stimuli—the posture of the trunk still retains its dominant role in regulation locomotion.

Thus, as Coghill has shown, trunk movements develop prior to independent limb movements; and the latter are dominated by trunk movements even after they have acquired a certain degree of functional independence.

2. Similarly, in early developmental stages of the *feeding reaction*, the trunk component—a short quick jump forward—becomes functional before snapping with the mouth appears. This characteristic forward jump can be evoked by a light touch upon a limb or adjacent parts before there is any evidence of a visual response. Somewhat later the jumping response appears when a bristle or similar object is moved back and forth at a distance of two or three millimeters in front of the young salamander's eyes. Under this stimulation the animal jumps forward toward the moving object, but without making any perceptible jaw movement. Still later, the performance includes actual snapping at an object which is moving in the field of vision.

Here, then, gross trunk movements develop first, the earlier ones in response to external contact, the later ones in response to movement within the visual field. Finally there ripens a mature, integrated behavioral pattern for catching a moving object in the mouth.

The process by which a specific response is differentiated out of mass activity is known as *individuation*. By this process the emerging behavioral pattern develops within and out of general integrated patterns. Behavior is integrated at every embryonic stage. The term *individuation* describes one of the two main aspects of the development of behavior. The other aspect of that development is *integration*—the process through which preformed patterns are organized to form a larger integrated whole.

There are, in fact, two main theories as to the nature of behavioral development. One holds that maturation proceeds by individuation; the other, that it is accomplished through a process of integration. The formulation of both of these theories is premature. Much more observation and analysis will be required before a complete and final genetic theory of behavior can be formulated.

Working toward this end, Carmichael (1934) observed the responses of fetal guinea pigs when a hundred specific areas of the skin were stimulated. He found that each of these receptor zones, when stimulated, elicited, from the first appearance of any response, a characteristic and individual reaction pattern. These patterns of response varied from one test to another according to the stage of development of the fetus, but at any given time each pattern could be described in terms of stimulus and response.

From his observations Carmichael worked out a developmental schedule of the behavior of the fetal guinea pig. A few examples, chosen at random from his list of a hundred, are presented below for illustrative purposes. In each instance there is given the receptor area stimulated, the age of the fetus at the time of the first appearance of the response, and the locus or general nature of the response.

Receptor area stimulated	Age of fetus at first response	Locus or nature of first response
Angle of lip	32 days	Neck and forelimb
Brow	40 days	Wink of unopened eye and pinna reflex
Hip	32 days	Trunk, forelimbs and hindlimbs
Elbow	34 days	Forelimb and digits
Tongue	36 days	Tongue movements

Among various points brought out by Carmichael's work the more significant for the study of behavioral development are these: There are definite stages in the behavioral development of the embryo. At each stage specific patterns of response (varying with age) appear when particular receptor areas are stimulated. Movements involving larger groups of muscles are the first to appear; these are followed by more specific muscular movements.

Another principle of behavioral development having psychological interest is the following. In the early stages behavior is controlled by *internal* bodily states and stimulations; later *external* stimulations become effective in the control of behavior. For example, Coghill (1936) has shown that, in the embryo toadfish, rhythmic integrated muscular contractions are observed before sensory structures become functional. These movements are endogenous in origin; they are accelerated by an increase in the quantity of carbon dioxide present in the solution. Since the sensory structures are not yet functioning, the effect of the carbon dioxide must come from within. The observation is important because it establishes the fact that chemical motivation is prior, genetically, to neural.

In a sense, as Coghill has shown, the development of the nervous system anticipates future forms of behavior. That is to say, at each stage of development more neural structures are present within the organism than are required for the immediate behavior. This overgrowth is especially marked in the neural mechanisms required for learning. In general, the higher the animal ranks in order of intelligence and the greater its capacity for psychological development, the more extensively do the central neural mechanisms develop prior to the motor mechanisms.

With this brief survey of the genesis of behavior in the embryo, as a background, we go on to the study of emotional development in the infant. At what stage of infant development does emotional behavior first appear? How can the earliest emotional responses be distinguished from non-emotional activities?

UNDIFFERENTIATED EMOTIONAL EXCITEMENT

Stratton (1928) drew an important distinction between diffuse, undifferentiated excitement, on the one hand, and specific differentiated forms of emotional behavior, on the other. Excitement, he said, plays a basic role in human adult behavior. Excitement may be the precursor or the successor of any specific emotion. General excitement may turn into fear, anger, sexual emotion, or some other specific emotional state; and these, again, may leave an aftermath of general excitement.

Excitement may also stand alone—when stimulation of the organism is excessive or from an unfamiliar situation or when the outcome of an impending event is unknown. For example, at a football game before the players have come onto the field, excited behavior can be seen among the spectators.

In Figure 23 Stratton has pictured diffuse, undifferentiated, excitement as the basic form of human emotion. The diagram shows the more highly differentiated emotions of fear, anger, affection at the top and the less differentiated emotional states (moods) at the bottom.

Stratton recognized that human emotional states are subjectively of two kinds: *pleasant*, shown at the right, and *unpleasant* at the left. It is to Stratton's credit that he recognized these two variables underlying emotion—excitement and the hedonic dimension—and, further, that he distinguished between diffuse, undifferentiated excitement and the specific forms of emotional reaction. These two basic dimensions of motivation are recognized in the directive-activation theory of motivation (Figure 12, page 73).

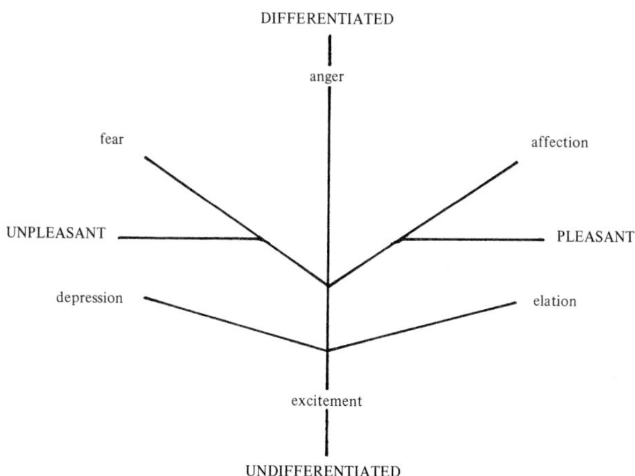

Figure 23. Excitement as a basic, undifferentiated emotion. *After* Stratton (1928).

Stratton did not stress the genetic aspect of his view. His paper was analytical. One can ask, however: How far are the differentiated emotional reactions determined by the genetic code? How far are the specific forms of emotional behavior acquired during ontogenetic development? According to what principles does emotional behavior develop? These and related questions will be considered below.

Diffuseness and Lack of Specificity in Early Behavior. One of the traditional views within psychology is that the newborn infant is a bundle of reflexes. Blanton (1917) illustrated this in summarizing observations of the neonate. She wrote:

> During the first twenty minutes of life may be observed sneezing, yawning, tears, sucking at nipple, fixation on light, putting thumb in mouth, jumping to loud sounds, grasping, crying with box-shaped mouth, crying with corners of the mouth pulled down, following a moving hand with the eyes, turning of the head in such a way as to get air when placed on the face, turning over when given a very slight advantage, complete erection of penis, and most indicative, perhaps, the cry of so-called anger immediately after birth, justifying perhaps Kant's so oft denied statement that the cry of a child just born has not the tone of lamentation but of aroused wrath. [482]

More recent observations, however, have raised a question concerning the adequacy of this view and revealed the diffuseness and generality of infant behavior rather than its specificity.

Pratt, Nelson, and Sun (1930), for example, have shown that the sensori-motor responses of the infant are not nearly so specific at birth as had formerly been supposed. Any one of several reactions may occur in the human infant after a given stimulation. Further, the same reaction may be evoked by a wide variety of stimulations. To illustrate the last point: These experimenters noted that stimulating the lips of the newborn infant was followed by sucking movements in over 90 per cent of the infants tested; but sucking was also produced by stimulating the cheeks, the eyes, the temperature sense, and the senses of taste and smell. Thus, although sucking is a specific response to stimulation of the lips, it is also elicited by many other kinds of stimulation. In fact, almost any mild stimulation may release the sucking response in the infant.

These investigators state that, while the infant is equipped with a variety of reflexes, the degree of their specificity has been much exaggerated. Moreover, many of the reflexes and emotional patterns which other investigators have described were not observed by them. For example, the newborn infant does not withdraw his hand precisely from a painful stimulation, but he is merely excited thereby; nor does he exhibit any of the much discussed emotional patterns of fear, rage, and love.

In short, behavior of the infant is not at all precise and specific; it consists largely of mass action—general or diffuse activity. This activity is greatest in those bodily segments near to the region stimulated and decreases in magnitude and frequency in rough proportion to the distance from the zone stimulated. This decreased frequency and intensity of response in the adjoining segments does not imply, of course, that activity within any given segment is well coordinated.

Specificity of behavior develops with growth and especially in response to the infant's social environment.

Essentially this same view was expressed by M. and I. C. Sherman (1929). They observed that the first overt bodily reactions of newborn infants are simple sensorimotor responses—strikingly undefined, uncoordinated, and aimless. Out of such vague, undifferentiated behavior there develop the characteristic adaptive processes of later life.

Some reflexes, it is true, are present in workable fashion shortly after birth. Examples are swallowing, closing the eyes upon stimulation of the cornea, and grasping a small stick placed in the hand. Sucking is present in nearly all infants after twenty-four hours; sometimes before this age sucking is difficult to elicit. Sneezing, the knee jerk, and the biceps and triceps reflexes, also, can be demonstrated in the newborn. Stimulation of the larynx or pharynx induces an immediate cough. The excretory processes are adequate at birth.

During the first few weeks the Babinski reflex is supplanted by the plantar reflex and does not again appear in adult life. If one stimulates lightly the sole of the infant's foot, the toes stretch upward and outward. This is the Babinski reflex. Later in life the same stimulation causes the toes to move downward and press together. This is the plantar reflex.

Despite these specific reactions in the infant, the gross bodily behavior of the newborn, according to the Shermans, must be characterized by such terms as *uncoordinated, undifferentiated, non-adaptive excitement.* The early behavior of the human infant is to a high degree diffuse, non-specific, general in character. This is the background upon which one must sketch the development of emotions in the human infant.

Bridges' Genetic Account of Early Emotional Development. In a comprehensive series of studies, Bridges (1930, 1931, 1932) reported her extended observations and tests of the emotional behavior of infants and young children. Her subjects were in the Montreal Foundling and Baby Hospital and in a nursery school. Because Bridges approached the study without any preconceived definition of emotion, her observations are of special interest and value.

According to Bridges, the first emotional response of the infant is a general agitation or excitement produced by a great variety of stimulating conditions. This diffuse excitement is an innate emotional response—perhaps the only one. During emotional excitement in the young infant, the arm and hand muscles are tensed; the breath is quickened; the legs make jerky kicking movements; the eyes are opened as if gazing into the distance, and the upper lid is arched. The stimulations which produce such agitation or excitement are: direct sunlight in the infant's eyes, suddenly picking up the infant and putting him down on the bed, pulling the infant's arm through his dress sleeve, holding the arms tight to the sides, rapping the baby's knuckles, pressing the nipple of the bottle into the mouth, the noisy clatter of a tin basin thrown onto a metal table or radiator, and so on.

Bridges described diffuse excitement as follows:

> Time after time on waking suddenly from sleep the infants were observed to wave their arms jerkily, kick, open and close their eyes, flush slightly, and breathe quickly and irregularly. Some grunted, some cried loudly for several minutes. The combined stimulation of light, of sounds, of damp or restricted bed clothes, and the change from sleeping to waking breathing-rate seemed to produce a temporary agitation and often distress. Waking apparently requires emotional adjustment.
>
> The hungry child before feeding would often show restless activity, waving, squirming, mouthing and crying at intervals. The infant who had been lying in one position for a long time and the tired child before falling asleep would also show emotional agitation. Their breath would come jerkily, uttering staccato

> cries of "cu-cu-cu-ah," and they would thrust out their arms and legs in irregular movements. At the moment the nipple was put into the hungry baby's mouth he again breathed quickly, occasionally cried, waved the free arm, and kicked in excited agitation. [325f.]

This diffuse emotional excitement can be differentiated from distress, or negative emotion, at an early age. It is difficult, Bridges writes, to distinguish between distress and general agitation in the newborn; but in a 3-week-old infant, *excitement* and *distress* are definitely distinguishable.

Bridges continues:

> The cry of distress, recognizable in the *month-old* baby, is irregular. There are short intakes of breath and long cries on expiration. The eyes are "screwed up" tight, the face flushed, the fists often clenched, the arms tense, and legs still or kicking spasmodically. The mouth is open and square in shape or, more usually kidney-shaped with the corners pulled down. The pitch of the cry is high and somewhat discordant, and the sounds something like "ah, cu-ah, cu-ah, cuaeh."
>
> Cries of distress were heard from month-old babies in the hospital on the following occasions; on waking suddenly from sleep, struggling to breathe through nostrils blocked with mucus, when the ears were discharging, when lying awake before feeding time, after staying long in the same position, lying on a wet diaper, when the child's buttocks were chafed, and when the fingers were rapped. The three main causes of distress at this age, therefore, seemed to be discomfort, pain, and hunger. [327f.]

The emotion of *delight*, according to Bridges, is also recognizable at an early age. The main characteristics of delight are these: open eyes and expansion of the face into a smile as contrasted with the puckering of the forehead and closing of the eyes in distress; movements of incipient approach rather than withdrawal; audible inspirations and quickened breathing; soft vocalizations lower pitched than those of distress or excitement; more or less rhythmic arm and leg movements which are free from restraint; prolonged attention to the object of interest; cessation of crying.

Although the details of behavior vary from child to child and with age, delight can readily be recognized by certain characteristic activities. Free and rhythmic movements, welcoming and approaching gestures, and smiles and vocalizations of middle pitch are the commonest features.

Observes Bridges:

> At *eight months* of age the child seems to take more delight than ever in self-initiated purposeful activity. He babbles and splutters and laughs to himself. Especially does he seem delighted with the noise he makes by banging spoons or other playthings on the table. Throwing things out of his crib is another favorite pastime. He waves, pats, and coos, drawing in long breaths, when familiar adults

swing him or talk to him. He will watch the person who nurses him attentively, exploring her, patting gently, often smiling. Here are perhaps the earliest demonstrations of affection. The child will also pat and smile at his own mirror image. But his behavior is rather more aggressive and inquisitive than really affectionate. [335]

According to Bridges, then, the first emotional behavior observable in the infant is a diffuse *excitement* that is dependent upon various kinds of stimulation. During the first few weeks *distress*, or negative emotional excitement, can be distinguished from the primal form of excitement and, somewhat later, *delight*, or primitive positive emotion, is recognizable.

These early forms of emotional behavior can be readily distinguished. In *distress* the infant cries, screams, wrinkles the brow, kicks and moves excitedly. In *delight* he smiles, laughs, coos and gurgles. In pure *excitement* there is a heightened level of general activity but without the complications of crying or smiling, etc.

These primitive forms of emotional behavior persist throughout life but the many specific forms of emotion that we recognize in adults are lacking in the neonate. These develop gradually. By the time an infant is 2 years old he has acquired a variety of emotional responses. In addition to general excitement, distress, and delight, the 2-year-old shows fear, disgust, anger, jealousy, joy, elation, affection for adults, and affection for children.

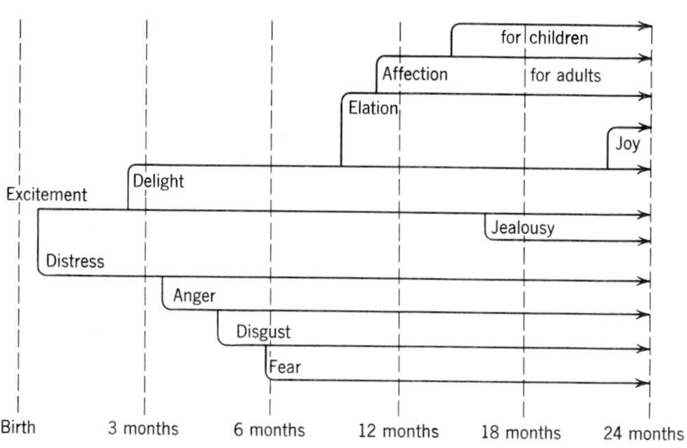

Figure 24. Early emotional development. The diagram shows the approximate ages at which different forms of emotional behavior emerge from more primitive forms during the first two years of life. *Modified from* Bridges (1932).

Figure 24 gives the approximate ages at which these different forms of emotional behavior develop. Bridges discussed in detail, and with many examples, the gradual growth of specific forms of emotional behavior out of the more primitive forms. The primitive forms of emotional behavior agree with the two basic dimensions of affectivity: the degree of excitement corresponds to the level of activation; distress and delight are obviously hedonic differences.

Bridges pointed out that emotional development and social development are intimately connected. In fact, she stated, emotional development might be treated as an aspect of social development. General characteristics of emotional development are: (1) decreasing frequency of intense emotional responses; (2) progressive transfer of emotional responses to situations which are socially approved; (3) gradual change in the nature of overt emotional responses in accordance with training and social pressures. Thus emotional and social development go along hand in hand.

HEDONIC PROCESSES IN EMOTIONAL DEVELOPMENT

It is a matter of theoretical interest that in the genetic account of emotion, *excitement* plays a dominant role. Excitement is present at birth and persists throughout life as a basic undifferentiated, diffuse, emotion. Excitement depends upon primary sensory stimulations as well as upon the perceptions, expectancies and memories of later life. Bridges' genetic account of emotional development recognizes a distinction between distress and delight. The neonate is able to cry, kick and scream; these reactions are generally accepted as objective indicators of distress. During the first two or three months of life the normal infant smiles, laughs, coos; these reactions are accepted by adults as marks of delight. Thus the basic distinctions among excitement, distress and delight can be made in early life before such emotions as fear, disgust and anger can be identified. The unpleasant emotions develop prior to positive states of elation and affection for adults and children.

In considering emotional development from the first beginnings, therefore, we should define *emotion* in the broadest possible terms to include all of the affective processes. To be technically correct we should speak of *affective* development. The affective processes include simple feelings of pleasantness and unpleasantness, moods, sentiments, as well as the more intense disruptive emotional states. *Emotional* development is an aspect of the total process of *affective* development.

The Role of Hedonic Processes in Behavioral Development. In early experiments on the food preferences of rats I observed the effects of suddenly changing one of the test foods—substituting a food that stood higher or lower in the preferential hierarchy (Young, 1933). Some of the results are presented in Figure 25.

In one series of preference tests crystalline cane sugar was used as a standard and the comparison foods were white flour, powdered whole wheat, butter-fat, milk. The percent choices, made by a group of three male rats, are shown as ordinates and successive blocks of tests as abscissas.

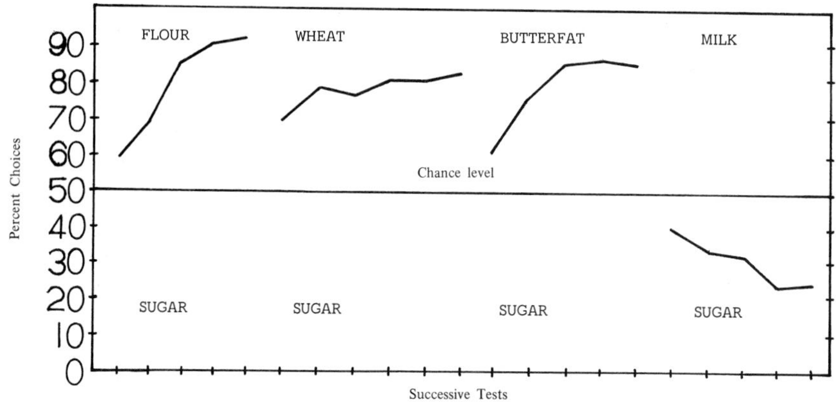

Figure 25. Preferential trends and hedonic shifts with a standard of sugar (sucrose) and varying comparison foods. *After* Young (1933).

Inspection of this graph reveals certain outstanding features: (1) In every group of successive tests the percents of choices reveal a preference. Sugar is preferred to flour, to wheat, and to butter-fat; milk is preferred to sugar. (2) In every group of successive tests there is a preferential trend, i.e., a more or less steady increase in the percent choices of the preferred food. This trend, in fact, is an important index of preference. The slope of the trend (I have found) is related to the *difference* in hedonic value between the two test foods. (3) When one test food was suddenly substituted for another there was an immediate change, from test to test, in the percent choices of both foods. These abrupt changes, I believe, are motivational in nature; they reflect the dynamic difference between the two incentives. (4) The more gradual preferential trend is a phenomenon of learning; it represents, with successive trials, the habituation effect of differential reinforcements. The abrupt changes are motivational and depend upon changes of hedonic values.

Expectancy Based on Hedonic Feedback. When rats run repeatedly to a pair of test foods presented on the preference apparatus and consistently select one and the same kind of food, they develop an *expectancy* that (in cognitive terms) they will encounter the same pair of foods on following runs and select the same (preferred) food with a similar hedonic feedback. If a novel and unexpected food is suddenly substituted for one of the pair, there is a discrepancy between expectation and reality. This discrepancy was clearly revealed in Figure 25.

In tests with single foods rather than pairs of foods there are similar effects when the hedonic value of the incentive is suddenly changed. An example of this was previously considered. See Figure 20 (page 131). Rats were thoroughly habituated to licking sucrose solutions of 1 or 4 or 8 or 32 percent concentration. After 11 days of acquisition all animals were offered an incentive of distilled water. There was an immediate and abrupt drop in the overall rate of licking when hedonic feedback was altered. Importantly, the levels of performance during extinction were inversely proportional to the original hedonic intensities during acquisition. An *expectancy* of a reward with a specific hedonic intensity had been built up during acquisition.

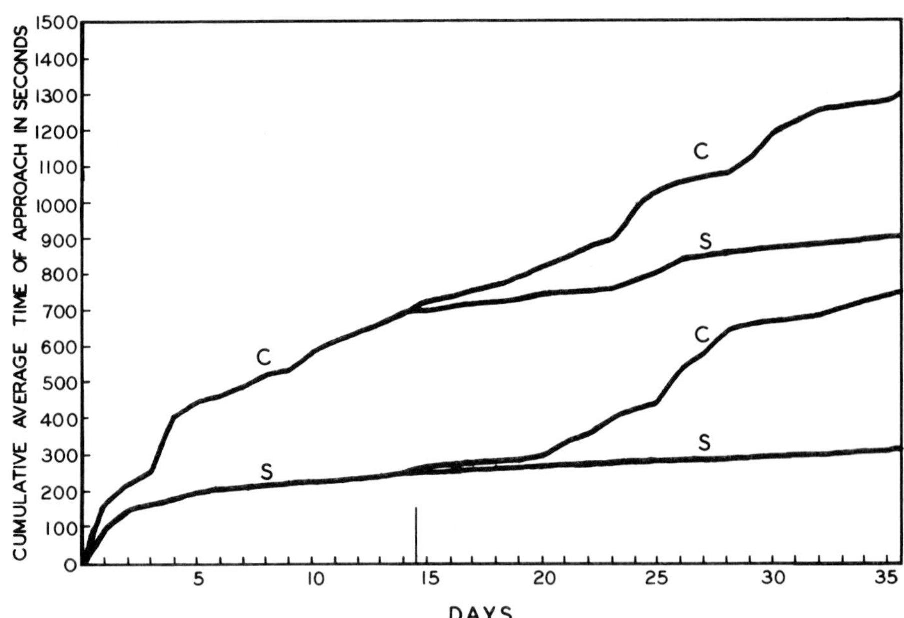

Figure 26. Cumulative average times of approach to casein (C) and sucrose (S) during successive days of testing. After 14 days of running, the original groups were subdivided and incentives were interchanged. Drawn from data of Young (1948).

In another experiment the influence of expectancy came clearly to light (Young, 1948). See Figure 26. There were two food incentives that differed widely in palatability: crystalline sucrose (S) and casein (C). Rats were trained to approach one of the incentives presented in an open field with food cup 38 cm from the threshold of the starting box. There were 14 rats in each group. For the first 14 days the rats in one group ran to an incentive of casein and the rats in the other group to an incentive of sucrose. After 14 days of habituation both groups were subdivided. Two groups of 7 rats continued to run for the original incentives. With the other two groups the incentives were interchanged. The animals originally running for sugar were offered casein; those originally running for casein were offered sugar.

The graph gives the cumulative average times of approach in seconds under the different incentive conditions. It will be seen that the rats were consistently slower in approaching casein. Casein was the non-preferred food. When the rats in the casein-incentive group, after day 14, were offered sucrose they immediately and repeatedly ran faster to the reward. This has been called an "elation" or "joy" effect! When the sugar-incentive rats were offered casein there was only a slight retardation in approach time for five or six days. Then there was a marked slowing down in the time of approach so that their approach times resembled those of the original (unchanged) casein-incentive group. Apparently the *expectancy* of a good (sugar) reward persisted for a while after the change of incentive had occurred and then the expectancy gradually yielded to a "disappointment" effect.

Crespi (1942, 1944) observed similar effects of altered feedback when he systematically varied the quantity of reward in terms of the number of food pellets presented as rewards to rats. In his interpretation he postulated an *emotional drive* shown by different degrees of *eagerness* in approaching the reward. Crespi's results show different levels of performance related to expectancy of a small or a large reward. There were effects of "elation" and "disappointment."

In general, the influence of hedonic intensity is shown immediately in performance. The hedonic effect leads to organization of approach or withdrawal patterns of behavior. When the rewarding situation is repeated the animal develops an expectancy of specific hedonic feedback-effects. Changes of hedonic intensity lead to changes in performance which should be interpreted in the light of expectancy based on previous experience.

Hedonic Organization and Development of Sexual Appetites. In a multidisciplinary analysis of sexual motivation, Hardy (1964) formulated an appetitional theory of sexual development in which hedonic processes and the expectation of pleasant effects play a dominant role.

Hardy agrees with F. A. Beach that the prevailing doctrine of sexual drive, based on an analogy to hunger and thirst, is inadequate. Hormones and physiological tensions are assuredly important but these factors do not completely explain the complex facts of human sexual development and motivation. Hardy stated some general principles of motivation and emphasized the importance of pleasantness from sexual stimulations in organizing and developing positive appetitional behavior. He pointed out that sexual appetites are based upon the pleasantness of tactual and specific genital stimulations. When stimulus-cues are repeatedly associated with pleasantness these cues arouse an expectation of positive hedonic effects. Specific forms of sexual behavior—masturbation, coitus, animal contacts, and others—appear to be organized and to develop on the basis of hedonic effects from sensory stimulations.

A doctrine of expectation based on the habituation to hedonic effects provides a sound basis for understanding the growth and continuance of sexual habits and appetites. Hardy takes account of habituation effects in relation to sexual appetites. The affective processes organize positive and negative dispositions which tend, with repetition, to become autonomous and lead to the expectation of further hedonic effects.

In his analysis, Hardy considers cultural and social factors, and differences in sexual codes and mores. Negative hedonic effects are derived from the frustration of sexual motives and from conflicts. These negative effects are analyzed from the point of view of Kurt Lewin and the approach-avoidance type of conflict. The opposing forces in a dynamic conflict vary in relative strength from situation to situation and from time to time. Interpersonal relations, of course, are complex.

Hardy's clear and cogent analysis of sexual motivation is, I believe, more realistic than Freud's doctrines of the libido and sublimation of an instinctive drive. The extension of hedonic theory into the realm of sexual motivation is worthy of careful consideration by psychologists. Of course, one must recognize that the human problems of living involve more than sex and a search for happiness. Hardy (1965) has replied to criticisms of his views.

TRENDS IN EMOTIONAL DEVELOPMENT

Empirical evidence is available that describes the course of emotional development during early and later stages of the human life cycle. A sample of this evidence is presented below.

Developmental Changes in Frequency and Causation of Crying. The reflex pattern of crying is present at birth. As a matter of fact the birth cry, incidental to the establishing of respiration, is about the first response that the infant makes to his new environment. Mothers universally regard the cry as a sign of distress but when viewed objectively it is just a reflex pattern.

Bayley (1932) gave sixty-one infants a variety of tests to determine the amount of crying during a test period of about an hour. She found that the percentage of time given to crying declined after the first month and reached its lowest point at about 4 months; after that the percentage of time given to crying increased with age up to 1 year. Subsequently there was a decrease in the frequency of crying to 18 months.

A partial explanation of these developmental changes lies in the fact that various factors which elicit crying vary independently in effectiveness as the child grows older. This is illustrated in Figure 27.

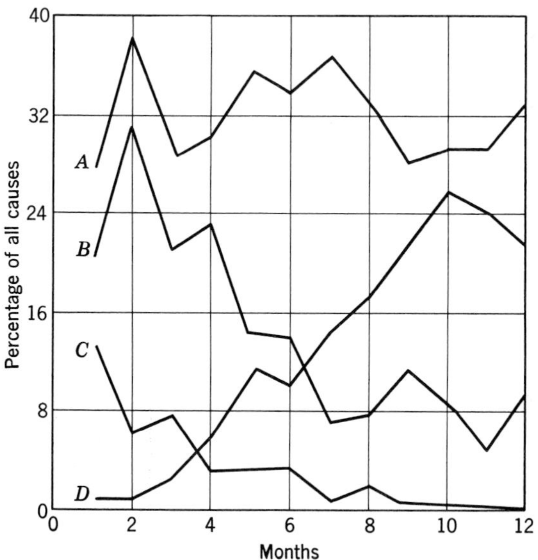

Figure 27. The causes of crying in infants. Developmental changes in four causes of crying: (*A*) Specific test situations. (*B*) Fatigue at end of a laboratory test. (*C*) Colic pains. (*D*) Strangeness of places and persons. *After* Bayley (1932).

Bayley listed the causes of crying in infants from birth to 12 months as follows: specific test situations employed by the experimenter; continued handling; fatigue at the end of a test period; internal conditions such as colic pains, sleepiness, and hunger; strangeness of the place and persons; being put down; interference with play activities; postural discomfort; "spoiled" behavior; adverse conditioning.

In the early months of infant development, crying resulted mainly from internal organic conditions which yielded pains and discomforts.

These internal conditions were recognized in various ways. For example, a colic pain was recognized by its continuity, recurrence, and relief when gas was expelled. Later the external environment rather than internal conditions became increasingly potent as a source of crying. A strange situation, an unusual method of handling the infants, and other environmental factors, became increasingly important. It is likely that places and persons cannot be experienced as strange until, through previous experience, infants have learned to perceive things as familiar.

The form of crying changed gradually from infancy to childhood. The early cries of the infant were tearless; tears did not appear until the second or third month. The weeping and sobbing of older children is an emotional expression in which tears are plentiful. In sobbing, the vocalization is reduced to a minimum; but younger children do not inhibit the vocal element in their weeping. The inhibition develops as a result of social training and experience.

Development of the Smiling Response. The smiling response is absent at birth but normally develops during the third, fourth, fifth, and sixth months. Like other reflexes of the infant, the smiling pattern is not rigidly attached to a fixed stimulus-pattern but is elicited by a variety of stimulations.

By the age of 6 months the smile becomes a normal response to social stimulation and is utilized in communication. Some students of infant behavior (Charlotte Bühler) believe that the infant's smile is a social phenomenon from the start, that smiling is *the* specific response of an infant to social contacts, to the voice and glance of the human being. Others (Arnold Gesell) believe that the smile in response to the mother's face is a kind of conditioned reflex. Innately the smile is a mark of satisfaction from being fed and placed in a warm crib. Repeated satisfactions of this kind build up expectancies that are associated with the face, voice and actions of the mother. Through conditioning, the social stimulation comes to elicit a response that was originally elicited by a non-social satisfaction.

The development of smiling during the first year of life was carefully investigated by Spitz (1946). He made repeated observations upon two hundred and fifty-one infants. The infants came from different environments: nursery, private homes, a foundlings home, a hospital delivery clinic, an Indian village. The infants were of different races: White, Negro, Indian. The subjects were thus a heterogeneous, randomly selected group.

To elicit smiling Spitz applied several kinds of stimulations. In one set of experiments the investigator presented a smiling or nodding face as the stimulus. The experimenter turned *en face* to the infant so that both eyes and the smiling mouth could be seen simultaneously. If the infant responded with a smile the experimenter turned his (or her) face slowly into profile, continuing either to smile or nod. If the infant stopped smiling, the experimenter turned the face back to its original position and tried again to provoke a smile. This kind of stimulation was tried with both male and female investigators to check upon a possible sex factor in the stimulus.

Spitz found that the human face, presented in front view, elicited smiling, especially with infants aged 3 months to 6 months. He next performed a series of experiments to discover whether the human face *in its human quality* was the stimulus that elicited a smiling response or whether the stimulus was some perceptual configuration *within* the human face. In these tests the human attributes were removed by using a black skull cap and a mask that retained only configurational factors such as eyes and mouth. The mask, of course, could not smile.

Previous observations had shown that movement of some kind must be present but movement of the smiling mouth could be replaced by movement of other facial muscles. Knowing this, the experimenter stuck out his tongue rhythmically through the mouth-slit of the mask. This stimulus pattern proved completely successful in provoking a smile from the babies. Then the experimenter, still retaining the mask, replaced tongue movements with nodding movements of the mask--covered head. The babies' reactions were the same: They smiled, laughed, crowed, according to the individual's inclination.

In another experiment a life-size puppet was presented as a stimulus object. This puppet was prepared by stuffing a bag roughly into the shape of a head, attaching a mask to it and covering the top with a skull cap. A body for the scarecrow was provided by hanging a dark shirt on a clothes hanger and fixing the artificial head to the collar of the shirt, so that it could be nodded. Spitz was surprised to find that the very first time the puppet was presented it had an effect identical with that of the experimenter himself bending over the baby and smiling. The babies greeted the nodding scarecrow by smiling, laughing, gurgling, or crowing exactly as they had responded to the experimenter's face. There were no signs of fear.

On the basis of many such observations Spitz concluded that it is not the human face, as such, that elicits smiling, but a configuration of elements in the facial stimulus pattern. The configuration consists of two eyes presented *en face* and not in profile, combined with a factor of motion. The motion can be produced by various facial muscles other than those used in the normal smile or by a movement such as sticking the tongue through the mask or by nodding.

Spitz confirmed the findings of other investigators that the smile is absent during the first 20 days of life and rarely appears during the first 60 days. The pattern matures during the third, fourth, fifth, and sixth months. For some reason, smiling as a response to the above forms of stimulation, disappears after the sixth month. The disappearance is gradual but becomes complete by the end of the eighth month.

The appearance and subsequent disappearance of the smiling response during the first year of life is shown in Table 5 which is based on the findings of Spitz. The age limits of this table are zones that merge imperceptibly into each other. The smiling response does not suddenly disappear after the sixth month but gradually, varying from infant to infant.

TABLE 5
Frequency of Smiling as Related to Age of the Infant

Age in days:	0-20	21-60	61-180	181-365
Smile present:	0	3	142	5
No smile:	54	141	3	142
Total subjects:	54	144	145	147

After Spitz (1946).

The significance of this gradual reduction in the frequency of smiling raises a question of interpretation. During the first 6 months the infants smiled indiscriminately at every adult offering the appropriate pattern of stimulation, and at masks and scarecrows. The smile appeared to be reflexive. During the second half of the first year the infants discriminated, smiling at some persons and not at others.

Although the smiling pattern is innate and universal, being found in infants in all times and places, this pattern comes to be used as a signal of social recognition and approval. The smile becomes a basic form of social expression. It is used to communicate positive affectivity.

The failure of an infant to smile is a symptom of organic defect or of some marked abnormality in social relations. Spitz described a child detained in prison and raised from birth in the prison nursery. The child's mother was emotionally disturbed. The child reacted to the presence of the mother by screaming instead of smiling and reacted in the same manner to other adults. During the time that the mother was emotionally unbalanced, the approach of any grownup, elicited a "reversed smiling response," i. e., screaming with marked negative affectivity.

In this case the intervention of a matron relieved the mother from her emotional tension, and this resulted in a completely normal smiling reaction within 1 week. The child undoubtedly perceived and recognized her mother but the facial configuration did not elicit smiling. The smiling response, therefore, depended upon some discrimination among persons.

Development of Anger. The emotion of anger is associated with behavior that can be described as hostile, destructive, retaliative. Such behavior is a normal result of frustration.

In the small child retaliative behavior is frequently observed. Thus, a boy of 3 violently mussed his freshly combed hair with both hands when his mother refused to give him permission to go to a playmate's home. A boy of 7 whose mother insisted that he dress himself before coming to the table rushed violently to the table, caught hold of the tablecloth and jerked it to the floor, breaking dishes and glassware. A child of 2, when thwarted by removal of his playthings, ran to the davenport, dragged off the cushions and flung them to the floor, screaming violently during the act. A boy of 3, although not an habitual thumb sucker, sucked his thumb conspicuously when frustrated by his mother. Apparently the act was retaliative since the mother had carefully trained him to avoid thumb sucking.

Such retaliative behavior is lacking in the newborn and rarely appears during the first few months of life. Retaliative behavior becomes more and more frequent as the child grows older.

In a careful study of the development of anger in young children, Goodenough (1931) first trained college-educated mothers to observe and record outbursts of anger in their own children. Attention was paid to the causes of anger, the manifestations, the duration, the time of occurrence, and other details. Altogether, forty-five children were observed. Their ages ranged from 7 months to 7 years and 10 months. A total of 2,124 outbursts of anger was recorded.

Percentages, based upon Goodenough's data, are shown in Table 6. The table gives the percentages of anger outbursts in which there was a display of random, undirected energy. It also shows the percentage of outbursts in which retaliative, aggressive behavior was definitely present.

The undirected energy displays were such as these: jumping up and down, holding the breath, stamping and kicking, throwing self on the floor, pouting, screaming, snarling, etc. The retaliative behavior took a good many forms: throwing objects, grabbing, pinching, biting, striking, calling names, arguing and insisting, etc.

The form of retaliative behavior was found to depend somewhat upon the age of the child. A small child may bite when frustrated; an older child may strike or throw something at the offender. Still older children retaliate verbally but the size and picturesqueness of a child's vocabulary varies with age and experience. A youth or adult may plot revenge; he seeks retributive justice—to get even.

TABLE 6
Development of Retaliative Behavior as Response to Frustration

Age in years	0-1	1-2	2-3	3-4	4-8
Percentage of outbursts with undirected energy					
Boys:	100.0	78.0	73.1	65.2	45.0
Girls:	86.9	78.7	83.3	29.6	29.0
Both:	88.9	78.4	75.1	59.9	36.3
Percentage of outbursts with retaliative behavior					
Boys:	0.0	9.4	10.4	25.7	30.0
Girls:	0.8	3.8	11.5	25.3	36.3
Both:	0.7	6.3	10.6	25.6	28.0

Data from Goodenough (1931).

The percentages in Table 6 show clearly that random, undirected energy displays become less frequent with advancing age, and behavior that is definitely retaliative and aggressive becomes more frequent. This transition from random emotional excitement to retaliative hostility marks the normal course of events in the development of anger in young children.

With older children and adults, anger is recognized and identified by the destructive, retaliative, hostile, aggressive actions directed against the frustrating person, object, or situation. With adults, however, hostility may be suppressed and not manifested openly as it is with small children.

Development of Fear. Jersild and Holmes (1935) studied the kinds of situations that elicit fear in children of different ages. They depended upon a variety of methods of gaining information about the fears of children: direct observations by parents and other adults; interviews with parents and teachers; interviews with the children concerning their fears; questionnaires to adults concerning present fears and fears of childhood; observations of children under controlled conditions; case studies. From the various sources they obtained a mass of information for analysis and interpretation.

A finding of general importance was that the relative frequency of specific fears varies markedly with age. This is illustrated by a small sample of the data in Figure 28.

The figure shows the relative frequency of fear in response to various situations at biyearly age levels. This figure is based upon records kept by parents over a 21-day period. In the study, nine hundred and fifty-three fear-inducing situations were recorded.

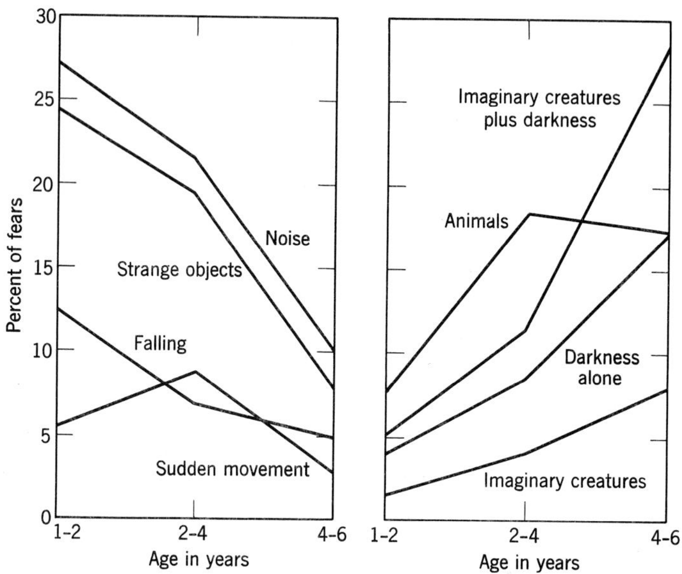

Figure 28. Percentage of all fears attributed to various situations as related to age. *After* Jersild and Holmes (1935).

A brief description of the fear-inducing situations follows:

1. Noise, mechanical or vocal, and agents or objects associated with noise, plus instances of noise combined with movement.
2. Strange objects, unfamiliar persons or situations; queer, deformed or ancient persons; also unfamiliar variations in otherwise familiar objects and persons.
3. Falling, loss of support, danger of falling, high or insecure places, or events associated with falling, danger, or loss of support.
4. Sudden, rapid, or unexpected movement, plus flashes, reflections, sudden disappearance of persons; also events combining noise with sudden, rapid, or unexpected motion.
5. Imaginary creatures, in connection with or apart from darkness or solitude, fear of ridicule, fears arising during dreams, fear of death, robbers, etc.
6. Animals, active or inactive, aggressive or passive.
7. Being alone in the dark, or darkness plus imaginary creatures.
8. Imaginary creatures, feared in connection with or apart from the factors of darkness or being alone.

Some of the above categories overlap. This is because the situations that elicited fear in children usually contained several factors in combination, such as darkness, noise, solitude.

A point that stands out clearly in the data is that the effectiveness of a given factor (or group of factors) in eliciting fear varies with age of the child. Some fear-inducing situations decrease in effectiveness with age; others increase. There are fairly consistent developmental trends. Age and experience thus make a marked difference in the kind of situation that induces fear in children.

Hormonal Regulation of Growth and Sexual Behavior. Hormones are substances produced in the cells of the body, especially in the ductless glands, that are circulated in the blood to all parts of the body. They regulate growth, metabolism, reproduction, activity and vigor.

Especially important as determinants of growth and behavior are secretions from the gonads (reproductive glands) and the pituitary body. The testis of the male, in addition to forming sperm cells that carry the paternal chromosomes, secretes hormones directly into the blood. The ovary of the female, in addition to forming egg cells that carry the maternal chromosomes, pours out hormones into the blood stream. In general, male hormones are called *androgens* and female hormones *estrogens*. These hormones regulate growth as well as sexual behavior. The pituitary gland and the gonads act reciprocally; the secretions of the pituitary stimulate gonadal secretions which, in turn, act to check the pituitary secretion.

It has been shown in experiments with chicks that the testes and ovaries can be successfully transplanted. A bird hatched as a female can have the ovaries removed and testes implanted. Then the body form and featheration of the rooster develop and along with this the typical copulatory behavior of the male. Similarly a bird hatched as a male can have the testes exchanged for ovaries. Then the body form and mating behavior of the hen develop. Thus the gland transplantation experiments have shown that both growth and behavior depend upon internal secretions from the gonads.

In human development the marked physical and mental changes that occur at puberty and during adolescence are, in both sexes, associated with increased activity of the reproductive glands. Some of the changes that occur in the adolescent boy are shown graphically in Figure 29, which is based upon the report of Kinsey et al. (1948). Between the ages of 12 and 15 most boys go through a period of rapid growth. Pubic hair appears; the beard commences to grow; the voice lowers; there is rapid increase in stature. Sex interest and sex activity are stepped up until, within a few years, most young men reach their maximal rate of sexual activity.

The Development and Shifting of Interests with Age. Interests are usually defined as activities that are pleasant, that are carried on "for their own sake." An individual's interests are activities he *likes*; his aversions are activities he *dislikes*.

Pleasant activities, upon repetition, become habituated and tend to be carried on automatically. But there remains an expectation or anticipation of pleasant feedback while carrying on an interesting activity.

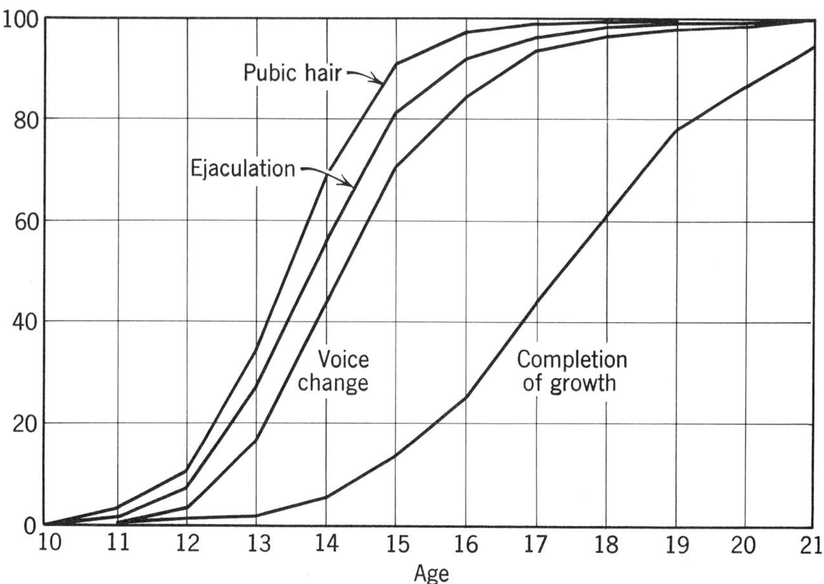

Figure 29. Physical developments in adolescence. The curves show physical developments in adolescence of the male: age at which pubic hair appears; age of first ejaculation; age of voice change; age upon completion of growth. *After* Kinsey et al. (1948).

Hedonic motivation plays a part in the development of interests and aversions, attitudes and motives. There are, of course, non-hedonic motivations that interact with hedonic processes. For example, a small boy looks at the colored pictures in a book and finds them pleasing, interesting. Later this boy is taught to read about the pictures. Since reading is a grown-up activity, there is a satisfaction in reading which is more than just looking at pictures. When the boy is older, other motivations enter. Some books satisfy his curiosity about the circumambient world; these books arouse interest because they answer questions. Other books take him into a make-believe world of magic and success; these are interesting, exciting, in their own right apart from the pictures. As a college student the young man will read books that are

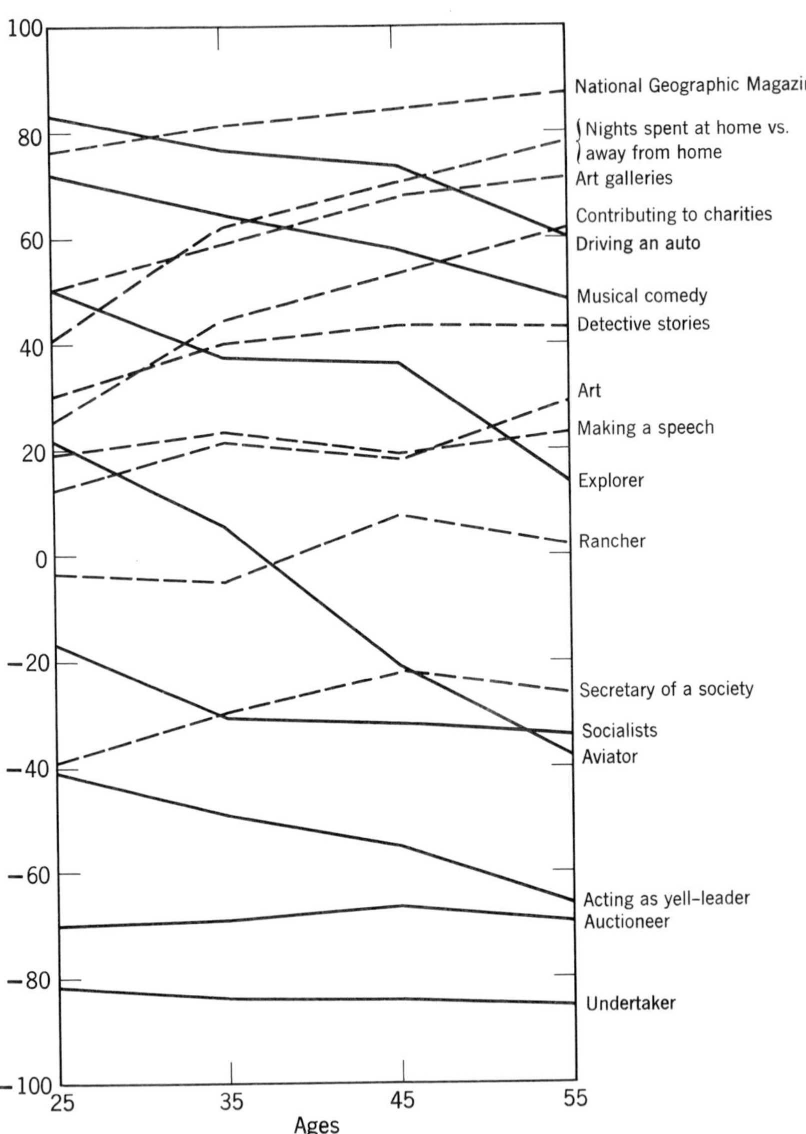

Figure 30. Change of interests with age. The curves are based upon a study of the interests of 2,340 men. The attitude index on the vertical at the left presents numerical differences between the percentage of a group liking and the percentage disliking the various items shown at the right. Indifference, when expressed, is ignored in computing the attitude index. For example, at age 25, 88 percent like and 2 percent dislike driving an auto; the attitude index in this case is 86 percent. At age 25, 3 percent like and 84 percent dislike the occupation of undertaker; the attitude index is −81 percent. The solid lines represent interests that decrease with age or remain about constant; the broken lines, those that increase. *After* Strong (1931).

dull, difficult, irksome, unpleasant. He reads them for the sake of passing a course, of being well thought of by teachers and fellow students, but especially he wants to pass the course!

Now pleasantness and unpleasantness are *affects*—subjective feelings. Viewed objectively, a man's interests are simply the things he does. If a man spends much time playing golf, then he is interested in golf. But a man also spends time sleeping, eating, eliminating, working on the job, etc.,,and these, too, must be regarded as among his objective interests or activities.

Observations upon the vocational interests of American boys and girls indicate that there are many shifts at the time of adolescence. For example, the desire to be a movie actor or actress usually declines with the onset of pubescence; interest in becoming a cowboy generally wanes at the same period. The interests of adults, by contrast, are relatively stable, but even here the changes of interests are more rapid between the ages of 25 and 35 than in succeeding decades of life.

Strong (1931) found that about 50 percent of the interests expressed by his subjects changed between the ages of 25 and 35, about 20 percent between 35 and 45, about 30 percent between 45 and 55. There was little fluctuation of interests between the ages of 55 and 65.

Figure 30 presents a sample of Strong's data to show certain fluctuations in interests between the ages of 25 and 55. Some of the items listed are liked at all ages, others are disliked at all ages. For example, the occupation of undertaker is generally disliked by young and old; the *National Geographic Magazine* is generally liked. The curves show many interests which increase with age (dotted lines) and numerous others which remain about constant or decrease (solid lines). Fields of activity which demand marked physical skill and daring show pronounced changes in popularity with age. For example, the interest in such occupations as aviator and explorer declines with age, doubtless because the younger men are physically more fit for these vigorous activities. Older men, again, dislike items suggestive of change or interference with the established order.

In general, interest in all occupations, including one's own, shows a decline with advancing years. Interests in activities which involve reading manifest an increase with age, whereas those which involve talking or writing decline with advancing years. It is worth noting that older men prefer amusements pursued alone rather than group activities. Also, as men grow older they become more discriminating in their likes and dislikes for people, showing an increasing preference for those with traits which they regard as desirable, and a growing aversion for those with qualities which they consider unworthy.

There was no appreciable difference, Strong found, in the *number* of items liked or disliked at the ages of 25, 35, 45, and 55. At age 25, 35 percent of all items were liked; 30 percent were disliked. At age 55, 34 percent of all items were liked; 31 percent were disliked. The older men, therefore, had as many likes and dislikes as did the younger ones, or at least indicated as many on the test blanks. The older men did not develop more interests with increased age, as one might expect, nor were they more catholic in their interests than the younger men. The interests of the younger men were simply different from those of their elders. This means, in general, that the acquiring of new interests goes hand in hand with the abandonment of old ones. It is plain that this must of necessity be the case, unless one's waking hours are to become a hodgepodge of diversified activities shifting kaleidoscopically with increasing speed as age advances.

Instead of asking why an interesting activity continues with advancing age it might be more instructive to inquire why, in so many cases, it finally ceases. Why, for example, does a boy actively engaged in stamp collecting lose interest in this hobby and stop collecting? As a man of forty he doubtless retains all the skills needed for stamp collecting, but the psychological organization has become inert. There is no dynamic determination to call it into function.

A fading interest is somewhat like a perseverating experience that gradually disappears.

EFFECTS OF EARLY EXPERIENCE UPON ADULT BEHAVIOR

Early experience has a profound effect upon adult behavior. Denenberg (1967) reviewed an extensive literature dealing with the effects of stimulation in infancy upon later emotional reactivity. In experiments with rats it has been found that stimulation during different stages in ontogeny (prenatally, during infancy, after weaning) can have significant effects upon the emotional behavior of adults.

W. R. Thompson, according to Denenberg, has shown that if the mother rat is made anxious (by sounding a buzzer previously associated with pain) during pregnancy, the pups are more emotionally reactive than pups of non-anxious mothers. Other studies have confirmed this finding of a prenatal influence. Handling rats in infancy increases exploratory behavior as measured by a number of different procedures and, independent of this dimension, handling also reduces emotional reactivity as measured in a wide variety of situations.

Several studies with mammalian species have shown that if the young are isolated they develop increased emotional responses to strange situations, poorer ability to solve problems, and poorer capacity for discriminative learning, than litter mates allowed a more stimulating infantile environment. Again, experiments upon mothering and gentling have demonstrated that stroking and petting the young animals affects their physical growth and behavior. When animals are petted and gentled during the early stages of development, they tend to become superior, physically and psychologically, to those that are ignored.

The following sections deal with some of the effects of early experience upon later behavior.

The Effect of Infant Feeding Frustration upon Adult Hoarding. Psychoanalysts harbor the belief that experiences in infancy and early childhood determine personality traits of adults. Through the study of dreams and free associations they have arrived at the view that the early experiences of feeding, toilet training, genital behavior, and social conflict within the family, affect adult patterns of behavior.

Supporting evidence for the psychoanalytical view comes from studies of primitive cultures. Tribes using similar practices in nursing, weaning, toilet training, and care of the young, appear to develop similar personality traits even though they live in different geographic and economic environments. Where the infants are nursed affectionately and weaned late, and where little attention is paid to toilet training, the adults are optimistic; they do not hoard food even though famines repeatedly occur. Where the infants are reared without affection, nursed briefly, and treated harshly in other ways, the adults become competitive, arrogant, aggressive, quarrelsome.

This emphasis upon the importance of infantile experience and early training, however, is based upon casual observations and impressions rather than upon any systematic array of scientific evidence. We would like to see data from controlled experiments upon infantile experience but such data do not exist. For social and humanitarian reasons valid data upon human subjects cannot be obtained. It is possible, however, to carry out controlled experiments with subhuman animals.

A pioneer experiment upon the problem of infant feeding frustration was carried out by Hunt (1941). He asked: Will feeding frustration during infancy alter the pattern of collecting food, or hoarding, in adulthood?

Hunt formed two equivalent groups of rats—experimental and control. At the time of weaning, the experimental animals were subjected to a 15-day period of feeding frustration. The frustrating was produced by a competitive and unpredictable system of feeding. The animals were fed in groups so that each rat had to compete for his share of the available food. To minimize inanition, rats that lost weight were given extra individual feedings. The rats were fed for 10-minute periods at irregular intervals varying from 9 to 36 hours. The control animals were placed at the time of weaning upon an unrestricted diet of food and water; they were not subjected to feeding frustration.

Following the 15-day period of feeding frustration all of the rats were maintained for 5 months upon an unrestricted adequate diet.

As adults the proclivity for hoarding was tested. It was found that when the rats were satiated there was no difference between groups in hoarding behavior. That is to say, when an unlimited supply of food pellets was available the infantile feeding frustration had no apparent effect upon hoarding. But when the food supply was restricted a difference between the groups appeared.

The adult rats were placed on a subsistence diet for 5 days; then given a controlled test of hoarding. After this feeding frustration it was found that the experimental animals hoarded two and a half times as many food pellets as their litter-mate controls. In other words, the early feeding frustration made a significant difference in the amount of adult hoarding of food pellets. The difference appeared when the adult animals were frustrated in a feeding situation.

In another experiment Hunt et al. (1947) repeated and extended the study of the effects of infantile feeding frustration upon adult hoarding. In each of three repetitions of the original experiment it was found that the rats that had experienced infantile feeding frustration hoarded more food pellets than their litter-mate controls. The odds against such a series of results being obtained by chance are better than 1 in 1,000. The *degree* of the effect, however, was less in the repeated experiments than in the original.

In general, it is reasonable to conclude that the amount of food hoarding exhibited by adult rats is dependent upon their early history. Rats that had to compete for food and were subjected to brief and unpredictable periods of feeding were, as adults, more prone to hoard food than their litter-mate controls that experienced no feeding frustration.

The Effect of Early Sensory Deprivation upon Emotional Behavior. Studies at McGill University on sensory deprivation have shown that the restriction of sensorimotor experience during early life has a profound effect upon adult behavior. One of these studies by Melzack (1969) showed that severe restriction of early experience in dogs (raised in cages that drastically reduced but did not eliminate sensory inputs) produced striking abnormalities in their behavior at maturity.

Two behavioral features, in particular, distinguished the restriction-reared dogs from their normally-reared littermates. First, when the animals were released from their restriction cages, they showed during the first few days, an *excessive behavioral arousal*. The dogs tended to "freeze" or to creep along the walls of the laboratory room. As they continued to make contact with the environment, however, they became increasingly active until the activity level greatly exceeded that of their control littermates. The high level of excitement, or activation, was commonly increased by almost anything new in their environment such as a slight modification in their home cage or the presence of an unusual inocuous object. Excitiment was revealed by "whirling fits." These fits were brought on by sudden excessive stimulations but they were also observed to occur spontaneously and even with some dogs before they were removed from their home cages. Sometimes the "whirling fits" were so violent that the dogs would crack their tails or break the skin on their heads against the walls of their cages.

Second, there was *impairment of selective perceptual processes.* It appeared to be difficult for the restricted dogs to attend selectively to environmental stimulations. They would dash from object to object in a room and rarely show sustained attention to any single object. The restricted dogs did not habituate to normal stimuli as rapidly as normally-reared dogs. The restricted dogs, moreover, exhibited a general impairment of sensory perception. They had difficulty learning a simple visual discrimination and often appeared to take little notice of auditory stimuli. Some restricted dogs even failed to perceive and respond normally to noxious stimuli such as a pin prick or a flaming match. The restricted animals also showed other behavioral abnormalities such as a high frequency of perseverative, stereotyped behavioral patterns.

In general, the severe restriction of early sensorimotor experience in dogs produced striking abnormalities in their behavior at maturity. Characteristically, restricted dogs showed a high level of behavioral arousal and at the same time exhibited an impairment of selective perceptual processes.

Neurophysiological studies indicated that when restricted dogs were first permitted to look at a novel environment through their open cage doors, their reticular and cortical EEGs showed a striking shift from predominantly low to high frequencies, and a shift back to low frequencies only after the door was closed. Melzack suggests that these neuroelectrical changes support the hypothesis that the behavioral effects of early sensory deprivation are due to a failure to filter out irrelevant information on the basis of prior experience, thereby producing excessive arousal in the central nervous system and a disruption of the perceptual discriminative adaptive processes.

The Emotional Effects of Separating Infant Monkey from Mother. Species of monkeys differ in contact behavior. Bonnet macaque monkeys (*macaca nemestrina*) huddle together for contact; pigtail macaque monkeys (*macaca radiota*) space out without contact. According to

Kaufman and Rosenblum (1969), the young of both species maintain close contact of infant with mother. Separating infant from mother disturbs a dyadic relation and produces profound emotional effects in the infant.

The loss of a mother produces a searching, agitated response. Substitute mothering relieves the distress, the extent depending partly on the degree of mothering provided and partly on the nature of the tie to the mother. If the loss of a mother is unrelieved, the infant soon lapses into a state of severe depression. Withdrawal appears to conserve the infant's resources and minimize the danger of injury.

Figure 31. A depressed pigtail infant monkey showing the characteristic bodily posture and face of "grief." *Courtesy of* I. C. Kaufman.

There is considerable similarity between the response of macaques to loss of mother and that of unfortunately bereft children. There is an initial stage of agitation and if help is not adequately supplied, this is followed by a stage of depression. The agitated stage in macaques with calls and cries and with searching behavior would ordinarily succeed in effecting a reunion with the mother. This agitated stage, if continued, is followed by depression with marked curtailment of movement. The body is rolled up with the face often hidden and there is a general reduction of interactions with others. Kaufman and Rosenblum suggest that this behavior serves to conserve energy and to reduce the likelihood of attack; the behavior may sustain life until relief might be obtained. The agitated stage involves energy expenditure to regain contact with the mother; the depressed stage conserves energy by inactivity. See Figure 31.

The depressed stage may persist relatively unchanged for five or six days after which the depression then gradually lifts. With one pigtail monkey the recovery from depression started with resumption of a more upright posture. There was a gradual increase of movement and a resurgence of interest in the animal's environment. There were slow, tentative exploratory movements which increased in frequency. Gradually the motherless infant began to interact socially with other animals. Finally, there was a reemergence of play. After one month the infant appeared to be alert and active most of the time, yet he was not typical of infants of that age, particularly with regard to play.

THE PROCESS OF EMOTIONAL DEVELOPMENT

Emotional development is simply growth and decline of the individual viewed in relation to emotional events. This broad statement sounds simple enough but it must be remembered that there are different views of emotional development. Further, the analysis of emotion can be made from different points of view: developmental, physiological, behavioral, intersubjective, and others.

One view is that emotional patterns of reaction are instinctive and modified by learning but Beach (1951) has argued that the distinction between instinctive behavior and learned behavior is not helpful in the experimental analysis of animal activities. Various patterns of response have been grouped together under the rubric of instinct, not because they share any positive characteristics, but because they have been arbitrarily excluded from a rather narrowly conceived category called learned behavior.

It is certain, according to Beach, that the so-called instincts do not belong together in a single class of behavior. After a review of the literature upon reproductive behavior he writes:

> We have seen that sexual behavior develops in various ways in different animals and may be controlled by different external and internal correlates in males and females of the same species. Parental behavior appears to be affected by a variety of factors ranging from the female's diet during immaturity to her previous experience in rearing young. Species differences are pronounced, and in any one species the behavior is governed by a complex combination of processes. This kind of evidence contraindicates categorization of mating and maternal behavior as unlearned or instinctive.

Indeed, Beach states, the term *instinct* might profitably be dropped from the scientific vocabulary. Instead of explaining by words we could better study the concrete instances of behavior and examine the various determinants of behavior.

It has been widely recognized that from conception till death there is continous interaction between intraorganic and environmental determinants of behavior. The term *instinct* is a descriptive label to indicate that some aspects of behavior are determined chiefly by the genes and the mechanisms of heredity. But "instinct" is not a specific explanation of anything.

The Evolutionary View. The genetic view of emotional development, of course, is tremendously important. Following Darwin, the late surgeon G. W. Crile (1915) stated his evolutionary view of emotion as follows:

> When our progenitors came in contact with any exciting element in their environment, action ensued then and there. There was much action—little restraint or emotion. Civilized man is really in auto-captivity. He is subjected to innumerable stimulations, but custom and convention frequently prevent physical action. When these stimulations are sufficiently strong but no action ensues, the reaction constitutes an emotion. A phylogenetic fight is anger; a phylogenetic flight is fear; a phylogenetic copulation is sexual love, and so one finds in this conception an underlying principle which may be the key to an understanding of the emotions and of certain diseases. [76]

As compared with the entire course of organic evolution, Crile continues to explain, man came down from his arboreal abode and assumed his new role of increased domination over the physical world but a moment ago. And now, while sitting at his desk in command of the complicated machinery of civilization, if he fears a business catastrophe, this fear is manifested in physical changes like those his primitive forebears exhibited in the ancestral battle for existence.

Crile points out that man cannot fear intellectually or dispassionately. Whether the situation which endangers him is a struggle for credit, position, and honor, or a physical battle with tooth and claw, he fears with the same vital organs. The inducing situation may be moral, financial, social, or physical, but the responses thereto are a wildly beating heart, accelerated respiration, increased perspiration, pallor, trembling, indigestion, dry mouth, and other components of the augmented sympathetico-adrenal discharge.

The impulses to defense and escape are born of innumerable injuries which have been inflicted during countless centuries of organic evolution. When the tooth and claw of an enemy sink deeply into unprotected tissue, the deep-lying receptors are stimulated and reflex avoidance is set up at once. Animals which lack escape patterns are likely to be devoured and, conversely, those best endowed with injury-avoiding mechanisms are the ones most likely to escape and leave offspring. Thus, Crile concludes, the development of injury-avoiding behavior can be explained on Darwinian principles.

Emotional Development through Conditioning. The Pavlovian concept of *conditioning* was taken seriously by John B. Watson who used the term in his account of emotional development. The phrase "conditioned emotional reaction" originated in some observations by Watson and Rayner (1920) in a well-publicized study of the fear reactions of Albert, aged nine months, to a white rat.

Albert at first showed no signs of fear when presented with a rat, rabbit, dog, monkey, masks with and without hair, cotton wool, a burning newspaper, and other objects. But when a loud noise was made by striking a steel bar, he behaved emotionally. Response: The infant started violently; his breathing was temporarily stopped and his arms were raised in a characteristic manner. On the second stimulation the same thing occurred and, in addition, Albert's lips began to pucker and tremble. On the third stimulation the child broke into a sudden crying fit.

At the age of eleven months and three days, the conditioning experiment was tried. A white rat was presented; as before there was no fear. The next time the rat was shown, a loud sound was produced by striking upon the steel bar. There was a definite fear response to the loud sound.

On the following days when the rat alone was presented Albert began to cry. At the first test he not only cried but also almost instantly turned sharply to the left, fell over on the left side, raised himself on all fours, and began to crawl away so rapidly that he was caught with difficulty before reaching the edge of the table. The fear response had become conditioned to a stimulus-object not originally producing it.

The response was generalized. It was found that Albert now showed fear when presented with a rabbit and with various other furry animals and objects made of or resembling fur.

Other forms of conditioned emotional reaction have been reported. Thus, H. E. Jones (1930, 1931) described the conditioning of a fifteen-month boy to a bell. The infant was given a weak electric shock which produced startle. When a bell was sounded, there was no startle. Then this bell and a shock were presented simultaneously; this was done repeatedly. At a final test it was found that the bell, when sounded alone, brought the startle pattern.

The Elimination of Fears in Children. Proceeding upon the basis of Watson's hypothesis of emotional conditioning, M. C. Jones (1924*a*) investigated the means of eliminating the fears of children. In her study an attempt was made to remove the fear of animals, which was shown by a boy, Peter, at the age of thirty-four months.

The boy came from a highly unsatisfactory home environment. When tested in the laboratory Peter was found to be afraid of a white rat, a rabbit, a fur coat, a feather, cotton wool, and similar objects; but he was not afraid of blocks and other toys which were free from fur. At the sight of a white rat (which had been placed in the crib from behind a screen) Peter screamed and fell flat upon his back. He was in a paroxysm of fear. It was decided to see whether such fear could be removed and whether the reconditioning would spread in such a way that the fear of other objects could also be removed.

Each day Peter and three other children (selected because they were fearless toward the rabbit) were brought into the laboratory to play. The rabbit was always present during part of the play period, and from time to time Peter was brought in *alone* to observe his progress in overcoming the fear.

There were more or less regular gains in emotional tolerance of the rabbit from an initial terror at the sight of the animal to a completely positive attitude with no signs of disturbance. To rate these changes in fear attitude, a scale of toleration was devised. The scale contained seventeen steps between the two extremes here reproduced:

(1) Rabbit anywhere in the room causes fear reactions.
(17) Lets the rabbit nibble his fingers.

During the first period of observation there was a distinct gain in emotional tolerance. Then Peter was ill with scarlet fever and spent two months in the hospital. On the way home from the hospital he happened to become terrified by a dog.

As Peter and the nurse entered a taxi at the door of the hospital, a large dog, running past, jumped at them. Peter and his nurse were both frightened, Peter so much so that in the taxi he lay pale and quiet while the nurse debated whether or not to return him to the hospital. Being threatened by a large dog when ill and in a strange place, and being also in the company of an adult who showed fear, was a most terrifying situation against which all the previous training had not fortified him.

After this illness and fright Peter was again tested in the laboratory. He was terrified at the sight of a rabbit.

It was then decided to try the method of direct conditioning. Peter was seated in a high chair and given food which he liked. The experimenter brought the rabbit in a wire cage as close as possible to him without arousing any response which might interfere with eating. Occasionally other children were brought into the room to facilitate the process of re-education. In this way the fear was gradually eliminated and positive responses to the rabbit were established. At one point in the experiment, however, Peter received a slight scratch from the rabbit which temporarily retarded the extinction of the reaction.

After prolonged training Peter became tolerant not only of the rabbit but also of other furry objects. There was no fear, for example, of cotton or of a fur coat or of feathers. Peter looked at them, handled them, and turned without fear to something else. He picked up a tin box containing frogs or rats and carried it around the room. He picked up a fur rug. He became positive to angleworms, mice, and other living things. In a word, systematic reconditioning completely eliminated many useless fears.

In another study, M. C. Jones (1924*b*) examined the relative merits of seven common methods employed to remove the fears of children. These methods are listed below:

Elimination through disuse.
The method of verbal appeal.
The method of negative adaptation (familiarity brings indifference).
The method of repression.
The method of distraction.
Direct reconditioning (presenting the fear-object with one which is desired).
Social imitation (playing with children who lack the fear).

Dr. Jones found that the last two—the methods of direct reconditioning and social imitation—were the most effective ones in eliminating the fears of children.

Throughout all this work upon the elimination of children's fears there is a normative point of view. It is tacitly assumed that certain fears are undesirable and that the child makes "progress" in eliminating them. The normative view is practically important and valuable in itself, but it should be remembered that scientific discription is factual and that the processes of conditioning can be studied without evaluation regarding the goodness or badness of emotional behavior.

The conception of conditioned emotional responses has played so important a role in current discussions of emotional development that the psychological theory of conditioned emotional patterns must be examined critically.

Critique of Watson's Hypothesis of Conditioned Fear Responses. Students of present-day psychology are familiar with Watson's (1929) account of the three primary emotional patterns—rage, fear, love—and the way in which they can be conditioned and strengthened. The process of conditioning was illustrated above by the acquisition of fear responses with the infant Albert.

According to Watson, fear is a complex pattern of response, including a quick catching of the breath, a clutching at random with the hands, a sudden closing of the eyelids, puckering of the lips, and then crying. In older children there is sometimes flight or hiding (but it is uncertain that this element of flight is innate).

This innate fear response is elicited by two main kinds of stimulation. (1) *Mechanical disturbance*: Sudden removal of support, as when the infant is dropped from the hands and caught by an assistant, arouses fear. Again when the infant is just falling asleep or ready to waken, a sudden push or slight shake or a quick jerk of the blanket upon which he is lying will occasionally produce the fear response. (2) *Loud sounds*: Striking a metal bar, or other intense and sudden sound, arouses fear.

The fear pattern, Watson stated, can be conditioned to stimulations which did not originally produce it. To illustrate, the infant at birth has no fear of darkness. He may become afraid of darkness, however, if a clap of thunder or other loud noise occurs while he happens to be in the dark.

The Watsonian doctrine of conditioned fear responses can be criticized on the following counts.

In the first place, Watson's theory that there are innate emotional response patterns, which can be attached through conditioning and removed through reconditioning, presupposes a particular view of emotion—the view that an emotion is a pattern of response. The arguments which are valid against the pattern-response theory of emotion (pages 241-2) are all valid arguments against Watson's theory.

In the second place, all three of Watson's basic patterns are complex. A careful reading of Watson's original description in the light of more recent knowledge shows that "fear" contains elements of the startle pattern, the Moro reflex, or one of these plus crying. There are also other independently varying bodily changes such as pallor, dilation of the pupil, respiratory changes, and creeping or running away. The escape impulse is somethimes but not necessarily present in the fear of infants; hence, escape cannot be regarded as an essential component of the fear response.

Thus, Watson's "fear" is exceedingly complex and it can be factored into other patterns and activities which are independently variable. At the present time psychologists have not agreed to designate any particular combination of response elements as "fear."

In the third place, Watson's description of the conditions which evoke "fear" is not completely adequate. Valentine (1930) states that loud sounds do not invariably produce fear, though usually they do. It is not merely the loudness but rather the *suddenness* and possibly the *character* of the sound which induces fear. Further, *movement* may be a factor, especially when it is sudden and unexplained. Movement certainly can arouse fear-behavior in older infants and young children. For example, Valentine's daughter at the age of 427 days showed great fear of a teddy bear when it was moved toward her; she turned away from the moving object and trembled in every limb. When the teddy bear was still, she picked it up and kissed it.

In this connection it is of interest to note that Hilgard and Marquis (1940) have criticized the doctrine of conditioned emotion on the ground that emotional development takes place in a complex social context which has never been dealt with in terms of the principles of conditioning. To illustrate: A child is playing in a room with its mother. The mother spies a mouse and, frightened, shrieks. According to the results of the experiment upon Albert, this child, being frightened by the loud noise, becomes afraid of the mouse, which is present when the noise occurs. But why does the child not fear the mother who is the source of the shriek and closely associated with this loud noise? The child, as a fact, runs to the mother for protection. The mother has prestige in the eyes of the child, and the object of the mother's fear is also the object of the child's fear. But these complex social factors and motivating conditions have not been fitted smoothly into the conditioning prototype.

In the light of these criticisms it is clear that the acute student of modern psychology will think twice before he accepts Watson's rather simple formulation of emotional development through conditioning. Despite our criticisms, however, Watson's work is important historically in that it has stimulated other investigations.

Emotional Conditioning. The way in which an adaptive response is formed out of an original state of emotional upset will be illustrated by reference to a motion-picture film prepared by Elmer Culler at the University of Illinois.[1]

The film shows a dog harnessed to a frame with the front paw resting upon a grill. Under these conditions a tone is first sounded and then a painful shock is given to the foot. The initial response to the painful shock is highly emotional: There are diffuse movements of the trunk, legs, head, and tail—a struggle as if to escape from the apparatus. The dog yelps. This response to the shock is correctly designated as *painful excitement*. Bridges' term *distress* could also be used to describe it.

During the emotional excitement the dog lifts his foot off the grill and thus terminates the painful electrical stimulation. With successive presentations of the tone and the shock the dog manages more and more quickly to lift his foot from the grill. The tone serves as a warning signal. After repeated presentations the dog lifts his foot in a calm,

[1] The film, which is entitled *Motor Conditioning in Dogs*, was prepared by Professor E. K. Culler in the Animal Hearing Laboratory of the University of Illinois. The film is distributed by the C. H. Stoelting Company, 424 North Homan Avenue., Chicago, Illinois 60624.

matter-of-fact manner and thus avoids the painful shock. There are no longer any signs of emotional upset. The final response is adaptive, pain-avoiding, non-emotional.

The course of emotional development with Culler's dog is from diffuse emotional excitement to specific, non-emotional adaptive response. The signs of emotion (struggling, diffuse motor activity, yelping) disappear gradually as the problem of avoiding the pain is solved. This picture of emotional development is very different from that given by Watson in terms of the attachment and detachment of preformed emotional patterns of response.

Conditioning of Processes in the Glands and Smooth Muscles. It has been repeatedly demonstrated that involuntary changes in glands and smooth muscles can be conditioned. The classical work of Pavlov upon the conditioned secretion of the salivary glands leaves no room for doubt on this point.

In this connection it is interesting to note that vascular changes can be conditioned. Menzies (1937) has shown that vasoconstriction can be conditioned to the sound of a bell, to the sound of a buzzer, to the subject's whispered repetition of a nonsense word, to movements and postures of various parts of the body, to a pattern of light. Also vasodilation can be conditioned to the sound of a buzzer at the same time that vasoconstriction in another part of the body is being conditioned to verbal stimulation. With verbal stimulation, whispered words are found to be just as effective as those pronounced aloud. Menzies' work is significant because it shows that the bodily processes controlled by the autonomic nervous system can be linked through ordinary conditioning to such activities as bodily attitudes, gestures, and implicit speech reactions. Such conditioned processes, Menzies found, have great stability and permanence.

There is little doubt, therefore that involuntary processes in the glands and smooth muscles can be conditioned. Visceral processes are part of the total reaction of the organism.

According to the classical theory, conditioning is restricted to preexisting responses such as salivation or the secretion of gastric juice. Problem-solving behavior has been regarded as showing a separate kind of learning in which reinforcement is produced by rewards and punishments.

Neal Miller (1969) has demonstrated that visceral responses can be conditioned through intracranial stimulations used as rewards. Miller's subjects were rats paralyzed by curare and rewarded by direct electrical stimulation of the medial forebrain bundle to provide positive activation in the brain. The animals were anesthetized and maintained on artificial respiration. Working with various preparations Miller was able to show instrumental learning of visceral responses, e.g., either intestinal contraction or relaxation, and either increase or decrease in rate of heart beat. The results indicate that peripheral vasomotor changes, which could not be produced by general changes in heart rate or blood pressure, can be learned, and that such responses can be specific to a given structure such as the rat's ear. Changes in kidney function and blood pressure were also conditioned by intracranial reward. Miller believes that there is only one kind of learning and that so-called involuntary responses can be modified through intracranial reward. The reward may strengthen any immediately preceding response.

These unusual results fit in well with the directive activation theory of motivation and learning. See page 69.

EMOTION AND ADJUSTMENT

Social and Cultural Factors in Emotional and Expressive Development. It is a fact that the growing child learns to conform to group standards of expressing his feelings just as he acquires the speech, habits, skills, and attitudes which characterize his culture. He learns what to fear, when to weep, when not to laugh, how to show his love according to accepted standards of correctness, whom to admire, how to show resentment within the bounds of good taste, and how to interpret the conventional facial and behavioral expressions of others.

Facial expressions, vocalizations, gestures, ways of acting—all are to a large extent voluntarily controlled. Consequently it is necessary to ask: How far, on the one hand, are the apparent emotional expressions acted out for the purpose of communication, to conform to group standards, or just to produce an effect upon others? How far, on the other hand, are such expressions involuntary and reflexive bodily changes which are physiologically determined?

As words differ from group to group but are stable within a given culture, so also the "correct" facial expressions, gestures, or behavioral patterns for a given situation vary from culture to culture. To illustrate the point we turn to a study by Klineberg (1938), who read several Chinese novels to discover the phrases which describe the socially approved or "correct" forms of expressive behavior. In his study two points stand out clearly.

First, when the Chinese language describes the *involuntary changes* of emotion in muscles and glands, the account is very similar to that in our own language. For example, in Chinese we read: "Everyone trembled with a face the color of clay"; "Every one of his hairs stood on end, and the pimples came out on the skin all over his body"; "A cold sweat broke forth on his whole body, and he trembled without ceasing"; "They stood like death with mouth ajar"; "They were so frightened that their waters and wastes burst out of them." In these and similar phrases we recognize at once the emotion of fear. Again, in the phrase, "He gnashed his teeth until they were all ground to dust," we recognize anger, or possibly agony. "He was listless and silent," suggests sorrow. "His face was red, and he went creeping alone outside the village," *in the context*, indicates shame.

In many such expressions, Klineberg found, the Chinese forms and the Western are identical. The explanation is that during emotional excitement there are involuntary changes in smooth muscles and glands and there are impulses to act, which are similar the world over. These are the biological constants of emotional excitement. And so far as language refers to these constants, a cross-cultural uniformity is to be expected just as a certain degree of uniformity is to be expected in diverse accounts of a thunder storm or a sunset.

A second point is equally important though very different. Gestures, facial expressions, ways of acting, which can be *voluntarily* controlled, become stereotyped within a cultural group as definitely as the spoken word. A few samples are here given to show the contrast between Chinese and Western phrases.

"They stretched out their tongues," is an expression of surprise which most of us would not recognize except for the context. "Her eyes grew round and opened wide," suggests surprise or fear to most of us, but to the Chinese it usually means anger. In the form, "He made his two eyes round and stared at him," the phrase can mean nothing but anger to the Chinese. An attitude of hatred is implied by, "He would fain have swallowed him at a gulp." (Compare the Western phrase, "I could eat you up"!) "He scratched his ears and cheeks," probably suggests embarrassment to us, but in the novel, *Dream of the Red Chamber*, it means happiness. "He clapped his hands," is likely to mean worry or disappointment.

There are all gradations of expression, Klineberg (1940) writes, between purely physiological reflex patterns and socially acquired expressions:

> At the one extreme we have the crying of the child in pain—an expression common to all individuals no matter what their culture. At the other extreme we have the language of emotional expression on the Chinese stage, in which standing on one foot means surprise, and fanning the face with the sleeve means anger. In this same category also we may put the custom of the Blackfoot Indians to express their mood by the color of the paint used on their faces. "If we felt angry, peaceful, in love, religious, or whatever the mood was, we painted our faces accordingly, so that all who should come in contact with us would know at a glance how we felt." Between these extremes we find every possible degree of cultural patterning. [196]

Certainly bodily changes (for example, tear secretion) occur universally in grief, great joy, and similar human emotions; but cultural factors enter in to determine the time, place, and even the amount of crying which is expected. With us a man is expected to restrain his sobs and tears in public places. The boy is taught that it is "unmanly" for a male to cry openly. But in China, Montenegro, and doubtless in other countries, men weep as readily as women on appropriate occasions.

In the mid-Victorian era and even later, the English gentleman at times would weep openly and conspicuously at theatrical performances, sermons, and other gatherings; this was accepted as socially correct. Thus, a gentleman, upon hearing a rendition of Dickens' *The Old Curiosity Shop*, might weep openly at the story of the death of Little Nell and no one in the audience would think anything of it. Today the styles in weeping have changed!

Most people express joy by a smile, but joy without a smile is also known. Among the Andaman Islanders there is no observable difference between their demonstrations of joy when meeting a long-absent relative and those of grief on the death of one of their number. In both cases the stranger might suppose some great sorrow had befallen them. Weeping is the correct form of greeting.

Thus, conventional expressions of "emotion" vary from culture to culture. It is important to distinguish, as Landis (1924) has done, between *social* and *emotional* expressions.

Two psychological problems are raised by the above evidence. First, what are the innate physiological constants in human emotion the world over? Second, how are the conventional modes of "emotional" behavior acquired by the individual in any given cultural group?

The second problem is one of social learning which is related to the problem of learning to speak one's language. The "emotional" behavior which is *learned* is psychologically similar to that of an actor who skillfully shows his anger, fear, love, disgust, shame, embarrassment, and other "emotion" on the stage. Such "emotion" may or may not be visceralized.

Characteristics of Emotional Maturity and Immaturity. As the individual advances from infancy to adult life the characteristics of his emotional behavior change radically. When his emotional development reaches a certain stage, we say that he is emotionally mature.

Although the phrase, *emotional maturity*, has been used by psychologists, e.g., by Hollingworth (1928), and Morgan (1934), this phrase has not yet been satisfactorily defined. The best way to approximate its meaning is to note changes in emotional behavior which take place as a child develops into an adult and to contrast the emotional responses of children with those of adults. The contrasts described below are based upon the analyses of Hollingworth and Morgan.

One important contrast between the emotional behavior of infant or young child and adult is in the *degree of frustration tolerance.* The infant is intolerant of discomfort and thwarting. Hunger pains, a bath that is too cold or too warm, the prick of a pin, restraint of free movement, uncanny sounds, a toy just out of reach—all these arouse an emotional display in the infant. The older child is more tolerant. Instead of crying like a baby at every mishap, he is able to withstand suffering and disappointment with fewer signs of disturbance.

A two-year-old kicks and screams when refused a second helping of some desired food. Adults take this for granted, for, as they say, "He is just a baby and he behaves like one emotionally." If, however, a six-year-old behaves in the same manner, he is regarded as "naughty." When a nine-year-old kicks and screams in this situation we say he is "spoiled." But such conduct from an adult would be regarded either as hysterical or as a sign of emotional immaturity. If an adult were to scream and kick because refused a second helping at dinner, a psychiatrist would be summoned!

In the ancient pubertal ceremonies of a certain primitive people, physical and mental hardships were inflicted as an ordeal. If the youth refused to submit to the ordeal or yielded to the grilling situation with outcries of fear or distress, he failed in his initiation to adulthood. Possibly some trace of this custom remains in the more modern fraternity initiation. That the capacity to endure pain and to face danger with fortitude is a criterion of emotional maturity is implied in the pubertal ordeal.

A second contrast between the emotional behavior of child and adult is a *decrease in the frequency and degree of emotional upset* as the individual grows up. An adult does not display outbursts of anger as frequently as a child nor does he weep so often. When the adult is emotionally aroused, his response is commonly less intense than that of children. If the adult pinches his fingers, he does not scream as loudly as possible. If insulted, he does not fly into a towering rage but limits the degree of response, keeping it within bounds. If his hat is blown off, he does not bellow.

As a physiological explanation of this contrast it may be said that the adult manifests a higher degree of cerebral control over subcortical behavioral patterns than does the child. This is largely the result of social training. Present-day American culture discourages the overt expression of weeping, anger, and fear; and encourages (or at least does not discourage) smiling and laughing. But on those rare occasions when an adult is genuinely horrified, terrified, or enraged, emotional outbursts do occur with all their primitive intensity. It must not be concluded, therefore, that the adult in our civilization has lost his capacity for emotional outbursts but only that under usual conditions he is better controlled by his cerebral machinery than is the child. The cerebral control of the adult is such that emotional behavior is less likely to arise than with children.

There is another factor. The adult frequently suppresses the outward manifestations of emotion. On this account he reveals emotion overtly with less frequency than does the child.

A third contrast between child and adult is a difference in the *impulsiveness or explosiveness of behavior.* The child "cannot wait" to express anger, joy, or fear. He must respond without delay. In anger he strikes; in joy, jumps up and down; in fear, cries out or runs away; in pain he cries or screams. The adult, in contrast, is able to delay his response and manifests less impulsiveness.

A fourth difference between the emotional behavior of child and adult if found in the *attitudes of self-regard.* Injury to the human ego awakens in the child a self-pity which is out of all proportion to the pity felt by sympathetic onlookers and comforters. This solicitude for self is keenly felt by the injured person.

Writes Hollingworth (1928):

> In childhood self-pity is unrestrained. The injury to the person strikes at the very center of the universe. The mature person approximates the "poor-you" attitude in pitying his own injuries and mishaps. He tries to feel no sorrier for himself than others would feel for him, and strives against sinking into the "poor-me" attitude, with its childish appeal for a sympathy from others which they cannot sincerely give. The emotionally mature person does not prey upon the amiability of his fellow men. [210]

This self-pity reflects the fact that the child is self-centered. As his knowledge of the world increases, he becomes less obviously egocentric. This may be due to the fact that manifestations of self-interest are socially disapproved and that the signs of self-pity are suppressed more in adults than in children.

Finally, *the child in contrast with the adult is more overt in his emotional manifestations.* If an adult is grieved, he refrains from weeping; if angered, he controls the facial muscles which express anger and the impulse to attack; if afraid, he assumes the anti-fear attitude of courage.

An adult may consciously experience an emotion but inhibit its outward manifestations. The child, by contrast, is usually overt, direct, and quite frank in his emotional behavior. How many times have parents of small children witnessed the following kind of a scene!

Sister: Mama! Bobby kicked me and hit me, and I didn't do anything to him. Boo-hoo, boo-hoo!

Brother: Nancy hit me first and I only got even!

Sister: Mama! Bobby kicked me and hit me and took my crayons away. He's just bad. Boo-hoo! Boo-hoo!

Brother: I don't care. So there (strikes).

Throughout this little drama there is the greatest openness of emotional demonstration.

Summing up the above points, it may be said that the child in contrast with the adult is: (1) less tolerant of discomfort and thwarting; (2) given to more frequent and intense outbursts of emotion; (3) more impulsive, explosive in behavior, and with less capacity to delay his response; (4) more given to self-pity and egocentricity; (5) more overt, direct, frank in his emotional displays. It is also true that adults differ among themselves in these respects, and for this reason the above contrasts should be kept in mind by students of temperamental differences in adults.

Tests of Emotional Development. The practical success of the Binet scale of intelligence plus the obvious importance of emotion in human life have led psychologists to attempt measures of "emotional age" and to discriminate age levels of emotional development. Weber (1930, 1932) and others have worked on the problem. Unfortunately the work has met with little success, mainly because the problem of emotional development had been obscurely formulated. Part of the difficulty lies in the fact that psychologists have not agreed upon the correct definition of emotion.

The papers by Weber report an attempt to devise a paper-and-pencil test of emotional age based on McDougall's psychology of emotion. The scores for emotional age were found to correlate positively with the Otis intelligence scores; the value of r was 0.775. It was concluded that intelligence weights the E. A. (emotional age) scores too heavily.

Bridges (1931) proposed a check list for estimating the level of emotional development. Her scale is made up of items which designate different ways children react to situations. The items are checked by someone who has personally observed the child's behavior. A sample of the items is reproduced below to illustrate the nature of the scale:

I. *The child has NOT or has*:
Cried at naptime
Cried when pushed, hit or teased by a child

II. *The child has NOT or has*:
Screamed, cried violently, and jumped about when hurt
Run away or withdrawn from dogs

III. *The child has NOT or has, when required to do something disliked:*
Lain on floor and kicked
Pouted and drooped lips
IV. *The child HAS or has not:*
Clapped hands in delight at things or events
Laughed at his own mistake
V. *The child has NOT or has:*
Wet clothes indoors while engaged in interesting occupation
Hurried through one occupation after another in excited interest
VI. *The child has NOT or has, when finding a task difficult:*
Wiggled in seat
Sucked thumb or fingers

Bridges' rating scale is divided into six sections, as listed below, each section containing thirty-five to forty-five items.

	Number of Items
1. Distress and tears	45
2. Fear and caution	35
3. Anger and annoyance	45
4. Delight and affection	45
5. Excitement and enuresis	40
6. Mannerisms and speech anomalies	35

In her discussion of this emotional rating scale, the emphasis is upon the close relation between *social* and *emotional* development. Bridges writes:

> Social situations both cause and control emotional behavior and even determine the nature of its development. In fact, emotional development might almost be considered as a form of social development. But since some emotional behavior is not prompted directly by social situations, and since emotional behcvior in general constitutes a separate psychological problem, it seemed desirable to think of the two aspects of behavior separately, but to study them conjointly in the children. [5]

It is obviously necessary to distinguish clearly between social and emotional expressions. The difference should not be obscured. Social expressions do conform increasingly to group norms as a child develops. Emotional patterns of expression, contrastingly, are more innately determined and more constant the world over.

Bridges reports that in preliminary trials with this scale it was found that *emotional* behavior varied with age less directly than *social* behavior. For this reason the scale has not been much used for exact measurements of the level of emotional development. But the scale is useful, Bridges states, as an instrument for differentiating children according to the degree of their general emotionality and to indicate particular trends.

In addition to this difficulty of distinguishing between social and emotional aspects of development there is one other difficulty with Bridges' scale. Her whole genetic theory of emotion implies that specific emotions can be distinguished from each other and that distress, delight, anger, fear, and the other emotions are differentiated from primitive excitement as the individual develops—but the discussion does not clearly and specifically show the criteria by means of which such differentiations can be made. Obviously, if one is to trace the development of anger, one must know how to recognize anger and how to distinguish anger from fear.

The genetic study of emotion needs to be carried forward. Possibly a few situations for arousing emotional behavior can be standardized, for example: taking away from the child a toy which is greatly desired, an uncanny noise made mechanically in a controlled situation, or an unexpected fall. Observers could record the child's patterns of response and behavior, as: crying, screaming, smiling, laughing, trembling, urination, excitement, attack, avoidance, or pouting the lips. With this approach changes in emotional response could be studied in relation to age and other conditions. More actual observations of emotional behavior, made under controlled conditions, are needed to advance our knowledge of emotional development.

The work of Dr. Arnold Gesell, at Yale University, on behavioral and social development is well known and should be examined in the context of emotional behavior.

Emotion and the Educative Process. Progress along the path of learning may be retarded by many minor emotional upsets, such as over-anxiety about examinations, resentment over extra-long reading assignments, and personal antipathy for an instructor. In addition, students may encounter more seriously disturbing emotional events, whose source is quite outside the college halls. For example, a young woman in one of the writer's classes learned of her brother's death in the siege of Bataan. The news came just before an important examination and quite naturally was so upsetting that her examination had to be postponed. Another student was so upset over a tempestuous love affair that she could not carry on with her accustomed habits of study.

It is not only in these ways that education and emotion are related. There is a more direct and fundamental relationship between the two.

On account of the importance of emotion in human life, educators have sought to find some means of training and developing the emotional side as well as the intellectual of the pupil. To this end the

American Council on Education in 1933 appointed a special committee to investigate the relation of emotion to the educative process. Prescott the chairman, and his collaborators took as thier main objectives to determine: (1) whether emotion has been unduly ignored in the stress laid upon the acquisition of knowledge and upon the development of skill in acquiring knowledge; (2) whether education should concern itself with the strength and direction of desires developed or inhibited by the educational process; (3) whether educators have overemphasized an attitude of neutral detachment (desirable in the scientific observer), thereby robbing American youth of enthusiasms and loyalties; and (4) whether there exist suitable educational devices by means of which emotional development can be accurately described, measured, and directed.

The findings of Prescott's committee (1938) are of great practical importance. In a letter of transmittal to the American Council on Education are these words:

> World political developments, new devices for swaying the emotions of entire nations simultaneously, emphasis on blind mass fervor, impatience with the scientific approach to national problems, all have driven home the lesson that the job of education is not done when knowledge is disseminated and increased. If the scholar, concerned with his primary business of knowledge, fails to deal with the whole man, particularly with the control of passion and the guidance of desire, he may properly be charged with contributory negligence when the democracy becomes either a mob or a regimented army, when freedom to learn or to teach disappears, when the neglected emotions submerge the life of reason, and so force recognition of their claim to a share in the lives of men. [vii]

The above statement has a distinctly modern ring. Certainly it is true that the human individual is very far from a coldly logical thinking machine. It is a wholesome sign, therefore, that educators are taking account of the non-rational factors of human nature and that present-day psychologists are placing an increasing emphasis upon the study of motivation and emotion.

In writings upon education one meets such phrases as these: *emotional education and training, emotional development, emotional stability, emotional maturity, direction of the emotions, emotional control, swaying the emotions*. To discuss these topics adequately, one must first have a clear idea of the nature of emotion and its relation to adjustment.

Emotion and Adjustment. In the routine of daily living one continually encounters petty annoyances and satisfactions, larger frustrations and successes. A friend inconveniences you by being late for an appointment; a fall on the ice embarrasses you before your friends; a letter containing an unexpected check arrives just in time to pay a bill; your seriously ill child takes a turn for the better; a bread-winner for four persons, you unexpectedly find yourself without a job.

In each of the above experiences there is frustration or relief from frustration. In each of them some conscious emotion or feeling is evoked, a disturbed psychological state indicating a need for adjustment. The relation, then, between emotion and personal adjustment is this: states of conflict and frustration (or relief from frustration) are *revealed* by one's emotional behavior. The individual's emotional reactions indicate the need for an adjustment and help the counselor to find the source of frustration.

This is why Shaffer (1936) has said that emotion is "a type of response that is of peculiar importance to problems of adjustment." We will present here a few cases which show the relation between emotion and personal adjustment.

All of us have had the experience of disliking some person or thing without knowing exactly why. An example of this, with an explanation of its psychological background, is the following taken from Hart's (1937) classic, *The psychology of insanity*:

> A man, walking with a friend in the neighborhood of a country village, suddenly expressed extreme irritation concerning the church bells, which happened to be pealing at the moment. He maintained that their tone was intrinsically unpleasant, their harmony ugly, and the total effect altogether disagreeable. The friend was astonished, for the bells in question were famous for their singular beauty. He endeavored, therefore, to elucidate the real cause underlying his companion's attitude. Skilful questioning elicited the further remark that not only were the bells unpleasant but that the clergyman of the church wrote extremely bad poetry. The causal complex was then apparent for the man whose ears had been offended by the bells also wrote poetry, and in a recent criticism his work had been compared very unfavorably with that of the clergyman. The rivalry-complex thus engendered had expressed itself indirectly by an unjustifiable denunciation of the innocent church bells. The direct expression would, of course, have been abuse of the clergyman himself or of his works. [73-74]

In this case the man revealed, by his emotional behavior concerning the church bells, a need for adjustment of a conflict over the clergyman and his poetry. A possible adjustment would have been for the man to make a re-evaluation of his own abilities as a poet, and regard his poetry less seriously. He might, instead, have attempted to write better poetry, or to disregard entirely the literary criticism of a simple country journalist. Any of these ways of resolving the conflict would have reduced the intensity of his emotional disturbance.

Feelings of failure and of inferiority are surprisingly common and constitute an important index of inadequate adjustment. A frequent cause of feelings of inferiority is the presence of some physical defect.

McKinney (1941) tells of a student with a physical defect in one of his legs, which caused him to walk with a limp. When talking with a counselor he insisted that he was of inferior stock. His evidence for this point was that he had always failed; people had always disliked him; his work had never come up to par. An unpleasant feeling of failure and inferiority colored nearly all his accounts of his activities.

In this case the source of frustration was obvious and probably could not be removed. The man's emotional behavior showed that his feelings of inferiority had spread from his physical defect to his self-image, his attitude toward work and his family. He needed to dissociate his attitude toward his physical defect from his evaluation of his abilities and achievements.

In both of these cases it is clear that emotional reactions are indicators of inadequate adjustments to frustrating situations.

Emotional Control and Dyscontrol. The phrase *emotional control* has several possible meanings. According to the commonest meaning, emotional control is the voluntary suppression of the outward expressions of emotion. The visceral processes are involuntary and may still be present. Thus, a man may control his words and actions but he blushes involuntarily, in embarrassment. Voluntary control is limited to the somatic mechanisms—facial expressions, vocalizations, gestures, and gross ways of acting.

The voluntary enactment of emotional behavior does not *necessarily* induce the associated visceral responses. Years ago William James interviewed actors asking them whether they *felt* the emotion they enacted on the stage. Testimony was sharply divided: some actors said they did and some that they did not *feel* the emotions they expressed. Perhaps some actors played the emotional role solely with their skeletal musculature; others threw themselves into the part, identifying themselves empathically with the character and the situation and allowing behavior to become visceralized.

According to another meaning of *emotional control*, the total response, though highly visceralized, remains integrated and free from outer disturbance. For example, an airplane pilot, realizing that his plane is out of control, may act with utmost precision and skill to regain control. Although he is in great danger and there is a high degree of visceralization, the overt behavior remains integrated. The behavior is highly motivated, well organized but free from upset. Emotional disturbance does not arise. How such total control of the response can be achieved, of course, is another question.

One way to avoid emotional upset is to acquire skill in meeting a situation and to gain knowledge and understanding. To illustrate: A 5-year-old boy was afraid to go to bed at night. There were shadows moving on the wall of his bedroom. His father explained that the shadows were there from branches of trees moving in front of a street lamp. The child was shown the branches moving in the wind. He was allowed to produce other shadows by moving the window curtains. When he understood the cause of the shadows and could control some of them the fear vanished. The fear came from lack of understanding and inability to meet the situation positively.

A logically possible (but rare) meaning of *emotional control* is the conscious avoiding of situations that produce emotion. Thus an adult may avoid dangerous occupations like auto racing and avoid anxiety; he may stay away from a dead animal that disgusts him; he may avoid public meetings where the speeches anger him; he may move out of town to avoid becoming infatuated with the wife of his friend, etc. In all such instances there is an active *avoiding of situations that are known to arouse emotion*. This is a yield-not-to-temptation kind of control. The situation is controlled so that emotion does not arise.

When all is said and done it remains obvious that individuals differ widely in the nature and degree of their emotional control. There are differences in frustration tolerance. An insult may throw one person into a towering rage while the same insult leaves another unperturbed. Some persons are *under-controlled*; others, *over-controlled*.

Pathological states induced by drugs, in psychoses, great stress, and similar conditions, may result in dyscontrol with the loss of sanity and rationality. Emotional dyscontrol is indicated by criminal acts—murder, rape, violent attack, and other behaviors. The situation calls for psychiatric help.

CONCLUSION

When we consider emotional development it is neccessary to take a longitudinal, or temporal, view of the life cycle of an individual. We must postulate a certain stability and permanence in the determinants of activity and experience.

There are various aspects of physical and mental development; and there are different views of emotional development. If we view emotion broadly as equivalent to affectivity, then we observe the formation, persistence and change of affective memories, attitudes of acceptance and rejection, interests, aversions, loyalties, preferential discriminations, values, motives, goal-orientations, and the like. These determinants of human feeling and action persist in time. They have a degree of stability though they change from time to time.

When we speak of an emotionally disturbed child or patient, however, we imply a persisting state of conflict, frustration, anxiety, hostility, or neurosis. Emotional disturbances which persist have important consequences in behavior and mental health. It is important to account for the conditions that cause persisting emotional disturbances and to examine the consequences of upsets. Psychological or psychiatric counseling may be required.

There is nothing sacrosanct or mysterious about emotional development. Emotional development depends upon the natural processes of maturation and learning through experience. Reflexive patterns such as smiling, laughing, crying, screaming, rage, fear, disgust, and others, appear during the normal course of growth. These patterns are modified through experience and training. Social learning constitutes an important part of human development.

From one point of view, the story of emotional development is an account of the conditions that arouse emotional disturbances. From another point of view, emotional development is seen as the acquisition of adaptive behavior that reduces, minimizes, escapes, avoids, eliminates, emotional upsets. Individuals solve problems and make adjustments through the acquisition of attitudes, habits, motives, interests and aversions, and other dispositions. In one sense: *Emotional development is simply the growth of techniques for dealing with frustrations, threats, and other causes of upsets.*

A READING SUGGESTION ON EMOTIONAL DEVELOPMENT

Textbooks on child psychology frequently contain references to materials on emotional development that are not considered in the present chapter. Jersild (1954) has chapters that deal with affection, joy, humor, and sex; fear and anxiety; anger and hostility. The book is matter-of-fact and very readable.

Educational psychologists concerned with the affective aspect of human development as well as the intellectual would do well to read the report of the committee on the relation of emotion to education by Prescott (1938). And some of the texts in educational psychology have important material on the emotional and motivational aspects of development. Cronbach (1954), for example, considers motivation and emotion in his excellent textbook.

Chapter V

Bodily Changes in Emotional Behavior

To assume that psychology is concerned only with the outwardly observable expressions of emotion, and physiology with the internal bodily mechanisms, is quite misleading. The separation between external and internal events is arbitary. All vital processes occur within a *biosphere* which contains the organism and the variöus environments encountered during an organism's life cycle. The separation, at the surface of the body, between organism and environment is convenient but arbitrary.

The true relation between external and internal events will be illustrated by a concrete example. Cannon (1929) has shown that during emotional excitement the number of red corpuscles (erythrocytes) per cubic millimeter of blood increases.

This change, called *emotional polycythemia*, is attributed directly to the action of the spleen. The spleen, a muscular organ, which contracts and expands, is a reservoir for red corpuscles. It renders to the organism the service of quickly increasing the number of circulating erythrocytes and later of storing them away again. Contraction of the spleen occurs in carbon monoxide poisoning, in hemorrhage, in the lessening of the oxygen content in the blood as during asphyxia and muscular excerise and following injections of adrenin and pituitrin, as well as in emotional excitement.

Figure 32 shows the course of emotional polycythemia. The curve is based upon averages of blood counts obtained from nine cats. The scale at the left indicates the number of erythrocytes in millions per cubic millimeter of blood. The base line shows passage of time. Before *O* the initial blood determination was made. Then a dog was allowed to bark at each cat for one minute—between *O* and *O'*. Subsequent blood counts were made at *O'* and at five-minute intervals thereafter, with the average result shown in the curve.

It is obvious from Fig. 32 that an environmental event (barking of a dog) is assoicated with a specific internal bodily change (increase of red blood corpuscles).

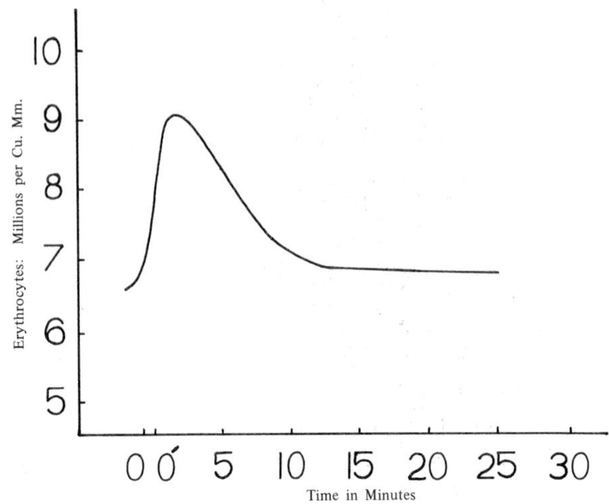

Figure 32. The course of emotional polycythemia. *After* Cannon (1929).

Cannon has interpreted this fact: Erythrocytes carry oxygen from lungs to the heart, brain, active muscles. In a biological emergency which might involve a vigorous struggle or a race for one's life, this process is serviceable in that it facilitates energy liberation within the organism. It is part of a general preparation of the body for strenuous activity.

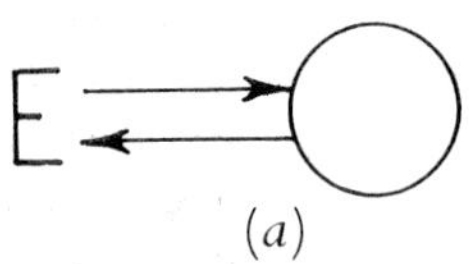

(*a*)

The relation between internal and external manifestations of emotion may be shown by a series of diagrams.

Behavior is a dynamic relation between the organism as a whole (*O*) and its environmental field (*E*). This relation may be symbolized: (*a*)

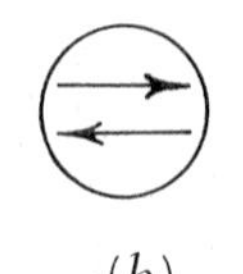

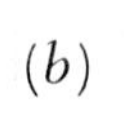
(*b*)

Internal bodily changes, contrastingly, may be represented as occurring inside the skin of the organism in this way: (*b*)

The figures imply a sharp separation of events inside and outside the skin of an organism. Actually, however, this separation at the surface of the body is made only for convenience in working with a complex problem. There is a physical continuity between organism and environment. The complete view may be symbolized in this fashion: (*c*)

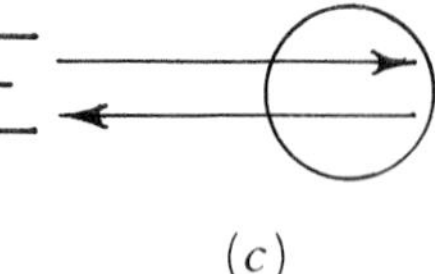

(*c*)

In an important work, Skinner (1938) argues for the establishment of psychology as a pure science of behavior, which behavior is to be investigated quite apart from and regardless of the processes going on inside the body. Distinct from a science of behavior should be a science of the nervous system, which starts from the direct observation of neural activity and which frames its theoretical conceptions on the basis of its own facts.

Skinner's pure science of behavior is concerned with the relations symbolized in the first diagram, and his science of the nervous system is included within the relationships represented in the second. Skinner's work has been described as a science of the empty organism; and the organism has been compared to a black box. From the standpoint of scientific methodology there is a value in restricting the sphere of one's science and working intensively in the area marked off for one's self. Skinner's research is an excellent illustration of this truth.

A somewhat similar limitation upon the scope of psychology has been made by those who rely mainly on the mathematical analysis of test scores rather than upon the facts of physiology. What goes on within the skin of an organism is said to be irrelevant so far as the validity of quantitative relationships is concerned. This point was emphasized by Woodrow (1942) in his presidential address before the American Psychological Association. Woodrow pointed out that quantitative laws in psychology can be formulated in terms of the inducing situation and the subject's response thereto. The situation-response relationships can be expressed by empirical equations which have a validity independent of any particular theoretical interpretation. Between the stimulating situation and the individual's response the psychologist may interpolate determining tendencies, mental sets, neural excitations, instincts, motives, and the like, to suit his fancy. The quantitative laws of psychology have a validity which is independent of these assumed explanatory processes and structures.

When we turn to the analysis of emotion the complete view, shown in the third figure, is essential. Emotion is revealed in overt behavior; but behavior is only one of its phases and aspects. Emotion is an internal bodily process, but this process is aroused through external events. The physiological processes have vital significance when considered in relation to external events.

The complete view is held by the ecologist, by the evolutionary biologist, the physiological psychologist, and many others. This view preserves the organism in its natural setting whether in the field or laboratory.

PERIPHERAL MANIFESTATIONS OF FEELING AND EMOTION

Many of the physiological changes that occur during specific feelings and emotions are observable at the surface of the body. Changes in respiration, heart beat, sweat secretion, tears, erection of dermal appendages, etc., are clearly apparent without the aid of instruments. But instrumental techniques have been extensively employed in experiments upon the peripheral manifestations of feeling and emotion.

Peripheral Signs of Emotional Disturbance. The literature upon the bodily changes of feeling and emotion is voluminous and highly technical. Lindsley (1951), after a survey of the literature, listed the main bodily changes that have been studied and described the techniques for recording them. The following list is based largely upon Lindley's summary.

1. *Electrical phenomena of the skin.* The phenomenon variously known as the galvanic skin response (GSR), psychogalvanic reflex, skin resistance, palmar resistance, palmar conductance, electrodermal response, and skin potential, is related to *sweating.* The effector mechanism for this reponse is the sweat gland membranes, activated by the sympathetic nervous system.

The activity of the sweat glands is augmented by a sudden noise, by a painful shock, by an odor, and by a word that is emotionally loaded through its associations (such as *love* or the subject's name). In some of the early studies the GSR was regarded as a dependable index of emotion. It has been shown, however, that the electrical conductance of the body is lowered during activities that require effort and controlled attention as well as emotion. Just analyzing a geometrical puzzle or turning impulsively from a problem in multiplication to one in division is sufficient to evoke a temporary GSR. The GSR is an index of activation. It does not distinquish pleasant from unpleasant arousals.

2. *Blood pressure and volume.* Changes in blood pressure and the GSR are probably the best indicators of facilitative and preparatory functions that are mediated mainly by the sympathetic nervous system. These changes occur also during emergency emotions of rage, fear, pain, and excitement. There are two measures of blood pressure: the *systolic* pressure is the maximal pressure reached during contraction of the heart muscle and the *diastolic* pressure is the minimal pressure during expansion. The difference between them is known as *pulse pressure.*

Blood pressure is usually measured by a sphygmomanometer which consists of a cuff placed about the arm of the subject and inflated until the mechanical pressure cuts off and then releases the circulation. When it is necessary to record continuous changes in blood pressure, the pressure in the cuff is raised to a point above the diastolic level but not to a point where it occludes the circulation. With this midpressure it is possible to measure changes in blood pressure but not, of course, the absolute level.

The volume of blood in some part of the body is regulated by vasoconstriction and vasodilation. If the finger, hand, or foot is enclosed in a rigid apparatus, which is then filled with water, changes in the volume of the body part can be recorded in terms of pressure changes produced by rise or fall in the water level.

The *plethysmograph* is an instrument for recording such changes in the volume of blood in a specific part of the body.

3. *Electrocardiogram and heart rate.* The usual method of determining the rate of heart beat is simply to count the pulse with watch in hand. The *electrocardiograph* is an instrument for recording the heart beat. Electrodes from the instrument are attached to the two arms of the subject or to either arm and the left leg or to the body wall near the heart. The electrodes pick up electrical potentials that accompany the cycle of the heart beat. The record obtained from the instrument is known as an electrocardiogram (EKG).

4. *Respiration.* Changes in the respiratory cycle are prominent in emotional conditions such as startle, fright, attempts at deception, states of conflict and anxiety.

The apparatus for recording respiration is a *pneumograph*—a flexible, air-filled tube that is placed around the thorax or abdomen of the subject and connected to a sensitive diaphragm that moves a stylus on a recording paper. The principal variables of respiration are rate, depth, and pattern. The ratio of inspiration to expiration is commonly expressed as the *I/E* ratio and sometimes (more meaningfully) as the *I*-fraction. The *I*-fraction expresses the ratio between duration of inspiration and duration of the total respiratory cycle: $I/I+E$.

5. *Skin temperature.* The temperature of the skin depends upon local vasoconstriction but also upon temperature of the blood and upon that of the body generally. Hence, indirectly, it depends upon a large variety of factors. It has been reported that emotional stress and persisting conflict are associated with a fall in skin temperature.

6. *Pupillary response.* In fear, rage, pain, and great excitement, the pupil dilates, indicating a response of the sympathetic nervous system. We all know, however, that the pupil has non-emotional functions. Constriction and dilation regulate reflexly the amount of light that is admitted into the eye.

7. *Salivary secretion.* The secretion of the salivary glands has been extensively studied by Pavlov and his associates in relation to conditioned reflexes but salivary secretion has been little studied in relation to emotion. The salivary glands and their blood vessels, however, are supplied by both sympathetic and parasympathetic nerves and their function is known to vary with emotional states. During some emergency emotions there is dryness in the mouth due to inhibition of the salivary secretion.

8. *Pilomotor response.* In various species, as Darwin has shown, emotional excitement is associated with erection of dermal appendages. When the cat is frightened her hair stands on end; when the porcupine is excited his spines erect; when the hen senses danger the feathers bristle. In man, the hair-raising reflex is vestigial but the hair-raising mechanism is still present. The "goose flesh" we experience when chilly is a pilomotor response. The wave of feeling sometimes experienced when a piece of chalk or the finger nail scrapes the blackboard is dependent upon a pilomotor response.

9. *Dermographia.* If a firm stroke with a dull rounded instrument and a constant pressure is made on the arm of the subject, the stroked area immediately appears blanched. In a few seconds it turns red and the redness then gradually disappears. Duration of the total response until the redness disappears is measured. The response may require 3 to 30 minutes or more. This measure, Lindsley writes, is probably a better index of autonomic balance or stability than of emotional susceptibility.

10. *Skin sweating.* The galvanic skin response is an index of palmar sweating

but in addition to this there are several types of chemical applications that reveal the distribution of sweating on the surface of the body. These chemical methods have a value in clinical diagnosis and possibly in future studies of emotional patterns of response in which both the sympathetic and the parasympathetic systems are activated.

11. *Analysis of blood, saliva, and urine.* Studies of the chemical constituents of the blood have shown that during emotion there are changes in the blood sugar level, adrenin content, acid-base balance, red cell count, and other factors. Changes in the acid-base balance of saliva, and in the sugar excreted in the urine, have been noted when samples are taken before and after emotional excitement.

12. *Gastrointestinal motility.* Studies of the motility of the stomach and intestine under emotional conditions have been made with animals and human subjects. Cannon demonstrated that the activities of the gastrointestinal tract of cats are inhibited during fear and anger. With human subjects the motility of the stomach and intestine has been investigated by having the subject swallow a tube containing a small bag which can then be inflated through the tube. Variations in pressure upon this bag, made by contractions and relaxations of the stomach wall, are transmitted mechanically to a recorder.

13. *Metabolic rate.* Basic metabolic rate (BMR) has been defined as the minimum heat or energy production required to keep the individual alive—to maintain respiration, circulation, digestion, muscular tonus, body temperature, glandular secretions, and other vital functions. One method of determining the BMR is to measure, by means of a *calorimeter*, the bodily heat produced. A more widely used method is to determine oxygen consumption through a test of respiration. Heat is produced by oxidation. The consumption of oxygen can be determined from the O/CO_2 ratio of inhaled and exhaled air.

The rate of oxygen consumption (BMR) generally increases during emotional excitement and during mobilization of the energies of the body for vigorous and prolonged action.

14. *Muscle tension.* It is well known that anxiety is associated with an increased tension in the skeletal muscles. Muscle tension can be recorded mechanically or indirectly by recording muscle potentials. Muscle tension is an important determinant of performance and regulates efficiency of action. It has been extensively studied in both emotional and non-emotional behavior.

15. *Tremor.* When antagonistic muscle groups are pitted against each other it is normal for a tremor to develop. In maintaing a posture, as in holding out an extended finger, a tremor of about ten to twelve oscillations per second develops. Muscle tremor is accentuated during emotional excitement, anger, fear, and grief. Luria recorded tremor mechanically by a pneumatic system; he studied tremor in relation to emotional conflict. In subsequent work more sensitive *tremographs* have been developed.

16. *Eye blink and eye movement.* Eye blinking suggests a kind of nervousness. It has been observed during anxiety and emotional tension. Movements of the lid and movements of the eyes can be recorded by placing electrodes appropriately in the region of the eyes and registering changes of potential. There has been little systematic study of blinking as related to emotion.

Respiration in Emotion. Everyone has observed the disturbances of respiration which occur during crying, laughing, startle, fear, and other states of excitement. The child in a tantrum sometimes holds his breath till he turns blue. In violent laughter expiration becomes spasmodic, and the breath forces the vocal cords to vibrate and emit sounds. In sudden fright there are various signs of respiratory involvement: quick gasping intake of air, holding the breath, dilation of the nostrils. These and other respiratory changes in emotion have been recorded and analyzed by physiologists and psychologists.

Respiration serves two main functions, both of which are disturbed during emotional excitement. The primary service of respiration, necessary to life, is to ventilate the lungs and thus to make possible a gaseous exchange between air and the blood. When there is an increased need for oxygen, as during vigorous muscular activity, this need is met by more rapid and deeper breathing, and by a lengthening of the inspiration phase relative to the total cycle of respiration.

The second and less vital service of respiration—an important factor in social behavior—is to supply the air pressure needed to vibrate the vocal cords. The lungs act as a bellows supplying and regulating the stream of air which in expiration passes between the cords, vibrating them to produce uttered sounds. The outcries of emotion as well as all sounds of speech and song are brought about in this manner by the vocal cords.

Although, as noted above, the ratio of inspiration (*I*) to expiration (*E*) is commonly employed in experimental studies that monitor respiration (the *I*/*E* ratio) the *I*-fraction is more meaningful. Woodworth (1938) recommended the simpler and more intelligible measure—the *I*-fraction. The *I*-fraction shows the proportion of the total respiratory cycle that is used for inspiring air. The fraction shows the ratio between the duration of inspiration (*I*) and the duration of the total cycle (*I* + *E*), that is: *I*/*I*+*E*.

Woodworth worked out a simple reduction table for converting the more unusual *I*/*E* ratios into *I*-fraction ratios. His table is based on the assumption that *I* and *E* have been so measured that they comprise the whole cycle. The relationship between the *I*/*E* ratio and the *I*-fraction is a simple arithmetical one.

Because all the air utilized by an organism is drawn into the lungs during inspiration and because inspiration is usually the active muscular phase of the respiratory cycle, the *I*-fraction indicates what proportion of time in the cycle is consumed by the necessary labor of inhaling air.

On the basis of experimental results Woodworth tabulated representative values of the *I*-fraction as follows:

Process	*I*-fraction
In speech	0.16
In laughter	0.23
In attentive mental work	0.30
In the resting condition	0.43
In excitement	0.60+
In posed wonder (in which the subject is asked to imagine a wonderful or surprising situation and to express his feeling by face and gesture)	0.71
In sudden fright	0.75

During speech only one-sixth (0.16) of the total respiratory cycle is taken up in supplying the oxygen necessary to sustain life. In this case the reduction of the *I*-fraction is obviously not an emotional concomitant. Rather it appears to be due to a quickening of the intake of air to avoid interruptions in speech, since vocalizing is dependent upon expired, not inspired, air. An even greater shortening of the inspiratory phase may occur in singing.

In quiet breathing somewhat less than one-half (0.43) of the time is used for inspiration, while in excitement inhalation is relatively prolonged (0.60+). During sudden fright a quick intake of air, followed by holding the breath, explains an even larger *I*-fraction.

What biological significance has the increased *I*-fraction occurring in emotional excitement? In times of stress when vigorous and prolonged action becomes necessary for self-defense or protection of the young, there is a need for more rapid and complete oxygenation of the blood to speed up metabolism and to counteract the chemical effects of fatigue. This increased oxygenation of the blood is accomplished partly by an increased *I*-fraction and partly by more rapid and deeper respiration, as noted earlier.

Incidentally, there is evidence that the *I*-fraction is increased if the subject attempts to tell a lie and to conceal the fact that he is lying. This is probably because the situation arouses a state of excitement and at the same time calls for a suppression of it. Lie-detecting will be considered in a following section.

Circulatory Changes in Emotion. Circulation of the blood, although continuous throughout life, is far from being constant in nature. Marked changes occur during sleep, exercise, mental activity and after eating, as well as during emotional excitement.

In emotional excitement, as all of us have observed, there are appreciable disturbances in cardiovascular processes. There is the blush of shame or embarrassment (dilation of blood vessels at the body surface), the pallor of fear (vasoconstriction), the rapid pounding of the heart in excitement or rage. We commonly describe emotional experiences with such familiar phrases as: "My heart was in my mouth"; "Everything went black before my eyes"; "My hands were like ice"; "My cheeks were burning." Such experiences are based upon circulatory changes in emotion.

In research upon emotion, laboratory measurements have been made of the following circulatory variables: (1) pulse rate and amplitude, (2) distribution of blood to the various parts of the body, (3) blood pressure, (4) chemical composition of the blood.

A few of the more common techniques and instruments for measuring the first three of these variables are described below. Some of the chemical changes will be noted a little later.

1. *Rate and amplitude of pulse*. The common practice of counting the pulse at the wrist gives only the more obvious changes of rate and rhythm. In the laboratory a graphic record of the pulse can be obtained which shows variations in amplitude and form of pulse wave as well as in rate. This is done by strapping to the radial artery of the wrist an instrument (sphygmograph) which presses against the artery and which by means of levers, writes a mechanical record of the pulse wave.

Another instrument (cardiotachometer) counts and records the heart beats continuously. In adjusting the instrument, two small electrodes are placed on the chest of the subject, one over the base of the heart and the other near its apex. The electrical changes, which can be referred to the beating heart, are amplified and recorded at some distance from the subject.

Laboratory workers have consistently found that during emotional excitement there is an increase in both rate and amplitude of pulse. Almost any exciting circumstance, such as anticipation of pain in the dentist's chair, an impending examination in the classroom, or winning an important prize, is likely to be associated with an acceleration of heart beat.

2. *Distribution of the blood*. Through constriction or dilation of the blood vessels in any given member of the body the volume of blood in that member is decreased or increased. The variations in volume of blood in the forearm can be measured by sealing this body part airtight in a large glass or metal tube. As the blood vessels constrict or dilate, the corresponding changes in volume are converted into variations of air pressure, which in turn are communicated through a rubber tube to a recording tambour. The graphic record obtained from the plethysmo-

graph reveals fluctuations in volume and variations in the pulse wave as well.

Actually, when the blood flows into the forearm it comes from other parts of the body. Dilation or constriction of the blood vessels in one part changes the total distribution of blood throughout the body. Local vascular changes are only symptoms of the total blood distribution at the time of observation.

In the earlier decades of experimental psychology plethysmographs were used to record the vascular changes during pleasant and unpleasant feelings. It was found that during pleasantness the arteries usually dilated; during unpleasantness they usually constricted. Perfect correlations, however, were not obtained, partly because of the limitations of the introspective technique but more largely because the opposition and contrast between felt pleasantness and unpleasantness depends upon central neural processes which are much more complex than the relatively simple constriction and dilation of the arteries and not univocally related to them.

3. *Blood pressure.* The most familiar method of measuring blood pressure is that of the physician, who binds a flat rubber bag around the arm, then pumps it up with air until the air pressure cuts off the arterial circulation. Now the air is slowly released from the bag until circulation is resumed, maximum and minimum blood pressure being read on an indicator. The *systolic* pressure is the maximum pressure obtained during a given heart cycle, and the *diastolic* pressure is the minimum. Although there are wide variations with conditions, a representative systolic pressure is 120 millimeters of mercury, and a representative diastollic pressure, 80 millimeters.

A typical study of circulatory changes during emotion is that of Scott (1930), who obtained graphic records of systolic blood pressure before, during, and after various emotional episodes. His subjects, 100 college men, witnessed a motion-picture film which presented three emotional episodes seperated by approximately ten minutes of neutral story:

1. To arouse sexual emotion there was the usual love scene followed by pictures of a nude girl dancing.

2. For "anger" a scene was presented in which the suitor, who was also the hero, was treacherously betrayed and rejected by his sweetheart, being finally flogged into unconsciousness and thrown out on the street.

3. "Fear" was portrayed by a scene showing the destruction of a city by earthquake. To this was added a sudden loud noise.

With sexual stimulation there was a consistent rise of blood pressure, only one man in the 100 reacting with a drop in pressure. This finding leads to the conclusion that sexual emotion is characterized by a rise in systolic blood pressure.

In his studies with "anger" and "fear" Scott did not find any striking difference between the vascular reactions in these emotions. Some subjects showed a rise and others a fall in blood pressure. Scott concludes: "Anger and fear have no characteristic vascular reaction." This conclusion is not final, however, inasmuch as we cannot know exactly what kinds of emotions were aroused by the film. On the one hand, the emotions would depend upon empathy–projecting one's self into the situation presented by the film. On the other hand, so far as we know, no one has yet succeeded in distinguishing fear from anger on the basis of vascular and glandular changes, despite much study of these emotions. However, see Ax (1953).

Changes in blood pressure have been utilized, also, in tests of deception. If a person tells a lie or tries to conceal something that is important to himself, such as a crime he has committed or a clandestine love affair, there is a sudden, sharp, brief rise in blood pressure.

In a pioneer study of deception, Benussi (1914) employed respiratory changes as an indicator of deception. Later Marston (1917) showed that a rise in blood pressure may betray a lie. In the present-day art of "lie-detecting," as it has been developed by Larson (1923, 1932), both respiratory and circulatory disturbances are recorded and analyzed.

In practice a man who, to illustrate, is suspected of stealing a horse, is connected to the recording instruments. He is then asked a series of questions, some of which are neutral and some pointed, as, "Did you steal the horse?" The interview is carefully planned in advance. If a question embarrasses the subject, there is an involuntary rise of blood pressure and an increased *I*-fraction–telltale signs.

Clearly, the lie-detector does not distinguish truth from falsehood. The instruments indicate involuntary emotional disturbances which must be carefully interpreted in relation to the questions asked during the interview.

The Galvanic Skin Response–An Index of Sweat Secretion. The fascination which the galvanic skin response holds for psychologists is due, according to Landis (1930), to two things. First, the psychologist would like to believe that at long last he has discovered some method by which he can detect and perhaps measure that kind of human experience commonly known as emotion. The second lure, which is probably the greater, is that in measuring the electrical changes of the body the psychologist makes use of instruments which give a semblance of physical exactness and precision to his research. Galvanometers, Wheatstone bridges–beautifully exact instruments–foster the delusion that emotion is a precisely defined psychological process simply because the instruments of measurement are exact!

When all is said and done, the galvanic skin response turns out to be a delicate index of the amount of secretion of the sweat glands. A slight increase in the activity of these glands moistens the surface with a weakly saline solution, the result of which change is to lower the electrical resistance of the body at the skin. Such a change of electrical resistance can be detected by the swing of a galvanometer if a weak current is passed through the body.

There are two electical effects: (1) a lowering of bodily resistance made manifest when an exosomatic current is passed through the body (the Féré effect); (2) an increase in the electric potential of the body (the Tarchanoff effect), the generation of an endosomatic current.

Action of the sweat glands, however, can be observed without electrical instruments, as Darrow (1932) pointed out. By pressing the finger tip against a glass plate and observing under low magnification the pore of a sweat gland, a globule of sweat can be seen to emerge from the pore and spread out upon the glass. If the sweat cannot evaporate, it returns into its pore.

Activity of the sweat glands is augmented by numerous sensory presentations such as perfumes, bad odors, loud noises, and by emotionally loaded words., e.g., the word "kiss" or the subject's name.

Some psychologists have regarded the galvanic skin response as a dependable indicator of affective processes. The claim, however, is not tenable in view of the fact that the galvanic skin response appears also in neutral activities such as analyzing a geometrical puzzle-figure or turning impulsively from a problem in multiplication to one in division.

Since it has been shown that the presence of the galvanic skin response indicates an augmented activity of the sweat glands, one may inquire: What useful role does sweat secretion play in behavior?

One service of sweat secretion to the body is that of cooling the skin by evaporation and thus helping to regulate body temperature. On a hot day or during vigorous exercise this is obviously an important function. In emergency situations, too, such as those existing when a cat is attacked by a dog or when a man is surrounded by savages, cooling the body is an important function.

The interpretation of the role of sweat secretion in terms of cooling the body is open to one criticism: Sweat glands are very numerous in the palms and soles of the feet, regions in which evaporation is frequently prevented by contact with solid objects or reduced to a minimum by a cupped position of the hand. Profuse sweating in the palms and soles can hardly be explained in terms of cooling of the body. Does such sweating have another function?

Darrow (1936) has pointed out that moisture on the palm enables the hand to get a firmer grip upon an object. The workman realizes this when he spits on his hand to obtain a better hold of a tool; and the office clerk realizes it when she moistens the fingers with a sponge to aid in counting papers. Moisture gives a firmer hold upon objects.

Among primates a firm hold upon the limb of a tree has obvious utility when an escape has to be made through the forest. The primitive man who can obtain a firm grasp upon a club or stone has an advantage in combat. Thus, the profuse sweating of palms and soles during emotional excitement has utility other than that of cooling the body. This interpretation fits in with the view of Cannon and the earlier view of Darwin that the bodily changes of emotion are biologically serviceable in the struggle for existence.

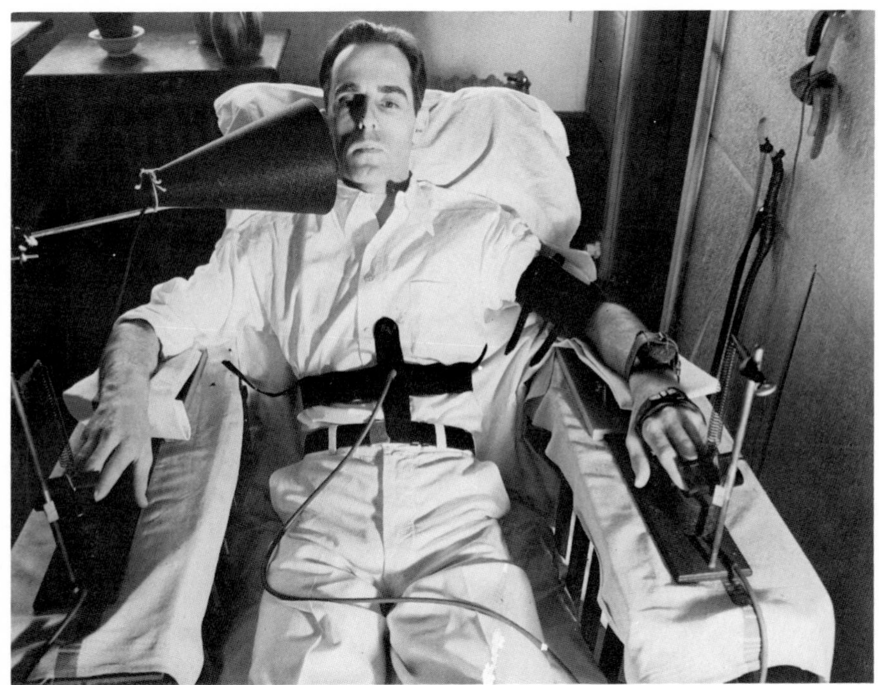

Figure 33. Subject adjusted for simultaneous recording of vocal responses, voluntary and involuntary movements of the hands, respiration, galvanic skin reflex, pulse rate, and continuous changes in blood pressure. *Courtesy of* Ralph R. Brown. (The subject is a normal person who was employed at the U.S. Public Health Service Hospital, Lexington, Kentucky, when this picture was taken.)

Simultaneous Recording of Bodily Changes in Emotion. In some investigations of emotion a great deal of information is gained from recording simultaneously several kinds of bodily changes. Figure 33 shows a subject seated in an easy chair with various kinds of recording apparatus attached. The view shows an arrangement for recording simultaneously the vocal response to a stimulus word, abdominal respiration, the galvanic skin response (GSR), pulse rate, changes in blood pressure, and two forms of reaction of the skeletal muscles (involuntary tremor and voluntary movement).

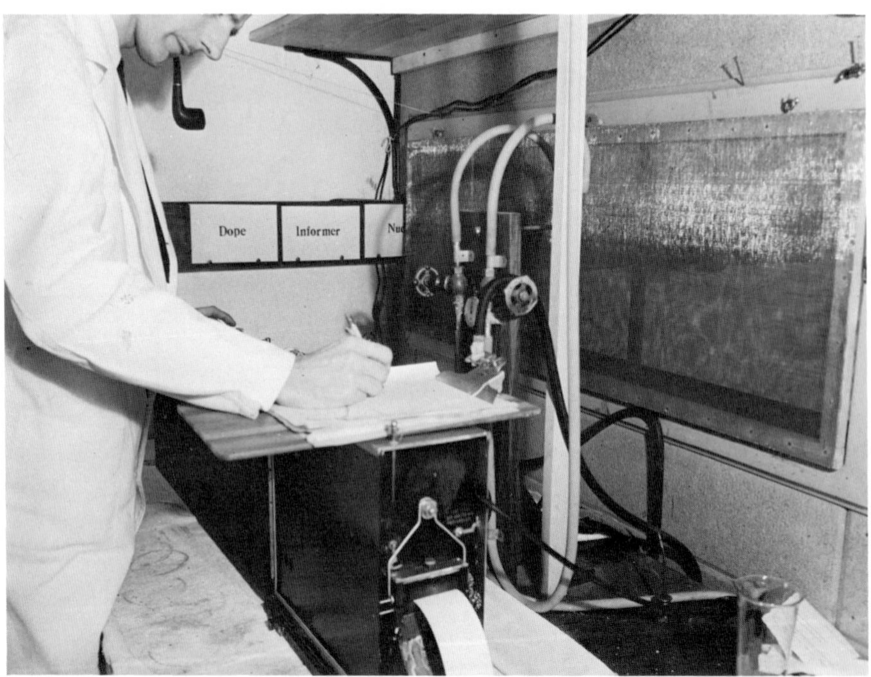

Figure 34. Photograph showing Darrow's photopolygraph, one-way observation screen, and other details. *Courtesy of* Ralph R. Brown.

Figure 34 shows Darrow's *photopolygraph*, in an adjoining room, arranged for presenting stimulus-words and simultaneously recording bodily changes. The various bodily changes are recorded photographically on a moving film. In front of the experimenter is a one-way screen for direct observation of the subject's behavior. Stimulus-words, presented to the subject one at a time, are visible on the wall.

In this kind of work it is necessary to have a normal, or control, period as a base before emotionally-loaded stimulus-words are presented to the subject.

Figure 35 shows part of a photographic record. Vertical cross lines in the photograph indicate successive units of time.

Studies with Taboo Words. The phrase "perceptual defense" was used by McGinnies (1949) to refer to a certain resistance against the recognition of words that are socially taboo.

In an important study, McGinnies exposed single words in a tachistoscope with exposure times too brief to permit complete recognition. In preliminary trials he determined the threshold times for recognition by exposing stimulus words for 0.01 second, 0.02 second, etc., until complete recognition and correct verbal report occurred. He obtained the threshold recognition time for each of his subjects.

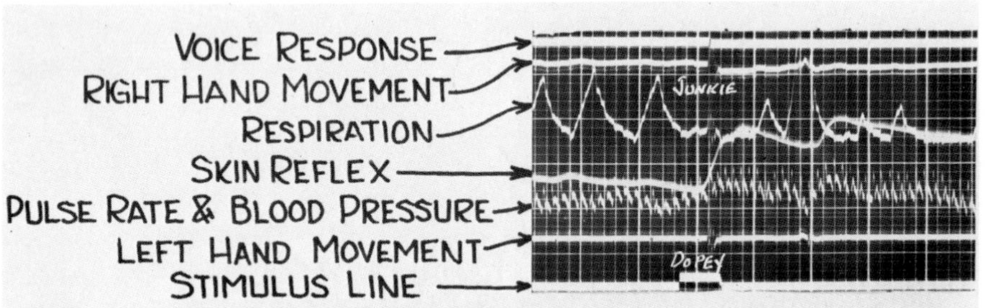

Figure 35. Part of a record from Darrow's photopolygraph showing the vocal response of a male subject to the word "dopey," respiration, galvanic skin reflex, pulse and blood pressure variations, and hand movements. *Courtesy of* Ralph R. Brown.

In the main experiment eighteen words were presented one at a time. Eleven of these words were neutral and seven of them were critical, i.e., affectively loaded, taboo words. The list follows with critical words in italics:

1. Apple	7. River	13. *Penis*
2. Dance	8. *Whore*	14. Music
3. *Raped*	9. Sleep	15. Trade
4. Child	10. *Kotex*	16. *Filth*
5. *Belly*	11. Broom	17. Clear
6. Glass	12. Stove	18. *Bitch*

The subjects were told that they would be shown some words which they might not be able to recognize at first. They were instructed to report whatever they saw or thought they saw on each exposure, regardless of what it was. They were asked to delay their report until a signal was given by the experimenter. The purpose of this delay was to allow about 6 seconds for the appearance and recording of the galvanic skin response (GSR).

Prior to exposures, electrodes were strapped to the palms of the hands for recording the GSR. The GSR is known to be a sensitive indicator of action in the autonomic nervous system.

McGinnies obtained two kinds of data for each exposed word. First, a record of the magnitude of the GSR and, second, a record of the subject's verbal response. There were, all together, sixteen subjects—eight male and eight female.

Average data for the group are presented in Figures 36 and 37. Fig. 36 shows the mean threshold time (in seconds) required for the recognition of neutral and critical (emotionally charged) words. The figure reveals that the recognition times are consistently longer for the critical (taboo) than for the neutral (non-taboo) words. The average difference between neutral and critical words is statistically significant.

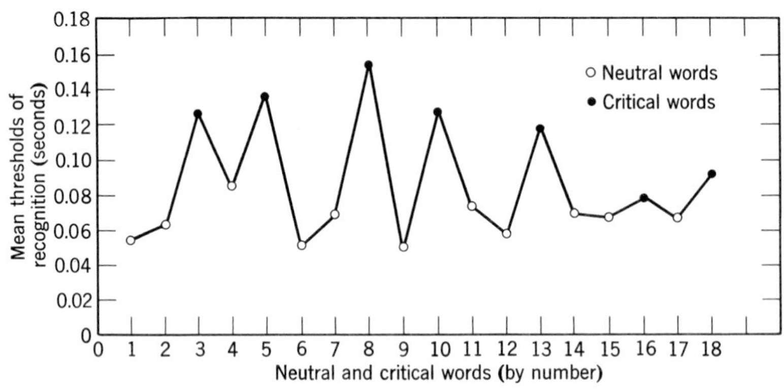

Figure 36. Mean thresholds of recognition (in seconds) for neutral and critical words. *After* McGinnies (1949).

Fig. 37 gives the mean micrometer readings on the instrument used to measure the GSR. These readings give an arbitrary index of the magnitude of the autonomic response. The readings were made with prerecognition exposures, i.e., with exposure times too brief to permit recognition of the word and verbal report. An interesting feature of these data is that the critical words evoked an affective response (GSR) with exposure times so brief that the words could not be recognized and correctly reported. This finding suggests that there is a resistance to recognition and/or reporting these taboo words. What is the nature of this resistance?

McGinnies calls this resistance to recognition "perceptual defense" and believes that the defense is a way of avoiding anxiety created by briefly exposed taboo words. Early in life the child is taught that certain words are naughty and must not be used in polite society. A child is likely to be familiar with some of the bad words but if he uses them, he is reproved. Words referring to sexual and excretory functions are taboo; there is a resistance against using them in polite society and they tend to arouse an emotional response.

The facts indicate that there are two aspects to the response to a word. There is a cognitive, discriminatory aspect shown by recognition and verbal report of a word. There is also an affective aspect of the total response shown by the GSR and the delay of verbal report. McGinnies' study indicates that an affective arousal may be present when exposure times are too brief to permit clear recognition and report of the word. Does the affective reaction occur before the cognitive? Does the affective reaction indicate some kind of blocking or inhibition?

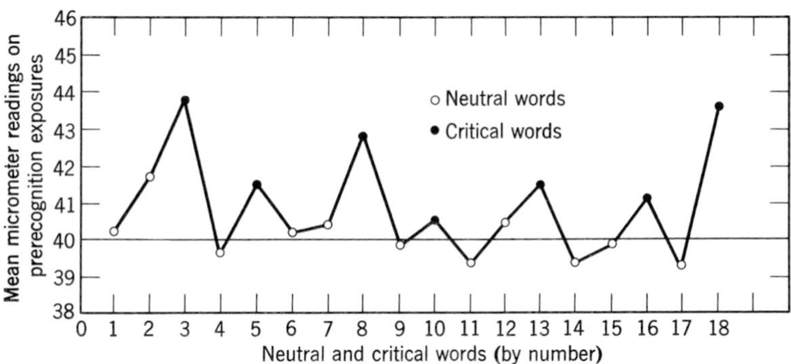

Figure 37. Magnitude of the galvanic skin response to neutral and critical words with exposure times too brief for recognition. *After* McGinnies (1949).

The Art of Lie Detecting. The art of lie detecting is a practical application of the experimental psychology of emotion. The art rests upon a sound principle: If a man has knowledge of guilt which he wishes to conceal, he will be emotionally disturbed when questioned about his criminal or immoral act. A guilty person may control facial expression voluntarily and tell lies with little outward sign of emotion but the lie detector records *involuntary* changes in pulse and blood pressure, respiration, and electrodermal response. When we say that these changes are *involuntary* we mean that they cannot be suppressed by the wish of the subject to hide them.

The lie detector is really an *emotion* detector. The difference between truth and falsehood is not a *psychological* difference but rather one related to logic and morals. What the instrument really detects is the presence or absence of emotional disturbance. If the subject feels embarrassed or ashamed or guilty while making a true statement, the involuntary changes in blood pressure, pulse, respiration, and the GSR, still occur. Again, if a subject can deliberately make a *false* statement with complete composure, the lie detector records no emotional disturbance.

The first lie detector, historically, was a pneumograph—an instrument for recording respiration. The sphygmograph—an instrument for registering changes in blood pressure and pulse—was later introduced; it is now commonly employed alone or with the pneumograph in lie detecting. The galvanometer is sometimes used alone. Any one of these instruments can be used as a lie detector but a combination gives added checks upon the involuntary changes of emotion. These instruments

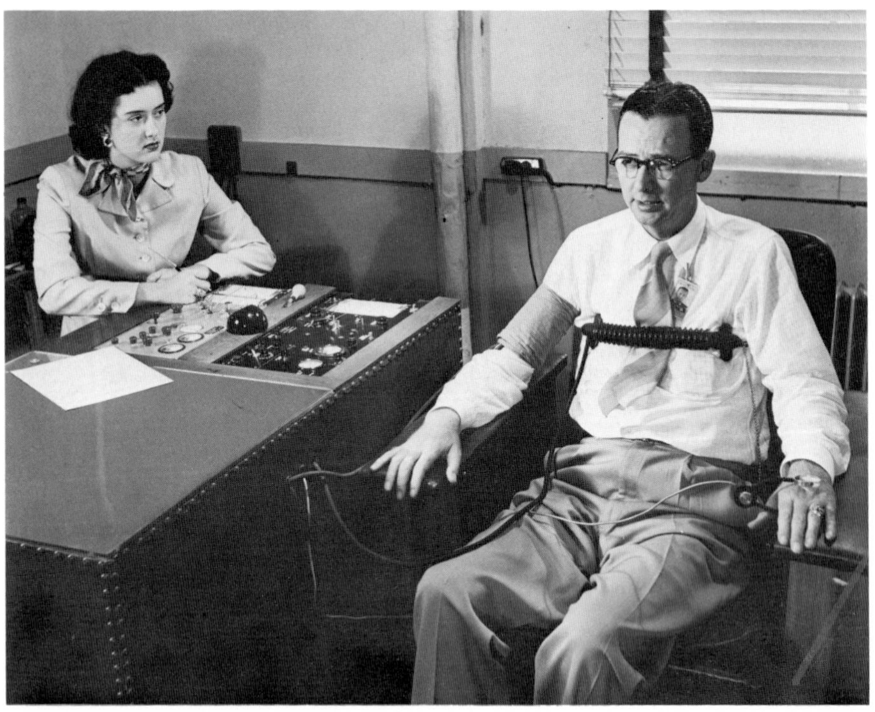

Figure 38. Subject taking a lie-detecting test. The desk contains two three-channel polygraphs. A sheet contains a previously prepared list of questions, and the examiner is shown writing on the chart the number assigned to the question she has just asked. The cuff on the subject's right upper arm is connected by a rubber tube to the instrument for recording changes in blood pressure, pulse pressure, and heart rate. The distendable, corrugated pneumograph tube about the chest is attached to the instrument for recording respiration rate and depth. The electrodes attached to the left hand and to the recording galvanometer of the polygraph serve to register on the chart the electrodermal responses—variations in the resistance of the skin to minute electrical currents introduced through the electrodes. *Courtesy of* Russell B. Chatham, Oak Ridge, Tennessee.

automatically write their curves on a moving tape with ink pens. See Figure 38.

In questioning a suspect, the examiner asks a number of control (neutral) questions and intersperses the critical items. For example, a farmer is suspected of arson; it is believed that he burned the barn of a neighbor and competitor. Control questions might include such items as: How long have you lived in Blanktown? How many children do you have? Critical items might be: Did you burn the barn? How did the fire start? If the lie detector consistently registers changes in blood pressure, pulse, respiration, GSR, for the key items and not for the controls, the subject is suspected of concealing knowledge of guilt. It is the *difference* between key and control items that is relied upon in the art of lie detecting.

The courts are generally unwilling to admit lie detector findings as evidence obtained under duress; but the result of a test may be so convincing that it leads to a confession. The test may be useful in helping detectives look for further evidence.

The methods of lie detecting, as discussed by Larson (1932) and Inbau (1942), are somewhat similar to those employed by psychiatrists to detect emotional complexes. The patient is made to relax and respond to selected stimulus words. If the words arouse emotion, involuntary bodily changes occur and can be recorded. The involuntary bodily changes are considered in conjunction with the meaning of the stimulus-words.

OBSERVABLE PATTERNS OF RESPONSE IN EMOTIONAL EXCITEMENT

According to a commonly accepted view, an emotion is a pattern of response. Thus, Watson (1919), although he recognized at least three other formulations, stated explicitly in his major definition that an emotion is a pattern-reaction: "*An emotion is an hereditary pattern-reaction involving profound changes of the bodily mechanism as a whole, but particularly of the visceral and glandular systems.*" Also, Bard (1934*a*) in a review of research upon the neurohumoral basis of emotion emphasized that "in his experimental work the physiologist (as distinguished from the student of subjective experience) considers emotions as behavior patterns." Ax (1953) claimed that fear and anger can be differentiated with human subjects in terms of the pattern of physiological changes.

The term *pattern* implies that the separate elements of response appear with a definite spatial form and in approximately the same sequence each time the inducing situation is present.

The patterns that appear during emotional excitement are more complex than simple reflexes. They appear with mechanical regularity when stimulating conditions are present. And, further, like reflexes the emotional patterns can be conditioned and extinguished. Emotional patterns are said to differ from simple reflexes mainly in complexity and generality. The former involve the bodily mechanism as a whole, particularly the glands and smooth muscles, whereas the latter are more restricted in scope.

No claim is made here that any of the following patterns *is* an emotion. The patterns are described as organic responses to stimulus-situations, which occur in or during emotional excitement. Many of the patterns are outwardly observable as "expressions" of emotions. All of them have a physiological–neuromuscular and biochemical–aspect.

Rage Patterns and Hostile Attack. With most animals there appear from time to time patterns of behavior which are unambiguous in their biological meaning–the rage patterns. The entire organism becomes integrated for a fight–for a vigorous, hostile attack upon an enemy.

Hostile behavior has developed through countless years of evolution. Nature has produced the claws and teeth of the tiger, the antlers of the deer, the spurs of the cock, the fangs of the snake, and the sting and poison sac of the insect as instruments of offense and defense. It is not surprising that internal organs are also organized for a serious life-and-death struggle.

That hostile behavior is primitive and depends upon deeply ingrained neural organization is shown by the fact that a pattern of hostile attack persists after the cerebral cortex has been surgically severed from the brain stem and spinal cord.[1] Reactions of hostile attack have been observed, according to Bard (1934*b*), in decorticate dogs by Goltz, Rothmann, Bard and Culler; in decorticate cats by Dusser de Barenne, Cannon and Britton, and others.

In the decorticate cat there is a remarkable exhibit of rage which includes lashing of the tail, arching of the trunk, protrusion of the claws and clawing movements, snarling or growling, hissing, turning of the head from side to side with attempts to bite, rapid panting with mouth open, movements of the tongue to and fro, along with numerous signs of vigorous sympathetic discharge; erection of the hair on the tail and back, sweating of the toe pads, dilation of the pupils, large increments

[1]That the nervous system is organized to provide for attack may be illustrated by the following unusual example. A number of years ago a turtle was found in Florida which had two heads and a single body containing only one stomach. A newspaper photograph of the monster showed the two heads fighting each other for possession of a morsel of food. Having two complete heads the monster possessed duplicate neural mechanisms for integrating the pattern of attack. And fighting occurred even though both heads were struggling to feed the same stomach!

in heart rate and arterial pressure, retraction of the nictitating membrane, and (as physiologically determined) an abundant secretion of adrenin and increased level of blood sugar—which level may rise to five times its normal concentration. Such manifestations appear in "fits," lasting from a few seconds to many minutes with intervening periods of quiet during which a "fit" can be evoked by the slightest disturbance of the animal, such as pinching the tail or the loose skin of the flank. See Figure 39.

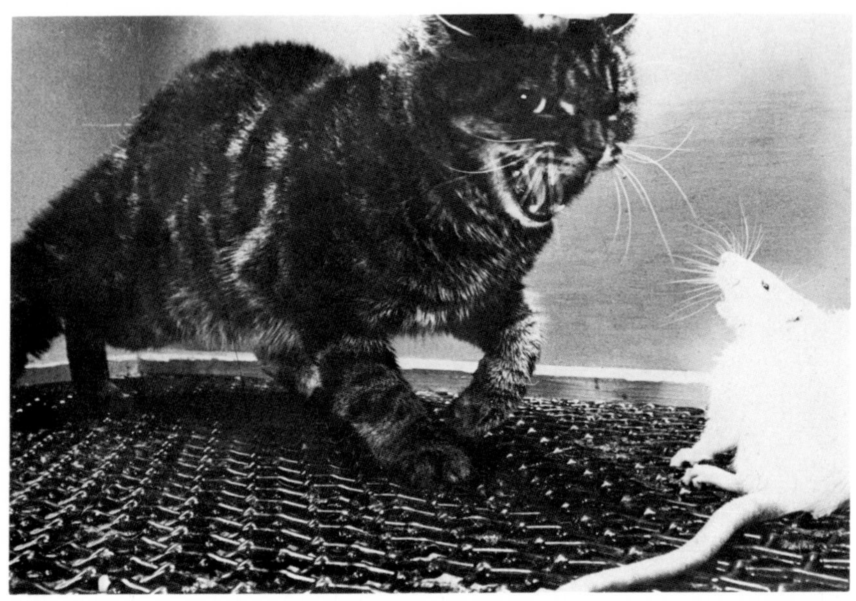

Figure 39. The pattern of rage and hostile attack in the cat, produced by intracranial stimulation of the hypothalamus. *Courtesy of* John L. Flynn, Yale School of Medicine, with permission of the Rockefeller University Press.

With decorticate dogs the pattern is quite similar. There are such manifestations as baring of the teeth, vicious biting and snapping, snarling or growling, struggling. These symptoms are readily elicited by stimulation, e.g., forcibly restraining the animal or rubbing his skin.

Decortication renders both cats and dogs unusually sensitive to patterns of hostile attack. In fact, *the rage patterns of animals are more easily elicited with decorticate than with normal animals.*

This form of attack has been designated "sham rage" on the assumption that the decorticate subject experiences no conscious emotion and, further, that the hostile attack is purely a reflex and not regulated by the cerebral centers as in normal animals. The phrase, however, serves only to confuse the picture by introducing an element of mystery. As *behavior*, "sham rage" is genuine rage.

Bard reported the observation of a real fight between one of his decorticate cats and another animal. During her decorticate career the cat shared a room with a varying number of normal and partially decorticate cats. Among her cage companions were several quarrelsome beasts that made a practice of striking whenever she came within range, the blows usually landing on her face or the top of her head. Bard noted that this decorticate cat held her ground, raising the forepart of her body and striking out with one or both forefeet. During pauses between attacks–which are characteristic of most forms of feline fighting–she kept one forefoot raised, with claws protruded ready to strike as soon as the combat was renewed. The striking was accompanied by retraction of the ears, growling, spitting, erection of the hair, and other signs of sympathetic discharge. Her blows, it is true, were not well directed toward her more resourceful opponent, but when the latter came close enough, the decorticate animal regularly gave more vigorous and more frequent blows. Bard states that gentle tapping of her nose evoked a hostile response of such a quality that it was advisable to wear gloves during the test.

The rage pattern in the decorticate cat differs from that of the normal animal mainly in being more undirected and automatic. It is noteworthy that the decorticate animal never retreated during one of these bouts. The normal animal has better coordination of movement, superior orientation toward the enemy; also he sometimes retreats.

Some components of the rage pattern, e.g., baring of the teeth, biting, and growling, are as truly reflexive in character as are sneezing, coughing, sucking, yawning, and the postural and righting reflexes. In the decorticate animal the rage response is prompt, uniform, and stereotyped, in contrast with that of the normal individual whose behavior is more regulated by the cerebral cortex.

After reviewing the experimental evidence, Bard concludes that the rage pattern is organized by central neural mechanisms which lie within an area comprising the caudal half of the hypothalamus and the most ventral and caudal fractions of the corresponding segments of the thalamus. Some elements of this pattern can be induced even in the spinal cat, still more in the bulbospinal or midbrain preparation; but only when the midbrain mechanisms are present can the elements be welded together to form the complete rage pattern. The cerebral cortex is not essential to the pattern.

Rage patterns, though all similar in many respects, differ from species to species according to the offensive equipment of the animal.

One should speak, therefore, in the plural of *rage patterns* rather than of a single pattern.

The Startle Pattern. Everyone has experienced the startle or quick muscular jerk which occurs immediately when there is an unexpected, intense, or sudden stimulation such as the bang of a gun.

The startle reflex involves skeletal muscles throughout the entire body. The pattern includes blinking of the eyes, forward movement of the head, a characteristic facial expression, raising and drawing forward of the shoulders, abduction and pronation of the upper arms, flexion of the fingers, forward movement of the trunk, contraction of the abdomen, and bending of the knees. A schematic representation of these muscular changes is given in Figure 40.

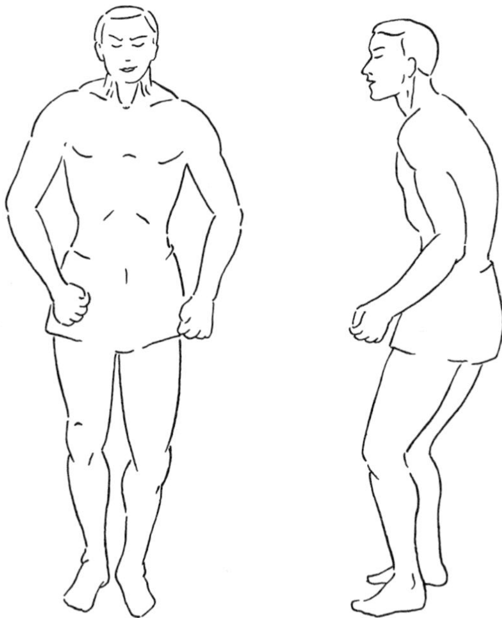

Figure 40. Schematic representation of the startle pattern. *After* Landis and Hunt (1939).

The most noticeable feature of the facial pattern is the closing of the eyes. There is a widening of the mouth as though in a grin, but only occasionally does this lead to baring of the teeth as in the rage pattern. The head and neck are brought forward and down, but the chin is tilted up so that the features are still directed straight ahead. The muscles in the neck stand out prominently.

Not all the elements of this pattern appear in every individual or in a given individual every time that he is startled. The eye-blink always occurs (except with some epileptics). The least constant element in the entire pattern is the pronation of the arms. Instead of pronation (palms of the hands down) there is frequently supination (palms upward).

The pattern as a whole is a general flexion, a protective contraction or shrinking of the individual. The response is usually, but not always, symmetrical.

The startle pattern was first described with scientific precision by Strauss (1929). It has been studied in detail by Landis and Hunt (1939), whose work is mainly followed in the present discussion.

Although it is possible to produce startle by non-auditory stimulations, such as an electric shock to the hand or a jet of cold water directed to hit between the shoulders, the shot of a revolver has proved to be most efficacious in laboratory work. The simultaneous application of other stimuli–discharge of a magnesium photoflash bulb or the application of an electric shock–increases the degree of startle; but the reaction evoked by a gun is intense enough for experimental purposes. The use of a gun, moreover, has this advantage that by using a gun of known caliber (0.22 and 0.32 were used) a rough standardization of loudness is attained. Laboratory workers have employed the gun consistently to evoke startle.

The main recording technique in the investigations of startle has been the use of high-speed motion pictures. The response has been photographed with cameras taking 64 exposures per second; for some parts of their investigation Landis and Hunt employed superspeed cameras giving as high as 300 to 3000 exposures per second. The films were later projected at the usual rate of 16 per second.

In some of the work, levers were attached to the back of the trunk and to the knees so that forward movement of these parts was turned into vertical movement of the levers and thus made more noticeable on the film. Abdominal contraction was measured by a pneumograph attached to a tambour which moved a recording lever.

These laboratory methods have been found necessary because of the great speed with which the pattern develops and vanishes. The response usually comes and goes in less than half a second. The range for the total response is 0.3 to 1.5 seconds.

Startle begins with the closure of the eyelids, both eyes reacting simultaneously. Next there is mouth movement. Then, at about the same time, a movement of the head and neck. The response sweeps downward to the shoulder, arm, hand and trunk, and knee.

The following are some of the data which show the time in milliseconds (1 millisecond = 0.001 second) needed for the response to start at different parts of the body:

	Range	Mean	S.D.
Eye-blink	20- 54	40	7
Widening of the mouth	52-140	69	17
Initiation of head movement	60-120	83	16
First neck muscle movement	75-121	88	13

The further down the body the response moves, the wider in general are the individual differences in reaction time. This is indicated by the following figures, which give the range of the interval (in milliseconds) between the shot and the first movement:

Shoulder movement begins after	100-150 milliseconds
Arm movement begins after	125-195 milliseconds
Hand movement begins after	145-195 milliseconds
Knee movement begins after	145-345 milliseconds

If the gun is discharged at intervals of one or two minutes, habituation may occur; but there are wide individual differences in the amount of habituation. The habituation effect develops in a direction which is the reverse of that followed in the characteristic spreading of the response: The lower body movements drop out first, then those of the trunk and arms, then head movements, and the eye-blink is the last of all to disappear.

With some subjects the anticipation of a noise reduces the amount of the response; in others it makes little if any appreciable difference. The blink reflex and the facial changes were always present, even in the responses of trained marksmen of the New York Police Department.

Tests with animals were made at the Bronx Zoological Park and in the laboratory. Although the pattern is not seen in reptiles and amphibia, it is clearly present in mammals. With animals in the Zoological Park the most noticeable addition to the human pattern appears to be flexion of the ears. The ears were frequently laid back close to the skull. Also the flexion of startle sometimes resulted in a crouching posture, with the legs braced as if to spring. The postural response suggests that startle has defensive utility. The startle pattern was observed in every one of the sixteen primates tested. With monkeys and chimpanzees the response was more widespread than in man, i.e., more elements were present.

In man, the startle pattern is most inflexibly patterned. It is a general reflex response of the skeletal muscles to a sudden stimulus. According to Strauss, the form of the pattern is independent of the direction of the sound source and largely independent of the posture of the subject at the time of stimulation.

The pattern is probably organized on a subcortical level. Landis and Hunt report that tests were made upon five primates which had cortical extirpations, and that in none of them was the pattern modified in any way.

Startle is similar to the rage pattern in that it is a general response of the whole organism. Startle is similar to other patterns, also, in that it can be broken down into component movements, such as the eye-blink and distinguishable changes in posture.

If we ask whether startle is a true *emotional* pattern, an interesting question arises. Some psychologists have assumed that activity of glands and smooth muscles is the fundamental criterion of true emotion; yet startle is a response limited to the skeletal musculature. Startle is a general reflex.

The startle pattern is completed in the fraction of a second, whereas the responses of glands and smooth muscles have a latency well over a second. Ordinarily startle is followed by secondary behavior, such as the development of observant postures, flight, defensive activity, and various signs of overstimulation or annoyance. Startle is frequently the precursor of glandular and smooth-muscle activity but, considered by itself, as we have noted, it is a general reflex of the skeletal muscles.

The Moro Reflex. Closely akin to startle, but distinguishable from it, is the Moro reflex of infants.

The startle pattern is primarily one of flexion, whereas the Moro reflex is one of extension. In the Moro reflex the arms are extended straight out at the sides, at right angles to the trunk, the fingers are extended and spread, the trunk is arched backward, and the head is extended.

Following the primary extension of the Moro reflex there is a secondary flexion which has been described as a "clasping" pattern, but it is doubtful whether this is a true clasping response or merely a slow return to the normal position.

One of the main characteristics of the Moro reflex is that it disappears during the early months of an infant's life. The following tabulation, taken from the work of Landis and Hunt (1939) gives a bit of evidence regarding the persistence of the Moro reflex. See Table 7.

Strauss (1929) believed that in very young infants the Moro reflex takes precedence over the startle pattern and that it is not until the Moro has disappeared that startle is found in the infant's behavioral repertoire. Landis and Hunt, however, are inclined to the view that both of these patterns are present together from birth—that they exsist side by side. The startle pattern occurs so rapidly that it is not ordinarily noticed, and the observer's attention is drawn to the slower, grosser, more obvious Moro reflex.

TABLE 7

Presence and Condition of the Moro Reflex in Relation to Age

Age Group	No.	Excellent	Fair	Decayed	Absent
14 days	3	2	1		
28 days	3		1	2	
2d month	6		2	3	1
3d month	9		1	6	2
4th month	6		1	3	2
5th month	5				5

In any event, the startle pattern and the Moro reflex are distinguishable organic patterns. Both are evoked by the stimulation of a loud noise. Hence, it is not the *kind* of stimulation but rather the *age* of the subject, as we have seen, which determines whether the Moro reflex or the startle pattern will be more obvious to an observer. This fact in itself is interesting from the standpoint of emotional development.

Patterns of Escape, Defense and Fear. The terms *escape* and *defense* designate forms of protective behavior in which the individual avoids a source of danger instead of attacking it. Animals exhibit a great variety of defensive reaction patterns. In considering the kinds of behavior through which an animal escapes from an enemy or defends itself against impending injury, a distinction must be drawn between reflexive patterns of response and persistent flight. For example, the turtle draws in its head, legs, and tail beneath protective armor. The clam closes its shell. The child swiftly withdraws his burnt fingers from the candle flame. Obviously these are all relatively simple protective responses.

In contrast are those more complex forms of directed activity in which an animal persistently avoids an approaching enemy. Birds take to wing. Fish dart away. The deer stands at attention momentarily, then turns and runs. Cattle stampede blindly.

In the present context our primary concern is with those simple patterns of escape and defense which are akin to reflexes rather than with prolonged purposive flight such as that of a man in a race for his life.

An unusual form of escape reaction has been described by Piéron (1928) in the behavior of certain crustaceans and insects. These animals will amputate a leg or claw when necessary to escape rather than be devoured by an enemy. To illustrate: Suppose that a crab has been tied to a stick by a wire which is attached to one of its claws. If left alone with food near by but out of reach, the crab will die on the spot, being unable to free itself. But if an octopus—the most dangerous of its enemies—is released near the crab, the latter will amputate its claw and escape. This response, which is known as *autotomy*, is induced by the visible presence of a deadly enemy. Species of crabs differ in their readiness to sacrifice a limb. In one species (*Grapsidae*) a sudden seizure of the animal is sufficient to cause the abandonment of its claws, and even a quick movement of the hand, as though to seize it, brings immediate autotomy; whereas with another species (*Carcinus*) only the actual sight of an octopus produces autotomy.

Self-amputation has been observed in various Orthoptera (an order of insects comprising the grasshoppers, locusts, crickets, and similar forms) when the situation requires an immediate escape. When one of these creatures is tied by the tibia, it will die without freeing itself, but it amputates its leg immediately and takes to flight when a dangerous enemy approaches.

More familiar than autotomy, to most of us, is the escape behavior of cats and dogs. Sometimes there is a slinking or creeping away; more often there is a wild dash, as when the terrified cat runs for a tree. Her behavior is adaptive in the sense that she makes for a particular tree, avoids obstacles between it and herself, and maintains a constant orientation away from the dog and toward the tree.

Continued flight does not have the mechanical rigidity and uniformity of a simple reflex; it is persistent goal-oriented activity. To be sure, the coordinated muscular contractions occurring in locomotion are reflexive, but the behavioral character and orientation of flight are regulated by the environmental setting. Normal flight, therefore, should be regarded as a form of purposive behavior rather than as a mechanically rigid reflex. But perhaps the bare undirected impulse to dash away—as the taking to wing of birds or the darting reaction of fish when startled—can be considered a reflexive pattern.

There is some evidence that even decorticate cats and dogs, when stimulated by loud sounds, exhibit a blind impulse to dash away. The decorticate animal runs blindly, colliding with objects in its path. The following observations bearing on this point have been reported by Bard (1934*a*, 1934*b*).

On the eleventh day after surgical decortication, it happened, by chance, that one of the decorticate cats was exposed to the sound made by steam escaping under high pressure. At the time, this animal was walking slowly about and licking the floor. The moment the stimulation occurred, she abruptly retracted and lowered her head, crouched, mewed, and then dashed off, running rapidly in a slinking manner with the head, chest, abdomen, and tail close to the floor. After blindly colliding with several objects in her path, she came to rest in a corner, crouching and mewing plaintively, with eyes wide open, pupils dilated, and hair of the back and tail standing erect. A few minutes after the noise had ceased, the cat resumed her previous behavior. Repetition of the noise a little later produced the same response. Similar avoiding behavior appeared again when a noise was made by water running from a tap through a narrow nozzle.

A second decorticate cat gave the same kind of response to the hiss of escaping steam. The response of a third animal was confined to crouching, retraction of the head, plaintive vocalization, and widening of the eyes and pupils. This animal never dashed off. With a fourth cat the only response observed when stimulated was a twitching of several muscles and erection of the hair.

Two of three decorticate dogs also manifested similar avoidance behavior. The response was a retraction of the head, crouching low to the floor, crawling on the abdomen or shivering. The third animal, interestingly enough, exhibited rage instead of fear when stimulated by loud sounds. Bard states that rage could be readily distinguished from fear both by its positive characteristics—baring of the teeth, growling, attack—and by the absence of an impulse to slink away or escape from the source of sound.

Although Bard designates these avoiding responses as *fear*, it is possible that the term *pain avoidance* would be more appropriate. The hissing or whistling noises which evoked the escape impulses were intense; they may have been above the pain threshold of decorticate cats and dogs. The possibility should be checked by further experiments in which pain thresholds of auditory stimulation are measured.

Bard's observations show that the blind impulse to dash away was not invariably present in decerebrate cats and dogs. But with every animal there were some signs of autonomic discharge, such as hair raising and dilation of the pupil, whether or not the animal dashed away. The observations leave us uncertain as to the precise definition of fear in decerebrate cats and dogs.

A similar uncertainty exists concerning the definition of the fear response in man. Writers who have described fear often mention the wide opening of the eyes with dilation of the pupils. This feature of fear is clearly shown in Figure 41*a*. But the ocular responses are only part of a more widespread response pattern.

Watson's description of the fear pattern, as I noted previously, contained elements of startle, the Moro reflex, crying, and sometimes, with older children, an impulse to escape. It is confusing, as Hunt (1939) pointed out, to group together discrete patterns under such terms as *body jerk* or *fear*. What is needed is further observation and analysis of specific patterns of response in the infant, child, and adult, without bias concerning what constitutes the emotion of fear.

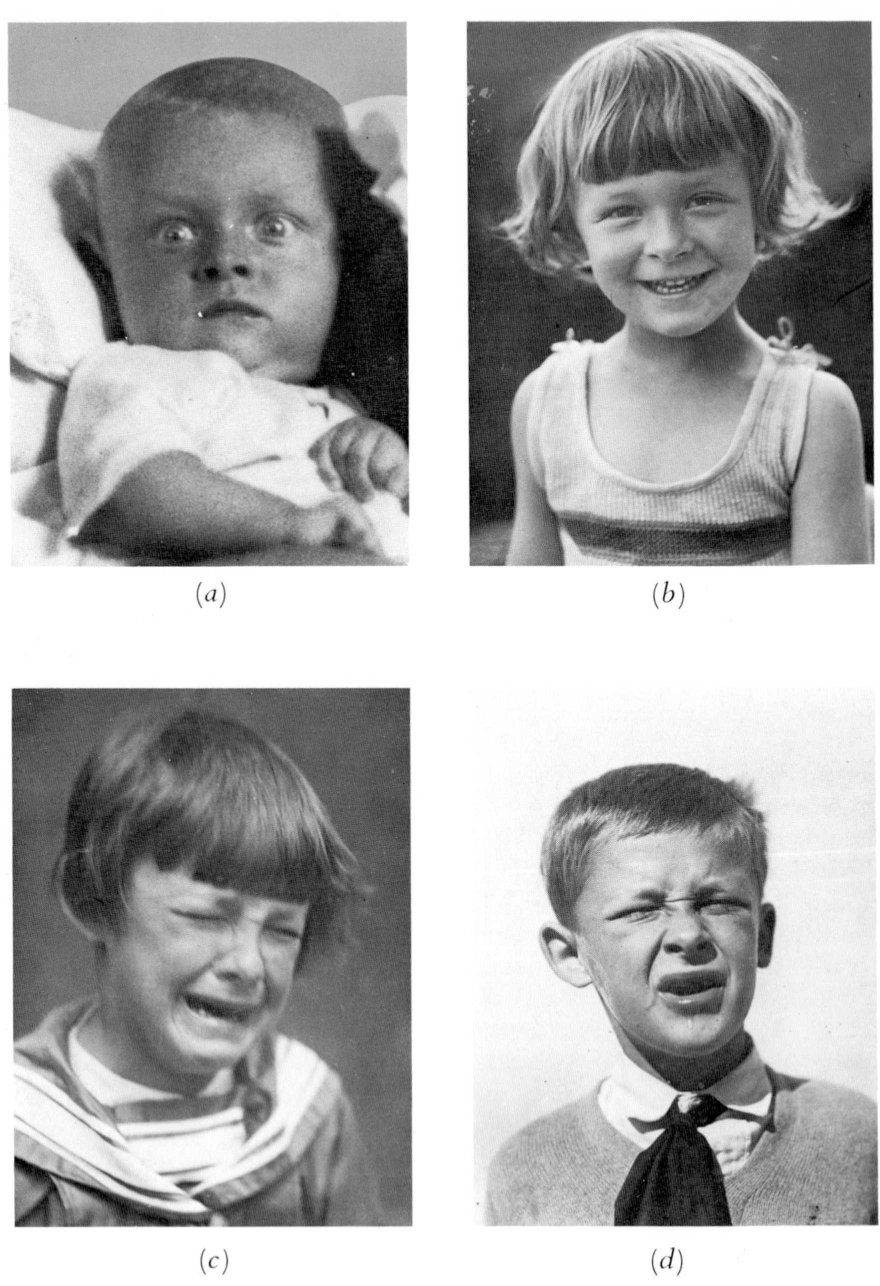

(*a*) (*b*)

(*c*) (*d*)

Figure 41. Facial expressions: (*a*) Fear. (*b*) Laughing child. (*c*) Crying child. (*d*) Disgust. *Courtesy of* Nadie Kohts, Moscow, U.S.S.R.. These expressions are discussed in following pages.

Organic Patterns of Sexual Response. An objective account of sexual behavior in animals includes a description of both male and female patterns of response. These patterns are reflexive in their original nature even though in man they may have become modified by social conditioning. The reflexive sexual patterns are clearly revealed in animal behavior. The ethologist, Tinbergen (1951), has described the interlocking reproductive patterns of male and female fish and birds. The male and female patterns of mammals are also interrelated.

Female Patterns. When a normal female cat is in estrus, as indicated by a swollen, congested condition of the genital organs and by the fact that males are strongly attracted to her, she behaves in a characteristic manner. This behavior has been described by Bard (1934*b*) as follows:

> Resting on forearms and chest with pelvis elevated and tail raised the animal executes alternate treading movements of the hindlegs and emits a curious low sound not heard at other times. This posture and this action are maintained for hours at a time even when the cat is left entirely alone. It can be said of such animals that they are bound by this pattern of behavior, for it is difficult, short of some excessive or unusual disturbance, to induce them to act in any other way. If now the vulval region be gently tapped or rubbed the treading is accentuated, and the pelvis is further elevated and the tail is raised until it is perpendicular to the vertebral axis. If a male be present and does not at once approach, the female is likely to go to him and roll playfully before him. When the male is aroused he attempts to hold the female by the loose skin of the back of the neck and this usually induces a certain amount of spitting and growling. [442]

In the decorticate cat essentially the same behavior can be evoked. Bard reports that on the twenty-ninth day after the final cerebral removal an animal came into heat.

Insertion of a thermometer into the vagina immediately induced loud growling, lowering of head and chest, elevation of pelvis and tail, and treading movements of the hind legs. Except for the growling, the pattern is identical with that shown spontaneously by normal cats in estrus. The behavior was maintained for the few moments during which the thermometer remained in contact with the genitalia. On removal of the instrument the cat rolled over onto her side and, with face upward, playfully rubbed the back of her head and neck against the floor. This sequence of events was repeated on again inserting the thermometer. Furthermore, the typical posture of estrus was assumed and the treading occurred whenever the vulval region was tapped gently or rubbed. Stimulation of other parts of the body failed to produce this behavior; it is significant that insertion of a thermometer into the rectum never evoked the sexual response pattern.

Fulton (1938) has stated that the patterns of sexual behavior are laid down in the spinal cord. While experimenting with spinal dogs he found that a gentle manipulation of the external genitalia of the female elicits contractions of the uterus and probably also increased vaginal secretions. Sherrington and Goltz reported that a spinal bitch was sucessfully impregnated and delivered a litter of normal puppies after the usual period of gestation.

Male Patterns. With spinal dogs and cats, the male exhibits an erection of the penis on gentle manipulation of the skin of the thighs or the genitals. The same has been reported in the spinal monkey. Ejaculation, also, may be brought about in the same way. In the spinal dog manipulation of the genitalia causes the animal to assume a copulatory posture. With humans, in some cases in which there has been an injury breaking the spinal cord, it has been reported that both erection and ejaculation can occur.

Earlier observations on the copulatory posture of the male frog during the breeding season indicate that once the posture has been developed, actual decapitation of the frog does not disturb the pattern.

In view of the above evidence it is correct to conclude that the behavioral patterns of both sexes are organized in the subcortical regions of the nervous system. In this respect sexual responses are very similar to those of rage, startle, and other patterns described in this chapter.

The innate nature of copulatory behavior in the rat has been demonstrated by Stone (1922, 1926). He reared male and female rats in separate cages until they were sexually mature. When a mating test was given, both male and female response patterns appeared at once.

The sexual behavior of man contains response patterns which are similar to reflexes. In the complex sexual activities of civilized man these patterns are often modified or inhibited through social customs and taboos. Esthetic and romantic interests color human sexual behavior; ethical and practical considerations complicate it.

These complications do not concern us here. Despite all cultural factors, such reflexive patterns as erection, copulatory movement, ejaculation, and uterine contractions can be found in fairly constant form throughout the world.

Beach (1956) demonstrated that there are two mechanisms in sexual activation—the one general and hormonal, the other specific and neural. Mating behavior is regulated reflexively as well as chemically.

Smiling and Laughing as Patterns of Response. When a child is told that he may have a vacation trip, he jumps up and down and claps his hands in joy. Smiling and laughing, he talks excitedly about the coming event. He is eager to start. Among the varied manifestations of joy two only will be considered in this section: The related patterns of smiling and laughing.

The smile and the laugh of joy differ in degree rather than in kind. A smile may increase to a broad smile and then burst into vigorous laughter; or, as frequently happens, a paroxysm of laughter quiets down into a smile or other mild expression of cheerfulness.

Smiling and laughing are similar in that both response patterns are evoked by the same general kind of situation. They are similar also in that both are processes in which there is a general relaxation of muscle tonus in the face as well as in other parts of the body.

Laughing differs from smiling in that it is accompanied by vocalizations. The mouth in laughter is widely opened; the vocal cords are adjusted for sound production and the air is forced out by rhythmic contractions of the muscles of respiration.

That smiling and laughing are innate patterns of human response may be illustrated by reference to the case of a ten-year-old girl who had been blind and deaf from birth. Being thus cut off completely from the visual and auditory stimulations of her social environment, she could not be influenced by the facial expressions and vocalizations of other persons. Goodenough (1932) observed the child an hour or more daily for a period of several weeks. Motion pictures and stills were taken; notes were made on the spot. See also the report on this case by McCarthy (1929). On one occasion a small china doll was dropped inside the neck of the child's dress and the immediate response was photographed. The body became tense, particularly the muscles of neck and shoulder; the mouth opened part way; the sightless eyes opened to their fullest extent and the eyebrows were raised. The left hand at once began to grope for the toy. Both the posture and the facial expression indicated what we ordinarily call startled attention.

In the present context we are interested in this child's behavior when, after a struggle, she at last succeeded in reaching the doll. When she got it out she threw herself back in the chair with feet drawn up under her and laughed loudly. Both the hand containing the doll and the empty hand were raised in an attitude of delight. There were peals of hearty laughter, which later faded away leaving a smile of pleased satisfaction.

In this instance there was an element of surprise which created a tension. Recovery of the doll released this tension and laughter occurred.

That surprise and tension-relief are present in the laughter of normal children may be illustrated by the response of the child to tickling. If the element of surprise is lacking, the child does not laugh while being tickled. When he attempts to tickle his own ribs, for example, there is no uncertainty, no surprise, and also no laughter. But the sudden thrust of the tickler, followed by a light contact, brings immediate laughter.

That smiling and laughing are innate patterns is indicated also by the fact that these responses can be elicited during the first year of infancy. In an observational study of smiling and laughing during the first year of life, Washburn (1929) employed ten or more stimulating situations. A sample of the kind of situation which she found to be highly effective in producing *smiling* is this:

> The child was placed in the dorsal position, in about the center of the table space, with feet toward the experimenter. The experimenter then leaned over, placing her hands on the table in the region of the subject's hips. The arms were kept stiff, thus controlling the distance which the experimenter leaned toward the child. The experimenter then "chirruped" to the child. The sound was caused by closing the jaws, opening the somewhat protruded lips, and drawing the air in through the closed teeth while contracting and relaxing the tongue three or four times. The experimenter then smiled and said, "Come on, then, give us a smile," repeating the whole three or four times, if the child did not smile at once. [470]

An example of the kind of social situation used to evoke *laughter* is presented in the following account:

> With the subject in the dorsal position, in the center of the table space, feet towards the experimenter, the experimenter grasped his hands in hers and held his arms out at the side, shoulder level, leaving the trunk exposed. The experimenter's head was then playfully shaken from side to side and rapidly ducked until it came into contact with the center of the child's body, when it was immediately withdrawn again. As the head was lowered, *"ah-boo"* was said, in a long-drawn-out manner. This was repeated at least three times, and more often if the response was increasing in vividness. If there was no response or a negative one, it was repeated later in the period, or the mother was substituted as stimulator. If the child preferred the seated position, the experimenter drew him toward the edge of the table, held his hands and arms out at the side, knelt in front of the table and proceeded as above bringing her head into contact with the child's body about half way between the arms and hips. [473-474]

In general, the situations which arouse smiling and laughing are *social* in nature. This point has been stressed by Kenderdine (1931) in her study of laughter in the pre–school child.[1] She reported that out of 223 situations in which laughter was observed, only fourteen or 6.3 percent occurred when the child was alone. The presence of other persons seems to be an essential element in the occurrence of laughter

[1]In a study of laughter I found (1937) that, with a group of 240 college students, laughing was attributed to social situations in 98 percent of the instances.

in children, although the mere presence of others does not mean that there will necessarily be an increased amount of laughter.

Kenderdine found that preschool children laughed most frequently in situations which involved motions—motions made by the child himself or those made by other persons or by toys. Next in effectiveness were situations regarded as socially unacceptable, such as kicking a person, belching, or other bad manners; and third, situations in which an element of humor was appreciated, as in a joke.

The facial expression of a joyful child is portrayed in Figure 41*b*. Laughter in the chimpanzee is shown in Figure 4 on page 16. There is an undeniable similarity between human and simian laughter.

For a detailed description of the pattern of laughing, I have selected from Darwin's (1872) classical work upon the expression of the emotions the facts in the following paragraph:

> The vocalization of laughter is produced by deep inspirations followed by short, interrupted, spasmodic contractions of the chest, and especially of the diaphragm. From the shaking of the body the head nods to and fro. Through contraction of the zygomatic muscles, the mouth is opened more or less widely with the corners drawn back and a little up; the upper lip is somewhat raised so that the upper front teeth are exposed; the cheeks are drawn upward. At the same time the orbicular muscles (those surrounding the eyes) are contracted above and below. This forms wrinkles under the eyes and, with older people, at their outer ends, which are highly characteristic both of laughing and smiling. The eyes are bright and sparkling owing to increased secretion of the lacrimal glands. The nose appears shortened, and the skin on the bridge becomes finely wrinkled in transverse lines, with other oblique longitudinal lines on the sides. There is a well-marked nasolabial fold which runs from the wing of each nostril to the corner of the mouth.

That the bodily pattern of laughing is organized on the subcortical levels of the nervous system is indicated by certain pathological evidence in which brain tumors have destroyed the normal functional relationship between centers in the hypothalamus and those in the cerebral cortex. These unfortunate patients are still able to laugh. They may laugh, however, in inappropriate situations.

One such patient, described by Lashley (1938) in a footnote of a paper dealing with neural centers of emotional patterns, used to laugh spasmodically when reference was made to his very distressing home situation. The patient not only denied any subjective feeling of amusement but claimed that he experienced sadness and depression during the spasms of laughter.

Patterns of Crying and Weeping. In human weeping during grief there is a disturbance of normal respiration. There are vocalizations which can be heard as sobbing or crying. Tears are plentiful. In grief there are other bodily changes as well. The "lump in the throat" can be referred to a contraction of smooth muscles in the alimentary canal at the level of the throat. The skeletal muscles are weak and flabby. The bodily posture is altered. The flexor muscles dominate the extensors so that we commonly speak of the person as being "bowed over" with grief. The grief-stricken widow, for example, walks with head and shoulders bent, her eyes fixed on the ground; her step falters.

Grief is a complex emotional state. In it one can recognize various bodily changes. Only two of these—the vocal-respiratory disturbance and tears—are discussed in the present section.

The order of events in the crying of a Japanese infant has been described by Borgquist (1906) as follows: (1) At the seventh week the mouth is drawn into a square shape; in the twelfth week a protrusion of the lower lip precedes crying. (2) Next the eyes are closed, and (3) the infant makes the vocal sound *â â â*. During the ninth week, (4) a reddening of the face is definitely observed. It begins in the face, spreads up over the top of the head, and simultaneously down toward the feet. In the ninth week, also, sobbing is clearly present. Finally, (5) there are tears. This infant shed tears within two days after birth, which is exceptionally early.

The vehemence of crying of infants is related to its duration. Bayley's (1932) judgments of vehemence and persistence show the following relationship:

PERSISTENCE			VEHEMENCE
	Slight whimpering	Moderate	Violent
Very persistent	4	85	204
Average	33	203	21
Intermittent	189	74	11

Although there is a subjective element in these estimations of vehemence, the judgments are probably dependable since they were made at the time of the crying. Differences are so gross that there can be little doubt that the most vehement crying is also the most persistent and that the least intense crying is intermittent (whimpering).

When an infant screams, his respiration is spasmodic and violent. During the respiratory disturbance the shoulders are generally raised. The screaming itself consists of prolonged expirations; there are short and rapid inspirations. The infant's mouth is widely opened and the lips are retracted to produce a squarish form, the gums or teeth being more or less exposed. The eyelids are firmly closed and the skin around the eyes is wrinkled, the forehead being contracted into a frown.

The musculature which gives the facial expression in weeping is described as follows. The facts of the description are taken from Darwin (1872):

> The corrugator muscles of the brow contract, drawing the eyebrows downward and inward to produce the vertical furrows of the frown and the simultaneous disappearance of the transverse wrinkles across the forehead. The orbicular muscles contract at the same time as the corrugators and produce wrinkles around the eyes. Then the pyramidal muscles of the nose (procerus) contract and draw the eyebrows and skin of the forehead still lower down, producing transverse wrinkles across the base of the nose. The muscles running to the upper lip contract and raise the lip. This action also draws upward the flesh of the cheeks producing a fold on each cheek from near the wings of the nostrils to the corners of the mouth and below.

An obvious characteristic of human weeping is the presence of tears; but tears are not essential to crying. Tears are absent in the crying of very young infants and often during the reflexive outcries of bodily pain when freed from the complication of a social factor.

In this connection it is interesting that Goodenough (1932) does not report tearful grief in the behavior of the blind and deaf girl which she observed. She gives, however, the following account of resentment in response to frustration:

> Mild forms of resentment are shown by turning her head, pouting the lips, or frowning; sometimes by crouching down into a little heap with head on knees, or by thrusting the thumb and index finger into the nostrils. . . . More intense forms are shown by throwing back the head and shaking it from side to side, during which the lips are retracted, exposing the teeth which are sometimes clenched. This is accompanied by whimpering or whining noises, rising at intervals to short high-pitched staccato yelps. In her most violent outbursts the entire body is thrown back and forth; the feet are twisted around each other or beat violently upon the floor; the vocalizations are intensified and as a rule become shriller in pitch; and the head and chest are beaten with sharp flail-like movements of the arm. These blows are usually struck with the open hand, but at times the clenched fist is used. [331]

In this case there are definite vocalizations but no tears. Tears are lacking also in the distress cries of many animals. The crying of the chimpanzee, for example, is tearless. See Figure 4 (page 16) and compare the chimpanzee with the crying child shown in Figure 41*c*.

Tears are by no means limited to the emotion of grief. Lacrimal secretion occurs in other kinds of emotion as well as under nonemotional conditions. In laughter, for example, the bright eye is due to lacrimal discharge; in the paroxysms of laughter and in great joy tears may be seen at times to roll down the cheeks. Although as a rule tears are more frequent and copious in weeping than during laughter, this difference in lacrimal secretion is one of degree rather than of kind.

Lund (1930) has noted that tears flow under the following non-emotional conditions: (1) irritation of the eyeball and lid through the presence of a foreign body; (2) irritation of the mucous membrane of the nose, for example, by a whiff of ammonia or by mechanical stimulation; (3) stimulation of the eye by infra-red or ultra-violet light; (4) during the discharge of various reflexes such as coughing, yawning, sneezing, retching.

In view of these facts it is suggested that the term *crying* be reserved for emotional distress in which vocalization occurs. There are different kinds of crying. Crying occurs during pain, grief, fear, surprise, and other conditions. Crying may or may not be tearful. The term *weeping* should be reserved for emotional distress in which tears are present. Weeping may be silent or nearly so, as when the individual sobs.

Weeping occurs in complex, typically *social* situations. According to Lund, it is not merely loss or bereavement which brings tears. Rather it is the presence of some alleviating or happy circumstance within an otherwise distressing situation which is the immediate occasion for tears. At a funeral, for example, tears flow when the speaker eulogizes the deceased by saying that he was a fine father to his children, a great-hearted citizen, and so forth. On the screen, weeping is occasioned by the reunion of lovers after some harrowing experience or by the generous and kind remark of a poor, crippled boy. There is regularly some beneficent or alleviating circumstance in the situations which evoke the tears of weeping.

Contrary to common belief, the deep depression of psychotic individuals is tearless. Lund found that tears of psychotics are the most plentiful in *mixed* emotional states—during the transition from a depressed to an exalted state.

The Disgust Pattern and Its Relation to Gastrointestinal Tone. The emotion of disgust, according to McDougall (1926), is shown by two impulses. First, there is an impulse to reject from the mouth or otherwise to avoid substances which are foul-smelling and often noxious. The second impulse of repulsion is excited by cutaneous contact with slimy and slippery substances. This impulse is a shrinking away of the body, accompanied by a throwing forward of the hands or by a "creepy" shudder.

Although shuddering may be regarded as a pattern of response occurring in disgust, the former of the two impulses (nausea and vomiting) will be taken up first and more in detail because it is a clear-cut pattern. In fact, it may be designated as the basic pattern in disgust.

Subjectively considered, disgust is experienced as a nausea or sickishness which in its extreme form is the act of vomiting. In moderate disgust the mouth is opened widely as if to let an offensive morsel drop out. There may be spitting, blowing out through the protruded lips, guttural sounds such as *ach* or *ugh*. In intense disgust the mouth is rounded to a shape identical with that occurring in the act of vomiting; the upper lip is strongly retracted, producing wrinkles beside the nose. There is retching or actual vomiting. Figure 41*d* pictures the facial expression of disgust in a boy.

Innately, nausea and vomiting are produced by the presence of irritating substances in the stomach. Later, through conditioning, the flavor, odor, appearance or even the conscious recall of these substances may induce incipient or actual vomiting.

The writer recalls that as a boy he walked through a vacant lot where he found the body of a rabbit covered with maggots and giving off the strong odor of decaying flesh. The experience was so sickening that he retched repeatedly. For months thereafter he avoided this lot and found himself nauseated when he went near the spot where the dead rabbit had been found.

Less intense experiences of disgust are common in everyday life. To a sensitive and highly civilized person it is disgusting to find a fly in the milk, a hair in the butter. The disgust may be due to the thought that these things contaminate the food with filth or that they might be eaten with it.

Certain topics of conversation are definitely taboo at the table, for example, such subjects as vomiting, diseases, and elimination. These topics are sickening to many individuals and for this reason are not discussed at the table in polite society. Of course, a topic which nauseates one person may not disturb another. There are marked individual differences.

Disgust has been studied experimentally by Brunswick (1924). To obtain a graphic record he trained subjects to swallow a rubber tube with a small deflated balloon tucked inside it, following the method of Cannon, and others. When the balloon was in place, it was inflated through the tube so as to press against the wall of the stomach or duodenum. The changes in air pressure due to gastrointestinal contraction and relaxation were graphically recorded. A similar technique was used in the rectum for recording changes of muscular tone.

To produce disgust, Brunswick used decaying rat flesh. A small piece of rat flesh was placed in a test tube which was corked and allowed to decay. At the proper time the experimenter brought out the tube, uncorked it, and placed the open end directly under the subject's nose. After a wait of ten to fifteen seconds to give the subject time to react to this stimulation, the experimenter announced: "This is a piece of rat flesh allowed to decay." The nature of the odor made the announcement plausible, and the statement sometimes intensified the subject's disgust. After another ten or fifteen seconds of delay the experimenter, with an intentionally shaky hand, allowed the end of the tube to touch the subject's nose. Brunswick states that this apparently accidental contact effectively increased the disgust.

The experiment demonstrates clearly that during the experience of disgust there is an *increase* of gastrointestinal muscle tone. In other unpleasant emotional states—such as those evoked by an unexpected turning off of the light, shooting a pistol in the dark, threatening with a pistol and then giving an unanticipated shot into the air, dashing water into the subject's face—in all these states the tone of the stomach is *decreased*. Disgust, therefore, includes an effect upon gastrointestinal tone which is opposite to that of other disagreeable emotions.

Brunswick suggests that this effect for disgust may be interpreted as the combination of a specific "disgust effect" plus a general "unpleasantness effect"; that opposed contraction and relaxation may occur in two different axes of the stomach, or in different groups or layers of muscle fibers, or in different parts of the gastric wall. Be that as it may, the important point is that the disgust-effect on gastrointestinal tone is different from that of other unpleasant emotions.

From the standpoint of the pattern-response theory of emotion one might well identify disgust with nausea, including incipient as well as overt vomiting. The question, *What disgusts us?* then becomes, *What environmental conditions evoke the nausea-vomiting type of response?* Another question is this: *How, through conditioning, is this innate response modified and attached to situations not originally producing it?*

Returning now to McDougall's view that in addition to the characteristic disgust response to foul odors and tastes there is also an instinctive revulsion against slimy contacts with worms, slugs, frogs, and the like, it is clear that if we identify disgust with the nausea-vomiting pattern, slimy contacts are disgusting only in so far as they arouse the tendency to vomit. In this connection one recalls Brunswick's finding that cutaneous contact with the tube of decaying rat flesh increased the disgust. If the nature of the object is not recognized, surprise or fear is more likely to be induced than disgust. On the other hand, if the slimy contact produces a shudder (as it may), this is a pattern of response certainly distinguishable from nausea and incipient vomiting.

The term *disgust* is sometimes applied to sexual situations, but it is an open question whether the word, so used, does not refer simply to an aversion to the sexual act, an attitude resting upon some unfortunate sexual experience.

Novelists, further, sometimes use the word *disgust* to describe the response to complex experiences such as seeing a master flog a slave or seeing a native island girl tortured for infidelity. The stories about cruel treatment of prisoners are said to disgust us. When such experiences produce sickishness or actual vomiting, then it is psychologically correct to refer to them as genuinely disgusting. But if a sickishness is not aroused, the term *horror* may more correctly describe the emotional upset.

Emotional Defecation and Urination. Involuntary evacuation of the bowel and bladder during emotional excitement has been repeatedly observed in many situations. Through early social training, the child learns to control the eliminative processes, but in extremes of fear or terror the sphincter control may be lost. Even in mild anxiety, such as stage fright before an important speech or performance, there is sometimes an increased urge to urinate or defecate.

With the rat, an emotional disturbance is produced when the animal is placed in an unfamiliar environment or when the subject is roughly handled by a stranger. This disturbance is shown by the increased frequency of urination and defecation.

Hall (1934) employed the frequency of elimination as an index of emotionality. He placed the rat in a circular enclosure, eight feet in diameter, with a food pan at the center. Ordinarily rats explore a novel environment; they explore beside the wall before running in an open field, but with Hall's apparatus they had to leave the wall to reach the food located at the center. At first there was much exploration in the outer zone of the apparatus, but with habituation to eating in the center this outer-zone activity decreased.

Throughout the course of the experiment, Hall measured the weight of food consumed and counted the number of fecal boluses evacuated on the apparatus during successive stages of the experiment. Figure 42 shows the grams of food consumed and the total number of feces passed by a group of twenty-six male rats. The data indicate that as strangeness of the environment wears off, the frequency of defecation in the situation declines. A similar result was obtained for the frequency of urination.

As long as the animal is excited enough to defecate or urinate frequently while exploring the apparatus, he will eat little food. In only 20 of the 728 possible concurrences did the rats defecate and eat within the same experimental period. Only after they had become sufficiently adjusted to the new apparatus to overcome the tendency to stay near the wall, and only after they had left off defecating and urinating, did they commence to eat.

Figure 42 shows the total number of grams of food eaten per day as the rats became habituated to the open-field feeding. As the strangeness of the environment decreased (in other words, as familiarity and degree of habituation increased), there was an increase in the amount of food consumed. The two variables are inversely related.

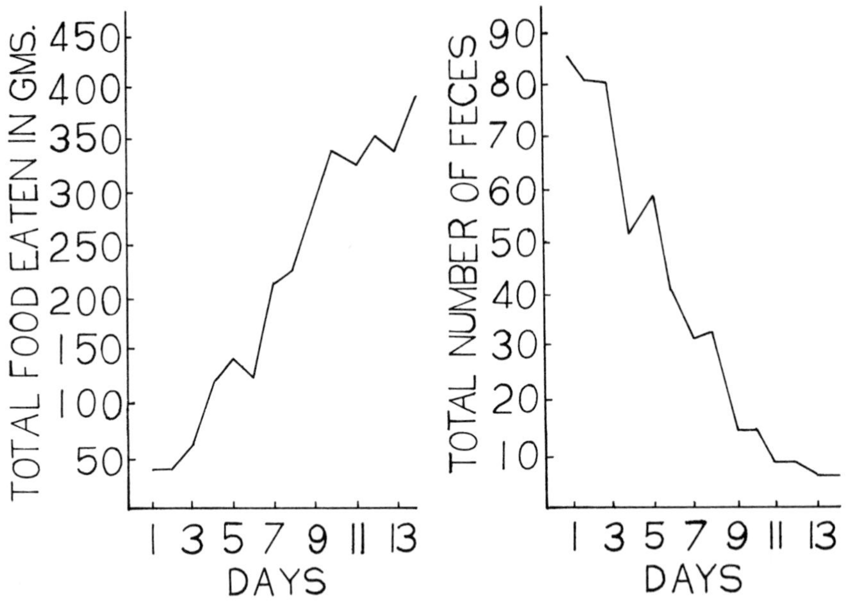

Figure 42. At the left, total grams of food eaten per day in the center of an open field. At the right, total number of fecal boluses passed per day in the field. N = 26 male rats. *After* Hall (1934).

Hall's open-field test of "emotionality" has given rise to a great deal of research especially on the genetic aspect of emotional responsiveness. For an introduction to the early history of Hall's work see Broadhurst (1969).

A question can be raised as to how far defecation and urination are indexes of general "emotionality." It is certain that in many complex human emotions these evacuative responses are absent. Perhaps emotional defecation is a symptom of affective disturbances in the fear-anxiety category. Further research upon this problem is indicated.

CRITIQUE OF THE PATTERN-REACTION DEFINITION OF EMOTION

On pages 181-3, I criticized Watson's view that an emotion is an innate pattern of response to specific stimulating conditions; and that emotional patterns can be conditioned and extinguished according to the principles of classical conditioning. Most of the objections to Watson's view apply also to the general concept that an emotion is an innate pattern of response to stimulation.

The pattern-reaction view of emotion makes a strong appeal to physiologists and physiological psychologists. There are obvious reasons for this: (1) The patterns of reaction described above are prominent components of emotional behavior. (2) Temporospatial patterns can be clearly observed in the field and in the laboratory and the conditions of their occurrence controlled. (3) The principles of emotional development that apply to simple reflexes and to instinctive patterns of behavior appear to apply also to the acquisition of complex emotional behaviors. (4) Behavioral patterns can be described in terms of stimulus and response. The pattern-reaction concept of emotion fits smoothly into the S-R paradigm. (5) The neural mechanisms that integrate some of the emotional patterns have been localized in subcortical regions of the central nervous system and have been described accurately.

These are sound advantages of an objective pattern-reaction definition of emotion. It is clear why Watson, Bard, and others, have defined emotion as a pattern of response to stimulation.

Difficulties with the Pattern-Reaction Definition of Emotion. In the foregoing sections we have considered some of the main patterns of reaction that appear in emotional behavior. Whether or not one holds to the pattern-reaction definition of emotion, he must faithfully describe and study the patterns that are observed. He must examine the conditions that elicit them, the way they develop, the neural mechanisms that control them, etc. The task of describing patterns of response is straightforward and scientifically important quite apart from any difficulties in defining emotion. Certainly no bias concerning the nature of emotion should interfere with the task of describing emotional patterns objectively. The patterns must be studied in their own right and in relation to the conditions that elicit emotional perturbations.

Despite these remarks I believe that the pattern-response concept does not adequately define emotion. There are several difficulties with the view that an emotion is an integrated pattern of response to stimulation:

1. The pattern-reaction definition of emotion provides no criterion for distinguishing between emotional patterns and non-emotional reflexes and instincts. Coughing, sneezing, hiccoughing, sucking, swallowing, blinking, etc., are well-integrated reflexive patterns. They are not ordinarily regarded as emotions. Why not? I do not know a satisfactory answer to this question. It is commonly assumed that emotional patterns involve visceral processes but visceral processes are also present in

coughing, sneezing, sucking, and other simple reflexes. Again, the startle pattern was described above with other patterns but Landis and Hunt regard startle as a general reflex of the skeletal muscles and not a true emotion. Startle is completed in the fraction of a second before visceral processes can get under way. Landis and Hunt regard visceralization as essential to emotion.

2. The pattern-reaction definition of emotion disregards the affective and dynamic aspect of all emotions. Viewed from this angle, the pattern-reaction definition appears to be incomplete. It ignores important facts relating to acute disorganization at the level of the cerebral cortex. I prefer to speak of patterns of response that occur *in* or *during* emotional disturbances.

It may be that the cerebral disturbance *releases* the emotional patterns. If this is true, the emotional patterns differ in origin from simple reflexes which are responses to peripheral stimulations.

3. Another difficulty is that of specifying precisely the grouping of elements into emotional patterns. The patterns of response that are observed in the laboratory do not correspond to the forms of behavior that in everyday life are described as emotions. For example, Watson claimed that "fear" is an innate pattern of emotion; but his description of "fear," as I noted previously, included more elementary patterns: crying, catching the breath, startle, possibly the Moro reflex, an impulse to crawl away, etc. Watson's "fear" is thus a complex of more elementary patterns. More precise definitions are required.

4. Finally, in everyday life we refer to pride, mother love, and the like, as "emotions"—but what reflexive patterns correspond to these complex affective states? Also we identify emotions by the forms of adaptive behavior that restore complacency. Flight reduces fear. Aggressive attack relieves anger. Sexual behavior reduces the emotion of lust. The adaptive behavior is well integrated but can we define *emotion* as organized, purposive activity? If we could, there would be no need for the concept of emotion.

Specific Patterns of Reaction as Fragments of Emotional Behavior. Delgado and Mir (1969) have described their work on intracranial stimulation with electrodes permanently implanted in the brains of rhesus monkeys. Different points in an animal's brain could be stimulated by radio control while the subjects lived within the permanent cage of a colony. Individual and social behavior were recorded and quantified by time-lapse photography; vocalizations were tape recorded and analyzed spectrographically; spontaneous and evoked electrical activity of the brain was recorded by telemetry. With these sophisticated techniques the typical patterns of response which recur and which can be observed, recorded, identified, were analyzed in space and time. Intracerebral activity was recorded and sometimes correlated with observed behavior.

The working hypothesis of Delgado and Mir was that emotional expression is composed of sequences of specific behavioral fragments that include autonomic responses, vocalization, facial expression, tonic and phasic motor activity, and that, depending on the cerebral area stimulated, these responses may be evoked as isolated fragments or as organized sequences. They proposed that activation of neuronal mechanisms by brain stimulations may have effects similar to activation by sensory inputs from the environment, and that direct stimulation of the brain permits the artificial manipulation of emotions as well as of emotional reactivity.

Aggressive behavior, for example, includes patterns of threatening display, vocalization, chasing, grabbing, and biting. These fragments of reaction are included within the full pattern of aggressive behavior which is well organized, purposefully oriented, and adapted to changes in the environmental situation. Again, penile erection in the rhesus monkey has been evoked by stimulation of the supraoptic region of the hypothalamus. But the effect seems to be automatic and without sexual meaning since other elements of complete sexual behavior are lacking.

In general, Delgado and Mir claim that emotional behavior and expression are composed of fragments which include autonomic responses, vocalization, facial expression, tonic and phasic motor activity; and that these fragments can be elicited as isolated units or as parts of complex, integrated, purposive activity. The specific patterns of reaction depend upon the activation of specific cerebral structures, determined by the decoding of particular sensory inputs. Brain stimulation may produce specific patterns or the more complete organized emotional behavior depending upon the place stimulated.

Delgado proposed that emotions may be identified by a series of characteristics: lack of voluntary control, positive or negative reinforcement, motivation and driving properties, lasting modifications of the responsive state, conscious interpretation of sensory inputs, social contagion, feedback, nonlinearity of the stimulus-response relation, disturbances of ongoing behavior, and dynamic sequences of behavioral categories. This is clearly an omnibus or shotgun type of definition. It is far removed from the definition of emotion as a specific pattern of response to stimulation.

Reflexes, Instincts, and Emotional Patterns. The concept of *pattern* applies to simple reflexes and complex instinctive sequences as well as to emotional expressions. A question can be raised, therefore, as to how emotional patterns differ from reflexes and instincts. Relative to this matter Jerram L. Brown (1969) has written:

> I offer a tentative definition: . . . instinct is the collection of mechanisms through which the effects of evolution on behavior are mediated. *Instinctive* would mean, essentially, evolved. However, since all behavioral mechanisms have clearly evolved, use of the term *instinct* would serve merely to emphasize the importance of evolution for the trait or difference in question. The temptation toward a false dichotomy between instinct and learning would, therefore, be reduced. A second consequence of this definition is that *reflex* is interpreted as a subcategory of instinct. The physiological mechanisms underlying reflexive behavior are thereby brought into the same sphere of discourse as those earlier assigned to instinctive behavior. The similarities between these two types of behavioral mechanisms are fundamental; the differences, secondary. Thus interpreted, the study of instinct can be seen as one of the central problems in behavioral biology. [1085, italics added]

Brown's definition raises a question as to whether emotional patterns should be regarded as reflexes, as instincts, or as different in some way from these categories. It is clear, as Darwin pointed out long ago, that the emotional expressions are products of evolution and that they have survival value in the struggle for existence. But Darwin was unable to point to the survival value of many emotional expressions; he sought to explain such expressions in terms of the constitution of the nervous system.

It seems to me that those emotional expressions which are clearly and obviously *emotional*—fright, rage, agony, weeping, laughing, etc.—indicate a perturbation of biologically adaptive behavior. These expressions indicate a disturbance of the organism in its inevitable attempts to cope with environmental problems and situations. Many emotional expressions, of course, *are* biologically adaptive, e.g., autotomy in the crab, but many lack biological utility except, perhaps, in so far as they serve to communicate environmental situations and personal needs to other organisms.

It may be futile to attempt to define certain patterns of response as emotional and others as non-emotional. The concepts of reflex and instinct apply to both. But apart from definition, the investigation of all integrated patterns of response and the conditions under which they appear and are disturbed is a matter of prime importance to behavioral science.

BODILY CHANGES PRODUCED BY THE AUTONOMIC NERVOUS SYSTEM

The visceral components of emotion are regulated by the autonomic nervous system. It is important, therefore, to examine the structure and functions of the autonomic system and the way it regulates the bodily changes of emotion.

The Visceralization of Response. An organism's response (R) to a situation (S) is partly somatic, partly visceral. The two components of the total response can be represented in this way:

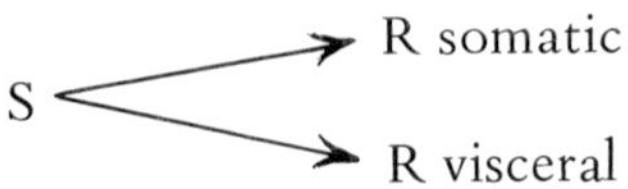

The total response is integrated, but there are degrees of visceralization.

What are the viscera? The term *viscus* (plural *viscera*) means a hollow structure such as the intestine, the tubes of the reproductive system, the blood vessels. The term is commonly used, however, to designate any soft organ located in the body cavities, such as the brain, heart, lungs, stomach, liver, etc.

Psychologists are agreed that emotional responses are highly visceralized. The blush of shame, the pallor of fear, the cold sweat of anxiety—these are visceral components of response which are outwardly observed and inwardly felt. The viscera are markedly aroused in emotional states such as rage, terror, horror, agony, laughing, and weeping.

Cameron and Magaret (1951) defined emotional reactions as: "*reactions whose non-specific visceral contribution dominates or determines them, or colors them distinctively*." This recognizes the central importance of visceral components of the emotional response. "Thus, climbing a fence in the course of a cross-country hike, and climbing it to escape a charging bull, may both involve visceral change; but in one the visceral participation is likely to be negligible, while in the other it is clearly dominant. The same distinction holds between dispassionate discussion and angry argument, between picking up one's valise on arriving at the railroad station and picking up one's child, between breaking up a radio for its parts and breaking it up as a reaction to what it says."

Cameron and Magaret emphasized the unity of the total emotional response of which the visceral component is just a part. If we try to think of some activity that is completely free from emotion, we will probably think of a routine, automatic action like knitting passively or twiddling one's thumbs. Possibly we will think of sleeping. In any event, non-emotional activity is relatively free from visceral changes; emotional activity is strongly visceralized. Thus, in the emotional displays of children we observe responses of the somatic muscles in crying, biting, striking, diffuse motor excitement, etc. We also observe the shedding of tears, the blush of anger, and other changes in glands and smooth muscles.

The patterns of response that appear during emotional disturbances contain both visceral and somatic components. In some patterns, such as the startle reflex, the somatic components appear first and constitute the pattern; visceral components may develop later and secondarily. In others, such as disgust, the visceral components are primary and the skeletal muscles adjust themselves to the primary antiperistaltic pressures.

Dominance of the Autonomic Functions. Although there are differences of opinion concerning the proper definition of emotion, there is unanimity on one point: Emotional processes involve visceral changes that are regulated by the autonomic nervous system.

The autonomic and cerebrospinal nervous systems control different organs but are interdependent in function. Changes in one system rarely occur without producing effects in the other. The perception of a threatening or enticing situation is a function of the cerebrospinal system that produces visceral changes through the autonomic system. The visceral changes, once they are aroused, feed back excitations into the cerebrospinal system. At all times—during sleeping and waking, during calm activity and emotional disruption—the autonomic and cerebrospinal systems function interdependently.

The cerebrospinal system supplies innervation to the striped muscles of the head, trunk, and limbs; the autonomic system supplies innervation to the smooth muscles and glands of the gastrointestinal, circulatory, respiratory, and urogenital tracts. In general, the cerebrospinal system sends its nerves to the somatic system of skeletal muscles and receptors at the surface of the body while the autonomic nerves are connected with smooth muscles, glands and other internal structures. The cerebrospinal system is directly concerned with adjustments of the organism to external reality; the autonomic with the essential processes of energy expenditure, metabolism and reproduction.

From the point of view of development, the autonomic system is prior and dominant. In evolution, the autonomic system is of ancient origin. In the developing embryo the autonomic nervous system is comparatively well organized prior to a comparable organization within the cerebrospinal system. Dominance of the autonomic begins prior to birth and continues throughout life. If cerebral control is lost during an emotional crisis, the autonomic functions continue (perhaps with disturbance) despite disorganization at the cerebral level. If the brain is damaged, the vegetative processes (that are essential to life) continue. Kempf (1920) has argued that the autonomic functions are dominant over those of the cerebrospinal system. But the two systems function interdependently during emotional and non-emotional activity.

Structural and Functional Divisions of the Autonomic Nervous

System. The autonomic nervous system is an aggregation of ganglia, nerves, and plexuses, through which visceral organs (smooth muscles and glands) receive their innervation. The system is made up entirely of *efferent* neurons, i.e., nerve cells organized to conduct impulses away from the central nervous system toward the visceral structures. There are, however, visceral *afferent* fibers, in close association with the autonomic nervous system, which carry excitations from the viscera back into the central nervous system.

From the point of view of anatomy the autonomic nervous system is composed of three divisions: (1) The *cranial* division is composed of fibers making their exit from the central nervous system at the base of the brain in several of the cranial nerves. (2) The *thoracicolumbar* division is composed of fibers emerging from the spinal cord at the level of the thorax and in the lumbar region. (3) The *sacral* division is composed of fibers emerging from the central nervous system at the sacrum, or pelvic level.

Fibers from the central nervous system bring impulses to ganglia where synapses are made with other fibers that carry impulses outward to the visceral structures. Those fibers bringing impulses to the ganglia are called *pre-ganglionic* fibers and those carrying impulses away from the ganglia to visceral structures are designated as *post-ganglionic* fibers. The fibers leading to the adrenal glands are different from the others in that they carry nerve impulses directly to the glands, without synapsing.

Although there are *three* structural divisions of the autonomic nervous system, there are *two* divisions when we consider the system from the point of view of function. The central division (thoracicolumbar), when considered from the physiological point of view, is commonly designated as the *sympathetic nervous system*. This system is a vast and complicated network related, in evolution, to a primitive network type of system. It functions as a unit. Neural excitations spread diffusely through the sympathetic network producing widespread and profound bodily changes in the smooth muscles and glands. The upper (cranial) and lower (sacral) divisions together constitute the *parasympathetic nervous system*. *Para* means "along the side of" or "beside." This designation is appropriate because the parasympathetic nerves are anatomically beside the sympathetic and, to a considerable extent, innervate the same effectors.

From the point of view of physiology, the sympathetic and parasympathetic nerves are functionally antagonistic. Where one kind of fiber excites, the other inhibits, and *vice versa*. See Table 8. The table shows, in the central column, some of the bodily structures that are excited by autonomic nerves. Effects produced by excitation of the sympathetic network are shown at the left. Effects of parasympathetic excitation are listed at the right. Some of the bodily structures are innervated only by sympathetic nerves; parasympathetic nerves have no effect upon them. This is true, for example, of the smooth muscles that erect the hair cells, the sweat glands, and the surface arteries.

A study of Table 8 shows that many of the bodily structures are innervated by both the sympathetic and the parasympathetic nerves.

TABLE 8
Autonomic Functions

Sympathetic Nerves	Bodily Structures	Parasympathetic Nerves
		Cranial
Dilates the pupil	Iris	Constricts the pupil
Inhibits secretion	Salivary glands	Facilitates secretion
Erects (pilomotor reflex)	Hair	
Augments secretion	Sweat glands	
Constricts	Surface arteries	
Accelerates	Heart	Inhibits
Dilates bronchioles	Lung	Contracts bronchioles
Secretes glucose	Liver	
Inhibits gastric secretion and peristalsis	Stomach	Facilitates gastric secretion and peristalsis
Constricts, giving off erythrocytes	Spleen	
Secretes adrenin	Adrenal medulla	
Inhibits smooth muscle activity	Small Intestine	Facilitates smooth muscle activity
Constricts	Visceral arteries	
		Sacral
Relaxes smooth muscle	Bladder	Contracts smooth muscle (empties)
Relaxes smooth muscle	Colon and rectum	Contracts smooth muscle (empties)
Constricts, counteracting erection	Arteries of external genitals	Dilates, causing erection
Contracts at orgasm	*Vasa deferentia*	
Contracts at orgasm	Seminal vesicles	
Contracts at orgasm	Uterus	

Where double innervation occurs the physiological actions of the two systems are opposed. Where the parasympathetic system facilitates, the sympathetic inhibits; where the parasympathetic system contracts, the sympathetic relaxes, etc. Both systems, however, function simultaneously in emotional processes and a visceral pattern results from the diffuse action of the sympathetic combined with some specific effect from a particular parasympathetic nerve.

It should be kept in mind that the sympathetic system acts diffusely to produce diverse and widespread effects. Excitations from the central nervous system spread through the central chains of ganglia and diffusely throughout the sympathetic network as a whole. The parasympathetic nerves, contrastingly, produce particular effects upon specific organs. The parasympathetic nerves send pre-ganglionic fibers directly to the organs that they innervate or, rather, to terminal ganglia close to or within these organs. Thus the third cranial nerve supplies the pupil; action through this nerve constricts the pupil, cutting down the amount of light that enters the eye. The seventh and ninth cranial nerves reach out to the salivary glands, to the mucous membranes and, through ganglia, to the lacrimal glands. The tenth cranial nerve (vagus) has a widespread distribution to heart, lungs, stomach, liver, pancreas, and intestine. The pelvic nerves supply the colon, rectum, bladder, and external genitals. By combining the diffuse action of the sympathetic system with the particular effects produced through the parasympathetic a variety of visceral patterns is possible.

Figure 43 is a schematic representation of the autonomic nervous system and the visceral afferent system. The figure shows at the left the central origin and peripheral termination of the sympathetic and parasympathetic nerves. It shows, at the right, the visceral afferent system that feeds back information about visceral changes into the central nervous system. Some of the more important visceral structures are listed in the illustration.

A detailed study of this chart is beyond our present concern. The reader interested in further details is referred to Lindsley (1951).

Cannon's Emergency Theory of Emotion. During a biological crisis, when an animal must fight or run for its life and when there is likelihood of bloodshed, profound and widespread bodily changes occur which mobilize the energies of the body for a vigorous and prolonged struggle. In fear, rage, pain, and emotional excitement there is a diffuse discharge across the sympathetic network which produces a variety of bodily changes. There is also increased secretion from the medulla of the adrenal gland. The sympathetic discharge and the adrenal secretion combine to produce bodily changes that are *serviceable* to the organism in a struggle for existence.

Summarizing the detailed findings of many experiments, Cannon (1929) wrote:

> Every one of the visceral changes that have been noted—the cessation of processes in the alimentary canal (thus freeing the energy supply for other

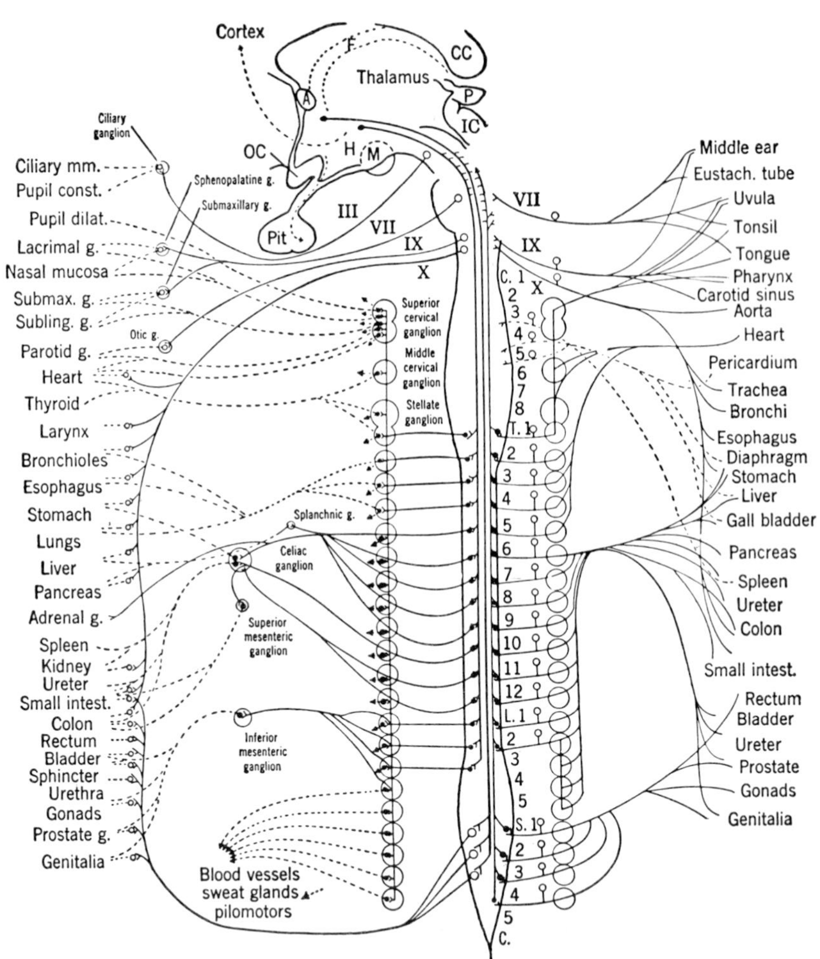

Figure 43. Schematic representation of the autonomic nervous system, showing the central origin and peripheral termination of *sympathetic* and *parasympathetic efferent pathways* on the *left* and the origin of *visceral afferent pathways* on the *right*. Cell bodies of pre- and postganglionic neurons of the parasympathetic system are symbolized by open circles; those of the sympathetic system, by solid circles. Arrows projecting from the sympathetic chain ganglia symbolize postganglionic fibers to blood vessels, sweat glands, and pilomotors. Dotted lines on the left of the figure represent efferent postganglionic fibers; those on the right are nonautonomic fibers of the phrenic nerve. Key: A—anterior commisure; CC—corpus callosum; F—fornix; H—hypothalamus; IC—inferior colliculus; M—mammillary bodies; OC—optic chiasma; P—pineal body; Pit—pituitary or hypophysis. *From* Lindsley (1951).

> parts); the shifting of blood from the abdominal organs to the organs immediately essential to muscular exertion; the increased vigor of contraction of the heart; the discharge of extra blood corpuscles from the spleen; the deeper respiration; the dilation of the bronchioles; the quick abolition of the effects of muscular fatigue; the mobilizing of sugar in the circulation—these changes are *directly serviceable in making the organism more effective in violent display of energy which fear or rage or pain may involve.* [225–226]

The bodily changes produced by a discharge across the sympathetic network are supplemented and, to a considerable extent, supported by chemical changes. The sympathetic nerve endings control effectors by releasing a substance, *sympathin.* The medulla of the adrenal gland also releases, directly into the blood, a similar compound, *adrenin.* Adrenin is said to be *sympathetico-mimetic* in that it produces or supports, chemically, many of the changes also produced by action of the sympathetic nervous system, such as speeding up of the heart and the rate of breathing, and constricting the sympathetic blood vessels. Adrenin in the blood has effects of its own: it counteracts fatigue and speeds up the coagulation of blood. Adrenin and the sympathetic nervous system cooperate in producing similar, though not identical, changes. Both effects—neural and chemical—have obvious utility in the struggle for existence. The bodily changes mobilize the energies of an organism and protect it against exhaustion and bleeding to death.

Cannon's emphasis upon the utility of the bodily changes in fear, rage, pain, and related emotions, agrees well with Darwin's claim that many of the outward expressions of emotion are signs of biologically serviceable acts. Cannon, in fact, carried Darwin's principle of utility inside the organism and thus supplemented and extended the Darwinian interpretation.

In a word, when an organism has to go on a wartime basis or is subjected to stress, the sympathetic nervous system mobilizes the energy reserves of the body and prepares for the emergency. When there is no emergency—in times of peace—the parasympathetic nerves control the conservative and upbuilding processes of anabolism. The peacetime functions are incompatible with the emergency emotions. Because of this interpretation, Cannon's theory is known as the "emergency" theory of emotion.

Critique of Cannon's Theory and Reformulation. Cannon's emergency theory of emotion has been severely criticized and modified so that it can no longer be regarded as an adequate account of emotion. A review of some of these criticisms is illuminating and gives a more adequate view of emotion. I will, therefore, briefly examine three criticisms and summarize the results.

1. Gellhorn (1943) demonstrated that the physiological basis of

emotion lies in the simultaneous excitation of *both* divisions of the autonomic nervous system and not in sympathetic excitation alone. In emotion there is increased secretion of the glands controlled by *both* divisions of the autonomic nervous system.

There is much evidence for parasympathetic activity during emotion: It is common knowledge that under strong emotion the bladder and rectum are involuntarily evacuated. Although Cannon assumed this to be an exceptional case, there is additional evidence of parasympathetic action during excited emotions.

Since Pavlov's pioneer experiments, it has been known that the pleasantness associated with intake of food is accompanied by parasympathetic excitation. Thus the sight and smell of food causes "psychic secretion" of saliva and gastric juice. The effect is absent after severing the vagus nerve. Again, sexual excitement leads not only to secretory and vasodilator effects in the genital organs but also to widespread parasympathetic effects in the gastrointestinal tract. One cannot assume, however, that pleasantness is associated with increased parasympathetic activity and unpleasantness with increased sympathetic activity. It is unfortunate that Cannon neglected the pleasant emotions with their parasympathetic effects and limited investigations to pain, hunger, fear, rage, and related unpleasant emotions.

During fear and general excitement parasympathetic activity, rather than sympathetic, is predominant, Gellhorn argued. Parasympathetic dominance leads to spasticity of the sphincters, increase in peristalsis, diarrhea, hyper-secretion of gastric juice. Even in mild excitement, such as that which may be produced by memory and imagination, the signs of parasympathetic excitation dominate sympathetic effects. The tears of grief, for example, are evoked by parasympathetic action.

Investigations of the circulatory changes accompanying emotional excitement have given evidence of both sympathetic and parasympathetic effects in emotion. The increased heart rate may be due to inhibition of tone in the vagus or to sympathetic impulses or to the secretion of adrenin or to all of these. There is multiple control.

Gellhorn concluded that various forms of emotional excitement (rage, "sham rage," fright) lead to excitation of the vago-insulin system as well as the sympathetico-adrenal system. Hormonal effects produced by nervous impulses include not only the secretion of the adrenal medulla but also the secretion of the pancreas and the pituitary glands.

2. Kling (1933), in agreement with Gellhorn, stated that Cannon's emergency theory of emotion is misleading. Cannon gave the impression that the sympathetic network alone is responsible for the major bodily changes in emotion, and further, that the parasympathetic

nerves are concerned mainly with upbuilding and conservative functions of the body.

Cannon also gave the impression that emotion is an occasional event just as biological crises and emergencies occur from time to time. Actually, Kling pointed out, *both* divisions of the autonomic nervous system are on duty 24 hours a day. There are, of course, marked changes in autonomic function during an emotional crisis, but the sympathetic and parasympathetic nerves play equally important roles in these emotional responses. In most emotions there is a balanced action between the two divisions of the autonomic nervous system. This balanced action results in characteristic patterns of bodily changes. The patterns differ from emotion to emotion and are produced by reciprocal innervation of the two divisions of the autonomic system.

In fear, parasympathetic symptoms are present as well as sympathetic. In sexual activity, both divisions of the autonomic system function together for, as we know, the sacral nerves lead to engorgement of erectal tissue and the sympathetic nerves lead to ejaculation. Further, the parasympathetic nerves become active during quiet emotional states of depression and exhaustion as well as in excited states.

Kling stated that individuals tend to express all emotions by habitual patterns of facial and somatic expression. Along with these habitual patterns there are characteristic patterns of vagotonic disturbance that differ from individual to individual. The habits of emotional expression involve *autonomic* processes and not merely the sympathetic network.

3. Arnold (1945) is another critic of Cannon's emergency theory of emotion. She questioned Cannon's statements concerning: (1) the role of adrenin, and (2) the role of the sympathetic nervous system.

After surveying research upon adrenal function, Arnold affirmed that cortin (the cortical hormone) rather than adrenin (the medullary hormone) is instrumental in maintaining muscular strength. Adrenin, in the intact organism, does *not* prevent fatigue, she stated. Adrenin has a depressing rather than a stimulating effect. The secretion of adrenin during fear or the injection of the drug adrenalin serves to diminish muscular activity and reduce muscular contractions.

Physiologically, adrenin has diverse effects: (1) Adrenin produces vasoconstriction and *reduced* blood flow. Actually the effect of adrenin has to be overcome by muscular activity before an increased blood flow can meet the augmented oxygen need of the skeletal muscles. (2) Adrenin increases the heart rate but without increasing the stroke volume and oxygen utilization. This would be a hindrance, rather than a help, to forceful action.

Other effects of adrenin, to which Cannon referred, are probably due to acetycholine (the parasympathetic hormone) rather than to adrenin.

The explanation of the energizing effect of adrenin after exhaustion can be found in Gellhorn's report that an increase in blood pressure caused by adrenin or by sympathetic stimulation automatically produces parasympathetic action. The total physiological evidence, in fact, gives little support to the view that adrenin has a dynamogenic action and much support to the view that it has depressant effects.

Arnold goes on to consider the psychological effects of fear. In every instance where the symptoms of fear are accurately described, Arnold stated, the level of somatic activity is reduced rather than increased. This reaction is in sharp contrast to anger, where the activation level is definitely raised. Introspective evidence indicates that extreme fear paralyzes action before the possibility of flight can be explored. Laboratory workers know that when animals are placed in an open field they don't run; they explore cautiously or "freeze." The fact seems to be that in mild fear muscular activity is reduced while in extreme fear it is prevented altogether.

The total evidence, Arnold stated, indicates that fear is enervating rather than invigorating. Fear can be useful to the organism, indeed, not because it prepares for action but because it forces caution. If completely fearless, the human race, as well as its animal progenitors, would have destroyed itself long ago. Fear came with the realization of impending danger, caution, and, perhaps, the dawn of consciousness. The penalty we pay for this increased awareness is retardation of action. The emergency theory of emotion, therefore, is not valid for the emotion of fear. Nor can the effects of fear be explained as adaptive reactions. They are disturbing, disruptive.

Cannon's theory of homeostasis was a logical extension of the emergency theory of emotion. Cannon assumed that every reaction following some environmental interference (as when a dog barks at a cat) is adaptive and has survival value. This view, however, neglects the disruptive and disorganizing effects of fear and other strong emotions.

Arnold wrote: "Amending Cannon's theory of homeostasis we would suggest, therefore, that during overactivity of the sympathetic division of the autonomic nervous system (in fear or cold) the balance of the organism is restored by a cholinergic *reaction* in the form of activity; and during parasympathetic overactivity (in anger or during fear) by a secondary sympathetic *reaction* with its adrenergic effects. If such a reaction is delayed or insufficient or if the original stimulus is protracted too long, the primary effects of overstimulation may become irreversible."

Arnold identified fear with sympathetic action but claimed that fear has enervating rather than energizing effects. She suggested that anger is accompanied by dominant parasympathetic action and fear by dominant sympathetic action. According to this hypothesis, every parasympathetic excitation, e.g., in anger, produces a sympathetic reaction with a discharge of adrenin, though it does not necessarily produce fear.

Arnold concluded that there are at least three different physiological states corresponding to three different emotions: *fear*, with predominantly sympathetic excitation; *anger*, with strong parasympathetic activity; and *excitement* or elation, with moderate parasympathetic activity. In addition to these emotional states there are two excitatory states which she hesitated to call emotions: (1) startle, and (2) an explosive or epileptoid reaction. Both of these reactions seem to represent a short circuiting which Darrow called "functional decortication."

The condition most favorable to efficient activity is found in a moderate stimulation of the cholinergic mechanism, resulting in facilitation of action by excitement without untoward secondary effects from adrenin. Neither anger nor fear can be shown to have an emergency function. Rather they are disruptive and represent obstacles to efficient action, the former by short-circuiting too large an amount of excitation into the parasympathetic and the latter by inundating the sympathetic system.

In summary, the above criticisms of Cannon's emergency theory of emotion agree on several points: (1) Emotion is a function of autonomic activity and not a function of sympathetic action alone. Both divisions of the autonomic system function simultaneously and reciprocally. In this reciprocal action different patterns of visceralization are produced corresponding to fear, rage and "sham rage," general excitement, sexual and other emotions. (2) In addition to adrenin there are physiological effects produced, in emotion, by hormones from the pancreas and the pituitary body. (3) The autonomic nervous system is on continuous duty 24 hours a day. Changes produced by a biological crisis and stress correspond to departures from normal function. (4) Cannon, like Darwin, has emphasized the utility of the bodily changes in emotion; but some of these bodily changes indicate disruption rather than adaptation.

In a reformulation of Cannon's emergency theory of emotion we should take account of the work of Selye (1956) upon the adjustments of the organism to stress. Stressful situations have profound physiological effects other than the bodily changes that occur during emotional states.

CONCLUSION

Emotional reactions may be viewed as sequences of bodily changes in the skeletal musculature associated with processes in the smooth muscles and glands. Some of these bodily changes are outwardly observable as emotional expressions and others are internal and hidden from ordinary view. Changes in pulse, blood pressure, respiration, sweat secretion, facial expression, vocalization, and other bodily processes, have been extensively studied in relation to emotional excitement. The outwardly observable manifestations of feeling and emotion depend especially upon processes in the nervous and endocrine systems.

The changes in glands and smooth muscles—essential components of every emotional upset—are evoked through action of the autonomic nervous system. Both divisions of the autonomic system (sympathetic and parasympathetic) are excited during emotional upsets.

The patterns of response that appear during emotional excitement are dependent upon innate bodily structures. Many of them have utility in the biological struggle for existence but some, e.g., laughing, weeping, rage, terror, agony, disruptive excitement, etc., indicate a perturbation of smoothly running adaptive behavior.

Under quiet, non-emotional, conditions the autonomic processes regulate internal functions related to digestion, respiration, reproduction, and other vital processes. During times of crisis and stress the autonomic processes mobilize the energy reserves of the body for prolonged and vigorous action.

Reading suggestions for Chapters V and VI are combined on page 286.

Chapter VI

Physiological Aspects of the Affective Processes[1]

Neurologists, endocrinologists, chemists, physiologists, psychologists, and other men of science, are all interested in the nature of emotional behavior. Current investigations of brain chemistry and behavior, of the neurophysiology of emotion, the physiology of affective and related processes, are highly technical and sophisticated. The studies are interrelated and there is an extensive literature.

In the present chapter we will examine some of the physiological aspects of affective processes and leave the follow-up work to experts.

Gross Anatomical Development and Organization of the Central Nervous System. In its embryonic development, the nervous system of man presents something like a synopsis of early evolutionary history. The first appearance of the nervous system in the embryo is a neural groove which forms along the dorsal (back) side of the organism. With growth, this groove closes over, first near the middle of the body, and from this region the closure proceeds in both directions. A neural tube is thus formed.

During the first few weeks of development, bulges appear at the head end of the tube and there is a folding back of one part over another. One of these head regions (the pallium) becomes the cerebrum in the adult organism; this structure grows to such size that eventually it covers over and hides from view all other portions of the brain.

A reconstruction of the brain of a human embryo at the age of five weeks is shown in Figure 44. Figure *A* presents a lateral view with some of the gross structures. Figure *B* is a median sagital section, showing the original tubular structure. This figure roughly resembles an adult brain with cerebral hemispheres lacking. The similarity is due to the fact that the pallium has not yet grown to such an extent that it covers the other structures.

[1]Parts of this chapter presuppose some knowledge of physiology and gross neural anatomy.

In the brain of the adult vertebrate the neural tube remains in the form of ventricles within the brain and a minute neural canal within the spinal cord. In the adult brain, however, the external parts visible to the naked eye are largely the bulges and folds which conceal from view what is left of the embryonic neural tube.

Figure *A* shows the diencephalon, a general region of the nervous system, just behind the pallium. In this region are the thalamus and the

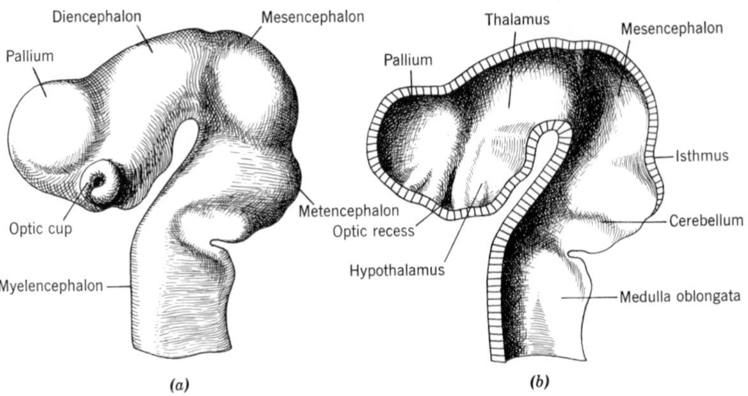

Figure 44. Reconstruction of the brain of a human embryo at the age of five weeks: (*A*) A lateral view. (*B*) A median sagital section. Drawn by Mrs. K. H. Paul from a figure originally in Prentiss, *A Laboratory Manual and Text-book of Embryology* (1915).

hypothalamus, represented in *B*. The hypothalamus of the adult brain and closely related neural structures contain coordinating centers for patterns of response which are displayed during emotional excitement.

The anatomical locations of the neural centers which coordinate patterns of emotional reaction are indicated further in Figure 45. This

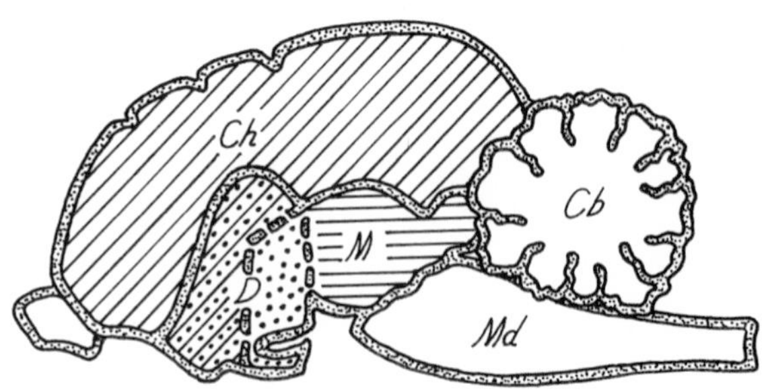

Figure 45. Diagram of the midsection of the cat brain. The parts distinguished by slanting lines can be wholly removed without destroying the rage pattern. The figure shows: the cerebral hemispheres (*Ch*); diencephalon (*D*); mesencephalon (*M*); cerebellum (*Cb*); and medulla (*M*). Modified from Cannon (1929).

diagram is based on the anatomy of the adult cat—an animal that has been extensively studied in researches upon emotion.

The location of the diencephalon is indicated by dots. As noted above, this region of the brain contains the hypothalamus and closely related structures. Most of the patterns of reaction that appear during emotional excitement have their coordinating centers in the hypothalamus and in parts of the nervous system which are located structurally and functionally at lower neural levels. The vertebrate nervous system is organized on the basis of loops or levels.

According to a principle of Hughlings Jackson, the nervous system is organized as a hierarchy of neural structures. The lower (phylogenetically older) neural structures are normally dominated by higher (younger) centers. This view fits in well with a great deal of current research regarding the relation between lower and higher centers. For example, surgical removal of the cerebral cortex renders the animal *more* rather than *less* sensitive to stimulations that elicit the rage pattern. The cerebral cortex, during non-emotional behavior, has a dominant regulatory influence over lower centers but during emotional excitement this cerebral control is weakened or modified in such a way that the emotional patterns are exhibited in behavior. In a sense, emotional behavior is more primitive than the patterns of behavior acquired by civilized man.

PHYSIOLOGICAL THEORIES OF EMOTION

Viewed historically, there has been a trend away from studies exclusively concerned with conscious emotions to studies concerned with human and animal behavior. Early physiological studies were concerned with bodily changes that could be readily observed at the surface of the body. Since many of these changes are regulated by the autonomic nervous system, attempts were made to explain emotions largely in terms of autonomic processes.

There has always been an interest in the central nervous system and its role in emotional behavior. Current theories are mainly concerned with the neurophysiology, chemistry and endocrinology of emotional processes.

There is today a growing recognition that emotional behavior is exceedingly complex. To understand emotion one must consider the organism as a whole, living within its biosphere, interacting with present and previous environments. Emotional behavior, to a high degree, is a product of biological evolution. It is this complexity which demands a multidisciplinary approach to the analysis of emotion.

Some of the leading theories of emotion are considered below:

The James-Lange Theory of Emotion. In his classic chapter upon the emotions, William James (1913) pointed out that profound bodily changes occur during emotional excitement. He quoted a Danish physiologist, C. Lange, to show that in grief, for example, there are such manifestations as the following: paralysis of voluntary movement, movement which is slow and heavy and without strength, a weak voice, neck bent with head hanging or "bowed down," eyes large in appearance, bloodlessness of the skin, mouth dry, and in nursing women diminishing of the milk. James quoted Darwin to present some of the organic symptoms of fear: eyes and mouth wide open, posture motionless or breathless, heart beating violently, paleness of the surface, cold sweat, hairs erect, breathing hurried, trembling of the muscles, mouth dry, arms protruded as if to avert some danger, and so on. During hatred, according to a quotation from Mantegazza, there are such bodily changes as these: withdrawal of the trunk, contraction or closure of the eyes, frowning, display of the teeth and contracting jaws, deep inspirations, automatic repetition of one word or syllable, redness or pallor of the face, dilation of the nostrils, standing up of the hair on the head, and so on.

If we go through the whole list of emotions and examine their organic manifestations, we but "ring the changes on the elements which these three typical cases involve." James was somewhat pessimistic about bringing law and order out of the mass of descriptive details in the literature of emotion. Nevertheless, he went on to a statement of his theory in a paragraph which, perhaps, has been more widely quoted and discussed than any other paragraph in the literature of emotion.

> Our natural way of thinking about these coarser emotions is that the mental perception of some fact excites the mental affection called the emotion, and that this latter state of mind gives rise to the bodily expression. My theory, on the contrary, is that *the bodily changes follow directly the perception of the exciting fact, and that our feeling of the same changes as they occur IS the emotion.* Common-sense says, we lose our fortune, are sorry and weep, we meet a bear, are frightened and run; we are insulted by a rival, are angry and strike. The hypothesis here to be defended says that this order of sequence is incorrect, that the one mental state is not immediately induced by the other, that the bodily manifestations must first be interposed between, and that the more rational statement is that we feel sorry because we cry, angry because we strike, afraid because we tremble, and not that we cry, strike, or tremble, because we are sorry, angry or fearful, as the case may be. Without the bodily states following on the perception, the latter would be purely cognitive in form, pale, colorless, destitute of emotional warmth. We might then see the bear, and judge it best to run, receive the insult and deem it right to strike, but we should not actually *feel* afraid or angry. [449–450]

James proceeds to argue for his theory. First, he points out, no one can doubt that psychological objects and situations do excite bodily changes through a preorganized mechanism and that in emotion these reverberations extend throughout the entire organism. Second, every one of these bodily changes is *felt*, acutely or obscurely, the moment it occurs. Third, if we fancy some strong emotion, and try to abstract from it the consciousness of its bodily symptoms, there is nothing left behind. "What kind of an emotion of fear would be left if the feeling neither of quickened heart-beats nor of shallow breathing, neither of trembling lips nor of weakened limbs, neither of goose-flesh nor of visceral stirrings, were present, it is quite impossible for me to think. Can one fancy the state of rage and picture no ebullition in the chest, no flushing of the face, no dilatation of the nostrils, no clenching of the teeth, no impulse to vigorous action, but in their stead limp muscles, calm breathing, and a placid face? The present writer, for one, certainly cannot . . ."

For James the essential point is that *an emotion is an awareness of bodily changes as they occur*. There is a situation which arouses bodily changes reflexively. The awareness of these changes constitutes the conscious emotion.

Three main features of the James-Lange theory of emotion are these: First, emotion is assumed to be a consciously felt experience. Second, the theory deals with the sequence of: (a) perception of an exciting fact, and (b) perception of involuntary bodily changes. Third, the theory implies a *causal* relation. Do we run *because* we feel afraid? Or do we feel afraid *because* we tremble, have an impulse to run, etc.? Taken literally, these questions imply mind-body interaction; and they raise some profound philosophical problems.

Wenger's Critique of the James-Lange Theory. The theory is widely known as the James-Lange theory of emotion but Wenger (1950) pointed out that the theory is really that of James. Textbook and other discussions of the theory usually follow James' striking presentation.

The Danish physiologist, C.G. Lange, in 1885, published a paper in which he emphasized the vasomotor disturbances as real outcomes of affective experiences. The vascular innervations, Lange wrote, produce secondary disturbances such as motor abnormalities, sensations of paralysis, disturbances of secretion and intelligence, etc. Lange regarded emotion as a *visceral* reaction.

Wenger extended and modified Lange's view. Wenger denies that an emotion *is* the awareness of bodily changes. He does not speak of visceral changes *induced by* emotion or of emotion *induced by* visceral changes. Rather, he regards the visceral response pattern itself *as* an emotion. Wenger writes:

> . . . Emotion would be continuous, because autonomic activity is continuous, while the state of homeostasis would be regarded as a state of emotion, and we would speak of increased or decreased emotion from this basic pattern. We would distinguish between emotions per se only insofar as we can differentiate patterns of visceral change, and we no longer would speak of visceral changes induced by emotion. Furthermore, all other reactions would be regarded as correlates or noncorrelates of emotional response. [5]

Wenger explains that there are indeed visceral patterns of response. Perhaps the clearest example of unique visceral patterning is the specific emotional complex found in sexual excitement. Three or four visceral patterns can be detected in sexual excitement. Wenger would accept the observed visceral patterns *as* emotions. He thus implies an objective patterned-reaction concept of emotion and deplores the views of James, Cannon, and others, who define emotion as a conscious experience.

Cannon's Thalamic Theory of Emotion. Cannon (1927, 1931) criticized the James-Lange theory of emotion and proposed an alternate interpretation.

According to Cannon, the excitations from peripheral receptors are relayed through the thalamus to the cerebral cortex. These incoming excitations over projection pathways contribute to the perception of the situations that induce emotion. Patterns of emotional discharge are organized in the thalamus. When an emotional pattern in the thalamus is excited there is a reflex discharge over motor pathways to the skeletal musculature and the viscera.

Cannon assumes that the cerebral cortex *exercises a continuous inhibitory action on the thalamic emotional centers.* Perception of an emotion-inducing situation produces a cerebral disinhibition and thus frees the thalamic centers from their normal restraint. When this disinhibition occurs the emotional expressions automatically appear. Subsequently, afferent impulses from the viscera and skeletal musculature arrive at the thalamus and are relayed upward to the cerebral cortex. These incoming impulses, according to Cannon, give an emotional *quale* to conscious experience.

In arguing for his theory Cannon made five points:

1. Surgical separation of the viscera from the central nervous system does not alter emotional expressions and behavior. Hence incoming excitations from the viscera are not essential to emotional reactions.

2. The same visceral changes occur in different emotional states and under non-emotional conditions. Again, responses of the viscera are too uniform to account for the variety of conscious emotions.

3. The viscera are relatively insensitive structures and hence could not serve to distinguish among conscious emotions as implied by the James-Lange theory.

4. Visceral changes are too slow to be a source of emotional feeling. They do not occur soon enough to account for affective tone.

5. Artificial induction of visceral changes typical of strong emotion does not necessarily produce emotion. This was shown in some experiments by Marañon upon the effects of injecting adrenin.

Cannon cited experiments by Bechterev, Woodworth and Sherrington, and Bard, which showed that surgical ablation of all brain structures anterior to the diencephalon does not remove emotional expressions. Bard (1934*a*, 1934*b*, 1950) demonstrated, by successive operations, that after bilateral removal of the entire cerebral cortex the cat and dog are capable of displaying behavior that closely resembles rage in normal animals. The decerebrate animals are hypersensitive. Stroking the fur, which to normal animals is indifferent or pleasurable, evokes displays of intense rage in decerebrate subjects. Transections below the level of the caudal hypothalamus abolish the pattern of rage.

Incidentally, the emotional reactions of decorticate animals are poorly directed with respect to the provoking stimuli. A normal animal exhibits better coordination and precision in fighting than does a decerebrate preparation. The intact animal responds with rage to visually perceived situations, such as the approach of a familiar enemy, but decerebrate animals are not aroused in this way. The telencephalon thus widens the range of conditions that are effective in producing rage and renders behavior more effective in combat.

Decorticate cats have been observed to purr and show the usual pleasure reactions of normal animals, as well as rage. Sherrington (1911) reported that decorticate dogs show disgust as well as rage. When presented with dog flesh for food the animals showed normal disgust, reacting negatively. Sherrington called these reactions *pseudo-affective* assuming that conscious emotion is dependent upon cortical processes and that decorticate animals could not *feel* rage and other emotions. This, of course, raises a moot question. Since animals cannot introspect, there is no way of knowing the conscious correlate of emotional expressions. "Sham rage" looks like genuine rage.

Cannon cited some clinical evidence, reported by Henry Head, on human subjects with unilateral lesions in the thalamic region. These subjects reacted excessively to emotional stimulations; reactions were both pleasant and unpleasant. Head attributed the phenomena to release from cortical inhibition. Also cortical dominance can be released by nitrous oxide ("laughing gas"). The drug weakens cortical inhibitions; the subjects laugh and weep.

In view of the total evidence Cannon suggests that James' section, entitled "No Special Brain Centers for Emotion," must be modified.

Grossman's Critique of the Thalamic and Emergency Theories of Emotion. Cannon's thalamic theory of emotion has been criticized on a factual basis by Grossman (1967). There are several factual objections to the theory:

First, complete removal of the thalamus has no effect on rage reactions of decorticate animals. This emotional response disappears only when the posterior and ventral portions of the *hypothalamus* are removed. The hypothalamus, however, has neither the specific sensory inputs nor the sensory projections to the cortex which Cannon's thalamic theory requires.

Second, if rage were elicited by the release of thalamic mechanisms from cortical inhibition, removal of the source of inhibition should produce a continuous, permanent, rage but this does not occur. Some (not all) stimuli elicit rage in decorticate subjects. Stimulation elicits rage from occasion to occasion, not continuously.

Third, rage responses have been elicited by stimulation of the hypothalamus, the cerebral cortex, and even the cerebellum. Such facts cannot be explained in terms of the release of cortical inhibition.

Again, Cannon's view of the emergency function of adrenin is probably incorrect. Cannon (1929) emphasized the utility of the bodily changes of emotion in a struggle for existence. He claimed that the secretion of the adrenal glands prepares the organism for vigorous activity as in a fight or a race for one's life. It is now known, however, that the adrenal glands secrete two hormones: epinephrine and norepinephrine. Grossman summarized the evidence to show that the effects of epinephrine are quite different from those mentioned by Cannon in support of his emergency theory of emotion:

Epinephrine depletes liver glycogen but also decreases glycogen stored in the muscles even when the concentration is too low to produce a rise in blood pressure. Also epinephrine tends to inhibit the utilization of glucose by slowing the transfer from extracellular fluids to tissue cells. Far from aiding the reconversion of lactic acid to glycogen, epinephrine seems to break down muscular glycogen and thus hinder rather than help the emergency reaction. The cardiovascular effects of epinephrine are complex but do not seem to be designed to "prepare the organism for a struggle." Epinephrine decreases the blood flow in muscles at rest and has similar effects on active muscle. Epinephrine accelerates the heart beat but this does not necessarily imply improved circulation since stroke volume may decrease with high acceleration. Therefore, all things considered, Grossman states, Cannon's view of the emergency function of adrenin (epinephrine) is probably incorrect.

There are, however, two secretions from the adrenal medulla: epinephrine and norepinephrine. These two hormones have different adaptive functions. According to Kety (1967), epinephrine is secreted primarily in situations of stress and uncertainty, in which flight or fight might be an appropriate response. According to Kety, this agent would have adaptive functions (as Cannon maintained). Norepinephrine appears to be secreted in those situations in which the outcome is inevitable or unavoidable and muscular activity would be inappropriate or useless. Norepinephrine in the brain plays an important adaptive role in mediating alertness and wakefulness, pleasure and euphoria, anger and fear. Norepinephrine also has an advantage in protecting the animal against the acute effects of hemorrhage.

Arnold's Appraisal-Excitatory Theory of Emotion. On page 108, I referred to Arnold's view that the pleasant and unpleasant feelings elicited by sensory stimulations are rudimentary appraisals (evaluations). This same appraisal theory applies to the complex cognitive processes that elicit emotions.

Arnold (1960, Vol. I, p. 182) defines emotion as "*the felt tendency toward anything intuitively appraised as good (beneficial), or away from anything intuitively appraised as bad (harmful). This attraction or aversion is accompanied by a pattern of physiological changes organized toward approach or withdrawal. The patterns differ for different emotions.*" [italics in the original]

The essential feature of Arnold's definition of emotion is an emphasis on appraisal, evaluation, estimation of the inducing situation. Something must be known (actually or in imagination) before it can be feared, hated, loved, desired. Understanding or estimation of a situation determines the emotion that will be aroused. For example, an encounter with a grizzly bear in the mountains elicits fear but the perception of a similar bear in the zoo is just an interesting, non-emotional experience.

Arnold agrees with James that the emotional response involves involuntary changes in viscera and skeletal muscles. The feedback from these peripheral changes, Arnold states, is appraised in terms of, "How I feel in this situation." According to the James-Lange theory, this feedback *constitutes* the conscious emotion. According to Arnold, it is the immediate appraisal or estimation of a situation that excites the emotional experience and the feedback.

When an emotion is aroused the subject is motivated for action. There is a desire to flee from danger, to attack an enemy, to entice a mate, or to make some other response that is appropriate to the situation. The desire or determining outlook (Nina Bull's "attitude") is an essential determinant of emotional behavior. According to Arnold, emotions are *motivating* processes. The emotional individual becomes integrated, organized, motivated for some kind of adaptive behavior. Arnold carefully considers emotional disorganization but regards this as a secondary phenomenon. Emotions are adaptive in a positive or negative direction.

This main emphasis in Arnold's theory is upon cognitive appraisal of situations or events as the source of feeling and emotion. This cognitive appraisal is mediated by cerebral processes. Hence cerebral excitation is the main cause of emotional behavior.

Arnold (1950) formulated an excitatory theory of emotion which is tied in with her emphasis on the cerebral processes of cognition and appraisal: Stimulation of the peripheral receptors sends afferent impulses through sensory relay stations in the thalamus to the cerebral cortex. At the cortical level the situation is evaluated and a specific attitude such as fear or anger is formed. The cortical attitude sends patterns of impulses to the sympathetic relay station or to the parasympathetic relay station or to both of these thalamic stations. The autonomic excitations then discharge to blood vessels and other visceral structures. Afferent impulses from these peripheral structures are sent back through sensory relay stations in the thalamus to the cortex where there is sensation from visceral changes. This sensory feedback from the periphery is evaluated at the cortical level and the feedback, as James postulated, transforms a purely cognitive experience into an emotion which is felt.

Arnold describes in detail the neural anatomy of structures involved in her theory but her assignment of functions to these neural structures is quite speculative.

Grossman (1967) criticized Arnold's theory on several counts: First, the cerebral cortex exercises a *dual* control over lower centers. Cannon emphasized the inhibitory influence and Arnold the excitatory. Both inhibitory (negative) and excitatory (positive) influences are known to exist. Moreover, some cortical areas are excitatory with respect to specific emotional targets and inhibitory with respect to other targets. Second, Arnold's postulate that specific cortical areas mediate particular types of emotions, such as fear and anger, is gratuitous; there is lack of evidence for this assumption. Third, Arnold and others have proposed classifications of emotions in terms of their sympathetic-parasympathetic components. But since autonomic changes are essential neither to the experience nor to the expression of emotion, it is unlikely that such changes can serve to determine the site of the cerebral representation of specific conscious emotions.

All things considered, therefore, it appears to me that the neurophysiology of emotion is still speculative and not well understood.

Lindsley's Activation Theory of Emotion and Motivation. In discussing the nature of motivation I referred to Lindsley's activation theory of emotion and to the fact that activation has been recognized by outstanding psychologists such as Hebb, Duffy, J. S. Brown, and others, as the basis of non-specific drive (page 67). I have noted elsewhere that Lindsley's activation theory takes account only of the excited, or sthenic, emotions such as rage, fear, terror, great excitment, etc., and that the theory is more properly regarded as a theory of motivation than as a general theory of emotion.

Activation can be viewed as a central neural process within the reticular formation of the brainstem and the diffuse corticothalamic projection systems. Lindsley (1951) has given a schematic diagram of gross neural structures to show the location of the reticular formation. See Figure 46 which should be compared with Bindra's diagram on page 65.

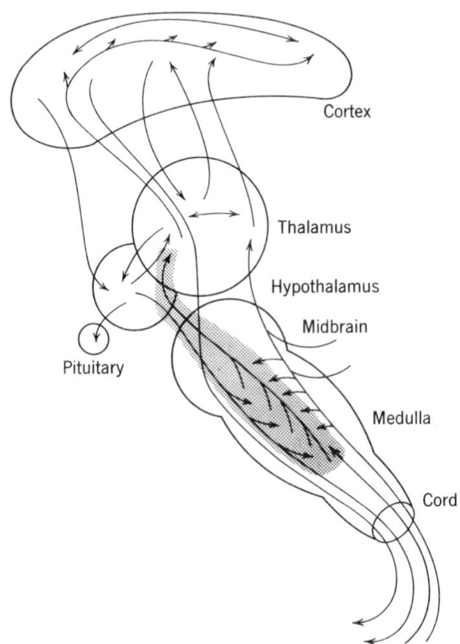

Figure 46. A schematic representation to show location of neural structures and probable pathways in the reticular formation. *After* Lindsley (1951).

The activating mechanism is composed of two interrelated systems: the brainstem reticular formation and a system of fibers that project through thalamic nuclei to the cerebral cortex. The reticular network is located at the levels of the medulla, midbrain, hypothalamus, and lower thalamus. The system contains many synapses and small neural systems.

It is known that afferent pathways from all receptors, including those from visceral and somatic structures, send collaterials into the reticular activating system. Impulses are there integrated and distributed to the hypothalamus where they excite the diencephalic waking center as well as non-specific thalamic nuclei through which they activate all parts of the cerebral cortex—sensory and nonsensory. Excitations via the diffuse projection systems tone up the cortex as a whole.

Arrows in Figure 46 indicate two-way conduction. There is conduction of neural impulses into the reticulum and upward, through diffuse projection tracts, to the cerebral cortex. There is also conduction downward from the cortex to the reticulum and outward to peripheral effectors, as shown by other arrows. The descending reticular system regulates spinal motor activity. It has a persisting influence in providing tonus for posture and tonic motor responses.

Lindsley's activation theory provides a sound physiological basis for understanding differences in the *intensity* of emotional excitement. One obvious weakness of the theory is that it does not take account of the diffuse positive and negative neural excitations that are known to exist and are reciprocally related. See page 72. Also the theory does not take account of specific patterns of emotional response.

Routtenberg (1968) reviewed the neuropsychological literature on affective arousal, particularly researches stemming from the work of Olds and associates. On the basis of experimental evidence Routtenberg postulated *two* arousal systems rather than a single activating system. Arousal System I includes the reticular activating system of the brainstem; this system maintains arousal of the organism and provides drive for the organization and activation of responses. Arousal System II includes the limbic and related systems; it provides control of responses elicited through incentive-related stimuli (food, sex, temperature, pain, etc.). The evidence indicates that two arousal systems are mutually inhibitory and reciprocally related. It is necessary to postulate reciprocal relations between the two systems, Routtenberg states, to explain the facts. But anatomical and physiological details, at the present time, are far from clear.

The directive-activation theory of motivation implies a dual control. See page 69. There is a GO system (positive, excitatory) and a STOP system (negative, inhibitory). Of course, one cannot identify pleasantness with GO and unpleasantness with STOP since a great deal of

GO-behavior and STOP-behavior is hedonically neutral. But there can be no doubt about the fact that some receptor stimulations (sweet tastes, fragrant odors, genital stimulations, etc.) are innately GO while other stimulations (bitter tastes, foul odors, pain stimulations, etc.) are innately STOP.

One must assume a neural mechanism that is fully adequate to explain the facts of hedonec regulation, algebraic summation of hedonic processes, hedonic integration, positive and negative forms of reinforcement, habituation, and related phenomena. The final explanation is not yet clear but the postulate of diffuse, non-specific, excitatory and inhibitory processes that are reciprocally related would seem, at least, to be required by the facts. Just where and how the positive and negative excitations are integrated is still not clear.

It must be recognized that intense positive and negative affective arousals are *occasional* events. Much everyday experience and behavior is hedonically neutral. The alert attentiveness which Lindsley described as associated with moderate or high levels of activation, can be a relatively neutral state hedonically.

In a word, although much positive activation is hedonically neutral, there are hedonically positive and negative arousals which summate algebraically to produce hedonically neutral activations. Positive and negative activations are reciprocally related.

The Circuit of Papez. After a thorough review of the physiological literature, Papez (1937) formulated a psychoneural theory of emotion. He described a complex neural structure, known as the Papez circuit, which mediates emotional behavior, emotional conciousness and its outer expression.

The emotive process, according to Papez, is built up in the hippocampus. When the hippocampus is excited, impulses are relayed via the fornix to the mammillary bodies of the hypothalamus. Excitations are also sent from the hippocampus to the anterior thalamic nuclei and onward to the cingulate gyrus of the cerebrum. Completing the circuit are fibers that conduct excitations from the cingulate gyrus to the hippocampus and amygdala. These structures, located in the mesocortex and archicortex, influence the cerebral cortex through excitations in the cingulate gyrus and in this way add emotional coloring to conscious experience. Papez describes this circuit as a harmonious mechanism, a reverberating circuit, which elaborates the central emotion and participates in both emotional consciousness and emotional expression.

The circuit is closely related to the midbrain reticular formation and to the limbic system. The circuit receives impulses from the reticular formation by way of the olfactory tubercle. The reticular formation, as we have seen above, is a primitive diffuse system of interlacing nerve cells and fibers which form the central core of each half of the brainstem. It occupies the central part of the medulla, pons, and midbrain tegmentum; and continues upward into the intralaminar and reticular nuclei of the thalamus and ventral thalamus. The reticular formation sends specific fibers to circumscribed areas of the cortex and also non-specific fibers, by means of collaterals, to several cortical regions.

The Papez circuit receives fibers from the limbic system which, in turn, receives fibers and excitations from the auditory, visual, gustatory, olfactory, somato- and viscero-receptor systems. The circuit is believed to integrate information from the limbic system. Possibly it provides a basis for the integration of positive and negative hedonic effects.

The limbic system, superimposed on the hypothalamus, serves as a regulatory system for autonomic functions. These structures integrate and coordinate visceral and bodily needs with sensory, including peripheral, events. The structures regulate innate activities concerned with searching, feeding, attack, flight, sex, and responses to most of the biologically basic situations that provoke emotions. (Papez does not define emotion assuming, perhaps, that we all know what an emotion is!)

In a paragraph reminiscent of William James' "stream of consciousness" and recalling the ancient tripartite division of mental processes into action, thought and feeling, Papez writes:

> It is thus evident that the afferent pathways from the receptor organs split at the thalamic level into three routes, each conducting a stream of impulses of special importance. One route conducts impulses through the dorsal thalamus and the internal capsule to the corpus striatum. This route represents "the stream of movement." The second conducts impulses from the thalamus through the internal capsule to the lateral cerebral cortex. This route represents "the stream of thought." The third conducts a set of concomitant impulses through the ventral thalamus to the hypothalamus and by way of the mammillary body and the anterior thalamic nuclei to the gyrus cinguli, in the medial wall of the cerebral hemisphere. This route represents "the stream of feeling." In this way, the sensory excitations which reach the lateral cortex through the internal capsule receive their emotional coloring from the concurrent processes of hypothalamic origin which irradiate them from the gyrus cinguli. [729]

In general, Papez argues that the cingulate gyrus is the seat of that dynamic vigilance by which experiences are endowed with emotional coloring. The theory postulates that the hypothalmus, the anterior thalmic nuclei, the gyrus cinguli, the hippocampus and their interconnections constitute a circuitous mechanism for elaborating the functions of central emotion, as well as participating in emotional behavior and expression. Papez's theory is thus much more extensive and inclusive than the foregoing theories of emotion.

MacLean's Concept of a "Visceral Brain." MacLean (1949), elaborating and extending Papez's theory of emotion, writes:

> The problem pertaining to emotional mechanisms is basically one of communication in the central nervous system. It may be assumed that messages from both without and within the organism are relayed to the brain by nervous impulses traveling along nerve fibers and possibly by humoral agents carried in the blood stream. Ultimately, however, any correlation of these messages must be a function of a highly integrated body of neurones capable of sorting, selecting and action upon various patterns of bioelectric activity. [338]

MacLean refers to the rhinencephalon as a "visceral brain." This structure is strategically situated for correlating information from internal and external perception. The "visceral brain" can bring into association not only oral and visceral sensations but also impressions from the sex organs, body wall, eye, and ear. In contrast to the neopallium, the "visceral brain" has many strong connections with the hypothalamus. MacLean regards the hypothalamus as the head ganglion of the autonomic nervous system. The "visceral brain" (mesopallium) coordinates impressions from all sense organs, intraorganic and peripheral, and through the hypothalamus regulates visceral responses along with the skeletal responses shown in fear, rage, and other emotions.

The mesopallium is transitional between phylogenetically old and new brains. The mesopallium contributes the affective component of awareness by relaying impulses to the cerebral cortex. Evidence indicates that only the cerebral cortex is capable of appreciating all the affective qualities of experience and combining them into such states of feeling as fear, anger, love, and hate. The cerebral cortex is involved in *experiencing* emotion; the hypothalamus in *expressing* emotion.

The "visceral brain," MacLean states, is not at all unconscious (possibly not even in certain stages of sleep), but rather eludes the grasp of the intellect because it cannot communicate in verbal terms. Perhaps one should say that the "visceral brain" is animalistic, illiterate, primitive. It does, however, have a kind of "organic language."

MacLean has a practical interest in emotions. In psychosomatic illnesses such as asthma, ulcerative colitis, peptic ulcer and hypertension, an emotional state of rage, fear, hostility, grief, resentment, or other, is clearly involved. From a therapeutic point of view, therefore, it is important to understand the neural mechanisms of emotion.

In general, MacLean's views agree with the widely accepted proposition that the affective, including emotional, processes are mediated by subcortical structures while the cognitive, intellectual, and evaluative, processes implicate the cerebral cortex. The anatomy of the central nervous system provides a clue to understanding the difference between what we *feel* and what we *know*.

The Neural Substrate of Affective Processes. Pribram and Kruger (1954) reviewed an extensive literature dealing with the structure and function of the rhinencephalon. Originally the rhinencephalon was thought to be concerned exclusively with smell and was described as an "olfactory brain." Now it is known that only one part of this structure (the olfactory bulb and closely connected neural structures) is concerned exclusively with olfaction. Other parts regulate emotional and social behavior.

The rhinencephalon, in fact, contains three structural systems. The first of these systems is concerned with olfactory discrimination. The second and third systems are implicated in emotional and social behavior. The second system has a variety of functions. It mediates visceral functions but cannot, according to Pribram, be regarded exclusively as a "visceral brain" because it is implicated in olfactory and gustatory reactions as well as social and emotional behavior. Hence one cannot assign any single function to this system. The third system, designated by Pribram and Kruger as the "allo-and juxtallocortical system," also has several interrelated functions. It is not exclusively concerned with emotion.

In general, there are diffuse excitations within these three structural systems. The diffuseness of excitations in these systems contrasts with the discreteness of organization and excitation of the afferent and efferent projection systems. Pribram and Kruger suggest that the affective and motivational aspects of psychological processes may *require* a diffuse rather than a specific neural substrate but the evidence for this is sparse.

Physiological psychologists appear to agree that the limbic and closely related systems provide the neural substrate for motivational and affective (including emotional) processes. Little is known, however, regarding the interrelations of functions of different parts of the limbic system and the relation between limbic structures and other portions of the brain.

The limbic system is a group of structures and regions in the forebrain that are interconnected with each other and with the hypothalamus. The limbic lobe is situated bilaterally at the base of the forebrain and is so called because it forms a "limbus," or border, around the brainstem. The limbic lobe runs practically the entire length of the cerebrum.

The major anatomical structures of the limbic system include: the *amygdala*, a large nuclear mass embedded deeply in the temporal lobe; the *hippocampus*, a long tubelike structure of cortical tissue embedded in the cerebrum; the *septum*, a nuclear region in the anterior medial depths of the forebain; the *olfactory projection fields*, regions which receive direct anatomical projections from the olfactory bulb; and several areas called the "old cortex" because they are more primitive in appearance than the neo-cortex.

Pribram's Comprehensive Account of Emotion. Pribram (1967*a*, 1967*b*), has presented an exceedingly broad and comprehensive account of emotion based upon a thorough analysis of the physiological and neuropsychological facts. In summarizing, Pribram states that his theory differs from most currently held views of emotion in five respects:

1. The theory is *memory-based* rather than based on drive or visceral processes. This means that to understand a particular emotion one must take account of previous experience and the present inducing situation. This view also implies that the cerebral cortex has an important role in instigating emotional behavior. Emotion, Pribram states, is relative to some plan or program that is under way rather than to the level of activation as in Lindsley's theory.

2. The theory regards *organized stability as the baseline from which perturbations occur.* Inputs that are incongruent with the baseline produce a disturbance. An important part of the baseline is the continuing activity of the viscera, regulated through the autonomic nervous system. A mismatch between expected and actual bodily changes in heart rate, sweating, presence of "butterflies," etc., is immediately sensed as a discrepancy which is the basis of visceral theories of James and Lange.

3. Emotion is a *perturbation*, an interruption, a disruption, of normal ongoing activity. The theory makes explicit the relation between motivation and emotion by linking both to ongoing, pre-behavioral organization, i.e., to a plan, program, or disposition. Pribram's theory implies an extension of the homeostatic doctrine from intraorganic events to the total organism-environment relation.

4. The theory defines emotion as e-motion, *a process that takes the organism temporarily out of motion* and effects control through the regulation of sensory inputs. The processes that occur when an organism is "out of" or "away from" motion are just as important and interesting scientifically as the normal activities of organisms carrying out plans.

5. There is *central control through the regulation of peripheral inputs*. Pribram's theory identifies two forms of regulation of sensory inputs. One form inhibits peripheral inputs while the organism determines what to do in a situation, what plan to follow. The other form enhances inputs thus making the organism attentive to critical aspects of the situation. Pribram spells out the details of this dual process.

In general, Pribram's comprehensive theory takes account of the total organism and its experiences (memories, plans, etc.) as well as the environmental situation. In this respect the theory is an advance over the peripheral theories of James and Lange, the thalamic theory of Cannon, and the neuropsychological theories of Papez and MacLean. The theory is of special importance in understanding human emotions.

Pribram's theory is closely related to the equilibrium-disequilibrium theories of motivation. Emotion, for Pribram, is a state of disequilibrium, a perturbation, disturbance, upset. It is not clear, however, as to how emotional perturbations differ specifically from non-emotional disturbances and from illnesses. But no one else is very clear about this matter.

CHEMICAL FACTORS IN EMOTIONS AND MOODS

Pribram (1967*a*) referred to an ancient doctrine that circulating humors are the cause of moods and emotions. The doctrine needs to be brought up to date and modified for it is known that circulating humors come up against blood-brain barriers which often make the humors ineffective centrally. Further, some humors are synthesized by the brain itself: norepinephrine, serotonin, histamine, dopamine, and others. It is known that unidentified chemical "releasers" are secreted into the venous portal system which bathes the base of the brain where it joins the pituitary gland—that master endocrive structure which controls the secretions of other endocrine glands.

Pribram pointed out that core structures in the diencephalon and mesencephalon are sensitive to a variety of chemical agents. Receptor sites have been identified that are sensitive to estrogenic steroids, circulating glucose, some amino acids or derivatives, osmotic equilibrium of electrolytes, androgenic and adrenal steroids, acetylcholine, epinephrine, and the partial pressure of CO_2. These chemical agents play an important role in the regulation of internal homeostasis. The chemical agents are circulated in the blood stream to and from certain target organs.

Schildkraut and Kety (1967) reviewed an extensive literature on biochemical factors in emotion. They pointed out that psychological and situational conditions can affect differentially the relative excretion of epinephrine and norepinephrine. Increased epinephrine excretion occurs in states of anxiety that involve a threat or that are unpredictable in outcome. Norepinephrine excretion occurs in states of anger or aggression or in situations that present a challenge. The increase of either epinephrine or norepinephrine or both is specifically adapted to the inducing situation. See also the paper by Kety (1967) on the psychoendocrine systems and emotion.

We are just beginning to understand the role of these chemical factors in behavior and as determinants of conscious experience but enough is already known to indicate their great importance in the regulation of motivational and affective processes.

Hormones and Behavior. We have seen that development of bodily form and sexual behavior depends upon the secretion of androgens and estrogens by the gonads (page 168). The gonadal hormones influence aggressive as well as sexual behavior.

Connor, *et al.* (1969) demonstrated that male and female rats differ in the type of aggressive behavior they reveal. Using a shock technique, Connor, *et al.*, induced "agonistic" behavior, shown by aggression and a persisting readiness to fight. These investigators found that neonatally castrated male rats showed female-like patterns of fighting behavior in shock-induced fighting situations. This would indicate that the neural substrate on which androgen acts in modulating aggressive behavior is organized in a female-like pattern. Exactly how castration produced this effect is unknown but it appears that at least part of the effect is due to some alteration in the functioning of the central nervous system.

Numerous studies of emotion have confirmed the extreme sensitivity of psychoendocrine systems to a wide variety of environmental manipulations, with activity of the pituitary and adrenal glands receiving an appropriate emphasis. For example, Brady (1967), and associates, have shown that epinephrine and norepinephrine are separate hormones induced by different environmental conditions. Brady believes that hormonal activity has a relation to durable emotional behavior and to the more stable aspects of feeling which include generalized mood states and affective dispositions.

Hormones affect not only moods and emotions but also the cognitive processes as well. Woolley (1967) pointed out that the hormone serotonin participates directly in the formation of emotion and also in the functioning of intellect.

The serotonin analogs in which the hormone-like action is prominent usually cause symptoms of excitement and agitation in normal persons. The analogs in which the antagonism to serotonin is prominent tend to cause mental depression. It is with the analogs that have marked serotonin-like effects that one can produce, in normal persons, visual and auditory hallucinations, sometimes accompanied by pleasure and often with mental aberrations. In general, Woolley concludes, there is considerable evidence that links serotonin with both emotional and cognitive functions.

Serotonin has a profound effect upon moods. But moods are also influenced by other factors: by intraorganic states of fatigue, sleepiness, pain, ill health; by physical environmental conditions such as temperature, humidity, the weather, music or noise; and especially by events within the social environment such as success or failure, victory or defeat, good news or bad news, reward or punishment, praise or reproof, etc. It is important to note the complexity and variety of the conditions that can influence a prevailing mood.

The Influence of Drugs upon Moods. Nowlis and Nowlis (1956), working with G. R. Wendt and others, made a careful study of conditions that influence moods. They examined the effects of moderate dosages of commonly used drugs such as amphetamines, antihistamines, and barbiturates, on the social, emotional and motivational behavior of college men. Over a 5-year period, 95 men were observed in approximately 2400 hours of controlled social observation and in about 4800 hours of relatively free activity in group work. There were self-ratings and objective behavior ratings by partners and other observers.

In this work the subjects did not know whether they were taking a drug or a placebo. They did not know what the behavioral effects of a drug might be. Although several methods of testing moods were tried, the most successful method was a check list of 100–200 adjectives. In making a rating the subject read the list rapidly, checking words that described his feeling, double checking words that indicated strong feeling, ignoring words that did not apply and crossing out words that definitely did not apply. See Nowlis (1953).

The check list gave a clear picture of the prevailing mood. For example, dramamine usually produced a definite increase in checking: *tired, drowsy, detached, sluggish, disinterested, dull, lazy, retiring, withdrawn;* and a decrease in *businesslike, genial, industrious, talkative, cheerful, energetic*. Benzedrine gave an increase in: *businesslike, talkative, capable, enterprising, independent,* and sometimes *nervous, jittery*; and a decrease in: *lazy, languid, nonchalant*. The ratings of partners and observers strongly confirmed the self-ratings.

Nowlis and Nowlis reported a social influence of seconal. In one experiment, four men in a group were tested together. The main hypothesis of the study, namely that a subject on seconal is more influenced by the mood of his partners than a subject on dramamine, received strong support. The mood of companions as well as the nature of the task and the drug itself influenced the ratings.

Drugs and Anxiety. Boissier and Simon (1969) have reviewed an extensive literature upon the psychopharmacology of emotion. They considered especially the relation of drugs to the forms and measurement of anxiety.

Fear, or fright, is an acute disturbance which is manifested in two ways either as an activation pattern with incessant movements or as a "freezing" pattern with immobility. The first pattern is exciting and energizing; the second is a form of inhibition. Anxiety, contrastingly, is a more persisting state involving the expectation or anticipation of harm. Anxiety is a mental state or condition rather than an acute manifestation. See page 82.

A major difficulty in the management of anxiety is that anxiety is not a simple state. There are different types of anxiety that react differently to different drugs. Hence there exists no unique reference drug for anxiety as such. Boissier and Simon write:

> . . . The anxiety of neurotics and psychosomatic patients is generally alleviated by minor tranquilizers (chlordiazepoxide or meprobamate type), barbiturates, or even alcohol; the anxiety of schizophrenics is eliminated or suppressed by the neuroleptics (or major tranquilizers); the anxiety of depressive patients can be removed after treatment by antidepressants alone (imipramine-like drugs). [898]

Fear can be provoked in animal subjects by a sudden noise, an electric shock, or a strange environment. This is followed by anxiety while the animal waits, more or less consciously, for a repetition of the disagreeable stimulus.

In general, *anxiety* is a psychological concept rather than a chemical entity but both psychological and chemical approaches are required in the study of anxiety and other motivational states and processes.

Chemical *versus* Cognitive Determinants of Affectivity. The labels that one attaches to a bodily state, describing how one feels, are a joint function of cognitive factors and physiological conditions of arousal. This assumption is supported by a series of experiments reported by Schachter (1970).

To illustrate: The physiological effects of injecting epinephrine are well known. We know that an injection of ½ CC of 1:1000 solution of epinephrine causes an increase in heart rate, a marked increase in systolic blood pressure, a redistribution of blood with a cutaneous decrease and with increased blood-flow to the muscles and cerebrum. Blood sugar and lactic acid concentrations increase and respiration rate increases slightly. These changes are similar to a state produced by sympathetic arousal. With the human subject the major subjective symptoms are palpitation, slight tremor, and sometimes a feeling of flushing and accelerated breathing.

Now by cleverly controlling the environmental situations, in a series of studies, Schachter was able to show that this epinephrine-induced state of sympathetic arousal was manifested in behavior and in experience as anger or euphoria or amusement or fear or (with informed subjects) as no mood or emotion at all. The subject's cognitive understanding of the inducing situation determined the feeling. Such results, Schachter states, are virtually incomprehensible if we persist in the assumption of an identity between physiological and psychological states, but they fall neatly into place if we specify the fashion in which cognitive and physiological factors interact.

Schachter reports some experiments with obese and normal-sized persons. The obese subjects misinterpreted their internal bodily state of hunger and were influenced to a greater extent than normal-sized persons by environmental conditions. With normal-sized persons the physiological correlates of food deprivation, such as gastric motility and hypoglycemia, are directly related to eating behavior and to the reported experience of hunger. With obese subjects the bodily state of hunger is less definitely related to food intake. External or non-visceral cues, such as smell, taste, and sight of other people eating, the passage of time, and so forth, affect eating behavior in obese subjects to a greater extent than in normal subjects.

These findings throw light upon a variety of studies with drugs in which blatantly opposite behavioral effects have been reported in the literature. LSD, for example, has been proved to be both hallucinogenic and nonhallucinogenic, a euphoriant, a depressant, and to have no effect at all upon mood. This nightmarish pattern of conflicting and nonreplicable results is familiar to anyone who has delved into the literature on the behavioral or emotional effects of many of the so-called psychotropic drugs. Years ago Marañon studied the effects of adrenalin. Some of his subjects described the physiological effects objectively; others *as if* afraid or *as if* happy; others described themselves as anxious; some as angry; others as euphoric.

In general, Schachter's experiments show the need for considering the organism-environment relation as a functional unity within which external and internal factors have interrelated and interdependent dynamic roles. Further, the experiments warn us about confusions which can arise when we deal with the relation between objective and subjective data.

VOLUNTARY AND INVOLUNTARY FACTORS IN EMOTIONAL BEHAVIOR

Although the organism is frequently considered apart from its environment, the distinction between organism and environment is arbitrary and can be misleading. Schachter's experiments show that it is futile to look for a *single* cause of an emotion. Some environmental factors have internal physiological effects and some physiological factors are psychologically effective. We must learn to see the organism-environment relation as a dynamic unity. This is especially obvious in the study of emotional behavior.

It has often but wrongly been said that changes produced by the autonomic nervous system are *involuntary* and that purposive behavior originating within the brain is *voluntary*. Let us examine the distinction between voluntary and involuntary behavior in relation to emotion.

Habituation and the Distinction between Voluntary and Involuntary Nervous Systems. According to a tradition, established since 1800 or earlier, the autonomic nervous system has been regarded as regulating *involuntary* processes of smooth muscles and glands while *voluntary* activities involving the skeletal musculature are controlled by the cerebrospinal system. Vanderwolf (1971) points out that, in the light of modern knowledge, this tradition is difficult or impossible to maintain.

One aspect of this tradition is the idea that autonomic processes are susceptible to classical (Pavlovian) conditioning while activities involving the skeletal muscle are conditionable only by instrumental, or operant, procedures. The facts do not support this idea.

It is difficult or impossible to elicit either autonomic or somatic reflexes in isolation. Increases of heart rate, for example, are associated with both voluntary and involuntary movement; decreases, with immobility. It has not been established that changes in heart rate occur independently of movement in the skeletal muscles.

Again, the voluntary and involuntary systems commonly function tegether. Solomon, Kamin and Wynne (1953) found a puzzling result in their experiments upon traumatic avoidance learning with dogs. Dogs were trained to respond to a signal by jumping over a hurdle to the other side of the shuttle box to escape an electric shock from a grid on the floor. The dogs readily learned to jump with about 1.0 to 1.5 seconds after the warning signal. Solomon, *et al.*, saw this acquired reaction as a response to the environmental signal. If the animals had been responding to an involuntary autonomic process (a fear drive?) the reaction time would be considerably longer–about 2.4 to 3.4 seconds.

What happened in this experiment was a gradual transition from emotional behavior that involved the autonomic nervous system to an habituated adaptive response that involved little sign of autonomic activity. During habituation the two nervous systems functioned together. There was a transition from autonomic to cerebrospinal control.

Even in the classical experiments of Pavlov the interdependence of skeletal and visceral processes must be assumed. As Hebb, I believe, pointed out, the animals must salivate in order to eat. And in the leg-flexing responses during aversive conditioning the paradigm of trial-and-error learning is more applicable than a model that implies conditioning of innate involuntary reflexes.

There is, in fact, only one kind of learning and not two kinds—classical and operant conditioning. Neal Miller (1969) has shown that heart rate, blood pressure, renal and peripheral blood flow, can all be altered by operant procedures! So the distinction between classical and operant forms of learning becomes a myth. The distinction is not supported by available evidence.

According to Brady, Kelly and Plumlee (1969), we cannot regard responses in the skeletal muscles as causally dependent upon autonomic effects nor *vice versa*. Rather, it would appear that cardiovascular and skeletal changes are more accurately represented as independently conditioned by the same environmental contingencies. There is only one form of learning.

In general, the distinction between voluntary and involuntary nervous systems and the implication that there are two corresponding forms of learning, is no longer tenable. The autonomic and cerebrospinal systems cooperate in producing adaptive behavior and both are influenced by contingent environmental stimulations.

More important than the distinction between voluntary and involuntary is the distinction between innate behavior, on the one hand, and stereotyped, automatic, behavior, on the other. The process of habituation is not well understood despite much research. The nature of habituation presents unsolved problems to the neurophysiologist.

The Neurophysiological Basis of Voluntary Movement. Vanderwolf (1971) has made a detailed review of the many studies that have a bearing on the neurophysiological mechanisms of voluntary movement. He considered experiments utilizing the techniques of ablation, intracranial stimulation, and electrical recording of brain waves, in so far as these experiments have some relation to the problem of voluntary movement. Actually, very little is known about the physiology of voluntary behavior.

Important in understanding voluntary behavior is the concept of *levels of function*. According to a suggestion of Hughlings Jackson the different motor activities can be arranged roughly in a scale extending from highly automatic movements such as respiration, cardiac and vasomotor activity, and simple somatomotor reflexes, to highly voluntary activities including speech, manipulation of objects, directed attention and locomotion. There are different *levels of function.*

The initiation, performance and termination of voluntary activities that involve walking, manipulations of objects, etc., are associated with activation of the ascending pathways from the diencephalon to the hippocampus and neocortex. The more automatic, habituated, responses, such as chewing, emotional expressions, and conditioned reflexes, are not directly dependent upon these ascending pathways.

Median thalamic lesions interfere with *voluntary* behavior more than with habituated *automatic* behavior. Rats with large medial thalamic lesions are grossly deficient in their ability to avoid painful shocks even though the animals are not paralyzed in the usual sense and possess adequate sensory and learning abilities as well as motivational capacity. The defect appears to be in the initiation of movement, in dysfunction of a mechanism that links perceptual, mnemonic, and motivational systems to the voluntary motor system.

There are points in the medial thalamus and in the posterior hypothalamus where electrical stimulation invariably produces motor activity of some sort, but the actual pattern of behavior varies–running, climbing, digging, etc. Stimulations with the same placement and same stimulation-parameters produce behaviors that vary with the environmental situation. There is thus an *environmental* regulation of voluntary movement.

How about the internal drive state? A given motivational state has a cluster of automatic responses that are unique to that drive state. Thus "feeling cold" is associated with vasoconstriction, shivering, a crouched posture, etc.; fear is associated with cutaneous vasoconstriction, an exaggerated startle response, patterns of urination and defecation, etc. Now voluntary movements do not form an integral part of such clusters, but can be temporarily coupled to any one of a large number of these dynamic reaction clusters.

In voluntary activity the organism is poised between two or more patterns of response. There are trigger mechanisms that can release one system or another. For example, when an animal is confronted by an enemy the response can be an aggressive fight or a flight from the threatening situation. The environmental situation normally influences the course of action.

Vanderwolf postulates that septal damage and electroconvulsive shock disrupt mechanisms which normally control activity in a movement trigger system. One of the main conclusions from his work on medial thalamic damage is that higher level motor control can be disrupted by lesions which leave perceptual-mnemonic processes relatively undisturbed. This point appears also in certain human neurological conditions. The perceptual-mnemonic systems that can trigger organized patterns and sequences at lower levels, exist at the highest cortical levels. Lesions of the septal nuclei produce complex behavioral changes without disturbing the perceptual-mnemonic systems.

At least two conclusions from the neurophysiological studies of voluntary movement follow: (1) There are considerable differences in the neural organization of voluntary and automatic (habituated) motor activities. (2) The structures in the medial diencephalon form part of a trigger mechanism that is involved in the initiation of voluntary movement.

What Is Voluntary Action? Vanderwolf's scholarly presentation does not answer the question.

First, I think it can be said that voluntary activity involves the possibility of choice. In human decisions there are often several courses of possible action. The subject feels that he is free to decide but actually he is influenced by considerations based on past experiences, and by his biases, moods, and temporary metabolic state as well as by the environmental situation.

Second, in human voluntary action the subject arrives at a plan, a determination or mental set to act in a particular way. In a specific instance the subject can usually give an account of the factors that influenced his decision. He can state his plan.

Third, involuntary actions are commonly determined by environmental events. Involuntary attention, for example, is produced by movement in the perceptual field, by certain intense stimulations such as loud sounds, by a novel change or unexpected event, etc. In contrast to these external determinants of perception and action is voluntary attention which implies a mental set or fixed determination to observe or act in a particular way.

The study of voluntary attention and action, in my opinion, resolves itself into an examination of the factors that influence and regulate behavior. In my food preference studies, for example, the rat has a choice. Independent evidence indicates that the food that elicits the more intense positive activation will increasingly dominate the choice. But, of course, the problem of describing the mechanisms of choice is much more complex than this. At every stage of development there is interaction between gustatory and intraorganic factors.

The Interactional View of Emotional Behavior. Tolman (1923), in describing persistent purposive behavior, emphasized the stimulus-response relationship. In defining emotion, he wrote, it is not the stimulus-situation *as such* nor the response *as such* that defines an emotion. Rather it is the response as affecting or calculated to affect the stimulus-situation that defines emotional behavior. Thus, in fear it is escape from the stimulus-object, in anger the destruction of it, and in love the encouragement or enticement of the stimulus-object which objectively characterizes the different emotions. It is the "response-as-back-acting-upon-the-stimulus" which distinguishes emotions as such.

Each emotion is characterized by a tendency toward its own particular type of adaptive behavior. The adaptive behavior appears as an adjustment to the emotional disturbance. Tolman's view clearly implies a dynamic interaction between organism and environment and his view stresses the adaptive behavior that can arise from an emotional upset.

Tolman's emphasis upon the adaptive value of emotion is similar to that of Arnold and Leeper. In presenting a perceptual-motivational theory of emotion Leeper (1965) asked: How are emotions distinguished from each other? He rejected as not fully adequate the views that emotions are distinguished on the basis of conscious experiences or as perceived patterns of bodily reactions or by the disruptive effects or by the lack of adequate adjustment.

These views, Leeper said, are partially correct but there must be some more basic means of recognizing and distinguishing emotions. Leeper wrote that emotional processes are distinguished from each other, and from other types of processes, on the basis of their *motivational* effects. Thus in fear one flees, in anger one strikes, in love one entices, etc. We recognize and distinguish emotions by their dynamic effects, by what the individual does while in an emotional state and situation. Emotions *are* motives, Leeper stated, and akin to the traditional motives and drives.

With this emphasis on motivation, Leeper considers the relation between emotional motives and cognitive events. He points to the important role of perception in the arousal and regulation of emotional behavior. Perception and emotion are commonly regarded as separate processes but actually they are closely interrelated. Darwin, as we have seen, recognized this relation long ago: If a dog approaches a stranger, his stance is that of hostility; but if the dog suddenly *perceives* his beloved master, hostility vanishes and the dog instantly becomes friendly. Perception of an environmental object produces the emotional behavior. See pages 83-5.

According to Tolman, Leeper, and other psychologists, then, an emotion is a *dynamic* relation between an organism and its environment. This is an *interactional* view.

The interactional view of emotional behavior can be contrasted with views that are more restricted, on the one hand, to the organism and, on the other hand, to the environment. E. J. Kempf, for example, regarded the autonomic nervous system as dominant over the cerebrospinal system. Tensions are built up in the stomach, intestines, rectum, liver, salivary glands, bladder, diaphragm, heart, lungs, prostate gland, external genitals, kidneys, and other organs. These tensions or "strivings" from the vegetative organs, regulated by the autonomic system, make primary demands upon the cerebrospinal system which is the slave of the autonomic system. See page 81.

Kempf's emphasis on the dominance of autonomic functions implies that the primary motivations arise within the organism. This view is just as extreme as that of environmentalists who attempt to write a psychology without reference to the role of internal bodily processes. Radical behaviorists of the B. F. Skinner type can write a psychology in terms of the organism-environment relation without troubling about what goes on inside the skin of the animal. The environmental situation is the prime determinant of behavior, including so-called emotional reactions.

The interactional view takes full account of all conditions that influence behavior, internal and external, but emphasizes the dynamic relation between organism and environment. Emotional behavior is always an interaction between external and internal factors; and the interaction takes full account of the past experiences, moods and motives of the subject.

An interactional point of view is implied in many of the common sense accounts of emotional behavior. As a single example consider the delightful account of Melzack (1967) who describes the laughter of his five-year-old daughter in response to tickling:

> I would like to begin this discussion by telling you about my daughter. She is five years old, plump and cute, and she loves to be tickled—by me or my wife, but not by strangers. She often asks me to tickle her, which I do gladly, and she laughs uproariously, squirms around in delight, and asks for more when I stop. If I tickle too hard, or change my expression and pretend to scowl, she tries to get away from me. If I persist, she becomes frantic in her attempt to escape, and her laughter may turn to tears. The moment my tickling movements become gentle again, or my scowl changes back to a smile, all is well, and the game continues as before. This description also applies to my four-year-old son, who is even more ticklish than my daughter. Sometimes it is not even necessary for me to touch him: all I have to do is extend my hand and say that I am going to tickle him, and that is enough to get him laughing. [60]

Now in this example there is: (1) an emotion-provoking sensory input; (2) a high level of arousal or excitement which pervades the whole of behavior; (3) a central mediating process—such as the daughter's interpretation of the scowl or of the intention of a stranger. And, of course, the emotional behavior depends obviously upon an *interaction* between the daughter and her social environment. Laughter—a characteristic pattern of response—is only part of the total picture. An emotion is more than a pattern of reaction.

CONCLUSION

The physiological theories of emotion start from facts of conscious experience or facts of behavior and attempt to give an account of the internal neural and chemical processes that accompany the psychological events. Confusion arises over the fact that there are two or more points of view. Consciously experienced emotion is *not* observed objectively in the nervous system; neither are the environmental situations that induce emotional behavior. An *interactional* point of view is necessary to do justice to the facts. There is a continuing dynamic interaction between organism and environment within an ecosystem.

An emotion involves the organism as a whole living within an ecosystem. Well-organized patterns of reaction (the final products of eons of organic evolution) appear during emotional behavior. Emotional behavior, however, involves considerably more than these integrated patterns. The emotional patterns are organized in the diencephalon and lower subcortical stations. The patterns become integrated into various forms of purposive behavior.

Visceral changes of emotion involve both divisions of the autonomic nervous system and not the sympathetic system alone. During a great deal of emotional behavior the autonomic and cerebrospinal systems function together in an integrated manner.

The view is unsound that the autonomic nervous system regulates involuntary processes and the cerebrospinal system voluntary activities. Voluntary behavior involves a trigger mechanism that can direct an organism's behavior in one direction or another. Choice can be determined by environmental events or by memory traces in the brain or by a prevailing mood or drive. Little is known about the distinction between voluntary and involuntary behavior. More important is the basic distinction between automatic, habituated, activity and behavior that is innately determined. The process of habituation needs further study.

The hormones and other chemical agents in the circulating blood have profound effects upon behavior and upon the more permanent moods and affective states as well as upon the processes of homeostatic regulation. The chemical approach to problems of motivation and emotion is of prime importance.

READING SUGGESTIONS ON BODILY PROCESSES IN EMOTION

For historical background and orientation I suggest a quick perusal of Darwin's classical work, *The Expression of the Emotions in Man and Animals* (1872). Although written 100 years ago, the book contains a wealth of observations (despite anecdotal material) which have permanent value. William James' chapter on emotion, in the second volume of his *Psychology*, is another classic written in a delightful style. An influential book that has aroused considerable research and criticism is W. B. Cannon's work, *Bodily Changes in Pain, Hunger, Fear and Rage; an Account of Recent Researches into the Function of Emotional Excitement* (second edition, 1929). Further, if anyone wants to delve into the theories of feeling and emotion during the remote past, I suggest Gardiner, H. M., Metcalf, R. C., and Beebe-Center, J. G., *Feeling and Emotion: a History of Theories* (1937).

There is a wealth of older experimental material that deals with the affective processes. References can be found in current textbooks on physiological and experimental psychology. I will mention three special sources of bibliography: Ruckmick, C. A., *The Psychology of Feeling and Emotion* (1936). Lund, F. H., *Emotions; their Psychological, Physiological and Educative Implications* (1939). Arnold, M. B., *Emotion and Personality* (1960, two volumes).

At the present writing the serious student of emotion is embarrassed by an explosion of technical information dealing with the chemistry, physiology, and psychology of affective processes. The research literature is of interest to chemists, physiologists, psychiatrists, psychologists, and others. The qualified student and research psychologist could well examine papers contained in the following works: Schildkraut, J. J. and Kety, S. S., Biogenic amines and emotion (article in *Science*, 1967, 156, 21-30). Glass, D. C. (Editor), *Neurophysiology and Emotion* (1967). Experimental approaches to the study of emotional behavior in *Annals of the New York Academy of Sciences*, 159, 3, 1969. The book edited by Perry Black entitled, *Physiological Correlates of Emotion* (1970), came to my attention after the present chapter had been completed. This book obviously contains valuable articles by experts and references to the experimental literature.

Historical Note upon the James-Lange Theory of Emotion. W. James' paper "What is an emotion?" appeared in *Mind* in 1884. C. Lange's paper was published in Danish in 1885 and translated into German by

H. Kurella in 1887 under the title *Ueber Gemüthsbewegungen.* James restated his theory in 1890 in his *Principles of Psychology*, Vol II, Chap. 25. Lange's article has been translated into English from Kurella's German edition in a volume edited by K. Dunlap: C. G. Lange and W. James, *The Emotions*, in the Psychology Classics Series (Baltimore: Williams and Wilkins, 1922). Some of the more important historical references are contained in Boring's *A History of Experimental Psychology* (New York: Century, 1929; 502-504, 532).

For an introduction to the criticism of this theory the student is referred to: W. B. Cannon, the James-Lange theory of emotions: A critical examination and an alternative theory, *Amer. J. Psychol.*, 1927, 39, 106-124; W. B. Cannon, Neural organization for emotional expression, in the *Wittenberg Symposium on Feelings and Emotions* (Worcester, Mass.: Clark Univ. Press, 1928; pp. xvi + 454). Cannon's theory has been criticized by E. B. Newman, F. T. Perkins, and R. H. Wheeler, under the heading: Cannon's theory of emotion, a critique, *Psychol. Rev.*, 1930, 37, 305-326. This criticism was answered by Cannon: Again the James-Lange and the thalamic theories of emotion, *Psychol. Rev.*, 1931, 38, 281-295. Citations of other experimental studies of the theory can be found in Bard (1934).

This theory has been discussed by Ruckmick (1936), *The Psychology of Feeling and Emotion*, in a chapter entitled: The James-Lange-Sergi Theory.

Chapter VII

Feeling and Emotion as Conscious Processes

When we speak of the physiological correlates or the substrata of emotion we imply that an emotion is something different from the observed bodily processes. Emotion, as we know it in everyday life, is, in fact, a conscious experience. Everyone, except perhaps the psychologist, knows what an emotion is! Fear, anger, rage, terror, horror, lust, embarrassment, agony, excitement, disgust, grief, jealousy, shame, humiliation, amusement, laughter, joy, sorrow, weeping, etc., *are* emotions. Trouble with the psychologist is that emotions are exceedingly complex experiences which must be analyzed piecemeal and from different points of view.

When Darwin (1872) wrote upon *The expression of emotions in man and animal*, the word *expression* implied that the true emotion was an inner consciousness which is revealed or "expressed" by physical signs. Although Darwin himself paid little attention to the strictly subjective aspect of emotion, his contemporaries pictured an emotion primarily as a conscious experience.

The human "expressions," whether of an emotion or of a less disruptive feeling, are muscular movements and glandular secretions—*objective* facts of nature. The conscious experience which is "expressed" is purely a *subjective* datum.

Recognizing this distinction, psychologists have devised two kinds of method for the experimental study of feeling and emotion: the method of *impression* and the method of *expression*. Both methods imply the primary importance of the conscious experience.

The various forms of the *method of impression* aim at getting a descriptive account of the conscious experience of the subject or of his evaluation of objects presented during the experiment. Typically the subject is presented with perfumes, colored surfaces, geometrical designs, or other materials. Following the "impression" the subject makes a report, in the form of a preference judgment or an aesthetic evaluation or a direct report or description of the felt experience. The form of the report varies with the aim of the experiment. The experimenter copies the subject's reports and later makes an analysis of the protocol.

The many forms of the *method of expression* are designed to obtain graphic records of bodily changes in respiration, pulse, blood pressure, blood volume, sweat secretion, etc. These graphic records are measured and analyzed by the psychologist in the hope of discovering some relation between subjective experience and its outer "expression."

In the two preceding chapters the bodily changes of emotion were examined for their own sake rather than as "expressions" of *felt* experience. In the present chapter *felt* experiences will be examined with little reference to bodily changes. The reason for this plan is that *felt* experiences and bodily changes are regarded as different aspects of a single natural event. The word *expression* implies a dualism of viewpoint but not necessarily a dualism of reality.

THE PHENOMENOLOGY OF SUBJECTIVE AND OBJECTIVE EXPERIENCE

Observation in the natural sciences involves certain features. Every observation involves some phenomenon which constitutes its object and every observation involves an observer. Usually the observer has a particular purpose or intent in making an observation but this is not necessary. The bodily processes of observing may be reduced to simpler physiological processes in the receptors, nerves, muscles, and other structures; but this physiological reduction is incomplete because it leaves out of account the phenomenon observed. Scientific observation is generally followed by a report which expresses in words or other symbols the phenomenon observed. Record is made of the object, event or relation which is observed.

Within psychology the method of observation is essentially the same as in other natural sciences. How then does psychology differ from physiology, physics, chemistry, and other objective sciences? In my opinion the traditional gulf between physical and psychological sciences exists only for those who have made it. All the sciences form a single system of organized knowledge. Each science is limited in scope.

Titchener (1912*a*, 1912*b*) argued that the method of observation is the same inside and outside of psychology. All observation, he said, involves clear experience followed by report. The difference between systematically controlled introspection, on the one hand, and physical observation on the other, lies in the point of view, or attitude, of the observer. For Titchener, the facts of observation are regarded as existential experiences (phenomena) that depend upon an experiencing organism.

Titchener's view is somewhat similar to that of the physicist, Ernst Mach. Mach (1910) wrote:

> A color is a physical object so long as we consider its dependence upon its luminous source, upon other colors, upon heat, upon space, and so forth. Regarding, however, its dependence upon the retina . . . , it becomes a psychological object, a sensation. Not the subject, but the direction of our investigation, is different in the two domains. [14-15]

The psychologist, however, deals with some phenomena that depend largely upon processes within the nervous system and that have no external physical existence. For example, if a subject takes the drug *peyote (Anhalonium Lewinii)* he observes vivid hallucinatory images and experiences distortions of perceived space; only gradually does he return to normal perceptions of phenomenal objects and events. Similarly, dream images and the true images of memory, imagination and thought, are largely dependent upon internal processes in the brain—memory traces laid down by previous experiences. All such experiences are called *subjective* in contrast to the *objective* observations of the physiologist and the physicist.

In simple terms, one can say that subjective experience is dependant upon the experiencing subject. Objective experience is regarded *as if* there were no observer. The objective world exists out there, in its own right, just as if there were no one to observe it. The physical world is believed to be independent of experiencing individuals despite the fact that all we know about it has been garnered from observations of phenomenal experiences—especially from the observations by men of science.

The biological sciences are mostly objective in their methods of observation, experimentation, and theorizing. The study of animal behavior, including human behavior, can be a strictly objective science. But when the psychologist regards the organism as a subject of experience he is inferring that the organism is conscious, i.e., capable of phenomenal experience similar, no doubt, to one's own. The psychologist's organism is an *experiencing individual* capable of perceiving, remembering, feeling, acting.

Views of the Individual and the World. In everyday life, various words are used to designate the human individual. The physician, concerned with matters of health, refers to the individual as a *patient*. The lawyer, trying to help a man write a will, refers to his *client*. The business man speaks of the individual as a *customer*; the clergyman, as a *parishioner*; the teacher, as a *pupil*; and so on. Academic people have other words. We read about the *economic man*, the *political man*, the *religious man*, etc. Students of biology, according to the context, refer to the individual as a *mammal*, a *primate*, of an example of *Homo sapiens*.

The basic sciences have different views of the individual and the world in which he lives.

1. From the *physical* point of view, a man is regarded as a *body* surrounded by other bodies in the physical world. All physical bodies are characterized by their properties—mass, volume, motion, chemical constitution, electrical potential, and the like. If a man jumps out of a plane, he falls to earth; when a parachute checks his fall he still moves in accordance with physical laws. He moves through space like other physical bodies. His falling through space is a kind of movement that is different from the autogenous activity that a psychologist calls behavior.

2. From the *biological* point of view, a man is an *organism* living within a physical environment. Like other organisms the human individual grows, reproduces, responds to stimulation, ingests and assimilates food, eliminates wastes, moves about within his environment, and adapts himself to changing conditions.

Angyal (1941) recognized that the line of distinction between organism and environment is artifical; the line is drawn for convenience only. He proposed that the realm within which the total biological process takes place be called the *biosphere*, that is, the sphere of life. "The biosphere includes both the individual and the environment, not as interacting parts, not as constituents which have independent existence, but as aspects of a single reality which can be separated only by abstraction." See page 200 (*c*).

3. From the point of view of *subjective psychology*, an individual is a *conscious subject*, aware of the world about him as well as of memories, thoughts, emotions and desires. The psychological individual *knows* about the world within which he lives, *reasons* about problems, and *dreams, loves, hates,* and *strives* to reach goals and to carry out intentions.

The world within which the psychological individual lives is described as a world of experience. The individual himself is part of his experienced world. He perceives himself, evaluates himself, builds concepts concerning his nature and existence. An individual's direct experience is sometimes called *phenomenal experience*, and the study of conscious phenomena is called the *phenomenological* approach.

4. From the *social* point of view, a man is a *person* living within a sociocultural environment. At birth the individual enters a world containing other persons—mother, father, nurse, siblings, playmates. He interacts with these persons and gradually develops traits of *personality*.

From his society he acquires attitudes, ways of speaking, of acting, of thinking, and of expressing feelings and emotions. He learns to manipulate tools, to draw, to read.

The cultural environment is more permanent than any person. Culture contains: (1) artifacts—buildings, clothing, tools, weapons, and other physical products of human activity; (2) symbols that preserve ideas from generation to generation—printed words, painted pictures and signs, carvings, and the like; (3) manners, styles, attitudes, and ways of acting that are transmitted directly from person to person. The patterns of culture can and do exist independently of behavior.

The above four views of the individual and his world are summarized in the following tabulation:

Point of View	Individual is named	World is named
Physical	Body	Physical world
Biological	Organism	Environment
Psychological	Subject	Experience
Social	Person	Sociocultural world

These fundamental points of view are frequently combined. Thus there are such compound terms as *psychophysical, biosocial, biochemical, psychophysiological, psychobiological sociopsychological,*etc. We do not need to choose among the views for they supplement each other. They are not contradictory and all are valid within limits.

Subjective and Objective Points of View. As we have seen (page 49), there are different points of view within psychology. Especially prominent is the basic contrast between subjective and objective points of view. There are different tacit assumptions, ways of regarding the world.

The whole system of physical science is evidence for the validity and utility of the objective way of regard. Within psychology, also, there is an objective approach which is unquestionably sound and definitely allied to the other objective sciences, especially to the biological sciences.

Traditionally, however, psychology has been concerned with the conscious experiences of individuals. After-images, dreams, hallucinations, memories and thoughts, feelings, desires, and other aspects of experience (which the physical scientist must ignore), are of great psychological interest. These conscious experiences, along with the whole of objective experience, depend for their existence upon processes within the brain of the experiencing individual. The subjective point of view regards the whole of experience as dependent upon processes within the biological organism.

With all points of view there are two factors. There is always an individual factor (*I*) and a world factor (*W*). The individual is part of the world within which he moves, lives, and has his being.

There is a large literature dealing with subjectivism, the method of introspection, mentalism, and related topics. This is no place to review it. But it must be noted, in passing, that many psychologists reject subjective data and regard the "introspective" method as invalid, and they abhor "mentalism."

In agreement with the *Zeitgeist* Bindra (1959) rejects subjectivism. He puts it this way:

> . . . the various activities must be defined without any reference to subjective states, such as "feelings of anger or anxiety," "desire for affiliation," and "emotion of rivalry." The verbal reports of experiential states are, of course, activities that must be studied like other activities, but such subjective experiences cannot be considered as representing psychologically valid categories for the analysis of behavior.

If we reject the subjective, or individual, point of view, however, we are closing the eyes to a world of fact. But if anyone wishes to close his eyes, there is nothing to stop him.

There are obviously different points of view within psychology. The eclectic is tolerant. His motto is: Live and let live. He recognizes that the phenomena of human experience are relative to points of view. And he is aware of the multiplicity of points of view.

Phenomenology of the Mind-Body Relation. One advantage of the phenomenological point of view is that we can consider problems that arise when viewpoints are shifted (Young, 1924). One such problem is the relation between mental and physical views of phenomena. In the field of emotion, for example, a persistent problem has been the question of how the bodily symptoms and conscious experiences are correlated. The psychology based on common sense assumes a causal interaction between mental and physical events. William James implied a causal interaction when he asked whether we feel sad because we weep, afraid because we tremble or whether (as common sense would have it) we weep because we feel sad, tremble because we are frightened, etc. The question about causation raises the classical mind-body problem.

The philosophical mind-body problem arises, however, only when we shift our point of view. We regard the flash of lightning and the clap of thunder as physical phenomena; and so they are. Lightning and thunder simply occur; they are natural, physical, events beyond our personal control. But from the point of view of an experiencing individual, the lightning is seen and the thunder heard. The perceptions are regarded as *caused by* physical events which can be described. The physiologist can describe the sequence of physical events in sense organs and nerves, but when he comes to the brain he does not find the thunder and lightning. To assume a *physical* cause for the phenomenal experiences it is necessary to shift from the psychological to the physical point of view.

If we start from the subjective point of view, contrastingly, we find that individuals are aware of making decisions, plans of action, commitments and pledges to do something in the future. Individuals believe that these determinations are efficient *causes* of action.

In a psychology based upon common sense these actions are regarded as intended activities or voluntary deeds. It is possible, by shifting to a physical point of view, to regard all muscular movements and their effects as physical processes. But again, the mind-body interaction implies a shift in point of view.

Now it is obvious that the strict and consistent behaviorist cannot discuss anything mental without abandoning his physical, objective, point of view. If he assumes that animals *consciously* perceive, feel, remember, etc., he is injecting subjective (anthropomorphic) concepts into his account of behavior. The strict physicalist, in describing behavior, avoids anything that might be called mental. Skinner is right about this but his psychology is limited.

Again, if we start from a consistent subjective point of view, it is clear that any existence outside of and beyond phenomenal experience (including the entire physical world) is assumed, not given to waking consciousness. The state of unconscious existence (during dreamless sleep, anesthesia, coma, etc.) is an inference, an hypothesis. The existence of an independently real world is *assumed* on the basis of phenomenal experiences.

Therefore, if we are consistently objective, the existence of experiences other than one's own is an hypothesis. If we are consistently subjective, the entire physical world is an hypothetical existence. The phenomenological approach recognizes diverse points of view. Shifts from one point of view to another are possible and shape the experience. The eclectic in psychology makes such shifts to throw light on problems.

In dealing with the practical problems of living, the psychiatrist and psychologist, as well as the man on the street, do not hesitate to shift from one point of view to another when the situation calls for a shift. Thus the psychiatrist gives physical treatment to the body, using drugs, surgery, and other physical means; he also uses psychotherapy based on words and on an understanding of the patient's emotional conflicts and frustrations, his hopes and fears, his ideas and attitudes, problems, and other factors that are clearly and definitely mental (based on an individual's phenomenal experience within his biosphere). The dual approach is necessary; and it works. One does not need to postulate two individuals—a mind and a body. In psychosomatic medicine a single individual is postulated. The single individual that one assumes to exist has many attributes that differ with the point of view from which the attributes are inferred. Thus the physical, biological and social attributes differ according to the point of view that is assumed.

For the psychologist the individual is at times assumed to be conscious and at other times unconscious. He dreams, imagines, thinks, perceives the world, remembers; he feels pleased and displeased, anxious, angry, affectionate, hateful, or in other mood; he decides upon plans for action and acts according to his decision; he has traits of personality and character, abilities and aptitudes, biases, habits, attitudes, and so on. This kind of an individual obviously has more functions and capacities than an organism viewed physically.

The phenomenologist is free to postulate several kinds of individuals: physical bodies, living organisms, social persons, minds, souls, and so on, but the principle of parsimony dictates that the postulate of a single individual, or being, viewed in different lights and from different points of view, is all that we necessarily have to assume.

My view is that of *biological monism*. I regard the individual as a living organism with chemical, physical, biological, psychological, social and possibly spiritual attributes. The special task of the psychologist is to consider the mental attributes. The study of behavior is an important methodological approach, but it is by no means the only approach to psychology. The study of conscious experiences is an important part of psychology.

AFFECTIVE PROCESSES AS CONSTITUENTS OF HUMAN EXPERIENCE

It is possible to study phenomena in many ways. Thus visual phenomena, as noted above, can be studied physically in relation to the theories of light or physiologically in relation to the theories of vision. Visual phenomena can also be studied descriptively without reference to any explanation. Thus the color pyramid represents the relations of hue, lightness and saturation when color quality is considered apart from perceptual meanings and significance. The color pyramid is a purely descriptive psychological construct; it presents factual relations among visual phenomena that may or may not require an explanation.

Similar constructs have been made for the senses of hearing, smell, taste and touch. These phenomenal qualities, abstracted from perceptual meanings, are called sensations. Physiologically, the sensations are regarded as processes in the receptors and nerves that depend upon receptor stimulations. The physiological view is objective. The view of a pure descriptive psychology is subjective. Both views are valid and they are closely related.

Sensation and Affection. Throughout the history of psychology attempts have been made to regard the simple feelings of pleasantness and unpleasantness as *sensory* processes or at least as attributes of sensation. C. Stumpf, for example, regarded pleasantness and unpleasantness as *Gefühlsempfindungen* (Titchener, 1908).

A recent example of the identification of affective qualities with sensory processes is found in the doctoral research of J. P. Nafe (1924), in Titchener's laboratory. Nafe argued that previous investigators (including the writer) had made their subjects *feel* without training them to be *observers* of feeling. If the affective qualities can be studied scientifically, Nafe argued, these affective qualities must be palpable. After a series of careful experiments Nafe concluded that pleasantness and unpleasantness *are* palpable components of conscious experience.

Ten years after publication of his thesis, Nafe (1934) restated his conclusion as follows:

> Pleasantness, as a psychological experience, consists of a pattern of discreet points of experience in the general nature of a thrill but usually less intensive. It is vaguely localized about the upper part of the body. Unpleasantness is similar but characteristically duller, heavier, more of the pressure type of experience, and is localized toward the abdomen or the lower part of the body. [1076]

I will not review the controversy that followed publication of Nafe's thesis that pleasantness is experienced as a bright pressure localized thoracically and unpleasantness as a dull pressure localized abdominally. Titchener accepted the finding. Prior to Nafe's doctoral dissertation Titchener had already placed bright and dull pressures on his system for touch qualities. See Young (1932*a*).

Nafe's research removed an inconsistency in Titchener's system of psychology. Titchener had long insisted that the basic method of science, including psychology, is observation of phenomena, from a specific point of view, followed by direct report. But he also claimed that when one attempts to observe the affective qualities *sui generis* one observes only sensory processes. He had previously argued that pleasantness and unpleasantness are non-sensory elements (components, constituents) of conscious experience. Pain, he said, is often experienced along with unpleasantness, but when one attempts to observe the unpleasantness *as such*, one finds only the pain sensation. There are, of course, several qualities of sensory pain. After Nafe's thesis, however, Titchener became a consistent sensationist.

One difficulty with regarding pleasantness and unpleasantness as *sensory* processes lies in the fact that there are no peripheral receptors for the affective qualities. Pleasantness and unpleasantness can be elicited in all sense departments—by odors, tastes, cutaneous and intraorganic experiences, colors and tones. Moreover, some stimulations elicit pleasantness and others unpleasantness, in all sense modalities, while under other conditions the same stimulations can be hedonically neutral, indifferent. Thus while pleasantness and unpleasantness are definitely elicited by certain kinds of receptor stimulations these affective qualities are accessory components of perception and are existentially and logically independent of any specific sensory quality. The affective qualities, I believe, are *non-sensory* constituents of phenomenal experience.

This view, of course, recognizes the fact that there is frequently an inevitable and compulsory association between sensory and affective qualities. Some receptor stimulations are consistently and uniformly pleasing; others, displeasing; others, indifferent. These are facts of human experience.

Affection and Meaning. Pleasantness and unpleasantness actually arise in many *meaningful* situations which are perceived, remembered, imagined, expected. Situations that involve reward or punishment, praise or reproof, victory or defeat, success or failure, etc., are commonly *felt* as pleasing or displeasing. And, of course, many everyday experiences are hedonically neutral. The affective qualities depend upon the *significance* or *meaning* of phenomenal situations, as distinct from the kind and intensity of receptor stimulations.

Titchener (1909) was much concerned with the nature of meaning. When the introspective methods are applied to the analysis of meaning (as in the famous controversy over imageless thought), Titchener and his students found only sensory and imaginal contents of experience. Titchener argued that these observed contents of experience "carry" the meaning. *The meaning of a perceptual pattern or of an idea resides in its sensory-imaginal context.* Otherwise the meaning itself does not exist within conscious experience, although meaning may be "carried" by brain habit. This view was not accepted by psychologists of the Würzburg school.

Now this view of meaning is quite similar to the view of affection that was taken by Titchener after the research of Nafe. In both the cognitive and affective processes only sensory and imaginal elements of experience are directly observed. The question arises, therefore, as to how *meaning* and *feeling* differ and how they are related. Let us consider several answers to the question:

Harvey A. Carr (1925), a functional psychologist of the Chicago school, took it for granted that the perceived object and the organic reactions that it elicits are the only observable contents that can be detected in the search for an affective element. Vague organic effects and reverberations, he said, are wrongly taken to be an affective element. In so far as these organic reverberations can be observed, they are sensory in nature.

In a textbook chapter dealing with the affective and evaluative aspects of human experience, Carr stated that the term *affection*, within psychology, refers to those aspects of experience on account of which we label them as pleasant or unpleasant. An experience which is judged to be neither pleasant nor unpleasant is said to be lacking in affective tone, indifferent.

Carr stated that pleasantness and unpleasantness are judgments—meaningful processes—based on normal reaction tendencies. Innately we are so organized that we normally react to certain stimulus-situations so as to enhance, maintain, or repeat them. Other situations arouse negative adaptive behavior—responses which minimize or rid us of their stimuli and which we do not repeat. For example, certain odors cause us to hold the breath or nostrils, flee from their vicinity, and avoid them in the future. Other odors cause us to take another whiff. A conscious experience is judged to be pleasant if it arouses the positive type of response and judged to be unpleasant if it arouses a negative reaction. Situations which arouse neither type of adaptive behavior are regarded as neutral, indifferent, lacking in affective tone. These judgments, based on our normal reaction tendencies, are verbalized as pleasant or unpleasant. As an individual develops, the judgments become modified by motivational and other influences.

The strength of Carr's judgmental theory of affection lies in the fact that innate positive and negative reactions to certain stimuli do assuredly exist; the reactions definitely occur and can be observed as behavioral processes.

Carr goes on to consider the nature of evaluation in relation to feeling. Pleasing things are regarded as good and valuable; they are desirable. Displeasing things are regarded as bad; they are undesirable and disapproved. A child identifies what is pleasant with good and what is unpleasant with bad. Later he has to learn that some pleasant things are bad and some unpleasant, good. There are, therefore, both hedonic and judgmental (cognitive) standards of evaluation.

Carr's judgmental theory of affective processes and values raises an important question: Can the conscious experiences of pleasantness and unpleasantness be reduced to meaningful judgments? Is there any difference between feeling and meaning, between affection and cognition?

Arnold (1960, Vol. I, p. 74) answers the second of these questions in the affirmative: there is a difference between affective and cognitive aspects of experience. She defines feeling as "*a positive or negative reaction to some experience. Pleasure and pleasantness are positive reactions, varying only in intensity. They can be defined as a welcoming of something sensed that is appraised as beneficial and indicates enhanced functioning. Pain and unpleasantness are negative reactions of varying intensity and can be defined as resistance to something sensed that is appraised as harmful and indicates impaired functioning. What is pleasant is liked, what is unpleasant, disliked.*" [Italics in original]

Central to Arnold's definition is the concept of appraisal, or evaluation, of an experience. Pleasantness and unpleasantness are rudimentary (not necessarily verbalized) appraisals of experience. There are, as Carr pointed out, built-in bodily structures that lead a naive organism to react positively toward some stimulations and negatively towards others. Fragrant odors, sweet tastes, sexual stimulations, lead to positive reactions and to *felt* experiences that are immediately appraised as pleasant. Foul odors, bitter tastes, painful stimulations, lead to negative reactions and to *felt* experiences that are immediately appraised as unpleasant.

But Arnold recognizes a second kind of appraisal that is definitely cognitive in nature and that depends upon cerebral processes. Thus man and subhuman animals *perceive* situations in their natural environments and "intuitively" appraise them in terms of danger, potential food, a mate, or something else. There is a *cognitive estimation* of the situation along with a more or less immediate reaction to it. This "intuitive" appraisal of situations is especially important in the causation of emotional behavior. In the second volume of her scholarly treatise, Arnold considers the neural anatomy of an *estimative* system.

Now Arnold's view of affective processes differs from that of Carr in that she regards the verbal reports "pleasant" and "unpleasant" as based directly upon *felt* conscious experiences while Carr regards these verbal reports as based upon innate positive and negative reaction tendencies. The two views are compatible when we recognize that *felt* experiences are subjective phenomena and reaction tendencies can be observed objectively (and also experienced).

But there is an important difference between these views. Carr's judgmental theory of affection blurs the distinction between affective experience and cognitive judgment. The implication is that *feeling* and *meaning* are psychologically equivalent or identical. Feeling must be regarded as a special kind of meaning.

I think that this implication is wrong and that a genuine difference exists between *felt experience*, on the one hand, and *cognitive meaning*, on the other. My bias goes back to a doctoral study, more than half a century ago, in Titchener's laboratory at Cornell (Young, 1918*a*, 1918*b*, and 1930). The experiment dealt with so-called "mixed feelings" or experiences in which pleasantness and unpleasantness presumably coexist. More than 2,000 attempts were made to please and displease a group of subjects simultaneously. Introspective reports were taken. The result was negative. There were no "mixed feelings."

The reports turned out to be of two types. In some reports the subjects described the presence or absence of *felt* pleasantness (or unpleasantness) and the qualitative and intensive hedonic changes during a brief experimental period. In another type of report the observers referred the *meaning* of pleasantness (or unpleasantness) to some object or situation. The affective quality was said to be "of," "from," "due to," "caused by," some perceived object or situation. In this type of report the "feeling" was commonly localized at the place of the object or referred to the object. But in the first type of report the affective quality tended not to be localized or referred. Some of the observers drew a distinction between, (1) pleasantness (or unpleasantness) as *felt* and (2) the awareness that an object had been or is (now or potentially) a source of feeling. With the first type of report, pleasantness and unpleasantness were never described as coexisting; the positive and negative affective processes were reported as varying in intensity and temporal course but not as *felt* simultaneously. With the second type of report there were some "mixed feelings" but one or more of the "feelings" was a cognitive meaning or judgment with the "feeling" referred to an object or situation.

In everyday life a distinction between feeling and meaning is commonly drawn. Thus when we say, "This is a pleasant day," we are making a cognitive judgment. The statement is ambiguous as to what is actually *felt* here and now. The statement may be purely verbal with no organic involvement. The cognitive judgment is certainly not equivalent to a controlled introspective report that pleasantness of a certain intensity and duration is *felt* here and now.

I concluded that pleasantness and unpleasantness *when actually felt with an appreciable degree of intensity* are dynamically opposed and do not coexist, at least under conditions of the experiment.

Now Beebe-Center (1932) regards pleasantness and unpleasantness as *concepts* characterizing experience. They are quantitative variables so related to each other that they may be represented respectively by the positive and negative values of a single algebraic variable. See Figure 11 (page 71). This variable he called *hedonic tone.* By regarding pleasantness and unpleasantness as concepts, Beebe-Center sidestepped the problem of determining the experiential nature of hedonic processes—whether hedonic tone is sensory, semantic, or an independent component of conscious experience.

Incidentally, the bipolar hedonic continuum has been found to represent accurately the dynamic relations of positive and negative reactions that can be objectively observed with laboratory rats. The hedonic continuum, therefore, is an example of a theoretical construct that can be formulated on the basis of subjective experience or on the basis of objective data from laboratory animals. Despite a wide difference in point of view toward phenomenal experience, there is a common theoretical interpretation.

Cognitive and Emotive Attitudes. Within conscious experience an important role is played by attitudes. Some conscious attitudes are purely cognitive; others are emotive.

In a scholarly review of the experimental studies of the thought processes, Titchener (1909) summarized the findings of introspective studies of conscious attitudes as follows:

> The attitude most frequently reported is that of doubt, with the cognate forms of uneasiness, difficulty, uncertainty, effort, hesitation, vacillation, incapacity, ignorance, and the opposite experiences of certainty, assent, conviction that a judgment passed is right or wrong. To the old-fashioned psychologist all these terms have an emotive ring, and it is worth noting that the same observers refer to surprise, wonder, astonishment, expectation and curiosity as emotions. But there is another group of attitudes that do not carry the emotive suggestion. These are described, in confessedly roundabout phrase, as remembrance of instructions, remembrance that one is to answer in sentences, recollection of the topic of past conversations, realisation that nonsense-combinations have been presented earlier in the experimental series, realisation that sense or nonsense is coming, realisation that a certain division will leave no remainder. Here we are in the sphere of intellection . . . . [101-102]

Thus some conscious attitudes are described in cognitive terms. Others are emotive.

Positive and negative behavioral tendencies and attitudes are commonly acquired on the basis of hedonic and cognitive experiences. Regulative attitudes may be latent or activated. Attitudes may be hedonically neutral (largely cognitive) or they may be strongly emotionalized. Affectively-toned attitudes color our conscious experiences.

Nina Bull (1951) emphasized the importance of attitudes as determinants of emotions. Through experience we have acquired a *Weltanschauung*—an outlook on life—which colors what we feel, think, and do.

Affection and Action. There is general agreement among psychologists that a positive affective process is shown by a tendency to accept and continue the stimulus conditions that elicit the response and a negative affective process is shown by a tendency to reject and terminate the stimulus conditions.

In a review of different approaches to the study of affectivity, W. A. Hunt (1939) made a pertinent generalization:

> It would seem fairly safe to assume that most psychologists today would agree that the concepts, pleasantness and unpleasantness, as used in psychology tacitly refer to general attitudes of acceptance and rejection and that the field of affectivity covers the investigation of these attitudes in their development and operation. . . . a brief summary would run something like this: The organism may either accept or reject a stimulus. The acceptance or rejection is carried out through appropriate bodily adjustments. These reactions are said to constitute the affective response and are assumed to be a functional entity of some kind. [824]

The attitudes of acceptance and rejection are expressed verbally by the phrases "I like it" and "I dislike it." These expressions, however, can refer to: (1) an immediate, contemporary, reaction tendency, or (2) a relatively stable disposition that has been acquired through experience and that can be reported without any affectivity.

Neal Miller (1963) pointed out that these positive and negative reactions indicate a GO-STOP principle. He postulated the existence of two fundamental mechanisms which he labeled the GO and STOP mechanisms. He reflected that this principle presents an alternative to the doctrine of reinforcement through drive reduction.

It is obvious that we cannot identify all GO reactions with pleasant and all STOP reactions with unpleasant. The motorist, for example, has learned to react to traffic lights in terms of GO-CAUTION-STOP. These reactions are thoroughly habituated, automatic, and do not indicate affectivity.

When we were considering the nature of motivation we emphasized the fundamental importance of the relation between positive and negative forms of activation and their relation to reinforcement. See pages 67 to 74. On the neurophysiological level, as Sherrington demonstrated, the simplest movement of a limb involves positive excitation of a muscle and simultaneous inhibition of the tonus of its antagonist.

The polarization between positive and negative phases of reaction is found, in fact, in many kinds of psychological processes: in sense feelings (pleasant-unpleasant); moods (cheerful-depressed); emotions (joy-sorrow); evaluations (good-bad); attitudes (liking-disliking); motivations (GO-STOP); expectations (hope-disappointment); and others.

THE QUANTIFICATION OF HEDONIC VALUES

For the quantitative study of hedonic values, functional reports and ratings are useful. A functional report in the form "I like it" or "I dislike it" reveals the attitude of the subject toward a particular stimulus-object or situation. Such a report is not analytical. It tells us nothing about the experiential basis of attitudes. It does, however, give significant information about bodily functions that are beyond the ken of introspective psychology.

To illustrate the utility of the functional type of report, consider the following experiments with odors and tones:

Hedonic Reactions to Odors. In an experiment with children and college students the hedonic reactions to odors were tested (Kniep, Morgan, and Young, 1931). Chemically stable substances were presented under standard conditions of instruction, ventilation, etc. Each subject was instructed to smell a substance and to report immediately whether he liked or disliked the odor.

Results are shown in Figure 47. Chemical names of the odorous substances are given at the base of the figure, in rank order for adults,

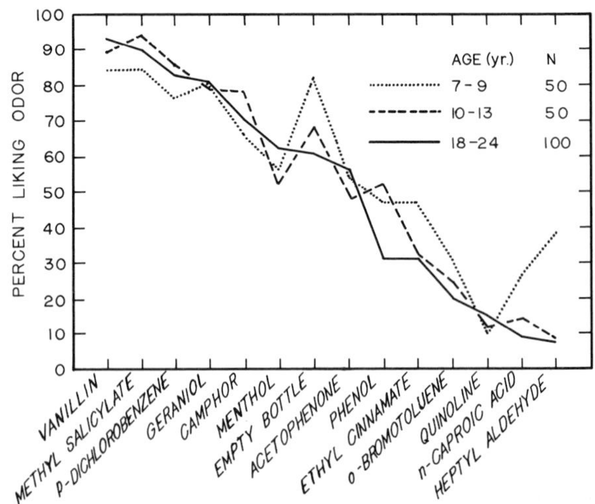

Figure 47. Affective reactions to odors for three age groups. *From* Kniep, Morgan, and Young (1931).

from the most frequently liked (vanillin, a synthetic vanilla) to the least frequently liked odor (heptyl aldehyde). The solid line shows percents of adults *liking* the odors. The other lines show percents of children *liking* the odors.

The curves for the three age groups are strikingly similar. Coefficients of correlation among the three age groups are exceedingly high—in the range of .91 to .96. These high coefficients indicate that whatever determines the hedonic value of these odors is relatively independent of age. Moreover, since most of the smells were unfamiliar to the subjects and since each odor was presented to a subject only once, it is reasonable to assume that these hedonic values are independent of prior experience. These data suggest that the likes and dislikes of odors depend upon some built-in bodily structures.

Incidentally, there appears to be an age difference in the hedonic reaction to an empty, sterilized, bottle—presented as a control stimulus in the context of odors. We have no explanation of possible age differences.

Hedonic Reactions to Tones. In another study a group of 39 adults rated the pleasantness and unpleasantness of relatively pure tones, using a graphic rating scale. The tones were produced electrically. Each tone sounded for 5 to 8 seconds after which the tone was immediately rated for a degree of pleasantness or unpleasantness.

Using part of the data collected by Singer and Young (1941*a*), Guilford (1954) plotted the chart of isohedons shown in Figure 48.

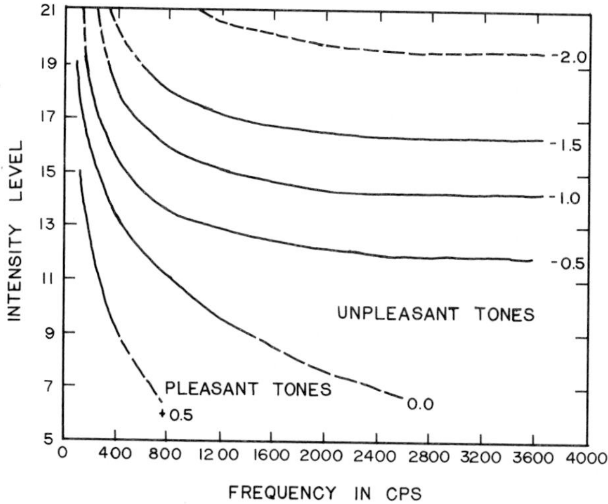

Figure 48. Isohedons in a stimulus-field of relatively pure tones. Plotted by Guilford (1954) from data of Singer and Young (1941).

Guilford (1939) had previously defined an isohedon as a line of constant affective value in a stimulus-field. This particular stimulus-field is defined by the frequency and energy of relatively pure tonal stimuli.

Note the locus of hedonic indifference—the curve marked 0.0. This curve starts with a tone of 100 cycles per second whose intensity level is at the arbitrary value 19 and ends, by extrapolation, with a tone of approximately 2,600 cycles per second whose intensity level is 7. Above and to the right of the locus of indifference are tones rated as unpleasant. Below and to the left are tones rated as pleasant. The isohedons are separated by steps of one-half sigma above and below the locus of indifference.

Tests of Interests and Values. Verbal materials differ from sensory presentations of odors, tones, tastes, and other sensory stimulations, in that their *meaning* depends on past experience which presumably is the basis of a subject's reaction to words. If a man enjoys playing golf, he will probably give a high interest rating to the word *golf*. If unfamiliar with the game, he might react to the sound of the word, or be quite indifferent to it.

Singer and Young (1941*a*) instructed their subjects to make immediate hedonic ratings of words and phrases that were listed on prepared sheets. Many of the verbal items were borrowed from Strong's Vocational Interest Blank. Examples are: *poker, chopping wood, hearing lectures in astronomy, energetic people, snakes, smoking a pipe, drilling in a company, fortune tellers*, etc.

The subjects gave immediate ratings of interest. On the basis of results for the group as a whole, percentages of pleasantness were computed. Examples of the lowest ranking items are: *people who chew loudly, street beggars, being confined in a hospital, girls who are gold-diggers*. Examples of the highest ranking items are: *playing baseball, musical comedy, singing, dancing.*

Pencil-and-paper tests of values are different in principle from tests of interest in that the subject is instructed to make a choice which, perhaps unconsciously, reveals the relative dominance of different evaluative tendencies and attitudes. As an example consider the study of values by Allport, Vernon, Lindzey (1960). Their test is based on the work of the philosopher Spranger who categorized six main kinds of human values: theoretical, economic, aesthetic, social, political, religious. See pages 105-7.

Values and interests are to a high degree culture-bound. They vary with time and place.

The Specificity of Affective Reactions. Is there a general trait that might be called *readiness-to-be-pleased*? Or are affective reactions specific to the kind of stimulus-situation presented?

It is widely recognized that temperaments differ in the level of cheerfulness: some persons are chronically cheerful and optimistic; others, depressed and pessimistic. A Pollyanna type of temperament might conceivably tend to rate odors, tastes, tones, activities, and other experiences as pleasant more frequently than a chronic grouch.

The data of Singer and Young (1941*b*) are ideally suited to a study of the problem of specificity in affective reactions. They instructed a group of thirty-nine subjects to make affective ratings of odors, tastes, tones, words and phrases, activities, and moods. Ratings were made with a scale that extended from *very great pleasure*, through *indifferent*, to *very great displeasure*. All told there were more than 54,000 individual affective ratings.

In the experiment, the subjects rated affectively the same presentations on two or more occasions. Correlations between different ratings of the same presentations were significantly high. We concluded that individuals are moderately consistent when called upon to rate the same stimulus-situations on different occasions.

But when correlations were tested between one sense modality and another or between one kind of presentation and another, the coefficients of correlation were exceedingly low; some were positive and some negative. There was no indication of a general trait of *readiness-to-be-pleased*. This means that affective ratings, to a remarkable degree, are specific. If John Jones rates the odor of camphor as "very pleasant," we cannot from this fact make any prediction as to how he will rate a particular tone of 1000 cycles per second, or a word or an activity or a mood. Affective ratings are highly specific to the stimulus-situation that is presented. With sensory presentations we found no general tendency to rate all presentations as pleasing or as displeasing.

Eysenck (1940, 1941*a*, 1941*b*), however, has reported the discovery of a general factor of aesthetic taste (T-factor). This may very well be a cognitive factor based on training and experience rather than a general affective factor. After reviewing the studies of Eysenck and other English psychologists, Peters (1942) commented that they all have made the stimulus error. "Stimulus characteristics, such as form, representativeness, classical, romantic, simple, complex, were treated as if they were variables of the physical stimulus with existence independent of any reacting subject." Peters warned us against the stimulus error.

In our studies we did find some evidence of a nonaffective judgmental factor which was most clearly evident in ratings of moods and verbal material but minimal with sensory presentations of odors, tastes, and tones. We can speculate that the affective ratings of sensory stimulations are largely dependent upon built-in neural connections and genuine affective arousals. Other ratings may be cognitive judgments that are more dependent upon past experience and training.

A conclusion similar to ours was reached independently, with another method, by Wechsler (1925) and Wechsler and Jones (1928) who concluded that, "Individuals tend to react in a specific rather than in a general way to emotional situations."

THE CONSCIOUS EXPERIENCE OF EMOTION

Most writers from Darwin to the present day have tacitly assumed that an emotion is a conscious experience that is "expressed." What can be said about the nature of the conscious emotion?

The Cognitive Basis of Emotion. Theorists have emphasized the fact that emotions are elicited by an experienced crisis or predicament. Many situations are threatening: an earthquake, a cyclone, a flood, a fire, an encounter with a maniac or wild animals, etc. Awareness of such situations produces fear. Other situations are frustrating: being confined in a prison cell, being insulted by a rival, failing in a business enterprise, interruption of one's work, etc. Awareness of such situations produces anger or possibly depression or some related emotion. Still other situations elicit joy and euphoria: acceptance by one's lover, sudden achievement of a fortune, victory in a contest, success in an undertaking, jokes that cause laughter, etc.

Now according to the theories of James, Arnold, Leeper, Schachter, and others, the cognitive awareness of an inducing situation is a basic part of the experienced emotion. The inducing situation may be perceived, remembered, imagined, or have some related cognitive basis.

On the level of complex human thought, feelings and emotions frequently arise. Festinger (1957), for example, pointed out that uncomfortable feelings arise from incompatible cognitive elements. Knowledge, opinions, beliefs, do not always agree with each other. Nonfitting relations among the cognitive elements give rise to uncomfortable feelings with pressures to reduce the cognitive dissonance by changes of behavior, of cognition, and circumspect exposure to new information and opinion.

There is also cognitive consonance: the believer is told what he already believes and this confirms his faith; the familiar melody comes to its expected end; the face of a friend is recognized; the expected pay check arrives on time. When all goes well and according to plan the expected event is pleasing. At least it is not dissonant on the cognitive level.

Schachter and Singer (1962) have demonstrated the great importance of cognitive determinants of emotional states. The physiological state produced by injection of adrenaline can be evaluated as joy or fury or fear or simply as a bodily state produced by the drug, depending on one's information and interpretation of inducing conditions. Schachter (1967, 1970) has argued that if we are to understand emotional states, we must consider cognitive, social, and physiological determinants. We cannot assume that the physiological state is an "unconditionally sufficient condition" to account for a psychological event. In other words, the study of emotional states must be approached from several different points of view. There are social, psychological, and physiological aspects.

The Awareness of Bodily Changes. William James (1890) wrote, "the bodily changes follow directly the perception of the exciting fact, and our feeling of the same changes as they occur *is* the emotion." From this it follows that an emotion is not a purely cognitive experience, but an awareness of such bodily changes as palpitation of the heart, cold sweat, trembling, tears, catching of the breath, vocalization, and others. "Without the bodily states following on the perception, the latter would be purely cognitive in form, pale, colorless, destitute of emotional warmth. We might then see the bear, and judge it best to run, receive the insult and deem it right to strike, but we should not actually *feel* afraid or angry." So far as the conscious emotion is concerned, James' view is that the awareness of peripheral bodily changes distinguishes emotional from non-emotional, purely cognitive, states. See page 260.

Implications of this theory, as Schachter (1970) pointed out, are: (a) that different emotions will be accompanied by recognizably different bodily states, and (b) that the manipulation of bodily states, by drugs or surgery, will also manipulate emotional states. These implications have, directly or indirectly, guided much of the research on emotion since James' day. According to Schachter, these implications have not been supported by current research. Schachter believes that an emotion cannot be defined as the awareness of a pattern of bodily changes.

In any event, we do perceive the bodily changes of emotion, mostly in sensory terms, and the organic sensation is an important part of the emotional experience.

Emotion as an Affective Experience. Titchener (1924) characterized the emotional experience as follows: It is a temporal process, a course of consciousness. It is suddenly initiated, arising abruptly and then quieting down. It is a highly complex consciousness, occurring in a total situation or predicament. It is an affective consciousness, being markedly pleasant or unpleasant. It is an insistently organic consciousness. Finally, it is a predetermined consciousness, proceeding to a natural terminus.

Titchener's account of the conscious emotion is comprehensive. If Titchener's statement be contrasted with that of James, a distinctive feature in Titchener's discussion is an emphasis upon the *affective* factor in emotion. For Titchener an emotion is a pleasing or displeasing experience as well as an insistently organic consciousness arising out of a predicament.

If we go back to Wundt's theory of feeling, we can note that an emotion is exciting or calming, pleasing or displeasing, tension-producing or relaxing. An emphasis upon the Wundtian *affective* elements is by no means incompatible with an emphasis upon organic sensation. The views of Titchener and James (so far as they are purely descriptive of the emotional experience) are supplementary rather than opposed.

The Dynamic Aspect of Emotional States. According to McDougall (1926), primary emotions are correlated with principal instincts. Thus fear is correlated with instinctive flight, anger with instinctive pugnacity, elation with instinctive self-assertion, tender emotion with parental instinct, lust with sexual instinct, etc. The subject is aware of these organized, instinctive, activities. McDougall's theory was influential during the early decades of this century, within social psychology, but his view of instinct has been thoroughly discredited.

We are well aware, however, of dynamic tendencies associated with emotional states: to "freeze" or run in fear, to strike or destroy in anger, to be aggressive or retiring when frustrated, to speak out or to withhold words, etc. These dynamic tendencies arise out of the emotional states.

In coping with life's situations there are often blocks, frustrations and conflicts. There are also times of joy, laughter and release from tension. An emotional upset is a perturbation of smooth, ongoing activity.

The emotional consciousness may be confused, aimless, a blur. Perhaps the upset will result in adaptive behavior, perhaps not. The subject may be aware of this disorganized, aimless, don't-know-what-to-do aspect of emotional states. Emotion, however, may also lead to planned, purposive, behavior. Anger is shown by an effort to throw off restraint. There is also a blind rage in which the angry man beats aimlessly at everything within reach or shouts. Again, the angry man may plan some retributive act and proceed step by step to a final attack.

VARIETIES AND DIMENSIONS OF AFFECTIVE EXPERIENCE

Anyone who considers the myriad varieties of human feelings must realize that emotion is only one form of affective experience. What are the forms, varieties, and dimensions of variation of affective experience?

Varieties of Affective Experience. One way to categorize the varieties of affective experience is to specify the conditions that elicit them. The following categories are arbitrary, but they are convenient and well established:

Sense feelings. The perception of odors, tastes, tones, temperatures, lights and colors, etc., often elicits positive and negative hedonic effects that are fused with the sensory processes and dependent upon receptor excitations. Hedonic processes elicited by stimulations of the receptors are called *sense feelings.* Sense feelings vary in hedonic sign (positive or negative), in intensity (strong or weak), and in temporal course (presence, intensive change, absence).

Intraorganic sense feelings. Bodily states of hunger, thirst, fatigue, drowsiness, eliminative tensions, and other intraorganic conditions, are associated with unpleasantness; their relief or satisfaction is associated with pleasantness. In various diseases there are pains, aches, cramps, chills, and other signs of malaise, which are distressful; relief from these conditions is a welcomed hedonic change. There are also positive sexual, and other, organic feelings. A person in sound health experiences positive organic feelings of comfort and well-being.

Activity feelings. Some activities are interesting, agreeable: plays, games and sports, dancing, etc. Other activities are monotonous, boring, disagreeable; we are averse to them. Studies may be dull or they may be bright, exciting, pleasant. Activity feelings are described as interests and aversions.

Sentiments and cognitively based feelings. Sentiments are affective experiences that have a cognitive basis. They rest upon past experiences. Memories, imaginations, anticipations, thoughts, often elicit feelings and emotions. Patriotic, religious, moral, aesthetic, intellectual and other sentiments, rest upon past experience and often on specific training or education. Many recalled experiences, of course, are relatively free from affectivity and sentiment.

Sentiments are usually enduring, persistent. But transient cognitive experiences—good or bad news, victory or defeat, success or failure, reward or punishment—also elicit feelings. Such transient experiences, however, are not regarded as sentiments.

In this connection the *aesthetic feelings* should be mentioned. Such visual factors as size, shape, color, position, balance, symmetry and, in music, melody, harmony, rhythm, and, in general, novelty, familiarity, and other perceived properties, contribute to aesthetic appreciation. Aesthetic judgements are complex. They involve a large cognitive element along with sense feelings.

Emotions. Emotions are complex affective arousals that originate in an organism's attempt to cope with the environment. Biologically basic activities–feeding, fleeing from danger, fighting, sexual behavior, care of the young, etc.–do not always run smoothly. The same is true with the pursuits of civilized man. Emotions arise when there is interference with or disturbance of these activities. Emotions arise also when there is sudden achievement of success in an activity with laughter. Emotions are acute, intense, disruptive, affective experiences.

Moods. Moods are typically less intense, less disruptive, and of longer duration than emotions. A mood may last for hours, days, or weeks. There are moods of cheerfulness, depression, anxiety, resentment, amusement, excitement, and the like. An emotion of anger may taper off into a mood of resentment or hostility. A mood of anxiety may build up into an emotion of fear or terror. It is not always possible to draw a sharp line of distinction between emotions and moods; but, in general, moods are chronic affective states and emotions are more acute disturbances.

The conditions that determine moods are complex. Nowlis (1953) has made important studies of the effects of drugs upon moods. It is common knowledge that moods vary with sickness and health, with the weather (temperature and humidity), and especially with environmental circumstances. In a small study I found that the moods of college students were strongly influenced by events in the *social* environment: grades, letters and money from home, the actions of friends, dates, and other social conditions (Young, 1937).

Affects. Psychiatrists, clinical psychologists, and others who are concerned with mental health and social welfare, refer to *affects* which may reach pathological intensity and become associated with dyscontrol of behavior. The affects include extreme anxiety, depression, manic excitement, rage, euphoria, apathy, and others. In neuroses there may be self-regarding affects of guilt, remorse, personal worthlessness and failure.

These abnormal affective states can be based upon brain lesions, drugs, endocrine imbalances, chemical and metabolic malfunction, or other physical traumata. They may also have a psychological origin.

Temperaments. Constitutional factors influence affective reactions. Temperaments are described as cheerful, apathetic, depressed, moody, vivacious, phlegmatic, sanguine, vigorous, lackadaisical, etc. Obviously, when we speak of temperaments we imply a view of human nature that covers a considerable period of time. Temperaments tend to be stable but they are known to change with traumatic experiences such as living in a concentration camp, endocrine disorders, and other conditions.

Dimensions of Affective Experience. The above categories of affective experience are convenient but not logically distinct. There are intermediate categories between any two classes of affective experiences. Several conditions that determine a specific feeling or emotion may be present together and in varying combinations and interactions.

Another way of looking at affective experience leads to the inquiry: What are the ways in which affective experiences vary? What are the dimensions of variability? Several dimensions of affectivity have been proposed and some of these will be considered in the following paragraphs:

Level of activation. In considering the directive-activation theory of motivation, I mentioned two variables: the level of activation and the positive-negative (including hedonic) variable (pages 69-74).

Lindsley (1951), on the basis of neural anatomy and his researches in electroencephalography, postulated a single linear dimension of activation. This is a motivational dimension which can be represented by a single vertical line. At the highest levels of activation are strong, excited emotions. At lower levels are alert attentiveness, relaxed wakefulness, drowsiness, light sleep, and at the lowest level, coma and death.

This continuum of *activation* applies to affective experiences. Some emotional states have a highly excited, agitated, level of activation; others are calm, quiescent. The emotions of infants as well as adults exhibit different levels of emotional excitement. The level of activation is independent of hedonic value. High excitement can be positive or neutral or negative in hedonic value.

The hedonic dimension. Hedonic quality is experienced at different levels of arousal. There are highly excited levels of pleasantness as, for example, when one receives an unexpected fortune. And there are calm, relaxed, pleasures as, for example, when one is enjoying Beethoven's Moonlight Sonata. There are highly excited unpleasant experiences, for example, during painful stimulations. And there are quiet depressed moods of disappointment. There are degrees of hedonically neutral, indifferent, activation produced by sensory stimulations of different intensities. Neutral levels of activation also vary with internal conditions of metabolism.

The interrelations of activation level and hedonic value are shown graphically in Figure 12 (page 73).

The dimension of tension-relaxation. Psychologists, so far as I know, agree upon the above two dimensions of arousal. There is less agreement about other affective dimensions. Wilhelm Wundt, for example, in presenting his famous tridimensional theory of feeling, proposed a third dimension: tension-relaxation. Expectation of an impending event,

Wundt argued, produces a feeling of tension; occurrence of the event produces a feeling of relaxation.

We are all familiar with anxiety tension, as during the critical illness of a loved one, when the outcome is uncertain; and the relief which is experienced when the crisis is safely passed or even when the illness results in death. Tension is experienced when we anticipate a pending event; relaxation, when the event is over.

Titchener (1908) rejected Wundt's claim that strain-relaxation is a dimension of *affection.* He reduced the affective elements to pleasantness and unpleasantness. The experiences of strain and relaxation are complex, Titchener argued, and based on sensory rather than affective qualities. There can be no doubt, however, that, whatever the existential basis of tension and relaxation, we sometimes feel strain and tension and at other times we are more or less relaxed.

Control and Dyscontrol. Nowlis and Nowlis (1956), after a thorough study of moods, suggested four dimensions of affectivity: (1) The level of activation. (2) The level of control. (3) Social orientation. (4) Hedonic tone. The first and last of these dimensions agree with the above. The other two are considered below.

The level of control is related to the degree of integration, or organization, present in experience and behavior. High control implies complete integration and cerebral dominance over subcortical emotional patterns. Low control implies disintegration at the highest functional level along with disorganization and confusion such as exists in the disruptive emotions. There are different levels of variation between complete control and dyscontrol. This variable is especially important when we consider persisting affective disturbances.

Some psychologists have emphasized that emotional behavior is disorganized, confused, aimless, disturbed, lacking in cerebral dominance and control. All agree that there are varying degrees of integration and disintegration—different degrees of emotional control. In some pathological states there is complete dyscontrol. The patient appears irrational and not responsible for his actions. In other states there is a very low level of cerebral dominance.

Emotional dyscontrol is a common phenomenon. It appears in many situations where values, interests, motives, attitudes and beliefs, are in conflict. Emotional outbursts are not fully under rational control. They may be completely irrational and uncontrolled.

Social orientation. Nowlis and Nowlis, on the basis of studies on the effect of drugs upon moods, suggested that there is a dimension of social orientation. A person may be socially orientated, non-socially oriented, or anti-socially oriented. We all recognize these differences and their practical importance.

More research is needed, however, to investigate variations in social orientation in relation to human feelings and emotions.

MOTIVATION AND THE AFFECTIVE CONSCIOUSNESS

In everyday life we commonly explain our actions by referring to what we feel, believe and desire. This type of explanation implies a subjective point of view toward phenomenal experience. To the strict behavioral scientist, as we have noted, explanations in terms of subjective experience (feelings, beliefs, motives, attitudes, etc.) must be ruled out of psychology. They are not valid, objective, categories.

I do not go along with strict behaviorism, but I welcome all the facts brought to light by behavioral methods. The subjective (individual) view of phenomena is valid. We are losing a trick in the scientific game if we ignore some of the available facts.

So let us consider the motivational aspect of conscious affective experience.

Satisfaction and Annoyance. The terms *satisfaction* and *annoyance*, as employed by Thorndike, Hollingworth, and others, signify something more than simple pleasantness and unpleasantness. These words imply motivational principles suggested by the concepts of need, appetite, drive, frustration, conflict, consummatory response.

How are satisfaction and annoyance related to each other? Hollingworth (1931) states that there are three views of the relationship between satisfaction and annoyance. These views are: (1) Satisfaction and annoyance are on a par in human nature; they are independent and equally basic processes. (2) Satisfaction is the elementary fact of human nature. Pleasure-yielding trends are basic, and annoyance arises through the interference or blocking of these trends. (3) Annoyance is the primary fact of human motivation. Satisfaction is not an additional process but merely the removal of annoyance.

Hollingworth is inclined to accept the third of these views. He writes: "The stimuli to men's active endeavors are always irritants, itches, aches, pains, distresses, cramps and tensions–the so-called 'disagreeables.' They are the prime movers to action. . . . The satisfaction of a motive is merely its removal."

According to this view, satisfaction is a form of relief. The view may be criticized by pointing out that there are *positive* forms of enjoyment as well as relief. Wholly apart from relief (which implies preexisting tension), the individual *enjoys* certain unsought sensory stimulations when and where they occur–perfumes, sweet tastes, musical tones. Further, various activities are interesting, i.e., pleasing: dancing, playing a game, carrying on a conversation with a friend. Such activities yield positive enjoyment that is more than relief from tension and stress.

Satisfaction, in fact, is of two forms: (1) *relief* from various pains, tensions, strains, irritants, etc., and (2) *enjoyment* of countless sensory stimulations, activities (interests), aesthetic experiences, etc. *Relief* is passive satisfaction and *enjoyment* is a pleasant experience in which the individual is more active. One *enjoys* success, achievement of a goal.

The Signs of Satisfaction and Dissatisfaction. In the report of an experiment upon training the preschool child to like or dislike taste stimuli, Gauger (1929) listed the observable characteristics of satisfaction and dissatisfaction as follows:

Satisfaction	*Dissatisfaction*
Chewing, smacking the lips	Making a wry face, frowning
Licking the lips	Trying to spit out the stimulus-object
Smiling	Tears in the eyes
Lighting up of the eyes	Speaking ("I don't like that")
Reaching for a stimulus-object	Coughing, gagging
Swinging the feet	Vomiting
Moving the head	Turning away the head
Waving the hands	Pushing away the stimulus-object
Sticking out the tongue	Not attending
Speaking ("That's good")	Retaining the stimulus-object as short a time as possible
Retaining the stimulus-object in the mouth as long as possible	Facial expression (looking "hurt," as if blaming the experimenter for a bad taste)

The lists are not complete and some of the characteristics fail to distinguish satisfaction from dissatisfaction. For example, swinging the feet, moving the head, and waving the hands may occur in satisfaction, indifferent activity, or dissatisfaction. The lists, however, raise the important problem of determining the objective signs of satisfaction and dissatisfaction, of pleasantness and unpleasantness.

A good many experiments have been performed in the hope of finding some peripheral *conditio sine qua non* of felt pleasantness and unpleasantness. As a matter of fact, there is simply no known peripheral criterion of pleasantness and unpleasantness which is valid in 100 per cent of the cases.

If we drop the quest for a peripheral *conditio sine qua non* of pleasantness and unpleasantness, we can summarize the various conditions which generate these feelings. A summary would run something like this:

Pleasant experience tends to occur when a desire is satisfied, when tension is released in such a way that the level of self-esteem is elevated, when sexual inhibitions are removed, or when some other motive is satisfied. If thirsty, a little water to drink is pleasing; if overheated, a cool breeze is pleasing; if the sexual appetite is aroused and intense, its satisfaction is pleasing. Play and sports which bring the companionship of others, the opportunity to converse and to listen, to display one's skills and gain recognition, bring pleasantness. In general, the satisfaction of a motive brings pleasant feeling.

Unpleasant experience, in contrast, tends to occur when a desire is frustrated, when tension is built up, when the level of self-esteem is lowered, when any appetite remains painfully intense and unsatisfied, when the tissues are being injured and the pain nerves excited, when one is prevented from doing or possessing what one wants to do or to possess. In a word, frustration, conflict, tension, pain, and injury tend to arouse unpleasant feeling.

Indifference exists when the conditions for evoking pleasantness and unpleasantness are absent.

Psychological Hedonism. The doctrine of hedonism, in its ethical and psychological forms, is as old as human thought. It is found in the writings of Aristippus, Epicurus, and other Greek philosophers. Ethical hedonism was developed in England by Hobbes, Locke, Hume, Bentham, John Stuart Mill, Spencer, and others. Thus Bentham wrote: "Nothing can act of itself as a motive but the ideas of pleasure or pain." And again: "A motive is substantially nothing more than pleasure or pain, operating in a certain manner."

Hedonic fact and theory enter American psychology in many places and in many ways. A hedonic principle is implied in Thorndike's law of effect, in Troland's principle of beneception-nociception, in Beebe-Center's account of pleasantness and unpleasantness, and in innumerable experiments on animal behavior that rely on reinforcement through rewards and punishments.

The *ethical* doctrine of hedonism maintains that pleasure or happiness is the sole or chief good in life and that human behavior can be evaluated as good or bad according to whether it enhances or impairs happiness. The *psychological* doctrine, in its current form, is a motivational principle: that pleasantness and unpleasantness are, in fact, determinants of human action and development.

The traditional pleasure-pain principle is quite general. "Pleasure" includes desire, satisfaction, enjoyment, sensual gratification, amusement. "Pain" includes punishment, unpleasant sensation, mental and emotional distress, trouble, effort. Experimental psychologists, however, have drawn a sharp distinction between sensory pain and unpleasantness. There are several qualities of sensory pain: the bright cutaneous pain, the dull muscular ache, the internal cramp, the "wicked" pain from the dentin of a tooth. Unpleasantness, as distinct from pain, arises from intense stimulations in all sense departments, from cognitive experiences, from the blocking of intended actions, from disease, and other sources.

Watson (1914) in launching his polemic against introspective psychology and mentalism, made an astounding statement:

> It is our aim to combat the idea that pleasure or pain has anything to do with habit formation or that harmfulness or harmlessness has anything more to do with the situation. It is perfectly natural in unreflective minds that the idea of good or bad or harmful or harmless should be called in to explain the habits we force upon animals and children. It is a bit strange that scientifically minded men should have employed it in an explanatory way.

A bit of personal history. At this point I think it might be in order to give a bit of personal history. I knew Watson personally and read some of his manuscripts while a graduate student studying with Titchener. I, too, had intellectual difficulties with the doctrine of psychological hedonism. The chief difficulty involved the mind-body relation. How can pleasant and unpleasant *feelings* (which are subjective) influence *behavior* (which is objectively observed)? Later I realized that there is no real problem here.

With an eclectic, multidisciplinary, approach to psychological processes it became clear that what one observes from one point of view can yield an understanding of what one observes from another standpoint. The problems of causation can be analyzed from either a subjective or an objective point of view. Subjectively we are aware of making decisions, of freedom to act, of psychological processes that determine our choice and actions. Objectively we observe many facts and principles of choice, preference, reinforcement, neurophysiological processes in thought, emotion, etc. The two views are congruent and supplementary. Neither pleasantness nor behavior is observed in the brain! A pseudo problem arises only when we shift points of view.

I was troubled also by the apparent teleological nature of hedonism and at one time I rejected the doctrine of psychological hedonism and held to physiological determinism (Young, 1922). But Tolman (1932) pointed out that goal-oriented behavior (appetitive and aversive) is a fact of objective observation. One can observe objectively the growth of purposive behavior. This applies to many experiments on learning, including my studies of food preference. There is, as Tolman said, a kind of natural teleology and one does not need to appeal to hormic forces or to subjective events to explain the development and persistence of purposive behavior.

In my *Motivation of Behavior* (1936), I formulated a view of "factual hedonism" which was simply the empirical law of effect rather than a theory of motivation. In *Motivation and Emotion* (1961), however, I stated a hedonic theory of motivation which has been elaborated in several theoretical papers (Young, 1952, 1955*a*, 1959, 1966, 1968*a*).

It is a fact that I was forced into acceptance of an objective theory of hedonism by a series of experiments upon the food preferences, appetites, aversions, dietary habits, and related processes, in laboratory rats. There was no mind-body problem while studying animal behavior because the rats could not make introspective reports of their feelings! And many of the hedonic principles of motivation which had been worked out with subjective methods were confirmed and substantiated by strictly behavioral methods!

Today I am convinced that the hedonic principle has a general validity that is independent of any particular point of view. In general, affective arousals regulate the pattern and course of behavior; they reinforce behaviors which are learned; they are prominent factors in organized and disorganized activities.

CONCLUSION

A phenomenological approach to the study of affective processes makes it possible to examine interrelations between subjective and objective facts. This approach is especially useful in the study of emotion because subjective and objective data are interrelated. Study of the relation of physical to mental facts requires that the student shift points of view. Such shifts are useful because observations from one point of view often supplement observations from other standpoints. An eclectic, multidisciplinary, approach is needed in the study of problems relating to feelings and emotions.

The physical stimulation of peripheral receptors is exciting, arousing. Occasionally some receptor stimulations are felt as pleasing and desirable; others, as displeasing and undesirable; many are experienced as hedonically neutral.

Feelings and emotions are elicited not only by receptor stimulations but by cognitive experiences: perceptions, memories, images. Cognitive processes, in fact, play a dominant role in the causation of emotional experiences. Cognitive experiences are especially prominent in biologically basic behaviors such as defense, feeding, mating, care of young, and related activities.

In coping with the environment organisms are sometimes successful and sometimes frustrated, blocked. Thwarting of purposive behavior can lead to emotional disruption and to behavior which, for the time being, lacks purposive direction. The subject may experience confusion and a blur.

There is general agreement among psychologists that the conscious emotion is characterized by awareness of bodily changes: respiratory, cardiovascular, glandular, muscular, and related physiological processes. In addition to organic sensation the emotional awareness is strongly affective—exciting or calming, pleasant or unpleasant, straining or relaxing. Commonly there is confusion, disorientation; and consciousness is a blur. An essential part of the total emotional experience is the cognitive awareness of an inducing situation. The emotion is outwardly expressed in behavior. There is commonly a dynamic tendency that arises from the affective disturbance.

The doctrine of psychological hedonism implies that positive and negative affective arousals are regulative and directive. This is shown in the determination of choice, in preference, and in the process of reinforcement that leads to habit formation. This regulative and directive aspect of behavior and development is apparent regardless of whether affective arousals are viewed subjectively, objectively, or in some other more specific way.

READING SUGGESTIONS ON AFFECTIVE EXPERIENCE

In the years following the behavioral revolution the dominant interest has been in physiological and behavioral studies. Consequently many of the best references on conscious feelings and emotions are found in pre-revolutionary decades. The studies of pleasantness and unpleasantness have been summarized by Beebe-Center (1932). A more general reference on feeling and emotion has been published by Ruckmick (1936). A history of theories of feeling and emotion is available in Gardiner, Metcalf, and Beebe-Center (1937). A scholarly summary of introspective studies of feeling can be found in Volume I of Arnold (1960). And there are the classical studies of Titchener (1908) and Lehmann (1914).

Interest in experimental aesthetics has continued from the time of Fechner to the present. Most of this work is ancillary to the present study and has not been considered. For a student interested in aesthetic motivation I suggest a perusal of D. E. Berlyne's (1960) *Conflict, Arousal, and Curiosity*, and a search for papers on specific topics by Berlyne and others. A recent book by Berlyne (1971), entitled *Aesthetics and Psychobiology*, contains a wealth of interesting material on experimental aesthetics.

Chapter VIII

Dynamic Determinants of Emotion

In any consideration of the factors which elicit emotions it is necessary to examine the underlying conditions. The present chapter will examine the more important dynamic determinants of emotion. The following chapter will take account of persisting conditions that predispose the individual toward emotional disturbances.

INTENSE MOTIVATION

If the intensity of stimulation by electric shock is gradually increased, from low to high, the activity level of an organism rises. Up to a certain point increased activation is indicated by faster movement, an increment in muscular strength, facilitation of performance, quicker learning and, in general, by increased efficiency in carrying out a task. But if the degree of motivation exceeds a certain critical point, emotional disruption occurs. For example, if a man, in a laboratory test, is sorting spools according to size, a weak electric shock for errors in discrimination may increase both the accuracy and speed of his performance; but if an intense shock is administered, he makes random and excessive movements with arms and legs, frowns, cries out in pain, and attempts to escape from the task at hand. Intense pain can disrupt almost any ongoing activity. With intense painful stimulation a man is said to "lose his head," "go to pieces," become "temporarily unbalanced," "disorganized."

In experiments reported below, the intensity of motivation was systematically varied. Laboratory animals were trained to make visual discriminations under varying degrees of electric shock, or punishment, for "errors." Although these experiments were concerned primarily with performance and learning in relation to motivation, they also illustrate an important point in the arousal of emotion.

The Yerkes-Dodson Law. In a series of experiments performed by Yerkes, Dodson, and others, an electric shock (pain-punishment) was used as an incentive to habit formation.[1] The intensity of shock was varied systematically, with weak, moderate, and strong currents being employed.

The experimental task confronting the animal was the discrimination between two brightnesses. The subject was given a shock for an arbitrarily defined "error."

There were two main experimental variables in the work of Yerkes and Dodson: (1) the degree of electric shock which was used as punishment for an "error" in discrimination; (2) the difficulty of the discrimination to be made.

Difficulty of the discrimination was varied by changing the relative brightness of the stimulus-fields. The *easiest* task was a discrimination between black and white. Black and white doors were presented side by side in a spatial arrangement determined by chance. If *black* is positive, the animal can escape through the black door to food; but if he enters the white door, he is given a shock through the feet for an "error." The discrimination was made *more difficult* by substituting two grays for the black and white. The difficulty was further increased by using two grays which were close together in brightness—very similar.

Various subjects have been used in work of this kind, including mice, chicks, kittens, and men. The general results of the work are presented schematically in Fig. 49.

The vertical line of the figure represents the number of trials required to learn a discrimination, the zero point being at the bottom and the maximal number of trials at the top. The base line represents degrees of electric shock (pain-punishment) from weak at the left to strong or intense at the right. Curve *A* presents the general result when the discrimination is easy; curve *B*, when it is moderately difficult; and curve *C*, when it is very difficult.

The figure is designed to bring out three main points. First, there is the fact of optimal motivation. For a task of any given degree of difficulty it is possible to find a degree of motivation which produces learning in the fewest number of trials. Up to a certain point, for any task, an increased degree of motivation speeds up the process of learning (reduces the number of trials required to learn). Beyond this critical point, further increases definitely retard the speed of acquisition. The optimal degree of activation is defined in terms of the experimental results. Results indicate that an optimal level of perform-

[1]The present brief discussion of the work of Yerkes, Dodson, et al., is based upon the writer's book, *Motivation of Behavior*, pp. 280-287, which may be seen for references to the literature.

ance exists for any task at a given level of difficulty and that an optimal or critical intensity of shock can be determined empirically.

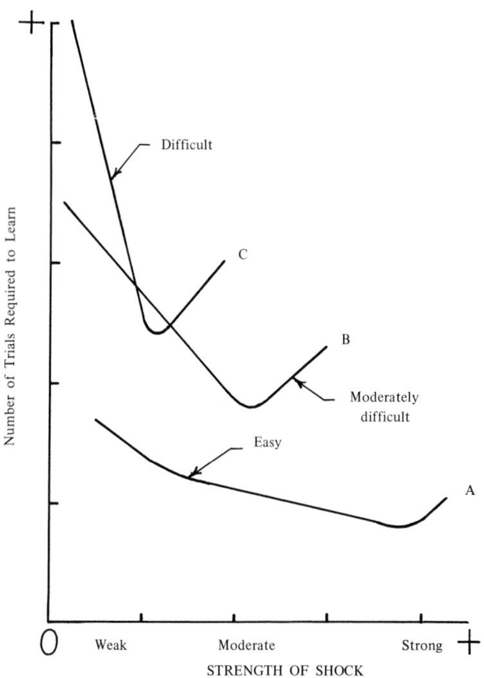

Figure 49. Schematic diagram to illustrate the Yerkes-Dodson principle.

The second point illustrated by the curves is one related to the dynamics of emotion. The level of performance in the task of visual discrimination is definitely lowered by intense, painful stimulations. The painful stimulations temporarily disorganize the activity in progress. When the degree of motivation is above the level that yields optimal performance, we can speak of over-motivation.

The third point is a principle known as the Yerkes-Dodson law. This principle relates the degree of motivation that yields optimal performance to the difficulty of the task. The principle can be stated as follows: *As the difficulty of a task increases, the strength of shock that yields optimal performance approaches the threshold value*. The principle is clearly shown in the generalized chart in Figure 49. This means that a *weaker* shock is required to give optimal performance on a difficult task than on an easy one.

If the Yerkes-Dodson principle turns out to have a general validity, there are several practical consequences. For example, if a bright boy and a dull boy are working on the same problems in arithmetic, these problems will be relatively easy for the bright boy and relatively difficult for the dull. If optimal performance is desired from both boys, weaker degrees of "punishment" (or possibly stronger "rewards") should be given to the dull child than to the bright. This is contrary to the out-dated practice of giving the stupid child a thrashing "to knock some sense into his head."

Again, the difficult task is more easily disrupted emotionally than the easy task. If a man is repairing a watch or engaged in some similar task that requires precision, steadiness, and fine coordination of muscular movements, or a task requiring difficult discriminations, he becomes upset emotionally by situations that would scarcely faze a ditch digger.

It may be assumed that for any task and any individual there is a breakdown point. If incentives, tensions, and pain are added together so that the level of activation is increased, smooth, coordinated activity is disrupted and emotional reactions appear.

Intensity of Stimulation. The Yerkes-Dodson law illustrates a principle that the psychological effect of electrical stimulation varies with the intensity of the stimulus.

Weak electric shocks are hedonically neutral or even positive. They can serve to inform a subject that his response is correct or erroneous. Moderate intensities are hedonically negative. They are aversive in that organisms do what they can to avoid them. Intense shocks are emotionally disruptive and disorganizing.

Now Ulrich, Hutchinson, and Azrin (1965) have shown that painful stimulations tend to elicit fighting and aggressive attack in many animals, including man. Hence aggression is one effect of intense painful stimulation. Aggressive fighting is commonly regarded as a form of emotional behavior.

FRUSTRATION AND EMOTIONAL BEHAVIOR

Frustration is an occasional event. From time to time some activity is blocked by a barrier or obstruction. The meal is delayed, the highway presents a sign "DETOUR 20 MILES." one loses his watch, work is interrupted, etc. Such events are experienced as blocking of purposive behavior along with annoyance, aggression and emotional disturbance. See the monograph by Cason (1930) on common annoyances, aversions and irritations.

A great deal of human activity, however, is free from frustration. Eating a meal, listening to enjoyable music, driving a car on the open highway, etc.—all can proceed without any interference. Many pleasant experiences are undisturbed. Human life also contains a good deal of purely automatic activity that runs its course habitually without interference—shaving in the morning, putting on a coat, walking to work, etc. But frustrations do occur! The following sections deal with the psychological effects of frustration and especially with the relation of frustration to emotional behavior.

Why Do Men and Other Animals Fight? The question is a timely one. To justify the destruction of human life in warfare, the militarist has argued that nature is red in tooth and claw, that evolution has resulted from the natural selection of the physically fit, and that without a struggle to the death the human race would degenerate. Actually, however, cooperation and socialization within a group are facts of nature just as truly as competition, fighting, and aggression. On the surface of things there is no obvious biological reason why men should not cooperate for the larger human welfare, seeking to eliminate the undesirables of disease, poverty, crime, and war.

In an ethical essay, Craig (1921) claimed that the militarist's argument for war does not agree with the facts of animal behavior. What, he asks, are the facts? In seeking an answer he refers to his observations upon birds. Craig has carefully observed the behavior of pigeons. He writes:

> . . . pigeons are a properly representative group: because, first, their behavior is typical; they quarrel and fight just about as much, or as little, as do the majority of birds. A healthy pigeon never allows another to trespass on his territory, or in any way interfere with his interests, with impunity. And, secondly, the pigeons are a "dominant" group; that is to say, the pigeon family is found all over the world, it has evolved into a large number of species, and the number of its individual members is enormous. All signs indicate that the pigeon family is in the most flourishing condition and in a state of rapid progressive evolution. If the members of such a group live and act in a manner contradictory to the militarist theory, this is sufficient to prove that the militarist policy is not necessary for the welfare or the evolution of a race.

Pigeons, of course, do fight. If the birds are crowded into quarters too small for them, they fight to a degree that is cruel and distressing. Each pair of birds insistently drives away the trespassers. But in nature they space out, keeping apart by moderate distances.

If a pigeon cote containing several compartments, each with its own door, is set up, the birds choose compartments for themselves. It sometimes happens that two males choose the same door. Each tries to enter and make the place his own. They can and do settle the difficulty by fighting for possession of the compartment.

With reference to fighting in the higher vertebrates, Craig's thesis is this: Fundamentally, fighting among animals is not sought after or valued for its own sake; it is resorted to as an unwelcome necessity, a means of defending the animal's interests. Further, Craig states that when an animal fights he aims not to destroy but to get rid of the enemy or of his interference. There is thus no true *appetite* for battle as there are appetites for food, water, mate, sleep, and elimination. Fighting is not a biological necessity in the sense that it is invariably required for continued existence of the individual.

This last statement suggests a possible answer to the initial question. The animal reveals in his behavior a number of specific motivating factors which lead him toward food, water, mate, to build a nest, to care for young, and so on. But fighting is not among these appetites in the sense that an animal must seek a fight in order to live. When his biological needs are met, he can survive indefinitely without fighting.

In support of this thesis is the following observation. In a well-known aquarium sharks are kept with small fishes. As long as the sharks are given sufficient food they do not attack and devour the other animals, but, in nature, as we know, the hungry sharks would quickly prey upon them.

Craig is doubtless right in claiming that fighting is not a biological necessity for the individual, but his thesis should be supplemented by at least two statements: First, animals and men inevitably do get in each other's way and do frustrate one another in actual life situations. It is hard to imagine a world completely free from mutual interference. It is especially true that animals do compete for food, mates, territory, shelter, and the other necessities of existence; and the brutal fact remains that countless organisms are carnivorous and continue to survive only by devouring other organisms. A second biological fact is that the process of evolution has produced a great diversity of organs for offense and defense—the spur, claw, tooth, quill, sting, sword, shell, and so on. This same process of evolution has laid down within the nervous system the structural organization which provides the bodily mechanisms necessary for attack and for the mobilization of those internal energies of an organism which are required in fighting.

Thus, the militarist's argument that the bodily mechanisms for fighting are widespread in the world and that they are fundamental in human nature is essentially sound. From this biological truth, however, it does not follow that men must inevitably destroy each other in battle.

Wars arise from *social* situations which preserve national patriotism instead of international cooperation and perpetuate political enmities and the struggle for face saving and power. Economic competition for the natural resources of the world is another cause of warfare, e.g., fishing rights on international waters. Economic competition between national groups creates problems which in the past have been solved on the primitive basis of brute force. The social situation is clearly at fault and must be changed, in the light of our knowledge of human nature, to meet the needs of men.

Painful Stimulation and Aggression. The causes of human aggression are complex and do not necessarily result in fighting. Fighting has always been an important human problem.

Other animals besides man fight their own kind. Scientists have done considerable amounts of research on aggression and fighting with animal subjects. Earlier work, like that of Craig, was largely descriptive. Recent research has examined the specific conditions that lead to aggressive fighting. Ulrich, Hutchinson and Azrin (1965) reviewed current research; they have emphasized the aggressive response to painful stimulation.

It is quite generally recognized that painful stimulation can lead to aggressive behavior and fighting. Small children are admonished not to hurt the "doggy" because it might make him bite. When animals are wounded they are more apt to attack than when free from pain. Further, research studies have shown that painful stimulation in the form of an electric shock or a blow or by other means, tends to induce fighting in laboratory animals.

If paired rats are confined to a relatively small chamber and given a shock through the feet, they tend to attack each other. Typically they stand erect with teeth and claws ready for attack. In addition to rats, paired snakes, turtles, chickens, and hamsters have been found to react to electric shocks with sudden movements of attack. Also cats, dogs, and monkeys, tend to fight when given a painful shock.

Ulrich, et al., relative to this matter, have written:

> . . . Placing a gopher snake and a rat snake together without shock.resulted in exploratory behavior with neither snake attending to the other. Once shock was delivered, however, both snakes immediately responded by striking at each other with mouths wide open. Such striking movements frequently resulted in one of the snakes being bitten. Turtles' reactions to shock, although much slower, do eventually result in attacks toward each other. The general reaction of paired chickens to shock is also one of attack. . . . Delivery of shock to a pair of hamsters produced a type of sterotyped fighting posture and attack similar to that of the rats. The only differences were that these fighting responses could be consistently elicited at lower intensities of shock than was required for the rats, and that the hamsters persisted longer in their fighting. . . . This persistence in fighting beyond the moment of shock presentation was also observed in cats. . . and in squirrel monkeys. . . Furthermore, both cats and monkeys often fought until forcibly separated, and unless precautions were taken they would frequently inflict serious physical injury. [113-114]

There is also inter-species aggression. Snakes, raccoons, monkeys, rats, hamsters, and cats, have all been observed to attack members of different species when given aversive stimulation. In most instances the form of fighting is that characteristic of the species but sometimes differences appear. When rats were paired with guinea pigs and shocked the rat did all the attacking. The guinea pig did not stand erect but simply withdrew. The rat assumed a semi-crouching posture with fore-paws raised only slightly off the floor. This brought the rat's head on a level with that of the guinea pig. But normally rats stand erect when fighting each other.

In general, many animals make an aggressive response to aversive stimulation. Not only painful shocks but also loud sounds, strong lights, and other intense stimulations, lead to escape from or reduction of the aversive stimulation. But painful stimulation also leads to direct aggressive behavior in the form of fighting.

There is a practical lesson that can be found in the laboratory studies with painful and other aversive stimulations. Aversive stimulations are commonly used for punishment as a means of controlling behavior. But it should be kept in mind that aversive stimulation in the form of pain can also lead to aggressive attack and fighting as a response of the punished organism.

FRUSTRATION, MOTIVATION AND EMOTION

Mandler (1964) prefers to speak of *interruption* of behavior, rather than frustration, as a principle cause of emotional behavior. As long as the psychobiological machine stays alive, Mandler states, it is compelled to execute successive steps of some plan. If the planned action is controlled within specific limits, it can be organized and integrated with other ongoing behavior. An interruption is often emotionally disruptive. Incidentally, Mandler speaks of both organized and disorganized forms of "emotional" behavior.

Most psychologists, however, use the term *frustration* to include all forms of thwarting, blocking of purposive behavior, including the interruption of planned action.

Some Forms of Frustration. There are many forms. The typical forms vary from age to age, as Symonds (1946) has pointed out in the following list.

> *Restricting of exploratory behavior.* The normal infant brings objects to his mouth; he grasps, touches, pulls, manipulates them. Parents find it necessary to restrict these activities to prevent injury, disease, fire. Inhibitions are imposed; these are frustrating to the normal exploratory activity of the infant.
>
> *Restriction of early sex experiences.* The infant explores his world including different parts of his body; he finds that manipulation of the genital organs yields pleasant feelings. Parents, in our culture, are alert and vigorous in thwart-

ing expressions of autoerotism. The frustrations centering around masturbation are reacted to with strong emotion, fantasy, and repression.

Rivalries within the family. When another baby is born the interest of the mother is diverted to the newcomer. The loss of attention and care is definitely frustrating to older children. Again, two children want to play with the same toy. One child (perhaps the younger and weaker) must give it up, but this is frustrating.

Early feeding frustrations. Children brought into guidance clinics are frequently found to have had unsatisfactory nursing experiences. Perhaps they were weaned too soon or had unsatisfactory bottle feeding. Weaning is a prototype of later forms of frustration.

Loss of love and support. If the mother works or if the home is broken, there is a widespread frustration bound up with loss of love, security, and support. The frustrations from loss of love have a profound effect upon personality development of the child.

Cleanliness training. Toilet training is a frustration of early childhood. It is also frustrating to have to wash the hands, behind the ears, and generally to keep clean.

Lessening dependence on the parents. As a child grows up he is expected to do more and more things for himself, to require less attention and care. The child is definitely frustrated by being forced to depend upon his own resources rather than upon the care of parents.

Frustrations from the school. In the schoolroom the child is required to sit still, to refrain from speaking and even whispering, to refrain from temper displays, to take care of materials in an orderly and cleanly manner. In a word, he is regimented to fit into the school situation. In addition to these thwartings, he is frustrated by failure in his work, through competition with superior pupils, and in other ways.

Adolescent frustrations. The adolescent must abandon childhood dependence for adulthood. He must acquire skills and attitudes for work. He must adjust himself to members of the opposite sex and to companions of his own sex. These adjustments involve repeated frustrations.

Adult frustrations. Economic necessity requires that the male adult earn a living and support a family. In times of high taxes or economic depression this involves marked frustrations. The professional man or woman maintains a status within his profession, club, and community, but not without repeated frustrations. Again, there are deprivations from death, financial failure, and other losses, that are severely frustrating.

In other words, from the cradle to the grave, people experience repeated frustrations but their form and nature vary from one period of life to another. We do not escape frustration by growing up. We just grow into new and different kinds of frustration.

Maier's Distinction between Frustration and Motivation. Some psychologists define motivation in terms of goal-oriented, or purposive, behavior. Others take a broader view and define motivation as the causal determination of behavior in all of its aspects and forms.

Maier (1949), holding to the narrower definition, thinks of motivation in terms of goal-oriented behavior. He contrasts motivated behavior with activity that lacks a goal. Many of the characteristics of abnormal and delinquent behavior, he states, must be attributed to the fact that the individual is frustrated, rather than to motivation. He distinguishes between those characteristics of behavior that must be attributed to frustration and those attributed to motivation.

In contrasting motivated behavior with behavior instigated by frustration Maier makes, among others, the following points (paraphrased):

1. Motivated behavior is variable, plastic; it leads to adaptation. Behavior that is instigated by frustration is stereotyped, rigid, unchanging in pattern. Tics, stereotyped movements, and similar rigid patterns, are attributed to frustration rather than to motivation.

2. When a motivated pattern has been well learned it can be altered by rewards and punishments, but a response due to frustration cannot be altered readily by incentives. Frustration fixates whatever responses are in progress at the time the frustration occurs even though these responses are non-adaptive. Once established, the abnormal patterns cannot easily be changed.

3. In motivated behavior the separate responses appear as means to an end. They are instrumental acts that lead towards the goal-response. Frustration-induced responses, contrastingly, are not instrumental but appear as ends in themselves.

4. In motivated behavior, discrimination, choice, and selection are possible. Frustration-instigated behavior, by contrast, has a compulsive quality with no possibility of choice.

5. In motivated behavior the goal-response is adaptive and satisfying to the subject. The frustrated subject reduces the degree of frustration by emotional expressions whether or not they are adaptive.

6. Motivated behavior, on the whole, is constructive and results in the organization of adaptive patterns. Frustration-instigated behavior is non-constructive and often destructive. Frustration leads to disorganized, emotional, non-adaptive activity.

7. A motivated individual is influenced by anticipation of the consequences of his action but a frustrated person makes whatever responses are available with little or no foresight.

8. When behavior is motivated, learning takes place that permits an increased differentiation and discrimination. Under frustration, by contrast, there is dedifferentiation (regression) and sometimes compulsive or mass action.

9. Motivated behavior is characterized by zest and eagerness. Behavior determined by frustration is often marked by resignation—the opposite of zest.

These and other contrasts were made by Maier to support his distinction between the effects of motivation and the effects of frustration. Abnormal behavior, Maier states, is frustration-instigated, and its characteristics should be referred directly to the fact of frustration rather than to motivation.

Maier applied the distinction between motivation and frustration to the interpretation of delinquent behavior in children. The symptoms of delinquency can be referred either to a need state or to frustration.

Consequently in the practical handling of such problems as stealing, lying, thumb-sucking, destructive behavior, whining, and the like, one must first determine how far such manifestations are due to a need and how far to frustration.

If the delinquent pattern has developed because it is satisfying, then the pattern should change when satisfaction fails or when dissatisfaction appears. If the delinquent pattern is an irrational manifestation of frustration, however, the behavior cannot be so readily modified. It will not be altered by the subject's realization of the consequences of his act. It is known that some deliquents repeat a non-adaptive pattern and are little changed by argument and awareness of the consequences of their behavior.

Thus there are, according to Maier, two kinds of determinants of delinquent behavior. First, delinquent traits such as stealing, lying, destructiveness, lack of dependability, and the like, might reflect unfulfilled needs. Possibly there is a need to be accepted or to maintain prestige, a need for love and security, or a need for possessing things, etc. The blocking of a need can lead to anti-social behavior. Second, delinquent behavior may be the result of frustration. If the delinquent pattern is not changed by realization of the consequences of action, or by rewards and punishments, but remains stereotyped, rigid, compulsive, irrational, then the pattern is determined by frustration and reflects frustration rather than motivation.

To the present writer it seems that Maier is quite correct in attributing certain manifestations of abnormal behavior to the fact that the organism is frustrated and others to the motivation that is blocked. By analogy, if a train is wrecked, there is an abnormal state of affairs. The explanation lies as much in the frustrating situation (broken rail) as in the energy transformations that moved the locomotive down·the track. Behavior, whether of man or machine, depends upon the total situation.

The only question that might be raised concerns the restricted definition of motivation. I have stated that *all* behavior is motivated, i.e., causally determined. Some of the determinants of behavior lie within the organism and others are within the environmental situation. Some forms of behavior are goal-oriented; others are not. All of the determinants and their interaction must be considered in explaining any bit of behavior. This broad view is more adequate, I believe, in the explanation of the total facts. With the broader view one can still take account of behavior that lacks a goal and of the effects of frustration.

Frustration as a Source of Drive. In psychological writings about frustration there is a double tradition. First, there is the tradition that frustration leads to improved performance and learning. For example, it is commonly stated that thinking is instigated by a problem. The problem is a frustrating condition that induces activity of the trial-and-error type. The result of thinking is solution of the problem. Second, there is the tradition that frustration leads to disorganization and impaired performance. For example, it is often affirmed that frustration is a condition that produces emotional disturbance.

Both traditions are psychologically sound. Under some conditions frustration leads to increased efforts in carrying out a task, to greater impetus, to a higher level of performance, and to problem solving. Under other conditions frustration is extremely disturbing, even emotionally disruptive. It is commonly assumed that for a given activity there is an optimal degree of motivation and that the total energy liberated through frustration may yield a degree of motivation either above or below the optimum, depending upon conditions.

It is important to ask, as Child and Waterhouse (1953) pointed out: Under what conditions does frustration raise and lower the quality of performance?

The difference between improved and impaired performance is not solely a matter of the severity and persistence of frustration but it varies also with the situation. To illustrate: A man stubs his toe and swears! Here frustration is relatively minor and the result is an emotional outburst. Compare this with the behavior of a prisoner who has succeeded in carrying through his plan for escape. The prisoner's frustration from loss of freedom was a major thwarting, but behavior was well integrated, persistent, and efficiently executed.

Brown and Farber (1951) recognized both the emotional and the non-emotional aspects of frustration but they were especially concerned with the fact that frustration generates a drive. They modified the Hullian system by introducing frustration as an intervening variable that influences the vigor and pattern of response.

With a primary drive, such as hunger or thirst, deprivation creates a need. Stimuli arising from the need-state are a source of persistent motivation. Frustration, however, produces an additional drive, one that is irrelevant to the basic need-state. The irrelevant drive from frustration combines with a primary drive to produce a combined effective drive. That is to say, frustration produces an increment in motivation. The increment can be recognized in terms of improved performance.

Frustration not only produces an increment in drive but also a unique stimulus pattern. The stimuli from frustration evoke either an innate response or an acquired tendency to respond.

The drive from frustration differs from other drives in the nature of the conditions that reduce it. According to Brown and Farber, frustration is reduced by increasing the strength of the stronger tendency so that it dominates behavior, or by decreasing the strength of the weaker tendency, or by allowing fatigue to dissipate the conflict state, or in some similar way. The reduction of frustration is obviously different from drive reduction through removal of a bodily need.

That frustration produces an increment in the strength of drive has been demonstrated also by some experiments of Marx (1956). His work shows that frustration depends upon the interference or conflict of excitatory tendencies. The degree of frustration varies independently of the bodily need-state.

In general, there is considerable evidence to show that frustration is a source of drive and that the drive from frustration combines with the drive from other sources. Whether the total drive facilitates or impedes performance depends upon the total level of motivation from all sources—need-states as well as frustrations.

Frustration and Aggressive Behavior. It is the thesis of Dollard *et al.* (1939) that whenever aggressive behavior appears the aggressive individual is frustrated in some way. In other words, aggressive behavior is motivated by frustration. The converse of this proposition is not necessarily true for, as we shall see, frustration can lead to other types of adjustment than aggression. Frustration can lead to regression or to resignation or to emotional upset without overt aggression.

The simplest and most direct form of aggressive behavior is a physical attack upon the frustrating object to destroy, injure, or remove it; but there are other forms of aggression. In polite society hostile aggression may take the form of a retaliative or derogatory remark. Words may be substituted for a direct attack on the tooth-and-claw level. Again, substitute aggression may take the form of burning in effigy or destruction of a symbol.

Two picturesque example from Dollard *et al.*, of the frustration-aggression relation are given below:

> 1. A college student was driving to a distant city to attend a football game. It was the Big Game of the season and represented an important event in the season's social festivities. He was accompanied by a girl whose good opinion he valued highly and whom he wished to impress with his extensive plans for a weekend of parties and amusement. They became very gay and hilarious during the course of the drive, and he was silently congratulating himself on the successful arrangements he had made. Suddenly a siren sounded behind him, and, when he stopped, the traffic officer reprimanded him severely and in a very insulting manner for "driving like a high-school kid." The sound of the siren and the officer's intrusion immediately destroyed both his rapport with the girl and the happy anticipation he had had. As soon as he was permitted to drive ahead, he began berating the manners of the officer and telling the girl that the police in that state were notorious for their bullying methods. During the remainder of

the drive he seemed to have difficulty with his car; he grated the gears frequently in shifting, refused to let other cars pass him, and made insulting comments about every policeman who came in sight (though, of course, slowing down whenever they appeared). The change in behavior here is not very baffling. The student was frustrated by being humiliated before his girl; his expectations of favorable response from her diminished. His behavior became aggressive because of his hostility toward the policeman, which he could not express directly and which kept bubbling up after the arrest.

2. A group of laborers . . . had gathered around a boarding-house table at six o'clock for dinner, as was their practice at the end of the day. On ordinary days they ate without much conversation but with a fair approximation of dignity and good manners. On the day in question, the group sat down at the usual hour but no waiters appeared. There were soon murmurs of protest to the general effect that, if the landlady were to stay home, dinner could be served on time; and threats were made that they might stop boarding at that house. Gradually the self-restraints usually governing behavior at the table disappeared and there was a rhythmic stamping of feet. Someone shouted, "We want food"—the rest took up the cry and produced a tremendous uproar. Hard rolls were seized from the table and thrown at the kitchen door, presumably in the direction of the landlady. Soon the object of their aggression appeared and explained the reason for the delay. Dinner was eventually served, and the unusual behavior gradually died down, but with many threats and mutterings. Frustration was induced by the inability to continue those responses habitually connected with sitting down at a table, and aggressive acts assumed the form of the breaches of etiquette, vociferous demands, shouted threats, and bread throwing.

Aggressive behavior in its primitive form is a direct attack. A man may attack the enemy with his fists, kick with his feet, slap, bite, shoot a gun, strike with a club, throw a stone, or in some other way aim to injure or destroy. The enraged animal growls, shows his teeth, and in other ways expresses hostility. The human subject feels the anger and, if not expressed, there develops a resentment with determination to seek revenge, to retaliate, to "get even" with the offender in some way. There is a primitive kind of retributive justice—an eye for an eye, a tooth for a tooth.

If direct aggression is not possible, the hostile action may turn against some innocent object or person. Thus a man, frustrated in his office by the boss, puts on a smile and says nothing; but when he comes home at night he kicks the cat, spanks his child, or complains about the food. The following amusing incident, told by a psychologist to his colleagues at a meeting of the American Psychological Association, illustrates *displaced aggression*:

An Englishman was hurrying to catch a London subway train already standing in the station. He started to put a coin in the glass coin-box beside the gate. Then he noticed that the coin (still in his fingers) was a half crown instead of a penny. He was in a dilemma that demanded immediate decision. He could drop

> the coin and catch the train or he could rescue the coin and risk missing the train. He took the latter course. Slowly and with difficulty he raised the coin from the coin-box, holding it tightly. Then the coin, nearly extricated, slipped between his fingers and fell back into the box. He had lost both the coin and the train! Doubly frustrated he walked down the platform. A short distance away was a man (a complete stranger), with one foot on a bench, tying his shoe. Impulsively and without pausing he gave the man a boot on the seat of the pants, saying, "Damn it, you are always tying your shoe!"

The remark was very bad logic—wholly irrational—but the action afforded a release of tension. The aggressive impulse, aroused by frustration, was directed against an innocent bystander. In a similar way a lynching mob, bent on violence, has been known to turn from one victim to another.

This is *displaced aggression*. The facts imply that when a man is frustrated there may be aroused a general hostility and readiness to attack or destroy. The man's hostile orientation may then be changed from one victim to another. We recognize this fact in daily life when we say that a man's ire is up, he is in an irascible mood, he is generally mad—so, look out! Hostility and aggression can be directed in this way or in that, by external circumstances.

Instances of displaced aggression imply that there is a general drive or tension produced by frustration and also an orienting factor that is directive and regulatory. When an individual is frustrated he must "let off steam" but the object of his aggression can be changed.

Frustration and Regression. Frustration, as we said, can also lead to regression. An example of regression due to frustration is found in a study by Barker, Dembo, and Lewin (1941) upon the play of children. They produced frustration by letting a child see but not play with some elegant toys.

Thirty children, ages 2 to 5 years, were given, individually, an opportunity to play with a standard set of toys. The toys were spread out on pieces of paper on the floor. Each toy was demonstrated to the child: "Look, here are some things to play with. Here is a teddy bear and a doll. Here is an iron to iron with, etc." All of the toys were shown. "You can play with everything. You can do whatever you like with the toys, and I'll sit down here and do my lesson."

One observer sat in the room and made notes on the play of the child. A second observer watched through a one-way screen while the child played for 30 minutes. The play was free, undirected.

In a *prefrustration* period all of the toys except crayons and paper were removed and incorporated into a more elaborate and attractive setting in another part of the room but concealed by a curtain. In the new setting was a big doll house, brightly painted and decorated. A child could enter the house through a doorway. Inside was a bed with a doll lying on it and a chair with a teddy bear sitting on it. An ironing board with an iron stood against one wall and a telephone, with dial and bell, was in the corner. Outside the house was a laundry line on which dolls' clothes hung. There was a rubber bunny near the entrance of the house and behind it a small truck and trailer. On the table were cups, saucers, dishes, spoons, forks, knives, an empty teapot and a large teapot with water in it.

When a child was shown the elaborate and attractive toys he immediately started to investigate them. Every child showed great interest in them; and every child was left free to explore and play as he wished.

In the *frustration* period the child was forced to play with the original, less attractive, set of toys and with the more desirable toys clearly visible behind a padlocked screen. After the child had played with the elegant toys, the experimenter collected in a basket all the materials that had been used in the original freeplay period. He spread them out on pieces of paper on the floor as they had been placed at the start. He then approached the child and said, "And now let's play at the other end," pointing to the "old" part of the room. The child went or was led to the other end of the room and the experimenter then lowered a wire partition and fastened it by means of a large padlock. The part of the room that contained the elegant toys was now visible through a wire mesh netting but physically inaccessible.

In the frustration period the child played for 30 minutes in sight of inaccessible and desirable toys. This constituted the frustration. Incidentally, there was a *postfrustration* period in which the child was again allowed to play with the elegant toys; but this was to satisfy the child, and had no experimental purpose.

The records were rated for constructiveness of play. The constructiveness scores were found to be higher, on the average, during the free-play situation than during the frustration period. In other words, a background of frustration decreased the average constructiveness of play with accessible toys. The decrease in constructiveness was measured. For the younger children (28 to 41 months old) the constructiveness scores showed an average regression of 9.6 months of mental age. For the older children (42 to 61 months old) the constructiveness scores showed an average regression of 21.5 months of mental age. For all thirty children combined the average regression was 17.3 months of mental age. A few children were *more* constructive in play when frustrated, but most regressed to earlier levels of play constructiveness.

Frustration in the play situation also aroused moods and emotions that, for the most part, were negative in affective tone. Frustration produced restlessness, aggressive actions, and other signs of unhappiness.

Barker, Dembo, and Lewin recognized a distinction between *retrogression* and *regression*. Retrogression is a return to a type of behavior characteristic of a previous stage of life history of the individual. In retrogression the individual repeats an actual pattern of behavior that characterized an early stage of his life cycle. Regression, by contrast, is a change to a more primitive pattern of behavior, regardless of whether the behavior actually occurred previously within the life history of the individual. This kind of change has also been called *primitivization.*

From the Darwinian point of view, primitivization can be understood in terms of evolution. If a child is frustrated and shows the rage pattern, or cries, this is regression to a biologically primitive pattern. Frustration constitutes a block or interference typically on the cortical level. When this occurs, there is regression to a primitive pattern, i.e., *primitivization.*

Other Adjustments to Frustration. We have seen that when a man is frustrated he may become hostile and aggressive. If he cannot directly attack the frustrating object, he may show displaced aggression as when a man, insulted by his boss, comes home and kicks the cat. We have seen that a child when frustrated may regress to a more primitive biological pattern or retrogress to a form of behavior that was present in his earlier years. There are other responses to frustration. One of these is resignation.

Resignation is simply the unhappy or apathetic acceptance of a situation when nothing can be done to remedy it. Refugees persecuted under the Nazi regime or unemployed persons during an economic depression may become apathetic in their outlook. An attitude of resignation implies extreme limitation of needs, no plan for the future, no hopes that can be taken seriously. The frustrating situation, in fact, is accepted as hopeless. Aggression is blocked; regression is useless and retrogression impossible. The unhappy situation is simply taken for granted apathetically. The subject, as we say, is resigned to his fate.

Resignation is a form of adjustment that may reduce or remove emotional tension. Some persons, however, may remain in an emotional state of disturbance, when frustrated, without making any adjustment.

Since frustration implies a blocking of organized behavior, it is normally associated with the signs of disorganization. Under some circumstances frustration brings increased postural tension. Commonly there is emotional excitement or anger or anxiety. The level of activity may be either raised or lowered by frustration depending upon circumstances. Frustration may lead to an output of excessive energy as when the individual attempts to surmount a barrier; but in the frustration of grief there is often a lowered output of energy as shown by a drop in the level of activity. Sometimes when a man is frustrated there is hesitation–faltering, loitering on the job, postponing action, slowness in decision, reluctance to resume a task. Occasionally there are meaningless responses–excessive, random, incoordinated activities. A combination of these manifestations may be present when a man is frustrated and fails to make some kind of adjustment.

CONFLICT AND EMOTION

Although the terms *frustration* and *conflict* commonly occur in psychological literature, a clear distinction between them is not always drawn. I shall use the term *frustration*, broadly, to designate any kind of blocking or thwarting of a motive, and the term *conflict* to refer to those forms of frustration in which two or more motivating factors are involved.

An example of simple frustration which is free from conflict is the following: A child, in trying to get a toy that is out of reach; he is frustrated by the environmental situation. His behavior, is oriented persistingly toward a single goal. He is well motivated. He becomes excited and cries (emotional behavior). But frustration does not necessarily lead to emotion. Some children when frustrated do not become emotional. They have higher degrees of frustration tolerance and find substitute ways to arrive at the goal.

An illustration of conflict between two motives is the following: I observed this conflict of motives in the behavior of my dog. To understand the conflict one should know that Prince had become habituated to following his master's auto for a few blocks when it left the yard. One day it happened that my wife brought the dog's food pan into the yard just as the auto left the garage. A conflict in behavior was very obvious. Prince first ran toward the food pan, wagging his tail; then he turned toward the auto and followed it, barking excitedly; again he ran toward the food, jumping and barking in excitement. A moment before Prince had been sleeping quietly beside the garage door. The two incompatible activities, aroused by the total situation produced a conflict with emotinal excitement.

This particular conflict was between two motives, both of which had positive valence. Lewin would call it an approach-approach type of conflict.

Types of Conflict. Lewin (1931, 1933, 1935), in developing his field theory of motivation, recognized that environmental objects have positive and negative valences. If a child moves toward a toy, the toy for that child at that time has a positive valence. If the child moves away from a strange dog, the dog has a negative valence.

Recognizing this basic positive-negative distinction in behavior, Lewin described three types of conflict. In the *approach-approach* type of conflict both goal-objects have positive valences. For example, if a man received two offers of jobs both of which are attractive, he has an approach-approach type of conflict. Dynamic conflict is based on the fact that it is impossible to move simultaneously in opposite directions.

In the *avoidance-avoidance* type of conflict the organism is caught between two undesirable courses of action. There are two negative valences. He is between the devil and the deep blue sea! For example, a man faces bankruptcy and loss of his home. He embezzles the company's funds to avoid the disgrace of failure. The alternatives—bankruptcy and embezzlement—are both undesirables. He would like to avoid both alternatives but the conflict is severe.

On the level of animal behavior, there is the situation of a rat in an apparatus with ice water on the floor. To escape the cold he jumps onto a platform. He is given a shock through the feet and returns to the ice water. The temperature is lowered and again he jumps onto the platform. He is in a situation with two negative valences! This is an avoidance-avoidance conflict.

Finally, there is the *approach-avoidance* type of conflict. For example, a child would like to leave the school room to play in the yard with the other children, but the teacher stands in the doorway perhaps with a switch in hand. The child would like to play in the yard (approach factor) but also is motivated to avoid any punishment by the teacher (avoidance factor). The conflict is between approaching one object and avoiding another.

All three types of conflict present behavioral problems that require solution.

Excitatory Gradients of Approach and Avoidance. Hull (1932, 1934) demonstrated that as a rat approaches a food reward in space and time, the excitatory level rises. Hull showed that as an animal approaches food in a goal box there is a speed-of-locomotion gradient. Rats run faster the closer they get to the goal. Also errors in learning a maze tend to drop out more quickly in the vicinity of the goal than in more remote places.

To measure goal gradients, Hull devised a straight forty-foot runway for timing the speed of locomotion as rats ran from a starting place at one end of the pathway to a food reward at the other. The path of this apparatus was broken into eight five-foot sections by valves of stiff cardboard which the rats lifted in running toward the food. These valves prevented retracing of the path, and also made electrical contacts which were used in timing the running speed. The results indicated clearly that a hungry rat runs faster and faster as he approaches the food. Just before he reaches the goal, however, the speed of locomotion is slightly retarded. Practice tends to speed up the animal in all sections of the runway and tends to level off the speed-of-locomotion gradient at relatively high speeds.

Similar gradients of excitation have been observed in avoidance behavior. If a rat is given an electric shock at one end of a runway, he quickly learns to avoid this end. The level of excitation in avoidance is greatest in the vicinity of the electric grill and decreases as the distance from the grill becomes greater.

J. S. Brown (1940), working with Neal E. Miller, put a harness on the rat and arranged a steel spring so that the strength of pull against the spring could be measured at any distance from the aversive stimulation. The harness consisted of two sturdy rubber bands passed through a swivel hook and around the animal's thorax and neck. The harness was fastened to an endless cord which moved over two pulleys. When it was desired to measure the rat's strength of pull at some point along the alley, a snap ring, firmly attached to a steel spring, was placed around the cord. A bead engaged the ring and, as the rat surged against the harness, a graphic record of the pull was obtained by means of a sliding marker.

With this procedure Brown demonstrated a strength-of-pull gradient. The force exerted by the rat decreased as the animal receded from the source of shock.

A considerable quantity of behavioral research upon conflict has been done in terms of the stimulus-response psychology of Hull and Miller. Gradients of approach and avoidance have been observed and measured. Different types of conflict have been studied experimentally. The influence of drugs upon behavior during conflict has been studied. This kind of work is central to the psychological study of motivation and important for its own sake, but is tangential to the central problems of feeling and emotion.

Dewey's Conflict Theory of Emotion. In 1894-95, John Dewey published two articles upon the theory of emotion. For 30 years, these papers had a negligible effect upon psychological thinking. This was partly because the intricate style and speculative argument made them difficult to read, and partly because psychologists at the time were preoccupied with the James-Lange theory of emotion and other matters.

Angier (1927) restated Dewey's conflict theory of emotion in simpler terms and pointed out the psychological significance of the argument. Dewey's reasoning, essentially, was as follows:

Whenever a series of reactions, required by the purposive set of the organism, runs its course to completion, the result is satisfaction and abolishing of the purposive set. If other reactions can be integrated with the activity in progress, and do not impede it, there is no emotion; but if the extrinsic reactions are so inconsistent with the activity in progress that they cannot be integrated with it, an emotion arises. For example, a man riding a bicycle is hurrying to an important engagement. He passes a friend and waves a hearty greeting. Waving the hand does not interfere with the bicycle riding. But if the friend stops the rider and engages him in a lengthy conversation, the cyclist, concerned over reaching his destination on time, is thrown into conflict and becomes emotionally disturbed by the delay.

Emotion arises when there is a resistance, an interference with the activity in progress. *Without* a conflict, there is no emotion; *with* it, there is. Fundamentally, Dewey argues, an emotion is a state of conflict.

In his first paper, Dewey (1894) pointed out that the so-called expressions of emotion are in reality reduced movements and postures which originally were useful and which have persisted as bodily attitudes. Thus, as Darwin claimed, an angry man bares the canine teeth, leans forward, and clenches his fists. The complete biological act would be biting, striking, and other forms of hostile attack. If the "expression" were complete, it would be an act that is serviceable in the struggle for existence. Similarly, the "expressions" of romantic love are the beginnings of the complete sexual act.

The integrated reactions that lead an organism to some biologically useful goal normally include the vegetative processes. These latter reinforce and facilitate the activity in progress. If the purposive act is frustrated, however, the vegetative processes, instead of reinforcing a useful act and making it more efficient, now interfere. The awareness of these vegetative changes absorbs the subject's consciousness. In other words, the consciousness of an instinctive act is not an emotion but emotion arises and is *felt* when there is some blocking or interference with the instinctive behavior.

In his second paper, Dewey (1895) developed further the conflict theory of emtotion, taking account of the dynamics and functional significance of the process. In addition to the upset or seizure, which is present in emotion, there are two other important phases. First, an emotion is a disposition towards some form of purposive behavior; it involves a purposive set or attitude. Thus, the emotional individual seeks to fight, to flee, to copulate, or to carry out some other purposive activity. Second, the emotional behavior is oriented towards some object. If one is angry, he is angry *at* someone or *on account of* something; if one is afraid, he is afraid *of* or *about* something. There is always an object *towards* or *against* which the individual is oriented. In pathological states of emotion which are objectless, such as certain anxieties and depressions, the individual, Dewey states, goes on at once to supply an object.

There is no reason to assume that biologically primitive acts (fighting, running from danger, etc.) and other purposive acts have a conscious emotional quality. When these acts are integrated and carried out without any blocking or interference, they are free from emotion. When there is interference with a purposive act there are organic repercussions and a feedback from the viscera to conscious states. Thus, the angry man becomes aware of his pounding heart, clenched fist, posture of attack. These are the conscious returns that symbolize a fight.

In summary: Dewey states that certain activities, formerly useful in themselves, have become reduced to mere action tendencies or bodily attitudes. As such, they serve to arouse useful actions and to realize ends. When a difficulty arises in adjusting the activity (represented by the attitude) to other activities, there is a temporary struggle, a partial inhibition of one or both activities, with visceral reverberations. The conflict state *is* or *constitutes* an emotion.

Critique of the Conflict Theory of Emotion. Dewey virtually defines emotion as a state of conflict. Without a conflict, there is no emotion; when conflict is present, there is emotion. A state of conflict *is* or *constitutes* an emotion.

If we take these statements literally, they are open to several fairly obvious objections. In the first place, conflicts are known to exist that are relatively free from emotional disturbance. The blocking of motor impulses—as when one starts to answer the door bell and the telephone bell ringing at the same time or when one hesitates between taking the right or the left path—produces a momentary conflict that is not emotional. It seems necessary to distinguish between emotional and non-emotional conflicts. In the second place, conditions other than conflict are known to produce emotion.

In the first edition of this book (Young, 1943) I listed four main causes of emotion: (1) Emotion is produced by intense stimulation, especially by pain. If sufficiently intense, pain can disorganize any purposive activity and make the individual emotional. (2) Frustration, as we have seen above, can cause emotional upset. Conflict is a special form of frustration which involves the clash of two or more motives within the individual; but the thwarting of a single motive can produce emotion. (3) Conflict is undoubtedly one of the conditions that cause emotion but it is not the only one. (4) Emotional disturbance is produced by the sudden release of tension as in joy and laughter and triumph and sudden success in an undertaking. The release of tension is often, but not always, associated with a response that is hedonically positive. The release from tension and conflict, no less than the conflict itself, produces emotional disturbance.

If the concept of conflict is extended from the immediately present behavior back into the life history of the individual, a significant relation appears between conflict and emotion. Unsolved conflicts and problems repeatedly and consistently produce emotional upsets. An emotion, in fact, may be taken as a sign of some persistent lack of adjustment. To understand the emotional upsets of an individual, the psychologist must take account of persistent attitudes, goals, interests, and sentiments, for these are basic determinants of feelings and emotions.

Physiological Conflict Theories of Emotion. More recent theories of emotion take account of physiological facts which were not known when Dewey formulated his conflict theory of emotion. These theories show the influence of Cannon's thalamic theory of emotion.

Hodge (1935) pointed out that the brain can respond to a situation which confronts the individual: (1) through efferent visceral excitation *via* the thalamic region, or (2) with specific skeletal movements and postures patterned in the cerebral cortex, or (3) by a combination of visceral and skeletal reactions determined in both the thalamic and cortical regions. Emotion is aroused, Hodge states, whenever the higher centers of the brain fail to provide a fitting response to the perceived situation or when some doubt, hesitation, or conflict is aroused as to one's ability to respond successfully. Thus: "*Emotional reactions are inversely proportional to the ability of the higher centers of the brain to meet a given situation.*"

A more specific conflict theory is that of Darrow (1935). After reviewing the experimental evidence, he states that the centers which regulate *excited* emotion are located in the hypothalamus. This is evidenced by the fact that, after surgical decortication, the animal still has a high capacity for emotional arousal; but, after the destruction of a certain area within the hypothalamus, erstwhile "wild" animals are changed into docile ones. (This last point was demonstrated by the surgical operations of Ranson and his associates upon monkeys.)

The role of the cerebral cortex is: (1) that of differentiating stimulus patterns, and (2) that of maintaining an appropriate inhibitory control over the subcortical mechanisms of excitatory response. These two functions become significant in any explanation of emotional excitement.

If circumstances arise which involve a threat to the physical or intellectual equilibrium of an individual and which necessitate an active, dynamic conflict, there is a release of the primitive autonomic (subcortical) mechanisms of *excited* emotion. An essential condition of emotion is that the cortical patterns precipitating the conflict shall be occasioned by perceptual or ideational "stimuli," demanding some action on the part of the individual. This limits the assumed conditions of emotional excitement to a neural state of dynamic conflict.

In a word, just as surgical decortication frees the lower centers from cortical control, so a conflict of impulses produces a functional decortication (or "excortication") which weakens or largely removes cortical inhibition, in this way rendering the individual more excitable emotionally. Darrow explains that this theory is limited to *excited* emotions. Another mechanism is involved in such emotional states as grief, sorrow, remorse, embarrassment, amusement. In these latter characteristically human emotions, however, the cerebral cortex plays the major role. These emotions are socially conditioned, and depend upon the subject's interpretation of his complex situation.

Motor Control and Verbal Behavior during Conflict. Luria (1932) studied human conflicts from the standpoint of disorganization of motor, including verbal, behavior. The situations he examined were vital to the subjects.

In one of Luria's studies subjects were students about to take a critical examination. It was in the spring of 1924 when the overcrowding of higher schools and universities, during the Russian revolution, made it necessary to cut down drastically the student enrollment. Every student had to appear before a commission that considered his academic activity. If the commission decided unfavorably, the candidate was expelled from the school and his plans for future education came to naught; if the decision was favorable, he could continue his academic career. Everything depended upon the outcome of the examination. It was no ordinary school exercise; it was called a "purge" or "cleansing."

Luria removed students from the waiting line and made psychological observations a few minutes before this all important examination. His method combined the recording of muscular movement with verbal responses. Stimulus words were presented one at a time and the subject was instructed to respond with the first word that occurred to him. In the list of thirty stimulus words some were indifferent: *day, pillow, gold*. Others referred to the traumatic situation: *examination, cleansing, commission*. At the instant that the subject responded verbally he squeezed a bulb with the right hand and also attempted to hold a weight steady with the left. Graphic records were obtained of the pattern of voluntary contraction and of steadiness. There was clear evidence that the pattern of normal motor control was disturbed.

Luria also found a blocking or obstruction of the associative processes. Verbal reaction times to indifferent words were lengthened if these words came in a period just after the critical words.

The gross behavior of a typical subject was described as follows: "Very excited, talking loudly, fidgeting in his chair, striking his hands on the table, continuously conversing in spite of being asked to keep quiet; scolding. He responds to the stimulus in fluctuating tones, sometimes in an ordinary voice and again very boisterously. Further investigations reveal a marked variability in the strength of the motor pressures; sometimes he strikes the dynamoscope. Toward the end of the experiment he says he cannot continue the experiment as he must wait his turn in the line."

Such emotional disorganization, according to Luria, is not a transient process. The individual is acutely disturbed but there is a chronic disorganization that outlasts the manifest emotion and that can be understood only in the light of the total situation.

A Minor Study of Hedonic Processes Arising from Conflict. In a small study, with four subjects, I examined the dynamic conflict of habituated movements in relation to affective processes (Young, 1928). The aim of the experiment was to test the hypothesis that a conflict of habituated motor impulses is felt as unpleasant. The general plan was to train the subjects to respond habitually to visual signals; then suddenly (without warning) to produce a conflict of habituated motor impulses by signaling for simultaneous incompatible movements.

The laboratory set-up was as follows: The subject sat on a table so that his feet dangled and could be moved freely with a forward or backward kick. In front of the subject were four miniature signal lamps. Two lamps, on the subject's left, signaled movements with the left foot; two on the right, movements with the right foot. Two of these lamps, located centrally at a distance from the subject, signaled forward kicks; two peripheral lamps, located nearer to the subject, signaled backward kicks.

At the start of the experiment it was necessary to habituate the subjects thoroughly to forward and backward kicks in response to the flashing signal lamps. Tapes attached to the shoes gave an objective record of gross movements. During habituation each subject was given

100 or more trials with single flashes. The trials were randomly distributed among the four signals and corresponding responses.

After habituation, critical tests were made. Without warning the two lights on the left (or the two on the right) were flashed simultaneously to signal incompatible forward and backward habituated kicks. Foot movements and verbal reports were recorded.

To give the experiment an affective setting the subjects were instructed to smell odors and report the pleasantness or unpleasantness of the smells. Several odors were presented for affective report both before and after the daily sessions with flashing lights. Also affective evaluations of leg movements (kicks) were occasionally requested immediately after the subject had responded to a light signal. Affective reports were always requested when conflicting signals were presented.

The affective reports showed that simple leg movements were hedonically indifferent or mildly pleasant. After habituation the forward and backward kicks were automatic, mechanical, and associated with little or no conscious feelings.

When the signals for conflicting habituated movements were given, the subjects, as expected, reported unpleasantness but there were also some unexpected reports of amusement along with smiling and audible laughing. The amusement and smiling were reported as mildly pleasant.

We did not anticipate reports of pleasantness but the explanation became obvious from the protocol. When the double signals were taken uncritically there was blocking, inhibition, uncertainty, and this was uniformly reported as the source of unpleasantness. But the incompatible signals created a situation that was perceived as impossible. The double signals were regarded as an error in procedure, a practical joke, an experimental failure. It was this cognitive appraisal or interpretation that was the source of amusement, smiling, laughing, pleasantness.

The signals for conflicting habituated movements, therefore, produced both a negative reaction (as expected) when the situation was taken uncritically and a positive amusement (not expected) when the situation was perceived as impossible, etc. *No response to the initial conflicting situation was hedonically indifferent.* I believe that the cognitive factor, the interpretation, was the source of amusement and pleasantness.

Then the experiment was continued with double signals on every trial. Of the six possible combinations with four lights, taken two at a time, four of the reactions are possible to execute by simultaneous kicks and two are impossible. After habituation all subjects took conflicting double signals as signs for no response. Both the unpleasantness produced by conflict and the pleasantness produced by release from conflict (amusement, laughter) disappeared with habituation. All responses to double signals became hedonically neutral.

Incidentally, the affective reports to odors, presented during the experimental sessions, while subjects were seated on the table, did not show any habituation or adaptation effect. The positive and negative ratings of the odors were relatively stable during this experiment.

RELEASE OF TENSION

Two emotional reactions with strong affective components are weeping and laughing. And there are persisting moods of grief and joy with occasional weeping or laughing.

Joy is typically a pleasant state in which there is smiling, laughing, excessive random activity. The joyful child when promised a trip to the circus, jumps up and down, claps his hands, laughs, in anticipating the event. His eyes are bright from increased lacrimal secretion. See pages 230-3.

Grief, with crying and weeping, presents a different picture. The head is bowed. The flexor muscles dominate the extensors in posture so that the body is bent over and sagging. There is frowning accompanied by weeping or sobbing. The activity level is low. See pages 233-6.

Why Do We Weep? As an event in human life grief can be recognized by weeping, sobbing, by tears, immobility, and a flexed bodily posture. The subject, while weeping, may report a "lump in the throat"—probably the experience of a smooth-muscle spasm in the alimentary tract at the level of the throat. The grieving individual may repeat, over and over again, some word or phrase which symbolizes the origin of his grief.

In grief the individual is frustrated by the loss of a loved one or of some valued object or opportunity. There are at least two factors in the grief: (1) awareness of the loss, and (2) appreciation of the value of that which is lost.

Lund (1930) found that weeping occurred in mixed emotional states rather than pure dejection. The grieving person is in a state of conflict; the tension from conflict is relieved by weeping. The discharge of tears typically occurs when a depressing situation gains a redeeming feature or when the tension of an unpleasant situation is somewhat relieved or alleviated. For example, a wife whose husband had died three days previously seemed to have been stunned by the blow, showing no outward signs of emotion except extreme depression; she broke down in tears when a friend brought a beautiful wreath. Again, the son of a physician had been run over in the street. The mangled body was taken to the hospital where an operation was performed. The boy died a few hours later. The physician wept for the first time when the boy's mother related a beautiful incident from the boy's behavior that morning.

Pure depressions such as those found in depressive psychoses are tearless, but patients not infrequently become lacrimose in a transitional state when passing from a depressed to an exalted phase. Lund concluded that the pathological conditions most favorable for tears are those of mild euphoria and mixed emotional states such as occur in paresis, multiple sclerosis, general arteriosclerosis, and pseudo-bulbar palsy.

Lund's remarks regarding the shedding of tears emphasize the fact that the emotion of grief is an acute manifestation of a conflict state. This conflict state, however, may be of brief duration or it may last for years. Everyone has heard a statement something like this, "John never got over grieving when his wife died." Such statements imply that the individual was not able to adjust himself to the world after the loss of his wife.

Normally a state of grief remains until the individual can make some readjustment to changed circumstances. Under some conditions a person may never become wholly reconciled to his loss. In the following case, described by Guthrie (1938), the individual took steps to perpetuate her grief. The behavior of the woman is abnormal.

A mother was overcome with grief at the sudden death of her young son during an influenza epidemic. Instead of making a gradual readjustment she took steps which made it difficult for her to forget the loss. The boy's possessions were left undisturbed in their places about the house, except for an occasional dusting. At dinner a place was regularly set for him as it had been during his life! Her conversation was devoted to the lost son. This state of affairs continued for a good many years.

The picture is complicated by the fact that the woman was unhappily married and had come to resent her husband's presence in the home. Also, she had an hysterical type of personality, evidenced by the fact that she had learned to get her way by crying and by other indirect means. She was not clearly aware of the motives behind her actions. In the present instance she used her grief to annoy her husband and to impress the world with her great loss, thus drawing attention and sympathy to herself.

Her inability to forget consisted in arranging her life so as not to forget. The acquiring of a new interest, or a move to a distant city or to another house, or even carrying on her routine in the same home would have helped this woman to forget her loss. A room with sad memories tends to lose those memories if one works in it with thought upon the work instead of upon the loss. But in this case the sorrowing mother actually took steps to conserve her state of grief.

This illustration has been described in detail because it clearly shows the relation between an acute emotion of weeping, on the one hand, and a perisitent affective state of grief, on the other. In everyday life the term *grief* is employed to designate: (1) the emotional process, and (2) the persistent state of non-adjustment. If, therefore, we speak of a widow as grieving for months or years over the loss of her husband, this can mean only that the widow has not made a readjustment. Readjustment, of course, may be easier said than done.

Why Do We Laugh? The question has been much discussed by philosophers and psychologists. Various answers have been given. Hayworth (1928) summarized these answers in a paper developing his own theory of the origin and function of human laughter. The following list of diverse conditions which evoke laughter is based upon Hayworth's discussion:

1. The *triumph* over a conquered enemy brings laughter. This is seen not only on the battle field but also on the playground, at the card table, in carrying out practical jokes, and in other situations.
2. Any *surprise* which brings a feeling of superiority is likely to evoke laughter, as an easy victory in cards or a foot race.
3. The act of *tickling* induces laughter, especially with children. The tickler assumes the role of an attacker. In a playful way he stimulates parts of the body which are supplied with protective reflexes—the soles of the feet, armpits, ribs, the solar plexus. There is usually some element of surprise or uncertainty in the situation. The tickler makes a thrust, then ends with a light touch.
4. Telling a *funny story* is an obvious and direct attempt to produce laughter. Story telling is an art in which tension is first built up and then suddenly released. The story has (or should have!) a point—unexpected turn or development.
5. Laughter is facilitated by a *sense of well-being associated with good health* of the individual or with social safety. If the subject is in excellent health, laughing is aroused by relatively slight provocations. Laughing may be analogous to sounds of contentment which are made by some animals, as purring of a cat.
6. Laughter is frequently aroused by *incongruous situations*. Incongruity covers a considerable portion of humor. It includes the humor of unusual costumes, of bad manners, of foreign customs. In all these instances there is an element of surprise or of novelty, combined with the awareness that there is no cause for alarm. This element of incongruity constitutes a large part of humor on the funny page, on the screen (e.g., the antics of Charlie Chaplin), in parlor jokes, funny stories, and so on.
7. Finally, *an individual sometimes laughs voluntarily* to cover up shyness or embarrassment, to show contempt or to conceal his thought. Such laughter is acted out for a purpose and is not to be regarded as the involuntary expression of emotion. some persons in social situations laugh at the slightest provocation in order to appear cheerful and agreeable. This kind of laughter is a *social* pose rather than a "spontaneous" manifestation of joy.

According to Hayworth's theory, laughter developed as a form of communication. Laughter was originally a vocal signal to other members of the group that they could relax with safety. After a tense situation, in which there is impending danger or prolonged strain, laughter is the signal that all is well. Through the smile or the laugh one flashes this meaning: "Have no fear of me; I like you and will not hurt you; the situation is safe."

Hayworth's theory recalls Darwin's view that joy and friendliness in animal behavior are the antithesis of hostile attack. The cheerful, friendly dog, for example, exhibits patterns of response which are directly opposite to those of angry aggression. Even though the friendly dog has no intention to communicate by wagging his tail, the friendly behavior is readily recognized by man and brute alike as the antithesis of hostility.

We believe that smiling, laughing, and various other manifestations of joyful emotion are best explained in terms of the release of tension. Voluntary laughter has a different explanation, for the individual may have a *determination* to smile or laugh or act in an agreeable manner. The pose of joyful emotion may closely resemble the involuntary emotional outbreak but, from the standpoint of motivation, the two activities are very different.

William James once asked a group of actors whether they *felt* the emotions they enacted on the stage. Testimony was divided. Some said they did and others that they did not actually *feel* the emotions. Perhaps the actors that felt the emotions were so closely identified with the part they played that there was visceralization; but visceralization is not a necessary component of enacted emotions.

> Incidentally, the expression and sound of laughter does not necessarily indicate joy. I recall the sounds of a "laughing" hyena which superficially resembled human laughter. I was strolling through the London Zoological Gardens when I heard the curious "laughing." Hurrying over to the cage I observed the conditions which produced this "laughing." The keeper held the animal's daily supply of meat just out of reach. The hyena, tantalized and while attempting unsuccessfully to get his food, "laughed." The onlookers, hearing and seeing the demonstration, were convulsed. But if we can judge from the situation, this "laughing" indicated annoyance, frustration, anger, rather than joyful emotion.

Perhaps a final word should be added about Freud's theory of wit and humor. Freud recognized that certain topics of conversation, relating to sexual and eliminative processes, are taboo in polite society. See the study by McGinnes (page 213). In the smutty story, laughter is produced by release of a suppressed thought or feeling. The story is told so as to escape the psychic censorship when the point is made.

Release from Tension and the Hedonic Processes. It is easy to assume that the tension produced by undesirable conditions is *felt* as unpleasant and that the release from such tension is *felt* as pleasant. This may be true in some instances but the assumption is not universally valid.

We know that the release from tension may be either pleasant or unpleasant. For example, if one is listening to election returns over the radio, the news of the success of one's candidate brings the reaction of joy; the news that the opposing candidate has won brings an unpleasant relaxation of sorrow and soberness. When the final outcome of the election is announced, there is release of tension but whether the release is pleasing or displeasing depends upon the returns.

In some situations the release of tension elicits laughing without joy or, perhaps, laughing and weeping alternately. Consider hysterical laughter. I recall witnessing the hysterical laughter of a middle-aged woman who was in a somewhat dangerous situation. Her house had caught fire. She was standing in the living room when the fireman started to remove the furniture. She objected to having an old oil painting taken down from the wall. The fire chief ordered the painting removed and asked the woman to leave the house. She refused and was forcibly taken out. As soon as she was outside the house, she emitted loud and prolonged peals of hysterical laughter. She did not weep. Surely this kind of laughing cannot be regarded as an expression of joy!

Of course, there are many reactions to stimulations that are intrinsically pleasing (positive) and others that are intrinsically displeasing (negative) when no tension or release from tension is present.

All things considered, therefore, it is wise to regard the release from tension as a dynamic condition that produces feeling and emotion (which can be either pleasant or neutral or unpleasant) while recognizing that hedonic processes also have other origins.

THE COGNITIVE BASIS OF EMOTION

In the foregoing sections we have examined dynamic determinants of emotion: intense motivation, painful stimulations, interruption and frustration in various forms, conflict, tension and the release from tension. These dynamic conditions *tend* to produce emotional reactions here and now.

It should be remembered, however, that emotional reactions arise within a psychological situation and that the kind of emotion aroused depends directly upon the environmental situation. There is a *cognitive* basis of emotion—in perception, memory and imagination.

Perception of a Situation. If one is forced to witness the distress of other creatures and is unable to relieve their suffering, the perception of a situation commonly arouses an emotion. Consider the following examples:

1. When the great dirigible, *Hindenburg*, burned at Lakehurst, New Jersey, the onlookers were horrified. They heard the cries of the victims and saw them leaping to their death. Nothing could be done to save them. It was a *horrible* accident.

The word *horror* correctly designates the emotion which arises when one witnesses a great tragedy or the torture of a loved one. The ruthless destruction of some valued object—the bombing of an ancient cathedral—may "fill one with horror."

2. Many people are emotionally disturbed when they see an animal in danger or in pain. Here is an example: A kitten had climbed up into the bed springs. Jimmy, aged five and a half, tried to catch her but in the attempt pulled her in such a way that the kitten's paw became caught in a spring. She hung by one foot, crying plaintively. Jimmy was much distressed by the outcry and called for help. At last a housemaid came to the rescue and crawled under the bed to extricate the kitten. While the kitten was being freed, Jimmy stood beside the bed crying and jumping excitedly. There was nothing he could do to relieve the distress of his pet. He was clearly disturbed emotionally by the situation. When at last the kitten was freed, Jimmy's excitement quickly subsided.

3. A housewife for the first time had to cook a live lobster by dropping the animal into boiling water. After much hesitation she dropped the lobster into the kettle and put on the lid. Then she left the kitchen weeping. Later she laughed and again wept. The emotional disturbance, aroused by causing pain and taking the life of an animal, lasted ten minutes or more and ended with the comment, "I don't want to cook any more live lobsters."

4. A girl of nine stood on the curbstone. Her dog started to dash across the street directly in front of an oncoming auto. "Oh," she exclaimed and at the same instant raised both hands as high as her head. The gesture, I believe, was a protective reflex. But the *pet* was in danger and not the girl!

The principle common to these examples is that an emotional disturbance is aroused in a person who perceives another creature in distress or danger. Perception of a situation is a direct determinant of emotion when danger, threat or suffering to some one or some thing is involved as a factor.

Sympathy, Empathy and Identification. I recall witnessing a vaudeville act in which no words were spoken. The actor simply came to the center of the stage and began to laugh. He laughed in different ways, louder and louder. At first a few people snickered. Then some laughed out loud. At the end of the act many people were laughing uproariously. There was no plot, no words, no conflicting tension to be relieved. Simply the perception of someone laughing.

McDougall (1920) has argued that the perception of an emotion in someone else tends to arouse the same emotion in one's self. Thus in a panic the perception of fear in others makes us afraid even though we do not know the source of danger. McDougall called this process the "sympathetic induction of emotion."

Floyd Allport (1924), however, criticized McDougall's doctrine of sympathetic induction of emotion on the ground that it presupposes an innate ability to perceive the emotions of others and to recognize them when they occur. Studies of facial expressions, Allport said, have shown a rather low degree of ability in recognizing emotions from facial expressions. Allport stated that it is not the direct emotional behavior of the person so much as the knowledge of the conditions affecting him that makes it possible for us to understand and sympathize with his state of mind. Again, Allport argued that the facts of life are against McDougall's theory. If, for example, we witness the anger of two men who are fighting, our *anger* is not necessarily aroused. Instead we may be interested, amused, or frightened, according to circumstances.

The nature of sympathy, however, needs further study. A child will weep sympathetically upon seeing his mother weep even when the cause of emotion is not known to the child.

It is common knowledge that emotions are aroused by reading a novel, watching a TV broadcast, following a stage play, hearing an impassioned address, reading a comic strip, hearing jokes and stories, etc. In all such situations it is the *meaning* or *understanding* of the situation that elicits the feeling. We identify ourselves with the characters or the situation and are emotionally aroused. We feel the anxiety, grief, resentment, anger, satisfaction, joy, and relief of the characters. There is thus a *cognitive* identification with others and their situations.

The term *empathy* (*Einfühlung*) has been introduced in psychology to designate the capacity for participating in another's feelings and ideas. Also we tend to project our feelings imaginatively into other persons and situations as well as into works of art and inanimate objects.

CONCLUSION

The dynamic conditions that produce emotional disturbances in man and animal include intense motivation, painful stimulation, frustration, interruption of a planned activity, the clash of conflicting motives, and the release of tension with a positive or negative hedonic effect. These determinants of feeling and emotion are interrelated. All operate within a psychological situation.

These *dynamic* determinants of emotion operate here and now, at a present time, and within a specific environmental situation. The more permanent conditions that predispose an individual to emotional reactions will be considered in the following chapter.

It should be kept in mind that feelings and emotions have a cognitive basis as well as a basis in physical stimulations. Perception, memory, imagination, all play a part in affective arousals. Also affective processes are aroused by printed matter, by radio and television broadcasts, by movies, oratory, and in other ways that depend upon understanding of words, upon knowledge, upon empathy.

Finally, it should be noted that emotional perturbations are only one outcome of frustration, pain, interruption, conflict and the release of tension. Emotional upsets lead to various forms of readjustment.

READING SUGGESTIONS

Frustration, conflict and stress are central topics in psychological researches on motivation. A carefully organized discussion of research studies on these topics, with many references to the literature, can be found in *Motivation: Theory and Research*, by Cofer and Appley (1964). Several experimental studies on conflict, made during the early 1960s, have been reprinted in *Current Research in Motivation*, by Haber (1966).

Many of the older works cited in the text have enduring value and contain useful references. The study of weeping by Lund (1930) is interesting. The paper on laughter by Hayworth (1928) contains references to earlier works. Incidentally, there have been more studies of laughter, wit and humor than of weeping and sadness. Cason's (1930) monograph on common annoyances, aversions and irritations, however, is of interest. Darrow (1935) reporting his conflict theory of excited emotions, has given a useful bibliography.

Chapter IX

Emotional Disturbance and Mental Health

If we consider the course of an individual's life during 24 hours or 24 days or 24 years, it becomes apparent that emotional outbreaks are sporadic and occasional events. Moreover, there are various kinds of feelings, moods, and emotions, that occur from time to time. An individual may have periods of depression or periods of elation or be in an apathetic mood for long stretches of time. Moods tend to recur. He may have feelings of love or hate or anger or anxiety or guilt or sadness or joy or something else.

An important point for the psychologist is that there are persisting, relatively stable, conditions that elicit a variety of affective reactions. These conditions are complex and differ from individual to individual with age, state of health, station in life, and other factors.

In the preceding chapter we have examined those dynamic conditions that *precipitate* emotions. In the present chapter we will examine those more permanent conditions that *predispose* an individual to react emotionally, and the problems of adjustment and health that are presented by emotional disturbances.

EMOTION AND HEALTH

An emotion has been defined as an acute affective disturbance that originates in the psychological situation and that is revealed in various ways—in conscious experience, in behavior, in bodily changes. This definition of emotion as a contemporary event was extended to include chronic conditions of disorganization which are occasionally revealed in emotional outbursts.

An extended view of emotion is essential in psychosomatic medicine, psychiatry, psychoanalysis, clinical psychology, and related disciplines in the field of mental health.

Proneness to Emotion and the State of Health. Stratton (1929) made a statistical study of anger and fear in relation to the history of diseases during early childhood and later. He instructed more than a thousand college students to keep a record, on a special form, of their emotions of anger and fear. For each student he obtained a score showing the frequency of emotional arousal.

Stratton also went to the University of California Health Department and examined the medical records of the students. The medical data had been obtained from examinations given at the time the students entered college. Each record contained a history of diseases prior to the physical examination.

Stratton correlated the incidence of diseases and the age at which they occurred with the scores that showed proneness to fear and anger. He summarized the statistical findings as follows:

> 1. Persons who at any time have been subject to severe illnesses tend in later life to respond more intensely to situations which arouse anger, and probably also to those which produce fear, than do persons who have been relatively free from disease.
>
> 2. Of persons who are alike in having had diseases, those individuals with a greater range or variety of diseases tend to respond more intensely to fear-producing situations than do those with a lesser range. The same is probably true for anger responses.
>
> 3. The period of life at which diseases occur is important for emotional behavior. With fear the results point to a greater significance of diseases during the ages of eleven to fifteen. For anger, there is clear evidence that persons subject to diseases in the first six years of childhood tend toward more intense emotional responses than do those whose diseases occurred in later age periods.

A possible interpretation of Stratton's result is this: Persons who have had a history of frequent and serious illnesses are more likely to be in a poor state of health *now* than are persons who have been relatively free from diseases in the past. In other words, we may assume that there is some degree of positive correlation between the previous and the present state of health. If we hold to this assumption, Stratton's result means that ill health tends to make one likely to have emotional upsets.

The result may be valid for emotions other than anger and fear. I have heard that when a person is suffering from dyspepsia he may become consistently grouchy, sober, depressed. In one instance known to the writer a person with chronic appendicitis became gloomy and dismal in his outlook upon life. After a surgical operation his condition became as cheerful and optimistic as it had been before the illness. Proneness to emotion and ill health are associated.

The question of why there is this association will be left open. But regardless of how Stratton's findings are interpreted, the fact is significant that a history of serious illnesses is associated with proneness to responses of fear and anger.

Psychosomatic Disorders. Behavioral scientists no longer think of an individual as a body plus a mind. They regard the individual as a biological organism with physical, chemical, biological, psychological, social, moral, and other attributes. A living creature presents many aspects.

When there is ill health the physician must seek out *all* of the causes. If a thorough physical examination fails to reveal the presence of organic disease, there remains the possibility of a psychogenic basis for the disorder. Even when organic disease is present, the symptoms may be exacerbated by psychogenic factors.

Several common forms of psychosomatic disorders are listed below:

Gastric ulcers. People in executive positions speak jokingly about a "two-ulcer" or a "ten-ulcer" job, implying that some kinds of employment with positions of responsibilty may cause gastric ulcers.

It is not only the anxiety and responsibility of one's work that causes ulcers. Feelings of resentment, anger and hostility have been shown to increase the motility and acidity of the stomach, and these conditions, in turn, tend to produce ulcers: A man with a gastric fistula was observed to have increased motility and acidity in the lining of his stomach at those times in his life when he was dominated by feelings of anger and resentment. The symptoms were particularly acute when he was discharged from a job on grounds of inefficiency. Contrastingly, feelings of contentment and well-being reduced his stomach motility and acidity.

Essential hypertension. One of the important affections of American adults is high blood pressure, or hypertension. It is well recognized that this disorder can result from various organic conditions, especially diseases of the blood vessels and kidneys. Many cases of hypertension, however, are found to be free from organic causes. "Essential" hypertension is regarded as psychogenic in origin. It is presumed to be caused by continuing action of the sympathetic nerves which accelerate the heart and constrict the blood vessels. Since anger also involves speeding up of the heart and constriction of blood vessels, it is obviously important for persons with hypertension to avoid anger and resentment.

It has been observed that many individuals with essential hypertension are of a submissive nature and often very dependent upon others. They frequently have domineering parents or bosses. A constant hostility or resentment occurs but, because of timidity, they rarely have outbursts of overt rebellion. Their blood pressures, usually high, are markedly lower following the relief that occasional periods of rebellion bring and rise again when they suppress their hostility. The relation between emotion and health is obvious in this condition.

Exophthalmic goiter. A serious thyroid disorder, exophthalmic goiter, sometimes appears to be caused by severe anxiety or at least to be exacerbated by it. A typical example is that of a stock broker who was in excellent health until his fortune was threatened by an economic depression and he finally failed in business. During the heavy strain, with its constant anxiety, he became increasingly nervous. Gradually he developed a pulsating enlargement of the thyroid gland, increased prominence of the eyes, palpitation of the heart, rapid respiration, and increased blood pressure. There were tremors in the fingers, a rapid loss of weight and strength, and a loss of control over impulses to act. He was broken in health as completely as in fortune. His symptoms were those of exophthalmic goiter.

In cases like this there are, in addition to the help from the physician's treatment, striking benefits derived from such things as success, happiness, and good luck; from a change of scene; from hunting and fishing; from optimistic friends.

Bronchial asthma. Another disorder sometimes attributed to psychogenic factors is bronchial asthma. Medical research has demonstrated that asthma is frequently caused by specific allergies to certain substances and can be cured by inoculation with these substances. When proper allergy tests have been found negative, climatic changes bring no relief, and the attacks of difficult breathing are regularly associated with certain emotional situations, then we are justified in assuming that the disorder may be caused or exacerbated by psychological conditions.

The factual basis of psychosomatic medicine is quite impressive. a leading clinical psychologist, R. W. White (1948), concludes:

> Psychosomatic medicine opens up the area where mind and body overlap, where it is no longer possible to distinguish between them. The physician of the future, whether he be general practitioner, specialist, or research worker, must be a psychosomatic physician. He must be able to describe with equal precision the tissue changes in organs, the neural pathways , and the emotional constellations that may have sent traffic over the neural pathways. The physician will be forced more and more to take account of man's emotional nature. In this he is but a part of the great twentieth-century revulsion against purely mechanistic and materialistic thinking. Neither the disorders of the body nor the disorders of the world can be cured without reference to problems of emotional adjustment.

STRESS AND NEUROSIS

The conditions that incite unpleasant emotions–pain, frustration, conflict, interruption of a plan, etc.–are also factors that produce stress. But stress is a broader, more comprehensive, concept than emotion. Persisting cold, hunger, fatigue, loss of sleep, disease, threat, and other conditions, produce stress. These same conditions, when persistent, *predispose* the individual toward repeated emotional outbreaks but do not necessarily *elicit* emotional reactions. They may, however, eventually bring about a nervous breakdown.

The Medical View of Stress. Hans Selye, as a young medical student, was impressed by the fact that most diseases are accompanied by nonspecific symptoms, such as fever. A specific disease has a specific syndrome but there is also a nonspecific syndrome that simply indicates that the individual is sick. The nonspecific syndrome can be studied independently of any specific disorder.

When some factor of stress is present the body reacts to it with a *general adaptation syndrome*. Writes Selye (1956):

> I call this syndrome *general*, because it is produced only by agents which have a general effect upon large portions of the body. I call it *adaptive* because it stimulates defense and thereby helps the acquisition and maintenance of the stage of inurement. I call it a *syndrome* because its individual manifestations are coordinated and even partly dependent upon each other.

The general adaptation syndrome manifests itself in three ways: (1) There is enlargement of the adrenal cortex. (2) There is shrinkage of the thymus, the spleen, the lymph nodes and all other lymphatic structures in the body. (3) There is bleeding, and deep *ulcers* form in the lining of the stomach and uppermost part of the gut. There are further symptoms of the reaction to stress such as loss of body weight, alterations in the chemical composition of the body, etc.

The general adaptive reaction to factors of stress is a physiological unit, involving the pituitary gland, the adrenals, the thymus glands, the stomach and the white blood corpuscles. These structures provide a unitary defense of the body against the diverse forms of damage from stressor factors.

According to Selye, stress is a fundamental medical and biological concept that has broad practical and philosophical implications. Stress is related to the maintaining of homeostasis and to resistance of the body against disease—but stress cannot be identified with disturbed homeostasis nor with the power of the body to fight disease. Injury to the tissues, infections from the attacks of bacteria, fatigue, hunger, thirst, pain , and similar conditions, as well as frustrations and threats, are factors that produce stress.

If we analyze stress from the developmental point of view, three stages are revealed. There is, to begin with, a normal level of resistance when no special stressor is present. When some stressor appears there is an *alarm reaction*. This is similar to what Cannon called the emergency reaction—a reaction that occurs when the animal's life is threatened. The alarm reaction is followed by a prolonged stage of *resistance* to the stressor. Finally, there develops a stage of exhaustion. These three stages—alarm reaction, stage of resistance, stage of exhaustion—occur whether the stressor is forced muscular work, drugs, infections, exposure to cold, threat, frustration, or something else.

During stress the adrenal cortex produces two types of corticoid hormone. One is pro-inflammatory and the other is anti-inflammatory. If bacteria attack a specific organ, there is always inflammation—redness, swelling, heat, pain, and interference with function. This inflammation is the general reaction of the body to a stressor at some specific place. Also leucocytes attack the invading bacteria and form an insulating layer of pus around the invaders.

Stress is an organic process but it may originate in environmental conditions. If a local irritation exists, general stress from the environment may either remove it or make it worse. The curative property of environmental stress was demonstrated by producing a local irritation in the back of a rat and then frustrating the animal by restraint of free movements. If a rat is forcefully immobilized, so that he cannot run around freely, he struggles and becomes angry. Selye found that stress produced by forceful immobilization of movement influenced the reaction of the body to local irritants that were experimentally introduced. When the irritant was weak the general stress from frustration produced a cure. When the irritant was strong the general stress was damaging. Thus it was found that stress produced by environmental frustration could either cure or aggravate a disease. Of course, overwhelming stress (such as that produced by prolonged starvation, anxiety, great fatigue, cold, combined with frustration) is capable of breaking down the body's protective mechanisms.

Selye believes that each individual has a certain quantity of *adaptation energy*. This is not the same as caloric energy (usually considered to be the fuel of life) because exhaustion occurs even when ample food is available. He believes that "every living being has a certain innate amount of *adaptation energy* or vitality. This can be used slowly for a long and uneventful life, or rapidly during a shorter and more stressful, but often also, more colorful and enjoyable existence." We hear about burning the candle at both ends.

Selye writes, in summary:

The three most obvious lessons derived from research on stress are: (1) that *our body can meet the most diverse aggressions with the same adaptive-defensive mechanism*; (2) that *we can dissect this mechanism* so as to identify its ingredient parts in objectively measurable physical and chemical terms, such as changes in the structure of organs or in the production of certain hormones; (3) that *we need this kind of information to lay the scientific foundations for a new type of treatment, whose essence is to combat disease by strengthening the body's own defenses against stress.* [Italics added]

Men under Stress. In times of war and other crises men may be called upon to endure hardship for long periods of time. A man may suffer from fatigue or exhaustion, hunger, loss of sleep, and pain, and also suffer persistent anxiety concerning the safety and security of others. Such factors may accumulate, producing acute stress.

During World War II two psychiatrists, Doctors Grinker and Spiegel (1945), examined the aviators in combat units who were called upon to fly in bombing missions. Their book, *Men under Stress*, gives a clear account of the stress of war conditions. The following illustrative materials are drawn from their account. The illustrations show how stress arises within a compact group such as the members of a bomber crew.

Cohesion and integration of the combat unit group. When the individuals of a group are faced with a common task or a common danger, differences in belief, attitude, and motivation cease to have significance. The group as a whole becomes integrated for the task ahead and it shows great cohesion. The combat unit, for example, is made up of men who fly the same plane and fight the same enemy; this fact produces a high degree of group integration.

The impersonal threat of injury from the enemy, affecting all alike, produces such a high degree of cohesion throughout the unit that personal attachments become intensified. Friendships are easily formed by those who might never have been compatible at home, and these friendships are cemented under fire. Out of mutually shared hardships and dangers are born altruism and generosity that transcend ordinary individual selfish interests. So sweeping is this trend that the usual prejudices and divergences of background and outlook, which produce social distinction and dissension in civilian life, have little meaning to the group in combat. Religious, racial, class, schooling or sectional differences lose their power to divide men. What effect they may have is rather to lend spice to a relationship now based principally upon the need for mutual aid in the presence of enemy action. Such forces as anti-Semitism, anti-Catholicism, and differences between Northerners and Southerners, are not likely to disturb interpersonal relations in a combat crew.

Common danger and common anxiety. Men in a fighting crew are dependent upon each other for survival. An error on the part of one can bring disaster to all. There is thus a common danger and a common anxiety.

Although fear of the aircraft and of human inefficiency are a constant source of stress, the greatest fear is attached to enemy activity. The enemy has only two forms of defense against combat aircraft: fighter planes and flak. The enemy's fighter aircraft are efficient and highly respected by the combat crew members; but they are not as great a source of anxiety as flak. Enemy planes are objects that can be fought against. They can be shot down or outmaneuvered, but flak is impersonal, inexorable, and, as used by the Germans, deadly accurate. It is nothing that can be dealt with—a greasy black smudge in the sky until the burst is close. Then the flak is appreciated as gaping holes in the fuselage, fire in the engine, blood flowing from a wound, or the lurch of a ship as it slips out of control. Fear of enemy activity is seldom concrete until the flier has seen a convincing demonstration of what damage can be inflicted, and how little can be done to avoid it. After a series of such demonstrations, the men are fully aware of what can happen, and the expectation of a repetition produces fear that is difficult to shake off. This load of apprehension constitutes the chief emotional stress during combat. Almost everyone has to make a conscious effort to deal with it. The extent to which a man is able to control it determines his success as a combat crew member.

Common bereavement heightens common anxiety. Grinker and Spiegel point out that the men of the combat group have common grief. The loss of one of their buddies heightens a common anxiety.

The death of a buddy is felt as keenly as the loss of a brother. The men suffer not only from the sense of bereavement, but from having seen the anguish of a bloody and painful death. They cannot look away when a ship flying on their wing receives a direct flak hit and bursts into flame. The sight of their tentmates bailing out with burning parachutes, or exploded out of a disintegrating ship, becomes stamped upon their memory. Empty beds in the tent at night reflect this memory, which does not disappear with the sending home of their buddy's clothes and personal effects. The grief persists. It is dulled by time, but new losses may add to it. The loss of friends arouses increased anxiety. What happened to a buddy may well happen to one's self, since all are so much alike. This double load of grief and anxiety is part of the heritage of emotional stress that is incidental to combat.

Anxiety tension disturbs sleep. Combat service is fatiguing. Rest and sleep become of great importance but unfortunately the tension and anxiety of the situation carry over into the night. Insomnia is common on the night before a mission. Refreshing sleep becomes of greatest importance but sleep is often seriously disturbed.

The men are likely to be awakened in the middle of the night for briefings for early morning missions. Going to sleep may be difficult because of emotional tension from the previous day's mission, not yet worn off. Varying amounts of insomnia are routine among combat crews. It is possible to walk into any barracks or tent containing fliers supposedly asleep and find several pacing the floor or smoking cigarettes. Some give up entirely the idea of obtaining any sleep on the night before a mission and prefer gambling, drinking or talking to tossing in their bunks until it is time to get up. Others would like to sleep but are continually disturbed by slight noises or by their crewmates talking in their sleep. A restless sleep broken by dreams of combat occurs frequently among fliers who have been in combat for more than a few missions. It is not unusual for such dreams to be accompanied by vocal or physical activity. Frequently a man's tentmates awaken the dreamer from a nightmare to quiet him so that the others can go to sleep. In this atmosphere of tension a long, refreshing sleep is a rarity and its absence increases the mounting fatigue. Only quick and short-acting sedatives are practical for fliers who need to be alert on the next day's missions. The anxiety thus carries over into the night and becomes relatively stable.

The Problem of Morale within the Group. It is not surprising that under great emotional stress there should be a strong personal desire to escape and go home. Additional motivation is required to keep the men fighting. The morale of a group is more than the simple sum of individual motivations of the men before they entered combat. Morale is the resultant of interpersonal relationships. It is dependent upon the loyalty of men to each other, to their leader, to their group as a whole. The men are fighting for each other; guilt feelings develop if they let each other down. They seem to be fighting *for* each other or *for* someone rather than *against* an enemy. The personal fate of any one man becomes of secondary importance. The spirit of self-sacrifice, so characteristic of the combat personality, is at the heart of good morale.

Leadership is important in the maintaining of the morale of the group. The leader must be technically competent, strong in character and decisive. There can be no question of his courage. He must have sound judgment concerning the limit of tolerance under conditions of combat, must hold the affection of his men, and must give every consideration to the creature comforts of those under his guidance.

War Neuroses Develop. It is not surprising that under prolonged stress, such as that experienced by fliers during the war, nervous breakdowns should occur. Combat stress results in psychological deficiencies from which no one is immune.

The unending strain eventually produces distress signals. Enthusiasm and eagerness give way to a weariness of battle, which is then endured because there is no way out. Transient fears turn into permanent apprehensions. Anxiety has a tendency to spread until it is continuous or is aroused by trivial sounds. Good muscular coordination is replaced by uncontrollable tremors, jerky manipulations and tension. Constant tension leads to restlessness that is intolerant of repose and never satisfied by activity. Sleep dwindles and gives way altogether to insomnia punctuated by fitful nightmares. Appetite is reduced and gastric difficulties appear. Although air sickness is rare, nausea and vomiting after meals, especially breakfast, are fairly common, as is a functional diarrhea. Frequency of urination, headache, and backache are common signs of the body's reaction to emotional stress. With the growing lack of control over mental and physical reactions come a grouchiness and irritability that interfere with good relations among the men. Some give way easily, and are always in a quarrel or argument. Others become depressed and seclusive, and stay away from their friends to avoid dissension, or because they feel ashamed. Thinking and behavior may become seriously altered. Forgetfulness, preoccupation, constant brooding over the loss of friends, and combat experiences impair purposeful activity. The behavior of the men becomes not only asocial but completely inappropriate and bizarre.

To avoid stigmatizing the flier these reactions are roughly grouped under the undiagnostic term of "operational fatigue." The symptoms do not fall into clear-cut diagnostic categories. The most frequent symptoms of "operational fatigue" (war neuroses) in men who have returned to the U.S.A. are: restlessness, irritability and aggressive behavior, fatigue on arising and lethargy, difficulty in falling asleep, subjective anxiety, easy fatigue, exaggerated startle reaction, feelings of tension, depression, personality changes and memory disturbances, tremor and evidences of sympathetic overactivity, difficulty in concentrating and mental confusion, increased alcoholism, preoccupation with combat experiences, decreased appetite, nightmares and battle dreams, various psychosomatic symptoms, irrational fears (phobias), suspiciousness.

Some Factors Producing Stress. The above account shows both the complexity of the manifestations of stress and the close relation between the physical and psychological determinants. Some of the factors producing stress were described by Darrow and Henry (1949) in a study concerned with submarine personnel.

Suppose a man in a submarine awaits a depth bomb that can sink the ship. He senses danger but there is little to do about it. Anxiety develops. His heart rate increases, blood pressure rises, hormones from the adrenal glands are secreted into the blood, muscle tonus is heightened, sweating is accelerated, there is hyperglycemia, and other bodily changes occur which are characteristic of the alarm reaction.

If the submariner could engage in strenuous activity, these physiological changes would be useful; but the situation of awaiting a depth bomb in a submarine neither requires nor permits violent expenditure of energy. The internal processes are inappropriate and emotionally disturbing. The submariner may become irritable, disagree with a superior officer, develop nausea and loss of appetite (sometimes reported many days after a depth bombing), and other signs of "operational fatigue."

Physical stressors in the submarine situation include: oxygen deficiency, excessively high or low external temperatures, high or low humidity, mechanical vibrations, changes in air pressure, strong odors, dazzling or flickering lights, persistent loud sounds, etc. Such factors have physiological effects apart from anxiety and other psychological factors. Psychological stressors include: boredom, low morale, loss of interest in one's job, and especially anxiety. A persisting anxiety is a stressful factor that can exist even when the physical conditions of survival are satisfactory.

Some of the factors that produce stress have been studied in the laboratory. With animal subjects most of the work upon "experimental neurosis" has involved factors of stress. With human subjects it is obviously impossible to duplicate in the laboratory the stressful situations of real life.

Lazarus, Deese, and Osler (1951) reviewed research on the psychological effects of stress upon performance. They found that investigators produced stress in two main ways. First, stress has been produced by forcing subjects to fail in one way or another. The problem given to the subject may be one that has no solution; the subject may be interrupted before completion of his task; false norms, that indicate failure, may be used. Failure is a threat to the self-esteem of the subject and to the achievement of his goal. Second, stress has been produced by complicating the subject's task. Distractions in the form of shocks, noises, flashing lights, etc., as well as verbal disparagement, have been employed to make the task difficult and stressful.

One general result of these studies is that a moderate degree of stress may facilitate performance but a high degree is disruptive and damaging. This generalization agrees with the findings in many experiments upon human and animal motivation. It also recalls the statement of Selye that mild stress has a curative property but intense stress is damaging to health.

Experimental Neurosis. Nervous breakdowns have been repeatedly observed during World Wars I and II. In the midst of bursting shells and flying shrapnel, men inhibited the strong impulse to escape to a safer place. A stern sense of duty and an attitude of courage kept many men at the front. Also, they were compelled by military regulations to remain in places of danger. Some developed paralyses, aphasias, amnesias, and other symptoms which necessitated withdrawal to a hospital far behind the lines even though they were physically uninjured. Most of these men were not malingering but simply unable to endure the strain of a terrifying situation. They suffered from shell shock.

Nervous breakdowns, long known in man, have quite recently been produced and studied experimentally in laboratory animals. Neurotic behavior, resembling that of human beings, has been produced experimentally in dogs, cats, rats, sheep, pigs, goats, chimpanzees, and other animals. In all instances the neurotic behavior has been elicited by a stressful situation involving the frustration of some basic motivation such as the need to escape from pain or from a terrifying situation.

The Russian physiologist, Pavlov (1927), was probably the first to report "experimental neurosis" although Lashley (personal communication) had observed neurotic behavior in rats prior to Pavlov.

Several kinds of situations produce experimental neurosis. The more important situations that cause nervous breakdowns in man and animal (according to an unpublished manuscript by O. H. Mowrer) are the following:

Threat to one's existence or security. During the heavy floods in Leningrad, in 1924, water unexpectedly entered the living quarters of the dogs that were used as subjects in experiments upon conditioned reflexes. Before attendants could reach the scene, the water had risen to such a height that the animals could keep their heads above it only with difficulty. To remove the animals through the low doors of their cages it was necessary for attendants to submerge the dogs' heads briefly. During the terrific storm—amid breaking waves, crashing trees, rising water against the walls of the laboratory—the animals had to be removed quickly by making them swim in small groups from their kennels into another laboratory about a quarter of a mile away. Here they were kept on the first floor, huddled together indiscriminately. The excitement strongly inhibited the animals. Most strikingly, they did not fight or quarrel; they remained quietly huddled together, which behavior is unusual with dogs in a group.

All of the animals were saved but after the storm it was discovered that several of them had completely lost their conditioned reflexes to visual and auditory stimuli. The learned responses had been so completely eliminated that only extensive training could restore them. One dog that seemed normal in behavior and that had not lost his conditioned reflexes, responded with intense fear when a loud bell (previously used in the experiments) was sounded near him. Pavlov believed that the loud sound produced an emotional disturbance equivalent to restoration of the flood experience. To test this hypothesis he produced a mock flood by letting water trickle under the door into the room where the dog, on the raised stand, could see it. When the animal noticed the stream of water trickling along the stone floor, it fell into extreme agitation—panting, yelping, trembling. The experiment ended with an impairment of behavior that Pavlov attributed to functional weakening of the nervous system through shock. The shock had produced an artificial or "experimental" neurosis.

A difficult discrimination when motivation is strong. An experimental neurosis may occur in situations which require the animal subject to make a difficult discrimination when the motivation is strong. For example, one of the dogs in Pavlov's laboratory was being trained to discriminate between a luminous circle and an ellipse of about the same area. Both forms were projected on a screen. The circle was made the signal for food and the ellipse a sign that no food would be given. The animal was hungry. At the start of the training the discrimination was easy: The axes of the ellipse were in the ratio of 1:2. As training continued, the elliptical form was made more and more circular by changing the ratio of the axes to 2:3, 3:4, 4:5, and so on progressively.

When the ratio 8:9 was reached, the dog, which formerly had stood quietly in the harness, began to struggle and howl, salivating indiscriminately to the presentation of both circular and elliptical forms. The dog tore off with its teeth the apparatus used for mechanical stimulation of the skin and bit through the tubes connecting the animal's room with that of the observer. It barked violently, contrary to its usual manner. In short, there appeared various symptoms of an acute nervous breakdown. The animal developed a seemingly foolish fear (phobia) of certain geometrical figures and, to a less extent, a fear of the experimental situation in which these forms had been encountered.

In this kind of situation the animal is in a situation which calls for sensory discrimination up to a very limit of its capacity. The subject is highly motivated by a state of hunger; the reward of food depends upon the discrimination that is made. As the discrimination becomes increasingly difficult, the making of a "correct" choice becomes unbearable and a breakdown occurs.

Incidentally, Pavlov's finding recalls the Yerkes-Dodson principle that a *difficult* task is disrupted by a weaker shock than an *easy* task. In Pavlov's situation the motivation was strong and constant and the difficulty of the task was gradually increased until finally there was a complete breakdown of behavioral organization.

This type of neurosis is similar to that which occurs on the human level when a man who is highly motivated, having much at stake, is forced to solve a problem and make a choice which is too difficult for him. During the stress and strain of the human conflict a breakdown may occur.

Pain as a signal for food reward. Pavlov demonstrated that a conditioned salivary reflex can be established as a response to almost any kind of signal, even to painful electric shock. In one experiment a weak electric shock was used as a signal for food and conditioned salivation was established. The dog showed no signs of defense reaction against the shock but rather turned his head, licked his lips, and produced a conditioned salivary secretion.

Then the shock was increased in strength until finally it became very intense. The shock continued to evoke a conditioned reflex. The reaction to an intense shock, as a signal for food, remained stable for many months. But there was a limit. After repeated presentations of intense shock there appeared an abrupt and complete breakdown in behavior. No trace of the alimentary reaction could be found. There was violent defense against the painful stimulation. And even weak currents failed to elicit a conditioned salivary reflex.

The noteworthy feature of experimental neurosis under these conditions is the suddenness of the breakdown. Prior to the crisis, the dogs showed no sign of fearful anticipation; their behavior was organized and controlled. The animals appeared to be quite oblivious to the painful nature of the shock so long as it was a signal for food. Then, quite suddenly, the acquired reaction disappeared and pain-avoidance behavior dominated the scene.

The abruptness of the transition has a counterpart in certain human neuroses: A man who has been regarded as a stable and dependable citizen suddenly deserts his wife, abandoning his job, and disappears from the community. Prior to this fugue he had enacted a cheerful, normal, role in a situation which was mainly unpleasant to him. No one knew that he was poorly adjusted to his wife, threatened by financial failure, and unable to face the disgrace of impending divorce and bankruptcy. Quite suddenly under the stressful situation a total nervous breakdown occurred.

Conditions that Produce Experimental Neurosis. Cook (1939) made a survey of the conditions that produce experimental neurosis. In addition to the above, he mentioned the following:

A neurosis may develop in conditioning experiments when the interval of delay between foresignal and food (or shock) is gradually increased beyond a critical value. For example, in one experiment the delay between foresignal and food was gradually increased by adding five-second increments to the interval employed. Under these conditions the animal became generally excited when the two-minute interval of delay was reached and at the end of a three-minute delay, as Pavlov stated, the dog became "quite crazy," violently and unceasingly moving all parts of the body, howling, barking, and squealing intolerably. Further, toward the last of the experiment there was a constant flow of saliva during the presentation of any stimulation, all signs of a delayed reaction having vanished.

A neurosis may appear when a transition between excitatory and inhibitory conditions is suddenly made. For example, in one experiment a cutaneous rhythm at the rate of twenty-four stimulations per minute was rewarded with food, and a rhythm at the rate of twelve per minute was not rewarded. When it was arranged that the twenty-four-per-minute rate would immediately follow the twelve-per-minute rate *at the same point on the skin*, all the positive conditioned responses which had been acquired during the experiment disappeared completely. It was found, however, that conditioned responses could be slowly restored by retraining. In this instance the rapid transition from exciting to inhibiting conditions is believed to be the basis for the loss of conditioned reflexes.

Neurotic symptoms sometimes appear when an inhibitory stimulation is changed by the experimenter into an excitatory one. To illustrate, in one experiment the clicking of a metronome at the rate of 120 beats per minute was made the positive signal for food, and clicking at the rate of 60 beats per minute was kept negative. After the animal had become accustomed to these signals, the experimenter began rewarding the 60-per-minute (previously negative) rate. When the change was made, the responses to the formerly positive rate decreased and disappeared. Concurrently, certain other conditioned reflexes that had been acquired during the experiment were lost.

To these conditions I might add a brief reference to some observations made during one of our experiments on food preferences. Need-free rats had been making series of preferential discriminations between pairs of saline solutions presented for choice. When they were offered a choice between a pair of hypertonic solutions (3% NaCl vs. 6% NaCl) they preferred 3% NaCl. Then the rats were made thirsty. The thirsty animals rejected completely both saline solutions. Suddenly the running-back-and-forth on the preference tester was completely inhibited. For days it was impossible to do any preference testing and we thought that the rats had been ruined as subjects for the experiment. Running the shuttle pattern was for a time completely suppressed, inhibited. Eventually, however, when again need-free, the rats made normal preferential discriminations and ran the shuttle pattern. But recovery was slow and with sporadic bursts of running at a high rate. See Young and Falk (1956) and page 141.

In general, experimental neuroses are produced in laboratory animals under these conditions: (1) the subject is strongly motivated; (2) the subject is frustrated, in conflict, painfully stimulated, in need, or facing some difficult discrimination or threat to adaptive behavior; (3) there is no escape from the situation, or (4) under these conditions the experimental situation is arbitrarily and unpredictably changed in some way by the experimenter.

Some Further Studies of Neurotic Behavior. Following Pavlov's pioneer work upon "experimental neurosis" other investigators have studied behavioral breakdowns in animals. Only a few of the many available studies can be mentioned.

Maier (1939), in his work upon experimental neurosis in the rat, produced behavioral breakdowns by placing the animals in a situation that involved conflict. Using the Lashley technique, he forced rats to jump a gap to a goal box. There were two goal boxes, side by side, with geometrical figures on the doors. If the animal discriminated correctly, the door would be open and the animal could jump through it to a food reward; if the animal made an error, the door would be locked and the animal would receive a bump on the nose and a fall as punishment. When the problem was difficult or insoluble, many animals developed neuroses.

Maier demonstrated both active and passive phases of the disordered behavior produced by conflict. During the active phase a rat rushes about violently, exhibiting convulsive movements and sometimes tics. He jumps in a curious manner. During the passive phase the rat is quiescent. His body may be rolled up into a ball or moulded by the experimenter into some posture which he maintains for several minutes. After the passive phase there is a return to a normal level of activity.

Liddell (1938), working in the laboratory barns at Cornell University, produced neuroses experimentally in sheep. Among other things, he found that neurotic behavior, once established, was relatively stable.

One animal exhibited symptoms of neurosis during 9 years until its death at the age of 13.5 years. Two other animals remained in a neurotic state for 6 years. When the sheep were removed from the laboratory situation and from the painful shocks that had been used to produce neurotic behavior, they appeared to be normal in every respect. When they were returned to the labortory and placed upon the threatening apparatus, their over-reaction and other abnormalities of behavior developed within a few days of experimenting. In other words, the "rest cure" was effective so long as the animals were removed from the situation that produced the traumata but the neurotic symptoms returned when the animals were again placed in the apparatus.

Further studies, that have a bearing upon the therapy of neuroses, were carried out by Masserman (1947). He trained cats to close a switch that rang a bell or turned on a light and then dropped a pellet of food into the food box. When the cats had learned to work the apparatus, they were subjected to sudden blasts of air at the moment of feeding. After several repetitions of the air blast, neurotic behavior developed and became well established. Various therapeutic procedures were then tested.

In one procedure the hungry cats were *forced to face the situation* by being placed in the apparatus and slowly pushed towards the food box by means of a movable partition. When the animals reached the scene of the former air blasts they went into an emotional state bordering on panic. Some of the cats, seeing the food in the box, made a dive for it and managed to eat; this put them on the road to recovery. Others were terrified, ate nothing, and left the apparatus in a state worse than that before the trials. In another procedure the cats were *retrained*. They were petted, stroked, and fed by hand when placed in the apparatus. When treated in this way they gradually learned to depress the switch, to tolerate the air blasts, and to eat in spite of it. If the retraining was hurried, the cats were thrown into neurotic excitement and further retraining became difficult. In still another method the animals were *left in the cage to work out their own solution*. They were in conflict between fear of the air blasts and hunger. As the hours went by, the cats became increasingly hungry and active. They would cautiously approach the switch and touch it lightly. When the bell sounded and the light flashed the cats would retreat, even when there was no air blast. As hunger became intense they grew bolder. Finally, being very hungry, they would eat the food. Reintroduction of the air blast sometimes renewed the neurotic behavior but with time the cats learned that even the blast of air was harmless and they would eat in spite of it.

Tests of Neurotic Tendency. At the time of World War I, it was recognized that soldiers who are prone to nervous breakdowns should be discovered early to prevent them from reaching the front. Under the stress of battle, amid bursting bombs and the hardships of warfare, some individuals had nervous breakdowns necessitating their removal from the scene of action.

A committee, headed by Professor R. S. Woodworth, devised a check-list of questions which aimed to detect those individuals likely to develop neuroses in warfare. The signing of the armistice, on November 11, 1918, prevented the use of Woodworth's test under conditions of actual warfare.

Following the war, however, other tests of neurotic tendency were devised. One of the best known was that of L. L. and T. G. Thurstone (1930), consisting of a list of 223 questions, each of which is to be answered by the subject with *yes, no*, or *doubtful*. For each item, a neurotic and a non-neurotic response was assumed to exist. For example, to the question, *Do you get stage fright*? the neurotic answer is *yes*; and to the question, *Can you stand criticism without feeling hurt*? the neurotic answer is *no*.

Although the maximal neurotic score would equal the number of questions, i.e., 223, the actual scores obtained from one group of college freshmen ranged from 5 to 134. A numerically low score on the inventory indicates relative freedom from emotional strain and anxiety, i.e., an emotionally well-adjusted and stable temperament.

Subsequently, Taylor (1953) described a test of manifest anxiety. In developing the test she selected fifty items from the Minnesota Multiphasic Personality Inventory that clinicians had judged to be indicative of chronic anxiety. These fifty items were supplemented by 225 additional items judged to be non-indicative of anxiety. The score on the critical items indicates the relative degree of manifest anxiety.

Figure 50 combines two graphs presented by Taylor. The solid line shows the frequency distribution of scores for 1971 university students and the broken line presents scores for 103 psychiatric patients. The difference between median scores of these two groups is highly significant and proves that psychiatric patients show more manifest anxiety than the group of college students.

Fright and Anxiety. A distinction is commonly drawn between fright (an acute emotional reaction) and anxiety (a persistent foreboding or presentiment of harm). The anxious person anticipates pain or failure or humiliation.

According to Mowrer (1939), a stare of anxiety is motivating. An individual tries to reduce his anxiety and whatever reduces anxiety is reinforcing. See page 82.

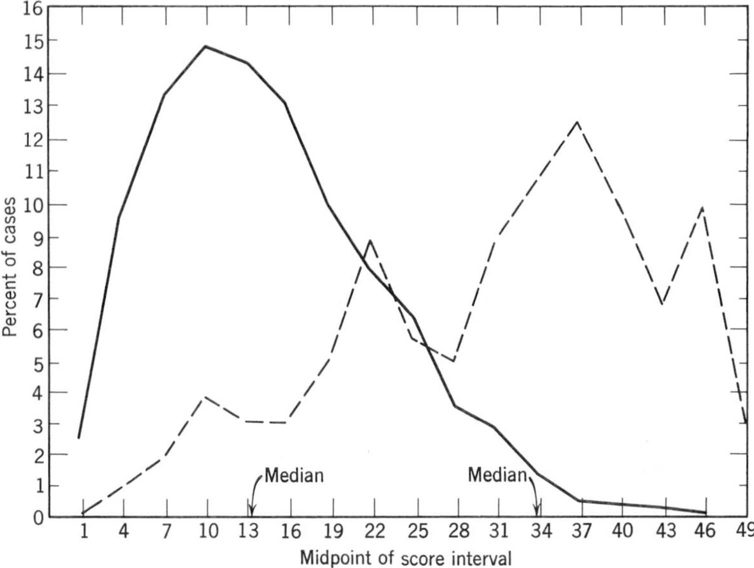

Figure 50. Frequency distribution of manifest anxiety scores. Solid line graph shows frequency polygon for 1971 university students. Broken line graph gives distribution of scores for 103 psychiatric patients. *After* Taylor (1953).

Fright is shown by heightened activity along with an impulse to escape or by immobility and "freezing." Both types of reaction are adaptive in a threatening situation.

Anxiety is medically important because it is known that symptoms of physical illness rest upon persistent worries. For example, the symptoms of exophthalmic goiter, or Graves' disease, sometimes appear directly after a severe shock or some long-drawn-out and worrisome strain.

The surgeon Crile (1915) described the case of a broker who was in excellent health until, in the panic of 1907, his fortune and those of many others were in jeopardy for almost a year. He finally failed in business. During the heavy strain, with its constant anxiety, he became increasingly nervous. Gradually he developed a pulsating enlargement of the thyroid gland, an increased prominence of the eyes, marked increase in perspiration, palpitation of the heart, more rapid respiration with frequent sighing, and increased blood pressure. There were tremors in the fingers and in other muscle groups, a rapid loss of weight and strength, frequent gastrointestinal disturbances, and a loss of normal control of his impulses to act. He was broken in health as completely as in fortune. His symptoms were those of exophthalmic goiter. They resembled closely the bodily signs of fear, and actually they followed in the wake of an intense anxiety.

Whatever the primary exciting cause of exophthalmic goiter may be, whether a chronic focus of infection, a tumor growth, or some other factor the medical profession may have determined, it is certain that an unusual business worry, disappointment in love, bereavement, the prolonged illness of a loved one—any shock or persistent anxiety—may markedly exacerbate the symptoms and in some cases appear to be an exciting etiologic factor of the disease. This relationship is suggested by the close resemblance between the symptoms of Graves' disease and the outward expressions of great fear.

Graves' disease, Dr. Crile writes, may be increased by giving thyroid extract or by experiences of fear. It may be diminished by removing part of the thyroid gland (or by partially interrupting the blood and nerve supply thereto) or by a complete rest. Any agency that can dispel anxiety will benefit the patient. The physical symptoms have, in part, a psychogenic basis, and they can sometimes be removed by psychotherapeutic means.

Dr. Crile writes: "The striking benefits of good luck, success, and happiness; of a change of scene; of hunting and fishing; of optimistic and helpful friends, are at once explained by this hypothesis. One can also understand the difference between the broken body and spirits of an animal in captivity and its buoyant return to its normal condition when freed."

One often hears the advice, "Don't worry." This advice is sound enough from the standpoint of mental hygiene; but often it is impractical since the bodily changes of anxiety are involuntary and little affected by a determination not to worry. When a student is awaiting an important examination, he does worry. When a patient is awaiting the entrance of the dentist with his instruments of torture, he worries despite his determination not to do so.

The technique of distraction—attending to some other activity—may temporarily reduce anxiety. The knowledge that there was an escape from the pain reduced the patient's anxiety and he thought, "If the pain is no worse than this, I can take it."

In some fortunate cases it is possible to reduce anxiety by changing the situation so as to remove the threat or the source of worry.

It is medically important to distinguish between those mental states which produce no physical symptoms and those which do. In simple words, some mental states of an individual are pathogenic in the sense that they lead to ill health; others are not.

Anxiety states are sometimes treated with drugs (Boissier and Simon, 1969). On this see page 277.

Emotional Stability and Frustration Tolerance. Some persons fly into a towering rage at the slightest provocation. Others respond to the same situation in a matter-of-fact way; they are the more stable emotionally.

Individuals differ markedly in their tolerance of pain and frustration. As Guthrie (1938), writing of nervous breakdowns, has put it:

> Probably any man could be placed in a situation which would bring on such collapse. Some situations are intolerable for any human beings. Central American prisons in the old days, solitary confinement in verminous dungeons, torture, cumulative misfortune can put any man in the condition which we describe as nervous breakdown. But there are great differences in what different individuals can tolerate. [231]

When painful, distressing factors are added together, the cumulative effect will sooner or later break down anyone.

The proneness to emotional upset as well as to nervous breakdown varies with age, habituation to an environmental situation, physiological state, and many other factors. An adult can tolerate much more frustration than a child, without showing emotion. The hardened soldier can tolerate without emotional upset more hardship than the new recruit; the veteran with composure can witness a horrible accident that would upset the newcomer. Fatigue, hunger, cold, loss of sleep, and similar conditions, make the individual–especially the child–more ready to respond emotionally. But if these factors could be held constant, constitutional differences in emotional stability would still appear.

TEMPERAMENT

Characteristic differences in the mode of emotional response were recognized before Galen, the philosopher, formulated his classical doctrine of the four basic human temperaments. The term *temperament* refers to the persistent type of affective reaction made by an individual. For example, we recognize that some individuals are chronically cheerful; others are sober and depressed; some are relatively apathetic; others moody. Some individuals are active, excitable, hyperkinetic; others are calm, quiet, hypokinetic.

Temperamental Differences among Infants and Animals. Differences in temperament can be recognized at an early age. Washburn (1929), in a study of smiling and laughing among infants, grouped the infants into these types:

1. Ambi-expressive (equally cheerful and sober)
    a. Parvi-expressive (serene, tranquil)
    b. Multi-expressive (excitable, emotionally labile)

2. Risor-expressive (cheerful)
3. Depressor-expressive (sober)

This classification of the temperaments of infants implies two main variables: (1) the factor of activation shown by the prevailing level of activity; and (2) The hedonic factor, shown by positions along the hedonic continuum from cheerful, through neutral (or balanced), to depressed and sober.

Temperamental differences have been recognized among non-human subjects. Hall (1941) defined temperament as "*consisting of the emotional nature, the basic-needs structure, and the activity level of an organism*. Such traits as timidity, aggressiveness, sexuality, spontaneity, variability, speed of reaction, and activity are examples of temperamental traits."

Hall reports that experiments upon animals have been carried out for: fearfulness, timidity, emotionality, and wildness; aggressiveness and savageness, including the inheritance of wildness and savageness; activity; and miscellaneous traits such as persistence and speed of reaction. There are some temperamental traits which have been largely ignored by experimenters. Among these, Hall states, are: variability, reaction strength, docility, dominance, tidiness, cooperativeness, friendliness, grief, boisterousness, spontaneity, and gregariousness.

Future research will have to decide how far the last-mentioned traits can be classified as *temperamental* and how far under some other heading such as *social behavior* or *personality*.

The Endocrine Glands in Relation to Temperament. In medieval physiology temperaments were supposed to be determined by the proportions of humors in the body. Today it is widely recognized that secretions of the endocrine glands exert a profound effect upon human temperaments.

Collecting evidence from many sources, Hoskins (1933) has pointed to some of the psychological effects of glandular imbalance. (1) In *thyroid* deficiency the effects vary widely from case to case. The subjects are rather commonly depressed in mood, the depression sometimes extending to a genuine psychosis which is scarcely distinguishable from the manic-depressive psychosis in the depressive phase. The patient shows a dissatisfaction with life, a distrust of his fellow man, and general unhappiness. In the myxedematous type of thyroid deficiency and irritability an over-sensitiveness to annoyance appears. (2) In *parathyroid* disorders the patient may become "touchy," flying into ungovernable rage at the slightest provocation, such as an unfriendly look or a mildly critical comment. Under treatment with parathyroid extract, supplemented by calcium and sunlight, a striking improvement has been reported. (3) *Pituitary* deficiency and behavior problems are definitely associated. In one study of pituitary disorder the aberrations of behavior were such manifestations as moroseness, bullying, disobedience, lying, thieving, and vagrancy. (4) Suprisingly, in women the psychological effect of *ovarian deficiency* is not particularly shown in the sexual sphere. Erotic desire often manifests no diminution and may even be increased. It is true, rather, that a deprivation of the ovarian hormones during the normal reproductive years results in a nervous tension and irritability. Commonly coupled with this are attitudes of self-pity and egoism and of hyperemotionalism. (5) In the male the effects of *castration* vary from individual to individual. If castration occurs early in childhood, normal male aggressiveness fails to develop. If castration is performed after puberty, a certain degree of masculinization may persist throughout life. But the emotional reactions of eunuchs are said to be defective. In one group they were reported to be cold and passive in the face of dire poverty, ugly in temper and moody, and to indulge in homosexual practices as well as in other sexual perversions.

If we inquire about the more normal relationship between endocrine glands and emotional behavior, we recall at once Cannon's emergency theory of the *adrenal glands*. Cannon pointed out that the adrenal secretion produces a curious assortment of bodily changes which have one common value—utility in times of stress and during highly motivated behavior.

The *sexual glands*, when they reach maturity, normally bring into behavior the complex manifestations of sexual appetite and the associated emotions. With the onset of puberty, as Hoskins has put it, the maid "trims her sails to catch the breeze of masculine fancy according to the customs of her generation. The wiles of Eve come unbidden to her aid. Unwittingly she assumes her role in nature's great drama and the race goes on. Her less sophisticated sister falls in with the plot unresistingly. Her blushing reticences at once mark her for chivalrous regard of her future mate and reveal her as swaying to the rising tide of her hormones."

That such vital events as puberty, menstruation, pregnancy, lactation, and menopause have a profound effect upon the appetitive and emotional life of women is known to everyone.[1] The analysis of these and other organic conditions in relation to emotional disturbances is an important field of investigation for the physiological psychologist.

[1]While writing these lines, I noticed an adolescent housemaid, a girl of fourteen, who had repeated crying spells in the kitchen over the loss of a fifty-cent piece. The crying was so persistent that the girl was suspected of being emotionally immature. Later it turned out that this girl was painfully menstruating at the time of the loss. Her general state no doubt predisposed her to the spells of crying.

Magnesium-deficient Diets and Abnormal Behavior. When newly weaned rats are placed on a diet which is deficient in magnesium but adequate in other respects, they become hyperexcitable. According to the observations of Kruse, Orent, and McCollum (1932), the hyperexcitability becomes progressively more pronounced until the eighteenth day of deprivation, when any sudden disturbance throws the animals into a fright that is followed by a convulsive seizure. During the early stages of magnesium deficiency the rats are apprehensive and show alarm at the noise of crumpling paper or the opening of a door or a moving shadow. Almost any slight sound or movement will terrify them.

This emotional disturbance is only part of the behavioral display of rats which have been maintained upon a magnesium-low diet. The convulsive seizure, which finally leads to death, is spectacular:

> The excitable animal, startled by sound, races at rapid speed in a wide circle until it finally falls on its side. The entire body of the animal is now rigid, with head stretched back, fore limbs extended at three upper joints and flexed at the metacarpophalangeal joint, and hind limbs extended backward. So fixed are the jaws that often the tongue is perforated by the clenched teeth. The skin presents a waxy appearance. All respiratory movements cease during the attack and return with relaxation of the musculature. Priapism may appear at this time and persist until death.
>
> This stage of spasticity is succeeded by a period of relaxation lasting only a very short time. While still lying on its side, the animal exhibits twitchings in various regions, or paddles rapidly with all extremities. Coincident with this behavior, the animal's eyeballs become more prominent, the ears stiffen and project backward against the side of the head, and the fur stands erect. Then reappears a tonic spasm in which the rigid body assumes a typical position, with fore limbs pressed tightly against the thorax, fore paws clenched, and hind extremities extended. This spastic condition may give way to clonic contractions in which the fore limbs are extended from the body. Next the animal may suddenly leap into the air, at the same time spinning laterally several times; or it may "curl up" with marked flexion of all extremities; or it may do neither. There is marked cyanosis. Associated with the convulsive seizure is regurgitation of the stomach contents into the esophagus and mouth, as sacrifice experiments during this period have shown.
>
> Within a short time the animal rears from the dorsal or lateral recumbent position in an attempt to stand, but its extremities will not support it. The animal buries its head in its outstretched fore limbs and propels itself forward entirely by its hind limbs, which, however, are so extended with paws hyperextended that the dorsal, not the plantar, surface bears the weight. Instead of forward motion, fine tremors may appear over the body. Throughout this stage the eyeballs are retracted.
>
> Following the convulsive stage comes a recovery phase, doubtless dependent on exhaustion. . . . [522-524]

The convulsive siezure described above is definitely an abnormal manifestation. The account suggests at least two points of general psychological interest.

First, the *emotional* disturbance is only one manifestation of the total physical state of the organism. There are many purely physical symptoms of the deficient metabolic state (not here described), and there are *non-emotional* signs of disturbance in behavior. The account is interesting because it shows how difficult it is to draw a distinction between emotional and non-emotional symptoms of a deficient metabolic state. A second point of interest is this: The case shows that there is a well-defined type of convulsive seizure associated with a specific dietary deficiency of magnesium. In other words, there is a uniform relation between abnormal behavior and a dietary lack. Incidentally, this convulsive seizure is somewhat similar to that of neurotic rats, produced through extreme frustration and conflict.

In an experiment upon magnesium deficiency, Scott, Verney, and Morissey (1950) reported that rats maintained upon a magnesium-deficient diet *avoided* foods that contained magnesium despite the fact that the mineral was essential to their health and ultimate survival!

The Psychiatric Approach to the Analysis of Temperament. One way to study differences of human temperament is to examine the emotional reactions of psychopathic individuals. The psychiatrist has recognized a number of pathological states of a strongly affective nature. The distinctions he has drawn can serve as guides to the analysis of temperamental differences in normal persons.

Very tentatively the following list of abnormal affective states is offered for study. The list is based upon the work of MacCurdy (1925), but his finer distinctions are here ignored.

1. In *manic psychoses* the patient is elated, restless, and distractible. The manic temperament is akin to the cheerful, active, alert individual of normal life.

2. In *depression* the patient appears sullen, inactive, and unresponsive. Some normal persons also are sad and gloomy in their behavior and outlook upon life. Perhaps they are the normal counterpart of patients who suffer from depressive psychoses.

There are also patients who vary from depression to mania (*manic-depressives*) just as there are normal persons who are moody—who have marked ups and downs of mood.

3. There are pathological states of *apathy* characterized by lack of affective reactions. In functional dissociation, for example, a patient who formerly took care of her mother, with normal feelings, became completely indifferent about her mother's death and spoke about her mother in a cold, matter-of-fact way. Apathy has its normal counterpart, perhaps, in the individual who appears to be without feelings and heedless of the feelings of others.

4. Chronic *anxiety states* in the abnormal, especially in psychoses associated with the fear of death, are in some respects similar to normal anxieties and worries.

5. States of *perplexity and confusion* in psychopathic patients are, perhaps, in some ways akin to the normal cognitive confusion and conscious blur of certain emotions and moods of normal life.

The affective states of abnormal individuals are in the above ways similar to normal affectivity. The study of abnormal persons thus offers an opportunity for the psychological study of temperaments because normal temperamental differences appear in exaggerated form and intensity in many psychopathic states.

EMOTION AND MENTAL HEALTH

There is a close relation between persisting emotional disturbances and mental health. We have seen how nervous breakdowns arise from stress and how emotions are elicited by frustration, conflict, pain, release of tension, and related conditions. The conditions that produce tense and unpleasant emotions are also factors that contribute to stress. These conditions give rise to problems of adjustment in normal life as well as to a possible impairment of health.

Medical men and women are concerned with all the conditions that affect health. In the following sections we will examine some of the dynamic concepts that have grown out of the work of Sigmund Freud. Then we will consider emotional experiences in relation to psychotherapy in general.

Freud's work has had a profound influence upon dynamic psychology. Consider the following processes:

The Nature and Etiology of Phobias. A phobia is the persistent fear of a specific object or situation. High-sounding names have been invented to designate phobias: *pyrophobia* (fear of fire), *odontophobia* (fear of teeth), *selenophobia* (fear of the moon), *doraphobia* (fear of fur), *thanatophobia* (fear of death), and so on. But these names add only the air of profundity to our understanding of what is acutally involved psychologically. High-sounding labels explain nothing.

To illustrate a specific phobia, a case reported by Bagby (1922) will be cited:

> A man suffered from a phobia of being grasped from behind, the disturbance appearing early in childhood and persisting to his fifty-fifth year. When walking on the street he was under a compulsion to look back over his shoulder at intervals to see if he was closely followed. In social gatherings he arranged to have his chair against the wall. It was impossible for him to enter crowded places or to attend the theater.

> In his fifty-fifth year he returned to the town in which he had spent his childhood. After inspecting his old home, he went to the corner grocery and found that his old boyhood friend was still behind the counter. He introduced himself and they began to reminisce. Finally the groceryman said this, "I want to tell you something that occurred when you were a boy. You used to go by this store on errands, and when you passed you often took a handful of peanuts from the stand in front. One day I saw you coming and hid behind a barrel. Just as you put your hand in the pile of peanuts, I jumped out and grabbed you from behind. You screamed and fell fainting on the sidewalk."
>
> The episode was remembered and the phobia, after a period of readjustment, disappeared. [17]

In commenting upon this case and another (in which a young woman developed an irrational fear of running water) Bagby states that phobias have these features in common: (1) The phobia originates in a traumatic episode during which the subject reacts with intense fear. (2) There is often an element of guilt or unpleasantness in the original experience which prevents the subject from talking about it. This presumably leads to repression, i.e., to protective forgetting, for typically the subject is unable to recall the psychological origin of his phobia. (3) The symptoms of fear may disappear when it becomes possible for the subject to recall the traumatic experience.

A phobia, Bagby notes, may persist for many years. It is called out repeatedly by a particular kind of object or situation having features in common with the object or situation which originally evoked the emotional display.

Another instance of a phobia, well known to the writer, is the following. A young woman, convalescing from a critical illness, was carried out of central China in a palanquin—a coffin-like conveyance. For days she was carried by coolies over mountainous paths and across dangerous bridges. At the end of the journey she was thoroughly shaken by the jogging steps of the coolies and frightened by the repeated exposures to danger and especially by being confined within the small compartment without any possibility of escape. After that experience there developed a fear of being enclosed in small spaces (*claustrophobia*).

The phobia is revealed when the subject is enclosed in a space from which there is no immediate escape. If, for example, the train on which she is riding goes into a tunnel, an unaccountable fear develops. If, while in a beauty parlor, her head is placed in an electric drying machine, this same fear arises. Being enclosed in an elevator is a source of fear. Today, years after the original fear, there is a marked response of fear whenever she is enclosed in a small space. The phobia remains despite the fact that its origin is clearly known to the subject. No attempt, however, has been made to remove this fear.

A phobia is not an acute emotion but rather a predisposition to a particular type of emotional response. The fact that a phobia may persist for years indicates that the individual has not become adequately adjusted to the situation which originally induced the fear response. When adjustment can be made, through aided recall or other psychological means, the phobia may disappear.

Obsessions and Compulsions. An *obsession* is a fixed idea or feeling that the subject cannot explain. For example, a patient complained of an idea that constantly recurred despite efforts to banish it. The patient was a young married woman who happened to look at another woman across the street and who watched her most of the time. Quite suddenly the patient discovered that she could not get the thought of this other woman out of mind. She seemed forced to think of her but did not know why nor was she able to stop the thought. This obsession was accompanied by a feeling of apprehension and depression for the greater part of the time during four years. No analysis of this obsession was made.

Obsessions are commonly associated with compulsive actions. A *compulsion* is an irrational impulse to carry out some act. Ordinarily the subject is unaware of the cause of his compulsive act.

An example of compulsive action is described in Bernard Hart's (1937), *The Psychology of Insanity*: A lady felt compelled to examine in the most careful manner the number of every bank note that came into her possession. She did not know why she acted in this way. The impulse was uncontrollable and she was distressed by this foolish behavior.

A Freudian analysis revealed the following details of the patient's history. Some time previously the lady had fallen in love with a certian man whom she had met in a country hotel. One day she asked him to change a bill for her. He complied with her wish and, putting the bill in his pocket, remarked that he would never part with it. The remark aroused a hope that her affections were reciprocated, and she longed to know whether he would keep his word. The man departed, however, without making further advances, and the lady finally realized that her hopes were in vain. Money which came to her hands recalled the scene as the hotel and feelings associated with it. The lady tried to forget the unhappy experiences and to banish the thoughts from her life. She was unsuccessful. After a while the painful experiences no longer affected her consciousness directly but there remained an exaggerated preoccupation with the numbers on bank notes.

According to Freud, the cure for obsessions and compulsions rests upon the discovery of the unconscious motivation. The patient must, in some way, be made aware of the causal experiences and relive them emotionally. It may then be possible to make a re-evaluation of past experiences and a readjustment of attitudes.

Repression and Dissociation. Modern psychoanalysis has been called "depth" psychology because it deals mainly with processes that are out of reach of conscious awareness, that originated in remote emotional experiences of the individual. The term *preconscious* refers to an area of past experiences—ideas, feelings, wishes—that can be readily recalled. For example, one can recall his name and the conversation with a friend an hour ago. The term *unconscious* refers to a realm of past experiences where recall is impossible except with the aid of special techniques. This unconscious realm contains motivations, persisting conflicts, and attitudes, that affect behavior in various ways.

Freud, as we know, emphasized unconscious motivation. He taught that slips of the tongue, forgetting appointments, losing objects, breaking things seemingly by accident, awkward movements, and other phenomena of everyday life, are motivated by determinations of which the subject is not consciously aware. Even dreams, day dreams, and flights of fantasy, are causally determined by unconscious motivations. All behavior according to Freud, is motivated.

We may voluntarily *suppress*, or inhibit, impulses and experiences that we regard as unworthy and want to forget. Thus we refuse to think about a cutting remark that someone made or we inhibit an impulse to tell a dirty story. *Repression* is something different from simple suppression or inhibition. Repression is a process that places experiences beyond the awareness of the individual so that he cannot voluntarily recall them. Feelings of anxiety or guilt or impulses of hostility and sex may become repressed. The individual becomes unconscious of the nature of his basic motivations and emotional conflicts. He may exhibit bizarre symptoms, however, as long as the unconscious motivation is present.

Repression implies *dissociation*—a functional splitting or disintegration within the personality. Janet's classical case of dissociation (technically known as a somnambulism because it resembles ordinary sleepwalking) has been described by Bernard Hart (1937) in *The Psychology of Insanity*:

> A French girl, Irène, had nursed her mother through a long illness that culminated in death. The trying experiences and painful events produced a profound shock upon the patient's mind. Then a somnambulism developed. Irène, engaged in sewing or in conversation at the moment, would suddenly cease her occupation and commence to live over again the painful scenes of her mother's death, enacting each detail with the power of an accomplished actress. While the drama was in progress she appeared to hear nothing that was said to her and to be oblivious of her environment. She was living in a world of fantasy. Quite suddenly Irène, seemingly unaware of the fact that anything unusual had

happened, would return to her former occupation. After an interval of perhaps several days another somnambulism, similar in most respects to the previous ones, would abruptly appear and vanish. During the apparently normal intervals between somnambulisms the patient was unaware of what had occurred and, moreover, unable to recall the system of ideas and feelings connected with her mother's death. She remembered nothing of the illness nor of its tragic end. She discussed her mother's death without feeling and was reproached by relatives for her callous indifference.

In this and similar instances of dissociated functioning the usual explanation is that a psychological system of painful experiences, through repression, has become dissociated from the main mental system. When functional dissociation is complete there is a splitting of experiences so that one mental system does not have memory access to the other. The repressed system asserts itself from time to time but between eruptions it remains unconscious. Dissociation and repression are nature's crude way of solving a conflict and freeing the individual from an intolerable situation.

The conditions that lead to repression and dissociation, according to Cameron and Magaret (1951), are these: (1) An unsolved personal conflict in which something of great importance is at stake. (2) Anxiety based upon the anticipation of punishment or misfortune. (3) A threat to one's self-esteem or prestige, i.e., an ego factor.

Sublimation *versus* Reorientation. Freud postulated a *libido*—a kind of free-floating psychosexual energy that can be channeled in this or that direction. If an individual's sexual urges are blocked, his *libido* may motivate creative work in art, religion, social welfare, science, philosophy, or other socially approved activity. An old maid, for example, may sublimate her *libido* by taking care of pets.

The difficulty with the concept of *libido* is that it is out of line with what is positively known about sexual motivation. There are no vital forces that flow through the nerves. The concept of a general energizing and alerting of the organism, however, is definitely tenable in the light of current physiology; but nonspecific activation cannot be identified with the Freudian *libido*. See pages 67-74.

It is obvious that one kind of activity can be substituted for another. For example, going to the movies may substitute for a glamorous and exciting life one would like to lead. Reading books about travel, exploration, and adventure may substitute for the real thing. Such substitutions do not imply any sublimation of the *libido*. They imply only a reorientation—a change of direction or goal.

There are many instances of reorientation that can be described without recourse to Freudian terms. For example, a child reaches for his father's gold watch and starts to play with it. The father realizes that the watch is in danger, but knows that if he takes away the glittering object without substituting another, the child will cry. Instead of taking the watch, he offers the child a toy, demonstrating its merits and how it works. Playing with the toy becomes substituted for playing with the watch, without any sign of emotional disturbance. This redirecting of the child's activity implies a shift of bodily set but there is no mysterious shifting of *libido*.

A question remains as to the nature of the energy or force that underlies all behavior. I have argued that the postulate of a single kind of energy—physical energy—is sufficient for psychological purposes. An organism may be bound, however, by the nature of its excitation, to some particular kind of activity such as hostile attack, or sexual advance, or fear avoidance.

In the primary appetites—such as those for water, food, air, rest, sleep, elimination—the need and tension are quite specific. There is no evidence that a thirst for water can be quenched by writing poetry! Reading the best of poetry may temporarily distract one from the existence of a growing bodily need and urge but it does not alter the primary motivation.

Sexual motivation is different from thirst in that sexual activity is not necessary for survival of the individual. It has significance, obviously, for survival of the species. Kinsey, Pomeroy, and Martin (1948) have shown that there are various kinds of sexual outlet. If one outlet is blocked, another may be found. There is no scientific evidence, however, for a free-floating psychosexual energy, *libido*, that can be channeled in this way or in that.

CORRECTIVE EMOTIONAL EXPERIENCES IN PSYCHOTHERAPY

The practical importance of emotion, in relation to health, is seen clearly in the field of psychotherapy. A man who is suffering from a persisting anxiety may be helped if he can freely express his feelings and emotions. The aim of psychotherapy is to aid him in expressing his emotions.

According to White (1948, 1956), psychotherapy is not an intellectual process. It has been wrongly said that the way to bring about readjustment is to help the individual *understand* his own problems. It is insufficient, however, merely to help him become aware of his motivations and frustrations on a cognitive level. There is certainly a value in intellectual understanding but this is not enough to effect a cure.

Psychotherapy operates in the sphere of emotion. The main aim of psychotherapy is to provide corrective emotional experience by relaxing the subject's defenses and permitting him to reappraise his anxieties. In the major methods of psychotherapy the subject is encouraged to *feel*, to express his emotions. See page 3.

This point will be illustrated by reference to three of the main forms of psychotherapy:

1. In *non-directive counseling* the counselor does not intervene by asking questions, by giving information or advice, or by directing the course of a conversation. He simply listens to what the client has to say, recognizes his feelings, and points them out. The counselor is constantly reacting to the *feeling* side of an interview rather than to the cognitive content. For example, if a student remarks that his study habits are bad and that he is not really so stupid as his grades indicate, it would be natural in a conversation to ask what the grades are. But in nondirective counseling the counselor might reply: "You are disappointed with your grades; you feel concerned lest they be taken as a true measure of your ability." If the client asks a direct question that shows anxiety, the counselor replies: "You feel anxious over a certain matter." If he asks for advice, the counselor replies that the client would like to have someone settle the question for him.

Non-directive counseling, as developed by Dr. Carl Rogers (1951), takes it for granted that the client will grow in his own directions, that he will remove obstacles and make changes in his attitudes and motives, that will result in changed behavior. The counselor is not an all-knowing adviser but rather a sympathetic listener who lets the client take the lead in the corrective process and who simply points out feelings. When the counselor is successful in recognizing feelings the client expresses more and more feelings. The client has probably never in his life had a listener who paid so much attention to his feelings. As a result, it commonly happens that within a single hour the client discusses matters that have not been mentioned previously to anyone. He expresses and recognizes feelings, gets a release from tensions, and of his own accord works toward a solution.

2. The goal of *psychoanalysis*, as developed by Freud and others, is the uncovering and resolving of major emotional difficulties that usually go back to the patient's childhood or infancy. This goal is reached through several stages and by the use of special techniques such as free association and dream analysis.

Psychoanalysis is distinguished from counseling by the techniques of free association, dream analysis, and others. The patient is made to relax upon a couch and told to report everything that occurs to him without change or omission. He is asked to assume a passive attitude toward his trains of thought, to eliminate conscious control over his mental processes and merely to report them. In this process there occur resistances and blockings, thoughts that are too unpleasant or too indecent to mention. The psychoanalyst notes these blockings and tries to get the patient to express his embarrassment and anxiety, and to explain the periods of silence. According to Freud, repressed memories and fantasies are strongly loaded with emotion. They are not easily expressed but may be expressed indirectly and in distorted form in dreams and fantasies.

The method of free association aims to reveal unconscious motivations and conflicts that underlie emotions. Freud interprets emotions to the patient and finds that troublesome problems, typically, date back to early emotional experiences. The problems involve repressed sexuality, hostility, or anxiety. These basic affects imply repression which has persisted, generating neurotic symptoms.

One feature of a complete psychoanalysis is known as the transference neurosis. In attempting to lift repressions and to make the patient aware of unconscious motivations, Freud discovered an unexpected fact. The patient, instead of attending to his own conflicts and emotions, commonly began to manifest personal feelings toward the physician. He might show an interest in the doctor's affairs, becoming cordial, grateful, enthusiastic about the treatment; or there might develop a negative transference in which the patient would become hostile and uncooperative. The transference neurosis typically develops after the more superficial defenses have been relaxed. It is a stage through which the patient passes during the course of treatment. Before the psychoanalysis is complete, of course, the transference neurosis is removed and the patient prepared to face the world alone.

A complete psychoanalysis requires a considerable amount of time and hence is costly. The patient usually comes an hour a day, five days a week, for one, two or even three years. Because this is time consuming for the patient as well as the psychoanalyst there have been attempts to shorten the process.

3. The *abbreviated psychoanalysis*, as developed by Doctors Alexander and French, is based upon the need to shorten and simplify the complete method of Freud and to gain more flexibility. Instead of holding to a fixed procedure, Doctors Alexander and French have varied the techniques widely. They introduced a principle of flexibility that makes it possible to vary procedures according to the needs of the patient.

The psychoanalytic procedure, as pointed out above, requires the patient to relax upon a couch and to talk without restraint; free association then reveals the emotional blockings. In the brief method the therapist may depart from this procedure by engaging the patient in direct conversation, argument, or even making challenging interpretations, as demanded by the situation. Of course, this requires skill and experience to know what method should be used and when. The details of procedure are varied to suit the particular situation. In the briefer method, also, the transference relationship is controlled. Freud's method tends to develop a childlike dependence of the patient upon the analyst; the briefer method treats the patient as a grown-up and discourages dependent relations. The transference neurosis may be discouraged and avoided, if that seems wise. In the briefer methods, again, the analyst may encourage the patient to engage in activities outside of the analysis. It is important to keep in mind that the patient finally must solve his problems in the real world and that experiences gained in the transference relationship are only preparations and training for life's conflicts. In addition to encouraging the patient to take active steps of some kind, the therapist occasionally makes contact with his spouse, employer, or a friend. A change in their attitudes may aid in speeding up the patient's recovery.

In general, it can be said that all three of the above methods—nondirective counseling, complete psychoanalysis, abbreviated psychoanalysis—have certain features in common. All emphasize the importance of corrective emotional experience in therapy. All require the individual to express his feelings and emotions. All point to affective experiences and aid the individual in recognizing and interpreting them. Again, in these basic forms of psychotherapy there is always a unique personal relation between the individual and the therapist. The therapist is permissive in the sense that he makes no censorious judgments upon the patient's actions and feelings; he is interested and friendly, and he is a source of encouragement. In this personal relationship there develops a transference neurosis in which the individual shows emotionalized attitudes—affection, hostility, fear—toward the therapist. These attitudes are carefully handled and treated so that the patient can face his problems alone when treatment is terminated. Finally, all methods of psychotherapy aim at the development of new behavior. Emotional maladjustments and neuroses are acquired through experience; they are learned. What was learned in early life through traumatic experiences cannot be instantly changed. Re-education, reorientation, change of attitude and habit, take time. There is no radical intervention, like surgery, to produce a quick cure.

In addition to the above methods there are many technical aids to psychotherapy: hypnosis, the use of drugs, re-education, the assignment of tasks, play therapy, psychodrama, and other forms of group therapy; but the consideration of these techniques is beyond the scope of this book. Clinical psychology is rapidly developing and expanding.

CONCLUSION

Emotion has been defined as an affectively disturbed process or state of psychological origin. This comprehensive definition includes not only the temporary manifestations of emotion in conscious experience and behavior but also the persisting emotional disturbances of individuals.

Practical problems are related to more or less stable conditions that elicit emotional outbreaks. These enduring conditions include persisting attitudes, habit systems, motives, interests, aversions, conflicts, beliefs, loyalties, commitments, and other psychological factors. Hence any study of the role of emotion in human life must examine emotional problems of individuals from a longitudinal and developmental point of view.

There are wide individual differences in temperament and in emotional stability. Some persons are easily aroused to anger, fear, love, pride, feelings of guilt, etc.; others are unperturbed by critical situations. Tests of individual differences in neurotic tendency and tests of manifest anxiety have been developed to detect persons liable to develop neuroses.

Emotional disturbances have been examined in relation to mental health. Especially important are neuroses that develop during times of stress—in war time and during crises in civilian life. A neurosis is a persistent disturbance within the individual that is revealed by various symptoms: tics, hyper- and hypoactivity, amnesia, functional paralysis, insomnia, chronic changes in the vegetative processes, as well as by repeated outbreaks of emotion. Emotional behavior is thus only one of the manifestations of neurotic disorganization.

Experimental studies of neuroses with animal subjects have shown that there is a limit to the amount of pain, frustration, and stress that an animal can tolerate without a breakdown. For every individual there is a breakdown point of endurance—a limit to frustration tolerance.

According to Freudian psychology, unacceptable feelings may be repressed and remain dissociated and unconscious as a source of neurotic symptoms. Psychoanalytic techniques aim to bring such repressed experiences into the light of clear consciousness. The recall and re-living of past emotional crises helps the individual to make a readjustment—to gain peace of mind, complacency, and to restore mental health.

In general, psychotherapy supplements physical medicine. Psychotherapy operates in the sphere of emotion combined with cognitive processes.

READING SUGGESTIONS

The disciplines that deal with emotional disturbance in relation to health are well established; each has a large literature. These disciplines include psychiatry, clinical psychology, psychopharmacology, psychosomatic medicine, psychoanalysis, and others. For orientation, an excellent history of medical psychology by Zilboorg and Henry (1949), is available. Cameron and Magaret (1951) have published a helpful work on behavior pathology. White (1956) has given us a useful textbook on abnormal personality (2nd ed.).

For the study of special topics in the field of mental health it might be well to consult *The Encyclopedia of Mental Health*, a six-volume work edited by A. Deutsch (1963). Special topics can be explored through *Psychological Abstracts* or by following up references given in this text. For example, good English translations of Pavlov's (1927, 1928) work on conditioned reflexes are available.

Chapter X

Social and Personal Determinants of Feeling

In approaching the study of social and personal determinants of feeling, one must keep in mind the three basic aspects of all psychological processes. First, there is the *cognitive* aspect (knowing, believing, understanding) which rests upon perception, memory, creative thinking and related functions. Second, there is the *affective* aspect (feelings, moods, sentiments, emotions) which includes the whole gamut of experiences in so far as they affect or influence individuals. Third, there is the *cathectic* aspect (arousal, activation, action) which is the readiness of individuals to do something within the psychological situation.

If we are to understand the social behavior of man, we must understand not only the structure of the social environment, and other social sciences, but also the world as it is apprehended and comprehended by individuals. Each individual has developed his own weltanschauung.

It is sometimes said that psychology deals with individuals and sociology with groups. The statement is misleading for two reasons. First, psychology is concerned with individuals who are members of groups and whose behavior cannot be understood apart from the social setting. A man's ways of acting, language habits, traits of personality, attitudes, motives, conflicts, neuroses—all developed within a social setting and cannot be correctly understood apart from that setting. A second reason why the statement is misleading is that some behavioral scientists prefer to study the group as a psychological unit rather than to study separate individuals. From the point of view of group dynamics it can be said that the group—for example, a football team—behaves as a unit within which the responses of one member influence the behavior of the group as a whole.

The human individual is an organism living in a sociocultural environment. His conduct is influenced both by the characteristics of protoplasm and by the characteristics of the environment within which he lives. In other words, human behavior has both biological and social determinants.

Importance of the Cultural Environment. It is axiomatic that if we wish to understand present behavior, we must know the psychological history of the subject.

The importance of *cultural* factors in determining beliefs, attitudes, motives, and consequently affective reactions, is a point stressed by Klineberg (1940). On the basis of several studies he cited the following facts:

Among the Murngin of Australia, if twins are born, the mother kills one of them because it makes her feel like a dog to have a litter instead of a single baby. With the Negroes of the Niger Delta, the rule is that both the mother and the twins are put to death. Occasionally the mother is allowed to live, but her life is little better than a living death for she becomes an outcast and must live the rest of her days in the forest. Less than a thousand miles from this group live the Bankundo of the Congo Valley, among whom the mother of twins is an object of veneration. She is entitled to wear a special badge and her name is changed to "Mother-of-twins."

With such wide differences in beliefs, attitudes, and practices, it is not surprising that an event such as the birth of twins is greeted in one area with joy and in another with unpleasant emotions–grief, humiliation, fear for one's life.

The influence of cultural factors upon behavior is also seen in attitudes toward death. In most known cultures death is a source of grief. In some, however, it is an occasion for rejoicing. Certain groups of Siberian natives and of Eskimos as well as of Fiji Islanders are said to be anxious to die before they become too old. These people believe that the present life is a prelude to an everlasting existence in which the individual will possess the bodily and mental powers he had when leaving this life. If a man lives until decrepit, he remains so in the hereafter. For this reason a son may kill his parents, secure in the conviction that this is doing them a great favor. A sincere belief in immortality may thus determine one's feelings and emotions regarding death.

Whether a particular belief is scientifically true or false is psychologically irrelevant. If a person believes something to be true, he will act in accordance with his belief. Therefore, any serious attempt to understand the affective life of primitive peoples must rest upon an analysis and understanding of their culture–their beliefs, attitudes, and practices.

Importance of an Individual's Past Experience. I recall that when I was a small boy a housemaid asked me not to play on the piano *My Old Kentucky Home* because, she said, that particular piece made her feel sad and weep. She explained that a man to whom she had been engaged used to sing this song, sang it at their final parting, and that this song reminded her of him. In this instance, her love motive had been thwarted, and this particular song tended to arouse the whole conflict of unrequited love. The song recalled the past and reinstated a persisting conflict along with its conscious emotion. In this particular case, incidentally, there was also an element of self-pity (the *poor-me* attitude).

Again, I recall that, as a boy, it was my duty to turn out the lights and raise the window just before getting into bed for the night. One night, after the lights had been turned off, I was lifting the window when a gun fired with a loud BANG just below the window. A neighbor called out, "What happened! There he goes!" I could hear someone running. The experience was so terrifying that for years after the emotional incident the raising of that particular window in the dark brought back the fear. I would not admit this to my brothers who slept in the same room, but attempted to hide the fear. Only moving to another house eventually solved the problem by removing the conditions that produced the fear.

It is obvious from the above, and from many similar examples, that a previous emotional crisis predisposes an individual to a particular form of emotional reaction. This is a basic principle of affective memory. To understand a present emotion one must know something about the individual's past emotional experience—as well as his beliefs, attitudes, motives.

In this connection we might recall the study by Schachter (1970) and the experiment by Schachter and Singer (1962) upon cognitive and social conditions of the emotional state. They found that by manipulating cognitive and social conditions the subjects could be made to experience anger, euphoria, amusement, fear, or no emotion at all, when precisely the same physiological state had been aroused through injections of epinephrine.

THE NATURE OF ATTITUDES

An attitude may be defined as a readiness of the individual to react toward or against a psychological object in a particular way with a certain degree of intensity. The different points in this definition are considered below:

1. An attitude is a readiness of the individual to react. This readiness is a relatively permanent reactive disposition that has been acquired through experience and that is regulative and directive.

2. Attitudes are polarized. They are toward or against, pro or con, approving or disapproving, accepting or rejecting, favorable or unfavor-

able, liking or disliking. In a word, attitudes are polarized between positive or negative.

3. The object of an attitude exists within an environmental situation. A person may have an attitude toward or against almost anything: a certain person, a specific kind of food, a musical composition, a political party, a religion, a skin color, an idea—almost anything, in fact, under heaven or earth. That is to say, the object of an attitude is psychological.

4. The definition states that an attitude is a readiness to react in a particular way. There are attitudes of love or hate, of fear or courage (anti-fear), of friendliness or hostility, of resentment, disgust, curiosity, amusement, etc. There are different ways of reacting, different forms of orientation.

The psychoanalyst, Horney, once put it this way: We can react *towards* people with friendliness and love or *against* people with hostility and hatred or *away from* people with fear and anxiety. I might add that we can also react *along with* people in cooperation and helpfulness. Some ways of reacting are biologically grounded and common to all men; others are specific and based on the sociocultural environment.

5. Attitudes differ in degree of intensity. One may approve weakly or disapprove strongly. One may love or hate intensely, Thus there is a quantitative, intensive, attribute of attitudes.

6. It should be pointed out that the attitudes of individuals can be latent or activated. Suppose, for example, someone asks you a question: Do you approve of communism? Do you like carrots? Do you enjoy jazz music? All such questions activate latent attitudes.

A latent attitude differs, of course, from a latent motive or plan of action. If I have determined to take a trip next week, the determination from time to time arouses tension within me and ultimately the intended course of action occurs. I take the trip. A latent attitude, contrastingly, is more like a latent habit system which underlies acts of skill but appears only when the situation calls it forth. Attitudes, like habits, are learned; they are acquired through experience. Thus a white child growing up in the South acquires the attitudes toward blacks that are held by his parents.

7. From the point of view of social psychology, it is obvious that similar attitudes are held by groups of people. Also that attitudes of people in a group can be measured and changes of attitude can be observed.

The Measurement and Changes of Attitudes. A frequently used technique for measuring attitudes is the test devised by Thurstone (1928, 1932) and Thurstone and Chave (1929). In a test of this type the subject is instructed to indicate by a check mark the statements in a printed list with which he agrees and to indicate those with which he disagrees. For example, in a test of attitudes toward war there are twenty-two statements of opinion about war—some favorable and others unfavorable. Here is a sample:

( ) Compulsory military training in all countries should be reduced but not eliminated.
( ) The misery and suffering of war are not worth its benefits.
( ) War brings misery to millions who have no voice in its declaration.
( ) Because right may be more important than peace, war may be the lesser of two evils.
( ) There is no progress without war.

From the responses of subjects to such statements of opinion a score is computed which is a numerical index of attitude toward war.

Attitude measurements have been popular, in part, because of a common belief that a person's behavior can be predicted if his attitudes are known. But the relation between attitude and behavior is actually ambiguous.

LaPiere (1938) has shown that the attitudes as expressed verbally by individuals may or may not indicate predispositions to react in a definite way to a specific situation. Since this ambiguity exists, it is impossible to predict behavior from verbal statements of attitude. LaPiere clinched the point by reference to a study of the causes of antagonism against the Armenians on the part of non-Armenian residents of Fresno County, California.

> The 879 separate explanations which were secured were highly standardized. The most popular was that the Armenians are "dishonest, lying, and deceitful"; in supplementary interviews, bankers, credit men, and merchants were found almost invariably to give this as their explanation. The second explanation in point of popularity was that the Armenians lived parasitically on the community and accounted for the major burden of charity, both private and public; when questioned, directors of charitable institutions and of public relief and professional social workers supplemented this finding. The third explanation was that the Armenians were a cantankerous lot, always going to law with some grievance or other; the District Attorney and his staff, local judges and their staffs, and private lawyers heartily endorsed this interpretation.
>
> These, then, are the three common ideologies by which the people of Fresno County explain their antagonism to the Armenians. An examination of the actual experiences of the people of the community with Armenians, however, shows the following facts: Over the years the Armenians have as a group a better credit rating with the Fresno Merchant's Association than have non-Armenians. The records of the County Hospital and the County Welfare Bureau revealed on the average that the Armenian member of the community requires only 20 percent as much charity and relief as the non-Armenian member. An audit of

> civil and criminal court records indicated that the Armenian almost never gets involved in a criminal action and that he is considerably less likely to go to law or to be dragged into law in civil-court cases than is the non-Armenian. What the ideologies of the non-Armenians are related to, what has occasioned them, and to what extent they affect behavior toward Armenians cannot be deduced from this study. One point, however, has been disposed of: The ideologies have no direct relationship to past experience. [181]

The ideology which is tapped by verbal statements is one thing; the objective facts in a situation are something else. Psychologically considered, it may be that the ideology is only a rationalization of certain more basic factors which are not admitted or which have not been made clearly conscious to the individual.

Changes of Attitude and Motive. In the summer of 1940, I read the views upon peace and war which had been stated by a distinguished professor or law in an eastern university. These views convinced me that the United States should remain neutral in any European war. Several days later I read the views of the president of the same university. Again I was convinced that from a more far-seeing standpoint it was to our contry's interest to aid England and France in the war rather than to remain neutral. Such shifting of opinion shows how mistaken we are when we believe that our attitudes are wholly the result of independent thought.

Shifts of motivation are frequent in everyone's experience. An instance of such vacillation is that of a colored maid who had applied for a job. At home that night her husband told her that it was not necessary for her to work, and after this she declined the job. The next day, however, she talked again to the prospective employer and, realizing her need for cash, accepted the job. In the evening she returned home. In home surroundings, bombarded by persuasive arguments from her husband, she declined the proposed job by telephone. Despite all this she decided to work and actually appeared for duty the next morning. This woman showed no greater degree of motivational shifting than the average person would show under the influence of similarly conflicting motives.

The following example has been given by a social psychologist: A group of farmers in a village of northern Wisconsin met in the afternoon and, under the influence of a persuasive speaker, voted to call a milk strike. In the evening this same group met again to hear a speaker with opposite views. After the evening speech, the farmers voted unanimously not to strike.

We all know that attitudes and motives can be changed by a speech, a film, a newspaper report, a radio broadcast, or by some bit of information from another source. The practical question, however, is: *To what extent can attitudes and motives be changed?*

There are in the literature of the field a number of experiments dealing with changes of attitude. For example, Thurstone (1931) has demonstrated that motion-picture films produce measurable effects upon the attitudes of children. The film, *Son of the Gods*, has been considered friendly in its interpretation of Chinese culture. This film was shown to school children in Geneva, Illinois. One week before and the day after seeing the picture, the children filled in a statement scale about the Chinese. Following the presentation they were found, to a significant degree, to be more favorably inclined toward the Chinese. Another film, *Welcome Danger*, has been criticized by the Chinese for portraying an unfriendly manner of dealing with them. This film was shown in West Chicago. One week before and the day after seeing the picture, the children filled in the same scale about the Chinese that was used in Geneva. Although the change of attitude was less than that produced by the first film, *Welcome Danger* left the children slightly more unfriendly toward the Chinese than they had been at the start.

Do such vacillations and changes imply that a scientific study of attitudes is impossible? Indeed not! Obviously, it is important to study the factors which change attitudes and the extent to which these factors are effective. Various techniques are now available for measuring attitudes and for analyzing the conditions which can change them.

How Do Attitudes Differ from Motives? Faris (1925, 1928) distinguished between *latent* and *kinetic* attitudes. He defined an attitude as a tendency to act in a certain way: "The term designates a certain proclivity, or bent, a bias or predisposition, an aptitude or inclination to a certain type of activity."

This definition is comprehensive. However, Faris drew a distinction between attitudes and wishes:

> An attitude exists as a tendency even when latent; a wish is always more or less dynamic or kinetic. A man may be said to have an attitude toward coffee. If he be very fond of coffee he may come to wish for coffee on occasion. Having had three cups, and enjoyed them all, he still has an attitude, the same attitude, toward the object, coffee; but he does not, let us hope, wish for any more. He may wish later. He has an attitude, but no wish. [279]

Stated in other words, a man's coffee attitude may be favorable (positive) at all times, but his wish for coffee varies with the period of coffee deprivation—with the recency and completeness of appetitive satisfaction.

This distinction which Faris draws is clearly that between attitude and motive. The distinction is exemplified by the two questions: *Do you like coffee*? and *Do you wish coffee*? The first refers to attitude; the second to motive. If a man were satiated upon coffee, he would be indifferent or averse to taking any more at the time but still he would report that he *likes* coffee, his attitude being positive but motivation lacking.

This same distinction has been drawn in a slightly different way by Gordon Allport (1935) in a critical review of the immense literature upon attitudes. Allport defined an attitude as: "A mental and neural state of readiness, organized through experience, exerting a directive or dynamic influence upon the individual's response to all objects and situations with which it is related."

Allport stated that an attitude may or may not be motivating. Raising the question, *Have attitudes motive power*? he distinguished between two types of attitudes: one which is so organized that it actually *drives*, and the other which merely *directs*. Both types, he said, are conditions of readiness and both enter into the determination of conduct. This statement implies that a "readiness for response" has two meanings: (1) passive direction or regulation, and (2) motivation, or active initiation of behavior.

In Chapter II, I made a similar distinction between the direction and activation of behavior (page 67). A psychological determinant can be latent or activated. And this applies to attitudes as well as to motives (determinations to carry out a specific course of action). Both attitudes and motives can be latent or activated; and both are regulative and directive.

One difference between these concepts is that a motive has a goal or terminus. When a predetermined act has been consummated the motive for that act no longer exists. But an attitude is not necessarily an intent to act. Attitudes can be quite general and not specific.

We describe attitudes in terms of what we *believe*, how we *feel*, what we *think*, what we *would wish* to have happen. This is not a specific determination to act in relation to a goal-situation. Hence, both attitudes and motives can be latent; both are activated by situational stimulus-cues; both have relative permanence and stability within the human mind; both are predispositions of a sort.

Attitudes and motives must be described in terms of concrete environmental situations. Both imply a relation between an individual and his external world. In this fundamental respect, attitudes and motives must be distinguished from neurophysiological processes within anatomical structures.

Place of the Concept of Attitude in Behavioral Science. Regarding the importance of the concept of attitude in social psychology, Gordon Allport (1935) wrote: "The concept of attitude is probably the most distinctive and indispensable concept in contemporary American social psychology. No other term appears more frequently in experimental and theoretical literature. . . . [It] has virtually established itself as the keystone in the edifice of American social psychology."

There was a time, however, in the history of social psychology, when the transmission of culture was explained in terms of imitation and suggestion. Later McDougall's doctrine of instinct was introduced as an explanatory concept—until the anti-instinct movement of the 1920s and 1930s made psychologists leery of the term. But in contemporary behavioral science the concept of attitude serves as a basic explanatory principle.

Within behavioral science the study of attitudes raises many problems. These problems are studied from different points of view: in differential psychology, dynamic psychology, developmental psychology, and in other areas of investigation.

Biological and Cultural Determinants of Attitudes. How far are attitudes biological and how far cultural in origin?

This question was raised by Allport and Schanck (1936). In an attempt to answer it the following exercise was given to Harvard and Radcliffe students. The students were instructed in this way:

> In greater or less degree the law condones the taking of a human life under the following circumstances. Assuming that the circumstances of the combat always give fair play to both combatants, arrange these situations in the order of greatest justification for the killing at the top of the list to least justification at the bottom, following your own feelings as a guide.
>
> 1. In defending the safety of one's family.
> 2. In protecting one's property against trespassers.
> 3. In defending the honorable reputation of a member of one's family.
> 4. In defending one's property against burglars.
> 5. In defense of one's own life.
> 6. In fighting for one's country.
> 7. In order to protect one's own honor or reputation.
> 8. In order to save the life of another human being. [197]

This exercise was presented to classes in social psychology during a period of five years. The rank order for the justifiability of homicide remained the same year after year for nearly all the situations listed. Only for those situations dealing with "honor" was there any variation.

The rank order of the eight items for the total group is indicated below.

	200 Men	110 Women
Defense of self	1	1
Defense of family	2	2
Defense of another	3	3
Defense of country	4	4
Defense of honor of family	5	6
Defense of honor of self	6	5
Defense of property against burglars	7	7
Defense of property against trespassers	8	8

Allport and Schanck concluded that biological factors which determine the attitude toward homicide rank ahead of cultural factors. Preserving one's life ranks first and preserving the life of the family and others is rated ahead of defense of country, honor, property. It is interesting to note that the defense of honor ranks higher than the defense of property.

Words and Deeds in Relation to Attitude. The disparity between words and deeds is brought out by Emerson's line, "Do not say things. What you are stands over you the while, and thunders so that I cannot hear what you say to the contrary."

The phrase, "Actions speak louder than words" implies that non-verbal behavior reveals attitudes more correctly than verbal behavior does. A man, to illustrate, may give lip service to ethical principles which he does not apply in his business dealings. Or, again, a man may express an attitude of hostility against the Japanese and yet go on using and purchasing their manufactured products. Words and deeds frequently do not agree. This fact is especially apparent in the rationalizations or alibis which a man fabricates to defend some act of which he is ashamed. The implication, however, that deeds more truly than words reveal the individual's attitude, needs to be considered further.

Deeds themselves frequently distort and conceal an attitude as completely as words do. Both verbal and non-verbal behavior are modified, as Murphy, Murphy, and Newcomb (1937) pointed out, by considerations of courtesy, expediency, and various other forms of social pressure. For example, a young woman who for years had maintained the attitude, instilled by her mother, that gum chewing was the height of vulgarity, chewed gum when it was offered her by a young man whose attentions she desired. Further, she took a long walk in the country on a rainy day with the same young man (though she disliked walking in the rain) because he expressed enthusiasm for being out in rainy weather.

From the psychologist's standpoint, verbal and non-verbal behavior have essentially one and the same relationship to attitudes. Both the spoken word and the non-verbal deed are significant parts of behavior. Both reveal attitudes, conceal attitudes, and depend in a similar manner upon attitudes.

The postulate of an attitude as a psychological reality and all our knowledge concerning it rests upon the observed facts of behavior, both verbal and non-verbal. In the writer's opinion, words both conceal and reveal attitudes more than deeds do; but instead of opposing words to deeds, the psychologist should look to both, and from both attempt to construct the psychological structure and organization of the individual.

Stereotypes in Social Evaluation. We all have mental pictures of a doctor, a missionary, a college professor, a preacher, a senator, a capitalist, a laborer, and so on. The cartoonist selects certain features of each type, exaggerates them, and uses these features as symbolic of the type. Thus, the doctor is shown as a man with a beard, and a bag in his hand; the missionary is represented as carrying an umbrella and a Bible; the college professor is typefied by a cap and gown, a bulging forehead, and glasses; the preacher is represented by a clerical collar and coat. Just a few details stand for the whole, and the observer is left to fill in the picture according to conventional views.

Prominent individuals, too, are represented by certain outstanding features. Thus, Theodore Roosevelt was shown with large teeth, a heavy mustache, glasses, and a big stick. Franklin D. Roosevelt was shown as a man with a high forehead, a large jaw, and a smile. The Hitler stereotype was build around a small dark mustache and a lock of hair conspicuously draped over the forehead.

Pictorial stereotypes are only one form of "pictures in our heads." Our ideas about persons, institutions, races, etc., are also highly conventionalized. Examples of this can be drawn from a study by Katz and Braly (1933) upon racial stereotypes. These investigators gave a hundred Princeton students a list of eighty-four words descriptive of traits from which the students were asked to select the ones typical of Germans, Italians, Negroes, Irish, English, Jews, Americans, Chinese, Japanese, Turks. The instructions provided for the addition of other terms if the ones listed were not adequate.

The results of the experiment revealed that there were racial stereotypes in these students' minds. Table 9 gives the number of times the five most frequent traits for each nationality or race were selected by the hundred students.

The study of Katz and Braly indicates that some stereotypes are more definite than others. Definiteness is shown by the extent to which the subjects agree with each other upon the descriptive terms. The most definite picture is that of the Negroes. The Germans and Jews also evoke fairly definite and consistent patterns of response, while the Japanese, Chinese, and Turks call forth the least clear-cut stereotypes.

TABLE 9

Racial Stereotypes (*From* Katz and Braly)

Germans		Italians		Negroes	
Scientifically minded	78	Artistic	53	Superstitious	84
Industrious	65	Impulsive	44	Lazy	75
Stolid	44	Passionate	37	Happy-go-lucky	38
Intelligent	32	Quick-tempered	35	Ignorant	38
Methodical	31	Musical	32	Musical	26
Jews		**Americans**		**Chinese**	
Shrewd	79	Industrious	48	Superstitious	34
Mercenary	49	Intelligent	47	Sly	29
Industrious	48	Materialistic	33	Conservative	29
Grasping	34	Ambitious	33	Tradition-loving	26
Intelligent	29	Progressive	27	Loyal to family	22

Irish		English	
Pugnacious	45	Sportsmanlike	53
Quick-tempered	39	Intelligent	46
Witty	38	Conventional	34
Honest	32	Tradition-loving	31
Very religious	29	Conservative	30
Japanese		**Turks**	
Intelligent	45	Cruel	47
Industrious	43	Very religious	26
Progressive	24	Treacherous	21
Shrewd	22	Sensual	20
Sly	20	Ingorant	15

Social evaluations and artistic judgments are also stereotyped in many cases. A study in which stereotypes were shown to determine judgments of literature was made by Sherif (1935). In this experiment, passages from Robert Louis Stevenson were presented to Harvard and Radcliffe students for ranking in an order of liking or disliking. Under each passage was the name of a fictitious author. The deception was not suspected by the students. One month previously, however, these same students had expressed preferences for the writings of the sixteen authors whose names appeared under the passages. These evaluations were utilized by Sherif in his experiment.

The correlations between preferences for Stevenson's passages and the previously tested preferences for the authors whose names were assigned to them are shown below:

Average correlation for 22 Harvard students	0.33
Average correlation for 17 Radcliffe students	0.45
Average correlation for 10 Extension Course adults	0.30
Average correlation for 8 School of Education students	0.31
Average correlation for total (57) students	0.36

Students who reported that they deliberately covered up the author's name or ignored it showed no significant correlation.

The experiment indicates that our biases in favor or disfavor of certain writers tend to modify our appraisals of works allegedly written by them. A mediocre literary passage is rated more highly if attributed, for example, to Shakespeare than if a less well-known name is attached to it. The name of a favored author tends to pull up the rating of a passage, and conversely the name of a less favored author tends to pull it down.

We may like or dislike a *word* with little or no understanding of the reasons for the bias. For example, Stagner (1936) found that a vast majority of the population disliked the stereotyped term *fascism* although they accepted a large number of the specific policies which identify fascism: breaking up labor unions, attacking radical political parties, holding prejudice against persons of different nationality or racial origin, and so on.

From the above studies of stereotypes we may conclude that evaluative attitudes are dependent upon past experience in the social environment and are not infallible guides to correct conduct.

SELF-REGARDING ATTITUDES AND MOTIVES

An individual appraises himself in relation to others. Although he may not be clearly aware of the evaluative process, he comes, in numerous spheres of activity, to behave as if he were superior or equal or inferior to those associated with him. He recognizes himself as holding some status and playing a role in each of the groups to which he belongs.

Evaluation of one's self (the self-image) plays a tremendously important part in human feelings and emotions. This fact will appear clearly in the following sections.

Attitudes of Inferiority and Pride. In the earliest years of life, self-evaluating attitudes begin to form. These attitudes change, with circumstances, throughout one's life. The developing child continually sees and hears himself compared with others: John is bigger and stronger than you. He can fight better; he can knock you down. Harry can run faster. Dick can throw a ball farther. Jim has a finer house, a bigger yard, nicer clothes. Joe's folks drive a better car; your folks have only a jalopy. Bill's father owns a store, but your father is just a janitor. It goes on and on.

It may be the other way around. Perhaps *you* are one of the bigger, stronger ones in your group; you can fight better, run faster than others; or you have a bigger house and car, nicer toys and yard equipment. In street fights, on the playground, in the class room, at home, this self-*versus*-other comparison goes on endlessly. The result is that the child makes an evaluation of himself in relation to other children.

Factors of wealth and social standing being approximately equal, the biggest and strongest boy in the group and the prettiest and most resourceful girl are likely to acquire well-developed attitudes of self-confidence and to become leaders. However, the acquirement of special skills or abilities helps to build up positive attitudes of self-regard, even when the former qualities are missing.

If the child happens to have some obvious defect—obesity, short stature, an unsightly birthmark, a crippled limb, deafness—other children make him repeatedly and painfully aware of it. An attitude of inferiority is thus formed which persists indefinitely. The child's attitude of inferiority results from the frustration of a normal social impulse—to belong to a group and to participate in its activities with one's share of importance and self-expression.

Alfred Adler pointed out the psychological importance of attitudes of inferiority as factors which regulate the development of personality. Such attitudes are often at the root of persistent non-adjustments. But an inferiority attitude may also lead the individual to great achievements. History provides well-known examples of men with defects who, in attempting to compensate for them, have achieved greatly: Demosthenes, with a speech impediment, became an orator; Lord Byron, who had a club foot, wrote immortal poetry; Steinmetz, a cripple, became a wizard of electricity; Kaiser Wilhelm, who had a withered arm, became a military leader.

In less spectacular ways, too, attitudes of inferiority play an important part in human life. A few instances of attitudes of inferiority and pride in college students will be cited from the *Social Psychology* of Lawrence G. Brown (1934).

The first example is that of a girl who, in a so-called *truth session*, was disturbed by remarks about her physical appearance. Note that, even when writing the present account, this young lady is emotionally blocked, as shown by the fact that she refers to "this particular feature" without once telling whether it is her nose, her chin, or some other feature.

When I was a girl in my teens I went on a camping trip. . . . Unfortunately the week chosen for our outing was a disagreeable one. . . . The second day found us sitting on a soaked ground. It had rained continuously. That night in our attempt to forget the penetrating dampness and chill we sat about talking quite frankly. Girls now call them "truth sessions." I couldn't seem to enter into the mutual criticism; in fact, I didn't feel well. One particular girl in the group was unusually pretty and she was not at all backward about criticising others and in a censorious manner. When it came to my turn I was thoroughly gone over. The thing that cut deepest was the stinging remark made by the pretty girl pertaining to one of my features which she described as "horrid." I had hitherto been a carefree happy-go-lucky person, hardly aware of the presence of any of my features so far as looks were concerned. Well, that night I went to bed, for the first time in my life worrying about myself, feeling like asking everybody to forgive me for living. . . . I was sick bodily and mentally. Such was the state of mind I possessed when I fell sick with scarlet fever. I caught it from our chaperon who had been ill a week or so with scarlet rash. Some of the other girls caught cold and developed a scarlet rash, but only two of us were quarantined. I was sick for the next few months. During my illness I frequently raved about my appearance and especially this particular feature. I remember feeling that this feature made up the biggest part of my face. At night the thing possessed me like a devil and I struggled with it. It seemed a gruesome monstrosity. In the daytime I was more submissive, more resigned to the fact that I was hopeless, mentally as well as socially.

When recovering from my illness my mental state certainly did not help me along. It was immaterial to me whether I got well or not. I felt as if I had been ignorantly unaware of my defects, of my shortcomings. How utterly stupid I had been! It seemed like a revelation to me—a revelation of myself. I felt that I was an outcast among the girls. Our doctor told me afterwards that this inferiority complex was due to the fact that my mind readily absorbed and accepted the criticism offered by the girls because the incipient illness and weakened physical condition allowed the impression made to become firmly rooted. My mother, father and our doctor tried to reason with me and to change my depression and pessimistic state of mind.

When starting back to school I hated to meet people. I was as careful as possible to keep several yards distant from my school mates when talking to them, thinking my "deformity" would be less noticeable. So sensitive was I that rather than meet people I would cross the street or go down the alleys to avoid them. If ever I caught anyone looking at me I immediately suspected them of making fun of me. Again and again my face felt as if this bad feature comprised the larger part of it. I became aloof, cold, and seemingly indifferent. I would shake my head when called on in class rather than trust myself to speak. Every situation was painful and embarrassing to me. When people came to our home I ran to my room, and remained there until they went away. Coupled with a proud disposition this awareness of inferiority was a terrible combination. . . .

Before that fateful camping trip I was jolly and carefree. Afterwards I became serious-minded, super-sensitive, pessimistic, unhappy. I was quite another person. All through the rest of my high school days I continued to hold my head high, be aloof, in order to hide my feeling of inferiority. . . . [222-223]

This girl's reaction to the *truth session* was abnormally intense. She was very serious and unable to laugh at her defect.

The next illustration shows how an attitude of social inferiority can be based upon poverty and lack of social standing.

The most pronounced definition of myself came to me when I was about ten or eleven years of age. My father was employed in a factory which produced coaches and hearses. It was not a large factory but they made a very sturdy product. My father was a master on a lathe in this shop but earned very small wages. Since our family was large, we lived in considerable poverty.

It was necessary to pass this shop on the way home from school and I often went in and watched dad turn out something on his lathe, but most of all to see the shavings fly. The owner of the factory had a son the same age as me. I went to school and played in the factory with him. We soon became great chums and finally one evening he invited me to his home for dinner.

My mother consented to my going and I dressed in the best clothes I had which were terrible. I had paid little attention heretofore to my chum's clothes or looks, but his to play in were better than my best. When his mother greeted me at the door she was greatly astonished that I was to be the guest that evening for dinner. Her attitude toward me was one of indignation. And to be sure, I looked like a bull in a china shop in her delicate and orderly home.

It was my first experience with anything like this; there I came to realize just who I was. A feeling of inferiority grew on me. I felt how out of place I looked there. I realized my family's poverty and it was brought home to me that I was not of the same class as the people with whom I was dining. I immediately learned my place and no longer played with this old playmate. [241]

The final illustration portrays the development of feelings or pride and superiority. It shows how the level of self-esteem may be raised by comparing one's self with other persons.

When I was in the lower grades of school I developed quite a superiority complex. There were a great many foreign children, mostly Greeks and Hungarians from the lime plant families, attending the small town school which I also attended.

I started to school when I was five years old which fact made me quite proud of myself and very confident that I was that much more intelligent than the usual run of children. The foreign children in the first grade were much older and larger than the American children.

The foreign children were rather self-conscious, bashful, timid, and backward. They couldn't talk much English, didn't know their A. B. Cs, couldn't count or write or read, and I could do all of these things. I began to wonder why it was that I knew so much more about those things than they did. I looked down upon them and felt sorry for their ignorance.

When a Hungarian boy about ten years old would stand up and try to read and would stumble because he couldn't pronounce a word, I would raise my hand and fairly jump out of my seat to show the teacher that I knew how. I would laugh at him and feel very superior to all those big boys who were so much older and bigger and still didn't know as much as I did.

At recess we would get together and talk and tell about our parents, our homes, and our playthings. Many foreigners lived in small one-room or two-room houses set in rows by the quarry. They would say to me, "Oh, do you live in that big white house?" I would think how envious they must be. I used to go with my father to the lime plant occasionally and then I would go to visit in these shanties. I would act as if it were doing them a great favor to have me enter their homes. I thought how happy they must be to have me come to see them. It seemed to be my delight to tell about "my" house. I think I liked to feel better than other children.

I thought that my father was superior to theirs because he didn't have to work in the quarry. After school at night I would take five or six children into the store with me and line them up in a row, and then give them each a piece of candy. I can still feel my delight and the condescending manner I had when I did this. My father would tell my mother how unselfish I was which made me very proud of myself. But I think that I liked the superior feeling it gave to me.

I imagined that all the children must be jealous of me and that they all would like to be like me. When I came to school with a new dress on I took their compliments as something due to me. When my mother came to visit school I felt so proud, because not many mothers came, as the foreign women couldn't talk English. When my teacher praised me I thought all children looked at me enviously. [224-225]

Attitudes of inferiority and superiority, acquired in the early years, play an important part in shaping personality and in the whole of one's life. It is important, therefore, to understand how inferiority attitudes and extreme superiority attitudes, like those just described, can be moulded into patterns more likely to make for success and happiness. Children with inferiority attitudes can be placed in the companionship of less competent children to give them the experience of success and attitudes of self-confidence. Also, they can be helped to acquire new skills and abilities, to give them a sense of importance among others of their age group. They can also be re-educated to a different set of standards for success, by which standards they find themselves equal or superior to others in their group. Persons with extreme superiority attitudes, too, can be helped to re-evaluate their skills and abilities. Contacts with persons having greater skill and more desirable social and personality traits may help in the process of re-education.

Self-Appraisal and the Level of Aspiration. The individual's evaluation of himself plays a major role in human behavior. This evaluation rests upon the experiences of success and failure in all areas within which success is important. If a man plays an occasional game of tennis for relaxation, a poor score may not especially disturb him, for tennis is only a matter of minor importance to him. He makes no claim of being highly skilled in this area of sport. His neighbor, who competes in the local tennis tournament every year, would feel very inferior if he made the same score. The poor tennis player, however, will certainly have other fields of activity in which success is important to him, within which he strives to gain a sense of success, and to win. Perhaps these areas include golf or music, the maintaining of a beautiful garden, and, most of all, the business and professional competence or the particular skill that is necessary for success in his work. Whatever it is, if the area is regarded as his own, experiences of success within that area lead him to attitudes of self-confidence and failure to feelings of inferiority.

An effective way of protecting one's self-esteem is to shift the area within which one professes competence. The field of competition is often limited on the basis of age or experience. Thus, in a foot race, if a six-year-old boy runs against a nine-year-old and loses, he is less likely to experience a sense of failure than in races with boys of his own age and size.

After a certain amount of experience with an activity, an individual is able to make a fairly accurate appraisal of his own ability. Ordinarily—unless he has a preformed sense of superiority or inferiority—his judgment is moderately close to the actual level of performance. In special skills—reading french, typewriting, shooting at a target, singing, playing badminton or golf—one learns to evaluate his degree of competence and to answer with fair exactness the question, *How good am I in this kind of activity*?

There is a range of proficiency within which an individual knows that his ability lies. On the one hand, if the quality of performance is below this range or toward its lower limit, the individual is likely to gain a sense of inferiority from failure. If the quality of performance, on the other hand, approaches or exceeds the upper limit of the proficiency range, he gains an experience of success.

It commonly happens that the individual sets for himself a *level of aspiration*. This goal usually represents a compromise between his evaluation of ability and a desire to achieve a high level of performance. If the subject in an experiment is instructed to set a goal for himself, this constitutes a threat to his level of self-esteem. In case he places the goal too high, there is a likelihood of failure and of consequent self-depreciation. The subject, therefore, attempts to meet this threat by manipulating the level of his aspiration to a point somewhere near his ability to achieve, as well as by a determination to perform as well as possible.

A great deal of experimental work has been done on the level of aspiration. For some early references see the papers by Frank (1941) and Rotter (1942).

Awareness of Self in Emotional Processes. The self-evaluative attitudes are aroused in a wide variety of feelings and conscious emotions. The awareness of self, in one form of another, enters as a causal factor into experiences designated as self-consciousness, embarrassment, timidity, shyness, boldness, shame, the sense of guilt or of innocence, self-assertion, self-abasement, pride in one's self, and the like.

These experiences are so numerous and so complexly interrelated that no attempt will be made here to distinguish among them. Instead, a series of illustrations will be given in which the *self* factor plays a prominent and obviously important part.

Stage fright is the common name for an experience which occurs when a novice is obliged to speak or perform in public. There are some actresses, singers, and public speakers who always suffer some degree of stage fright before every public appearance. The classical account of stage fright, in psychological literature, is that of the Italian physiologist, Mosso (1896),who introduced his book upon *Fear* with these words:

> Never shall I forget that evening! From behind the curtains of a glass door I peered into the large amphitheatre crowded with people. It was my first appearance as a lecturer, and most humbly did I repent having undertaken to try my powers in the same hall in which my most celebrated teachers had so often spoken. All I had to do was to communicate the results of some of my investigations into the physiology of sleep, and yet, as the hour drew nearer, stronger waxed within me the fear that I should become confused, lose myself, and finally stand gaping, speechless before my audience. My heart beat violently, its very strings seemed to tighten, and my breath came and went, as when one looks down into a yawning abyss. At last it struck eight. As I cast a last glance at my notes, I became aware, to my horror, that the chain of ideas was broken and the links lost beyond recall. Experiments performed a hundred times, long periods which I had thought myself able to repeat word for word—all seemed forgotten, swept away as though it had never been.
>
> My anguish reached a climax. So great was my perturbation that the recollection of it is dim and shadowy. I remember seeing the usher touch the handle of the door, and that, as he opened it, I seemed to feel a puff of wind in my face; there was a singing in my ears, and then I found myself near a table in the midst of an oppressive silence, as though, after a plunge in a stormy sea, I had raised my head above water and seized hold of a rock in the centre of the vast amphitheatre.
>
> How strange was the sound of my first words! My voice seemed to lose itself in a great wilderness, words, scarce fallen from my lips, to tremble and die away. After a few sentences jerked out almost mechanically, I perceived that I had already finished the introduction of my speech, and discovered with dismay that memory had played me false just at that point where I had thought myself most sure; but there was now no turning back, and so, in great confusion, I proceeded. The hall seemed enveloped in mist. Slowly the cloud began to lift, and here and there in the crowd I could distinguish benevolent, friendly faces, and on these I

> fixed my gaze, as a man struggling with the waves clings to a floating spar. I could discern, too, the attentive countenances of eager listeners, holding a hand to their ear as though unwilling to lose a single word, and nodding occasionally in token of affirmation. And lastly, I saw myself in this semicircle, alone, humbled, discouraged, dejected—like a sinner at confession. The first greatest emotional disturbance was over; but my throat was parched, my cheeks burned, my breath came in gasps, my voice was strained and trembling. The harmony of the period was often interrupted in the middle by a rapid inspiration, or painfully drawn out, as the chest was compressed to lend force to the last words of a sentence. But to my joy, in spite of all, the ideas began to unfold of their own accord, following each other in regular order along the magic thread to which I blindly clung without a backward glance, and which was to lead me out of the labyrinth. Even the trembling of the hands, which had made me shake the instruments and drawings I had from time to time to exhibit, ceased at last. A heaviness crept over my whole body, the muscles seemed to stiffen, and my knees shook.
>
> Towards the end I felt the blood begin to circulate again. A few minutes passed of which I remember nothing save a great anxiety. My trembling voice had assumed the conclusive tone adopted at the close of a speech. I was perspiring, exhausted, my strength was failing; I glanced at the tiers of seats, and it seemed to me that they were slowly opening in front of me, like the jaws of a monster ready to devour me as soon as the last word should re-echo within its throat. [1-4]

Mosso's stage fright, though unusually intense, is similar in form to other kinds of embarrassment. During the experience of stage fright the performer anticipates failure or humiliation. Even though the audience is interested and sympathetic the emotionally excited speaker anticipates that his talk may not have the desired effect. He has a high level of aspiration. Perhaps he expects too much—to make a "hit" or to be recognized as "brilliant" or "scintillating." Possibly someone is present in the audience who is felt to be secretly resistant or even hostile to the speaker. Experienced speakers avoid stage fright by lowering their level of aspiration somewhat, demanding less of themselves, doing their best and then accepting in a matter-of-fact way whatever acknowledgment there may be.

A variation of this emotional disturbance, made possible by the development of radio broadcasting, is commonly known as "mike fright."

Timidity and Self-consciousness as Forms of Embarrassment. The term *embarrassment* is used broadly to cover a variety of affective disturbances which occur in social situations. Stage fright is only one form of embarrassment. If one has "made a fool of himself in public" or committed a *faux pas*, or caught in some questionable act, he is said to be embarrassed. The timid child or self-conscious adolescent is embarrassed in social situations. Feelings of shame, remorse, and guilt, which will be described presently, are feelings of embarrassment. The emotion of embarrassment is always one which arises in a *social* situation.

Everyone has observed the reaction of shyness or timidity in children. A caller enters the living room. The timid child hides behind his mother's skirt or behind some piece of furniture. Perhaps he peeks out cautiously at the visitor. If the guest remains and acts in a friendly manner, the timid behavior gradually disappears. Timid behavior is akin to fear, for it is an unknown and threatening element in the social situation to which he responds by hiding or some other form of escape. The timid child is said to be "self-conscious." This phrase implies that an awareness of self is a factor in the situation producing shyness.

If a speaker is introduced with flattering words and overstatements, he, too, is made "self-conscious." He blushes in embarrassment. He is "aware of himself." Adverse criticism in front of others produces a similar embarrassment combined, however, with unpleasantness or anger instead of the pleasant self-consciousness resulting from flattery. Self-consciousness, in the literal sense of awareness of one's self, occurs in a wide variety of affective and non-affective experiences.

Shame, Remorse, and Feelings of Guilt. Very different from shyness and stage fright, but still based upon the self-other relationship, are those forms of embarrassment which arise when an individual has carried out some act contrary to the moral standards of his group or in violation of his personal principles. The terms *shame, remorse, feeling of guilt*, and others, are used to designate this group of emotions.

Children, as all mothers know, are born without a sense of shame, just as animals are. Before they can experience shame, they must learn what is considered proper and what improper within their social world. The conditions which induce feelings of shame—whether in the child or among primitive people or civilized adults—are variable, depending upon the mores of the group.

The evolution of the bathing suit, through the past two generations, well illustrates changing mores in dress and bodily exposure—and modified attitudes as to what should induce feelings of shame. Men of today might feel embarrassment wearing the satin knee breeches of George Washington's day or the shawl that Lincoln used to wear about his shoulders.

If it is customary for the women of a tribe to cover the face, a woman feels ashamed when she is discovered without a veil. Among many primitive peoples it is customary for female breasts to be exposed, with no accompanying self-consciousness or feelings of shame; but in cultures which require that the breasts be covered, a feeling of shame is elicited when they are inadvertently exposed. There are savage tribes who wear no clothing at all and who feel no embarrassment over this exposure unless some exponent of Western culture teaches them to wear clothes.

Among the Buka people in Melanesia, there is a feeling of shame between brother and sister such that they are ashamed to talk to each other unless other people are present; if a man's sister calls to him to come and take some food from her, he will probably pretend not to hear her. Illustrations of situations which elicit shame could be multiplied indefinitely, from both our own and primitive cultures.

Inasmuch as sexual behavior is usually regulated by the mores of various cultures, thus—through taboos and restrictions—sometimes frustrating a powerful motive, it is not surprising that feelings of guilt and remorse should frequently arise in the area of sexual conduct. The following illustration presents the case of a freshman in an eastern university who, having been taught that autoerotic practices are morally wrong, experienced a sense of guilt over his own autoerotic habits.

> John is a boy eighteen years of age. During his fourteenth, fifteenth, and sixteenth years he masturbated habitually. Since then he has indulged in this activity only occasionally. He believes that one who has done "this deed" has degraded himself morally, and that such a person can not succeed or prosper. All of his failures he explains in terms of this belief. He does not make a fraternity; it is because of his habit. He is not liked by young women; the explanation is simple: he has degraded himself. Thus the young man has lived for years in a state of resigned self-condemnation. [222]

Such feelings of guilt are accentuated by the exaggerated statements of misinformed parents and teachers regarding the ill effects of masturbation. There is a common belief that autoerotism is damaging to the sex function, that it causes insanity, or is a sign of moral degradation in the individual practicing it. Pullias (1937), from whose paper the above case study is taken, questioned seventy-five young men regarding their beliefs about autoerotic practices. He found a widespread belief that such practices are damaging. The following figures summarize his findings:

Some type of serious damage	62
Serious physical damage	33
Serious mental damage	28
Serious moral damage	18
Serious social damage	9
Harmful (kind of harm not specified)	6
A direct cause of insanity	12
Not seriously harmful	5
No response	8

The numbers at the right indicate the frequencies of positive response within the group of seventy-five subjects. Since some of the young men stated a belief that masturbation has several effects, the figures overlap and are not meant to be added.[1]

Feelings of shame, remorese or guilt are likely to be associated with the violation of taboos and customs. If one accepts the view that it is a virtue to suppress the sexual appetite, this is likely to bring a sense of guilt. Discovery in any immoral act is likely to bring shame.

Feelings of shame or guilt arise, of course, in a great variety of non-sexual situations. For example, if a man is caught cheating in an examination or at cards, he feels ashamed of himself. If a boy is seen being cruel to an animal or mean to a young child, he may feel guilty. Thieves, murderers, and other types of criminals, suffer from the compunction of a "guilty conscience." There are all gradations in intensity of these feelings of guilt and remorse.

As a group these feelings are commonly indicated by blushing (vasodilation) and downcast eyes, combined with some attempt to make amends–apologies, explanations, restoration or repair of property, etc.–in an effort to restore one's self to the good graces of a disapproving person or group. According to Freud, there is a "superego"–an ideal self. Ideal behavior may be violated.

A relatively permanent sense of guilt sometimes develops in the sphere of abnormal behavior. A patient in a psychopathic hospital, for example, was convinced that he had committed the "unpardonable sin." The exact nature of this sin was very vague to him. Nevertheless, he appeared to be experiencing a profound sense of guilt and self-reproach. With head bowed and a despondent countenance he rocked back and forth in his chair, repeating over and over: "All the evil in the world I have done. I am responsible for all the sin and trouble in the world. I am to blame for it all. . . . " This patient was in a pathological state of conflict from which he suffered a profound sense of guilt and remorse.

I am not sure that feelings of guilt and shame are unique to man. When a dog or cat is scolded for some misdeed, e.g., eliminating on the parlor rug, the animal may show a slinking, avoiding, behavior when the

[1]The notion that autoerotic practices lead to insanity is definitely incorrect. There is, however, a danger of sexual excess and of developing solitary sexual habits which will later interfere with the satisfaction of the heterosexual relationship. Still, it should be understood that more harm results from severe mental conflict, from anxiety and remorse over violating one's moral and religious code with its consequent lowering of self-esteem, than from any direct physical consequences of the practice. Autoerotism is known to be quite frequent in situations offering no other forms of sexual satisfaction.

An excellent treatment of the problem of masturbation and of other sexual problems from the standpoint of mental hygiene can be found in McKinney (1941). See also Landis and associates (1940). More recent references are available.

master scolds him. It is easy to interpret this behavior as shame or guilt but, of course, we don't know what the animal consciously feels.

Ego-involvement. During the second year of his life, when words begin to be used, the baby talks about himself in the third person: "Baby wants this" or "John wants that." It is later that words like *I, me,* and *mine* develop; the use of *we* comes later than *I*. References to the self and all personal pronouns are learned along with other words and by the same process of acquisition.

When a child first refers to something as *mine*—whether a toy, a pet, a piece of clothing, a parent, or a house—there is said to be ego-involvement. This manner of speech implies some knowledge of the individual as distinct from other individuals and things.

The child claims some place as his own. It may be a play yard or a room in the house or a bed. Even animals claim a territory as their own and defend it against intruders. Adults, too, recognize certain places as their own.

Sherif and Cantril (1947) have described the facts in this way:

> The space may be some corner of a room where we have a favorite chair, it may be some glade in the woods to which we make recurrent visits, it may be a barrel in the woodshed we like to sit on in the evening after dinner. Whatever it is, we come to feel that that space is not only ours but it is a part of us. If it is pre-empted by someone else, destroyed, or intruded upon, *we* are annoyed, we feel that *our* privacy, *our* selves have been violated, injured or insulted.

In the normal adult, ego-involvement has developed very far. A man is ego-involved with his family, automobile, home town, profession, church, political party, with various goals and values, etc. He is ready to fight for his property, his rights, his beliefs and convictions. If he has taken a stand, a proposition becomes *his* to defend and he will be loyal to it.

Ego-involvement gives an emotional tinge to certain courses of action. It gives interest and zest to pieces of property, systems of belief, plans for action, or whatever it may be that the individual accepts as belonging to himself.

Ego-involvement is a form of identification. But *identification*, as a psychological concept, has at least three meanings: (1) In one sense a child is said to identify himself with his father or with an older boy or with some individual who serves as a model. Hero worship implies identification in this sense. (2) In another sense we identify ourselves with the characters on the stage or in a novel. We put ourselves in their place and experience their feelings. This has been called empathy. (3) Finally, identification means ego-involvement in the above sense. A man is identified with his clothing, his automobile, his home town, his club, etc. These are *his* things.

Attitudes of Liking and Disliking Persons. What makes us like certain persons and dislike others? What characteristics of an individual (traits of personality, actions, attitudes) induce positive attitudes and what negative? Are there any differences between men and women in the factors which determine their attitudes of liking and disliking persons? These and similar questions were studied for college students by Thomas and Young (1938).

The subjects were 676 students in the elementary psychology course at the University of Illinois. Each student was given a printed form which instructed him to list the initials of a few persons who were the *most liked*, and, in another column, the initials of a few who were the *most disliked*. The sex of each person was indicated on the blank. Then the individuals were ranked in an order of preference by a method which provided for the equal ranking of two or more persons.

A statistical analysis of the results showed that, on the average, 2.7 times as many names were listed in the column headed *like* as in the column headed *dislike*. This was true for judges of both sexes. Also, the persons whose initials were listed tended to be of the same sex as the student who did the listing—a fact which probably indicates that one's acquaintances tend to be of the same sex as one's self.

The person who was ranked as the *most highly liked*. however, was usually a person of the opposite sex. This fact is not surprising for college students in the mating years! Again, the order in which the names were listed tended to agree with the order of ranking which was subsequently made. This indicates that we tend to think first of the most liked in listing the persons liked, and of the most disliked, in listing the persons disliked.

On the second page of the printed form the students were instructed to give the reasons for liking and disliking the persons already listed. Special interest attaches to the reasons given. The alleged reasons for liking and disliking persons were tabulated and the frequency with which each was mentioned was determined.

All told, seventy-four different "reasons" for liking and disliking persons of the same and opposite sex are presented in Tables 10 and 11. The tables speak for themselves and need no further comment.

Transformations of the Self-system. The beliefs and attitudes of an adult concerning his own nature are by no means stable. They change with circumstances and there are wide differences, from time to time, in the self concept. Several illustrations of transformation in the self-system will underscore the fact that any definition of the self is arbitrary and relative to circumstances.

First, in all societies it is normal for a child to become an adolescent and grow into adult status. Not only does adolescence mark a transfor-

TABLE 10

ALLEGED REASONS FOR LIKING AND DISLIKING PERSONS
From Thomas & Young (1938)

Why women *like*:

WOMEN Trait	N	MEN Trait	N
intelligent	134	intelligent	154
cheerful	123	considerate	102
helpful	103	kind	79
loyal	101	cheerful	70
generous	94	mannerly	70
sweet	84	conversational	62
entertaining	84	handsome	61
kind	82	sense of humor	61
good sport	79	congenial	55
common interests	77	interesting	54
congenial	77	common interests	53
sense of humor	73	entertaining	50
considerate	72	generous	46
understanding	65	friendly	45
friendly	63	good sport	44

Why women *dislike*:

WOMEN Trait	N	MEN Trait	N
conceited	111	conceited	122
deceitful	73	selfish	33
selfish	70	unmannerly	30
loud	43	overbearing	27
self-centered	40	deceitful	24
snobbish	40	uninteresting	22
affected	32	unintelligent	21
unmannerly	32	self-centered	19
overbearing	31	untruthful	19
inconsiderate	28	boastful	16
meddlesome	26	dishonest	16
unintelligent	24	ill-tempered	12
insincere	23	unfair	12
silly	20	weak	12
jealous	19	bold	11

TABLE 11

ALLEGED REASONS FOR LIKING AND DISLIKING PERSONS
From Thomas & Young (1938)

Why men *like*:			
MEN		WOMEN	
Trait	N	Trait	N
intelligent	130	beautiful	129
cheerful	101	intelligent	90
friendly	91	cheerful	56
common interests	90	congenial	55
congenial	87	sex-appeal	53
helpful	83	friendly	46
loyal	78	kind	46
sense of humor	70	good sport	41
generous	64	helpful	33
good sport	50	considerate	29
honest	46	understanding	28
kind	43	conversational	26
considerate	39	common interests	25
sincere	35	companionable	24
idealistic	32	sense of humor	23

Why men *dislike*:			
MEN		WOMEN	
Trait	N	Trait	N
conceited	170	conceited	48
self-centered	48	gossips	31
unintelligent	46	snobbish	25
deceitful	42	deceitful	21
overbearing	37	unintelligent	20
dishonest	37	loud	16
selfish	35	selfish	16
loud	33	affected	14
snobbish	32	silly	14
unmannerly	32	talkative	14
boastful	29	overbearing	12
personal injury	26	dishonest	9
untruthful	24	inconsiderate	9
ill-tempered	21	hypocritical	7
officious	21	ill-tempered	7

mation of the body of a child into that of an adult but the social roles and responsibilities of the adolescent become increasingly like those of an adult. The youth is forced to reformulate his beliefs concerning his nature and place in the group. The transformations in the concept of the self, at the time of adolescence, are so radical that it is correct to say that a new *self* has emerged from an old. There is a complete metamorphosis.

Second, in times of stress there are often radical changes in behavior, attitude, and personality, bound up with changes in self-evaluation. We sometimes say that a person "does not act like himself" or "a different self has appeared." For example, during World War II, prisoners arriving in German concentration camps attempted to preserve their independence and self-respect but this became impossible with the brutal treatment of the Gestapo. The prisoners were subjected to horrible experiences that completely altered their personality and their definition of the self. In time, people in these camps lost their old allegiances and identifications. In order to survive they gradually accepted new allegiances and identifications, more in conformity with standards and practices of the Gestapo. The older prisoners regressed to a childlike relationship in which they cooperated with the Gestapo, took on their ideology, and continued an unhappy existence. Self-respect was gone; a new ego system emerged. There was radical change in perception and in belief and evaluation of the self. A record of the terrible conditions in these camps is preserved in first hand interviews of survivors and reports obtained by Boder (1949).

Further examples of transformation in the definition of self can be found in persons suffering some physical change, as in alcoholism, disease, or surgery. Under the influence of alcohol a man may become temporarily freed from his inhibitions. Normally he may be a controlled and serious individual but when drunk he becomes jovial, free and easy with his remarks, "a different person." Again, a patient suffering from a mental disease hears hallucinatory voices and sees visions; his behavior becomes so fragmented and bizarre that we commonly say he is "beside himself," "out of his mind," "unbalanced." Behavior and traits of personality are so radically altered, by the diseased condition, that the man no longer acts like the same person. Finally, consider the effects of a surgical operation known as *pre-frontal lobotomy*. In this operation connections are severed between the frontal association areas of the brain and lower neural centers. The operation reduces anxiety and leaves the patient more serene and less self-conscious. The operation changes the temperament of the individual to such an extent that he acts like a different person.

From the above illustrations it is clear that the definition and characteristics of the self are dependent upon physical, biological, psychological, and social conditions, and that the characteristics of the self can and sometimes do change radically with circumstances.

Deficit Motivation and Self-actualization. Maslow (1955), who is looking for a "humanly usable theory of human motivation," argues that the deficit theory of motivation is inadequate. He writes: "If the motivational life consists essentially of a defensive removal of irritating tensions, and if the only end product of tension reduction is a state of passive waiting for more unwelcome irritations to arise and in their turn, to be dispelled, then how does change, or development or movement or direction come about? Why do people improve? Get wiser? What does zest in living mean?"

As distinct from *deficit motivation* there is *growth motivation.* In itself growth is an exciting and rewarding process. There is positive motivation towards fulfilling ambitions, like being a good doctor, becoming a skilled violinist or carpenter. In any field of activity the development of creativeness is more than removing a deficiency. There is positive motivation towards understanding people, learning about the universe and about one's self. There is a positive ambition simply to be a good human being.

The highest form of positive motivation, Maslow (1954) states, is self-actualization. To understand what he means by this we must consider his view that human needs arrange themselves in a hierarchy.

On the lowest level of the hierarchy are physiological needs for food, water, oxygen, sex, etc. These basic needs are urgent and until they are met other needs are simply non-existent or they are pushed into the background. If the physiological needs are gratified, there then emerges a new set of needs—needs for safety.

The child needs a predictable, orderly world in which he can feel safe. In our society the normal adult is rarely motivated by a need for safety because in a peaceful, smoothly running society the members feel safe from wild animals, extremes of temperature, criminal assault, murder, tyranny, etc. The healthy adult is generally satisfied in his need for safety.

If both the physiological and safety needs are fairly well gratified, there will emerge higher order needs for love, affection and belonging. The man who is well fed and safe will keenly feel the absence of friends or sweetheart or wife or children. He will experience a need for affectionate relations with people in general. He will want to belong to certain groups and to hold a place of respect in them. Within our society, Maslow states, the core of much maladjustment is found in the failure of the situation to meet the needs for love, affection and belonging.

If all of the above needs are gratified, there develops another motivational cycle based upon the need for esteem. In our society there is a felt need for competence, mastery, adequacy, achievement, status, recognition, importance, appreciation, prestige. In other words, there is a need for the esteem of others.

Finally, when all of the above needs are met there often emerges a new kind of restlessness and discontent. There is a need for self-actualization. Very simply, this means that a man needs to do and to become what he is fitted for. A musician feels the need to make music; an artist must paint; a poet must write if he is to have peace of mind. A man *must* do what he *can* do. This is the need for self-actualization.

Maslow qualifies his need hierarchy hypothesis somewhat. He points out that there are other needs not placed in the hierarchy such as the need to know and the aesthetic needs. He states that the need hierarchy is not the same for everyone. Nevertheless, needs do arrange themselves in a hierarchical order such that when one is satisfied another emerges. With the emergence of a new need there is another motivational cycle. And the highest need of all is for self-actualization.

In contrasting deficiency motivation with growth motivation, Maslow states that there is an important difference: In need gratification there is a climax, a consummatory goal response, which is followed by a period of relative freedom from the need. With growth motivation, contrastingly, this phenomenon is absent. The more one gets, the more one wants; the wanting of self-actualization is endless. The goal is never attained.

Self-actualization as Prime Human Motivation. Maslow's recognition that self-actualization is the highest need in the hierarchy of human motives is related to the postulates of Goldstein and Rogers.

Kurt Goldstein (1939,1947) postulated that the organism is a unit which functions as a whole and that its motivation is unitary. The prime motivation of the human organism is *to realize its capacities*. The impression that there are special drives or motives appears only when one considers the activities of the organism as isolated from their relation to total behavior. Goldstein writes: "Any explanation is doomed to failure which attempts to reduce human motivation to a number of *isolable factors*, capacities, drives, etc., to *separate* forces which interact only secondarily with each other."

The basic trend of the organism to realize its capacities, as much as possible, is seen in both normal and abnormal persons. As a single example of the trend consider patients suffering from hemianopsia—a total blindness of corresponding halves of the visual field in both eyes due to lesions in the occipital lobe of the brain. The everyday behavior of patients with hemianopsia often fails to reveal that they are blind in half of the visual field. Patients with hemianopsia are subjectively aware of impaired vision but they see objects in their entirety and not only halves of them. Their visual field is arranged around a center as it is with normal people. The region of clearest vision lies *within* this field—not (as one might assume) on the margin of the preserved half of the field that corresponds to the location of the fovea. If such a patient wants to see an object, he deviates the direction of his eyes a little to bring the object into the center of the preserved field of vision. This is the only way that he can recognize objects. The object must be placed in a field and surrounded by other parts of the total field containing other objects.

The apparent goal of the organism, in hemianopsia, is to have vision as good as possible, to realize the capacities that already exist. This trend towards realization of capacities is a tendency shown by the organism as a whole. It is shown by many other forms of behavior—normal and abnormal.

A view similar to that of Goldstein was expressed by Carl Rogers (1951), whose name is associated with the technique of client-centered therapy. He agrees that the organism has one basic tendency and striving—to actualize, maintain, and enhance the experiencing organism. Behavior moves in the direction of greater independence or self-responsibility—of increasing self-government, self-regulation. As Rogers puts it: "*The organism has one basic tendency and striving—to actualize, maintain, and enhance the experiencing organism.*"

This tendency to self-actualization occurs, as with all behavior, within a world perceived and known by the individual, i.e., within a psychological world. Self-actualization, Rogers states, is a prime human motivation.

LOVE, HATE, AND SEXUAL MOTIVATION

The word *love* is commonly used in a broad sense to designate any attitude of liking a person, object, situation or activity. Thus a man is said to *love* his home, his work, his religion, even his smoking jacket and slippers, or his fishing tackle. All of us have heard about the small boy who, when asked to distinguish between *liking* and *loving*, replied: "I *like* my mother but I *love* ice cream."

In psychological literature the term *love* is used in several senses to mean an attitude or a motive or a state of conflict. The term sometimes designates a mood or an emotion. In any event, the term needs to be clearly defined when used by the psychologist.

As a social or interpersonal relation, love is described by such terms as *admiration, benevolence, attachment, devotion.* In Webster's Collegiate Dictionary there are several definitions of *love.* Two of these are relevant to the present discussion: "An unselfish concern that freely accepts another in loyalty and seeks his good" and "The attraction based on sexual desire: affection and tenderness felt by lovers." Thus there are non-sexual and sexual forms of love.

The non-sexual forms of love include love of parents for children and of children for parents; love of brothers and sisters for each others; love of friends; love of mankind. The attitude toward a long-cherished pet is sometimes a genuine love attitude, too. Non-sexual love attitudes are based upon somewhat different factors for each relationship, but there is usually a basis of giving and receiving acts of kindness, helpfulness, and generosity. This is well illustrated in the care and feeding of an infant by its mother, with the intimate physical contacts entailed in nursing, bathing, dressing, and other care. Caressing and fondling figure largely in establishing love attitudes. A sharing of play is often an important factor in developing the mother-child or father-child love attitudes.

In the sexual form of love the affectionate behavior of an individual is normally directed toward a member of the opposite sex. Commonly the relationship is a reciprocal one, each of the pair revealing, in his behavior, his love for the other. All the factors mentioned above as bases of non-sexual love may also be factors in sexual love, but here caressing, kissing, and similar affectionate demonstrations play a more important role than in non-sexual relations. It is said that the basis of sexual love is "physical and mental attractiveness." The arousal of sexual appetite through the senses, and its normal consummation is the completed sexual act.

An attitude that is opposed to love is that of hate. The term *hate* is commonly used in as broad a sense as *love.* It is used, roughly, as the equivalent of *dislike.* Thus a child may say, "I *hate* castor oil."

Attitudes of hate may be based on either non-sexual or sexual factors. Thus if a military ruler of a city treats the citizens cruelly or in an overbearing manner, frustrating innumerable desires for independent action and security, and for freedom and dignity, the citizens will come to hate him, i.e., develop attitudes of intense dislike and antagonism based upon their frustrations.

The frustration of any strong motive, sexual or non-sexual, is likely to leave the individual with a negative attitude toward the frustrating individual or circumstances. There are various forms of sexual frustration. Thus if a husband or a wife turns to another mate and leaves his partner unsatisfied, there may develop attitudes of bitterness or hatred toward the mate. There are a good many forms of sexual and personal frustration which will be considered below. In most forms of frustration there is a factor (perhaps unconscious) of self-interest or self-regard.

Jealousy. Jealousy is a complex affective disturbance in which there are tendencies to attack the intruder who threatens to win away one's love object. Jealousy may be based upon non-sexual or sexual motives. The non-sexual type occurs in children, among adolescent chums, and in other non-sexual relationships. Sexually-based jealousy is present in the triangular love situations of adults.

A typical situation in which jealous behavior appears is that produced by the arrival of a new baby in the family. The attention, care, and affectionate demonstrations of the mother are now diverted from the older child to the newcomer. The jealous child responds by making an attack upon the baby.

Jealous behavior will be illustrated by citing the case of Joseph Wright, a six-year-old boy, described by Foster (1927):

> He was born while his father was overseas during the first World War. At that time the mother made her home with relatives. She frankly admits that she showered affection and caresses on the baby, filling her life with the baby's needs in order not to think about the possible fate of his father. When the baby was a year old the father returned. Upon entering the home he greeted the mother demonstratively, paying no attention at the moment to Joseph. The baby showed a temper which could not at once be quieted. For a long time after this he resented the affectionate attention which was shown to his mother by the father. Noting this, both parents adopted the practice of including him in their demonstrations of affection. When another son was born, Joseph again showed marked jealousy and on several occasions tried to injure him, once throwing a steel tool from the automobile kit at him. To overcome this the parents tried to see that both shared alike in everything. But at the present time, if Richard is ill and receives special attention, Joseph produces a cough or some other symptom that brings him attention also. [75]

In such situations the first child has come to accept the attention, care, and affection of the mother as his due. An "intruder" who disturbs this relationship is attacked as if he were a love-thief. I have known a small child to attack the newly arrived baby with a monkey wrench! The attack is a hostile one produced by the love frustration. Generally speaking, jealousies of this type need not become so serious as this one did, if the parents realize how difficult an adjustment the older child is having to make, and are careful to include him, so far as practicable, when caressing or caring for the new baby. On jealousy among children see also the studies by Sewall (1930) and Smalley (1930).

When the object of desire is someone else's property or honor or position, rather than the love or affectionate care of some other person, the terms *envy* and *covetousness* are more appropriate. For example, a man would like to own the beautiful new automobile in which Mr. Neighbor rides. His wife desires a fur coat as elegant as the one Mrs. Neighbor is wearing. Their child desires the bicycle which Jimmy Neighbor is riding. Psychologically, envy and jealousy are similar, as in both there is a desire for something not quite one's own; but *envy* is easily distinguishable from jealousy, since, with the latter, the object of desire is the love or affectionate care of some person rather than property or status.

An important form of jealousy is *sexual jealousy* in which there is a definite factor of sexual motivation. During the mating season, males sometimes get into a fight for possession of a female. For example, at the mating time the female elephant seals climb out of the sea onto the rocky beach and await the arrival of the males. When two or more dominant males arrive there is often a life-and-death struggle for possession of the harem. The strongest and fittest males leave offspring; the weakest are eliminated. Such sexual selection goes on in various animal species. Darwin pointed out that the antlers of the deer, the spurs of the fighting cock, the superior size and strength of the male, have been developed in the vital struggle for mates as well as in defense of self, mate and offspring.

There is also a gentler, more aesthetic, side to sexual selection. The beautiful plumage of the peacock, of the male pheasant and of many other male birds, has been evolved to charm or entice the female. The female, according to Darwin, selects the most attractive and charming male, who in turn becomes the father of an oncoming generation. Through this kind of selective mating, a type of male is developed which is increasingly attractive to the female of the species.

Returning now to the consideration of jealousy, we note that human jealousy is akin to its crude biological counterpart. When a rival intrudes and threatens to take possession of the loved individual, the jealous person is caught between two impulses: to make renewed love advances to the loved person and to attack the intruder. In some cultures the jealous man may challenge his rival to a duel or start a fist fight or even plunge a knife into his back or shoot him.

In modern polite society open attack upon the rival is taboo. Consequently the jealous individual may substitute slanderous or depreciating remarks; he may maneuver his competitor into appearing disadvantageously before the fair object of their love; or in more subtle ways he may reveal an attitude of hostility toward the rival lover.

A persistently jealous person is in a state of conflict. Various attitudes and motives may be implicated. The conflict may be between impulses of hostile attack upon the rival and love advances. Possibly the conflict involves social taboos against open attack and overt sexual advances. Possibly the loved object wavers in an attitude of loyalty and this induces anxiety lest the lover by lost.

In any event, jealousy is a complex affective state of conflict. There are various outcomes and resolutions of persisting jealousy.

Loss of Love. The emotional reaction to the loss of a loved one varies greatly with circumstances and especially with the particular interpersonal relationship that is involved. If a child dies, the parents grieve. If a lover is unfaithful and deserts her (or his) mate, the attitudes of self-evaluation usually become involved; a person may feel inferior in some way when a lover is untrue.

In *bereavement* the mate is lost through death or by permanent separation. The death of a mate blocks habitual forms of sexual satisfaction, but the grief of the widowed person has a far broader basis than sexual frustration alone. The bereavement involves loss of the interchange of affection and companionship, loss of someone to talk to, to share work with, to perform personal services for, to receive help of various kinds from, and so on.

If the deceased is of some other relationship than mate–child or parent, for instance–the grief is free from the augmenting factor of sexual frustration. But, assuming the relationship with the deceased spouse to have been, besides other things, a source of sexual satisfaction, the bereavement includes, along with all the other losses mentioned above, a frustration of the sexual urge. This sexual frustration may be felt later on more than during the first crushing grief of the bereavement period.

The more highly cherished the mate and the more sudden and complete the loss, the greater is the resulting emotional shock. In bereavement the emotional disorganization is sometimes so severe and so permanent that the subject goes into a neurotic condition. One such instance, drawn from cases collected by Lawrence G. Brown (1934), is presented here.

> As time went on, Mary and I became very much in love with each other. By the time the next September rolled around we were thinking of our future. We decided it would be a good thing for me to spend a few years in college to prepare me better for providing for our future happiness. She promised faithfully to wait for me until I was finished with my education and I did the same for her. When the time came, I entered college.
>
> The first year was great. I went home every weekend to see her and everything was going along smoothly. We were certain of our love. We would sit

by the hour planning and dreaming of our future home. I can still remember it very vividly, even so far as to the placing of the furniture. We delighted in having petty arguments over where a certain chair would be put and who would have a certain room. We often remarked in a joking way that our happiness was too perfect to last. We were both in paradise. Then, suddenly, like a flash the blow came. One day I noticed that she was looking ill. I asked her what the trouble was but she said she felt all right. I was not satisfied with this, so I took her to a doctor. The doctor said she had sugar diabetes, but not serious. She was under the doctor's care and we both thought that she was getting along fine. She picked up in weight and was looking much better. We did not go anywhere and were cautious in every move. One Sunday night she wanted to go to a dance; I did not want to go on account of her condition but she argued that she was all right now, so I took her word for it and we went to the dance. We had a wonderful time. When I left her that night she was full of pep and seemed the good old Mary. The next morning I was called by her mother; she told me that Mary was very ill and I should come right over. I went directly to her home and found her in her bed unconscious. She had lost consciousness some time during the night and was found by her mother in that state. I was at her side constantly, but was not able to help her. I just sat there and prayed that she might pull through. The doctors did all they could, but to no avail. Wednesday morning she died, never regaining consciousness. I was in the room when she passed away. I damn near went mad watching, staring at her, seeing her slip farther away—and I was helpless. The room—I shall never forget it. Her father and mother, the doctor and myself watching her draw her last breath. We were like stone. My hands clenched so hard that the finger nails went into the palm of my hand. She turned black, first her legs, then her arms; then she was black all over. I could see death taking her away from me. Words fail me when I attempt to describe it. When the doctor pulled the sheet over her head I passed out. I was like a mad man for over a week. Locked myself up in my room allowing no one to enter except my mother to bring food. They did not let me go to the funeral, I was in such bad shape. In my sleep I could see the accusing finger pointing to me and saying "You are guilty. You killed her." Mother tried to console me, but it could not be done. I thought of suicide. Oh! I thought of everything trying to forget. In my sleep I would dream about her alive and happy, then her ghastly dead face would loom up. I would wake up screaming and sweating like a lunatic. Finally I became strong enough to go out. The first thing I got was a quart of whiskey. I got drunk and went back to the bootlegger's place and stayed there that night. Drunk all night. I went home the next morning and I could see on my mother's face the night she had spent. That started everything. I did not draw a sober breath into my body for three weeks. Finally they called a doctor and I was given shots to put me to sleep. When I gained consciousness I felt that I wanted to die. The doctor explained to me that it was not my fault that Mary had died. This eased my mind slightly . . . [300-301]

No comment is necessary on this extremely intense emotional upset by the loss of love.

Romantic Love. A happier form of emotional disturbance is the conflict found in romantic love. The state of "being in love" is one of conflict which may last for an indefinite period. The lovers are more or less activated sexually and also inhibited.

Mutual caressing arouses the lovers. Physical contacts—holding hands, dancing, kissing, embracing, petting—are sexually arousing. The biological completion of love making is sexual union. But in our traditional culture, sexual union outside of wedlock is taboo. The taboo is based on various rational and irrational considerations, chief of which is the likelihood of impregnation and the birth of a child without legal father and suitable home conditions for its rearing. Young people are deterred from sexual promiscuity by knowledge of this danger and by a fear of social ostracism if an unwanted and illegitimate baby is born. Lovers have a fear of pregnancy, fear of venereal diseases, fear of social ostracism. There are also religious and moral teachings about the sanctity of the home and about good and bad conduct. All of these sex-inhibitory influences tend to heighten the state of conflict.

Consequently, in romantic love the lovers are at once aroused and inhibited sexually. The persisting state of conflict evokes the emotional disturbance known as "being in love," which is felt by the two individuals. The more strongly an individual is excited by sexual stimulation and the more completely this biological urge is frustrated, the greater will be the emotional disturbance.

Various factors can complicate the conflict state of romantic love. One of the lovers may have suspicion or knowledge that there is a rival; this introduces an element of jealousy. Signs of disinterest on the part of one lover may make the outcome of the romantic relationship uncertain and produce anxiety. Usually the ego of both lovers is strongly involved. Each of the lovers identifies himself with the other and becomes proverbially blind to the other's defects.

The conflict state of "being in love" is resolved in various ways. In marriage there are normally attitudes of trust and confidence in the fidelity of the partner and hence no state of conflict. Of course, infidelity in marriage can produce an intense conflict state which may lead to separation, divorce, and rarely to suicide and murder.

The conflict state of "being in love" may terminate in separation and desertion of one of the partners. Tragedy may bring persistent unhappiness and lowering of self-esteem. Romantic love, as everyone knows, may or may not end happily. Poets and novelists have filled literature with the stories about lasting love.

Sexual Motivation and Emotion. In presenting a directive-activation theory of motivation, I made the point that dynamic states differ in two important variables: the level of activation and hedonic tone (pages 72-4). This distinction applies to appetitive and aversive behavior, to emotions, and, in fact, to all affective processes, including sexual reactions.

Now the sexual appetite (desire, lust) is a potent form of human motivation and similar in many ways to the sexual motivations observed in non-human animals. The sexual appetite of both sexes, when uninhibited, normally leads to sexual union. During preliminary stages of sexual play the level of excitement rises until ejaculation occurs in the male and a physiological equivalent occurs in the female. The orgasm marks the climax of the sexual appetite, for the time being, through appetitive satisfaction.

From the subjective point of view, the sexual act is definitely pleasurable. This fact insures the carrying on of the species. Normal intercourse leaves a relaxed, contented mood. But sometimes, especially in women, the orgasm is not attained and a state of nervous tension and excitement remains. Failure of complete satisfaction may lead to the growth of attitudes of resentment.

Elsewhere I referred to the views of Hardy (1964) on the role of hedonic processes in the organization and development of the sexual appetite (page 159). There is little doubt that affective processes play a dominant role in human sexual behavior.

What is a sexual emotion? The answer is in part a matter of how we define emotion. If we take a broad definition of emotion and regard all affective processes as emotional, then sexual excitement and sexual relief are clearly emotional events. But other appetites, e.g., for food or water, are rarely designated as emotions. Appetitive behavior and emotional behavior can be clearly distinguished if one wishes to do so.

If we follow the view that emotion is a disturbed affective state of psychological origin, then sexual behavior becomes emotional to the extent that disturbance of normal activity is involved. From this point of view, there can be no doubt that such states as jealousy, loss of love, romantic love (described above) are emotional disturbances. They are sexual emotions in so far as sexual motivations are frustrated, in conflict, or satisfied.

In any event, the problem of a precise definition of emotion is less important than the apprehension of psychological reality!

FEAR AND ANXIETY

In preceding chapters reference was frequently made to fear, fright, terror, phobia, anxiety, and related emotions. There can be no doubt that these terms refer to an important family of emotional reactions in men and animals.

Bayley (1928), in a study using the psychogalvanic technique, suggested that there are two main kinds of fears. The first is an innate startle reaction induced by loud sounds, shocks and jars to the body, an unexpected fall, and possibly by sudden visual movement. The second is a more general bodily disturbance which depends upon inadequate understanding and control of a situation that is immediately appraised as threatening or dangerous. The first kind of fear is a reaction to sensory stimulation; the second, involves cognition. Bayley's second kind of fear refers to the environmental situation that elicits fear rather than to the pattern of response, as the basis for distinguishing fear from other emotions. She regards fear as a general disturbance which must be understood by its behavioral and experiential manifestations.

The fear reaction is premonitory of some danger that is not very clearly perceived or known. In nature there are many protective reactions associated with fear: a clam simply closes its shell, there is autotomy in the starfish, withdrawing from a painful stimulation, closing the eyelid, etc. Such protective reactions are reflexive; they are only part of a total response of an organism to a threatening or potentially dangerous situation.

There are all gradations in the intensity of the fear reaction from the weakest apprehension of threat to the severest disruptive terror.

A phobia, as we have seen elsewhere, is a predisposition to respond with intense fear to a particular kind of object or situation. A phobia is based upon a traumatic, typically unpleasant experience which is repressed, often with feelings of guilt or remorse.

Anxiety is different from phobias and other fears in that it is a persistent state, a chronic foreboding of pain or injury or illness or disgrace or humiliation or death. The anxious person usually recognizes the source of his impending misforturne and worry. There are, however, pathological states of chronic anxiety in which the individual seeks out or imagines some source for his fear.

This whole family of emotional processes is of tremendous human and practical importance. So let us ask: What are the signs, or signals, of danger that induce fear? What makes us afraid?

What Are the Signals of Danger? In a very early study, G. Stanley Hall (1897) determined the main source of fear within a group composed of 500 boys and 600 girls. The girls reported a total of 1765 "well-described fears" and the boys a total of 1116. The sources of fear were classified, with the result shown in Table 12. Our chief interest in the table lies in the relative frequency of the different danger signals mentioned by the children.

In a more recent study Jersild, Markey, and Jersild (1933) interviewed 400 children about their fears. The group was composed of twenty-five boys and twenty-five girls in each age group of five to twelve years, inclusive. The instructions were there: "*Tell me about things that scare you, things that frighten you. Tell me what makes you*

TABLE 12

SOURCES OF FEAR IN CHILDREN
After G. Stanley Hall (1897)

	Girls	Boys
Thunder and Lightning	230	155
Persons	190	129
Reptiles	180	123
Darkness	171	130
Death	102	74
Domestic animals	96	57
Rats and mice	75	13
Insects	74	52
Ghosts	72	44
Wind	61	35
End of the World	53	11
Water	53	62
Robbers	48	32
Mechanism	47	31
Blood	44	14
Heights	40	43
Self-consciousness	40	28
Noises	36	10
Buried alive	32	5
Imaginary things	24	23
Drowning	20	19
Clouds	15	4
Solitude	15	4
Places	14	2
Meteors	12	6
Shyness	8	9
Fairies	7	0
Ridicule	6	1
Totals	1765	1116

afraid. Tell me more about that. What else makes you afraid? What else scares you? What else? What else?

A few of the children tried to hedge in their answers to this questioning, but most of them came directly to the point.

After the questioning had been completed, the sources of fear were classified by the investigators. To illustrate, all the particular animals which were mentioned as sources of fear were classified under the heading "animals." In Table 13 only the first-mentioned sources of fear are considered, The source of fear first mentioned by each child was assumed to be one which was definite and certain.

TABLE 13

SOURCES OF FEAR
After Jersild, Markey, and Jersild (1933)

Type of Fear Object	Age Groups			
	5-6	7-8	9-10	11-12
Bodily injury and physical danger	5.1	4.0	14.0	15.2
Animals	27.3	22.0	11.0	11.1
Bad people, robber, kidnapper, etc.	12.1	6.0	6.0	5.1
Supernatural, mysterious	20.2	26.0	18.0	20.2
The dark, being alone, strange sights, deformities	11.1	11.0	14.0	20.2
Nightmares, apparitions	6.1	15.0	8.0	6.1
Scolding, guilt, failure	0.0	0.0	4.0	4.0
Illness, injury, death of relative	0.0	1.0	3.0	3.0
Startling events and noises	1.0	4.0	3.0	3.0
Frightening gestures with noises, tales	5.7	7.0	10.0	5.1
Scary games	1.0	0.0	2.0	0.0
All other sources	10.4	4.0	7.0	7.0

The four columns in the table show the percentage distribution of the various fear-objects for each of four age groups. Since there were 100 children in each of the four groups, the percentages are comparable and can be used to trace differences which depend upon age.

The older children show a relatively greater fear of bodily injury and physical danger. The older children likewise show more fear of uncanny and strange circumstances such as the dark, being left alone, lights and shadows, deformities. Other fear-objects reported more frequently by older than by younger children are: fear of scoldings and reprimands which give a sense of guilt or failure; fear that relatives might become sick or die; fear of startling events such as thunder and lightning; fear of sudden noises. Younger children show fear of animals much more frequently than do older ones. Younger children also report more fear of bad characters such as robbers and kidnappers. No outstanding sex differences were discovered, nor were the differences found to be significantly related to intelligence quotients.

In appraising studies of this type, one must assume that the results are relative to the culture within which the study was made. Children are taught what to fear and what not to fear but the objects of fear vary with the environmenal situation of the child–with place and time.

Changes in Fear Attitudes with Age. Changes in fear attitudes with advancing age have been repeatedly observed. The data in Table 13 suggest that the sources of fear may differ with the age of the child. Various studies of the development of fear have been made.

H.E. and M.C. Jones (1928) presented subjects with a live snake and observed their responses to it. The test was made with a group of fifty-one children and ninety adults. It was found that up to the age of two years children showed no fear of snakes. At three and a half there was commonly a cautious response to the reptile. At this age the children paid close attention to the movements of the snake and were somewhat on guard in approaching it. A definite fear of snakes was more frequently observed in children beyond the age of four than in younger children. Adults revealed a more pronounced and definite fear of snakes than children. Tests with college students indicated that they were more frequently afraid of snakes than were small children. Incidentally, no sex differences were found in these tests. In general, the fear of snakes developed progressively in the child from year to year (as observed in a laboratory rather than a field situation.)

As a child gains in understanding and control of his environment the sources of fear change. To illustrate: If a child sees water trickling through the base of a dam, he may be interested in the observation; but an adult, realizing that the dam might break and cause a deadly flood, is frightened by the same observation.

On the development of fear see the study of Jersild and Holmes (1935), described on page 166.

ANGER, VIOLENCE AND AGGRESSION

Fear and anger are perhaps the most commonly mentioned examples of basic emotions, although weeping in grief and laughing in joy are close competitors. Fear and anger are widespread throughout the animal kingdom; both are related to defense and attack in the struggle for survival. The herbivorous animals survive if they can escape their predators.

In man, anger is associated with aggression, violence, destruction. A quarrel among children (or adults) may end in a fight. There are depreciating remarks. The vocal exchange becomes louder and louder and ends in shouting personal and insulting remarks. Tempers rise and the quarrelers come to blows. An angry person becomes destructive, breaking furniture and other objects. A man in a towering rage is violent; he may attack, injure, or even kill his antagonist.

On the social level the result of a quarrel is strained or broken interpersonal relations. Persons who have had an altercation may not speak to each other. A hostile, antagonistic, frame of mind remains.

Hostility is not limited to individuals but spreads to the groups with which individuals are identified. A man is identified with his family, community, nation; with his team, club, race, occupation, labor union, religion. He is loyal to these groups and promotes their welfare rather than that of opposing groups. Frustration and conflict among groups may lead to group aggression—to strikes and war.

Conditions Which Arouse Expressions of Anger. In everyday life there are many frustrations, conflicts, irritations and annoyances which lead to retaliative behavior and outbursts of anger.

> Gates (1926) has reported a study in which, during one week, fifty-one women students kept records of their experiences of anger or extreme irritation. Among the many concrete causes of anger were mentioned: unjust accusations, insulting and sarcastic remarks, contradictions, criticisms, scoldings, unwelcome advice, others who "know too much," being bossed by parents or friends, being teased, having work left undone by someone, having to wait for friends, not being invited to a party, being shoved or stepped on, having hat pushed off, having one's seat taken, the sight of others being rude or unjust, disobedience of children, having a request refused, spilling the ink, being locked out, wrong phone number, having a radio or typewriter that doesn't work, umbrella or fountain pen or money lost, clothes injured, glasses or watch broken, hair that wouldn't stay up, light that went out, making a fumble in dressing or sewing, dog that refused to obey, elevator or bus too slow, study or sleep interrupted, store not open, physical pain, unsatisfied hunger. This list recalls Cason's (1930) classification of annoyances and irritations.

Gates found that *persons* rather than *things* were reported as the cause of anger in 115 out of 145 instances. Thwarting an impulse of self-assertion was the most frequently mentioned cause of anger. A depreciating or insulting remark or incident which lowered the level of self-esteem usually aroused anger or at least an attitude of resentment.

The impulses which were experienced or expressed during anger, according to the reports, were these:

Impulses	*N*
To make verbal retort	53
To do physical injury to offender (to slap pinch, shake, strike, choke, push, step on, scratch, shoot, beat, throw out of window, kill, tear to pieces, throw something at, spank)	40
To injure inanimate objects	20
To run away, leave the room[1]	12
To cry, scream, swear	10

The figures at the right indicate the frequency with which an impulse was mentioned. Other impulses which have frequencies of less than ten are not listed above. The list shows that retaliative behavior is the most frequently mentioned. Emotional diffusiveness (crying, screaming, swearing) is relatively infrequent with mature individuals.

Retaliative Behavior during Anger. Retaliative behavior was mentioned by Goodenough (1931*b*) as the most frequent manifestation of anger in the developing child. As the child grows older the initial diffuse emotional excitement becomes, during anger, increasingly retaliative. See pages 165-6.

A five-year-old boy at the dinner table played with his food, eating nothing except the mayonnaise on his lettuce. He asked for a second helping of salad dressing and was told to eat first the vegetables and meat upon his plate. To make matters worse the maid brought in the salad dressing and held a spoonful of it over his lettuce. When the dressing was taken back to the kitchen, the child cried; it was something he wanted, and the sight of the desired object, followed by its withdrawal, was strongly frustrating. He said in an angry voice, "I'll throw my plate on the floor," and held the food-covered plate in the air as if to throw it. This behavior was observed by those present without comment. Presently he thought better of his action and put the plate down on the table with the words, "anyway, I won't eat my lettuce."

This last remark was retaliative inasmuch as the boy's parents had wanted him to eat and refusing to do so was a way of "getting even" with them. Note also the destructive impulse appearing in the boy's retaliative behavior.

[1]Avoidance during emotional excitement is ordinarily regarded as a sign of fear; but on the basis of these reports we conclude that avoidance may also occur in anger as a mark of resentment. This form of avoidance, however, is not an impulsive escape from a dangerous object but rather a deliberate act of retaliation.

The resentment and retaliative feelings children harbor toward thwarting adults are brought out beautifully in the following lines. They are part of an endless chant of a four-year-old boy, a declaration of independence from adults and an impulse to harm those who thwart him.[1]

He will just do nothing at all,
He will just sit there in the noonday sun.
And when they speak to him, he will not answer them,
Because he does not care to.
He will stick them with spears and put them in the garbage.
When they tell him to eat his dinner, he will just laugh at them,
And he will not take his nap, because he does not care to.
He will just sit there in the noonday sun.
He will go away and play with the Panda.
And when they come to look for him
He will put spikes in their eyes and put them in the garbage,
And put the cover on.
He will not go out in the fresh air or eat his vegetables
Or make wee-wee for them, and he will get as thin as a marble.
He will do nothing at all.
He will just sit there in the noonday sun.

Retaliation may take the form of performing some act which has been forbidden by a person in authority. For example, a boy of three violently mussed his freshly brushed hair with both hands when his mother refused him permission to go to a playmate's home. A boy of seven whose mother insisted that he dress himself before coming to the table rushed violently to the table, caught hold of the cloth, and jerked it to the floor, breaking the dishes and glassware. A child of two, when thwarted, ran to the davenport, dragged off the cushions and flung them to the floor, screaming violently during the act.

The hostile behavior that results from frustration and painful stimulation has been discussed with further details in a previous chapter and will not be reviewed here. See pages 325-8.

Anger and Aggressive Behavior. Aggressive behavior is not necessarily emotional. Aggression is often planned, rational, calm, intrinsically motivated. But anger is a basic emotional reaction. Anger occurs when an action or plan is frustrated, when seom desire is blocked, or pride injured by an insult. The thwarting of aggressive behavior can itself heighten anger and lead to rage.

In warfare the aggressive action against an enemy is planned, deliberate, rational. The planners and the men at the front may or may not

[1]These lines, recorded by a young mother, are quoted from *The New Yorker* as condensed in *The Reader's Digest*, 1940, 36, 73.

experience genuine anger. Actually, however, the course of warfare may occasion almost every emotion that is possible to human nature.

The recurrence of great wars, each more devastating than the last, engenders a growing opposition to the display of hostile emotions in combat. As Cannon (1929) has put it:

> War has become too horrible; it is conducted on too stupendous a scale of carnage and expenditure; it destroys too many of the treasured achievements of the race; it interferes too greatly with consecrated efforts to benefit all mankind by discovery and invention; it involves too much suffering among peoples not directly concerned in the struggle; it is too vastly at variance with the methods of fair dealing that have been established between man and man; the human family has become too closely knit to allow some of its members to bring upon themselves and all the rest poverty and distress and a long heritage of bitter hatred and resolution to seek revenge.

This was written after World War I and before World War II.

The problem of eliminating human warfare is too complex to be solved by any one man. The elimination of war will require the cooperation of many persons who are specialists in the social disciplines: government, law, history, economics, political science, psychology, education, military science, and other fields. The psychologist's role in this cooperative endeavor is to portray human nature accurately and to show how human behavior can be controlled and modified.

CONCLUSION

To understand the feelings and emotions of individuals it is necessary to consider their weltanschauung as well as the particular environmental situation that elicits an affective reaction. To a high degree feelings and emotions are idiosyncratic, depending upon the particular situation that induces them. The cultural and social environments of civilized man, as well as past individual experiences, play dominant roles in determining attitudes, moods, sentiments, emotions and motives.

Underlying all affective processes are attitudes, habits, beliefs, motives, and the dynamic interplay of such determinants. These determinants always operate within a cognitive framework, or structure.

Of major importance are attitudes of self-regard and the self-seeking motivations. Self-regarding attitudes of individuals are often generalized to include the groups to which an individual belongs. Frustrations and conflicts arise in intergroup relations, as well as interpersonal relations, in dealing with particular environmental situations. The importance of cognitive determinants of emotions has been recognized by Arnold, Lazarus, Leeper, Pribram, Schachter, and many other psychologists.

Man shares with other animals the basic biological needs, motives and emotions which are revealed in civilized life in accordance with cultural and social restrictions. Among such basic biological determinants are the need to escape from danger and to defend one's life, the need for mating and care of young, the capture and ingestion of food, defense of territory and of property.

In this final chapter we have considered: basic attitudes, motives, feelings and emotions arising from self-regard; love, and sex; fear and anxiety; anger, violence and aggression. Equally important, and considered in other chapters, are humor and laughter, joy and sorrow, weeping, disappointment, grief, shame, feelings of guilt, and others. The outward manifestation of all feelings and emotions differs with the sociocultural environment and with an individual's past experience. But there are basic, biologically grounded, patterns of activity that are common to all mankind, in all places and times, and that are shared with other creatures struggling to survive on the planet Earth.

READING SUGGESTIONS

For a background in anthropology I recommend C. Kluckhohn's *Mirror for Man* (1949). An important work on emotion is: C. E. Izard, *The Face of Emotion* (which appeared after completion of the present manuscript). The book contains data on the cross-cultural studies of facial expressions during emotional behavior.

There is an immense literature on social psychology. For orientation I suggest G. Murphy's article entitled, "Social Motivation," in G. Lindzey (ed.), *Handbook of Social Psychology* (1954). A special work of merit is J. W. Atkinson's *Motives in Fantasy, Action, and Society* (1958).

The twentieth volume of the *Nebraska Symposium on Motivation* (1971-1972) will contain papers on the special topic of aggression.

General Conclusion

If there is one general conclusion which emerges more conspicuously than any other from this survey of feelings and emotions, it is that these processes are exceedingly complex. They are so complex that to discover a semblance of order within the observed facts the man of science must consider them from several different points of view and must clearly demarcate each line and area of approach. This I have done in the faith that the more views we have of any complex event the greater will be our understanding.

Perhaps the most basic postulate I have made is that an emotion is a unitary event in nature which can be described in diverse ways from different points of view. Several points of view are of primary importance to the student of psychology. First, there is the standpoint of the experiencing individual. An emotion is a conscious experience—at least with human beings—which is expressed outwardly in behavior. Feelings and emotions are *conscious* events which can be reported and the conditions of their occurrence analyzed. Second, there is the behavioral point of view. Animals, including human beings, reveal clear-cut expressions of emotion in behavior. Patterns of emotional behavior can be observed objectively and the intraorganic and environmental conditions of their occurrence can be determined. Third, the physiologist, and in particular the neurophysiologist, can observe and study the internal bodily changes that occur during emotional excitement. This aspect of emotion is highly important in any attempt to understand how the bodily mechanism works during emotional crises. Fourth, there is the standpoint of psychobiological developement. In the nineteenth century Darwin taught us to view man and his emotions as a product of organic evolution. Eons of development have occurred before birth. The frustrations, conflicts, satisfactions, hopes and fears, that arise during an individual's life cycle leave an imprint that modulates human action. But the modulation starts from innate capacities. Finally, there is the viewpoint of social psychology.

No single view of emotion is fully adequate. An eclectic approach is needed to avoid superficiality. Highly important in any account is an understanding of an individual's cognitive frame of reference—how he views the world and his place in it, his beliefs, attitudes, and motives. Equally important is a knowledge of psychodynamics—of the stresses, strains, and forces that underlie and control the course of human action.

What Is an Emotion? An emotion may be defined as a strongly visceralized, affective disturbance, originating within the psychological situation, and revealing itself in bodily changes, in behavior, and in conscious experience. This definition can be extended to include the persisting conditions that determine emotion. When, for instance, we speak of an emotionally disturbed child we imply a persisting state of disturbance within the individual.

This extended definition has utility in studies of emotional development. It is useful in considering questions like these: What produces emotional disturbances? What is their influence upon health? How does an individual make adjustment to emotional conflicts? What is the end result of emotional disturbance in terms of adjustment and development? What is the role of emotion in social behavior?

The extended definition is useful in the field of psychodynamics. Here a distinction must be drawn between the phenomena of emotion and underlying dynamics. As a phenomenon, emotion is initiated by perception, memory, fantasy, expectation, or other psychological event; it is *psychological* in origin. So far as we can observe or feel an emotion it is a contemporary event. In terms of the underlying dynamics (which we infer), an emotion is produced by frustration, conflict, painful stimulation and other factors of stress, by expectation, release of tension, and related dynamic conditions.

Within the broad context of the present study, an emotion, as process, is both cause and effect, both a determinant and an event that is determined. The emotional process is determined by a variety of conditions and circumstances. As students of emotion and motivation we must search for these determinants. They are found in the dynamic interplay of motivating conditions. The emotional process is also a causal factor in the organization of attitudes, motives, sentiments, traits of personality, and similar dispositions.

The emotional process is thus a central figure in psychology. Motivation is beyond doubt the broader concept. I have argued that all behavior is motivated in the sense of being causally determined but no one has argued that all behavior is emotionally disturbed! To understand a particular feeling one must turn to the motivating conditions as well as to the underlying bodily state and to past experience of the subject.

Can Emotions Be Distinguished by Their Intraorganic Sources? It is easy to assume that different emotions can be distinguished and classified in terms of their intraorganic sources. But if we limit consideration to the physiological drives and biochemical conditions, we soon discover that this approach is limited and not fully adequate.

In the primary appetites—hunger, thirst, fatigue, somnolence, the sexual appetite, air hunger, the eliminative appetites, etc.—the immediate source of motivation is intraorganic. But emotions have a wider field of origin than that: in emotions there is always an environmental factor (present or past) in the causation. Emotions arise from the total psychological situation, including both intraorganic and environmental factors.

Emotional disturbances arise from extreme excitement, from frustration and conflict, from stress and pain, as well as from satisfaction. If we attempt to define an emotion in terms of its specific underlying appetite, we run into difficulties the nature of which was illustrated by sexual emotions. There are emotions of sexual excitement and satisfaction but there are many kinds of sexual frustration: jealousy, loss of mate, the conflict of romantic love, etc. Differences among these and related emotional states can best be described in terms of the inducing situations and not simply as frustrations of the sexual appetite or denials of love.

How, then, can these forms of emotion be distinguished from each other if not on an intraorganic basis? The answer is that they can be distinguished in terms of the inducing situation and the response of the organism. In fear, the external situation is one which threatens harm (pain, injury, death, social humiliation) and the organism's response is an escape or an attempted escape. If escape is blocked, the fear can become intensified into terror. In anger, some motive is frustrated and this frustration is met by hostile attack. The organism turns toward the frustrating agent to remove or destroy it. If he is highly motivated but unable to reach the enemy, anger heightens into rage. In the agony which results from injury or in milder forms of painful excitement, the organism makes aimless, uncoordinated movements.

Thus, it is the situation-response relationship which enables us to distinguish different forms of emotional behavior, and not merely the internal bodily state. This principle can be further illustrated by another group of affective processes—the *social feelings and emotions.*

Feelings of inferiority and personal pride rest upon the individual's comparison of himself with others in some respect. Feelings of remorse and the sense of guilt rest upon the individual's evaluation of his conduct in terms of standards derived from the social group. Feelings of shame are relative to the customs and taboos of the culture in which he lives. Feelings and emotions of embarrassment depend upon violating the rules and customs in a social situation. These and other social feelings are mentioned to show that basic distinctions are made in terms of the social situation and the individual's response thereto and not in terms of the intraorgabic processes.

In general, if we wish to distinguish the different forms of emotional behavior, a common-sense analysis of the inducing situation and the individual's reactions thereto, is closer to psychological reality than a strictly physiological or neurological view. Feelings and emotions are commonly described in cognitive, meaningful, terms. The course of emotional development is described in terms of past experience—previous emotional events and crises which may have resulted in the formation of beliefs, attitudes, habits, traits of personality, motives, and related dispositions.

Organization and Disorganization in Behavior and Personality. I have emphasized the view that an emotion is a *disturbed* process or state within the individual. This was recognized a century ago by Darwin in his evolutionary account of emotional expressions. According to Darwin, bodily structures and functions have been evolved because of their adaptive utility in the struggle for existence.

The struggle for survival does not always run smoothly. There are two aspects: success or failure; adaptive behavior or injury and death. Darwin saw many forms of behavior, including emotional expressions, as having adaptive value but he also recognized that some emotional expressions have no obvious adaptive utility. They are expressions of disturbed activity.

Nature is replete with examples of persisting adaptive behavior which is relatively free from disturbances: the beaver persists in building a dam; animals travel miles to the watering places and to the salt licks; birds persist in building a nest until completed; birds feed their young and migrate to avoid the cold and food shortages of winter and profit from other feeding grounds in spring and summer. But nature is also replete with examples of attack and defense, of fighting with tooth and claw, of injury, bloodshed, and death. Adaptive behavior is thwarted and disorganization, disruption, is expressed in the outcries of pain and struggle.

The countless activities of everyday life are usually well organized. The individual carries them out in a smoothly integrated manner. Occasionally, however, organized activity is disorganized by circumstances within the psychological situation. This disruption of behavior is not necessarily emotional in character; a non-emotional distraction or disorientation may disturb the activity in progress. The disruption is an emotional one if the individual is so acutely upset that his behavioral disorganization is accompanied by a disturbance in the functioning of bodily structures regulated by the autonomic nervous system—heart and blood vessels, lungs, the sweat glands, the salivary and gastric glands, the adrenals, and others.

Emotional behavior is *disturbed* behavior. It may be more or less disturbed, varying within wide limits from the mildest annoyance or satisfaction to the most severe emotional seizure.

Emotional disorganization shows itself in behavior in a variety of ways. It may appear as a disruption of the activity in progress when emotion arises, as vocalization and aimless movement, as interference with the process of learning, as a loss of precision in carrying out skilled activities, as a well-marked series of changes in the functioning of glands and smooth muscles which are brought about through the autonomic nervous system, and, in general, as a regression from cerebrally controlled activities to those which are regulated at lower neural levels.

When emotion is regarded as a persisting state, rather than an event or process, a temporal dimension of analysis is brought into the picture. During his life cycle the individual develops relatively stable interests and aversions, attitudes, habits, traits of personality, sentiments, motives, and other dispositions, which serve to regulate and control his activities. His frustrations, painful experiences, conflicts of motives, and other thwartings, develop states of persisting stress and disorganization that may affect his health.

From the point of view of mental hygiene it is important to regard the developing personality in the light of persisting states of disorganization—anxieties, feelings of guilt and remorse, attitudes of personal inferiority, etc.—and to look for possible adjustments that can be made between a person and his social and physical environments.

The Individual and Social Problems. The investigation of the individual is a central task of psychology. In spite of the diversity of facts, psychological interpretations converge upon the individual as the chief object of investigation. There are not two individuals, a mind plus a body, but only one. This single individual possesses the attributes which the available facts compel the psychologist to impute to him.

The study of emotion throws light upon the individual. The individual feels pleased and displeased, experiences rage, fear, disgust, joy, grief, and other emotions. These emotions are revealed in conscious experience, in behavior and through internal bodily changes.

The affective development of an individual is simply that phase of his development which is determined by the influence of affective processes. The story of an individual's affective development includes the history of his interests, aversions, aesthetic tastes, from infancy to adulthood, and an account of the factors which have produced them, of conflict states and neuroses, of attitudes and motives including prejudices and tender spots within the personality. Affective development is simply the development of the individual insofar as it is related to the affective processes.

This development normally proceeds within a sociocultural setting. An individual's character and personality are determined by continual interaction between the developing organism and its environment.

In western society man is confronted with important social problems that have arisen from the technological revolution. We know what they are: the threat of nuclear war and total destruction, the exploding human population which brings poverty and hunger, the problems of racial conflict and conflicting national interests and needs, crime and violence in the cities, the pollution of the physical environment, the threat of government by dictators who are unstable or insane, and others.

In facing these problems a humanist must have a realistic appraisal of the needs, desires, feelings and emotions, of people. It is important to realize that human nature is rational only in part and that the ultimate destiny of man on this planet may depend on whether or not reason and sanity can dominate behavior.

A constructive solution of any human problem requires a realistic appraisal of human nature. An understanding of emotion and its role in behavior, therefore, is a matter of prime importance. Such an understanding, at least, can help to make us tolerant of the weaknesses and limitations of others.

References

Allport, F. H. *Social psychology*. Boston: Houghton Mifflin. 1924.

Allport, G. W. Attitudes. In C. Murchison (Ed.), *A handbook of social psychology*. Worcester, Mass.: Clark University Press, 1935. Pp. 798-844.

Allport, G. W., & Schanck, R. L. Are attitudes biological or cultural in origin? *Character and Personality,* 1936, 4, 195-205.

Allport, G. W., Vernon, P. E., & Lindzey, G. *Study of values.* Boston: Houghton Mifflin, 1960.

Angier, R. P. The conflict theory of emotion. *American Journal of Psychology,* 1927, 39, 390-401.

Angyal, A. *Foundations for a science of personality,* New York: The Commonwealth Fund, 1941.

Annals of the New York Academy of Sciences: Experimental approaches to the study of emotional behavior. Vol. 159, 3, 621-1121. Edited by P. D. Albertson, M. Krauss, K. Sussell, & E. Tobach. New York: Published by the Academy, July 30, 1969.

Arnheim, R. Untersuchungen zur Lehre von der Gestalt: Experimentell-psychologische Untersuchungen zum Ausdrucksproblem. *Psychologische Forschung,* 1928, 11, 2-132.

Arnold. M. B. Physiological differentiation of emotional states. *Psychological Review,* 1945, 52, 35-48.

Arnold, M. B. An excitatory theory of emotion. In M. L. Reymert (Ed.) *The second international symposium on feelings and emotions.* New York: McGraw-Hill, 1950.

Arnold, M. B. *Emotion and personality: Vol. I. Psychological aspects: Vol. II. Neurological and physiological aspects.* New York: Columbia University Press, 1960.

Arnold, M. B. *Loyola symposium on feelings and emotions.* New York: Academic Press, 1970.

Atkinson, J. W. *Motives in fantasy, action, and society: A method of assessment and study*. Princeton, N. J.: van Nostrand, 1958.

Ax, A. F. The physiological differentiation between fear and anger in humans. *Psychosomatic Medicine,* 1953, 15, 433-442.

Bagby, E. The etiology of phobias. *Journal of Abnormal and Social Psychology,* 1922, 17, 16-18.

Bard, P. The neurohumoral basis of emotional reactions. In C. Murchison (Ed.), *A handbook of general experimental psychology.* Worcester, Mass.: Clark University Press, 1934. (a)

Bard, P. On emotional expression after decortication with some remarks on certain theoretical views. *Psychological Review,* 1934, 41, 309-329; 424-449. (b)

Bard, P., Central nervous mechanisms for the expression of anger in animals. In M. L. Reymert (Ed.), *Feelings and emotions: The Mooseheart symposium in cooperation with the University of Chicago.* New York: McGraw-Hill, 1950.

Barelare, B., & Richter, C. P. Increased sodium chloride appetite in pregnant rats. *American Journal of Physiology,* 1938, 121, 185-188.

Barker, R., Dembo, T., & Lewin, K. Frustration and regression, an experiment with young children. *University of Iowa Studies: Studies in Child Welfare,* 1941, 18, No. 386.

Bayley, N. A study of fear by means of the psychologalvanic technique. *Psychology Monographs,* 1928, 38, No. 4.

Bayley, N. A study of the crying of infants during mental and physical tests. *Journal of Genetic Psychology,* 1932, 40, 306-329.

Beach, F. A. Instinctive behavior: Reproductive activities. In S. S. Stevens (Ed.), *Handbook of experimental psychology.* New York: John Wiley and Sons, 1951.

Beach, F. A. Characteristics of masculine "sex drive." In M. R. Jones (Ed.), *Nebraska symposium on motivation, 1956.* Lincoln, Nebra.: University of Nebraska Press, 1956.

Beebe-Center, J. G. *The psychology of pleasantness and unpleasantness.* Princeton, N. J.: Van Nostrand, 1932.

Bellows, R. T. Time factors in water drinking in dogs. *American Journal of Physiology,* 1939, 125, 87-97.

Bentley, M. Is "emotion" more than a chapter heading? In C. Murchison, & M. L. Reymert (Eds.), *Feelings and emotions: The Wittenberg symposium.* Worcester, Mass.: Clark University Press, 1928.

Benussi, V. Die Atmungssymptome der Lüge. *Archiv für die gesamte Psychologie,* 1914, 31, 244-273.

Berlyne, D. E. *Conflict, arousal, and curiosity.* New York: McGraw-Hill, 1960.

Berlyne, D. E. *Aesthetics and psychobiology.* New York: Appleton Century-Crofts, 1971.

Bindra, D. Organization in emotional and motivated behavior. *Canadian Journal of Psychology,* 1955, 9, 161-167.

Bindra, D. *Motivation: A systematic reinterpretation.* New York: The Ronald Press, 1959.

Black, P. (Ed.), *Physiological correlates of emotion.* New York: Academic Press, 1970.

Blanton, M. G. The behavior of the human infant during the first thirty days of life. *Psychological Review,* 1917, 24, 456-483.

Blatz, W. E. The cardiac, respiratory, and electrical phenomena involved in the emotion of fear. *Journal of Experimental Psychology,* 1925, 8, 109-132.

Boder, D. P. *I did not interview the dead.* Urbana, Ill.: University of Illinois Press, 1949.

Boissier, J. R., & Simon, P. Evaluation of experimental techniques in the psychopharmacology of emotion. *Annals of the New York Academy of Sciences: Experimental approaches to the study of emotional behavior.* New York: Published by the Academy, 1969. Pp. 898-914.

Borer, K. T. Disappearance of preferences and aversions for sapid solutions in rats ingesting untasted fluids. *Journal of Comparative and Physiological Psychology*, 1968, 65, 213-221.

Borgquist, A. Crying. *American Journal of Psychology*, 1906, 17, 149-205.

Brady, J. V. Emotion and sensitivity of psychoendocrine systems. In D. C. Glass (Ed.), *Neurophysiology and emotion*. New York: The Rockefeller University Press, 1967. Pp. 70-95.

Brady, J. V., Kelly, D., & Plumlee, L. Autonomic and behavioral responses of the rhesus monkey to emotional conditioning. *Annals of the New York Academy of Sciences: Experimental approaches to the study of emotional behavior*. New York: Published by the Academy, 1969. Pp. 959-975.

Bridges, K. M. B. A genetic theory of the emotions. *Journal of Genetic Psychology*, 1930, 37, 514-527.

Bridges, K. M. B. *The social and emotional development of the pre-school child*. London: Kegan Paul, Trench, Trubner, & Co., 1931.

Bridges, K. M. B. Emotional development in early infancy. *Child Development*, 1932, 3, 324-341.

Britt, S. H. *Social psychology of modern life*. New York: Farrar, & Rinehart, 1949.

Broadhurst, P. L. Psychogenetics of emotionality in the rat. *Annals of the New York Academy of Sciences: Experimental approaches to the study of emotional behavior*. New York: Published by the Academy, 1969. Pp. 806-824.

Brown, J. L. Neuro-ethological approaches to the study of emotional behavior: stereotypy and variability. *Annals of the New York Academy of Sciences: Experimental approaches to the study of emotional behavior*. New York: Published by the Academy, 1969. Pp. 1084-1095.

Brown, J. S. *Generalized approach and avoidance responses in relation to conflict behavior*. Unpublished doctoral thesis, Yale University Library, 1940.

Brown, J. S. *The motivation of behavior*. New York: McGraw-Hill, 1961.

Brown, J. S., & Farber, I. E. Emotions conceptualized as intervening variables: With suggestions toward a theory of frustration. *Psychological Bulletin*, 1951, 48, 465-495.

Brown, L. G. *Social psychology: The natural history of human nature*. New York: McGraw-Hill, 1934.

Brunswick, D. The effects of emotional stimuli on the gastro-intestinal tone. *Journal of Comparative Psychology*, 1924, 4, 19-79 & 225-287.

Bull, N. The attitude theory of emotion. *Nervous and Mental Disease Monographs*. New York, 1951.

Burright, R. G., & Kappauf, W. E. Preference threshold of the white rat for sucrose. *Journal of Comparative and Physiological Psychology*, 1963, 56, 171-173.

Cabanac, M. Physiological role of pleasure. *Science*, 1971, 173, 17 September, 1103-1107.

Cameron, N., & Magaret, A. *Behavior pathology*, Boston: Houghton Mifflin, 1951.

Cannon, W. B. The James-Lange theory of emotions: A critical examination and an alternative theory. *American Journal of Psychology*, 1927, 39, 106-124.

Cannon, W. B. *Bodily changes in pain, hunger, fear and rage: An account of recent researches into the function of emotional excitement*. New York: Appleton-Century, 1929. (Second edition)

Cannon, W. B. Again the James-Lange and the thalamic theories of emotion. *Psychological Review*, 1931, 38, 281-295.

Cannon, W. B. Hunger and thirst. In C. Murchison (Ed.), *Handbook of general experimental psychology*. Worcester, Mass.: Clark University press, 1934.

Carmichael, L. An experimental study in the prenatal guinea pig of the origin and development of reflexes and patterns of behavior in relation to the stimulation of specific receptor areas during the period of active fetal life. *Genetic Psychology Monographs,* 1934, 16, 337-491.

Carr, H. A. *Psychology: A study of mental activity*. New York: Longmans, Green & Co., 1925. Pp. 287-308.

Cason, H. Common annoyances: A psychological study of every-day aversions and irritations. *Psychology Monographs,* 1930, 40. No. 182.

Chandler, A. R. *Beauty and human nature: Elements of psychological aesthetics.* New York: Appleton-Century, 1934.

Child, I. L., & Waterhouse, I. K. Frustration and the quality of performance: I. A theoretical statement. *Psychological Review*, 1953, 60, 127-139.

Claparède, E. Feelings and emotions. In C. Murchison, & M. L. Reymert (Eds.), *Feelings and emotions: The Wittenberg symposium.* Worcester, Mass.: Clark University Press, 1928.

Cofer, C. N., & Appley, M. H. *Motivation: Theory and research.* New York: John Wiley & Sons, 1964.

Coghill, G. E. *Anatomy and the problem of behaviour.* New York: Macmillan, 1929.

Coghill, G. E. Integration and motivation of behavior as problems of growth. *Pedagogical Seminar,* 1936, 48, 3-19.

Conner, R. L., Levine, S., Wertheim, G. A. & Cummer, J. F. Hormonal determinants of aggressive behavior. *Annals of the New York Academy of Sciences: Experimental approaches to the study of emotional behavior.* New York: Published by the Academy, 1969. Pp. 760-776.

Cook, S. W. A survey of methods used to produce "experimental neurosis." *American Journal of Psychiatry,* 1939, 95, 1259-1276.

Courts, F. A. Relations between muscular tension and performance. *Psychological Bulletin,* 1942, 39, 347-367.

Craig,W. Why do animals fight? *International Jouranl of Ethics,* 1921, 31 264-278.

Craig, W. A note on Darwin's work on the expression of the emotions in man and animals. *Journal of Abnormal and Social Psychology,* 1921-2, 16, 356-366.

Crespi, L. P. Quantitative variation of incentive and performance in the white rat. *American Journal of Psychology,* 1942, 55, 467-517.

Crespi, L. P. Amount of reinforcement and level of performance. *Psychological Review,* 1944, 51, 341-357.

Crile, G. W. *The origin and nature of the emotions.* Philadelphia: Saunders, 1915.

Cronbach, L. J. *Educational psychology.* New York; Harcourt, Brace, & Co., 1954.

Cronbach, L. J., & Davis, B. M. Belief and desire in wartime. *Journal of Abnormal and Social Psychology,* 1944, 39, 446-458.

Cullen, J. W., & Scarborough, B. B. Effect of a preoperative sugar preference on bar pressing for salt by the adrenalectomized rat. *Journal of Comparative and Physiological Psychology,* 1969, 67, 415-420.

Darrow, C. W. The relation of the galvanic skin reflex recovery curve to reactivity, resistance level, and perspiration. *Journal of General Psychology,* 1932, 7, 261-273.

Darrow, C. W. Emotion as relative functional decortication: The role of conflict. *Psychological review,* 1935, 42, 566-578.

Darrow, C. W. The galvanic skin reflex (sweating) and blood pressure as preparatory and facilitative functions. *Psychological Bulletin,* 1936, 33, 73-94.

Darrow, C. W., & Henry, C. E. Psychophysiology of stress. In *Human factors in undersea warfare.* Washington, D. C.: National Research Council, 1949. Chapter 20.

Darwin, C. *The expression of the emotions in man and animals.* London: John Murray, 1872.

Dashiell J. F. Are there any native emotions? *Psychological Review,* 1928, 35, 310-327.

Davis A. *Let's eat right to keep fit.* New York: Harcourt, Brace, Jovanovich, 1970.

Davis, C. M. Self-selection of diet by newly weaned infants. *American Journal of Diseases of Children,* 1928, 36, 651-679.

Davis, C. M. Results of the self-selection of diets by young children. *Canadian Medical Association Journal,* 1939, 41, 257-261.

Delgado, J. M. R., & Mir, D. Fragmental organization of emotional behavior in the monkey brain. *Annals of the New York Academy of sciences: Experimental appraoches to the study of emotional behavior.* New York: Published by the Academy, 1969. Pp. 731-751.

Delgado J. M. R., Roberts, W. W., & Miller, N. E. Learning motivated by electrical stimulation of the brain. *American Journal of Physiology,* 1954, 179, 587-593.

Denenberg, V. H. Stimulation in infancy, emotional reactivity, and exploratory behavior. In D. C. Glass (Ed.), *Neurophysiology and emotion.* New York: Rockefeller University Press, 1967. Pp. 161-190.

Deutsch, A. (Ed), *The encyclopedia of mental health.* New York: Franklin Watts, 1963. (Six volumes)

Deutsch, J. A., & Jones, A. D. Diluted water: An explanation of the rat's preference for saline. *Journal of Comparative and Physiological Psychology*, 1960, 53, 122-127.

Dewey, J. The theory of emotion: I, Emotional attitudes. *Psychological Review,* 1894, 1, 553-569.

Dewey, J. The theory of emotion: II, The significance of emotions. *Psychological Review,* 1895, 2, 13-32.

Dockeray, F. C. *General psychology.* New York: Prentice-Hall, 1936.

Dollard, J., Doob, L. W., Miller, N. E., Mowrer, O. H., & Sears, R. R. *Frustration and aggression.* New Haven: Yale University Press, 1939.

Duffy, E. An explanation of "emotional" phenomena without the use of the concept "emotion." *Journal of General Psychology,* 1941, 25, 283-293.

Duffy, E. The psychological significance of the concept of "arousal" or "activation." *Psychological Review,* 1957, 64, 265-275.

Duffy, E. *Activation and behavior.* New York: John Wiley & Sons, 1962.

Dunbar, H. F. *Emotions and bodily changes: A survey of literature on psychosomatic interrelationships, 1910-1933.* New York: Columbia University Press, 1935.

Epstein, A. N. Oropharyngeal factors in feeding and drinking. In C. F. Code (Ed.), *Handbook of physiology: Section 6, Alimentary Canal; Food and water intake, Vol. I.* Washington, D. C.: American Physiological Society, 1967. Chapter 15, pp. 197-218.

Eysenck, H. J. The general factor in aesthetic judgements. *British Journal of Psychology,* 1940, 31, 94-102.

Eysenck, H. J. "Type" factors in aesthetic judgements. *British Journal of Psychology,* 1941, 31, 262-270. (a)

Eysenck, H. J. The empirical determination of an aesthetic formula. *Psychological Review*, 1941, 48, 83-92. (b)

Falk, J. L. *Determining changes in vital functions: Ingestion.* In R. D. Myers (Ed.), *Methods in psychobiology: Laboratory techniques in neuropsychology, Vol. 1.* London: Academic Press, 1971. Chapter 10, pp. 301-331.

Faris, E. The concept of social attitudes. *Journal of Applied Sociology,* 1925, 9, 404-409.

Faris, E. Attitudes and behavior. *American Journal of Sociology,* 1928, 34, 271-281.

Festinger, L. *A theory of cognitive dissonance.* Evanston, Illinois: Row, Peterson, 1957.

Foley, J. F. Judgment of facial expression of emotion in the chimpanzee. *Journal of Social Psychology,* 1935, 6, 31-67.

Foster, S. A study of the personality make-up and social setting of fifty jealous children. *Mental Hygiene,* 1927, 11, 53-77.

Frank, J. D. Recent studies of the level of aspiration. *Psychological Bulletin,* 1941, 38, 218-226.

Freeman, G. L. Postural tensions and the conflict situation. *Psychological Review,* 1939, 46, 226-240.

Fulton, J. F. *Physiology of the nervous system.* New York: Oxford University Press, 1938.

Gardiner, H. M., Metcalf, R. C., & Beebe-Center, J. G. *Feeling and emotion: A history of theories.* New York: American Book Company, 1937.

Gates, G. S. An observational study of anger. *Journal of experimental psychology,* 1926, 9, 325-336.

Gauger, M. E. The modifiability of response to taste stimuli in the pre-school child. *Columbia University Contributions to Education, No. 348.* New York: Columbia University, 1929.

Gellhorn, E. *Autonomic regulations: Their significance for physiology, psychology and neuropsychiatry.* New York: Interscience Publishers, 1943.

Gibson, J. J. A critical review of the concept of set in contemporary experimental psychology. *Psychological Bulletin*, 1941, 38, 781-817.

Glass, D. C. (Ed.), *Neurophysiology and emotion: Proceedings of a conference under the auspices of Russell Sage Foundation and The Rockefeller University.* New York: The Rockefeller University Press, 1967.

Goldstein, K. *The organism: A holistic approach to biology derived from pathological data in man.* New York: American Book Company, 1939.

Goldstein, K. *Organismic approach to the problem of motivation.* New York: Transactions of the New York Academy of Sciences, 1947, 9, 218-230.

Goodenough, F. L. The expression of the emotions in infancy. *Child Development,* 1931, 2, 96-101. (a)

Goodenough, F. L. *Anger in young children.* University of Minnesota, Institute of Child Welfare Monograph Series, No. 9. Minneapolis, Minn.: University of Minnesota Press, 1931. (b)

Goodenough, F. L. Expression of the emotions in a blind-deaf child. *Journal of Abnormal and Social Psychology,* 1932, 27, 328-33.

Green, H. H. Perverted appetites. *Physiological Review,* 1925, 5, 336-348.

Grinker, R. R., & Spiegel, J. P. *Men under stress.* Philadelphia: Blakiston, 1945.

Grossman, S. P. *A textbook of physiological psychology*. New York: John Wiley & Sons, 1967.
Guilford, J. P. A study of psychodynamics. *Psychometrika,* 1939, 4, 1-23.
Guilford, J. P. System in the relationships of affective value to frequency and intensity of auditory stimuli. *American Journal of Psychology,* 1954, 67, 691-695.
Guilford, J. P. *Personality*. New York: McGraw-Hill, 1959.
Guthrie, E. R. *The psychology of human conflict: The clash of motives within the individual.* New York: Harper & Brothers, 1938.
Guttman, N. Operant conditioning, extinction, and periodic reinforcement in relation to concentration of sucrose used as reinforcing agent. *Journal of Experimental Psychology,* 1953, 46, 213-224.

Haber, R. N. *Current research in motivation.* New York: Holt, Rinehart, & Winston, 1966. Chapter 7, Conflict, pp. 508-561.
Hall, C. S. Drive and emotionality: Factors associated with adjustment in the rat. *Journal of Comparative Psychology,* 1934, 17, 89-108.
Hall, C. S. Temperament: A survey of animal studies. *Psychological Bulletin,* 1941, 38, 909-943.
Hall, G. S. A study of fears. *American Journal of Psychology,* 1897, 8, 147-249.
Hardy, K. R. An appetitional theory of sexual motivation. *Psychological Review,* 1964, 71, 1-18. (See also: K. R. Hardy. Sexual appetite and sexual drive: A reply. *Psychological Reports* 1965, 17, 11-14.)
Harriman, A. E. The effect of a preoperative preference for sugar over salt upon compensatory salt selection by adrenalectomized rats. *Journal of Nutrition,* 1955, 57, 271-276.
Harris, L. J., Clay, J., Hargreaves, F. J., & Ward, A. Appetite and choice of diet: The ability of the vitamin B deficient rat to discriminate between diets containing and lacking the vitamin. *Proceedings of the Royal Society, Series B (biological sciences),* 1933, 113, 161-190.
Hart, B. *The psychology of insanity*. New York: Macmillan, 1937. (Fourth edition)
Hayworth, D. The social origin and function of laughter. *Psychological Review,* 1928, 35, 367-384.
Hebb, D. O. On the nature of fear. *Psychological Review,* 1946, 53, 259-276. (a)
Hebb, D. O. Emotion in man and animal: An analysis of the intuitive process of recognition. *Psychological Review,* 1946, 53, 88-106. (b)
Hebb, D. O. *The organization of behavior: A neuropsychological theory.* New York: John Wiley & Sons, 1949.
Hebb, D. O. Drives and the C. N. S. (Conceptual Nervous System). *Psychological Review,* 1955, 62, 243-254.
Higginson, G. D. The after-effects of certain emotional situations upon maze learning among white rats. *Journal of Comparative Psychology,* 1930, 10, 1-10.
Hilgard, E. R., & Marquis, D. G. *Conditioning and learning.* New York: Appleton-Century, 1940.
Hilliard, A. L. *The forms of value: The extension of a hedonistic axiology* New York: Columbia University Press, 1950.
Hodge, F. A. The emotions in a new role. *Psychological Review,* 1935, 42, 555-565.
Hollingworth, H. L. Effect and affect in learning. *Psychological Review,* 1931, 38, 153-159.

Hollingworth, L. S. *The psychology of the adolescent.* New York: Appleton-Century, 1928.

Hoskins, R. G. *The tides of life: The endocrine glands in bodily adjustment.* New York: W. W. Norton, 1933.

Howard, D. T. A functional theory of the emotions. In C. Murchison & M. L. Reymert (Eds.). *Feelings and emotions: the Wittenberg symposium.* Worcester, Mass.: Clark University Press, 1928.

Hull, C. L. The goal gradient hypothesis and maze learning. *Psychological Review,* 1932, 39, 25-43.

Hull, C. L. The rat's speed-of-locomotion gradient in the approach to food. *Journal of Comparative Psychology* 1934, 17, 393-422.

Hunt, J. McV. The effects of infant feeding-frustration upon adult hoarding in the albino rat. *Journal of Abnormal and Social Psychology,* 1941, 36, 338-360.

Hunt, J. McV., Schlosberg, H., Solomon, R. L., & Stellar, E. Studies of the effects of infantile experience on adult behavior in rats. I, Effects of infantile feeding frustration on adult hoarding. *Journal of Comparative and Physiological Psychology,* 1947, 40, 291-304.

Hunt, W. A. Ambiguity of descriptive terms for feeling and emotion. *American Journal of Psychology,* 1935, 47, 165-166.

Hunt, W. A. A critical review of current approaches to affectivity. *Psychological Bulletin,* 1939, 36, 807-828. (a)

Hunt, W. A. "Body jerk" as a concept in describing infant behavior. *Journal of Genetic Psychology,* 1939, 55, 215-220. (b)

Inbau, F. E. *Lie detection and criminal interrogation.* Baltimore: Williams & Wilkins, 1942.

Irwin, O. C. The organismic hypothesis and differentiation of behavior. *Psychological Review,* 1932, 39, 128-146; 189-202; 387-393.

Izard, C. E. *The face of emotion.* New York: Appleton-Century-Crofts, 1971.

James, W. *The principles of psychology.* New York: Holt, 1913. (First edition, 1890)

Jersild, A. T. *Child psychology.* New York: Prentice-Hall, 1954. (Fourth edition)

Jersild, A. T., & Holmes, F. B. Children's fears. *Child Development Monographs,* 1935, No. 20.

Jersild, A. T., Markey, F. V., & Jersild, C. L. *Children's fears, dreams, wishes, daydreams, likes, dislikes, pleasant and unpleasant memories.* New York: Teachers College, Columbia University, 1933.

Jones, H. E. The retention of conditioned emotional reactions in infancy. *Journal of Genetic Psychology,* 1930, 37, 485-498.

Jones, H. E. The conditioning of overt emotional responses. *Journal of Educational Psychology,* 1931, 22, 127-130.

Jones, H. E., & M. C. A study of fear. *Childhood Education,* 1928, 5, 136-143.

Jones, M. C. A laboratory study of fear: The case of Peter. *Pedagogical Seminar,* 1924, 31, 308-315. (a)

Jones, M. C. The elimination of children's fears. *Journal of Experimental Psychology,* 1924, 7, 382-390. (b)

Kanner, L. Judging emotions from facial expression. *Psychological Monographs,* 1931, 41, No. 3.

Kappauf, W. E., Burright, R. G., & DeMarco, W. Sucrose-quinine mixtures which are isohedonic for the rat. *Journal of Comparative and Physiological Psychology,* 1963, 56, 138-143.

Katz, D., & Braly, K. Racial stereotypes of one hundred college students. *Journal of Abnormal and Social Psychology,* 1933, 28, 280-290.

Kaufman, I. C., & Rosenblum, L. A. Effects of separation from mother on the emotional behavior of infant monkeys. *Annals of the New York Academy of Sciences: Experimental approaches to the study of emotional behavior* . New York: Published by the Academy, 1969, 159, 3. Pp. 681-695.

Kempf, E. J. *Psychopathology.* St. Louis: C. V. Mosby, 1920.

Kempf, E. J. Physiology of attitude: Emergence of ego-organization. *Medical Record,* 1935, 141, 136*f*; 142, 15*f*. (Published in fourteen successive parts)

Kenderdine, M. Laughter in the pre-school child. *Child Development,* 1931, 2, 228-230.

Kety, S. S. Psychoendocrine systems and emotion: Biological aspects. In D. C. Glass (Ed.), *Neurophysiology and emotion.* New York: The Rockefeller University Press, 1967.

Kinsey, A. C., Pomeroy, W. B., & Martin, C. E. *Sexual behavior in the human male.* Philadelphia: W. B. Saunders, 1948.

Klineberg, O. Emotional expression in Chinese literature. *Journal of Abnormal and Social Psychology,* 1938, 33, 517-520.

Klineberg, O. *Social psychology.* New York: Holt, 1940.

Kling, C. The role of the parasympathetics in emotions. *Psychological Review,* 1933, 40, 368-380.

Kluckhohn, C. *Mirror for man: The relation of anthropology to modern life.* New York: McGraw-Hill, 1949.

Kniep, E. H., Morgan, W. L., & Young, P. T. Studies in affective psychology: XI Individual differences in affective reaction to odors. XII. The relation between age and affective reaction to odors. *American Journal of Psychology,* 1931, 43, 406-421.

Koh, S. D., & Teitelbaum, P. Absolute behavioral taste thresholds in the rat. *Journal of Comparative and Physiological Psychology,* 1961, 54, 223-229.

Kohts, N. *Infant ape and human child.* Scientific memoirs of the Museum Darwinianum in Moscow, 1935. (In Russian)

Kruse, H. D., Orent, E. R., & McCollum, E. V. Symptomatology resulting from magnesium deprivation. *Journal of Biological Chemistry,* 1932, 96, 519-539.

Laird, D. A. Changes in motor control and individual variations under the influence of "razzing." *Journal of Experimental Psychology,* 1923, 6, 236-246.

Landis, C. Studies of emotional reactions: II. General behavior and facial expression. *Journal of Comparative Psychology,* 1924, 4, 447-501.

Landis, C. Psychology and the psychogalvanic reflex. *Psychological Review,* 1930, 37, 381-398.

Landis, C., & associates. *Sex in development.* New York: P. B. Hoeber, 1940.

Landis, C., & Hunt, W. A. *The startle pattern.* New York: Farrar & Rinehart, 1939.

LaPiere, R. T. The sociological significance of measurable attitudes. *American Sociological Review,* 1938, 3, 175-189.

Larson, J. A. The cardio-pneumo-psychogram in deception. *Journal of Experimental Psychology,* 1923, 6, 420-454.

Larson, J. A. *Lying and its detection: A study of deception and deception tests.* Chicago: University of Chicago Press, 1932.

Lashley, K. S. The thalamus and emotion. *Psychological Review,* 1938, 45, 42-61.

Lazarus, R. S., Deese, J., & Osler, S. F. Review of research on effects of psychological stress upon performance. *Research Bulletin, 51-28, Human Resources Research Center.* Lackland Air Force Base, San Antonio, Texas, December 1951.

Leeper, R. W. A motivational theory of emotion to replace "Emotion as disorganized response." *Psychological Review,* 1948, 55, 5-21.

Leeper, R. W. Some needed developments in the motivational theory of emotion. In D. Levine (Ed.), *Nebraska symposium on Motivation, 1965.* Lincoln, Nebra.: University of Nebraska Press, 1965. Pp. 25-122.

Leeper, R. W. The motivational and perceptual properties of emotion as indicating their fundamental character and role. In M. B. Arnold (Ed.), *Loyola symposium on feelings and emotions.* New York: Academic Press, 1970.

Lehmann, A. *Die Hauptgesetze des menschlichen Gefühlslebens.* Leipzig: C. R. Reisland, 1914.

Lewin, K. Gesetz und Experiment in der Psychologie. *Philosophische Zeitschrift für Forschung und Aussprache,* 1927, 375-421. Berlin-Schlachtensee: Weltkreis Verlag.

Lewin, K. *Die psychologische Stiuation bei Lohn und Strafe.* Leipzig: S. Hirzel, 1931.

Lewin, K. Environmental forces. In C. Murchison (Ed.), *A handbook of child psychology.* Worcester, Mass.: Clark University Press, 1933.

Lewin, K. *A dynamic theory of personality: Selected papers.* New York: McGraw-Hill, 1935. (Translated by D. K. Adams & K. E. Zener)

Liddell, H. S. The experimental neurosis and the problem of mental disorder. *American Journal of Psychiatry,* 1938, 94, 1035-1041.

Lindsley, D. B. Emotion. In S. S. Stevens (Ed.), *Handbook of experimental psychology.* New York: John Wiley and Sons, 1951.

Lindsley, D. B. Psychophysiology and motivation. In M. R. Jones (Ed.). *Nebraska symposium on motivation, 1957.* Lincoln, Nebra.: University of Nebraska Press, 1957. Pp. 44-105.

Lund, F. H. The psychology of belief. *Journal of Abnormal and Social Psychology,* 1925-1926, 20, 63-81; 174-196.

Lund, F. H. Why do we weep? *Journal of Social Psychology,* 1930, 1, 136-151.

Lund, F. H. *Emotions: Their psychological, physiological and educative implications.* New York: Ronald Press, 1939.

Luria, A. R. *The nature of human conflicts, or emotion, conflict and will.* New York: Liveright, 1932. (Translated from Russian by W. H. Gantt)

MacCurdy, J. T. *The psychology of emotion, morbid and normal.* New York: Harcourt, Brace, & Company, 1925.

MacLean, P. D. Psychosomatic disease and the "visceral brain": Recent developments bearing on the Papez theory of emotion. *Psychosomatic Medicine,* 1949, 11, 338-353.

McCarthy, D. A note on vocal sounds. *Pedagogical Seminar,* 1929, 36, 482-484.

McCleary, R. A. Taste and post-ingestion factors in specific hunger behavior. *Journal of Comparative and Physiological Psychology,* 1953, 46, 411-421.

McClelland, D. C. *Personality.* New York: William Sloane Associates, 1951.

McClelland, D. C. *Studies in motivation.* New York: Appleton-Century-Crofts, 1955.

McClelland, D. C., Atkinson, J. W., Clark, R. A., & Lowell, E. L. *The achievement motive.* New York: Appleton-Century-Crofts, 1953.

McDougall, W. *The group mind.* New York: G. P. Putman's Sons, 1920.

McDougall, W. *An introduction to social psychology.* Boston: Luce & Co., 1926.

McGinnies, E. Emotionality and perceptual defense. *Psychological Review,* 1949, 56, 244-251.

McKinney, F. *Psychology and personal adjustment: Students' introduction to mental hygiene.* New York: John Wiley & Sons, 1949. (Second edition)

Mach, E. *Contributions to the analysis of the sensations.* Chicago: Open Court Publishing Company, 1910. (Translated by C. M. Williams)

Maier, N. R. F. *Studies of abnormal behavior in the rat: I. The neurotic pattern and an analysis of the situation which produces it.* New York: Harper & Brothers, 1939.

Maier, N. R. F. *Frustration: The study of behavior without a goal.* New York: McGraw-Hill, 1949.

Malinowski, B. *Sex and repression in savage society.* New York: Harcourt, Brace & Company, 1927.

Malinowski, B. Man's culture and man's behavior. *Sigma Xi Quarterly,* 1941, 29, 182-196.

Mandler, G. The interruption of behavior. In D. Levine (Ed.), *Nebraska symposium on motivation, 1964.* Lincoln, Nebra.: University of Nebraska Press, 1964. Pp. 163-219.

Marston, W. M. Systolic blood pressure symptoms of deception. *Journal of Experimental Psychology,* 1917, 2, 117-163.

Martineau, P. *Motivation in advertising.* New York: McGraw-Hill, 1957.

Marx, M. H. Some relations between frustration and drive. In M. R. Jones (Ed.), *Nebraska symposium on motivation, 1956.* Lincoln, Nebra.: University of Nebraska Press, 1956.

Maslow, A. H. *Motivation and personality.* New York: Harper & Brothers, 1954.

Maslow, A. H. Deficiency motivation and growth motivation. In M. R. Jones (Ed.), *Nebraska symposium on motivation, 1955.* Lincoln, Nebra.: University of Nebraska Press, 1955.

Masserman, J. H. *Principles of dynamic psychiatry: Including an integrative approach to abnormal and clinical psychology.* Philadelphia: W. B. Saunders, 1947.

Melzack, R. Brain mechanisms and emotion. In D. C. Glass (Ed.), *Neurophysiology and emotion.* New York: Rockefeller University Press, 1967.

Melzack, R. The role of early experience in emotional arousal. *Annals of the New York Academy of Sciences: Experimental approaches to the study of emotional behavior.* New York: Published by the Academy, 1969, 159, 3. Pp. 721-730.

Menzies, R. Conditioned vasomotor responses in human subjects. *Journal of Psychology,* 1937, 4, 75-120.

Miller, G. A., Galanter, E. H., & Pribram, K. H. *Plans and the structure of behavior.* New York: Holt and Company, 1960.

Miller, N. E. Some reflections on the law of effect produce a new alternative to drive reduction. In M. R. Jones (Ed.), *Nebraska symposium on motivation.* Lincoln, Nebra.: University of Nebraska Press, 1963.

Miller, N. E. Psychosomatic effects of specific types of training. *Annals of the New York Academy of Sciences: Experimental approaches to the study of emotional behavior.* New York: Published by the Academy, 1969, 159, 3. Pp. 1025-1040.

Miller, N. E., & Kessen, M. L. Reward effects of food via stomach fistula compared with those of food via mouth. *Journal of Comparative and Physiological Psychology,* 1952, 45, 555-564.

Mook, D. G. Oral and postingestional determinants of the intake of various solutions in rats with esophageal fistulas. *Journal of Comparative and Physiological Psychology,* 1963, 56, 645-659.

Morey, R. Upset in emotions. *Journal of Social Psychology*, 1940, 12, 333-356.

Morgan, J. J. B. *Keeping a sound mind.* New York: Macmillan, 1934.

Mosso, A. *Fear.* New York: Longmans, Green & Company, 1896.

Mowrer, O. H. A stimulus-response analysis of anxiety and its role as a reinforcing agent. *Psychological Review,* 1939, 46, 553-565.

Murdock, G. P. *Our primitive contemporaries.* New York: Macmillan, 1935.

Murphy, G. Social motivation. In G. Lindzey (Ed.), *Handbook of social psychology*. Vol. II. Cambridge, Mass.: Addison-Wesley, 1954.

Murphy, G., Murphy, L. B., & Newcomb, T. M. *Experimental social psychology: An interpretation of research upon the socialization of the individual.* New York: Harper & Brothers, 1937.

Murray, H. A. *Explorations in personality: A clinical and experimental study of fifty men of college age.* New York: Oxford University Press, 1938.

Murray, J. A. H. *A new English dictionary on historical principles: Founded mainly on the materials collected by the Philosophical Society.* Oxford & New York: Macmillan, 1888. (Article, "Emotion")

Nafe, J. P. An experimental study of the affective qualities. *American Journal of Psychology,* 1924, 35, 507-544.

Nafe, J. P. The pressure, pain, and temperature senses. In C. Murchison (Ed.), *A handbook of general experimental psychology.* Worcester, Mass.: Clark University Press, 1934.

Nowlis, V. The development and modification of motivational systems in personality. In M. R. Jones (Ed.), *Current theory and research in motivation.* Lincoln, Nebra.: University of Nebraska Press, 1953. Pp. 114-138.

Nowlis, V., & Nowlis, H. H. The description and analysis of mood. *Annals of the New York Academy of Sciences,* 1956, 65, 345-355.

Nutrition Reviews, The Editors of. Self-selection of diets. *Nutrition Reviews,* 1944, 2, 199-203.

Olds, J., & Milner, P. Positive reinforcement produced by electrical stimulation of septal area and other regions of rat brain. *Journal of Comparative and Physiological Psychology,* 1954, 47, 419-427.

Olds, M. E., & Olds, J. Approach-avoidance analysis of rat diencephalon. *The Journal of Comparative Neurology,* 1963, 120, 259-295.

Papez, J. W. A proposed mechanism of emotion. *Archives of Neurology and Psychology*, 1937, 38, 725-743.

Patrick, J. R. The effect of emotional stimuli on the activity level of the white rat. *Journal of Comparative Psychology,* 1931, 12, 357-364.

Pavlov, I. P. *Conditioned reflexes: An investigation of the physiological activity of the cerebral cortex.* New York: Oxford University Press, 1927. (Translated by G. V. Anrep)

Pavlov, I. P. *Lectures on conditioned reflexes: Twenty-five years of objective study of the higher nervous activity (behaviour) of animals.* New York: International Publishers, 1928. (Translated by W. H. Gantt)

Perky, C. W. An experimental study of imagination. *American Journal of Psychology,* 1910, 21, 422-452.

Peters, H. N. The experimetnal study of aesthetic judgments. *Psychological Bulletin,* 1942, 39, 273-305.

Piéron, H. Emotions in animals and man. In C. Murchison & M. L. Reymert (Ed.), *Wittenberg symposium on feelings and emotions.* Worcester, Mass.: Clark University Press, 1928.

Pratt, K. C., Nelson, A. F., & Sun, K. *The behavior of the newborn infant.* Columbus, Ohio: Ohio State University Press, 1930.

Prescott, D. A. *Emotion and the educative process: A report of the committee on the relation of emotion to the educative process.* Washington, D. C.: American Council on Education, 1938.

Pribram, K. H. The new neurology and the biology of emotion. *American Psychologist,* 1967, 22, 830-838. (a)

Pribram, K. H. Emotion: Steps toward a neuropsychological theory. In D. C. Glass (Ed.), *Neurophysiology and emotion.* New York: The Rockefeller University Press, 1967. (b)

Pribram, K. H., & Kruger, L. Functions of the "olfactory brain." *Annals of the New York Academy of Sciences,* 1954, 58, 109-138.

Pullias, E. V. Masturbation as a mental hygiene problem: A study of the beliefs of seventy-five young men. *Journal of Abnormal and Social Psychology,* 1937, 32, 216-222.

Rapaport, D. *Emotions and memory.* New York: International Universities Press, 1950. (Menninger Clinic Monograph Series, No. 2, 1942. Unaltered edition, 1950)

Richter, C. P., & Barelare, B. Nutritional requirements of pregnant and lactating rats studied by the self-selection method. *Endocrinology,* 1938, 23, 15-24.

Richter, C. P., & Eckert, J. F. Increased calcium appetite of parathyroidectomized rats. *Endocrinology,* 1937, 21, 50-54.

Richter, C. P., Holt, L. E., & Barelare, B. Vitamin B_1 craving in rats. *Science,* 1937, 86, 354-355.

Richter, C. P., Holt, L. E., & Barelare, B. Nutritional requirements for normal growth and reproduction in rats studied by the self-selection method. *American Journal of Physiology,* 1938, 122, 734-744.

Rogers, C. R. *Client-centered therapy: Its current practice, implications, and theory.* Boston: Houghton Mifflin, 1951.

Rotter, J. B. Level of aspiration as a method of studying personality: I. A critical review of methodology. *Psychological Review,* 1942, 49, 463-474.

Routtenberg, A. The two-arousal hypothesis: Reticular formation and limbic system. *Psychological Review,* 1968, 75, 51-80.

Rozin, P. Thiamine specific hunger. In C. F. Code (Ed.), *Handbook of physiology: Section 6, Alimentary Canal; Food and water intake, Vol. I.* Washington, D. C.: American Physiological Society, 1967. Pp. 411-431.

Rozin, P., & Kalat, J. W. Specific hungers and poison avoidance as adaptive specializations of learning. *Psychological Review,* 1971, 78, 459-486.

Ruckmick, C. A. *The psychology of feeling and emotion.* New York: McGraw-Hill, 1936.

Russell, R. W., & Younger, J. The effects of avitaminosis-A on visual intensity difference thresholds in the rat. *Journal of Experimental Psychology,* 1943, 32, 507-512.

Schachter, S. Cognitive effects on bodily functioning: Studies of obesity and eating. In D. C. Glass (Ed.), *Neurophysiology and emotion.* New York: The Rockefeller University Press, 1967. Pp. 117-144.

Schachter, S. The assumption of identity and peripheralist-centralist controversies in motivation and emotion. In M. B. Arnold (Ed.), *Loyola symposium on feelings and emotions.* New York: Academic Press, 1970. Pp. 111-121.

Schachter, S., & Singer, J. E. Cognitive, social, and physiological determinants of emotional state. *Psychological Review,* 1962, 69, 379-399.

Schildkraut, J. J., & Kety, S. S. Biogenic amines and emotion. *Science,* 1967, 156, 21-30.

Schlosberg, H. A scale for the judgment of facial expressions. *Journal of Experimental Psychology,* 1941, 29, 497-510.

Schlosberg, H. The description of facial expressions in terms of two dimensions. *Journal of Experimental Psychology,* 1952, 44, 229-237.

Schlosberg, H. Three dimensions of emotion. *Psychological Review,* 1954, 61, 81-88.

Schumann, F. Beiträge zur Analyse der Gesichtswahrnehmungen. *Zeitschrift für Psychologie,* 1900, 23, 1-32.

Scott, E. M., & Quint, E. Self-selection of diet: III. Appetites for B vitamins. *Journal of Nutrition,* 1946, 32, 285-292.

Scott, E. M., & Verney, E. L. Self-selection of diets: VI. The nature of appetites for B vitamins. *Journal of Nutrition,* 1947, 34, 471-480.

Scott, E. M., Verney, E. L., & Morissey, P. D. Self-selection of diet: XI. Appetites for calcium, magnesium and potassium. *Journal of Nutrition,* 1950, 41, 187-201.

Scott, J. C. Systolic blood-pressure fluctuations with sex, anger and fear. *Journal of Comparative Psychology,* 1930, 10, 97-114.

Selye, H. *The stress of life.* New York: McGraw-Hill, 1956.

Sewall, M. Some causes of jealousy in young children. *Smith College Studies in Social Work,* 1930, 1, 6-22.

Seward, G. H., & J. P. Internal and external determinants of drives. *Psychological Review,* 1937, 44, 349-363.

Shaffer, L. F. *The psychology of adjustment: An objective approach to mental hygiene.* Boston: Houghton Mifflin Company, 1936.

Shand, A. F. *The foundations of character, being a study of the emotions and sentiments.* London: Macmillan, 1920.

Sheer, D. E. Emotional facilitation in learning situations with subcortical stimulation. In D. E. Sheer (Ed.), *Electical stimulation of the brain: An interdisciplinary survey of neuro-behavioral integrative systems.* Austin, Texas: University of Texas Press, 1961.

Sheffield, F. D., & Roby, T. B. Reward value of a non-nutritive sweet taste. *Journal of Comparative and Physiological Psychology,* 1950, 43, 471-481.

Sherif, M. An experimental study of stereotypes. *Journal of Abnormal and Social Psychology,* 1935, 29, 371-375.

Sherif, M., & Cantril, H. *The psychology of ego-involvements, social attitudes and identifications.* New York: John Wiley & Sons, 1947.

Sherman, M. The differentiation of emotional responses in infants. I. Judgments of emotional respones from motion picture views and from actual observation. II. The ability of observers to judge the emotional characteristics of the crying infants, and of the voice of an adult. *Journal of Comparative Psychology,* 1927, 7, 265-284 & 335-351.

Sherman, M., & Sherman, I. C. *The process of human behavior.* New York: W. W. Norton, 1929.

Sherrington, C. S. *The integrative action of the nervous system.* New Haven: Yale University Press, 1911.

Shuford, E. H., Jr. Palatability and osmotic pressure of glucose and sucrose solutions as determinants of intake. *Journal of Comparative and Physiological Psychology,* 1959, 52, 150-153.

Simonov, P. V. Studies of emotional behavior of humans and animals by Soviet physiologists. *Annals of the New York Academy of Sciences: Experimental approaches to the study of emotional behavior,* 1969, 159, 3. New York: Published by the Academy, 1969. Pp. 1112-1121.

Singer, W. B., & Young, P. T. Studies in affective reaction: II. Dependence of affective ratings upon the stimulus-situation. *Journal of General Psychology,* 1941, 24, 303-325. (a)

Singer, W. B., & Young, P. T. Studies in affective reaction: III. The specificity of affective reactions. *Journal of General Psychology,* 1941, 24, 327-341. (b)

Skinner, B. F. *The behavior of organisms: An experimental analysis.* New York: Appleton-Century, 1938.

Smalley, R. E. II, The influence of differences in age, sex, and intelligence in determining the attitudes of siblings toward each other. *Smith College Studies in Social Work,* 1930, 1, 23-40.

Smith, K. On the inter-relationships among orgainization, motivation, and emotion. *Canadian Journal of Psychology,* 1958, 12, 69-73.

Sokolov, E. N. Neuronal models and the orienting reflex. In M. A. B. Brazier (Ed.), *The central nervous system and behavior: Transactions of the third conference.* Josiah Macy, Jr. Foundation, 1960. Pp. 187-276.

Solomon, R. L., Kamin, L. J., & Wynne, L. C. Traumatic avoidance learning: The outcomes of several extinction procedures with dogs. *Journal of Abnormal and Social Psychology,* 1953, 48, 291-302.

Spitz, R. A. The smiling response: A contribution to the ontogenesis of social relations. *Genetic Psychology Monographs,* 1946, 34, 57-125.

Spranger, E. *Types of men.* Halle: M. Niemeyer, 1928. (Translated from the fifth german edition by P. J. W. Pigors)

Stagner, R. Fascist attitudes: Their determining conditions. *Journal of Social Psychology,* 1936, 7, 438-453.

Stellar, E. Hunger in man: Comparative and physiological studies. *American Psychologist,* 1967, 22, No. 2, 105-117.

Stone, C. P. The congenital sexual behavior of the young male albino rat. *Journal of Comparative Psychology,* 1922, 2, 95-153.

Stone, C. P. The initial copulatory response of female rats reared in isolation from the age of twenty days to the age of puberty. *Journal of Comparative Psychology,* 1926, 6, 73-83.

Stratton, G. M. Excitement as an undifferentiated emotion. In C. Murchison, & M. L. Reymert (Eds.), *The Wittenberg symposium on feelings and emotions.* Worcester, Mass.: Clark University Press, 1928. (a)

Stratton, G. M. The function of emotion as shown particularly in excitement. *Psychological Review,* 1928, 35, 351-366. (b)

Stratton, G. M. Emotion and the incidence of disease: The influence of the number of diseases, and of the age at which they occur. *Psychological Review,* 1929, 36, 242-253.

Strauss, H. Das Zusammenschrecken: Experimentell-kinematographische Studie zur

Physiologie und Pathophysiologie der Reaktivbewegungen. *Journal Psychologie und Neurologie,* 1929, 39, 111-231.

Strong, E. K. *Change of interests with age.* Palo Alto: Stanford University Press, 1931.

Strouthes, A. Thirst and saccharin preference in rats. *Physiology and Behavior,* 1971, 6, 287-292.

Symonds, P. M. The dynamics of human adjustment. New York: Appleton-Century, 1946.

Symonds, P. M. *Dynamic psychology.* New York: Appleton-Century-Crofts, 1949.

Taylor, J. A. A personality scale of manifest anxiety. *Journal of Abnormal and Social Psychology,* 1953, 48, 285-290.

Teitelbaum, P. Motivation and control of food intake. In C. F. Code (Ed.), *Handbook of physiology: Section 6, Alimentary Canal; Food and water intake, Vol. I.* Washington, D. C.: American Physiological Society, 1967. Pp. 319-335.

Thomas, W., & Young, P. T. Liking and disliking persons. *Journal of Social Psychology,* 1938, 9, 169-188.

Thurstone, L. L. Attitudes can be measured. *American Journal of Sociology,* 1928, 33, 520-554.

Thurstone, L. L. The measurement of change in social attitude. *Journal of Social Psychology,* 1931, 2, 230-235.

Thurstone, L. L. The measurement of social attitudes, *Journal of Abnormal and Social Psychology,* 1932, 26, 249-269.

Thurstone, L. L., & Chave, E. J. *The measurement of attitude: A psychophysical method and some experiments with a scale for measuring attitude toward the church.* Chicago: University of Chicago Press, 1929.

Thurstone, L. L., & Thurstone, T. G. A neurotic inventory. *Journal of Social Psychology,* 1930, 1, 3-30.

Tinbergen, N. *The study of instinct.* Oxford: Clarendon Press, 1951.

Titchener, E. B. *Lectures on the elementary psychology of feeling and attention.* New York: Macmillan, 1908.

Titchener, E. B. *Lectures on the experimental psychology of the thought processes.* New York: Macmillan, 1909.

Titchener, E. B. Prolegomena to a study of introspection. *American Journal of Psychology,* 1912, 23, 427-448. (a)

Titchener, E. B. The schema of introspection. *American Journal of Psychology,* 1912, 23, 485-508. (b)

Titchener, E. B. *A text-book of psychology.* New York: Macmillan, 1924.

Tolman, E. C. A behavioristic account of the emotions. *Psychological Review,* 1923, 30, 217-227.

Tolman, E. C. *Purposive behavior in animals and man.* New York: Appleton-Century-Crofts, 1932.

Tolman, E. C. Motivation, learning and adjustment. *Proceedings of the American Philosophical Society,* 1941, 84, 543-563.

Troland, L. T. *The fundamentals of human motivation.* Princeton, N. J.: Van Nostrand, 1928.

Ulrich, R. E., Hutchinson, R. R., & Azrin, N. H. Pain-elicited aggression. *The Psychological Record,* 1965, 15, 111-126.

Valentine, C. W. The innate bases of fear. *Journal of Genetic Psychology,* 1930, 37, 394-420.

Vanderwolf, C. H. Limbic-diencephalic mechanisms of voluntary movement. *Psychological Review,* 1971, 78, 83-113.

Washburn, R. W. A study of the smiling and laughing of infants in the first year of life. *Genetic Psychology Monographs,* 1929, 6, 397-537. No. 5 & 6.

Watson, J. B. *Behavior: An introduction to comparative psychology.* New York: Holt, 1914.

Watson, J. B. A schematic outline of the emotions. *Psychological Review,* 1919, 26, 165-196.

Watson, J. B. *Psychology from the standpoint of a behaviorist.* Philadelphia: J. B. Lippincott, 1929. (Third edition)

Watson, J. B., & Rayner, R. Conditioned emotional reactions. *Journal of Experimental Psychology,* 1920, 3, 1-14.

Weber, C. O. The concept of "emotional age" and its measurement. *Journal of Abnormal and Social Psychology,* 1930, 24, 466-471.

Weber, C. O. Further tests of the Wells emotional age scale. *Journal of Abnormal and Social Psychology,* 1932, 27, 65-78.

Wechsler, D. On the specificity of emotional reactions. *American Journal of Psychology,* 1925, 36, 424-426.

Wechsler, D., & Jones, H. E. A study of emotional specificity. *American Journal of Psychology,* 1938, 40, 600-606.

Weinberg, A. M. The axiology of science. *American Scientist,* 1970, 58, No.6, 612-617. (Nov.-Dec.)

Wenger, M. A. Emotion as visceral action: An extension of Lange's theory. In M. L. Reymert (Ed.), *The Mooseheart symposium on feelings and emotions.* New York: McGraw-Hill, 1950.

White, R. W. *The abnormal personality: A textbook.* New York: Ronald Press, 1948. (Second edition, 1956)

Wilkins, L., & Richter, C. P. A great craving for salt by a child with cortico-adrenal insufficiency. *Journal of the American Medical Association,* 1940, 114, 866-868.

Woodrow, H. The problem of general quantitative laws in psychology. *Psychological Bulletin,* 1942, 39, 1-27.

Woodworth, R. S. *Dynamic psychology.* New York: Columbia University Press, 1918.

Woodworth, R. S. *Experimental psychology.* New York: Holt, 1938.

Woolley, D. W. Involvement of the hormone serotonin in emotion and mind. In D. C. Glass (Ed.), *Neurophysiology and emotion.* New York: The Rockefeller University Press, 1967.

Young, P. T. An experimental study of mixed feelings. *American Journal of Psychology,* 1918, 29, 237-271. (a)

Young, P. T. The localisation of feeling. *American Journal of Psychology,* 1918, 29, 420-430. (b)

Young, P. T. Movements of pursuit and avoidance as expressions of simple feeling. *American Journal of Psychology,* 1922, 33, 511-525.

Young, P. T. The phenomenological point of view. *Psychological Review,* 1924, 31, 288-296.
Young, P. T. Conflict of movement in relation to unpleasant feeling. *American Journal of Psychology,* 1928, 40, 394-400.
Young, P. T. Studies in affective psychology: IX. The point of view of affective psychology. *American Journal of Psychology,* 1930, 42, 27-35.
Young, P. T. The relation of bright and dull pressure to affectivity. *American Journal of Psychology,* 1932, 44, 780-784. (a)
Young, P. T. Relative food preferences of the white rat. *Journal of Comparative Psychology,* 1932, 14, 297-319. (b)
Young, P. T. Relative food preferences of the white rat, II. *Journal of Comparative Psychology,* 1933, 15, 149-165.
Young, P. T. *Motivation of behavior: The fundamental determinants of human and animal activity.* New York: John Wiley & Sons, 1936.
Young, P. T. Laughing and weeping, cheerfulness and depression: A study of moods among college students. *Journal of Social Psychology,* 1937, 8, 311-334.
Young, P. T. *Emotion in man and animal: Its nature and relation to attitude and motive.* New York: John Wiley & Sons, 1943. (First edition)
Young, P. T. Studies of food preference, appetite and dietary habit: VIII Food-seeking drives, palatability and the law of effect. *Journal of Comparative and Physiological Psychology,* 1948, 41, 269-300.
Young, P. T. Emotion as disorganized response: A reply to Professor Leeper. *Psychological Review* 1949, 56, 184-191.
Young, P. T. The role of hedonic processes in the organization of behavior. *Psychological Review,* 1952, 59, 249-262.
Young, P. T. The role of hedonic processes in motivation. In M. R. Jones (Ed.), *Nebraska symposium on motivation, 1955.* Lincoln, Nebra.: University of Nebraska Press, 1955.
Young, P. T. The role of affective processes in learning and motivation. *Psychological Review,* 1959, 66, 104-125.
Young, P. T. *Motivation and emotion: A survey of the determinants of human and animal activity.* New York: John Wiley & Sons, 1961.
Young, P. T. Hedonic organization and regulation of behavior. *Psychological Review,* 1966, 73, 59-86.
Young, P. T. Palatability: The hedonic response to foodstuffs. In C. F. Code (Ed.), *Handbook of physiology: Section 6, Alimentary canal: Food and water intake, Vol. I.* Washington, D. C. American Physiological Society, 1967. Pp. 353-366.
Young, P. T. Evaluation and preference in behavioral development. *Psychological Review,* 1968, 75, 222-241.
Young, P. T. Feeling and emotion. In B. B. Wolman (Ed.), *Handbook of general psychology.* Englewood Cliffs, New Jersey: Prentice-Hall. (in press)
Young, P. T. *Hedonic regulation of behavior and development.* (Unpublished book manuscript deposited with Archives of the History of American Psychology. The University of Akron, Akron, Ohio 44325.)
Young, P. T., & Chaplin, J. P. Studies of food preference, appetite and dietary habit: III. Palatability and appetite in relation to bodily need. *Comparative Psychology Monographs,* 1945, 18, 1-45.
Young, P. T., & Christensen, K. R. Algebraic summation of hedonic processes. *Journal of Comparative and Physiological Psychology,* 1962, 55, 332-336.

Young, P. T., & Falk, J. L. The relative acceptability of sodium chloride solutions as a function of concentration and water need. *Journal of Compartive and Physiological Psychology,* 1956, 49, 569-575.
Young, P. T., & Greene, J. T. Quantity of food ingested as a measure of relative acceptability. *Journal of Comparative and Physiological Psychology,* 1953, 46, 288-294.
Young, P. T., & Madsen, C. H., Jr. Individual isohedons in sucrose-sodium chloride and sucrose-saccharin gustatory areas. *Journal of Comparative and Physiological Psychology,* 1963, 56, 903-909.
Young, P. T., & Schulte, R. H. Isohedonic contours and tongue activity in three gustatory areas of the rat. *Journal of Comparative and Physiological Psychology,* 1963, 56, 465-475.
Young, P. T., & Shuford, E. H., Jr. Quantitative control of motivation through sucrose solutions of different concentrations. *Journal of Comparative and Physiological Psychology,* 1955, 48, 114-118.
Young, P. T., & Trafton, C. L. Activity contour maps as related to preference in four gustatory stimulus areas of the rat. *Journal of Comparative and Physiological Psychology,* 1964, 58, 68-75.

Zilboorg, G., & Henry, G. W. *A history of medical psychology.* New York: Norton, 1941.

Index of Authors

Index of Subjects